BYZANTIUM AND VENICE

BYZANTIUM

AND

VENICE

A study in diplomatic and cultural relations

DONALD M. NICOL

Published by the Press Syndicate of the University of Cambridge
The Pitt Building, Trumpington Street, Cambridge CB2 1RP
40 West 20th Street, New York, NY 10011-4211 USA
10 Stamford Road, Oakleigh, Melbourne 3166, Australia

First published 1988
First paperback edition 1992
Reprinted 1994, 1995, 1999

British Library cataloguing in publication data
Nicol, Donald M. (Donald MacGillivray), *1923*–
Byzantium and Venice: a study in diplomatic
and cultural relations.
1. Venice. Foreign relations with
Byzantine Empire, ca 450–1453. Byzantine
Empire. Foreign relations with Venice,
ca 450–1453
1. Title
327.45′31′0495

Library of Congress cataloguing in publication data
Nicol, Donald MacGillivray.
Byzantium and Venice: a study in diplomatic and cultural
relations / Donald M. Nicol.
p. cm.
Bibliography.
Includes index.
ISBN 0-521-34157-4
1. Byzantine Empire – Relations – Italy – Venice. 2. Venice (Italy) –
Relations – Byzantine Empire. 1. Title
DF547.18N53 1988
327.495045′31 – dc 19   88–5019

ISBN 0 521 34157 4 hardback
ISBN 0 521 42894 7 paperback

Transferred to digital printing 2002

CONTENTS

v

non ut aligenas, immo ut aborigines Romanos genus Veneticorum nostra serenitas reputat ...

(Emperor Isaac II in 1189)

(The Venetians are) morally dissolute, vulgar and untrustworthy, with all the gross characteristics of sea-faring people ...

(Kinnamos, *Epitome rerum*, p. 280)

PREFACE

Constantinople and Venice, the two richest and most romantic Christian cities in the early Middle Ages, were separated by the many nautical miles of the Aegean and Adriatic seas. To sail from one to the other might take six to eight weeks. Yet they were bound together by long tradition, by mutual needs of defence, by commerce and by culture. Venice was born as a province of the Byzantine or East Roman Empire, linked by the ties of a remote provincial city to its capital in Constantinople, the New Rome. It grew into an ally, came of age as a partner and matured as the owner of extensive colonial possessions within the disintegrating structure of the Byzantine world.

In theory Byzantium and Venice were friends, however distant. Their relationship went back to the fifth century. In practice they were often at variance. They differed in language, in the form of their Christian faith, and above all in politics. Byzantium, the heir to the ancient Roman tradition, never forsook the idea of universal *imperium*. Venice was less demanding, more subtle and more realistic. Venice was a republic, hedged about by aspiring western kingdoms and empires which were nearer and more threatening than Byzantium. The Venetians lived by the sea and the trade that went by sea. The Byzantines preferred the dry land. They had an imperial navy but no great merchant fleet. Their ruling class regarded trade as rather beneath their dignity. Since Constantinople was the centre of the world, at the point where Europe and Asia meet, they expected the trade of the world to come to them. They never mastered the intricacies of capitalism and a market economy. The Venetians were traders by nature and by necessity. The wealth of Byzantium attracted their merchants like a magnet. The Venetians disapproved of monarchy, though they had an innate love of pomp and ceremony, of ritual and pageantry; and for these accoutrements of their courtly and cultural life they turned to the Queen of Cities, to Constantinople. Venice was like a sunflower, its roots firmly planted in the Latin west, yet constantly bending over to catch the rays of light from the Greek east.

Many books have been written about Byzantium and many about
Venice. Many scholars have devoted their researches to one or another
aspect or period of the association between the two. So far as I am aware,
no one hitherto has tried to set down the whole history of that association
during the thousand years from the foundation of the Venetian republic
to the fall of the Byzantine Empire in 1453. A Greek scholar of the
nineteenth century remarked that the Venetians, being in some sense
heirs to the Byzantine bureaucracy, had too many officials and, as a
consequence, too many archives. The abundant Venetian documents concerning trade and the commercial interest of Venice in Byzantium would
fill another book. I have dwelt mainly on the diplomatic and cultural
exchanges between Byzantium and Venice; though I have tried to see
trade as a vital factor in the love–hate relationship that developed between
the two centres of such different cultures. The book might have been
entitled *Constantinople and Venice*. But this would have obscured the
fact that Constantinople was the hub of the wheel of a wider world
which the Venetians half admired and half despised, and which in the
end they sought to appropriate, to exploit it for their own profit and
honour.

The Bibliography will indicate to whom I owe acknowledgments.
Above all, I am indebted to the original sources, Greek, Latin and other,
for the long history of Byzantium and Venice. Among modern historians
I would like to express my gratitude especially to the late Freddy Thiriet
who died while I was at work on this book; and to Sir Steven Runciman,
who gave me the idea and the licence to write it and would have done
it so much better.

D.M.N.
London, 1987

ABBREVIATIONS

ActAlb — *Acta et Diplomata res Albaniae mediae aetatis Illustrantia*, ed. L. de Thallóczy, C. Jireček, E. de Šufflay

ActAlbVen — *Acta Albaniae Veneta Saeculorum XIV et XV*, ed. J. Valentini

ASI — *Archivio Storico Italiano*

B — *Byzantion*

BF — *Byzantinische Forschungen*

BS — *Byzantinoslavica*

BZ — *Byzantinische Zeitschrift*

CFHB — *Corpus Fontium Historiae Byzantinae*

CMH — *Cambridge Medieval History*

CSHB — *Corpus Scriptorum Historiae Byzantinae*

DAI — Constantine Porphyrogenitus, *De Administrando Imperio*

DOP — *Dumbarton Oaks Papers*

DR — Dölger, F., *Regesten der Kaiserurkunden des oströmischen Reiches*, I–V

DVL — *Diplomatarium Veneto-Levantinum*, ed. G. M. Thomas and R. Predelli

GRBS — *Greek, Roman and Byzantine Studies*

JHS — *Journal of Hellenic Studies*

MGH — *Monumenta Germaniae Historica*

MM — Miklosich, F. and Müller, J., *Acta et Diplomata graeca medii aevi sacra et profana*

MPG — Migne, J. P., *Patrologia Graeca*

MPL — Migne, J. P., *Patrologia Latina*

OCA — *Orientalia Christiana Analecta*

OCP — *Orientalia Christiana Periodica*

PLP — *Prosopographisches Lexikon der Palaiologenzeit*, ed. E. Trapp

REB — *Revue des Etudes Byzantines*

RHC — *Recueil des Historiens des Croisades*

ix

RHSEE	*Revue Historique du Sud-Est Européen*
RIS	*Rerum Italicarum Scriptores,* ed. L. A. Muratori *et al.*
ROL	*Revue de l'Orient Latin*
RSBN	*Rivista di Studi Bizantini e Neoellenici*
RSI	*Rivista Storica Italiana*
SGUS	*Scriptores rerum Germanicarum in usum scholarum*
TM	*Travaux et Mémoires*
TTh	Tafel, G. L. F. and Thomas, G. M., *Urkunden zur älteren Handels- und Staatsgeschichte der Republik Venedig*
VV	*Vizantijskij Vremennik*
ZRVI	*Zbornik Radova Vizantološkog Instituta*

Map I. Byzantium and the Aegean Sea

Map II. Italy and the Adriatic

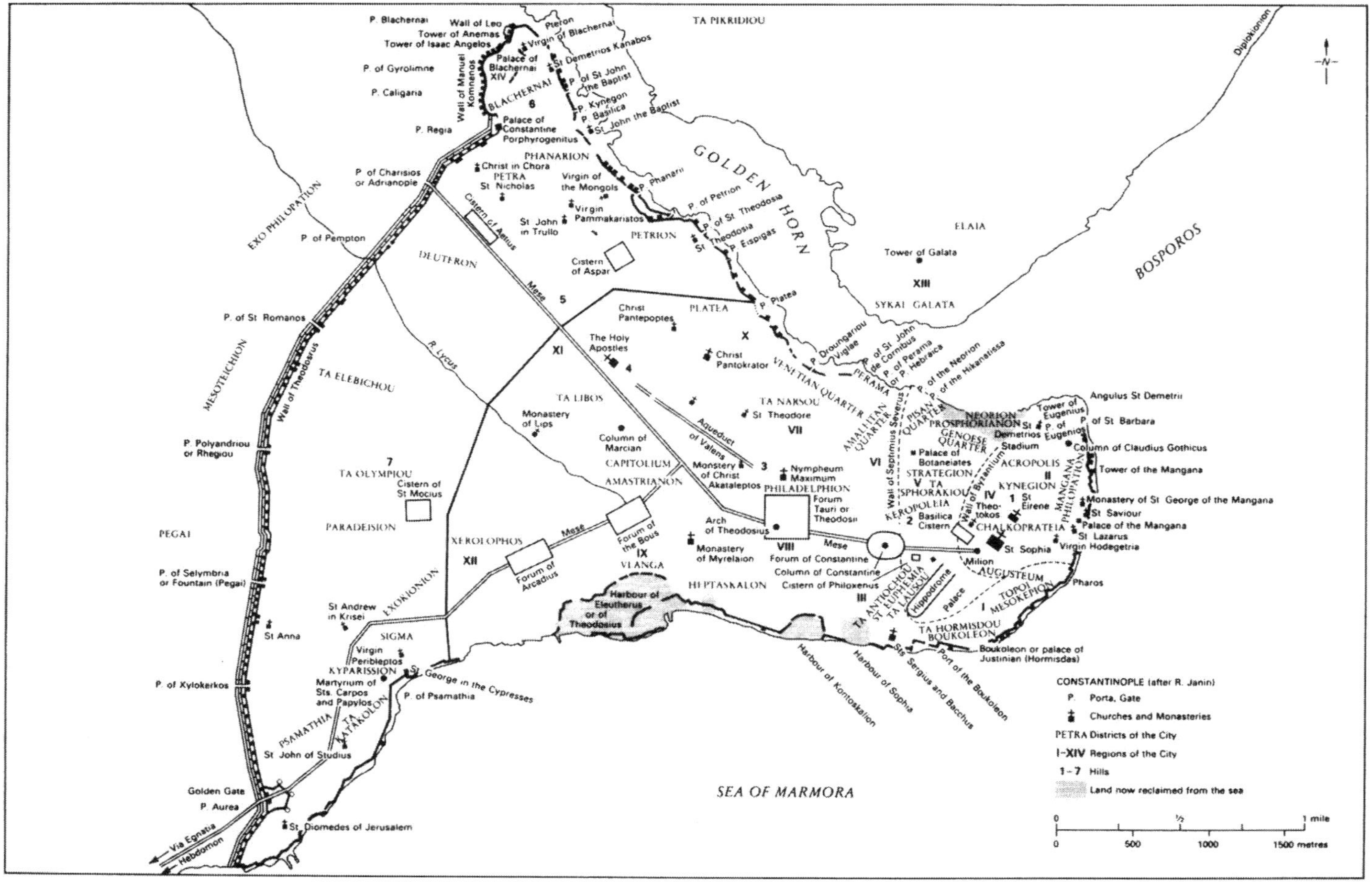

Map III. Constantinople

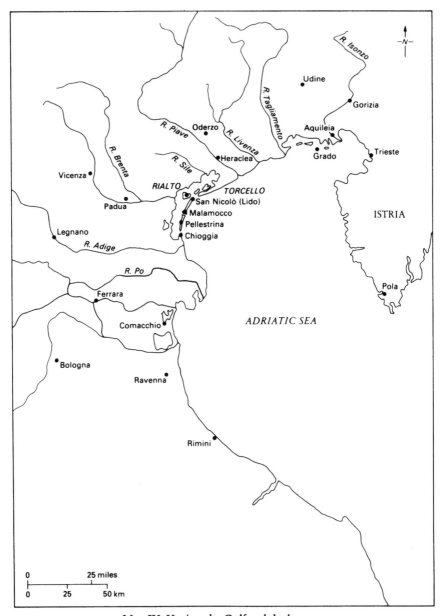

Map IV. Venice, the Gulf and the lagoons

1

VENICE:
THE BYZANTINE PROVINCE

THE imperial province of Venetia and Istria at the head of the Adriatic Sea was as old as the Roman Empire. It had been the tenth of the eleven regions of Italy marked out by the first emperor Augustus. Encircled by the foothills of the Alps on the north and itself encircling the sea, its southern border in Italy was fixed by the river Po, to the south of which, on the Adriatic shore, lay the imperial naval base of Classis or Ravenna. Its main cities were Padua, Aquileia and between them Opitergium or Oderzo. It was a mainland province whose inhabitants saw no promise in the muddy islands and lagoons on to which they looked. Fish could be caught there and salt could be collected. But no one could have foreseen that the islands would have a greater future than the continent. It was said in later years that the Veneti or Venetici were so called both in Greek and in Latin because they were a praiseworthy people.[1] It was a scholarly but fanciful etymology. For in truth the original Veneti were neither Greek nor Latin but Illyrian.

By the fourth century AD, when Constantine the Great became the first Christian Emperor of the Romans, the christianisation of Venetia had already been assured by the establishment of a bishopric at Aquileia. The province lay much nearer to Rome than to the new capital of the civilised world set up by Constantine on the site of the ancient Byzantium. But it was still a mainland province of the undivided Roman Empire. It survived as such for only some seventy years after the foundation of Constantinople. In 403 the Goths came down upon it. The Emperor Honorius fled to the fortress of Ravenna. Aquileia was destroyed and the Veneti took refuge in the offshore islands. Their own historians in a later age associated this event with the first beginnings of their city of Venice on the group of islands of the Rivo Alto or Rialto. They dated

---

[1] Paul the Deacon, *Pauli Historia Langobardorum, MGH, Script. rer. Langobardorum* (Hanover, 1878), II. 14: p. 81; John the Deacon, *Cronaca veneziana*, ed. G. Monticolo, *Cronache veneziane antichissime*, I (Rome, 1890), p. 63.

its origin precisely to 25 March 421, at midday.[1] They anticipated the truth by some 400 years. The settlement of the Veneti in the islands of the lagoons was not yet permanent. The mainland was still their home. Aquileia was repopulated, only to be destroyed again by the Huns of Attila in 452. The Huns, here as elsewhere, came and went. But the Goths stayed. They had made themselves indispensable and hence immovable as part of the Roman military machine. In 476 their leader Odoacer deposed the last of the line of Roman Emperors in the west and made himself effective ruler of the Gothic Kingdom of Italy. There was now only one Emperor of the Romans and he reigned at Constantinople, the New Rome.

The Gothic King Odoacer and his successor Theodoric recognised this fact. Theodoric made his capital at Ravenna and asserted or pretended that he was merely the viceroy of the Eastern Roman or Byzantine Emperor at Constantinople. For some years the arrangement worked. Justinian, however, who came to the throne in 527, thought that it had gone on long enough. He was inspired by the vision of a restored and reunited *imperium romanum* covering the length and breadth of the Mediterranean. It took years of bitter, expensive and destructive war to realise that vision. But in the end, by about 555, North Africa had been won back from the Vandals, part of Spain from the Visigoths and Italy from the Ostrogoths. The Mediterranean was, as Justinian boasted, a Roman lake once again; and at its most northerly point the province of Venetia and Istria and with it Ravenna had reverted to the rule of Rome, or rather of the New Rome from which the liberation of Italy had been directed. Justinian was proud that these furthest outposts of his empire had been recovered and he advertised his pride by enriching the churches of Ravenna, where his mosaic portraits are still to be seen. Other great cities of Italy, such as Milan and Rome itself, had been reduced to ruins in the course of their liberation from the Goths. But Ravenna was built anew as the seat of an imperial governor who was without any pretence the official deputy of the one true Emperor of the Romans.

The Veneti had sometimes supported and sometimes suffered from the war of liberation. They had been overrun by the Goths and then by the Franks who had taken their chance to come over the Alps and occupy much of northern Italy. The coastal cities of Venetia, however, seem to have been Roman again by 539; and they had sent ships to help in the blockade of Ravenna in that year. In 551 they had ferried a stranded army of mercenaries to join forces with the imperial troops

[1] R. Cessi, *Documenti relativi alla storia di Venezia anteriore al mille*, I: *Secoli V–IX* (Padua, 1942), no. 1, pp. 1–2.

at Ravenna.[1] By then the inland as well as the maritime province of
Venetia had been restored to Roman rule. It was later believed that Justinian's general Narses, who achieved the final defeat of the Goths, marked
the Venetian contribution to his success by building two churches on
the islands of Rialto.[2] Justinian wanted the world to believe that his
conquering armies had merely restored the old order of things. The *pax
romana* reigned again. It was as if the barbarians had never been and
nothing had changed. The older provinces of Venetia and Istria, together
with the neighbouring provinces of Pannonia and Dalmatia, were simply
and quickly reincorporated into the imperial administration with their
own governors.[3] The only innovation, though it is a striking one, was
that provincial governors were not now to be appointed by decree of
the emperor. They were to be elected from among their inhabitants by
the choice of their bishops and leading citizens. The overall government
of Italy was committed to a prefect or viceroy of the emperor, the first
of whom was Narses, with his capital at Ravenna.[4]

The earliest Venetian chroniclers speak highly of the just and pious
character of Narses and with admiration of the enormous wealth which
he amassed from the spoils of war. It was this, we are told, which excited
the envy of the Emperor Justin, who succeeded Justinian in 565, and
of his wife Sophia, who taunted Narses with being a eunuch and invited
him to wind wool in the women's quarter of the palace. Narses was
relieved of his office and left Ravenna for Naples. If the chroniclers are
to be believed, he took his revenge by calling on the Lombards to leave
the barren hills and dales of Pannonia and come to take possession of
the rich and fruitful land of Italy. He was replaced as prefect at Ravenna

---

[1] Procopius, *De Bello Gothico*, ed. J. Haury (Leipzig, 1905), ii. 29; iv. 24, 26: II, pp. 287–8,
617, 632–5. S. Romanin, *Storia documentata della Repubblica di Venezia*, 2nd edn, I (Venice,
1912), pp. 54–5, 56; H. Kretschmayr, *Geschichte von Venedig*, I (Gotha, 1905), p. 412 (cited
hereafter as Kretschmayr, I).

[2] *Chronicon venetum quod vulgo dicunt Altinate*, ed. H. Simonsfeld, *MGH*, *Script.*, XIV
(Hanover, 1883), p. 47; ed. R. Cessi, *Origo Civitatum Italiae seu Venetiarum* (*Chronicon
Altinate et Chronicon Gradense*) (Rome, 1933), pp. 69–70. The two churches were said to
have been those of St Theodore (the Doge's chapel) and of Saints Geminianus and Menas.
But the tale is clearly false. See O. Demus, *The Church of San Marco in Venice* (Washington,
D.C., 1960), p. 21 n. 71.

[3] E. Honigmann, ed., *Le Synekdèmos d'Hiéroklès et l'opuscule géographique de Georges de
Chypre* (Brussels, 1939), no. 559.

[4] J. B. Bury, *History of the Later Roman Empire*, II (London, 1923), pp. 281–6; E. Stein,
Histoire du Bas-Empire, II (Paris–Brussels–Amsterdam, 1949), pp. 612ff.

by Flavius Longinus.[1] The vengeance of Narses is probably a myth. But it is a fact that the Lombards, whom he had employed as mercenaries, descended on the north of Italy only three years after the death of Justinian. Later tradition also has it that the new Prefect Longinus visited the city of Venice, which had already sprung up in the lagoons, and negotiated on behalf of his emperor the first treaty between Venice and Byzantium. The Venetians were not asked to take any oath of loyalty to the emperor, only to acknowledge him as their overlord and to express their devotion to his cause. In return they would be assured of security and protection for their merchant ships sailing as far as Antioch and in all parts of the empire.[2] This is no more than patriotic fiction. The emancipation of Venice from Byzantine control, let alone the foundation of a city of Venice, were still in the distant future in the year 568; and it seems improbable that many Venetian merchants were yet venturing as far afield as Antioch.

Yet it was in that year that the Lombards began their invasion and occupation of Italy, an event that was to cause the final breakdown of the old order so laboriously restored by Justinian. Most of the mainland province of Venetia became a part of Langobardia or Lombardy. Its inhabitants once again took to the offshore islands as refugees. This time their migration was to be permanent. They took with them the name of their province of Venetia and, for a while, retained some footholds on the mainland in Istria on the east and around Padua, Altino and Oderzo in the west. But Aquileia was destroyed yet again in 569 and its people fled to the harbour town of Grado. In the early years of the seventh century the Lombards encroached still further. Padua was taken in 603, Concordia in 615, and their citizens took to the islands of Caorle and Malamocco. Venetia Maritima became a huddle of island refuges. Istria held out against the Lombards but it was cut off and communications by land with other parts of the empire were disrupted. When Oderzo and then Altino fell in 640 almost the last remnants of Roman or Byzantine rule on the mainland were gone. The people of Oderzo fled to Cittanova (*Civitas Nova*), which later came to be called Heraclea or Heracliana.

---

[1] Paul the Deacon, II. 5: p. 75; John the Deacon, pp. 60-2; Constantine Porphyrogenitus, *De Administrando Imperio* (*DAI*), ed. Gy. Moravcsik and R. J. H. Jenkins, *CFHB*, I (Dumbarton Oaks, Washington, D.C., 1967) II, *Commentary* (London, 1962), I, c. 27, p. 115. On Longinus, who was prefect from c. 568 to c. 572, see T. S. Brown, *Gentlemen and Officers. Imperial Administration and Aristocratic Power in Byzantine Italy, AD 554-800* (British School at Rome, 1984), p. 268.

[2] *Chronicon venetum* (*Altinate*), ed. Simonsfeld, pp. 44-8; ed. Cessi, pp. 74-8.

Those of Altino settled on the island of Torcello.[1] Yet Venetia in its new form remained a province of the Byzantine Empire. It was governed by a *magister militum* or military official answerable to the Prefect of Ravenna who, for the time being, upheld what was left of Roman authority in this far-flung outpost. Those who had no option but to live under the Lombards felt left out. In 590-1 some of the bishops wrote to the Emperor Maurice to express their feelings. 'Although for our sins,' they said, 'we are at present subjected beneath a grievous foreign yoke, yet we have not forgotten your pious government under which we formerly lived in peace and to which, with the help of God, we wish wholeheartedly to return.'[2]

There was little that the emperors in Constantinople could do to save the situation in Italy. The heirs of Justinian were not his equals and they faced the impossible task of paying the cost of his visionary enterprise from a treasury that he had emptied. At the same time they had to contend with enemies and invaders nearer home, with the Persians in the east and with the new flood of barbarians from across the Danube frontier, the Avars and the Slavs. The Emperor Maurice came to the throne in 582 after a victorious campaign against the Persians, which he pursued for another nine years. Maurice was a soldier and he took a soldier's view of what could be done to save the western provinces. They must be placed under martial law. Carthage in North Africa and Ravenna in North Italy were now to be governed by imperial deputies of a new kind with the title of Exarchs. The old distinction between the civil and the military administration was abolished. The Exarchs of Ravenna, whose authority extended to the province of Venetia and its islanders, combined the functions of a general with those of a magistrate. The civilians under his command must be conscripted to defend their own patch without expecting the imperial army to come to their rescue. The officer in charge of the Venetians held the military rank of *magister militum* and he seems at first to have been based on the island of Torcello, which early established itself as the market and commercial centre of the island settlements. After 640 the seat of the military government was moved to Cittanova, of which there is now no trace. It was a sensible move since the city had been founded by the people of Oderzo, which had

---

[1] On the Lombard conquest of the mainland and Venetian settlement of the islands, see C. Diehl, *Etudes sur l'administration byzantine dans l'Exarchat de Ravenne (568-751)* (Paris, 1888), pp. 46-51. For the origin of the name Heraclea (Heracliana) later given to Cittanova, see T. S. Brown, A. Bryer and D. Winfield, 'Cities of Heraclius', *Byzantine and Modern Greek Studies*, IV (*Essays Presented to Sir Steven Runciman*: 1978), 30-8.

[2] *Gregorii Papae Registrum Epistolarum*, ed. P. Ewald, I, 1 (Berlin, 1887), in *MGH, Epist.*, I, pp. 17-21; reprinted in Cessi, *Documenti*, I, no. 8, pp. 14-19.

formerly been the administrative centre of Venetia and the residence of a *dux*.[1]

It was left to another soldier–emperor in Byzantium to complete the work that Maurice had begun on the eastern frontier. Heraclius, son of the Exarch of North Africa, achieved more than any Roman Emperor before him by driving off the Persians from Constantinople in 626 and then utterly destroying their army at Nineveh in the heart of their own territory. The Persian Empire, the ancient rival and only equal of the Roman Empire, was ruined. Jerusalem was recovered. The True Cross was taken in triumph to Constantinople. It seemed as if the balance of power between east and west had been decisively tipped. Like Justinian, Heraclius now felt free to turn his mind to other areas of his empire. But whereas Justinian had found freedom only by patching up a treaty with the Persian king, Heraclius had laid the Persians low for ever. The mood of confidence and euphoria which his great victory induced was soon to be shattered; and perhaps Heraclius is to be blamed for not having foreseen that the defeat of the Persians left the way open for the Arabs. But for a moment before his death in 641 it was possible for him to see his empire as a whole stretching from Italy to the Euphrates.[2]

As the son of a former Exarch of Carthage, Heraclius understood the significance of these military enclaves in the west. He appointed as his Exarch in Ravenna an officer called Isaac who had served under him on the eastern frontier. It was probably Isaac who kept the emperor aware of the new developments in the province of Venetia and of the necessity of maintaining a strong naval establishment in the islands at the head of the Adriatic as an alternative base for the imperial fleet at Ravenna.[3] An inscription in the church now called Santa Maria Assunta at Torcello provides the earliest contemporary evidence for the continuing concern of Byzantium for Venice in the seventh century. It records that, in the twenty-ninth year of the reign of Heraclius (639), this church of St Mary the Mother of God was founded on the order of the Exarch Isaac as a memorial of his own achievements and those of his army. The building was completed by the local *magister militum* Maurice, then resident governor of the province of Venetia, and consecrated by its bishop Maurus. The governor Maurice was buried in the church. This

---

[1] G. Ostrogorsky, *History of the Byzantine State* (Oxford, 1968), pp. 80–3; Diehl, *Etudes sur l'administration byzantine*. For the geographical extent of the Exarchate of Ravenna, see P. Goubert, *Byzance avant l'Islam*, II, 2: *Rome, Byzance et Carthage* (Paris, 1965), pp. 39–48.

[2] Ostrogorsky, *History*, pp. 92–105.

[3] On the Exarch Isaac (625–43), see L. M. Hartmann, *Untersuchungen zur Geschichte der byzantinischen Verwaltung in Italien (540–750)* (Leipzig, 1889), pp. 14–15, 115; Hartmann, *Geschichte Italiens im Mittelalter*, II (Gotha, 1900), pp. 208–14; T. S. Brown, *Gentlemen and Officers*, pp. 149, 265.

precious lump of stone gives the lie to the tale later told that Venice had achieved political autonomy by the seventh century. The link with Byzantium and with the old Roman order of the world was still strong. In 639 the *Provincia Venetiarum* was still Byzantine territory governed by a master of soldiers answerable to the Exarch of Ravenna. It was a province made up of islands, of which, at that time, Torcello was evidently the most prosperous; though its governor was soon to make his permanent residence at Cittanova or Heraclea.[1]

The dedication of the cathedral at Torcello to 'the Mother of God', the Theotokos, demonstrates the religious Orthodoxy of the Christians of Venetia. The Council of Ephesos in 431 had confounded the heretics by declaring that Mary was the Mother of God and not simply the Mother of Christ. The definition had been accepted by the church universal, in west and east. In the seventh century the refugees in the Venetian islands may have built their houses of perishable mud and wattle; but they built their churches of stone and brick. The church provided the essential element of stability and continuity in their shattered lives. The leadership of the church, however, was not so easily resolved in the unsettled circumstances. When the Lombards had attacked Aquileia in 569, its bishop Paulinus had taken the relics and treasures of his church to Grado, among them the body of the martyr Hermagoras. When the coast was clear he went back to Aquileia. Ten years later, in 579, a new cathedral was built at Grado. By the eleventh century the Venetians claimed that the Emperor Heraclius had presented its bishop with the throne of St Mark, which had been brought from Alexandria to Constantinople by St Helena, the mother of Constantine. No such throne now exists. The so-called *Sedia di San Marco*, now in the Treasury of St Mark's, has no connexion with Heraclius or with the Evangelist and is more likely to have been a reliquary than a chair, unless its incumbent was a dwarf.[2]

St Mark was locally believed to have been the apostle of the northern Adriatic district and the founder of the church at Aquileia. Aquileia therefore claimed the status of an apostolic foundation and a patriarchate older

[1] V. Lazzarini, 'Un' iscrizione torcellana del sec. VII', reprint in *Scritti di paleografia e diplomatica* (Venice, 1938), pp. 120–131; A. Pertusi, 'L'iscrizione torcellana dei tempi di Eraclio', *ZRVI*, VIII (1964) (*Mélanges G. Ostrogorsky*, II), 317–39. Cf. Cessi, *Documenti*, I, no. 14, pp. 24–5.
[2] Paul the Deacon, II. 10: p. 78; John the Deacon, pp. 62–3; *Chronicon venetum (Altinate)*, ed. Simonsfeld, p. 49; ed. Cessi, p. 83; Dandolo, *Andreae Danduli Ducis Venetiarum Chronica*, ed. E. Pastorello, *RIS*, XII/1 (Bologna, 1938), p. 93. Cf. *DR*, I, no. 185. Brown, Bryer, Winfield, 'Cities of Heraclius', 35; A. Grabar, 'La Sedia di San Marco à Venise', *Cahiers Archéologiques*, VII (1954), 19–34; D. G(aborit)–C(hopin),'in *The Treasury of San Marco in Venice*, Exhibition Catalogue, The British Museum (Olivetti, Milan, 1984), pp. 98–105.

even than the apostolic church of St Mark at Alexandria. Fiction was piled upon fiction to support this claim. St Hermagoras (probably Hermogenes), whose relics were removed to Grado in the first exile, was said to have been a disciple of St Mark, along with St Fortunatus, of whom there were three versions and three sets of relics. The story that Heraclius gave the Evangelist's throne to Grado was no doubt meant to suggest that the Patriarch of Grado had his support. Rivalry between the ancient See of Aquileia and the upstart See of Grado had by then a long history. The Church of Aquileia stubbornly opposed the doctrinal decisions made at the Fifth Oecumenical Council at Constantinople in 553, decisions which the Church of Rome had supported. Pope Gregory the Great denounced its clergy as deviationists. The Bishops of Aquileia, once the sad victims of Lombard oppression, then turned to the Lombards for sympathy and protection.[1]

This schism between the 'Lombard' bishops of Aquileia and the 'Roman' bishops of Grado, though doctrinal in origin, had political consequences of long duration. It was a reflexion of the territorial schism between the Venetian mainland and the islands, a political division that persisted long after the doctrinal quarrel had been resolved at a synod at Pavia in 695. Two bishops presided over Christians of two divergent political interests, one nominally at Aquileia, the other at Grado, and each claiming the title of Patriarch. The Exarch of Ravenna had to keep the peace, through his deputy and governor in Heraclea. No help or support came from Constantinople after the death of Heraclius in 641. The Arab invasion of the eastern provinces of the Byzantine Empire began in the 630s, and within twenty years Syria, Palestine and Egypt were lost to the Christian world. They were the empire's richest provinces, in foodstocks, raw materials and manpower, as well as being the seats of three of the five recognised spiritual leaders of the Christian Church, Alexandria, Antioch and Jerusalem. The Arab conquests, compounded by the infiltration and settlement of the Slavs in the Balkans and Greece, inaugurated the dark age of Byzantium. In the west Ravenna held out against the Lombards and under its protection the islands in the lagoons of Venice continued to pay at least a nominal allegiance to the Emperor of the Romans. But before long the Arabs from North Africa were to begin their damaging raids first on Sicily and then on the coasts of southern Italy.

In 660 the Emperor Constans II, grandson of Heraclius, profited from a lull in the Arab onslaughts to visit his western provinces, beginning with Greece. From there he took a large army over to Italy. It was

[1] Kretschmayr, I, pp. 21–7; Demus, San Marco, pp. 10–11, 30–3; R. Cessi, 'Venice to the eve of the Fourth Crusade', in CMH, IV/1 (Cambridge, 1966), pp. 252–3.

the first time for many years that an emperor had visited Italy. Having seen Naples and Rome, where he was graciously received by the pope, Constans settled in Sicily. The Greek chroniclers allege that his intention was to move the capital of his empire to Syracuse, as though he had despaired of Byzantium. The western chroniclers relate that his purpose was to drive the Lombards out of Italy. Both accounts are probably distorted. Constans had other and personal reasons for leaving Constantinople. His visit to Italy is, however, evidence of the fact that he still saw the empire of east and west as one; and he certainly made a tentative effort to make war on the Lombards from Taranto. He may well have meant to use Syracuse as an operational base from which to attack the Lombards in Italy and resist the Arabs from North Africa. His true intentions will remain obscure. For in 668 a conspiracy contrived his murder. The rebels proclaimed an Armenian, Mezezios, as emperor. It was the Exarch of Ravenna, loyal to the house of Heraclius, who came to put down the rebellion and execute the leading conspirators.[1]

In the course of the seventh century the refugee communities on the Venetian islands developed into permanent settlements, whose leading families began to evolve their own political and administrative institutions. The life of the church was perpetuated through the succession of its bishops. Civic life went on through the appointment of tribunes, originally military officers subordinate to the *magister militum*. The tribunes had put down local roots as a landowning aristocracy before the migration from the mainland; and later Venetian chroniclers hailed them as the pioneers of the independence of the citizens. In theory they were no more than district officials subject to the Byzantine administration at Ravenna and so in the end to Constantinople, though in fact they exercised a large measure of political authority in their locale. John the Deacon, writing in the early 11th century, reports a momentous event in the constitutional history of Venice which he dates to the time of the Emperor Anastasios II (713-15) and of Liudprand, King of the Lombards (712-39). This was the appointment of the first *dux* or Doge of Venice. 'All the Venetians', he writes, 'together with the patriarch and the bishops in common council, determined that henceforth it would be more dignified to live under *duces* than under tribunes; and after much deliberation they nominated the illustrious Paulicius and set him up as *dux* at Heraclea.' Paulicius then negotiated a treaty with the Lom-

[1] Theophanes, *Chronographia*, ed. C. de Boor, I (Leipzig, 1883), pp. 348, 351; Cedrenus (Skylitzes-Kedrenos), *Compendium historiarum*, ed. I. Bekker, *CSHB* (1838), pp. 762-3; Paul the Deacon, v. 7-13: pp. 147-50; John the Deacon, pp. 80-4. Ostrogorsky, *History*, pp. 121-3; Brown, *Gentlemen and Officers*, pp. 66, 270.

bard king Liudprand which gave Venice independence and immunity from further attack.[1]

The story reads well, but it is half fiction. Paulicius, or Paul, was not a Venetian. He was a Byzantine official with the title of *dux* who was Exarch of Ravenna in the time of Liudprand. With the help of the *magister militum* Marcellus he marked out the boundaries of what remained of Venetian territory on the mainland. His demarcation was later accepted by Liudprand's successor Aistulf.[2] The myth that Paulicius was the first native Doge of Venice dies hard. In the days of Anastasios II, however, Venetia was still a Byzantine province. How long this could be so remained to be seen. There were those among the Venetians who welcomed the arrangement and saw in their connexion with the Exarchate their own salvation from the Lombards. There were others who resented it and looked to the day when they would cease to be provincials dependent on a distant empire which seemed in any case to be in poor shape. Matters were brought to a head in the second decade of the eighth century.

In 726 the Byzantine Emperor Leo III declared himself to be an iconoclast. Four years later he proclaimed his beliefs to be official. A decree went out from Byzantium that the creation and veneration of religious images was forbidden and that all existing icons must be destroyed. In Constantinople and the eastern provinces the decree could be enforced by the emperor's agents and there were many who supported and obeyed it. In the west, however, and especially in Italy, there was more shock than sympathy and the decree proved to be unenforceable. The pope protested; the towns of Italy rallied round him, for it was rumoured that the emperor had ordered his arrest and murder if he refused to obey the law. A mood of rebellion against Byzantium spread in Italy, encouraged by the Lombards. Paulicius, the Exarch of Ravenna, was assassinated in 727. The Venetians joined in the revolt. Their soldiers, locally recruited, turned against their *magister militum*. The tribunes and the clergy chose as their own leader Orso or Ursus, a native of Heraclea, who adopted the title of *dux*. The revolt was promptly and savagely suppressed. But the Emperor Leo tactfully conceded a measure of local autonomy to what he described as 'the province of Venetia conserved by God'. He recognised Orso as the first native governor or *dux* of Venice and granted him the Byzantine title of *hypatos* or consul. This was a first step towards the emancipation of Venice from the Exar-

---

[1] John the Deacon, p. 91. On the tribunes, see Brown, *Gentlemen and Officers*, pp. 56–7.

[2] Hartmann, *Untersuchungen*, pp. 21–3, 124–7; Kretschmayr, I, pp. 44–5, 418–19; R. Cessi, *Storia della Repubblica di Venezia*, 2nd edn, I (Milan, 1968), pp. 15–18. The identification of Paulicius with the Exarch Paul (c. 723–c. 727) is questioned by Brown, Bryer, Winfield, 'Cities of Heraclius', 31 n. 44.

chate of Ravenna, although *magistri militum* continued to be appointed alternately with the local *duces* for a few more years. No concession was made, however, with respect to the obedience of the province to Byzantine authority.[1]

The Lombard net meanwhile closed tighter. In 732 the Exarch of Ravenna was temporarily driven out by Lombard pressure. The Venetians loyally gave him asylum in their islands and provided ships to recover his city.[2] But in 751 the Exarchate was finally overrun and engulfed in the Kingdom of Lombardy. The province of Venice stood alone under the management of its own *dux*. The days of the *magistri militum* were over. It was perhaps inevitable that these events should provoke a struggle for power among the leading families in the islands. In 742 the people of Malamocco had rebelled against the administration in Heraclea and elected as their own *dux* a son of Orso called Teodato (Deusdedit). Local loyalties fuelled the fires of conflict among the islanders. Some were for and some were against maintaining their link with the Byzantine Empire, but the conflict among them was as much a matter of rivalry between families and between island communities. Certainly the enmity of Malamocco for Heraclea was brought about by family jealousies.[3] There was jealousy also in the church. In 774–5 a new bishopric was created at Olivolo (Castello) on the Rialto group of islands. It was set up by and under the protection of the *dux* of Malamocco. Its cathedral was dedicated to St Peter. The fact that its first bishop, Christopher, bore a Greek name suggests a Byzantine influence in its creation, though it cannot be proved. What is more provable by events is the jealousy which this upstart bishopric aroused in the older diocese of Grado. The struggle for power between Malamocco and Grado was long and bitter. But it was essentially a local feud, a storm in a teacup, engendered and prolonged by ecclesiastical rivalry and domestic intrigue among the contending families and their islands. The larger world beyond the islands was not affected or concerned, except when the rival parties sought to enlist the support of the Lombards, the Franks, or the Byzantines.[4]

Yet the Venetians retained a powerful sense of loyalty to Byzantium in the second half of the eighth century. It was especially strong during

---

[1] *Imperialis iussio* of Leo III and Constantine to the province of Venice, in Cessi, *Documenti*, I, no. 21, pp. 31–2; *DR*, I, no. 293. Kretschmayr, I, pp. 45–9, 419–20; R. Cessi, *Le origini del ducato veneziano*, Collana storica, IV (Naples, 1951), pp. 155ff.; Cessi, 'Venetiarum provincia', *BF*, II (1967), 91–9.

[2] Paul the Deacon, VI. 54: p. 184; John the Deacon, p. 95. O. Bertolini, 'Quale fu il vero oggiettivo assegnato da Leone III "Isaurico" all' armata di Manes, stratego di Cibyrreoti', *BF*, II (1967), 38–42, 46.

[3] Kretschmayr, I. pp. 48–50; Cessi, in *CMH*, IV/1, pp. 254–6.

[4] John the Deacon, p. 99. Kretschmayr, I, pp. 52–4.

the regime of the Doge Maurizio Galbaio and his son and grandson. The Galbaii were one of the old romanised families of Heraclea, who claimed descent from the Emperor Galba. Maurizio was honoured with the Byzantine titles of *hypatos* and *stratelates*, the Greek equivalent of the Latin *magister militum*; and he was pleased to style himself consul and imperial *dux* of the province of Venetiae. He also co-opted his son Giovanni as his colleague in authority, a practice which he learnt from the emperors in Constantinople who ensured the succession for their own families by crowning their eldest sons. No doubt the Doge Maurizio had authority from Byzantium to imitate this example, which was followed again when Giovanni co-opted his own son, Maurizio II, as Doge. The office of *dux* had never been hereditary in the Byzantine administration. There were many who hoped that it would not become so in Venice.[1]

Giovanni succeeded his father in 787. In the same year the first period of iconoclasm came to an end in Byzantium. A council of bishops held at Nicaea and summoned by the widowed Empress Eirene declared that traditional Orthodox belief in the matter of religious imagery was, after all, correct and that the iconoclasts were in heresy.[2] The popes and the western part of the church universal had said so all along and were thus pleased that the Byzantine church had seen and admitted the error of its ways. But in the sixty years since Leo had first propounded and enforced the heresy much had happened in the western world. The popes had felt unable to trust or to rely upon emperors who offended not only against the faith but also against the rights of the Roman Church, as Leo had done by detaching some of its provinces. They felt too that no material help against the Lombards was likely to come from emperors in Constantinople who could hardly hold their own eastern frontiers against the Arabs and the Bulgars. The popes therefore turned for comfort and support to the rising power of the Kingdom of the Franks. After the fall of Ravenna in 751 Pope Stephen II had asked the emperor to send an army. No army came. Disillusioned, the pope appealed to Pepin III, King of the Franks, and crossed the Alps to confer with him. In the spring of 754 he consecrated Pepin and his sons Charles and Carloman and bestowed titles on them. The Byzantine Emperor had failed to act as champion and defender of the papacy against the Lombards. The part would now be played by the Frankish king. A Byzantine embassy that went to the court of Pepin in 756 was informed that all the imperial territory in northern and central Italy, including Ravenna, now belonged

---

[1] J. B. Bury, *History of the Eastern Roman Empire* (London, 1912), pp. 321–2; Kretschmayr, I, pp. 51–2, 420; Brown, *Gentlemen and Officers*, p. 170.

[2] Ostrogorsky, *History*, pp. 177–9.

to the throne of St Peter. The papal state of Italy had been born. The Donation of Pepin was enshrined in the forged document known as the Donation of Constantine.[1]

The alliance between the papacy and the Franks challenged the Byzantine claim to the government of northern Italy. The Emperor Constantine V hoped to undermine it by winning the Franks to his side. But the spectacular victories over the Lombards first of Pepin and then of Charlemagne demonstrated that the Franks and not the Byzantines were masters of the situation in that part of the world; and the popes would do no business with Constantine, who was an even more fervent iconoclast than his father Leo. Charlemagne completed the conquest of the Lombard kingdom in 774 and went on to conquer Istria in 788. The province of Venetia was all that was left to the Byzantine Empire, and it was a province deeply divided. The arrival on the scene of the Franks aggravated the already existing divisions. Some saw in it the means of their salvation, or at least of the righting of their supposed wrongs and the fulfilment of their ambitions. Others, like the Doge Maurizio and his family, stayed loyal to Constantinople for all that its emperor was a condemned heretic. By the time that iconoclasm was renounced by the Empress Eirene in 787 affairs in northern Italy had acquired a momentum of their own which the Byzantines could no longer check or control. The islands of Venice seemed to be at the mercy of the Franks. Byzantine sovereignty over them had been (tacitly) accepted in the treaty which the pope had made with Pepin in 754. But when Pepin's son annexed Istria in 788 he intervened directly in Venetian concerns by transferring its bishops to the jurisdiction of the See of Aquileia. Venetian merchants were expelled from the ports of the former Exarchate. When John, the Patriarch of Grado, proclaimed his allegiance to Charlemagne, the Doge Maurizio had him hunted down and murdered as a traitor. The feuds between the ruling families and the islands of Venice were now more than ever fought under the banners of the Frankish and the Byzantine factions.[2]

On Christmas Day in the year 800 Pope Leo III placed a crown on the head of Charles the Great. In the pope's mind a new empire had been created. The old Empire of the Romans, then presided over by a woman, the Empress Eirene, was now rejuvenated under the aegis of an emperor from the west. This was the culmination of the policy of Pope Leo's predecessors in fostering their alliance with the Kingdom of the Franks. Whether Charlemagne himself saw eye to eye with the

[1] M. V. Anastos, 'Iconoclasm and imperial rule 717–842', in *CMH*, IV/1 (1966), pp. 75–6; Ostrogorsky, *History*, pp. 169–70. *DR*, I, no. 318; Cessi, *Documenti*, I, no. 28, pp. 44–5.
[2] Kretschmayr, I, pp. 53–4.

pope in this interpretation of the event is matter for debate. But the Byzantines were shocked and offended. The coronation of a second emperor struck at the very roots of Byzantine political theory. In the world of Charlemagne and Eirene it was axiomatic that the divine order depended on the preservation of a single *imperium romanum*; and just as there was only one God in heaven so there could be only one emperor on earth. On this point the pope was in agreement. By crowning Charlemagne he had effectively transferred the single sovereign authority in the world from Constantinople back to its origins in the west. The Byzantines were justified in questioning the right or the power of a Bishop of Rome to make or unmake emperors. But the insult to their pride stung them more deeply than the constitutional issue.[1]

In 802 ambassadors from Charlemagne and the pope went to Constantinople to see if a settlement could be reached. They are said to have been empowered to arrange a marriage between the new western emperor and the Empress Eirene.[2] It would have been a remarkable union. But Eirene was violently deposed in October of the same year; and her successor Nikephoros elected to bury his head in the sand of the Byzantine imperial myth in the hope that the problem in the west would go away. At the level of political theory and constitutional rights it would have been possible to come to some arrangement with Charlemagne, as was in the end to be proved. But at the level of political power and territorial rights it was a fact that Charlemagne ruled over an acreage of the globe almost as large as if not larger than that of the shrunken Byzantine Empire, while his eastern frontiers encroached upon the western provinces of that empire. This was all too obvious at the head of the Adriatic Sea. The Franks had taken possession of Istria and of northern Dalmatia even before 800. They might at any moment decide to occupy or to propose a protectorate of the islands of Venice. They knew that many of the islanders would have welcomed them, if only to achieve their own selfish purposes.

The welcoming party for the Franks came at last to power in Malamocco in 802. The Doges Giovanni and Maurizio II were sent into exile taking their Bishop of Olivolo with them. The coup had been planned and led by a former tribune, Obelerio, who now installed himself as

---

[1] F. Dölger, 'Europas Gestaltung im Spiegel der Fränkisch–byzantinischen Auseinandersetzung des 9. Jahrhunderts', in *Byzanz und die europäische Staatenwelt* (Ettal, 1953), pp. 282–369; W. Ohnsorge, *Das Zweikaiserproblem im früheren Mittelalter* (Hildesheim, 1947); Ohnsorge, *Abendland und Byzanz* (Darmstadt, 1958), especially pp. 1–49; R. Jenkins, *Byzantium. The Imperial Centuries, AD 610–1071* (London, 1966), pp. 105–16; Ostrogorsky, *History*, pp. 182–6; K. Leyser, 'The Tenth Century in Byzantine–Western Relationships', in *Relations between East and West in the Middle Ages*, ed. D. Baker (Edinburgh, 1973), pp. 33–4.

[2] Theophanes, *Chronographia*, ed. de Boor, I, p. 475.

Doge in Malamocco. He had acted more from personal jealousy than political realism. But the pro-Frankish faction were on his side. In the fashion that seemed to have been set he appointed his brother Beato as his colleague in power. One of their accomplices was the Patriarch of Grado, Fortunatus, who had gone to Charlemagne's court to seek the restitution of his bishoprics, which had been transferred to Aquileia. He got little comfort from the Franks. In Constantinople, however, the overthrow of the loyalist party by Obelerio was interpreted as rebellion. The rebels may have toyed with the idea of setting up a state independent of Franks and Byzantines alike. They forbade Fortunatus, as the friend of Charlemagne, to return to his church at Grado. But they soon found that they could not go it alone. At Christmas in 805 their leaders, Obelerio and Beato, went to see Charlemagne armed with rich gifts and high hopes. He set the seal of his authority on their usurpation of the province or duchy of Venice. They could hold it as a fief of his empire. In February 806, when he apportioned his empire among his sons, Charlemagne assigned Venetia, Istria and Dalmatia to Pepin, in his capacity as King of Italy.[1]

What had appeared to be a local rebellion in a distant province had now developed into a much more dangerous threat to Byzantine interests. The Emperor Nikephoros could no longer bury his head in the sand. He sent a fleet up the Adriatic to fly the Byzantine flag and restore order. Its admiral was the patrician Niketas. No imperial navy had been seen in those waters since the fall of Ravenna. The sight made a great impression. There was no resistance. The small Frankish fleet based at Comacchio at the mouth of the Po pretended not to notice; and Niketas anchored his ships in the lagoons of Venice without interference. He was an intelligent man and he had full powers to negotiate a settlement. He wisely decided that it would be better to sanction than to oppose the consequences of the coup d'état. Obelerio was confirmed in office as Doge and honoured with the Byzantine title of *spatharios*. His brother Beato, however, was taken as a hostage to Constantinople, and with him went the Bishop of Olivolo. The Patriarch of Grado, Fortunatus, was nowhere to be found. He had already fled to his friends the Franks. Venice was thus reconstituted as a province of the Byzantine Empire under its own *dux* or Doge, whose position was now legally ratified. Niketas completed his business by making a truce with Pepin, King of Italy. It was signed in Ravenna and was to run until August 808. Pepin, whose fief was supposed to include Venice, could not compete with the Byzantine navy. He was ready to sign his part of a mutual

[1] Bury, *History of the Eastern Roman Empire*, p. 323; Kretschmayr, I, pp. 54–6.

agreement. He would see to it that the province was protected from the mainland if the Byzantines would help to protect Istria against raids from the Slavs in the interior.[1]

The truce ran its course. Obelerio's brother Beato was allowed to go back to Venice from Constantinople, adorned with the title of *hypatos*. This was perhaps a mistake. Obelerio was not content to be a lackey of Byzantium. He welcomed Beato back as his colleague and strengthened his position by co-opting a third brother, Valentino, as co-regent. The news was reported to the emperor, and in the autumn of 808 another Byzantine fleet sailed up the Adriatic. It was commanded by Paul, *strategos* or military governor of the theme of Cephalonia in the Ionian Sea. Paul handled matters less tactfully than Niketas. The ducal triumvirate were not pleased to see him and stirred up as much trouble as they could; and he went out of his way to antagonise the Franks. In the spring of 809, having spent the winter in Venice, Paul launched an unprovoked attack on the harbour of Comacchio. He was beaten off after a skirmish with the garrison and forced to make new terms with the Franks before sailing away south to his own headquarters. Pepin was understandably annoyed by this example of Byzantine duplicity. When Paul and his fleet had gone, he answered a call for help from the Doge Obelerio and his colleagues, who saw their power slipping from them. The finer points of the intrigues and rivalries of the islanders in the lagoons were lost on Pepin. He came down with a heavy hand on Venetians of all persuasions. His army attacked them from the mainland, his ships from the sea. Heraclea and other settlements were captured and sacked, and finally Malamocco fell. The fighting went on for six months. It might have gone on longer if the *strategos* Paul had not reappeared on the scene with his Byzantine fleet. He had come not to rescue the Venetians from the consequences of their own folly but to deter the Franks from plundering the coast of Dalmatia. Pepin withdrew, but not before he had imposed the payment of an annual tribute on the wretched Doges Obelerio and Beato, who were now virtually his prisoners. He died a few months later, in July 810.[2]

Pepin's intervention changed the course of history for Venice. The islanders had for the most part sunk their differences in the resistance to his attack; and in the end the victory went to them. But it was not

---

[1] *Annales Regni Francorum 741–829*, ed. F. Kurze, MGH, SGUS (Hanover, 1895), *a.* 806, 807, pp. 122, 124; John the Deacon, pp. 103–4; Dandolo, p. 131. Bury, *History of the Eastern Roman Empire*, p. 324; Kretschmayr, I, pp. 56, 422.

[2] *Annales Regni Francorum*, ed. F. Kurze, *a.* 809, 810, pp. 127, 130; John the Deacon, pp. 104–5; Dandolo, p. 132; Constantine Porphyrogenitus, *DAI*, I, c. 28, pp. 119–21. Kretschmayr, I, pp. 56–8, 422.

a victory for the old warring factions among them, nor for the Doges
who had provoked the attack and the destruction of their earliest settlements. The victims and the refugees collected on the still sparsely popu-
lated islands of Rialto; and it was there, when the dust had settled, that
they began to rebuild their society and its institutions. The soil of Rialto
was fertile; there were settlers enough to cultivate it and to fill its islands;
and it already had a spiritual centre for their new hopes and ambitions
in the bishopric of Olivolo, with its church of St Peter. The loss of
Heraclea and of Malamocco and the discovery of Rialto as the new political and ecclesiastical centre of the Venetian people purged them of their
past and inspired them with a fresh sense of unity and independence.

The importance of this encounter between Franks and Venetians and
its consequences were for long remembered in Constantinople. The
Emperor Constantine VII Porphyrogenitus, writing in the middle of
the tenth century, gives a stirring account of the Venetian resistance to
Pepin's invasion. It derives from Venetian sources. It does not belittle
Venetian heroism. But it is naïvely slanted to show where the loyalties
of Venice really lay. When Pepin first tried to cross over from Alviola
on the mainland to the island of Malamocco, we are told that the Venetians
laid down spars and blocked the crossing. Pepin, baffled by this
manoeuvre, said to them: 'You are beneath my hand and my providence,
since you are of my country and my domain.' The Venetians, however,
replied: 'We want to be servants of the Emperor of the Romans and
not of you.'[1] If they had been unanimous in this opinion things might
never have come to the crisis of the year 809–10. Constantine Porphyrogenitus recorded what he was able to discover almost 150 years afterwards. But at the time the crisis of Venice was seen in another light
in Constantinople. It was a signal to the Byzantine government that
it could no longer postpone the day when it must come to terms with
the Frankish Empire in the west. The Venetians were the indirect agents
of the first agreement between the Eastern and the Western Emperors.

In 810 the Emperor Nikephoros sent an ambassador to Pepin. He
was the *spatharios* Arsaphios. He reached Italy to find that Pepin had
died in July. He went on over the Alps to see Charlemagne at his palace
at Aachen, where he was received in October. The terms agreed between
Arsaphios and the Western Emperor showed a remarkable appreciation
of reality. Far from holding out for his rights as Emperor of the Romans
everywhere, Charlemagne promised to relinquish his claim to the Byzantine province of Venetia and to hand it back to the Byzantine Emperor
together with the provinces of Istria, Liburnia and the towns on the

---

[1] *DAI*, c. 28, p. 121.

Dalmatian coast which the Franks had occupied. The *quid pro quo* was that the Byzantines should recognise his right to the title of emperor. The terms were formally set out in a letter which he gave Arsaphios to take back to Constantinople. He also handed over the Doge Obelerio, whom he had been holding in custody, to be taken to Constantinople to be punished for his treachery 'by his rightful lord'. In the spring of 811 Arsaphios went back to Venice. With the consent of the people he declared Obelerio and Beato to be deposed from office and solemnly confirmed the election, in the name of his emperor, of a new Doge of Venice. His name was Agnello Partecipazio, and he had been a hero of the resistance to the Franks. The seat of his government and of the new age which now seemed to dawn for Venice was Rialto.[1]

Arsaphios had done his work well. He sailed back to Constantinople with the disgraced Obelerio as his prisoner. Beato too was banished from Venice and sent to Zara on the Dalmatian coast, though their youngest brother Valentino was allowed to stay since he was thought to be too young to make trouble. The terms of the treaty which Arsaphios took with him had still to be ratified in Constantinople. The clause relating to Charlemagne's imperial title might well have proved difficult for Nikephoros to accept. But he was killed fighting the Bulgars on his northern frontier in July 811. The new emperor, Michael I, was more accommodating and also under greater pressure. His secretariate devised a formula which would save face on both sides. In return for handing over Venice and the other territories that Pepin had occupied, Charlemagne was to be recognised as emperor, though not as Emperor of the Romans. His status would be that of an emperor in abstract, holder of a unique and personal distinction graciously conferred upon him by the one true Emperor in Constantinople. As Constantine Porphyrogenitus was to put it in later years: 'This Charles, the elder, was sole ruler over all the western kingdoms and reigned as an emperor in Great Francia.'[2] That Charlemagne was ready to accept this formula is not too surprising. Unlike the pope who had crowned him, he believed that his title of emperor could only be validated by reference to the source of all imperial power in Constantinople. This much he had achieved.

In ratifying the terms of this first treaty between the Emperor whose power was universal and eternal and an emperor whose status was personal and provisional, the Byzantines seem to have been more anxious about matters of protocol than about the defining of frontiers. Yet agreement was also reached on these more practical considerations. In 812 another embassy from Constantinople went to Aachen. It was led by

---

[1] *Annales Regni Francorum, a.* 810, 811, pp. 132–4; John the Deacon, pp. 105–6. *DR,* I, no. 371.
[2] *DAI,* c. 26, p. 109.

Michael, Bishop of Philadelphia, accompanied by Arsaphios, now raised
to the higher rank of *protospatharios*, and by one Theognostos. Having
hailed Charlemagne in Greek and in Latin as *basileus* and *imperator*,
the ambassadors got down to business. The question of territorial rights
over the Byzantine provinces at the head of the Adriatic was discussed
and settled in detail. The settlement was based on that made by the
admiral Niketas with King Pepin five years before, but it provided a
clearer definition of where the frontiers lay and of how they would affect
the passage of travellers and goods and the payment of customs dues.
So far as concerned Venice it was agreed that the province should remain
under Byzantine jurisdiction, while continuing to pay tribute to the Frankish King of Italy. The text of the treaty was signed by Charlemagne.
The second copy was signed in Constantinople by Michael I's successor,
Leo V, and confirmed by Charlemagne's successor in 814.[1]

   This document, though drawn up between two powers far greater
than Venice, secured the new foundations for development which the
Venetians had already laid when they abandoned the wreckage of their
past and centred their hopes for the future on the islands of Rialto. They
were still legally tied to Byzantium and still tributaries of the Franks.
But they were not the property of either. The treaty of 812 guaranteed
their protection against enemies from the mainland, fixed their boundaries
with the Kingdom of Italy, and above all recognised the rights of their
merchant ships to sail freely about their business. These benefits had
been achieved not through the efforts of the Venetians themselves but
through Byzantine diplomacy; and for a while the Venetians were duly
grateful. They had gained the liberty to evolve in their own style with
the minimum of dependence on either of the great powers that might
have hemmed them in. Their submission to Byzantium assured their
immunity from harm in Italy. This was in fact the last direct intervention
of Byzantium in the affairs of Venice, but it was to have an enduring
effect on relations between the ancient empire on the Bosporos and the
emerging city–state in the lagoons.

---

[1] *Annales Regni Francorum, a.* 812–14, pp. 136–40; *DR*, I, no. 385. Kretschmayr, I, pp. 56–9;
   Cessi, *Storia*, I, pp. 29–34. On the embassies sent from Constantinople to Venice and to
   Charlemagne, see T. C. Lounghis, *Les Ambassades byzantines en Occident depuis la fondation
   des états barbares jusqu'aux Croisades (407–1096)* (Athens, 1980), pp. 159–62.

2

VENICE:
THE BYZANTINE PROTECTORATE

THE continuing interest of Byzantium in Venice cannot be explained solely in terms of the emperors' claims to universal *imperium*. The bubble of Justinian's imperialistic dream had been pricked first by the Lombards and then by the Franks. Sicily, parts of south Italy and some of the Dalmatian coast were still in Byzantine control at the beginning of the ninth century. Venice was a remote corner, isolated except by sea. It might be argued that Byzantine interests there had been preserved by the accident of the clash between the empires of east and west about 800. The settlement that came out of that confrontation laid certain mutual obligations on Venetians and Byzantines alike. Thereafter the Emperors in Constantinople expected that the Venetians would do their duty by sending ships to reinforce the Byzantine navy in south Italy when required; their expectations were often realised. But there were other factors that connected the interests of Byzantium and Venice.

The earliest Venetian chroniclers were well informed about Byzantine affairs, though they tended to interpret them in their own way. John the Deacon has as much to say about the Emperors of Constantinople and their families as he has about the Lombard or Frankish kings. Constantine Porphyrogenitus, on the other hand, who was writing half a century earlier, knew a surprising amount about the history and topography of Venice. He was aware that its inhabitants, originally called Enetikoi, had at first lived on the mainland in Concordia and other cities before they crossed over to the islands. The strongly fortified city in which the *dux* or Doge resided in the tenth century was surrounded by six miles of sea into which twenty-seven rivers flowed. But Constantine knew that the earliest seat of the Doge had been at Cittanova or Heraclea. He enumerates and names the other islands and settlements – the Lidi from north to south, from Grado (Kogradon) with its metropolitan church containing many saints' relics to Loreo (Lauriton), including Malamocco (Madaukon), Alviola (Hēvola) and Chioggia (Klougia); the islands behind the Lidi, Torcello, Murano and Rialto, 'which means

20

the highest point'; and the cities on the mainland.[1]

Constantine further records that the annual tribute payable by the Venetians to King Pepin was still being paid in his day, though at a diminishing rate.[2] More significant, however, is his qualification of the island of Torcello as 'the great trading station' or emporium of Venice. For this confirms that even in the tenth century Torcello was still the principal market in the lagoons as it had been four centuries earlier. Neither Heraclea nor Malamocco had usurped its place in this respect and the days of Rialto as the centre of Venetian trade and commerce were yet to come. Trade was undoubtedly one of the mutual interests between Venice and Byzantium. The Venetians took naturally to the sea. Cassiodorus, when secretary to the Gothic King Theodoric in 537, had poetically likened them to seabirds nesting in their islands, their settlements and houses protected by only the frailest of bulwarks against the expanse of sea. He praised them for their skill in navigation, for their egalitarian society and for their self-sufficiency; and he observed that they were blessed with two natural sources of wealth, their fish and their saltpans. Men could do without gold but not without salt.[3] In Cassiodorus's day Venetian seamen were already being employed to ferry wine and oil from Istria to Ravenna.[4] They quickly adapted to the larger role of middlemen between east and west. Byzantine merchants would bring luxury goods from the east to the market at Torcello and Venetian traders would then distribute them in the west, in Italy, France and Germany. The means of exchange was barter. The Byzantines would take payment in the form of timber for shipbuilding, of slaves, of metal, or of salt and fish, which were the two staple products of Venetian waters. But by the ninth century if not earlier Venetian ships were sailing as far afield as Syria, Palestine and Egypt. For a time, though not for long, they stopped trading there, in obedience to a decree of the Emperor Leo V that his Christian subjects should avoid travelling to the Holy Land and Muslim-occupied countries.[5]

Apart from trade the Byzantines held Venice to be important to them as a kind of early-warning station. In another remote corner of their

---

[1] Constantine Porphyrogenitus, *DAI*, I, c. 27, pp. 116–19; II, pp. 91–3. H. Kretschmayr, 'Die Beschreibung der venezianischen Inseln bei Konstantin Porphyrogennetos', *BZ*, XIII (1904), 482–9.

[2] Constantine Porphyrogenitus, *DAI*, I, c. 28, p. 120; II, p. 93.

[3] *Magni Aurelii Cassiodori Variarum Libri XII*, ed. Å. J. Fridh, Corpus Christianorum Series Latina, XCVI (Turnholt, 1973), VII, xxiv, pp. 491–2. Cessi, *Documenti*, I, no. 2, pp. 2–4.

[4] Cassiodorus, XII, xxvi, pp. 494–5.

[5] Dandolo, p. 144; T. L. F. Tafel and G. M. Thomas, *Urkunden zur älteren Handels- und Staatsgeschichte der Republik Venedig*, Fontes Rerum Austriacarum, Abt. II: Diplomata, XII–XIV (Vienna, 1856–7) (*TTh*) I, no. III, p. 3.

map they maintained a similar outpost at Cherson in the Crimea. Their
agents there, like their representatives at Venice, could report on the
movement and activities of the inhabitants of the huge land masses behind
their coastline. There was, however, a difference between the two. Cherson was constituted as a theme or military district of the empire under
the command of a *strategos* who was directly responsible to the emperor.[1]
In the same way Dalmatia, Durazzo (Dyrrachion), Nikopo-
lis, Cephalonia and the Peloponnese (Morea) were, or were to be, constituted as themes, each governed by its own *strategos*. Venice was much
more loosely tied to Constantinople. But being an essentially maritime
province it could provide a different kind of service for the empire by
sending its own ships and men to fight alongside the imperial fleet in
the Adriatic when called upon to do so. It was in the interest of both
parties to preserve a respectful if distant relationship.

The Venetians for their part were gratified to be counted as members
of a larger family which could provide them with greater rewards and
richer pickings than the Franks. Their Doges were for the time being
content to act as Byzantine officials, probably taking small salaries from
Constantinople, and rising through the gradations of the Byzantine court
dignities which the emperors saw fit to grant them. It gave them a sense
of belonging to a grander world from which they were eager to adopt
much of their culture and finesse. The office of *dux* or Doge was not,
of course, unique to Venice. The Byzantine governors of other parts
of Italy in the eighth and ninth centuries, such as Calabria and Sardinia,
held the same title and received the same dignities and remuneration
for their services. The *dux* of Calabria was honoured as an imperial *spatharios* or *protospatharios*. The governor of Sardinia was entitled *hypatos
et dux*.[2] In accordance with Byzantine practice such titles and honours
were granted *ad personam*. They were not held by hereditary tenure
in one family. The Doges of Venice often offended against this principle
by co-opting their sons to office. But they could point to the example
of the Byzantine Emperors, who did the same. Their absolutist tendencies
were, at least in theory, controlled by two annually appointed tribunes,
also subject to Constantinople. By sending their sons to be honoured
at the Byzantine court, by contracting marriages with Byzantine ladies,
the ruling families of Venice showed their admiration and respect for
an older civilisation, from which they were to acquire many of their
own social customs. The one lesson that they had no wish to learn from

[1] Constantine Porphyrogenitus, *De Thematibus*, ed. A. Pertusi, Studi e Testi, 160 (Vatican
City, 1952), pp. 98–100, 182–3.
[2] A. Pertusi, 'L'impero bizantino e l'evolvere dei suoi interessi nell' Alto Adriatico', in V.
Branca, ed., *Storia della civiltà veneziana*, I (Florence, 1979), p. 59.

Byzantium was constitutional theory. That they were to evolve on their own and in their own unique fashion. The evolution was long, violent and painful. But the Republic which in the end took shape, though gilded with a Byzantine façade, owed little to the political system of the East Roman Empire.

From 810 to 836 Venice was ruled by members of the family of Partecipazio. Agnello, the first of them (811–27), had risen to power on the wave of reaction against his pro-Frankish predecessors. It was he who laid the foundations of the city on the Rialto, whose islands had been settled in the time of the Galbaii when the bishopric of Olivolo was created. His residence was on the site of the later Doge's palace. Alongside it arose a chapel dedicated to the Greek saint Theodore, built by a wealthy Byzantine called Narses. Perhaps he was really the admiral Niketas, masquerading under a Greek name that was more familiar to Venetian chroniclers.[1] The Emperor Leo V, who came to the throne in Constantinople in 813, took an active interest in the foundation of the new city. Agnello had cause to be grateful to the Byzantines. He saluted Leo's accession by sending his elder son Giustiniano to his court, where the Emperor decorated him with the title of *hypatos* or consul. Eight years later he celebrated the accession of the new Emperor, Michael II, by sending his grandson to Constantinople, where he seems to have taken a Greek wife called Romana.[2]

Giustiniano was his father's appointed colleague and eventual successor, though while he had been away in Constantinople in 814 his younger brother Giovanni had tried and failed to usurp his place. Giovanni fled first to Zara, then to the Franks and then to Constantinople; and Giustiniano, thanks to Byzantine influence, became Doge of Venice in his own right in 827. His full title was: *imperialis hypatus et humilis dux provinciae Venetiarum*.[3] The word *humilis* indicated his loyal subservience to the Byzantine Emperor. Subservience brought its rewards. About 819 the Emperor Leo V presented a number of holy relics to the new city of Venice: a piece of the True Cross, the Virgin's veil, some fragments of Christ's raiment and the body of St Zaccaria (Zacharias), the father of St John the Baptist. It was a public demonstration of the emperor's favour. The convent of St Zaccaria, built to house the saint's relics, was endowed by the same emperor and erected by Byzantine

---

[1] G. Saccardo, 'L'antica chiesa di S. Teodoro in Venezia', *Archivio Veneto*, XXXIV (1887), 91–113; Kretschmayr, I, pp. 86–7; Demus, *San Marco*, p. 21.

[2] John the Deacon, pp. 106, 107; Dandolo, pp. 142, 144. *TTh*, I, no. IV, p. 4.

[3] Such is the signature on his last will and testament in 829: Cessi, *Documenti*, I, no. 53, p. 99; Kretschmayr, I, pp. 60–1.

masons sent from Constantinople at his expense.[1] Every Christian church must have its relics and every city its patron saint. St Zaccaria was eminent enough; but the Doge's chapel was already patronised by Theodore the warrior saint; and best of all the throne of St Mark had long before been given to the bishopric of Grado by Heraclius. It had been assumed that the Church of Venice would come under the jurisdiction of the Patriarch of Grado. But in 827, at the synod of Mantua, an assembly of western bishops, under Frankish influence, declared that the ancient See of Aquileia was the proper Patriarchate of Venice. The intrigues of the ambitious Fortunatus, Patriarch of Grado, had much to do with their decision. He did not live to see his patriarchate relegated to a parish of Aquileia, for he died in 825.[2]

It was certainly neither by accident nor by coincidence that the body of St Mark was brought to Venice from Alexandria in 828, the year after the synod of Mantua. Grado might have the throne of St Mark but Venice would have his body. The translation of the relic was an act of blatant piracy committed by Venetian sailors who, only a few years before, had assured the emperor that they would not travel to the lands of the infidel. The deed was justified long afterwards by reference to a prophecy made by an angel to St Mark himself, to the effect that his corpse would one day rest in Venice. The generally accepted version of the story, as depicted in mosaic in the later basilica of St Mark, tells of the enterprise of two merchants of Venice who, with the help of two Greek monks, spirited the body away from its shrine in Alexandria by bribing its guardians and substituting the body of a lesser saint. When they got it on board their ship they protected it from the prying eyes of Arab port officials and from its own propensity to emit a rare odour of sanctity by covering it with haunches of pork. The Arabs, being pious Muslims, were appalled by the sight and stench of pig, and the ship made off with its precious cargo. It was all but wrecked on its miraculously rapid voyage back to Venice, but the saint was there to wake its captain and avert disaster. The merchants were afraid that they might be punished for their illegal visit to Egypt. They were assured that no charges could be brought against men who had performed so sacred a mission.[3]

The tale is no doubt embellished with fictitious details. But the fact of the robbery is incontrovertible and it is clear to see that it was motivated

[1] Dandolo, p. 142 (wrongly ascribing the donation to the time of Agnello). *TTh*, I, no. 1, pp. 1–3; *DR*, I, no. 399; Cessi, *Documenti*, I, no. 52, pp. 92–3.
[2] Cessi, *Documenti*, I, no. 50, pp. 83–90. Kretschmayr, I, pp. 63–6; Demus, *San Marco*, pp. 20–2, 33–5.
[3] The story of the Translation of the relics of St Mark is in *Acta Sanctorum Bollandiana*, III, 25 April, pp. 353ff.

as much by politics as by piety. It was a calculated stab at the pretensions of the Patriarchate of Aquileia. Not that the holy relic was intended to adorn the church at Grado. It was at first placed and kept in a secret chamber alongside the Doge's modest palace. In his will the Doge Giustiniano bade his widow build a basilica of St Mark; and this building, the first of its kind, was erected between the palace and the chapel of St Theodore in the time of his successor, in 832. But for many years to come the body of the saint was kept in its hiding place beside the seat of power. It was the symbol not of the Patriarchate of Grado, nor of the bishopric of Olivolo, but of the city of Venice.[1]

No Byzantine reaction to this act of piracy is recorded. No Byzantine source mentions the event. The acquisition of relics, by whatever means, was thought to be a Christian duty. In the course of time the Venetians amassed an impressive collection. The relics of St Sabas were taken from Constantinople at the end of the tenth century. Those of St Barbara were brought from Constantinople, quite legitimately, a few years later. The church of Grado, which became the episcopate of Venice and whose bishop resided at Olivolo, found its own patron saint in Nicholas of Myra, whose corpse was stolen from its shrine in Asia Minor in 1100. The remains of St Nicholas's uncle Nicholas were found and removed to Venice at the same time, along with those of St Theodore the Martyr. The relics of St Stephen the First Martyr were filched from Constantinople soon afterwards; and those of the martyr Isidore were translated from Chios in 1125.[2] These were all saints of the Greek and not the Latin persuasion and their presence was to add another link to the chain between Venice and the Byzantine world. But St Mark was unique. Until his body was brought to Venice in 828 the patron saint of the Doges had been another saint of Greek or Byzantine origin, Theodore Stratelates, the holy warrior who guided the hand of the *dux* or military governor of a Byzantine province. Earlier in the ninth century the pro-Byzantine faction had tried to make the church of Venice still more Greek by placing the relics of Sts. Sergios and Bacchus in the new cathedral at Olivolo. They were two saints who had shown particular favour to Justinian and Theodora. The attempt was not popular. The cathedral was already dedicated to St Peter and two Byzantine saints could not compete with him. But the warrior saint Theodore was quickly upstaged by St Mark as

---

[1] Kretschmayr, I, pp. 64–7. The will of Giustiniano Partecipazio is in Cessi, *Documenti*, I, no. 53, pp. 93–9.

[2] The body of St Sabas was bought from its custodians by Pietro Barbolano (Centranico), the later Doge (1026–32): Marino Sanudo, *Le vite dei Dogi di Venezia*, ed. G. Monticolo, *RIS*, XXII, pt IV (1900), pp. 138–9. On the relics of St Barbara: Dandolo, p. 202; *TTh*, I, no. XX, p. 41. On the relics of Saints Nicholas, Stephen and Isidore, see below, pp. 71–3, 76, 79.

patron of the city and the state. His chapel ceased to be the Doge's church. His name was almost forgotten and eclipsed by that of the apostle and evangelist whose symbol was the lion.[1]

In the reign of the Emperor Michael II, who succeeded Leo V in 820, the Arabs began to look further afield for plunder and conquest in the Mediterranean. The island of Crete was captured and turned into a pirates' nest by Arabs who were refugees from their own ruler in Spain. Others from North Africa crossed over to Sicily where they established themselves with the help of a Byzantine admiral, Euphemios, a pretender to the throne, who was murdered in 828. The Byzantines were unable to dislodge them. In 827 they made a determined attack on Syracuse, the capital of Sicily. Michael II sent an urgent request to the Doge Giustiniano Partecipazio to send some ships to reinforce the Byzantine fleet. This was the first of several such requests, all of which were answered. The Venetians evidently felt bound to respond to the call to support the Byzantine navy when there was trouble in Italian waters. Their first intervention was fruitless. The Arab blockade of Syracuse continued. In 828, again at the request of the emperor, they sent another flotilla to Sicily to join forces with a Byzantine fleet. The Arabs were driven into the interior of the island, but again the Venetians went home without scoring a decisive victory. In the meantime Giovanni Partecipazio had been allowed to go back to Venice from his exile in Constantinople; and his brother Giustiniano, who was in poor health, agreed to have him as his colleague and heir apparent. This could have happened only with the consent of the emperor and may perhaps have been a form of reward for the loyalty of the Venetians to his cause against the Arabs.[2]

Giovanni Partecipazio reigned as Doge for only five years. He was not liked, and in 836 he was forced to abdicate and was imprisoned in a monastery. The faction that prompted the rebellion failed, however, to secure the nomination of their own candidate as Doge. Instead the Venetians elected Pietro Tradonico. He was a native of Istria and a neutral party in the perennial feuds and contentions of the old Venetian families. His nomination must have been ratified, if it was not inspired, by the Byzantine government. In 840 an ambassador from Constantinople went to Venice to invest him with the imperial title of *spatharios*. Pietro Tradonico was thus brought within the Byzantine family. He soon gave evidence of his loyalty to the head of that family. Yet he made it clear too that he had a mind and a policy of his own. Under Tradonico's regime the theory of Venetian allegiance to Byzantium was subtly reinter-

---

[1] Dandolo, p. 168. Demus, *San Marco*, pp. 20–2.
[2] John the Deacon, pp. 109–10; Dandolo, pp. 144–8. *TTh*, I, no. v, p. 4; *DR*, I, no. 412. A. A. Vasiliev, *Byzance et les Arabes*, I (Brussels, 1935), pp. 61ff., 80–2.

preted. In matters of foreign policy Venice began to act as a free agent
with regard to its neighbours and its suzerains.[1]

The emperor who decorated him as *spatharios* was Theophilos, son
of Michael II, who had come to the throne in 829. His reign was marked
by diplomatic successes and military failures. Perhaps no emperor with
the resources available in the early ninth century could at the same time
have held the Arabs at bay in Asia Minor and in Sicily. The field of
operations was too extensive. In August 838 the Arabs in the east captured
the cities of Ankyra and Amorion. It was a major disaster. Theophilos,
made ill by anxiety, sent to the rulers of the west to beg for help, to
the Frankish court of Louis the Pious at Ingelheim and even to the
Ummayad Caliph of the Arabs in Spain. The Arabs in Sicily, however,
had occupied still more of the island and were using it as a base for
raids on the coast of Italy. About 838 they surprised the garrison in
Brindisi, burnt the town and sailed back to Sicily. In 839 they returned
and captured Taranto, where they installed a large army. It was the
Arab occupation of Taranto that prompted Theophilos to send his
embassy to Pietro Tradonico in Venice in 840. The envoy was Theodosios
the patrician (almost certainly to be distinguished from the bishop Theodosios Baboutzikos sent from Constantinople to Ingelheim). He stayed
for most of the year in Venice and persuaded the Doge to join in a
campaign against the Arabs in the south. He probably needed little persuasion. The Venetians had no desire to see the south of Italy in Arab
hands and the Adriatic infested with Arab pirates. Sixty ships were
equipped and manned for war and sent off to the south. Nearly all of
them were destroyed off Taranto. Their soldiers and sailors were killed
or captured. If each ship carried 200 men, the Venetians had suffered
12,000 casualties. They could not afford such losses.[2]

The Arabs at once advanced with fire and sword up the Adriatic Sea,
first along the Dalmatian coast where, at Easter in the year 841, it is
recorded that they burnt the village on the island of Cherso in the Gulf
of Quarnero (Kvarner). From there they sailed over to pillage Ancona
and the Italian coast as far north as the mouth of the Po. On their return
voyage they seized a number of Venetian ships that were making for
home. In 842 they appeared once more in the Gulf of Quarnero and

---

[1] John the Deacon, pp. 113–14; Dandolo, p. 150. *TTh*, I, no. VI, p. 4; *DR*, I, no. 437 (dating
the embassy to 838). Kretschmayr, I, pp. 92–3; E. Lentz, 'Der allmähliche Übergang Venedigs
von faktischer zu nomineller Abhängigkeit von Byzanz', *BZ*, III (1894), 65–70.

[2] Vasiliev, *Byzance et les Arabes*, I, pp. 144ff., 177–84, where the date of these events is established, as well as the distinction between the Theodosios who went as envoy to Venice
and the Theodosios who went to Ingelheim. Cf. Lentz, 'Allmähliche Übergang', 69–70;
Lounghis, *Les Ambassades byzantines*, pp. 167–9.

again defeated a Venetian fleet near the little island of Sansego.[1] These first attempts at naval warfare by Venice, whether in co-operation with the Byzantines or on their own initiative, were scarcely crowned with success. But they taught the Venetians, and especially the Doge Tradonico, that they could no longer rely on the protection of the Byzantine navy. They must when necessary act independently, irrespective of their nominal allegiance to the emperor. Many believed that the disaster at Taranto had happened because the Greek admiral and his ships had run away, leaving the Venetians to fight alone. It was a sign of the changing mood in Venice that, after the engagement at Sansego, the Doge made a truce of his own with the Arab leaders without troubling to inform the emperor in Constantinople or his agents.

The same spirit of private enterprise inspired the making of the first treaty between Venice and the Franks, the oldest surviving document of Venetian diplomacy. It was signed at Pavia in February 840 by Charlemagne's grandson Lothair and the Doge Pietro Tradonico and is known as the *Pactum Lotharii*.[2] The initiative came from the Doge; the treaty was drawn up at his request and on his suggestion ('suggerente ac supplicante Petro, gloriosissimo duce Veneticorum'). It was to run for five years. Venice would continue to pay a yearly tribute to the Frankish Kingdom of Italy and would undertake to protect that kingdom by sea against the attack of Slav pirates. In return Venice's neutrality would be respected and its security from the mainland guaranteed. Venetian merchants would be assured of their freedom to trade by land, as would those of the Franks by sea. In September 841 Lothair signed another pact confirming the Venetians in undisputed possession of their territories as they had been defined in the time of Charlemagne by agreement with 'the Greeks'.[3]

These two documents opened the door for the progressive emancipation of the Venetians from outside dictation and control, whether from the west or from Byzantium. They remained tributaries of the Kingdom of Italy and theoretically servants of the Byzantine Empire. But the wording of the documents is revealing. Pietro Tradonico was proud to display his Byzantine title of *spatharios*. But the title is no longer qualified by the word 'imperial'. Nor does he, as his predecessors had done, describe himself as 'humble' (*humilis*). Instead he is 'the most glorious' *dux* of the Venetians. In later Venetian documents of state one can distinguish

[1] John the Deacon, pp. 114–15; Dandolo, p. 150. Vasiliev, *Byzance et les Arabes*, I, p. 183; II/1 (Brussels, 1968), pp. 10–11; Lentz, 'Allmähliche Übergang', 71–2.
[2] Cessi, *Documenti*, I, no. 55, pp. 101–8.
[3] Cessi, *Documenti*, I, no. 56, pp. 108–10. Kretschmayr, I, pp. 94–5, 431–5; Lentz, 'Allmähliche Übergang', 72–4, 81–2.

the protocol thought appropriate for those directed to Byzantium and those directed elsewhere. In the former the Doge no longer describes the emperor as his lord (*dominus noster*). He is Doge 'by the grace of God' (*Dei gratia*, or *Deo auxiliante dux*). His dominions are not called the *provincia Venetiae* but the *ducatus*; and his documents are dated not by the regnal year of the emperor in Constantinople, nor by the Byzantine system of chronology, but by the western computation of the *annus domini*. This was a gradual development. Venetian documents exist from as late as 982 and 1035 which are dated in western style but also with due deference to the names and regnal years of the emperors in Constantinople.[1]

The Franks were quicker than the Byzantines to accept the fact of Venetian independence. In March 856 Louis II, Lothair's son, confirmed the right of Venice to possession of lands within the Frankish Empire on the basis of the treaty of 812. A year later Louis paid a state visit to Venice. It was a grand occasion. The Doge and his son met the young emperor and his wife at Brondolo, south of Chioggia, and brought them to Rialto where they were entertained in great style for three days. Louis stood as godfather at the christening of the Doge's granddaughter.[2] The Byzantines could never approve of the idea that provincials might wish to run their own lives. It was contrary to the principle of the divinely ordained and universally comprehensive empire. Those kingdoms and principalities that had come into being independently beyond the frontiers could be accommodated in Byzantine theory. They had their places in the hierarchical world order, or family of kings, which was presided over by its *paterfamilias*, the Emperor of the Romans in Constantinople. It was within his power to grant them honorary degrees of affinity to his sacred person. Thus Charlemagne had been honoured as a 'spiritual brother' of the Emperor Michael I in 812, though his successors, like Lothair, ranked no higher than 'spiritual sons'. But it was hard to know how to accommodate Venice, which was a *ducatus* and not a kingdom.[3]

It may be by chance that no records survive of diplomatic or official

---

[1] Bury, *Eastern Roman Empire*, p. 328; Lentz, 'Allmähliche Übergang', 84–5; R.-J. Lilie, *Handel und Politik zwischen dem byzantinischen Reich und den italienischen Kommunen Venedig, Pisa und Genua in der Epoche der Komnenen und der Angeloi (1081–1204)* (Amsterdam, 1984), p. 3.

[2] Dandolo, p. 154: '(Lodovicus) ... Iohanis ducis genitam de sacro fonte levavit'. Lentz, 'Allmähliche Übergang', 92–3; Kretschmayr, I, p. 95; Cessi, *Storia*, I, p. 53.

[3] F. Dölger, 'Die "Familie der Könige" im Mittelalter', *Historisches Jahrbuch*, LX (1940), 397–420; G. Ostrogorsky, 'Die byzantinische Staatenhierarchie', *Seminarium Kondakovianum*, VIII (1936), 41–61; G. Ostrogorsky, 'The Byzantine Empire and the Hierarchical World Order', *Slavonic and East European Review*, XXXV (1965), 1–14.

exchanges between Byzantium and Venice in the years between 842 and 867. They were years in which the Byzantine Empire began slowly but purposefully to re-emerge as a great power after the dark age which had set in with the Arab and Slav invasions. The process began under Michael III who succeeded Theophilos in 842. It was triumphantly continued by Basil I, founder of the Macedonian dynasty, who murdered his way to the throne in 867. The new era opened with the second restoration of Orthodoxy after the somewhat ineffectual efforts of Leo V and Theophilos to reintroduce iconoclasm. It continued with an increasingly successful offensive against the Arabs in the east. Relations with the west, or at least with the papacy, were embittered by the schism between the Churches of Rome and Constantinople, resulting from the deposition of the Patriarch Ignatios and the appointment in his place of the Patriarch Photios in 858. The dispute that followed was, like that between the temporal rulers of east and west, symptomatic of a much deeper divergence of ideologies. It was aggravated rather than soothed by the work of Christian missionaries among the Slavs who had settled in the lands that lay between the two worlds of east and west, in Moravia, Serbia, Macedonia and Bulgaria. The christianisation of the Slavs became a race between Frankish missionaries from Rome and the west and Byzantine missionaries from Constantinople and the east. Mutual accusations were made of spreading false doctrine in theology and practice among the innocent heathen. The charges levelled against the Franks by the great Patriarch Photios, although in substance true, made compromise and understanding more difficult.

The competition to win Christian souls among the pagans had a lasting effect on the Slav population of Dalmatia on the Adriatic coast and hence indirectly on Venice. In the early years of the ninth century, as Constantine Porphyrogenitus relates, the Croats and Serbs and their other Slav neighbours in Dalmatia had abandoned any pretence of allegiance to Byzantium.[1] The coastal towns which had been there before the Slavs arrived had been allotted to the Byzantine Empire in the treaty with Charlemagne of 812. But they too had become independent and subject to no authority but their own; and in the south an autonomous Serbian kingdom had come into being. The anarchy of the Slavs was a threat to Venetian trade, as well as to the towns on the Dalmatian coast. The Venetians used the numerous islands off that coast as stepping-stones on their trade route to the east. Their activities were endangered by Slav pirate ships nesting in the islands; and with the Arabs apparently entrenched in the ports of Bari, Brindisi and Taranto on the Italian side

---

[1] Constantine Porphyrogenitus, *DAI*, I, c. 29, p. 125; II, pp. 103–4.

of the water, the Adriatic Sea was no longer in Venetian or in Byzantine control.

In 866 an Arab fleet of thirty-six ships from Italy attacked the Dalmatian coastal towns of Budva and Kotor and went on to blockade Ragusa (Dubrovnik). The inhabitants appealed for rescue to Constantinople. One of the first acts of Basil I as emperor was to send 100 warships to Dalmatia under the command of his admiral Niketas Ooryphas. The Arabs, who had been laying siege to Ragusa for fifteen months, at once fled back to Italy.[1] The Byzantines had not shown their flag in these waters for many years. This was the first demonstration of the new and vigorous offensive policy of Basil I. Agents political and spiritual followed the flag into Dalmatia; and it was constituted as a new theme or military zone of the empire, covering the maritime towns and the islands. Basil wisely conceded that the towns should go on paying tribute primarily to the leaders of the various Slav tribes in their hinterland and only nominally to Byzantium. His spiritual agents, however, pacified the Slavs with the Christian message and made them less hostile to the Christian Roman Empire. The Serbs and the Slavs of the south were rapidly converted to Orthodox Christianity. The Croats in the north, however, were finally to be won over to the Roman form of the faith by missionaries sent to them by the papacy and the Franks. The conversion was swift but not at first total. The Slav tribe known as the Narentani (or Pagani) at first stubbornly refused to accept the faith. They were notorious for their piracy along the Adriatic coast. The Venetians had suffered much from them and had indeed tried on their own account to pacify the Narentani by making Christians of them. Towards the end of Basil I's reign in 886 they were at last persuaded to see the light and to follow the Serbian example by accepting the now fashionable Christian faith from Byzantium.[2]

The creation of the theme of Dalmatia provided military bases along the coast which would protect the sea route to and from Venice and assist in the reconquest of south Italy from the Arabs. The Venetians, who were no doubt grateful, none the less feared that Byzantine intervention in the Adriatic might be just as sporadic and unreliable as in the past; and they took what they thought to be necessary action to protect their own interests. Basil I, however, had an ambitious plan for restoring south Italy and Sicily to Christian rule. He envisaged a combined

---

[1] Ibid., I, p. 130; Constantine Porphyrogenitus, *De Thematibus*, p. 97; Theophanes Continuatus, v. 53: pp. 289–90 (*CSHB*). Vasiliev, *Byzance et les Arabes*, II, 1, pp. 10–13.

[2] Constantine Porphyrogenitus, *DAI*, I, c. 29, p. 126; c. 36, p. 164; II, pp. 141–2. J. Ferluga, *L'amministrazione bizantina in Dalmazia* (Venice, 1978), pp. 164–89; D. Obolensky, *The Byzantine Commonwealth* (London, 1971), pp. 97–101; Ostrogorsky, *History*, pp. 235–6.

operation of east and west, in which the pope and the Western Emperor Louis II would co-operate. His negotiations with the pope, whom he invited to send legates to Constantinople, foundered on the rock of St Peter. Basil had supposed that by reinstating the deposed Patriarch Ignatios and arresting Photios he would have mended the schism with the Roman Church. The pope's legates to Constantinople in 869–70, however, declared that the punishment of Photios was the prerogative of their master, whose universal jurisdiction over the Christian Church in east and west must be acknowledged by the emperor and his people. Basil's dealings with the Frankish Emperor Louis II seemed at first to be more promising.[1]

In 866 Louis had launched his own campaign to dislodge the Arabs from Italy. He had some success, but the city of Bari which they had made their headquarters was impregnable without the help of a navy. Louis was laying siege to it when ambassadors came to him from the emperor in Constantinople. Basil offered to send a fleet to blockade the city. He also proposed that this gesture might mark the beginning of a new era of understanding and co-operation between the eastern and the western worlds. He might even concede that Louis had a claim to the name of emperor; and he suggested that his own eldest son Constantine might marry Louis's daughter. The proposals were welcomed. In the summer of 869 the Byzantine admiral Niketas was ordered to make for Italy at the head of an imperial fleet of 200 ships augmented by others sent over from Ragusa and Dalmatia. When he reached Bari, however, he found that Louis had abandoned the siege and gone away. This seemed to the admiral to be a gross breach of trust. He turned his fleet around and made for Greece. The new era of understanding ended at that point. There was an angry exchange of letters between the two emperors. The proposed marriage alliance was dropped. The Arabs were expelled from Bari in February 871, though by Frankish forces. It was not restored to the Byzantine Empire until after the death of Louis in 875, when it became the capital of the new theme of Lagoubardia or Lombardy created by Leo VI.[2] Basil's grand design of co-operation between east and west was wrecked by the storm that blew up over the question of a counter claim to the title of Emperor of the Romans. Once again

---

[1] F. Dvornik, *The Photian Schism* (Cambridge, 1948), pp. 132–58; Ostrogorsky, *History*, pp. 234–5.

[2] J. Gay, *L'Italie méridionale et l'empire byzantin depuis l'avènement de Basile Ier jusqu'à la prise de Bari par les Normands (867–1071)* (Paris, 1904), I, pp. 79–101, 110–11; Vasiliev, *Byzance et les Arabes*, II, 1, pp. 14–21. *DR*, I, no. 487 (Basil I's letter to Louis II, spring 871); Lentz, 'Allmähliche Übergang', 96–8.

the Christian world was divided on a point of protocol which epitomised a much deeper ideological separation.

In times past the Venetians might have received a summons, as servants of the Byzantine Emperor, to play their part in the great plan to drive the Arabs out of Italy. There is no evidence that they were alerted or invited to send ships to Bari. What evidence there is suggests, on the contrary, that they had now decided to pursue their own policies, conduct their own wars and make their own treaties with Arabs and Slavs without feeling obliged to follow the lead of their Byzantine masters. While the siege of Bari was in progress, the new Doge Orso I took command of a fleet built and equipped by his predecessor Tradonico and sailed down to Taranto. Having inflicted a defeat on the Arabs there, he returned in triumph to Venice. A few years later, when the Arabs took their revenge by attacking Grado, the mere sight of the Venetian fleet approaching was enough to scare them off.[1] The Doge also felt empowered to conduct his own diplomatic negotiations with his Slav neighbours and with the Franks. The Pact which the Venetians had first made with Lothair in 840 was renewed with Louis II in 856 and with Charles III in 880. The Franks accepted that Venice was free to act as an independent power.[2]

The Byzantines were still not ready to do so. Tradition made it harder for them to admit, except under duress, that one of their provinces could be allowed such liberties. They were not under duress. The Venetians had not rebelled. Nor had they come out with a formal declaration of independence. Had they taken either of these actions they could legitimately have been condemned. The Emperor Basil I understood the niceties of the situation. He would have preferred his relationship with Venice to be more closely defined as that between master and servant. But he was tactful enough not to press the point. With the creation of the theme of Dalmatia and the collapse of his plan for co-operation with the Franks, Basil needed the friendship of Venice. In 879 he sent an embassy to the Doge Orso I. The ambassadors brought valuable presents from the emperor and they conferred upon the Doge the imperial title of *protospatharios*. The enhanced status of the dignity did not pass unnoticed. Previous Doges had accepted the humbler titles of *spatharios* or *hypatos*. Orso had been promoted in the ranks of the Byzantine family. He returned the compliment by sending twelve bells to Constantinople. The emperor was entranced with these exotic toys and may have installed

---

[1] John the Deacon, p. 119; Dandolo, p. 157. Lentz, 'Allmähliche Übergang', 98.
[2] Kretschmayr, I, pp. 95, 97, 432.

them in his newly built church of the Nea with its golden dome overlooking the Sea of Marmora.[1]

This happy exchange of courtesies opened a new chapter in relations between Byzantium and Venice. Basil's embassy had been the first sent to Venice for nearly forty years. Its significance for the Venetians was no doubt greater than for the Byzantines. But for them too it signified that Venice, now more of a city–state than a province, was in some sense still a member of their family. They retained a firm belief, inherent in their Roman imperial tradition, that the granting of court titles to foreign powers domesticated them and made them feel what they would be missing if they seceded from the family. The Doge Orso and his successors were no doubt flattered to be called First Sword-Bearers of the emperor in Constantinople, so long as the honour carried with it no binding obligations.

The Byzantine embassy to Venice in 879 can be seen as the Eastern Emperor's answer to the Western Emperor's state visit in 856. Byzantine Emperors did not make state visits to other countries. They expected foreign rulers to come to them at Constantinople, to be properly impressed, and perhaps overawed, by a reception in the imperial palace and a conducted tour of the Queen of Cities. In the tenth century the Doges revived the earlier practice of sending their sons to Constantinople. Venice had still much to learn from Byzantium and there was as yet no ill-feeling between the city and the empire to stifle the educational process. The comings and goings of merchants and traders between the two and the influx into Venice of Greek architects and craftsmen must have made for a feeling of interdependence; though Venetian merchants were not happy about the high customs dues they had to pay at Constantinople. By the end of the ninth century Venice had become by far the most profitable and lively emporium and clearing house in Europe for eastern and western goods. The common interest of Venetians and Byzantines was served and fostered by their common concern to keep the Adriatic Sea clear of Slav pirates and Arab marauders. What the city of Venice lacked, however, was political and social stability; and this was a gift which it could never acquire or buy from Byzantium.

---

[1] John the Deacon, pp. 125–6; Dandolo, p. 160; Sanudo, *Vite dei Dogi*, p. 121. On the high-ranking title of *protospatharios*, see A. P. Kazhdan and A. W. Epstein, *Change in Byzantine Culture in the Eleventh and Twelfth Centuries* (Berkeley–Los Angeles–London, 1985), pp. 22, 238. The story that the Doge Orso married a niece of Basil I, told by Romanin, *Storia documentata*, I (Venice, 1912), p. 198, derives from no known source, though it is repeated by such authorities as A. Pertusi, 'Venezia e Bisanzio: 1000–1204', *DOP*, XXXIII (1979), 11–12.

3

VENICE:
THE ALLY OF BYZANTIUM

THE growing population and the rising prosperity of the city on the Rialto brought a recurrence of the family feuds and jealousies that had bedevilled the original settlements of refugees in the other islands. Pietro Tradonico had done much to keep the peace between the rival factions for more than twenty years. But at the last he fell victim to a conspiracy. He was murdered outside the church of St Zaccaria in September 864. His successor, Orso I Partecipazio (or Badoer), was appointed only after days of fighting in the streets and mainly because he was thought to be a neutral party in all the sordid squabbles. It was with Orso that Basil I exchanged courtesies in 879 and it was he who secured the freedom of Venice from the Franks in 880. No less important for the future of his city were the constitutional reforms that he introduced. Venice was supposed to be governed by its people and their elected representatives as a democracy, a form of government which the Byzantines, for all their classical heritage, despised. In practice, however, the power of the Doge had become more and more absolute. The administration, the domestic and foreign policy were controlled by him and by the faction which had put him up; the authority of the tribunes appointed to curb his power had declined; and the practice of co-option of his sons had come near to creating a hereditary monarchy. Orso invented a new curb on his own authority and that of his followers by the institution of judges (*judices*) elected to be magistrates as well as counsellors to the Doge. He also reorganised the ecclesiastical structure of the islands. By securing the creation of five new bishoprics he thwarted the pretensions of the Patriarch of Aquileia and freed the Church of Venice from domination by the Patriarch of Grado. It was now that Torcello became a bishopric in its own right, as did Caorle, Malamocco, Heraclea and Equilo.[1]

The full sovereignty of Venice as a *civitas* or city–state was taken by Venetian chroniclers to date from the time of the Doge Pietro Tribuno

---

[1] Cessi, *Storia*, I, pp. 53–60; Kretschmayr, I, p. 96.

(888–912). John the Deacon records that it was Pietro who, in the ninth year of his office, began to build the city on the Rialto. Although not strictly true, the statement reflects the significance of Pietro's achievement in completing the emancipation of Venice from foreign interference and concentrating the patriotism of its people around their capital city. It is none the less a fact that Pietro Tribuno was the first Doge to fortify the islands of Rialto with walls and to protect them with an iron chain which could be thrown across the entrance to the Grand Canal. The work was undertaken after a sudden and devastating raid on Lombardy and Venice by the Magyars in 899.[1] Venice was taking on the characteristics of what erudite Byzantines would have called a *polis*, a walled city-state of the ancient Greek style. Yet Tribuno and his successors continued to respect the traditional contact with Byzantium. It must be assumed that they did so willingly and not under duress, since the emperors could hardly have enforced even a nominal subjection upon them. Tribuno was given the title of *protospatharios* by the Emperor Leo VI. His successor Orso II (912–32) sent his son Pietro to Constantinople where Leo entertained him, invested him as *protospatharios* and sent him home with many gifts. Pietro II Candiano (932–9) likewise sent his son Pietro to Constantinople, where he too was made *protospatharios* by the Emperors Constantine VII and Romanos Lakapenos.[2]

The tendency to equate the sovereignty of Venice with the sovereignty of its Doge was most clearly seen in the career of Pietro IV Candiano (959–76). He was the last in the line of the family of Candiano who, despite the safeguards introduced by Pietro Tribuno, had turned the *ducatus* more than ever into a hereditary monarchy. The first of them had been killed fighting the Slavs in 887. His son, Pietro II, was Doge from 932 to 939, and his grandson Pietro III from 942 to 959. Pietro IV was his great-grandson. Banished by his father for his disruptive activities, he busied himself as a mercenary and sometimes as a pirate in Italy. He married a niece of the newly crowned Emperor Otto I of Germany and began to fancy himself as a feudal monarch. He put his fancies into practice when, after the death of his father, he was elected as Doge and brought back to Venice from Ravenna. Through his marriage he had acquired, as his personal property, huge estates on the mainland which he held as fiefs from the Western Emperor. He made his son Vitale Bishop of Torcello and Patriarch of Grado. His regal behaviour and luxurious life style soon caused resentment among the Venetians who had recalled and appointed him; and though he had turned the Doge's palace into a fortress he was finally smoked out when the people set it and the district on fire. He and his son were murdered. The fire

---

[1] John the Deacon, pp. 130, 131; Dandolo, pp. 165, 167. Kretschmayr, I, pp. 103–4.
[2] John the Deacon, pp. 131–3; Dandolo, pp. 164, 168, 171. *TTh*, I, nos. VIII and IX, p. 5.

in 976 destroyed most of the centre of the new city of Venice. The Doge's palace was gone, as well as the chapel of St Theodore and the church of St Mark alongside it.[1]

There is no record that Pietro IV was ever honoured by the Byzantine Emperor. He would probably not have wished it. His interests, his friends and his property lay in Italy and the west. Yet when in 971 an embassy came to Venice from Constantinople, Pietro was quick to respond. It was sent by the emperor to lodge a formal protest against the continuing Venetian trade with the Arabs, which had been forbidden by his predecessors. He announced that any Venetian ships found to be carrying arms or timber for shipbuilding to Arab ports would be set on fire with all their crews and cargo aboard. The Doge professed to be horrified and agreed to put a stop to this traffic which brought help and comfort to the infidel. He issued a decree, in association with his son, the Patriarch Vitale, and the other bishops, clergy and people of Venice, forbidding his subjects to carry to the lands of the Saracens arms, iron, timber or any other goods which they might use to make war upon or to defend themselves against the Christians. Offenders were to be liable to a fine of 100 pounds of gold payable to the Doge. Those unable to pay would be executed. The decree was, or so the Doge affirmed, inspired by zeal for the Christian faith and prompted by a desire to appease the wrath of the Emperor of Constantinople who was at the time planning the recovery of the Holy Land from the infidel.[2]

The trade in question was evidently being done with the Arabs in the east. The Emperor who lodged the protest was John I Tzimiskes, who had usurped the Byzantine throne two years before, in 969. It was his declared intention to continue and complete the brilliant campaigns of his predecessor, Nikephoros Phokas, who had reconquered from the Arabs so many of the eastern provinces of the Empire. Nikephoros had won back the islands of Crete and Cyprus and a large part of Cilicia and Syria. John Tzimiskes led the Byzantine armies first into Mesopotamia and then further into Syria and into Palestine, capturing Damascus, Tiberias, Nazareth and Caesarea. He was within striking distance of Jerusalem when he died in January 976. His exploits might well be interpreted in Venice as a war for the liberation of the Holy Land from the infidel. The emperor himelf saw them in this light. The Venetian trade in arms of which he complained was probably being conducted not with the Arabs in Syria but in Egypt, where the first Fatimid Caliph had established himself in 969 and built the city of Cairo as his capital. The Fatimids had designs on Syria and John Tzimiskes had had to fight off

---

[1] Kretschmayr, I, pp. 108–15; Cessi, *Storia*, I, pp. 69–77.
[2] Dandolo, p. 179. *TTh*, I, no. XIV, pp. 25–30; *DR*, I, no. 738.

their attack on Antioch in 971. He cannot have been pleased that Christian Venice was supplying them with the means to accomplish their designs.[1]

It was during the reign of the Doge Pietro IV Candiano that the Roman Empire of the west was born again in new form. In 962 Otto of Germany was crowned emperor by the pope in Rome. He had driven the Magyars out of Lombardy and made himself the most powerful ruler in Italy. His coronation struck a second and more vital blow at Byzantine pride, for Otto, unlike Charlemagne, had no doubts or reservations about his status as Emperor of the Romans. The news was bitterly received in Constantinople. The Emperor Nikephoros Phokas was justifiably proud of the growing prosperity and strength of his own empire, and he had an unshakeable conviction of the uniqueness of his own imperial majesty. The world could not contain two Emperors of the Romans. Otto had naively proposed that an accommodation could be reached by a marriage alliance. His son might take a Byzantine princess to wife. The proposal had been taken to Constantinople by his envoy, Liudprand, Bishop of Cremona, in 968. It had been treated with derision and contempt. The emperor was made more indignant when he heard that Otto had attacked Bari, the Byzantine capital in south Italy. He informed the unfortunate Liudprand that his master was neither an emperor nor a Roman. He was no more than a jumped-up barbarian chieftain from the backwoods of Germany. But the problem could not be dismissed so easily. It was left to John Tzimiskes to approach it with greater tact and diplomacy. He saw that a rival empire in the west had come to stay and he agreed that an alliance between the two imperial families would help to dispel bitterness. He selected a relative of his own called Theophano as a bride for Otto's son, the young Otto II. She was not quite the blue-blooded princess that they had asked for. But she was acceptable and she was married in Rome in 972.[2]

The Venetians had found themselves caught between two empires before. In the days of Charlemagne and his sons the Byzantine connexion had still been strong. By the tenth century Venice appeared to have become a self-sufficient state not reliant on the charity or the protection of empires either in east or west. Its rulers and its people, however, could still not rid themselves of their besetting sin of civil war; and the emergence of a new imperial power close at hand gave hope of support to one faction or the other. The storm of the reign of the Doge Pietro IV was followed by a short period of calm under the saintly and pious Pietro Orseolo (976–8), who began to rebuild a city that had been gutted

---

[1] Ostrogorsky, *History*, pp. 284, 290–1, 297–8.
[2] Ibid., pp. 291, 296–7; Jenkins, *Byzantium. The Imperial Centuries*, pp. 284–95; Leyser, 'The Tenth Century in Byzantine–Western Relationships', pp. 43–6.

by fire. The Doge's palace and the church of St Mark rose in new form from the ruins; and among the Doge's benefactions to the church was an altar screen wonderfully worked in gold and silver which he had ordered from Constantinople.[1] The calm was soon disturbed. The widow of Pietro IV had escaped and taken refuge at the court of her uncle Otto together with her stepson Vitale, the Patriarch of Grado. The Candiano family hoped to interest the Western Emperor in restoring them to power in Venice. Otto wisely declined to help. But Orseolo was driven to abdicate in any case, and the exiles returned. Vitale Candiano became Doge, but only for a few months. He was followed by Tribuno Menio (979–91), a son-in-law of the late Pietro IV, and he proclaimed a general amnesty for all who had fled after the dreadful events of 976.[2]

More exiles returned. Their return made matters worse. The rival factions grouped around the leading families of the Morosini and the Coloprini. The former looked for support to Byzantium, the latter to the Western Empire. At one moment it seemed that Venice might become a vassal state of Otto II. Tribuno Menio would have preferred to take up the threads of contact with Byzantium. In the last year of his reign he sent his son Maurizio to Constantinople to be honoured by the Emperor Basil II.[3] But he was given no chance to formulate a foreign policy. In 991 he too was forced to resign and withdrew to a monastery. It was then as if the Venetians saw the folly of their feuding and took a firm decision to start afresh. They elected as their Doge the son of the saintly Pietro Orseolo who had abdicated in 978. Pietro II (991–1008) was only thirty years old but he came of a family that was generally respected and he had many talents. He was a statesman, tactful and persuasive in the domestic quarrels of his city, diplomatic but forceful in his dealings with others.[4]

He was rightly convinced that trade was the life blood of Venice. Trade required peace at home. It also required immunity from the fear of attack and the stimulus of ready markets. Attack might come from the Western Empire. The most lucrative markets were in the east. In 992 he contracted substantial agreements with the rulers of both empires. The treaty that he signed with Otto III was in essence a renewal of that made by Venice with Otto's father and grandfather in 987 and 967.

[1] John the Deacon, pp. 142–3. Nothing of this screen now remains. The famous Pala d'Oro was commissioned for the third and later church of St Mark. See below, Chapter 4, pp. 65–7.
[2] Kretschmayr, I, pp. 115–19; Cessi, Storia, I, pp. 77–80.
[3] John the Deacon, p. 148; Dandolo, p. 187.
[4] Kretschmayr, I, pp. 119–25; Cessi, Storia, I, pp. 80–3.

Otto III was no more than twelve years old in 992, but he was to become a firm friend of Pietro II Orseolo; and he would not now be tempted to annex Venice to his empire as his father had nearly done. Further privileges were to come to the Venetians from the young Otto III in later years, particularly in the matter of trading rights and facilities on the mainland.[1] But for the encouragement of overseas trade Pietro's contract with the Byzantine Emperor was of still greater significance. The Latin text of this document survives, although in a wretched and sometimes barely intelligible translation of the Greek original. It is in the form of a chrysobull issued by the Emperors Basil II and Constantine VIII dated March 992.[2] This was the style of document by which Byzantine Emperors were accustomed graciously to confer privileges upon foreign powers in return for services rendered to their empire or as a gesture of goodwill. It was unthinkable that an emperor could treat with a foreign prince or potentate on equal terms. A golden bull was not a contract between two parties of like status. It was a privilege granted from on high by God's vicegerent on earth to a lesser mortal who had solicited his favour. This the Doge would have understood.[3]

The preamble to the text of the document makes it clear that the process was initiated by Venice. John the Deacon reports that ambassadors from the Greeks as well as from the Arabs went to Venice in 991 to pay their respects to the new Doge. Pietro Orseolo no doubt took the opportunity to discuss with the Greek envoys the problems that the Venetian merchants were encountering in Constantinople; though the matter had been raised already by the Doge Maurizio. The merchants had complained that they were being overcharged at the port of entry. Their ships were being obliged to pay upwards of thirty *solidi* apiece on arrival with their cargoes at Constantinople, whereas it had for long been the case that each ship should pay no more than two *solidi* in customs dues. Inquiries were made and the emperors found that the complaint was perfectly

[1] Kretschmayr, I, pp. 126–35, 432, 440–1; Cessi, *Storia*, I, pp. 84–8.

[2] John the Deacon, pp. 148–9; Dandolo, p. 193. *TTh*, I, no. XVII, pp. 36–9; *DR*, I, no. 781. The best edition of the chrysobull of 992 is that by A. Pertusi, 'Venezia e Bisanzio nel secolo XI', in *La Venezia del Mille* (Florence, 1965), pp. 155–60; reprinted in V. Branca, ed., *Storia della civiltà veneziana*, I (Florence, 1979), pp. 195–8. Cf. Hélène Antoniadis-Bibicou, 'Note sur les relations de Byzance avec Venise', *Thesaurismata*, I (1962), 176–8; O. Tůma, 'Some notes on the significance of the imperial chrysobull to the Venetians of 992', *B*, LIV (1984), 358–66; R.-J. Lilie, *Handel und Politik* (Amsterdam, 1984), pp. 1–8, 326–7.

[3] H. F. Brown, 'The Venetians and the Venetian quarter in Constantinople to the close of the twelfth century', *JHS*, XL (1920), 69; F. Dölger, 'Die Kaiserurkunden der Byzantiner als Ausdruck ihrer politischen Anschauungen', in *Byzanz und die europäische Staatenwelt* (Ettal, 1953), pp. 9–33; F. Dölger and J. Karayannopulos, *Byzantinische Urkundenlehre*, I: *Die Kaiserurkunden* (Munich, 1968), pp. 94–7.

justified. Their chrysobull of March 992 laid down the tariffs and the regulations for the future. Each Venetian ship coming from Venice or from elsewhere should pay no more than two *solidi* on arrival at Abydos, the port of entry on the Hellespont, and only fifteen on departure. The total payable by each vessel would therefore be seventeen *solidi* or *hyperpyra*. The dues would henceforth be paid to and collected by the Logothete of the Dromos alone and not by any of his underlings. The Logothete was forbidden to detain a Venetian ship for more than three days and then only when there was good cause. He alone had authority to inspect and assess the nature and the value of Venetian cargoes, 'according to ancient practice'; and if disputes arose among the Venetians or with others the cases would be judged only by the Logothete and not by any other magistrate. The Logothete of the Dromos was one of the most important Byzantine ministers of state, combining the functions of postmaster-general with those of foreign secretary and chief adviser to the emperor on external affairs. He was a busy man and it is hard to believe that he could have had the time to examine every Venetian ship passing up and down the Hellespont. But the intention of the emperor's order is clear. The Venetians were a special case, to be spared the officious attentions of lesser fry in the civil service. The secretariate of the Eparch, the prefect of the city of Constantinople, was instructed to make sure that all other officials concerned with the collection of taxes, down to the lowest rank in the service, left the Venetians, their ships and their cargoes alone. They were answerable only to the Logothete and subject only to his supervision.[1]

The emperors professed that they were moved to make these concessions in consideration of the facts that the Venetians, though described as 'outsiders' (*extraneos*), were fellow Christians, loyal to the empire; that they had never forgotten their pledge to come to the emperor's aid whenever his armies were fighting in Italy (Lombardy); and that they had never failed in their duty to send their own ships to fight alongside the imperial fleet. In return the emperors hoped that the Venetians would continue to act as loyal servants in Italian waters when called upon. There was only one restrictive clause in the chrysobull. The concessions applied only to Venetian ships carrying Venetian cargoes. Any ship found to be carrying the wares of Amalfitans, Jews, Lombards from Bari or elsewhere would forfeit its entire load. This cannot have been

---

[1] On the Logothete of the Dromos, see J. B. Bury, *The Imperial Administrative System in the Ninth Century* (London, 1911), pp. 91–3; N. Oikonomides, *Les Listes de Préséance byzantines des IXe et Xe siècles* (Paris, 1972), pp. 311–12; Brown, 'The Venetians and the Venetian Quarter...', 68–70. The other officials were: the Cartularii, the Notarii Parathalassii, Limenarchi, Hypologi, Xylocalami and Commerclarii of Abydos.

a very troublesome restriction. Merchants from Amalfi trading with Constantinople did so in competition and not in co-operation with Venice. The new arrangement would help to ensure that the competition was won by Venice.

The references in the document to 'ancient practice' or former custom imply that similar regulations governing Venetian trade with Constantinople had been laid down in the past. Even the privilege of being answerable only to the Logothete is said to have been conceded in earlier times. Nor is it easy to measure the economic advantages which Venice gained from this agreement. The sums mentioned can hardly have been customs dues, since they were levied at a fixed rate on each vessel entering or leaving the Hellespont regardless of its size or the value of its cargo. They were rather fees payable for the right of passage through the straits to and from Constantinople. At least the Venetians had scored their point in the matter of overpayment of such dues, reducing their liabilities by almost 50%, from thirty to seventeen *solidi* for each ship. In the wider context of foreign relations, however, the chrysobull of 992 singled out Venice as a most favoured nation of Byzantium. There was no suggestion that the 'province' of Venice was in any way subservient or that its Doge was a vassal of the emperor in Constantinople. Nor were its people held to be his subjects. They were described as outsiders who, it was hoped, would continue to be loyal servants of the emperors as they had proved to be in the past.[1] The word 'servant', however, was not meant to be humiliating. The special status of Venetian merchants was indeed emphasised by the ruling that they were the special concern of one of the highest ministers of state and not to be bothered by the petty bureaucracy of minor officials. The chrysobull thus regulated the conduct of trade between Venice and Constantinople. But it was the first statement in writing of the nature of the relationship between the two as conceived by the Byzantine Emperors at the time.

It was signed by the two Emperors, Basil II and his brother Constantine VIII. This was a mere propriety, for everyone knew that Basil was effectively emperor on his own. He was the last of the great soldier emperors of the tenth century and most of his life was spent in warfare. The great crisis of his reign was the rebellion of Bulgaria. The year before signing his chrysobull for Venice Basil had led his first campaign against the rebels. But it was not enough. The Tsar Samuel of Bulgaria built up a vast empire of his own in the Balkans, stretching from Dalmatia to Macedonia to Thessaly and over to the Black Sea. In the west he captured the Adriatic port of Durazzo (Dyrrachion) and annexed much of Serbia

---

[1] On the interpretation of the word *extranei* in this document, see Lilie, *Handel und Politik*, p. 3 n. 6.

and Croatia. For more than fifteen years Basil II concentrated on the methodical conquest and extermination of this Bulgarian empire on his northern frontiers. His campaigns were conducted with a single-minded ruthlessness that earned him the title of the Bulgar-slayer. Samuel died in 1014, already defeated. The conquest of his empire was complete by 1018. Bulgaria was absorbed into the Byzantine Empire and its territory was divided into three new themes. Serbia and Croatia were restored to the rule of their native princes as vassals of the Byzantine Emperor. The theme of Dalmatia was reconstituted along the Adriatic coast; and Durazzo, restored to Byzantium, was put under the command of a *dux*.[1] While this long war against the Bulgars was in progress the Venetians embarked on an expedition of their own. Some of the coastal towns of Dalmatia had appealed for help against the pirates of Croatia. In May of the year 1000 the Doge Pietro II Orseolo led a great fleet out of Venice and down the Adriatic. It was a triumphal progress. The fleet was welcomed and feted at almost every town. The Slavs were pushed back from the coast. The days when Venice paid tribute to the Croats were over. The Narentan pirates were forced to admit defeat and to swear on oath to keep the peace. When he got back to Venice the Doge, in the manner of a Roman emperor of old, added another title to his name. He was now not only *dux Veneticorum* but also *dux Dalmatiae*.[2]

Some have explained this event as part of the overall strategy of the soldier Emperor Basil II in his campaign against Bulgaria. Basil, it has been said, called on the Doge to act as his ally in hemming the Bulgars in on the west and weakening their hold over the Croats and Serbs. As a reward the emperor granted him the right to call himself Duke of Dalmatia.[3] It is true that the fourteenth-century chronicler Dandolo gives some such impression. It is true also that the Doge sent his son Giovanni to Constantinople in 997, where he could have received instructions from the emperor to take back to his father.[4] But the only contemporary historian, John the Deacon, who gives the fullest account of the affair, gives no hint of a co-operative venture between Byzantium and Venice or of a concerted strategic plan to encircle the Bulgars. In his view, the Doge's expedition was a completely independent enterprise which put the Slavs in their place, brought deserved glory to Venice and made the Adriatic Sea safe for Venetian merchants to ply their trade. Each

1 Ostrogorsky, *History*, pp. 300–13; R. Browning, *Byzantium and Bulgaria* (London, 1975), pp. 73–5.
2 John the Deacon, pp. 155–60; Dandolo, pp. 196–9. *TTh*, I, no. XIX, p. 40. Kretschmayr, I, pp. 135–41; Cessi, *Storia*, I, pp. 91–3.
3 Jenkins, *Byzantium. The Imperial Centuries*, p. 322.
4 John the Deacon, p. 154; Dandolo, p. 196. *TTh*, I, no. XVIII, p. 40.

one of the towns on the coast made its own submission of homage to the Doge and he thus earned his title of Duke of Dalmatia. This sounds convincing. The Doge's triumphal progress down the Adriatic had nothing to do with the Byzantine Emperor's strategy. It was simply another and a splendid advertisement of the fact that Venice was now strong enough to take action on its own. In theory, however, Dalmatia remained under Byzantine sovereignty. The Venetians accepted this. They sent no governors or representatives to the towns which they had guaranteed to protect. The citizens of those towns continued to manage their own affairs; and in their churches the name of the Byzantine Emperor was commemorated before that of the Doge of Venice. Thus, when the Bulgarian war was over and the theme of Dalmatia was reconstituted, the Venetians were happy enough to pay lip-service to the principle of Byzantine sovereignty. They had made their point and had done what they thought was necessary. A restored Byzantine presence in the Adriatic could only make it safer for their shipping.[1]

Pietro II Orseolo steered a skilful and confident diplomatic course between the Eastern and the Western Empires. The young Otto III, who had transferred his capital to Rome, was the Doge's devoted friend and admirer. In 1001 he paid a curiously furtive visit to Venice.[2] His friendship was also sought by the Byzantine Emperor. Basil II was aware that Otto had been made susceptible to Byzantine influence and ideas by his Greek mother Theophano. It had often been proposed in the past that the problem of the two Empires of East and West could be eased if not solved by a marriage. Otto III was indeed the child of such a marriage. If he were now to marry a Byzantine princess of the blood imperial, the male issue of their union would surely qualify as the one true emperor of a single reunited *imperium romanum*. Basil II had never married and his brother Constantine had only daughters. But they were unquestionably heiresses of the imperial line that stemmed from Basil I, the founder of the Macedonian dynasty. One of these daughters, the princess Zoe, was now offered as a bride for the Emperor Otto III. Again it seemed as if providence was not in favour of such grand dynastic schemes. Zoe was escorted to Italy for her wedding only to learn, when she reached Bari, that her betrothed had died of a fever, on 24 January 1002.[3]

The Venetians would have gained by the happier outcome of this pro-

[1] Ferluga, *L'amministrazione bizantina in Dalmazia*, pp. 191–204.

[2] John the Deacon, pp. 160–4; Dandolo, p. 200. Kretschmayr, I, pp. 133–4; Cessi, *Storia*, I, pp. 89–91.

[3] Gay, *L'Italie méridionale*, pp. 295–8; G. Schlumberger, *L'Epopée byzantine à la fin du Xᵉ siècle*, II: *Basile II (989–1025)* (Paris, 1900), pp. 303–6. *DR*, I, nos. 784, 787.

ject. When it fell through, the Doge sent envoys to pay his respects and perhaps to offer his condolences to the emperor in Constantinople. At the same time he quickly declared his support for the new Western Emperor, Henry II of Bavaria, Otto's second cousin; and in November 1002 he was rewarded with a charter addressed to him as Duke of Venice and Dalmatia and confirming all the privileges formerly enjoyed by his people.[1] Two years later the Doge distinguished himself by another heroic naval action in the Adriatic, which earned him the gratitude of the Byzantine Emperor. Basil II had reorganised the administration and defence of his territories in south Italy, grouping them all together under one official who held the title of Catepano. He regarded this foothold in the west of his dominions as a precious legacy and one on which he hoped to build. But in April 1004 the Arabs from Sicily returned to the attack on Bari, where the catepano had his headquarters. The Emperor could spare no reinforcements, and the city was under siege all summer. When the news reached Venice, however, the Doge Pietro II brought a squadron of warships to the scene under his own command. In September the Venetians broke through the blockade, relieved the siege of Bari and, in co-operation with the Catepano Gregory, chased the Arabs away. The rescue operation may have been unsolicited, or it may have come in response to an appeal from Bari. John the Deacon writes that the Venetian ambassadors who had gone to Constantinople some months before had gone home, evidently by way of Bari, laden with gifts from the imperial Catepano. But in either event it was in the interest of Venice as well as of Byzantium to keep the south of Italy free of Arabs. It had been a gesture that demonstrated yet again the naval might of Venice as well as the Doge's concern to maintain his link with Byzantium.[2]

Basil II was properly grateful. He too wanted to maintain that link. If the Venetians would police the Dalmatian side of the Adriatic and come to his aid on the Italian side as well, they must be encouraged. The emperor invited Pietro Orseolo to send his son Giovanni to Constantinople. Giovanni was nineteen years old and had just been formally named as Doge with his father. He set out with his younger brother Otto. What the Emperor Basil had in mind was another diplomatic marriage to strengthen the link between Byzantium and Venice. The son of a Doge could not, of course, be offered the hand of a blue-blooded princess like Zoe, the disappointed bride of Otto III. But a suitably

[1] John the Deacon, p. 167. Kretschmayr, I, pp. 134–5, 432.
[2] John the Deacon, p. 167; Dandolo, p. 202. Gay, L'Italie méridionale, p. 369; Schlumberger, L'Epopée, II, pp. 307–22; Kretschmayr, I, p. 129. The Byzantine Catepano was Gregory Tarchaneiotes.

distinguished young lady was found in the person of Maria, daughter
of the patrician Argyropoulos. She was, it seems, one of the sisters of
the future Emperor Romanos III; though John the Deacon and Dandolo
believed that she was a niece or a sister of Basil II and of imperial stock.
This would be stretching the evidence. The marriage was celebrated in
the imperial chapel in Constantinople. The blessing was given by the
patriarch and the golden wedding crowns were placed on the heads of
Giovanni and Maria by the two emperors. There followed three days
of festivities in one of the palaces ('Yconomium'). Maria brought her
husband a substantial dowry which included a house or 'palace' of her
own in Constantinople where they stayed after the wedding. The emperor
had to hurry away to his war against the Bulgars. When he came back
he invested Giovanni Orseolo as a patrician and, at Maria's request,
gave her the holy relics of St Barbara to take with her to Venice. Maria
was loth to leave the civilised comforts of Constantinople and her parents
were sad to see her go 'as if into exile in a foreign land'. By the time
they boarded ship she was already some months pregnant.

The couple reached Venice safely. They were greeted by the Doge
with a reception the like of which had not been seen before. 'In truth,'
says John the Deacon, 'no one could recall such a show of rejoicing
in Venice as there was over this wedding.' Maria gave birth to a son
a few days later. The Doge assisted at the child's baptism and, since
he had been conceived in Constantinople, gave him the name of Basil
after the emperor. But the emperor's plans were again doomed to failure.
In 1006 a comet was seen in the sky, always a portent of disaster. It
was followed by a famine and then a plague, among whose many victims
were Maria, her husband Giovanni and their infant son. They died within
sixteen days of one another. They were buried in the monastery of St
Zaccaria. The Doge Pietro was inconsolable. He made his younger son
Otto Doge in place of Giovanni and retired into obscurity in a wing
of his palace. He died in 1008. Nothing was left to remind him of his
high hopes for his eldest son and his grandson conceived in Byzantium
and born in Venice, except for the relics of St Barbara, the Emperor's
gift to Maria Argyropoulaina. These he presented to the abbey of St
John, his son's namesake, on the island of Torcello.[1]

Long after Maria's death a cautionary tale was told about the Greek
wife of a Venetian Doge which seems to refer to her. It was related

[1] John the Deacon, pp. 167–70; Dandolo, p. 202. *TTh*, I, no. xx, pp. 40–1; *DR*, I, no.
794; George Cedrenus, *Compendium historiarum*, II, p. 452. Gay, *L'Italie méridionale*,
pp. 368–9; Schlumberger, *L'Epopée*, II, pp. 323–6. On the identity of Maria Argyropoulaina,
see J.-F. Vannier, *Familles byzantines. Les Argyroi (IXᵉ–XIIᵉ siècles)* (Paris, 1975), no. 15,
pp. 43–4.

by St Peter Damian, a fervent reformer of the evils of his time, who died in 1072. The moral of it was that the good Christians of the west should beware of the decadent and sybaritic ways of the east, lest the Orontes flow into the Tiber. Peter records with vindictive satisfaction how the Greek princess who came to Venice died a hideous death as a result of her self-indulgence. Distrusting the water supply of Venice, she had her servants collect rain water for her ablutions. Too fastidious to eat with her fingers, she carried her food to her mouth with a two-pronged golden fork. Disliking the stink of the lagoons, she filled her rooms with incense and perfumes. For such depravity and vanity she was a victim of the wrath of God, who smote her with a vile disease. Her body putrefied, her limbs withered, her bedchamber was permeated by such a stench that only one of her maids could bear it; and after a lingering illness of excruciating agony she passed away, to the great relief of her friends. It is a nasty tale, but it is eloquent of the difference in living standards between Byzantium and the west in the eleventh century. Maria's parents had been right to sympathise with their poor daughter going off to exile in a foreign land. To a lady brought up to the refinements of aristocratic life in Constantinople, Venice must have seemed rather barbarous. What Peter Damian and his like took to be signs of depravity were esteemed in Byzantium as marks of urbanity and civilised living. The princess Theophano who had married Otto II was believed to be burning in Hell because of all the baths she had taken during her lifetime. If eating with a fork or taking baths were thought enough to bring down the wrath of God, western society had still some way to go to match the cultured habits of Byzantium.[1]

Pietro II Orseolo and Basil II were both competent and energetic rulers who presided over an age of glory in their respective domains. But in character they had little in common. Pietro loved luxury, pomp and ostentation. Basil had a distrustful, withdrawn and puritanical nature. Both set standards of greatness which their immediate successors could not uphold. Basil II died in 1025. He had been about to lead a great armada for the liberation of Sicily from the Arabs, which would be the start of the reunification of Italy and the west with the true Empire of the Romans. After his death the Macedonian dynasty, which had

---

[1] Peter Damian, *Opuscula varia, Opusculum* L: *Institutio monialis*, c. XI, in *MPL*, CXLV, col. 744; Dandolo, p. 215. Cf. Sanudo, *Vite dei dogi*, p. 155. Kretschmayr (I, p. 156) and, more recently, Pertusi (*DOP*, XXXIII, 1979, 12) have taken the story to refer not to Maria but to Theodora, who married the Doge Domenico Silvio. But Theodora outlived Peter Damian and he could not have described her death. See D. I. Polemis, *The Doukai* (London, 1968), no. 19, p. 54 and n. 3. On Theophano's posthumous punishment, see Leyser, 'The Tenth Century', pp. 45–6.

endured for more than 150 years, was all but extinct in the male line.
A long decline set in, and the internal structure of the empire, whose
resources and boundaries had no doubt been overstretched by the soldier
emperors, began to disintegrate. The Byzantine Empire was an institution
whose people expected to be ruled by a supreme being. Emperors such
as Justinian, Heraclius, or Basil II could set their stamp upon whole
generations. In Venice it was not so. A great Doge like Pietro Orseolo,
with his luxurious ways and grandiose foreign policy, might excite more
envy than respect, more jealousy than loyalty. His son Otto who took
over from him had been named after the Emperor of the West and had
been a guest at the court of the Emperor of the East. He shared his
father's love of power and ostentation. He was not allowed to indulge
it for long.

In Byzantium the Macedonian dynasty ran its hereditary course first
through Basil's brother, Constantine VIII, and then through his niece
Zoe, who had so nearly married the Emperor Otto III, and finally
through her elderly sister Theodora, who died in 1056. The will of the
people prolonged the authority of the ruling family to its natural end.
They would not force the end of a dynasty that had brought such prosperity and prestige. The Venetians felt differently. They disapproved of the
attempt of Otto Orseolo to perpetuate his own family's power by nomi-
nating first one brother as Patriarch of Grado and then another as Bishop
of Torcello. The Patriarch of Aquileia, appointed by the Emperor Henry
II, revived the notion that Grado and all its treasures really belonged
to him. For a while Venetians of all opinions were united in their reaction
to this brigandage; and the pope at first refused to countenance it. But
a new emperor, Conrad II, persuaded him to change his mind. Those
who distrusted the Orseolo family now arrested the Doge Otto, shaved
his head, dressed him up as a monk and shipped him to Constantinople,
where he had once been so happy. It was not quite the end of his family's
bid for power. The Byzantine Emperor Romanos III, who had come
to his throne by marrying Zoe, was angry at this shabby treatment of
one who was related to him by marriage. For a while he withdrew the
privileges that had been granted to Venetian merchants coming to Constantinople. The Western Emperor Conrad was also displeased. The
Orseolo faction secured the downfall of the Doge who had replaced Otto.
His brother Orso, the Patriarch of Grado, took over and invited Otto
to come back as Doge. It was too late. He died before he could make
the journey. The Patriarch of Grado admitted that the game was up.
At least he seems to have foiled the schemes of his rival in Aquileia.
But the dynasty of the Orseoli was now ended. A new Doge with new
ideas was appointed. He was a rich merchant called Domenico

Flabianico (1032–43). The Macedonian dynasty in Constantinople was then drawing to its close in a twilight of popular respect. The dynasty of the Orseoli in Venice had to be told when to go and went only under compulsion.[1]

---

[1] Dandolo, pp. 205–8. Kretschmayr, 1, pp. 144–8, 443–4; Cessi, *Storia*, 1, pp. 94–101; Demus, *San Marco*, pp. 35–6.

4

VENICE:
THE PARTNER OF BYZANTIUM

THE native sources for the history of Venice in the middle years of the eleventh century are not plentiful. The Chronicle of John the Deacon ends in the year 1008. The Chronicle of Andrea Dandolo was not composed until the fourteenth century and derives many of its unverifiable and often distorted facts from lost sources and documents. The history of Byzantium in the eleventh century is by contrast well documented by a number of well-informed and sophisticated historians such as Michael Psellos, Michael Attaleiates, John Skylitzes and John Zonaras, even though Venice was not often in the forefront of their minds. So far as is known, the new Doge Domenico Flabianico, elected in 1032, had few formal dealings with Constantinople, though he bore the Byzantine title of *protospatharios*; and his successor, Domenico Contarini (1043–70), was entitled imperial patrician and *anthypatos*, as well as *magistros*.[1] He was the first of the Doges to be so honoured, and the title may be evidence of the value which the Byzantine Emperors set upon their continuing relationship with Venice. The arrest and exile of the last of the Orseoli may have caused a certain coolness between the two. It could not be allowed to last if Venice was to survive and prosper as an independent state.

In the wider context of European history the eleventh century was the age in which the balance of power began to shift decisively from east to west. At its beginning the Byzantine Empire under Basil II was greater in extent and richer in resources than any of its rivals or competitors. At its end the German Emperors of the West could freely boast of their superiority; the papacy, reformed and reinvigorated, had declared the Patriarch of Constantinople to be in schism if not in heresy; the Normans from south Italy had almost succeeded in overwhelming the empire; and the First Crusade had been preached and launched. The

---

[1] V. Lazzarini, 'I titoli dei dogi di Venezia', *Nuovo Archivio Veneto*, n.s., v/2 (1903), 281–2; R. Cessi, *Venezia Ducale*, II, 1: *Commune Venetiarum* (Venice, 1965), p. 37. Cessi, *Storia*, I, p. 110, and Demus, *San Marco*, p. 23, credit Contarini with the title of *protosebastos*.

decline of Byzantium after the death of Basil II was partly due to the radical changes in the social and economic structure of the empire brought about by its own prosperity. The rich had become richer through the years of conquest and expansion. They could no longer be constrained to live under the discipline of a form of martial law which had been devised to see their society through an age of grave crisis and emergency. The neat division of the provinces into military, economic and administrative units known as themes broke down, as did the centralisation of all authority in the person and the office of the emperor in Constantinople. To those living at the time, however, the symptoms of disintegration were not apparent. Michael Psellos did not feel that he was living in an age of decline. Constantinople was still by far the richest and most agreeable Christian city in the world; and for many years its people nourished their illusions by living on the capital of the glory and renown won for them by the Macedonian Emperors. Their eyes were opened and their complacency was shattered not by reflexion on their own short-comings but by their manifest weakness when faced by new and determined enemies from outside, the Normans from the west and the Seljuq Turks from the east.

The Venetians of the eleventh century were not drawn to Constantinople by admiration of its social structure or form of government. Indeed, after the fall of the Orseoli they abandoned one of the few monarchical practices which they may have learnt from Byzantium. No Doge thereafter was to co-opt a member of his family as his colleague in authority.[1] The relationship of Venice to Byzantium may have been affected by the sentiment of long tradition. But it was based more firmly on realism. Constantinople and the Byzantine ports of the eastern Mediterranean were the treasure houses of Venetian trade; and Venice needed Byzantium as an ally against the growing ambition of the Western Emperors. There were also many things to be learnt or acquired from Byzantium to make the city of Venice more splendid. The Venetians may not have admired its political system; but they were ardent admirers of its art and culture. The greatest monument to the Byzantine influence on Venice in the eleventh-century remains the church of St Mark. It stands on the site of the church first built in the ninth century which was destroyed by the fire of 976. The Doges Pietro I and II Orseolo had rebuilt it, though little is known of it in its second form. The third and still existing church of St Mark was begun by the Doge Domenico Contarini and continued and completed by his successors, Domenico Silvio (1070–84) and Vitale Falier (1084–96). There appears to have been no cogent reason for

---

[1] Cessi, *Storia*, I, pp. 102–5.

rebuilding the church. The motive was civic pride. The new building was a public demonstration of the new wealth and strength of Venice. But it was to Byzantium that its architects and interior decorators turned for inspiration. The church was modelled on that of the Holy Apostles in Constantinople, the great five-domed basilica built by Justinian which served as the mausoleum of Byzantine Emperors. The fact is well attested by contemporary sources and there can be no doubt that the master architect of the eleventh-century St Mark's was a Greek from Constantinople. Nothing could more obviously proclaim to all the Christian world the special relationship between Venice and Byzantium.[1]

The construction of the church was still in progress when Domenico Silvio became Doge in 1070. Silvio is said to have married a sister of the Byzantine Emperor Michael VII Doukas called Theodora and to have received the title of *protoproedros*.[2] The Byzantine historians are silent on the matter and the marriage is recorded only by later Venetian chroniclers. It was not much of a match. Michael VII, son of Constantine X, came to his throne when the Byzantine Empire was at the lowest ebb of its decline. He was the pupil and, as emperor, the creature of his father's minister Michael Psellos. Constantine X had allowed the defences of his empire to be dangerously run down and so had widened the growing gap between the civilian aristocracy of the capital and the military aristocracy of the provinces. The effects were felt on all sides but especially on the eastern and western frontiers. In the east the Seljuq Turks had swept away what was left of the Arab empire in Asia. In 1056 they had conquered Baghdad, centre of the Arab Caliphate for 300 years. The Seljuq Sultanate became a next-door neighbour of Byzantium and of the Fatimid Caliphate in Egypt; and its soldiers, fired by the zeal of holy war against the Christians, began to penetrate into Byzantine territory in Asia Minor. A wave of reaction against the complacency and feebleness of the government in Constantinople brought a soldier to the throne. In 1068 Romanos IV Diogenes married the widow of Constantine X and became emperor, much to the distaste of Michael Psellos and the civil aristocracy. Romanos was an experienced general, but with the demoralised and undisciplined army that he had to command he was unable to stem the tide in Asia Minor. On 19 August 1071 he was defeated and taken prisoner by the Seljuq Sultan at Manzikert on the Armenian border. He was allowed to return to Constantinople, only to find that he had been deposed by the aristocracy, who had acclaimed Michael VII as emperor in his place. Romanos was disgraced, blinded

---

[1] Demus, *San Marco*, especially pp. 69–100.
[2] Dandolo, p. 215. Lazzarini, 'I titoli', 282–3; D. I. Polemis, *The Doukai*, no. 19, p. 54.

and left to die. The gates of Asia Minor were wide open for the Seljuqs to march in and occupy the heartland of the Byzantine Empire.[1]

In the very same year as the disaster at Manzikert, on Palm Sunday 1071, the port of Bari was captured by the Normans. It was the last surviving stronghold of the Byzantine protectorate in south Italy. The Norman infiltration into Italy had begun earlier in the century as a trickle of roving adventurers. It had grown into a flood of determined and invincible invaders. The Normans in the west, like the Seljuqs in the east, had come to stay. In 1046 they found a leader of genius, Robert Guiscard. The popes felt menaced by these intruders and appealed for protection to the Emperors of East and West. But in 1053 Pope Leo IX was taken prisoner by the Normans. He died in captivity and his successor, despairing of any help from Constantinople, compromised by recognising the Norman conquest of Italy as a fact. Robert Guiscard became the pope's vassal, with the title of Duke of Apulia and Calabria and, with God's help, thereafter of Sicily. The Byzantines deeply resented this alliance of the papacy with the Normans. An army that they sent from Constantinople to Italy in 1060 achieved some limited and temporary victories. But the Norman Duchy was too well grounded morally and materially; and in 1061 its leader embarked upon the conquest of Arab Sicily as a holy war encouraged by the pope.[2]

In times past the emperors in Constantinople might have summoned the Venetian fleet to help rescue the cities of Byzantine Italy. There is no record that they did so on this occasion. It is possible, though it is nowhere documented, that Michael VII gave his sister in marriage to the Doge Silvio in a desperate attempt to provoke the Venetians to action. By then it was too late. Robert Guiscard made no secret of his ultimate ambition. The Normans, like the Venetians, admired the wealth and glory of Byzantium. In Italy they retained much of the Byzantine administrative system and the Greek titles and dignities that went with it. But their conquest of Byzantine Italy and Muslim Sicily was only a beginning. Robert's eyes were set on the centre and the source of all the wealth and glory, on the city of Constantinople. The Duke of Apulia would become the Emperor of the Romans. Michael VII had no weapon left but that of diplomacy. All that remained of the Byzantine army was concentrated in the east. Three times he tried to make a settlement with the Normans; and in 1074 it was finally agreed that Robert Guiscard should be nominated as defender of the empire in the west. His daughter was betrothed to the emperor's son Constantine. At the same time the

---

[1] Ostrogorsky, *History*, pp. 341–5.

[2] On the Norman conquest of south Italy, see F. Chalandon, *Histoire de la domination normande en Italie et en Sicilie*, I–II (Paris, 1907).

emperor made a proposition to the pope, Gregory VII. In return for
the promise of military aid against the Turks, he offered to mend the
schism between the Churches of Constantinople and Rome.[1] Michael
VII was the first Byzantine Emperor to tempt the papacy with the bait
of a Christian Church reunited under Rome. It was to become a familiar
ploy in Byzantine diplomacy in later years. He should have known that
it was an offer that he could never implement without creating uproar
among his people. But the pope was intrigued. In 1073 he sent as his
legate to Constantinople Dominicus, Patriarch of Grado, to bring back
a report on the state of affairs in Byzantium and the east.[2]

The pope knew that a Venetian would be able to learn more through
his contacts in Constantinople than any other western prelate. The
Patriarchs of Grado had by now won papal approval in their long struggle
for precedence with their rivals in Aquileia. Grado had at last been recognised as the premier patriarchate with the name of Nova Aquileia; and
in 1053 Pope Leo IX had formally named it head and metropolis of
all Venetia and Istria. Its bishops had taken to residing in Venice and
the Patriarchate of Nova Aquileia or Grado was in effect the Patriarchate
of Venice. Dominicus, whom the pope sent to Constantinople in 1073,
was very conscious of his rank in the church and no doubt a very suitable
legate for the purpose in hand; though the Patriarch of Antioch had
some years before taken exception to his use of the patriarchal title.
He had frostily observed that Dominicus had no right to it. Just as there
were only five senses in the body of man, so there were only five patriarchs
in the Church of Christ. Dominicus may not have cut such a figure
in Constantinople as he did in Italy. But the report that he brought
back fired the sympathy and the imagination of the pope. Gregory VII
announced that he would now raise an army in the west and lead it
in person to drive the infidel from Asia Minor. He would then preside
over a council in Constantinople to receive the grateful submission of
the Greeks.[3]

It was perhaps as well that this noble but fanciful gesture went no
further. Five years later Michael VII was deposed by a leading light
of the military aristocracy who was crowned as the Emperor Nikephoros

---

[1] Cf. P. Charanis, 'Byzantium, the west and the origins of the First Crusade', B, XIX (1949),
17–24.
[2] The letter, dated 9 July 1073, of Gregory VII to Michael VII appointing Dominicus as
his legate to Constantinople is printed in Acta Romanorum Pontificum a S. Clemente I
(an. c. 90) ad Coelestinum III (†1198), ed. A. L. Tăutu, Pontificia Commissio ad redigendum
CICO: Fontes, ser. III: 1 (Vatican City, 1943), no. 375, p. 786. Cf. S. Runciman, A History
of the Crusades, 1 (Cambridge, 1952), pp. 98–9.
[3] Kretschmayr, I, p. 446; S. Runciman, The Eastern Schism (Oxford, 1955), pp. 63–4; Demus,
San Marco, p. 36.

III. The pope looked on him as a usurper and excommunicated him. The Normans were not dismayed when he rejected Michael VII's arrangements with their leader; and they were delighted when, in July 1080, the pope authorised Robert Guiscard to enlist the help of all the faithful of St Peter in the task of reinstating the Emperor Michael, 'unjustly overthrown'. The Norman conquest of the Byzantine Empire now had the blessing of the pope, as a holy war to right the wrongs done to its lawful ruler. The Venetians were worried by this development. The way from south Italy to Constantinople lay, as it had lain since early Roman times, across the Adriatic Sea from Bari or Brindisi to the harbours of Valona or Durazzo (Dyrrachion) on what is now the Albanian coast. There the ancient Via Egnatia, the overland route to Thessalonica and Constantinople, could be joined. The Normans had already triumphantly proved the prowess of their navy in their campaigns in Italy and Sicily. The Venetians could not permit them to have the free run of the Adriatic. It was at this point that their activities became the joint concern of Venice and of Byzantium.

The Doge of Venice liked to be known as Duke of Dalmatia; and the Byzantine Emperor was still titular suzerain of the autonomous towns along the coast. Durazzo was garrisoned by imperial troops. But elsewhere the 'theme' of Dalmatia had disintegrated. The native Kings of Croatia who had been overawed by Basil II had ceased to behave as vassals of the emperors. They preferred to get their crowns and their royal warrants from the popes. Further inland, the rulers of Hungary were looking for ways to expand their kingdom to the sea; while the Slavs whom Basil II had brought within his boundaries were rising in revolt. The *pax romana* no longer held in the country between Venice and Constantinople. The arrival in Dalmatia of the Normans added to the confusion. Some of them had found their way there even before 1080. In 1074 a Norman count, Amico of Giovinazzo, captured the King of Croatia and attacked Dalmatia. The Byzantine Emperor was powerless to protect either side of the Adriatic. It was left for Venice to take action. The Doge reasserted his rights with an impressive display of naval might, sailing in triumph down the Dalmatian coast. Order was restored. The Normans fled. In February 1075 the Doge Silvio summoned representatives of four of the Dalmatian towns and made them swear that they would never again let Normans or other foreigners on to their land. The document recording this event reveals the new mood of Venice. The Doge was pleased to employ his Byzantine title of 'imperial *protoproedros*'. But he ignored the traditional forms of Byzantine protocol. The emperor's name is not mentioned, nor is the date given by the year of his reign, the month and the indiction, according to Byzantine usage. Venice was now a fully autonomous state exercising its sovereignty without reference to any higher authority.[1]

The Norman count who had so rashly invaded Croatia was probably a freebooter not in the pay of Robert Guiscard. The Venetians had quickly flushed him out. But the real Norman invasion across the Adriatic was now about to begin, as the prelude to the conquest of the Byzantine Empire. It was well timed. The empire was in chaos. Nikephoros III was too old to understand or to control the rivalries among those who aspired to succeed him. It seemed vital, if the empire were to survive at all, that the military aristocracy should produce an emperor who was a soldier. In the end they did, out of a welter of rioting, intrigue and civil war. The new emperor, crowned in March 1081, was Alexios I of the family of Komnenos. It had happened in the past that when Byzantium was almost overwhelmed by crisis a great emperor emerged to save the day. Providence had produced Heraclius to conquer the Persians and Leo III to defeat the Arabs. So it was with Alexios Komnenos. His rise to power and his career are the subject of one of the most celebrated works of Byzantine literature, the *Alexiad*, written by his erudite daughter Anna Comnena. As she says, when her father came to the throne the empire was at its last gasp and beset by enemies on every side.[2] In particular there were the Seljuq Turks in the east and the Normans in the west. But of the two in 1081 the Normans presented the more serious and the more immediate threat. For their invasion from Italy had the blessing of a pope who regarded Alexios as an excommunicated usurper.

To be able to concentrate his forces on repelling this threat, the emperor had to make his peace with the Seljuq Sultan in June 1081. It was a compromise forced by necessity. The Turkish Sultanate, now based at Nicaea almost within sight of Constantinople, was recognised as a sovereign state, with an agreed boundary between Christian and Muslim territory. Although Alexios had come to power with the support of the military and was himself a soldier, he knew that his empire could not survive by warfare alone. It needed money and it needed friends and allies. Since the loss of most of Asia Minor, the manpower of the army had to be made up of foreign mercenaries, many of them Normans and Turks; and they had to be paid at competitive rates. The navy, which

[1] *TTh*, I, no. XXI, pp. 41–3. Kretschmayr, I, pp. 158–9; Cessi, *Storia*, I, pp. 121–2; Ferluga, *L'amministrazione*, pp. 240–1; Pertusi, 'L'impero bizantino e l'evolvere dei suoi interessi nell' alto Adriatico', in *Le origini di Venezia* (Florence, 1964), 61; D. Mandić, 'Gregorio VII e l'occupazione veneta della Dalmatia nell' anno 1076', in A. Pertusi, ed., *Venezia e il Levante*, I, 1, pp. 453–71.
[2] Anna Comnena, *Alexiad*, ed. B. Leib (Paris, 1937–45) iii. 9:1, p. 130.

had been dangerously depleted, must be helped out by foreign ships. The recruiting of mercenaries and the payment of allies made the empire more than ever dependent on foreign relations and diplomacy. The Byzantines could no longer comfort themselves with the myth that their empire was the only power on earth around which everything else revolved. Alexios knew this. He looked for help from every quarter, from the Western Emperor, even from the pope, but above all from Venice. The Venetians were not mercenaries who had to be paid. They were still theoretically his servants, if not his subjects. They may not have seen things this way. But they too were anxious about the Norman threat to the freedom of their shipping in the Adriatic. And they were realists in an age of myths. They foresaw that, though they might not be paid as mercenaries, they might be handsomely rewarded for their co-operation with Byzantium.

Robert Guiscard led his army and navy across the sea in May 1081.[1] His objective was the harbour and fortress of Durazzo, the gateway to the Via Egnatia. His son Bohemond had already taken an advance guard and captured Valona on the coast to the south; and the Byzantine garrison on the island of Corfu had surrendered. Alexios at once sent an urgent message to the Doge, Domenico Silvio, asking him to mobilise the Venetian fleet and sail to the relief of Durazzo. His ambassador brought lavish gifts and promised great rewards, which would be confirmed in writing by an imperial chrysobull.[2] The Doge did not hesitate. There were many Venetian residents in Durazzo. He took command of fourteen warships and forty-five other vessels and made for the scene of action. The Norman fleet riding off Durazzo, though greater in numbers, could not compete with the superior tactics of the Venetians. Most of its ships were sunk. The Norman army, however, which had already disembarked, suffered no casualties and began to lay siege to the castle of Durazzo. Meanwhile the emperor was leading his own army overland from Constantinople. He arrived in October. A battle was fought outside Durazzo. It proved what the emperor had feared, that his bands of mercenaries of many races could not match the single-minded discipline of the Norman troops. Alexios was seriously wounded. He was forced to retreat across the mountains to try to regroup what was left of his battered army. Durazzo fell to the Normans a few months

---

[1] The main sources for the Norman invasion from 1081 to 1085 are: Anna Comnena, *Alexiad*, Books iii–vi: 1–11; William of Apulia, ed. Marguerite Mathieu, *Guillaume de Pouille, La Geste de Robert Guiscard*, Istituto Siciliano di Studi Bizantini e Neoellenici. Testi e Monumenti: Testi, 4 (Palermo, 1961), Books iv and v, pp. 204–59; Geoffrey of Malaterra, *De Rebus Gestis Rogerii ... et Roberti Guiscardi ...*, ed. E. Pontieri, *RIS*, v/1 (Bologna, 1927), Book iii, pp. 71–82.

[2] Anna Comnena, iv: 2: 1, p. 146. *DR*, 11, no. 1070.

later, in February 1082. Some versions of the event have it that the gates
of the city were opened to the enemy by a Venetian, who hoped to
be rewarded for his treachery by the hand in marriage of a niece of Robert
Guiscard. Others say that the traitor was from Amalfi.[1] The Norman
army then penetrated inland along the Via Egnatia as far as Kastoria
and down to Larissa in Thessaly. They might well have gone further
had not messengers from Italy arrived to summon Guiscard back to his
Duchy of Apulia. Byzantine agents had been at work stirring up trouble;
and the pope demanded his immediate return. The Western Emperor
Henry IV was at the walls of Rome. Leaving his son Bohemond with
an army in Macedonia, Guiscard hurried back to Italy.

The Venetians had promptly and willingly played their part as allies
of Byzantium at Durazzo. It was no fault of theirs that things had gone
wrong. While Guiscard was busy in Italy in 1083 they sent another
fleet. They could not dislodge the Norman soldiers from the castle of
Durazzo, but they took over the lower part of the city and their ships
spent the winter in the harbour. In the spring of 1084 they sailed down
to Corfu and expelled the Norman garrison. All that was left of the
Norman conquest was a tenuous foothold on the Albanian coast. Further
inland the Byzantine army had begun to drive the invaders back from
their positions in Thessaly and Macedonia; and a Byzantine navy had
at last appeared in the Adriatic. But Robert Guiscard was not one to
give in easily. As soon as he had settled his affairs in Italy he got ready
a huge fleet of 150 ships to return to the attack. Alexios once again
called on Venice to come to his aid.[2] Guiscard's first objective was
to recapture Corfu. But his ships were delayed by bad weather and then
attacked by a joint squadron of Venetians and Byzantines. The Venetians
were convinced that victory was theirs after two encounters, until Guiscard rallied the remnants of his fleet and caught them unawares. The
final victory went to the Normans, who went on to retake Corfu.

For Venice it was a disaster. Anna Comnena, whose account does
not always tally with that of western sources, put the Venetian dead
at 13,000.[3] Another 2500 were taken prisoner and horribly treated by
their Norman captors. Nine great warships had been lost, two had been
captured and seven sunk. The news of the victory which had suddenly
turned into so humiliating a defeat caused dismay and anger in Venice.
The responsibility was laid at the door of the Doge, Domenico Silvio.
He was made to abdicate and enter a monastery. Like every Doge before

---

[1] Anna Comnena, iv. 6: I, pp. 157–63; William of Apulia, iv. ll. 450–505: pp. 228–31; Geoffrey
    of Malaterra, c. xxviii, p. 74.
[2] Anna Comnena, vi. 5: II, pp. 51–2. *DR*, II, no. 1119.
[3] Anna Comnena, vi. 5: II, p. 53; Dandolo, p. 218.

him he had his political and family enemies. After the loss of so many ships and men they were not alone in thinking that he must go. But there was no revolution, no violence. Silvio's successor, duly and legally elected, was Vitale Falier (1084–96). In the longer term, however, the Norman victory proved to be of little consequence. The Byzantines had regained the initiative on the mainland and the Norman army on the coast was decimated by a deadly epidemic. In December 1084 Guiscard's son Bohemond was taken ill and had to be sent back to Italy. In July of the following year Guiscard himself caught the plague and died on the island of Cephalonia, which he was planning to occupy. The storm of the Norman invasion had blown itself out, at least for a time. The Emperor Alexios could breathe again. It seemed indeed as if God was on his side. For in the same year 1085 the Seljuq ruler Suleiman died and his Sultanate fell apart into a number of warring principalities.[1]

The Venetians expected their reward for all their sacrifices as allies of Byzantium. They had been promised great things when the emperor first appealed to them. They had lost many ships and many men in the cause; and their ignominious defeat off Corfu had damaged their reputation as masters of the Adriatic Sea. There seems to be no truth in the statement made only by Anna Comnena that they took their revenge on the Normans in a fourth naval battle.[2] The Venetian chroniclers would surely have reported such a victory if it were true. Although they had acted in their own interests as well as in those of Byzantium, they had earned a reward; and there is no doubt whatever that they received it. The text of the chrysobull which Alexios had first promised them in 1081 exists, albeit only in incomplete Latin versions contained in later documents and in a Greek résumé by the emperor's daughter Anna Comnena; and its exact date has been the subject of discussion. The problem has exercised many scholarly minds. The first editors of the document assigned it to May 1082, and this date has been generally accepted, not least by its most recent editor. Others, however, have proposed that it should be dated to the year 1084 or 1092. On balance the year 1082 seems to be correct. The reasons for moving it forward are either inadequate or misinformed. It has been argued that in May 1082, so soon after he had been wounded and forced to retreat from Durazzo, the emperor would hardly have been free to apply his mind to formulating so elaborate and important a document. But no doubt the text had been prepared in advance. For it is evident that it was in part a reward for services already rendered by the Venetians at Durazzo,

[1] Kretschmayr, I, pp. 160–4; Cessi, *Storia*, I, pp. 125–30.
[2] Anna Comnena, vi. 5: II, p. 54.

as the emperor says in its preamble, and in part an incentive to put them under further obligation to continue the good work.[1]

The content of the document, however, is rather more important than its date, for it was by far the most comprehensive and detailed charter of privileges hitherto granted to Venice by a Byzantine Emperor. It was also the most consequential, for it became the corner-stone of the Venetian colonial empire in the eastern Mediterranean, the prototype of a series of imperial chrysobulls for Venice in the next one hundred years. Alexios was in generous mood. The reasons for his generosity are stated at the beginning of the document. The Venetians are being rewarded for their loyalty in times past and especially for the great services rendered by their ships at Durazzo. The privileges which they have thus earned are then itemised as follows: 1. An annual grant of twenty pounds (of gold coins) is to be made for distribution among their churches as they see fit. 2. The Doge is to be honoured with the title of *protosebastos*, with a substantial stipend; and this honour is accorded not simply *ad personam*, as it would be in Byzantium: it is to be hereditary and handed on to his successors in perpetuity. 3. The Patriarch of Grado and his successors are to be similarly honoured with an annual stipend of twenty pounds and the title of *hypertimos* or most honourable.[2] 4. The church of St Mark in Venice is to receive three gold coins every year from each of the establishments owned by merchants from Amalfi in Constantinople and the empire. 5. The Venetians are to be allotted a number of shops, factories and houses in Constantinople in the market area of Perama, with free access to and egress from all the district stretching from the Jew's Gate to Vigla (the Watch Gate) with its warehouses and its three

---

[1] The Latin text of the chrysobull was originally published in *TTh*, I, no. XXIII, pp. 51–4. The latest and more critical edition of it is in S. Borsari, 'Il crisobullo di Alessio I per Venezia', *Annali dell' Istituto Italiano per gli studi storici*, II (1969–70), 111–31 (124–31: Appendices A and B). Cf. Lilie, *Handel und Politik*, pp. 8–16. On its date, see A. Tuilier, 'La date exacte du chrysobule d'Alexis I Comnène en faveur des Vénitiens et son contexte historique', *RSBN*, n.s., IV (1967), 27–48; E. Frances, 'Alexis Comnène et les privilèges octroyés à Venise', *BS*, XXIX (1968), 17–23; M. E. Martin, 'The chrysobull of Alexius I Comnenus to the Venetians and the early Venetian Quarter in Constantinople', *BS*, XXXIX (1978), 19–23; Anitra R. Gadolin, 'Alexis Comnenus and the Venetian trade privileges. A New Interpretation', *B*, L (1980), 439–46; O. Tůma, 'The dating of Alexius's chrysobull to the Venetians: 1082, 1084, or 1092?', *BS*, XLII (1981), 171–85; Lilie, *Handel und Politik*, pp. 8 n. 19, 331–5.

[2] The title of *protosebastos* was one of several invented by Alexios I and at this time ranked fourth in the court order after the emperor. E. Stein, *Untersuchungen zur spätbyzantinischen Verfassungs- und Wirtschaftsgeschichte*, Mitteilungen zur osmanischen Geschichte, II, 1–2 (Hanover, 1925), pp. 30–1. The title of *hypertimos* was bestowed on several bishops of the Byzantine church in later years, but the Patriarch of Grado seems to have been the first to receive it. H.-G. Beck, *Kirche und theologische Literatur im byzantinischen Reich* (Munich, 1959), p. 68.

landing stages on the Golden Horn; in addition the church of St Akindynos, which seems already to have been granted to the Venetians, is to
enjoy the annual revenue of the bakery alongside it. 6. The Venetians
will also be given possession of the church of St Andrew in Durazzo
with its property and revenues, except for the material stored there for
the imperial navy. 7. The emperor grants to Venetian merchants the
right to trade in all manner of merchandise in all parts of his empire
free of any charge, tax, or duty payable to his treasury. The names of
the towns are specified, as are the taxes from which the Venetians are
exempted and the titles of the customs and revenue officials from whose
authority they are free. 8. These dispensations are offered to the Venetians
as true servants of the emperor who have proved their goodwill towards
him and have promised to serve him and his heirs with all their might
for evermore. Wherefore no one, private citizen, church, or monastery,
is to question their rights to the properties assigned to them in Constantinople, even though some prior title might be advanced to the said warehouses and landing stages. The donation of them to the Venetians is
immutable and inviolable and it will be recorded in a *praktikon* or survey
which will in due course be filed in the imperial registry. 9. Anyone
who infringes the dispositions of this chrysobull shall without fail be
fined ten pounds of gold by the secretary for home affairs and be required
to pay four times the value of any goods that he has misappropriated
from the Venetians.[1]

The chrysobull which Basil I had issued for Venice in 992 envisaged
a passing traffic of merchant ships up and down the Hellespont to and
from Constantinople, though privileged to pay their dues only to the
highest official of the state. The chrysobull of Alexios Komnenos envisaged a permanent colony of resident Venetian traders on the Golden
Horn in the heart of Constantinople. Certain buildings, a church and
three landing stages were formally designated as Venetian property. In
addition, Venetian merchants were now to be exempt from the payment
of any dues whatsoever in Constantinople or any of the markets of the
Byzantine Empire, with the exception, as it later appeared, of the islands
of Crete and Cyprus. These provisions alone were enough to make them
feel that their sacrifices in the war against the Normans had not been
in vain. The privilege of free trade would put their competitors, Greek
or Italian, out of business in Byzantine markets. The merchants of Amalfi,
who had for long been established in Constantinople and who had been
singled out as competitors in 992, were now classed as tribute-paying

[1] Brown, 'The Venetian Quarter', 70–2; Borsari, 'Il crisobullo', 119–20. On the Amalfitans,
who had been the first Italians to have a trading concession in Constantinople, see M. Balard,
'Amalfi et Byzance (x^e–xiie siècles)', *TM*, vi (1976), 85–95.

subordinates of Venice. The Venetians had been given a monopoly, legally sanctioned and perpetually guaranteed.

The terms of the chrysobull were no doubt the result of some hard bargaining by Venetian agents in Constantinople. The emperor too must have spent long hours reasoning with his Patriarch over the alienation of churches and church property to Christians of the Roman rite. The wording of the document gives no hint of this. Like the chrysobull of 992 it purports to be a charter graciously and generously granted by the Emperor of the Romans as a mark of favour to those who have loyally served his cause. It is unfortunate that the text as it has survived tells only of the privileges granted to Venice. There must once have been a corresponding section setting out the reciprocal obligations of the Venetians themselves. For the emperor, though in generous mood, must have expected something from them in return. They are indeed described no longer as 'outsiders' but as 'true and faithful servants', loyal to the crown. It is as though they were in some sense still subjects of the emperor; and so far as concerned the law those residing in Constantinople were to be treated as such. As in all Byzantine documents of state the terminology of the text is taken from the past. Its style is formally archaic; and, as a chrysobull, it is not phrased as a contract between two parties. Perhaps Alexios saw this as a safeguard. It was a form of charter which, since it emanated from him alone, could be withdrawn at any moment for all its protestations of perpetuity. At the time he badly needed the continuing help and friendship of Venice. When order had been restored in the world he could modify the terms or cancel the arrangement, as his successor tried to do. If such thoughts were in his mind he deluded himself. His chrysobull gave the Venetians a foot in the door that led to the wealth of Byzantium. They made sure that its terms, far from being modified, were renewed and extended at intervals until the door was pushed wide open. On the other hand it was a document clearly designed to bring the Venetians back into the Byzantine orbit, as dependable allies if not as grateful subjects.

The *praktikon* or itemised survey of properties promised to them by the emperor does not survive. It is therefore hard to determine the precise limits of the Venetian colony as established in Constantinople in 1082. It may indeed be incorrect to speak of a colony or quarter in the sense of landownership at this stage. That was to come some fifty years later. What Alexios made over to the Venetians was a number of separate buildings and properties in the commercial area or market of Perama on the Golden Horn where, presumably, they already had the use of a wharf and business premises, as did other foreign traders in the city. The number of wharfs or landing stages exclusively for their use was now increased to three; and the warehouses, factories and shops within a prescribed area were declared to be freehold Venetian property. There is as yet no mention of a Venetian consul or representative. The chrysobull had been directed to the Doge and people of Venice. It was up to them to make their own arrangements for their properties and their residents in Constantinople, subject to the laws of the city.

Two years later, in 1084, the new Doge, Vitale Falier, sent three envoys to Constantinople at the emperor's request. Dandolo reports that he was honoured with another imperial chrysobull granting him jurisdiction over Dalmatia and Croatia and the title of *protosebastos*.[1] Dandolo may have invented the first of these privileges. But the second may be true, even though the title had already been conferred on Falier's predecessor, Domenico Silvio, in 1082 and on his successors in perpetuity. Silvio was still alive in 1084 and still, it appears, proudly styling himself *protosebastos*.[2] Better substantiated is the action that Vitale Falier took with regard to the Venetian real estate in Constantinople. In 1090 he made much of it over to the church. The abbot of the monastery of San Giorgio Maggiore in Venice and his successors became landlords of the buildings in Constantinople situated between the Gate of Vigla and the Gate of Perama. Other buildings were made over to the monastery of St Nicholas. In 1107 the Doge Ordelafo Falier formally ceded to the Patriarch of Grado the church of St Akindynos, which Alexios had confirmed as being a Venetian possession in his chrysobull. With the church went all its land, treasures, books and other properties, including its shops and its bakery; and the clergy of St Akindynos became the keepers and guardians of the standard weights and measures used by all Venetian merchants. This transaction saved the Doge and his heirs some money. For it was stipulated that the Patriarch of Grado was to have the usufruct of St Akindynos in place of his Venetian revenues and his annual stipend from the state. The Doge found it simpler and cheaper to farm out to the church much of the property that went with the all-important warehouses and wharfs in Constantinople; though he was careful to reserve

---

[1] Dandolo, p. 217. *TTh*, i, no. xxiv, pp. 54–5; *DR*, ii, no. 1109. Lilie, *Handel und Politik*, p. 10. The supposition (cf. Lazzarini, 'I titoli', 283–7) that the first Doge to be made *protosebastos* was Vitale Falier in 1084 and that the chrysobull cannot therefore be dated to 1082 is disproved by the evidence that the Doge Domenico Silvio already bore the title in 1083. *Famiglia Zusto*, ed. L. Lanfranchi, Fonti per la Storia di Venezia, Sez. 4. Archivi Privati (Venice, 1955), no. i, p. 6: 'Dominicii Silvii ducis senioris nostri et imperialis protonsevasto ...'. Cf. Borsari, 'Il crisobullo', 114; Lilie, *Handel und Politik*, pp. 8 n. 19, 335–6.

[2] *Famiglia Zusto*, no. iii, p. 13 (A.D. 1086): 'nos quidem Dominicus Silvius quondam Dei gratia Venetie dux et imperialis protonsebastos ...'. Cf. Borsari, 'Il crisobullo', 115.

for himself and his agents the use of the largest of the three landing stages, the Scala Maior.[1]

The Norman threat to Byzantium, which the Venetians had helped to thwart, seemed to die with the death of Robert Guiscard in 1085. The Venetians had seen it as a threat to their control of the Adriatic Sea. For this reason if for no other the Doge had gone to the relief of Durazzo. It was an important staging post on the maritime route to the east, with a large population of traders from Amalfi as well as from Venice. The emperor acknowledged this fact by giving the church of St Andrew in Durazzo to the Venetians and naming it as one of the cities in which they could trade duty free. The Amalfitans were not so privileged; they were treated as second-class citizens. Durazzo reverted to Byzantine rule in 1085, evidently with some reluctance. The Emperor had to ask the Venetians in Constantinople to intervene and advise their own people and the Amalfitans in the city to give it up.[2] Twenty years later the Normans were to try again to get it back. Bohemond, son of Robert Guiscard, had by then covered himself in dubious glory in the First Crusade. In 1105 he returned to Italy to prepare a crusade of a different kind, the second Norman conquest of Byzantium. It was to follow the route that he had taken before, and again the enterprise was blessed by the pope. In 1107, with a force of 34,000 men, he sailed over from Apulia, captured Valona and laid siege to Durazzo. This time, however, the Byzantines were ready for him. The empire was not the feeble and disintegrating institution that it had been in 1081. The Emperor Alexios had given it new life. He had annihilated the barbarous Pechenegs in the north; he had the measure of the Seljuq Sultan in the east; and above all he knew his Norman enemy from bitter experience in Constantinople and Syria. As a precaution, however, he called for support from Venice. The Doge, Ordelafo Falier, sent a fleet to join forces with the Byzantine ships off Durazzo and with the army which the Emperor himself commanded. In September 1108 Bohemond was forced to surrender. Better still, he was browbeaten into making a treaty with Alexios in his camp by the river Devol in Albania. The text of the treaty is recorded

[1] *TTh*, I, nos. XXII, XXV, XXXIII, pp. 43, 55–63, 67–74; *San Giorgio Maggiore*, II. *Documenti 982–1159*, Fonti per la Storia di Venezia, Sez. 2. Archivi Ecclesiastici–Diocesi Castellana ed. L. Lanfranchi (Venice, 1968), no. 69, pp. 168–75 (July 1090). Brown, 'The Venetian Quarter', 80–1; Chrysa A. Maltézou, 'Il quartiere veneziano di Costantinopoli (Scali marittimi)', *Thesaurismata*, XV (1978), 30–61, especially 32–42. On the church of St Akindynos, see R. Janin, *La Géographie ecclésiastique de l'empire byzantin*, I: *Le Siège de Constantinople et le patriarcat oecuménique*, III: *Les Églises et les monastères*, 2nd edn (Paris, 1969), p. 571.

[2] Anna Comnena, *Alexiad*, vi. 6: II, pp. 56–7. *DR*, II, no. 1126. A. Ducellier, *La Façade maritime de l'Albanie au moyen âge* (Thessaloniki, 1981), pp. 70–3.

in full by the emperor's admiring daughter Anna Comnena. Bohemond had to swear a solemn oath of vassalage as the liege man of the emperor. As a westerner he understood its implications all too well. It meant the end of his ambitions. He died in 1111. But the dream of the Norman conquest of Byzantium continued to haunt his heirs.[1]

Vitale Falier, who succeeded Domenico Silvio as Doge in 1084, had reaped the first benefits of the imperial chrysobull which gave his people such far-reaching investments from Durazzo to Constantinople to distant Laodikeia in Asia Minor. He had also lived just long enough to witness the completion of the new church of St Mark in Venice. The consecration of the church was attended by high and supernatural drama. When the day came to transfer the sacred relics of the saint to their new shrine they were nowhere to be found. They had always been hidden and the secret of their hiding place was supposed to be known only to the Doge and the highest dignitary of the church. Now they were lost. For three days the whole community of Venice, led by the Doge and clergy, fasted and prayed, until a miracle occurred. Part of a column supporting the church collapsed, leaving a hole in which the saint's sarcophagus was revealed. Some said that a hand was seen to be beckoning from it and that the saint's body lying inside was found to be whole and uncorrupted. This legend, like so many tales telling of the foundation and glory of Venice, was invented long afterwards. The only certain fact, substantiated by an inscription on the lead casket containing the relics, is that the mortal remains of St Mark were deposited in the crypt of the finished building on 8 October 1094. Later Venetian antiquarians and chroniclers, however, were not content with bare facts. They discovered that the builders of the church of the Holy Apostles in Constantinople, on which their own church was modelled, had unearthed in the earlier foundations the relics of Saints Andrew, Luke and Timothy. The Venetians could do better than the Byzantines. They could first lose and then find a whole Evangelist and make him reveal himself by a miraculous apparition.[2]

The famous Pala d'Oro for the high altar of the new church of St Mark was commissioned by Ordelafo Falier (1101–18), the Doge who had answered the emperor's call for help against Bohemond in 1108. It was made to order by Byzantine craftsmen in Constantinople in 1105; and it replaced the earlier altar screen made in the time of Pietro Orseolo

---

[1] Anna Comnena, *Alexiad*, xii. 1–2, 8–9; xiii. 1–12: III, pp. 50–4, 77–85, 87–139; Dandolo, p. 226. *DR*, II, no. 1238; *TTh*, I, no. XXXIII, pp. 74–5. Runciman, *Crusades*, II, pp. 47–51; J. Ferluga, 'La ligesse dans l'empire byzantin', *ZRVI*, VII (1961), 97–123.

[2] Dandolo, p. 219. Demus, *San Marco*, pp. 12–13.

in the tenth century. As it now stands, the Pala d'Oro is a much larger and more elaborate gallery of Byzantine enamels than that commissioned in 1105. Its lowest section, however, is probably of that date, though the figures displayed in it have been rearranged and some have disappeared. In the centre stands the Virgin, flanked on the left by the figure of the Doge Ordelafo Falier and on the right by that of the Empress Eirene, presumably the wife of Alexios Komnenos. Various explanations have been offered for this odd juxtaposition of figures. It has been suggested that the portrait of the Doge may originally have been that of the Emperor Alexios. Or that there may at first have been four persons represented, the emperor and his wife Eirene, and the Doge with the son and co-emperor of Alexios, John II. Less probably, the figure of the Doge could have been superimposed on a portrait of the Emperor John II, whose wife was also called Eirene, and who fell out of favour in Venice when he declined to renew his father's chrysobull. The portrait of the Doge, however, is clearly inscribed in Latin as that of Ordelafo Falier, even though its head was subsequently changed; and the portrait of the lady is clearly inscribed in Greek as 'Eirene the most pious empress'.

Technically it would not have been possible to superimpose the Latin inscription on the Doge's portrait on a Greek original. This fact rules out the suggestion that the figure was originally either Alexios or his son John. Yet the Doge, although only a *protosebastos* by title, is shown in the full regalia of an emperor, with sceptre, crown and halo. The most convincing explanation seems to be that the twelfth-century Pala d'Oro carried portraits only of Alexios Komnenos and his wife Eirene, the donors and benefactors of Venice. In 1105 protocol would surely have forbidden a portrait of the Doge standing alongside that of the emperor, as if they were equal partners. A hundred years later, however, matters were different. After the Fourth Crusade in 1204 the Doge of Venice assumed the almost imperial title of lord of three-eighths of Constantinople. The partnership between Byzantium and Venice had been shattered. At this point and in these circumstances the portrait of the emperor on the Pala d'Oro may well have been removed and that of the Doge inserted in its place. This could have been one of the consequences of the 'renovation' of the Pala which Dandolo sets in the year 1209. The procurator of the church of St Mark at that time was Angelo Falier, a descendant of the illustrious Doge Ordelafo who had commissioned the work in 1105. Angelo may have felt moved to take out and discard the portrait of the now discredited Byzantine Emperor and to replace it with that of his ancestor, somewhat clumsily copied from the original and so depicted with all the trappings of an emperor to which the Doges felt entitled after 1204. When and why the head of Ordelafo was later changed remains a mystery, but it may have been when the screen was next renovated, in 1345.[1]

The Pala d'Oro in its present form conceals the mystery of its origins behind the dazzling wealth and beauty of its later accretions. Yet it recalls and symbolises the relationship between Byzantium and Venice as it existed at the beginning of the twelfth century. It was a partnership in which the senior partner and giver of good things was Byzantium.

---

[1] Dandolo, p. 225. Demus, *San Marco*, pp. 23–5; W. F. Volbach, A. Pertusi, B. Bischoff, H. R. Hahnloser, *Il Tesoro di San Marco: La Pala d'Oro*, Fondazione Giorgio Cini (Florence, 1965); J. Deér, 'Die Pala d'Oro in neuer Sicht', *BZ*, LXII (1969), 308–44; S. Bettini, 'Le opere d'arte importate a Venezia durante le Crociate', in *Venezia dalla Prima Crociata alla Conquista di Costantinopoli del 1204* (Florence, 1965), translated (with all its inaccuracies, though with excellent illustrations) as S. Bettini, 'Venice, the Pala d'Oro and Constantinople', in *The Treasury of San Marco Venice* (The British Museum: Olivetti, Milan, 1984), pp. 35–64.

5

BYZANTIUM, VENICE AND
THE FIRST CRUSADE

THE remains of St Mark had lain in their new shrine in Venice for just over a year when a movement was launched in western Europe which was to have consequences that no one could foresee. In November 1095 Pope Urban II addressed the throng of clerics and laymen assembled for his Council at Clermont. He announced it as his will that the Christians of the west should march to the rescue of their brethren in the east, threatened as they were with extinction by the godless Turks. The whole of a reunited Christendom could then proceed to the liberation of the Holy Land. The idea of an armed pilgrimage, or a crusade, touched a chord in the hearts of his western audience; and as the word got around the response was overwhelming. The pope had proposed that the 'soldiers of Christ' should assemble at Constantinople. Within twelve months of the Council at Clermont thousands had set out, trudging overland in more or less disorganised bands. The pope had unwittingly unleashed forces in western society which it would be difficult to control.

The task of controlling them when they reached Constantinople fell on the Emperor Alexios Komnenos. The news of their approach filled him with horror and dismay. Nor was he clear about the pope's intentions. It was not long since the previous pope had denounced him as the excommunicated enemy of western Christendom and the target of a just war directed by that champion of the faith, Robert Guiscard. Since then the emperor had indeed made diplomatic efforts to win the sympathy and support of Pope Urban II, but for a limited purpose. His efforts had been well received, though his purpose had been misinterpreted. In March 1095 his ambassadors had presented his case to the pope at the Council at Piacenza. He had asked for help in the form of limited numbers of mercenary soldiers. By then his campaign against the Seljuq Turks was going well. The Sultanate was divided in civil war. The tide was in the emperor's favour. With more troops at his command he might take it at the flood. He would pay them well and they would fight alongside the many Franks already in his service. Perhaps his mistake was to play on the fancies of western Christians by suggesting that, with their help, the Holy Land might be freed from the infidel. The price that he had to pay was the First Crusade, not a welcome and manageable body of mercenaries but, as his daughter Anna was later to describe it, a mass movement from west to east of 'all the barbarians between the Adriatic and the Pillars of Hercules'.[1] The Byzantines had grown accustomed to small numbers of Venetian and other western residents in Constantinople. They did not much care for their rude and noisy ways. They had never expected to see the 'Franks' in such overwhelming multitudes; and it was no comfort to learn that some of their leaders were Normans, among them Bohemond, son of Robert Guiscard.

This is not the place to rehearse the story of the First Crusade, except in so far as it affected relationships between Byzantium and Venice. The first hordes of pilgrims from the west led by Peter the Hermit were wiped out by the Turks in Asia Minor. The crusading armies of knights that followed them were rather better disciplined and the emperor prevailed upon all but one of their leaders to take an oath of loyalty to him. He promised to assist them in every way on the understanding that they would restore to him any places which they captured on their long march to the Holy Land. In May 1097 crusaders and Byzantines co-operated in laying siege to Nicaea, the capital of the Seljuq Sultanate in Asia Minor. The city was taken after seven weeks and was garrisoned by Byzantine troops. The crusaders then pressed on across the high plains of Anatolia, and by the autumn they had reached Antioch in Syria. Their conquest of Antioch in June 1098 was a brilliant if hard-won victory. But it led to their first serious clash with the Byzantines. Bohemond, who made himself master of the city, refused to consider handing it over to the emperor in accordance with his agreement since, in his view, the emperor had broken his promise by not sending help when help was needed. Bohemond stayed put in Antioch while the rest of the crusaders, led by Raymond of Toulouse, who had hoped to gain Antioch for himself, marched on towards Jerusalem. The Holy City, the goal of their endeavours, fell to the crusaders in July 1099. They had endured a long and bitter assault in the heat of summer. They relieved their feelings and displayed their fanaticism in a merciless massacre of all the Muslim and Jewish inhabitants. Raymond of Toulouse, who had piously declined to be crowned as king in the city of Christ, was once again outwitted. The title of Defender of the Holy Sepulchre was conferred on his rival, Godfrey of Bouillon.

The Latin Kingdom of Jerusalem, then effectively constituted, was

[1] Anna Comnena, *Alexiad*, x. 5: II, p. 209.

only one of several independent principalities established by the knights of the crusade on what had once been Byzantine territory. But it was the loss of Antioch which most distressed the emperor. He sent troops and ships to isolate it. In 1101 Bohemond was taken prisoner by the Turks. He was quickly ransomed by his colleagues; but after the crushing defeat of the crusaders at Harran in 1104 he decided to return to Europe to take his revenge on the Byzantines who, he believed, had basely betrayed him and undermined the cause of the holy war. Such was his excuse for following the trail blazed by his late father Robert Guiscard, bringing his men across the straits from Italy to Durazzo. He was thwarted and humiliated. By terms of the treaty imposed upon him in 1108 Bohemond became the emperor's vassal. As such he was allowed to keep Antioch. He died three years later. His nephew Tancred, however, whom he had left in charge of Antioch, refused to accept that the emperor's terms applied to him. The Norman threat to Byzantium in the Balkans might be over but the Norman possession of Antioch remained a nagging problem and a cause of dissension between Byzantines and crusaders for another thirty years.

The Doge of Venice had willingly come to the emperor's aid against Bohemond at Durazzo in 1107. What happened in the Adriatic Sea was of more immediate interest to the Venetians than events in Syria and Palestine. They had been slow to join the bandwagon of the crusades. A new Doge, Vitale Michiel, had been elected in 1096, and he had been loth to commit himself to the cause. The emerging commercial republics of Pisa and Genoa were quicker off the mark. The Pisans and the Genoese, though as yet little involved in Byzantium and the eastern Mediterranean, had been active in defending the western shores of Italy against the Arabs in the eleventh century. In 1087 they had joined forces with the Romans and Amalfitans in a large and successful expedition sponsored by the pope to North Africa, from which they made a handsome profit in plunder and trade concessions. The Genoese were the first to send a flotilla to the east to support the crusade. Theirs was a private initiative, though the pope had invited them to help; and they were rewarded with promising commercial privileges in Antioch.[1] The larger fleet from Pisa, which set out in 1098, had a more public and official nature, for it was carrying the Archbishop Daimbert whom the pope had appointed as his legate in the east. Daimbert was shortly to become Patriarch of Jerusalem and his influence brought many more rewards to the merchants

[1] K. M. Setton, ed., *A History of the Crusades*, 1, 2nd edn (Milwaukee–London, 1969), pp. 52–3; Lilie, *Handel und Politik*, p. 339.

of Pisa in the crusader states.[1] The news that others were already making profits out of the crusade concentrated the minds of the Venetians. They had been reluctant to act until they saw how matters developed. They had their interests in Constantinople to consider. They were also anxious about the effect of a holy war against the infidel on their lucrative trade with the Muslims, especially with the Fatimids of Egypt. But by 1099, with Antioch and Jerusalem both in Christian hands, the outcome of the crusade was unexpectedly hopeful. The Venetians could no longer stand on the sidelines. They equipped the largest fleet that had yet been sent from Italy to the Levant.[2]

It is a curious fact that the only major source for the first Venetian intervention in the crusade is the account of the translation of the relics of St Nicholas of Myra from Asia Minor to Venice. It was written some fifteen or twenty years after the event. The patriotic monk who composed it clearly thought that the acquisition of another saint for his city was of greater significance than the holy war being waged in the east. He was after all a monk of the Benedictine monastery on the Lido dedicated to St Nicholas. He relates how the Doge Vitale Michiel, fired with zeal for the crusade, prepared a fleet of about 200 ships which set out from Venice in the summer of 1099. It was under the command of the Doge's son, Giovanni Michiel. Its spiritual leader was the Bishop of Olivolo (Castello), Enrico Contarini. They sailed down the Adriatic, round the Peloponnese and on to Rhodes where they would spend the winter. When the Byzantine Emperor heard of their arrival there he sent messengers to persuade them to go no further. Most of them paid no heed to the emperor's demands and the rest were won over by the eloquence of their bishop.

While they were at Rhodes a fleet of fifty warships from Pisa arrived. They were flying Byzantine standards and pretending to be a squadron of the Byzantine navy. The Venetians were alarmed and humbly asked them not to provoke hostility between fellow Christians. The Pisans replied with arrogant abuse. The Venetians were finally driven to putting thirty of their own ships to sea; and in a bloodless victory they captured twenty-eight of the Pisan vessels with the loss of only four of their own. Nearly 4000 Pisans were taken prisoner. The Byzantine officials in Rhodes demanded that the prisoners should be sent to the emperor to be executed. This the Venetians refused to do. Instead they let them

---

[1] Runciman, *Crusades*, I, pp. 112, 219, 299ff.; J. Prawer, *Histoire du Royaume latin de Jérusalem*, I (Paris, 1969), pp. 258–64.

[2] S. Runciman, 'L'intervento di Venezia dalla prima alla terza Crociata', in *Venezia dalla Prima Crociata alla Conquista di Costantinopoli del 1204* (Florence, 1965), pp. 1–22, especially pp. 6–11.

all go free, except for thirty-six who volunteered to stay with them, on condition of a promise that the Pisans would stop trading in Byzantine waters and never again make war on Christians. In the spring the Venetian fleet left Rhodes and made first for Myra across the water in Asia Minor. (Had they gone first to Smyrna, as the narrator says, they would have made a very long detour.) There they ardently sought and miraculously discovered the remains not only of St Nicholas but also of his uncle Nicholas and of St Theodore the Martyr. Taking this precious cargo on board they sailed on to the Holy Land whence, after performing heroic deeds, they went back to Venice. Their arrival in the lagoons was nicely timed to coincide with the feast of St Nicholas of Myra, on 6 December 1100.[1]

There is much that is credible in this story and much that stretches credulity. The Pisans had in fact been assisting Bohemond in his illegal blockade of the Byzantine port of Laodikeia (Lattakieh) in Syria.[2] But the details of their battle with the Venetians off Rhodes are questionable; and their alleged promise to stop trading in Byzantine waters is anachronistic, since no Pisan merchants are known to have challenged the Venetian monopoly of Byzantine trade as early as 1100. The story is, however, presented as that of a venture whose motive, unusually for Venice, was religious and not commercial. It begins with an act of reverence to St Nicholas in his church on the Lido. It ends with the solemn interment of his mortal remains in that church for evermore. It is a work of piety and told in the manner of such works, a pilgrim's tale rather than an objective historical narrative. But it is also a work of propaganda of a less edifying type. The Bishop of Olivolo, then known as Castello, who led the expedition was the acknowledged primate of Venice. In 1094, five years before he set out, the body of St Mark had made its miraculous apparition in the new church dedicated to him in Venice. St Mark had always been the patron of the city, the symbol of the state, whose shrine was in the Doge's chapel. The bishopric of the church of Venice stood in need of a patron saint to call its own. St Nicholas of Myra, protector of those who sail the seas, was the obvious choice. His church on the Lido had been built by the Doge Domenico Contarini, father of the Bishop Enrico. It would be a double act of piety to adorn it with the relics of its saint.

It was unfortunate that the church of Bari already housed what was

[1] *Translatio Sancti Nicolai*, in RHC, Hist. occ., v (1895), pp. 253–92; Dandolo, pp. 221–4; *Annales Venetici breves*, in MGH, Script., xiv, p. 70; Albert of Aix, *Historia Hierosolymitana*, in RHC, Hist. occ., iv (1879), pp. 519–22. Kretschmayr, i, pp. 215–16, 455; Cessi, *Storia*, i, pp. 137–9; Lilie, *Handel und Politik*, pp. 340–1.
[2] Runciman, *Crusades*, i, pp. 300–2.

claimed to be the body of St Nicholas. It had been brought there from Myra by some merchants in 1087 and the crypt of the great church built for it was consecrated by Pope Urban II in 1089. The fact was substantiated by two pious accounts of the translation of St Nicholas to Bari. The Venetians were seldom daunted by facts when they conflicted with the legendary glory of their city. The real St Nicholas, yet to be found, would reveal himself to them, as St Mark had done. And so it came about. When they broke into the sanctuary and excavated the altar of the church at Myra they found three coffins. One contained the uncle of St Nicholas, the second St Theodore; but the third was empty. The custodians, when threatened with violence, stuck to their story that the third body had already been removed by some men from Bari, though there was a local tradition that the Emperor Basil I had once tried and failed to take St Nicholas to Constantinople. The Bishop of Venice prayed loud and long for a miracle. He was rewarded by an odour of sanctity coming from another tomb in the church. It was hacked open and inside it, to the great delight of the Venetians, lay the remains of St Nicholas. There was no doubt that this was the real Nicholas. Beside him lay the palm branch, still green and new, which he had brought with him from Jerusalem. The bishop and the Doge's son attested that he was authentic. There was also an inscription in Greek which they left in its place in Myra to be found later on by a pilgrim. This was perhaps dubious evidence. But the surest guarantee of the truth lay in the circumstance, readily believed by those present, that the body of St Nicholas had revealed its own whereabouts by a form of apparition, just like St Mark. The people of Bari could cling to their illusions. The real St Nicholas belonged to Venice. The monk of his monastery on the Lido joyfully celebrated the twin blessings of his city, with its Lion, of St Mark, which brought it victory in war, and its Sailor, St Nicholas, who feared no storm by sea. The Greek Bishop of Myra was understandably upset when he heard of the robbery and of the damage done to his cathedral. He compared the barbarity of the Venetians with that of the Turks. The Venetians were a little abashed. They gave him back one of the reliquaries which they had found in the altar and, by way of conscience money, 100 gold bezants to pay for the damage.[1]

When they had done their business at Myra the Venetians, as the monk relates, sailed on to the Holy Land and performed heroic deeds

---

[1] *Translatio S. Nicolai*, pp. 267, 281, 290–1. A. Pertusi, 'Ai confini tra religione e politica: la contesa per le reliquie di San Nicola tra Bari, Venezia e Genova', *Quaderni medievali*, v (1978), 6–58; Pertusi, 'Venezia e Bisanzio', 6–7; Cessi, *Storia*, I, pp. 144–5; Lilie, *Handel und Politik*, pp. 341–5.

before going home with their trophies. Their heroism as valiant crusaders
was less apparent then their jealous attention to self interest. They
dropped anchor at Jaffa in June 1100. Godfrey of Bouillon, Defender
of the Holy Sepulchre, was glad to hurry from Jerusalem to welcome
them. He was badly in need of naval support. But the Venetians would
not give him their services for nothing. They agreed to help the cause
for two months, until 15 August. In return they demanded the right
of free trade in all Godfrey's dominions, a market and a church in every
town so far liberated, and one-third of every town that they helped to
capture from the infidel. On these terms they consented to assist in the
conquest of Haifa, Acre and Tripoli. In the event their fleet was delayed
off Jaffa partly by contrary winds and partly by the death of Godfrey
and the election of his successor, Baldwin of Edessa. Time was short
and a compromise was reached. The Venetians would limit themselves
to joining in an assault on Haifa before their contract ran out in August.
It was successful. Haifa was stormed and captured. Its Jewish and Muslim
populations were massacred and the Venetians were allotted one-third
of the city. That was the end of their co-operation. Leaving some merchants and sailors in Haifa they set out for home, still carrying the relics
of their saints. It was to be ten years before another Venetian fleet sailed
for Syria.[1]

Meanwhile the Genoese, who had been the first Italians on the scene,
combined heroism with business, helping Baldwin to capture Arsuf and
Caesarea in 1101 and Acre in 1104. The Venetian merchants moved their
market to Acre and set up a small trading colony in Antioch. It seemed
as though they were content to let their commercial rivals from Pisa
and Genoa have a free hand in exploiting the new markets in the crusader
states. They were still reluctant to become involved. They were aware
that the Byzantine Emperor was far from sympathetic towards the establishment of those states and concerned about the turn which the crusade
had taken. The Venetians did not want to alienate either the emperor
or the Fatimids of Egypt, with both of whom they were still actively
doing business. The certainties of their existing, stable markets in Constantinople and Alexandria were more important than the uncertain possibilities of much smaller and less stable markets in Syria and Palestine.[2]
But they were also preoccupied with affairs nearer home at the beginning
of the twelfth century. The King of Hungary had marched into the neighbouring Kingdom of Croatia and from there descended on the coastal

---

[1] *Translatio S. Nicolai*, pp. 272–8. Kretschmayr, I, pp. 216–17; Runciman, *Crusades*, I, pp. 312–
17; Runciman, 'L'intervento di Venezia', pp. 11–12.
[2] Runciman, *Crusades*, II, pp. 73–4, 87–8; Lilie, *Handel und Politik*, pp. 345–6.

cities of Dalmatia. Hungarian domination of the Dalmatian coast endangered Venetian freedom of passage in the Adriatic. It was a direct challenge to the Doges' title of Duke of Dalmatia. The challenge was met by Venice with characteristic determination. The Byzantine Emperor too was rightly apprehensive of the rising power of Hungary in the Balkans. To bring it within the Byzantine family he arranged for his son and heir to marry a Hungarian princess. The Venetians on the other hand had to fight for their rights in Dalmatia. The struggle went on for ten years. In 1125 they forced an agreement of sorts on the Hungarian King, Stephen II. But the problem remained with them for the rest of the twelfth century.[1]

There were nevertheless moments when the Venetians felt that they could not let developments in the east pass them by. One such moment came in 1110 when the Doge Ordelafo Falier led a fleet to Palestine. He arrived in time to lend support to Baldwin of Jerusalem who was laying siege to the town of Sidon. His ships dispersed the Fatimid fleet and Sidon fell to the Christians in December. The Venetians had their reward in the form of new trading concessions in Acre, a more lucrative market than Sidon, and one which the Genoese thought they had already cornered.[2] But with a war in Dalmatia on their hands they could not afford to emulate the Genoese by maintaining a more or less permanent naval presence in the Holy Land; and their regular commercial traffic with Constantinople was in any case more vital to their interests. They cannot have enjoyed hearing that the emperor in Constantinople had been negotiating with Pisa. In October 1111 Alexios issued a chrysobull to the Pisans which for the first time accorded them a privileged status within the Byzantine Empire. His motives were political and diplomatic rather than economic. By flattering the Pisans he might dissuade them from giving comfort to his enemies, notably to Bohemond's nephew Tancred who persistently refused to surrender his title to the city of Antioch. In any event, the emperor could not ignore the growing importance of Pisa and Genoa in the crusader states. Anna Comnena reports that earlier in 1111 a number of Genoese, Pisan and Lombard ships had tried to force a passage up the Hellespont to Constantinople. The Byzantine navy had turned them back. They may have been no more than pirates. But the episode underlined the truth that the new Italian powers were a force to be reckoned with in Byzantine waters.[3]

[1] Kretschmayr, I, pp. 218–20, 457–8.
[2] Dandolo, p. 228. Runciman, *Crusades*, II, pp. 92–3; Prawer, *Royaume latin de Jérusalem*, I, p. 276.
[3] Anna Comnena, *Alexiad*, xiv. 3; II, p. 154ff. Cf. Lilie, *Handel und Politik*, pp. 361–2.

The privileges which Alexios granted to the Pisans in his chrysobull must have seemed disturbingly reminiscent of those which the Venetians themselves had obtained thirty years before. Yet they were not on the same scale. The Pisans were to be welcomed as merchants in Byzantine markets. But they were required to pay customs duties, even if only at the rate of 4% instead of the normal 10%. More disquieting for Venice was the clause granting to Pisa a commercial quarter and a landing stage in Constantinople. It seemed to endanger what had hitherto been a Venetian monopoly in the heart of Byzantium.[1] A formal embassy from Venice is known to have gone to Constantinople in 1112, led by the Patriarch of Grado. Its purpose was to solicit Byzantine support against the Hungarians in Dalmatia. But the delegation may also have wished to see how the Pisans were exploiting their newly won privileges in the city.[2] There is no record that the Genoese were granted any like privileges in the Byzantine Empire by Alexios. Their time was to come some forty-five years later. But the seeds were being sown of the rivalry between the Italian republics which was to be one of the most potent causes of the malaise of Byzantium. Was it to register their displeasure that the Venetians committed yet another act of vandalism, stealing some of the relics of St Stephen the First Martyr from a church in Constantinople? The Doge Ordelafo Falier certainly made much of giving the robbery his official blessing. It was he who laid the relics to rest in the monastery of San Giorgio Maggiore, to become one more tourist attraction in his own city.[3]

In the summer of 1118 Ordelafo Falier was killed fighting at Zara in Dalmatia. The Emperor Alexios Komnenos died at almost the same moment, on 15 August 1118. Ordelafo had been Doge for sixteen years. He had had to contend with many political problems and natural disasters. As a result of the crusade and of his war with Hungary relations between Venice and Byzantium seemed to have been soured; and the elements had been unkind to the fabric of his city. A series of flood tides and storms had inundated the lagoons and completely swept away the old town of Malamocco. Two fires, whipped up by gales, did irreparable damage on the islands of Rialto; and in 1117 an earthquake brought churches and houses crashing down.[4] Ordelafo will always be remembered, however, as the Doge who nationalised the shipbuilding industry of Venice by his foundation of the Arsenal. For the future his successors

---

[1] *DR*, II, no. 1255. Lilie, *Handel und Politik*, pp. 69–76, 356–62.
[2] Dandolo, pp. 229, 230; *TTh*, I, no. XXXIV, pp. 75–6. Kretschmayr, I, p. 222.
[3] Dandolo, p. 227. Kretschmayr, I, p. 222.
[4] Dandolo, p. 225. Kretschmayr, I, pp. 221–2, 458–9.

would not have to rely on the unco-ordinated labours of family firms and private companies to provide for the needs of trade and war at sea. Private enterprise in shipbuilding was still encouraged. But the work of all the craftsmen required for the construction and maintenance of ships in an emergency could henceforth be concentrated in one great complex of docks and shipyards, the Arsenal, to the east of the city.[1]

The Emperor Alexios Komnenos had reigned for nearly thirty-seven years. He too had faced many difficulties. The inundation that swept over his dominions was a human flood. He had managed to hold the Normans, the Pechenegs and the Turks at bay. But the crusaders presented a new problem. Before 1096 the Byzantines had been able to deal with the western powers as separate kingdoms and principalities, sometimes friendly, sometimes hostile. The Venetians were useful allies in the midst of them all. After the First Crusade, however, the westerners were in the midst of the Byzantine world. They came to be seen as one dangerous and disruptive block, collectively known as the Latins and irremovably entrenched on or around Byzantine territory. The case of Antioch, still unlawfully held by Bohemond's successors, was symbolic of the mistrust between Greeks and Latins.

Alexios was succeeded by his eldest son John II Komnenos. The succession was not undisputed. The princess and historian Anna Comnena in particular intrigued against her brother in the hope that her own husband would wear the crown. But John was a match for all his dynastic opponents. The empire that he inherited was a stronger and healthier institution than it had been when his father became emperor. His foreign policy had indeed to take account of the Turks in Asia Minor, of the crusaders in Syria and Palestine, and of renewed restlessness among the barbarians on the Danube and the Serbians in the Balkans. But there were no enemies at the gates as there had been in 1081. There were, however, dissidents and troublemakers within the gates of his empire. Among them, in the new emperor's opinion, were the Venetians. In 1119 the new Doge of Venice, Domenico Michiel, sent envoys to Constantinople to pay his respects and to ask that the charter granted to his people by Alexios I be confirmed and renewed. John II refused.[2]

---

[1] Kretschmayr, I, p. 185; F. C. Lane, Venice. A Maritime Republic (Baltimore–London, 1973), pp. 45–8.

[2] Dandolo, p. 232; Historia Ducum Veneticorum, MGH, Scriptores, XIV, p. 73; TTh, I, no. XXXIX, p. 78. On John II Komnenos (1118–43), see Ostrogorsky, History, pp. 375–80; F. Chalandon, Les Comnènes. Etudes sur l'empire byzantin aux XIe et XIIe siècles, II: Jean II Comnène (1118–1143) et Manuel Comnène (1143–1180) (Paris, 1912); M. Angold, The Byzantine Empire, 1025–1204 (London, 1984), pp. 150–9.

He was quite within his imperial rights to do so. A chrysobull issued by one emperor was not necessarily binding on his successor. There had been differences between Byzantium and Venice over the question of the Hungarian occupation of Dalmatia. Nearer home there had been incidents which suggested that the Venetians in Constantinople regarded themselves as being above the law and beyond the control of the local authorities. They had stolen relics from a church. They were intolerably insolent not only to the common people but also to those of rank and quality among the Greeks. Such conduct had to be punished. The Venetians must be reminded that their privileges were conditional upon their behaving as loyal and law-abiding servants of the crown. It has sometimes been argued that John II refused to renew his father's charter to the Venetians because he was concerned about their stranglehold on Byzantine trade. There is no evidence that economic considerations dictated his decision. For him as emperor it was simply a matter of law and order, of restating the fact that Byzantium was the senior partner in the arrangement.[1]

The Venetians were at first uncertain how to react. Their merchants and agents did not at once pack their bags and leave. Some of them were still trading in Constantinople three years later, though on much less favourable terms.[2] Gradually, however, they resolved to take retaliatory action. Their resolve was strengthened when they heard that the emperor was negotiating a treaty with the King of Hungary, thereby recognising Hungarian claims to Dalmatia. They were moved to action by a desperate plea for help addressed to them in 1120 by Baldwin II of Jerusalem. The Christian cause in the east had suffered a disastrous setback in the battle known as the Field of Blood. The Prince of Antioch had been killed. Baldwin's appeal was endorsed by the pope. The Venetians were cast in the role of crusaders. They would answer the call. But who could blame them if, on their way to the east, they took the opportunity of avenging themselves on the Byzantines who had so wronged them? Many months passed before their fleet was ready to sail. In August 1122, however, a great armada, commanded by the Doge, put out from Venice. There were more than a hundred ships of war and cargo ships, carrying about 15,000 men. They seemed to be in no hurry to get to Palestine. Having shown their flag and done some

---

[1] John Kinnamos (Cinnamus), *Epitome rerum ab Ioanne et Alexio Comnenis gestarum*, ed. A. Meineke, *CSHB* (1836), p. 281. Chalandon, II, p. 156; Angold, *Byzantine Empire*, p. 154; Lilie, *Handel und Politik*, pp. 367–8; cf. Ostrogorsky, *History*, p. 377.

[2] Documents relating to Venetian traders in Constantinople in R. Morozzo della Rocca and A. Lombardo, eds., *Documenti del commercio veneziano nei secoli XI–XIII*, I (Rome, 1940), nos. 41, 42, 45, 46, pp. 43–9 (dating from February 1119 to January 1121).

plundering on the Dalmatian coast, they sailed on to the island of Corfu. During the winter the Doge besieged its castle. But the Byzantine garrison held out. In the spring of 1123 an urgent message came to him from Jerusalem to say that King Baldwin had been captured by the Muslims. Reluctantly he abandoned his siege and made for Acre. In a single encounter off Ascalon the Venetians sank or seized almost all of the Egyptian navy. It was a memorable triumph and it gave heart to the crusaders, who now offered great temptations to the Doge and his men to stay and continue the fight. Early in 1124 a treaty was drawn up. In return for their services the Venetians were to be given, among other rewards, a street, a church, baths and a bakery in every town in the Kingdom of Jerusalem and to be exempted from all taxes and dues. Once again it was clear that the Venetians would not serve the cause for love. They were realists. The promise of a martyr's crown for dying in battle against the infidel was less attractive to them than the promise of material rewards in the way of trade.

It had been decided that the first objective should be the city of Tyre, the last town on the coast north of Ascalon that was still held by the Muslims. The Venetians sailed north while the crusaders marched along the coast. The siege of Tyre began in February 1124 and in July its Muslim garrison surrendered. There had been talk of next attacking Ascalon. But the Venetians now felt that they had fulfilled their obligations in Palestine and they announced that they were leaving.[1] They had in fact other business to do. Corfu had resisted them. They would take their revenge on the Byzantine Emperor elsewhere. In October they reached Rhodes and raided the island, on the pretext that the inhabitants refused to give them provisions. The fleet wintered at Chios; and there the chance was taken to add another saint to the Venetian collection. The relics of St Isidore the Martyr were looted from their shrine to be carried away to Venice. Early in 1125 the Doge led his ships on a leisurely cruise for home, stopping at the islands of Kos, Samos, Lesbos and Andros to plunder and destroy. Their last port of call in Byzantine territory was the town of Modon or Methoni on the south-west tip of the Peloponnese. In later years, after the Fourth Crusade, Modon was to be much prized and well defended as one of the 'chief eyes of the Republic' in the colonial empire of Venice. But in 1125 they demolished its walls, robbed its people and carried away their livestock. Back in the Adriatic the Doge sailed along the Dalmatian coast, relieving a number of towns

[1] Kretschmayr, I, pp. 224–8, 455–6; Runciman, *Crusades*, II, pp. 143–52, 166–71; Prawer, *Royaume latin de Jérusalem*, I, pp. 305–8; Lilie, *Handel und Politik*, pp. 368–72.

of their Hungarian garrisons. In June he steered his fleet in triumph and in safety into Venice.[1]

It had been a glorious expedition, bringing comfort to the Christians in the Holy Land, punishing the Byzantines and outwitting the Hungarians. The Doge had set out flying the banner of St Peter given him by the pope. But it was the last occasion in the twelfth century on which the Venetians pretended to be crusaders. They had now got all they wanted out of Palestine. They had secured their interests in the two main ports of entry, Acre and Tyre, and they had extracted numerous privileges from the Kingdom of Jerusalem. They were much more concerned about their relationship with Byzantium. It had become so bitter that, if Dandolo is to be believed, the Doge decreed that Venetians should be cleanshaven and stop wearing beards like the Greeks. In 1126 he applied more pressure on the emperor by sending a raiding party to the island of Cephalonia. An incidental consequence of their plundering was the acquisition of yet another Greek saint. The body of St Donatos, once Bishop of Photiki in Epiros, was stolen and taken to Venice.[2] The main consequence, however, was a change of heart in the Emperor John II. In August 1126 he relented and signed a chrysobull confirming all the rights which his father had conferred on the Venetians in 1082. Their raids on his islands had been more of a nuisance than a danger. But with the other commitments that he had in hand, especially in Asia Minor, the emperor could not afford to become involved in what might be a prolonged war by sea with the greatest naval power in the Mediterranean. Better to make his peace with that power in the hope that he could call on its help as an ally.

His chrysobull of 1126 begins with the emperor's expression of that hope.[3] He dwells on the ancient loyalty, friendship and service rendered to Byzantium by the Venetians, lightly passing over their recent offences against himself and his empire. He is now ready to renew their former privileges as merchants on the understanding that they will mend their manners and behave as his allies and servants. The honours and stipends

---

[1] Fulcher of Chartres, *Historia Hierosolymitana*, ed. H. Hagenmayer (Heidelberg, 1913), pp. 655–8, 669–72, 693–8, 728–30, 745–6, 758–61; William of Tyre, *Historia rerum in partibus transmarinis gestarum*, in *RHC, Hist. occ.*, I/1, pp. 545–76; Dandolo, pp. 233–5; *Historia Ducum Veneticorum*, pp. 73–4; *Translatio Isidori*, in *RHC, Hist. occ.*, V, pp. 321–34. Kretschmayr, I, pp. 228–9; Chalandon, *Les Comnènes*, II, pp. 157–9; Lilie, *Handel und Politik*, pp. 372–3. The Venetians also collected the 'sacred stone on which the Saviour sat' while they were at Tyre. *Translatio Isidori*, p. 330; Dandolo, p. 234.

[2] Dandolo, p. 236. The relics of St Donatos were placed in the church at Murano in the diocese of Torcello, which was dedicated thereafter to SS. Maria e Donato.

[3] The Latin text of the chrysobull of 1126 is contained in that issued by Manuel I in 1147. *TTh*, I, no. XLIII, pp. 95–8; *DR*, II, no. 1304; Dandolo, p. 237. Kretschmayr, I, pp. 229–30; Brown, 'Venetian Quarter', 73; Lilie, *Handel und Politik*, pp. 17–22, 373–5.

of the Doge and the patriarch are confirmed as well as the trading rights and properties of Venice in Constantinople. There is no sign that the emperor extended their rights and privileges. They were to be content with exactly what they had before. Not long afterwards it was conceded that Venice should also enjoy free trade in Crete and in Cyprus. But this was not in the terms of the chrysobull of 1126.[1] Some of them had evidently complained that the 10% tax or *kommerkion* on their trans-actions, from which they had been expressly exempted by the charter of 1082, had for some time past been charged to the accounts of the Byzantine merchants with whom they were trading. This was due to a misunderstanding and the emperor went out of his way to correct it. Neither Greeks nor Venetians doing business with each other any-where in his dominions, whether buying or selling, were required to pay the *kommerkion* or any other tax on their transactions.[2] The chryso-bull ends with a solemn reminder to the Venetians that their concessions carry certain reciprocal obligations. They are bound by oath and in writ-ing to serve the emperor and his empire. The emperor had thought it prudent to relent, but he had not surrendered to Venetian intransigence. He stood on his dignity. The Venetians were no doubt glad that this was the end of the matter, though secretly they must have felt that the emperor's hand had been forced by the actions of their heroic Doge Domenico Michiel. They were accustomed to the peremptory tone of imperial chrysobulls. They themselves had been accused of arrogance. It was in the interest of both parties to sink their pride and end their quarrel.

One can only assume, since the evidence is lacking, that the Venetians moved back at once into their former trading stations and markets in Constantinople and elsewhere. Certainly they played no further part as crusaders in the east. Some of their ships privately contracted to carry troops or passengers from Italy to Acre, before sailing on to do more important and more profitable business in Alexandria or in Constanti-nople. But Venice had nothing to do with the Second Crusade or with the crusading expeditions to Egypt in the later twelfth century.[3] The Doge Domenico Michiel died much honoured and lamented in 1130. He did not live to see the creation of a new kingdom in the west, when Robert Guiscard's nephew, Roger of Hauteville, received a crown as King of Sicily from a grateful pope. The revival of Norman power in Sicily and south Italy was noted with deep concern not only by the Venetians, jealous as always of their mastery of the Adriatic Sea, but

---

[1] *DR*, II, no. 1305. Cf. Lilie, *Handel und Politik*, pp. 374–5.
[2] On the matter of the *kommerkion*, see Lilie, *Handel und Politik*, pp. 17–22.
[3] Runciman, 'L'intervento di Venezia', pp. 17–20.

also by the German Emperor in the west and by the Byzantine Emperor
in the east. John II must have felt that there were Normans to the right
of him and Normans to the left of him. Antioch was still claimed as
a Norman inheritance, though its prince, Bohemond II, was killed in
1130 leaving only an infant daughter; and now another descendant of
Robert Guiscard had been proclaimed a king in Sicily. But John II was
talented in diplomacy as well as in war. Events in eastern Europe and
the Balkans caused him to delay settling his accounts with the widowed
Principality of Antioch. First he had to deal with the Cumans, who
had stormed across the Danube into Thrace in 1122. After his decisive
victory on that front he had to contend with the Serbians, who were
encouraged to rebel by the King of Hungary. Having married a Hungarian princess, John was able to exert some diplomatic influence on her
relatives and their rivals for the throne. These affairs of war and foreign
policy were rather more important than his tiff with Venice. But they
held him back from the even more important business of reconquering
Asia Minor from the Turks and Antioch from the crusaders. Not until
1130 was he free to turn to these problems in the east. He was triumphantly successful on both counts. Victorious campaigns in Anatolia
and Cilicia brought his armies to the borders of Syria. In 1137 Antioch
surrendered after a siege and its new prince, Raymond of Poitiers, swore
allegiance to the emperor.

These were great achievements, fully in line with the ambition which
John had inherited from his father, of reincorporating all of Asia Minor
into the Byzantine Empire and restoring the former frontier between
Christianity and Islam at the Euphrates. But the days were past when
the Byzantines could act alone as defenders of the faith in the east without
reference to western Christendom. Raymond of Antioch, who had married the daughter of the late Bohemond II, soon objected to his status
as a vassal of the Byzantine Emperor. The new Norman Kingdom of
Sicily proved to be an even greater challenge to the old order of things.
In the last years of his life John II tried to meet it by making friends
with its other and nearer natural enemy, the German Emperor Lothair
II. Lothair had already invaded Italy and knew that he could count on
Byzantine support in his conflict with the Normans. When he died,
it was arranged that Manuel, the youngest son of John II, should marry
a relative of his successor, Conrad III of Hohenstaufen. This alliance
between the Empires of East and West which had for so long been
estranged opened up possibilities of co-operation in Italy and Sicily,
in the Balkans and in the crusader states. There might even be a new,
joint crusade to the Holy Land. The Venetians had been asked and had
readily agreed to assist in the discomfiture of the Normans in Italy.

The Emperor John had also encouraged the support of the Pisans by renewing their trade privileges in 1136. But his wider ambitions were left unfulfilled and his accounts with the Normans unsettled; for he died of blood poisoning after a hunting accident in Cilicia in April 1143.[1]

[1] Kretschmayr, I, pp. 230–3; Runciman, *Crusades*, II, pp. 210–24; Ostrogorsky, *History*, pp. 377–80; Angold, *Byzantine Empire*, pp. 155–9; Lilie, *Handel und Politik*, pp. 376–91. For John II's chrysobull to Pisa of 1136, see *DR*, II, no. 1312.

6

THE PARTING OF THE WAYS

AS he lay on his deathbed John II nominated his youngest son Manuel Komnenos as his heir. His two older sons, Alexios and Andronikos, had recently died and he had no confidence in his third son Isaac. It fell to Manuel, young though he was, to lead his father's army back to Constantinople, there to secure his position as emperor. His coronation by the patriarch set the seal of legitimacy on his succession to the throne. Manuel shared his father's conviction of his unique status as Emperor of the Romans, claimant to a sovereignty that had once been, and would again in God's good time become, universal. Yet he was personally attracted by many aspects of western, Latin life and culture; and he was enough of a realist to see that the Byzantines could no longer bury their heads in the sand of their own mystique and hope that the westerners, the German Emperor, the Normans, the Italians, the papacy and the crusaders would melt away. To cement his alliance with the Germans against the Normans of Sicily, John II had arranged that Manuel should marry Bertha of Sulzbach, sister-in-law of Conrad III. Manuel's admiration for western culture was shaken when she reached Constantinople in 1142. Bertha was plain and dull and stubborn. In the end, however, Manuel took her to wife and she became his empress with the less Teutonic name of Eirene. The Eastern and Western Empires were now united against their common enemy, the Norman Kingdom of Sicily; and Manuel was able to return to the east to continue the campaign that had been interrupted by his father's death.

In 1144, the year after his accession, the crusaders suffered a serious setback when Edessa was captured by the Muslims. The news of this disaster prompted the preaching and mounting of the Second Crusade. The leading participants were King Louis VII of France and the German Emperor, Conrad III, to whom Manuel was now related. They came their separate ways but they and their armies had of necessity to pass through Constantinople. Manuel treated them with the same tact and propriety that his grandfather had shown to the first crusaders. That

their expeditions came to grief was no fault of his, though inevitably
he was blamed. With the Emperor Conrad out of the way, the Normans
saw a chance of striking at the Byzantine Empire. In the summer of
1147, while Manuel was busy seeing the crusaders on their way to the
east, a Norman fleet from Otranto attacked and captured Corfu, placing
a garrison of 1000 men in its citadel. It then sailed round the Peloponnese
to Euboia, back to the Ionian Islands and into the Gulf of Corinth.
Thebes and Corinth itself surrendered with hardly any resistance and
the Normans went back to Italy with a heavy load of plunder and prisoners. They had got nowhere near Constantinople. They had merely
raided the western fringes of the empire like pirates. But they had captured
Corfu and they might well use it, as their ancestors had done, to invade
the Greek mainland and make for the heart of Byzantium. They must
be driven out of the island. The Venetians were of the same mind. Once
again the interests of Venice and of Byzantium coincided on the question
of the control of the Adriatic Sea.[1]

It can hardly have been by accident or oversight that Manuel had
let four years of his reign pass without confirming the privileges that
his predecessors had accorded to Venice. Perhaps the Doge had to make
representations. Two legates from Pietro Polani are known to have been
in Constantinople on other business in September 1147. Legally the
privileges of the Venetians required formal ratification by the emperor,
for all that they had been guaranteed in perpetuity by Alexios I. On
the other hand, Manuel had shown no sign of questioning or withdrawing
them. Both parties had been engaged in diplomatic exchanges with the
other western powers, with the Normans and with the German Emperor.
Both were uncertain about the outcome of their diplomacy. The Norman
raid on Greece and the capture of Corfu brought them together. Manuel
at once called on the Venetians to help, as they had so often done before;
and in October of the same year he issued a chrysobull confirming all
the privileges granted to them by his father and his grandfather. It seems
probable that the Doge declined to commit himself to answering the
emperor's call for help until he had been assured of his reward. His
ambassadors to Constantinople brought that reward back to Venice in
the form of the imperial chrysobull of October 1147. Its terms were
in all respects the same as those of 1126, with special mention being

---

[1] Kinnamos, p. 92; Niketas Choniates, *Historia*, ed. J.-L. van Dieten, *CFHB*, XI/1 (Berlin–
New York, 1975), pp. 72–6. Chalandon, *Les Comnènes*, II, pp. 317–21; Ostrogorsky, *History*, pp. 381–3; Angold, *Byzantine Empire*, pp. 159–69. Manuel's dealings with the western
powers are fully discussed by P. Lamma, *Comneni e Staufer. Ricerche sui rapporti fra Bisanzio
e l'Occidente nel secolo XII*, I–II, Istituto Storico Italiano per il medio evo. Studi storici,
fasc. 14–18 (Rome, 1955, 1957). Cf. D. Abulafia, *The Two Italies* (Cambridge, 1977), pp. 80–
4, 141–2.

made of the fact that Venetian merchants were to be permitted to trade
tax free in the islands of Crete and Cyprus, which had been excluded
in the charter of 1082.[1]

The Doge responded swiftly by preparing a large fleet to go to the
rescue of Corfu. By the spring of 1148 it was ready to sail. The emperor
was so pleased by this evidence of loyal co-operation that he extended
still further bounty to Venice. In a second chrysobull, dated March 1148,
he made provision for a substantial enlargement of the Venetian quarter
in Constantinople, adding to it a number of new properties and a fourth
landing stage. This he did at the request of the Venetians and in anticipation of the successful outcome of their help against the Normans. In
return they agreed to put their fleet at his service for a period of six
months, until the end of September.[2] Things did not go quite as the
emperor had planned. He had meant to lead his own army to the relief
of Corfu while his ships joined forces there with the Venetians. But
he was delayed, first by an invasion of the barbarous Cumans from across
the Danube, and then by the arrival in Thessalonica of the German
Emperor Conrad, returning disheartened and defeated from his crusade
to the Holy Land. It was a useful encounter, for on Christmas Day
1148 the two emperors struck up an alliance against the Normans, sealed
by a marriage contract. A joint campaign against the King of Sicily was
planned for the following year. Meanwhile the immediate task of expelling
the Normans from Corfu remained to be achieved. The admiral of the
Byzantine fleet which had sailed there was killed and the commander
of the land forces had to take on the double role of general and admiral.
The Venetian fleet was delayed on account of the death of the Doge,
Pietro Polani. The Emperor Manuel finally arrived to take overall command. But even with the support of the combined navies of Byzantium
and Venice his army made little headway. The Normans had the advantage of the commanding height of the citadel of Corfu, and they were
able to rain down showers of arrows and rocks on to their attackers.
It seemed incredible that they had contrived to capture the place so effort-
lessly a year before. Their king, Roger II, staged a diversionary ploy
by sending some ships round Greece and up the Hellespont, to the walls
of Constantinople and the Bosporos. They were caught by the Greeks
and Venetians as they came back round Cape Malea. Not until the summer of 1149 did the Norman garrison on Corfu surrender to the emperor.

[1] Dandolo, p. 242; *TTh*, I, no. XLIX, pp. 107–9 (September 1147), no. LI, pp. 113–24 (wrongly
dated October '1148'); *DR*, II, nos. 1356, 1365. Chalandon, *Les Comnènes*, II, pp. 321–2;
Lilie, *Handel und Politik*, pp. 22–4.

[2] *TTh*, I, nos. L, pp. 109–13 (March 1148), LXXI, pp. 189–94 (text in chrysobull of Isaac II
of 1187); *DR*, II, no. 1373.

They had despaired of a relief force ever coming to their aid. Their commander and a number of his officers entered the emperor's service. The
Venetian ships went home. Manuel led his troops on a punitive campaign
against the Serbians and Hungarians whom the Norman king had incited
to rebellion; and at Christmas 1149 he was free to return to Constantinople to celebrate a triumph.[1]

During the long siege of Corfu an incident had occurred which showed
how shallow was the friendship between Venetians and Greeks. Their
soldiers fell to brawling and fighting in the market place of the city where
they were quartered. Very soon they were engaged in mortal combat
with their weapons in their hands and calling on their unarmed fellow
countrymen to join in the fight. Some of the more senior Venetians
tried to intervene but things had got too far out of hand. The Byzantine
commander did his best to control his men but his efforts only brought
more Venetians pouring out of their ships to help their comrades. Realising that it was a racial conflict that would end in a pitched battle, he
sent in his own bodyguard of crack troops. The Venetians were dispersed
and ran back to their ships. They took their revenge by attacking and
burning some Greek cargo ships from Euboia which were lying off a
little island between Ithaka and Cephalonia. They then managed to seize
the emperor's flagship, decked it out with its gold-threaded hangings
and purple carpets and brought aboard an Ethiopian negro whom they
acclaimed as Emperor of the Romans in a burlesque coronation ceremony.
It was a calculated act of mockery and a personal affront to the Emperor
Manuel, who was known to have a swarthy complexion. Manuel was
furious and never forgave the Venetians for this insult. He contained
his anger until they had served his purpose. But he must have wondered
whether he had been wise to encourage still more of such people to
settle in Constantinople.[2]

Manuel had intended, once he had recovered Corfu, to carry his war
into the Norman kingdom by invading Italy. He had made his pact
with the Emperor Conrad with this in mind. He had hoped to join
Conrad in Italy before the winter came on. But Conrad was not there,
and the revolt of the Serbians changed Manuel's plans. Part of his army
and his fleet were, however, sent ahead with orders to establish a base
at Ancona. They got no further than the estuary of the Vjosa river in
Albania. There they stayed, partly due to the incompetence of their commander, but also because the Venetians persuaded them to disobey their

---

[1] Kinnamos, pp. 96–101; Niketas Choniates, pp. 77–9, 82–9; *Historia Ducum Veneticorum*,
p. 75; Dandolo, p. 243; *DR*, II, no. 1374. Chalandon, II, pp. 321–33; W. Heyd, *Histoire
du Commerce du Levant au Moyen Age*, I (Leipzig, 1885), pp. 198–200.
[2] Niketas Choniates, pp. 85–7.

emperor's orders. They were afraid, or so it is said, that if the campaign in Italy succeeded they would be the losers. The emperor would no longer need their support and would disregard their interests.[1] The truth of this allegation cannot be proved. Manuel certainly meant to use Ancona as a base for his operations in Italy. It was a convenient headquarters for a combined German–Byzantine campaign, though the Venetians may have thought that it was uncomfortably close to their own waters. In any event, their fears were allayed by an act of God. The Byzantine fleet was damaged by a storm that blew up in the Adriatic. The survivors turned for home and reached Constantinople in the winter of 1150.

These incidents were symptoms rather than causes of the growing estrangement between Byzantium and Venice. The two Greek historians who describe them, Niketas Choniates and John Kinnamos, disliked the Venetians, not without reason; for they made themselves unpopular by their arrogant behaviour. The Emperor Manuel had extended the limits of their quarter in Constantinople after they had complained that the strip of land along the Golden Horn allotted to them by his father and grandfather was no longer big enough for their needs. The number of Venetian merchants and businessmen residing in the city had evidently grown, though the figure of 10,000 given by Venetian sources may be an exaggeration.[2] Alexios I had granted them the freehold of a number of buildings and wharfs in a designated area by the Golden Horn. Manuel's chrysobull of 1148 implies that the whole area with all the buildings in it was made over to the Doge and people of Venice as their colony in the city. The emperor hoped that it would be a ghetto in which the Venetians would be confined. The residences and activities of other foreign merchants, from Pisa, Amalfi and later Genoa, were likewise confined to certain areas, though on a smaller scale. One cause of conflict was that the Venetians were not content to be so restricted. Several of them acquired properties in other parts of the city and so created problems of public order and security; for they made unruly and objectionable neighbours.

The properties originally made over to them in 1082 had stood within the strip of land along the Golden Horn stretching from the Jews' Gate (Porta Hebraica) to Vigla or the Porta Viglae, to the east of the later Phanar quarter. The centre of it was the Embolum of Perama where stood the

[1] Kinnamos, p. 102.
[2] On the numbers of Venetians in Constantinople, see P. Schreiner, 'Untersuchungen zu den Niederlassungen westlicher Kaufleute im byzantinischen Reich des 11. und 12. Jahrhunderts', *BF*, VII (1979), 175–91, especially 182–4. Lilie, *Handel und Politik*, pp. 290–3; Angold, *Byzantine Empire*, p. 196.

warehouses and business premises of the Venetian merchants. The sea wall of Constantinople ran through the middle of it, with houses abutting it on either side. Perama (or Zeugma) was the place from which the ferry crossed the Horn at its narrowest point over to Sykai or Galata. Access through the wall from the shore side to the landward side was by three gates, the Gate of Vigla or the Droungarios, the Gate of St John called *de Cornibus*, and the Jews' Gate or Hebraica (also called the Gate of Perama), which was the limit of the district at its south-eastern end. Inside the wall and running parallel with it was a street with houses and shops on either side. The Embolum or business centre was probably near the Jews' Gate; and a number of churches stood in the area, notably that of St Akindynos, which the Doge had made over to the Patriarch of Grado in 1107 and which housed the standard weights and measures of Venetian merchants.[1]

Manuel's chrysobull of 1148 redefined the boundaries of the quarter in which Venetians were permitted to reside. They are set down in writing in the text of the document according to a survey that had been prepared. He extended them somewhat beyond the Vigla Gate in the north and beyond the Jews' Gate at the other end, as far as the Gate of St Mark and beyond. Many of the buildings and churches named in the document cannot now be identified. But the fourth landing stage which the Venetians acquired seems to have been that known as the Scala Sancti Marciani.[2] Manuel had readily agreed to make allowances for the growing population of Venetians in Constantinople and other cities of his empire. But they must be made aware of their legal status and of their obligations. He divided them into two categories: the permanent residents whom he designated by the Latin title of *burgenses*, or bourgeois, and those who were there only on transitory business. The former had citizens' rights and duties on condition of their taking an oath to conduct themselves as servants of the emperor, as they were enjoined to do by terms of his chrysobull.[3] That there was still some sense of reciprocal obligation appears from a document which mentions thirteen Venetian

[1] Brown, 'Venetian Quarter', 74–80; A.-M. Schneider, *Mauern und Tore am goldenen Horn zu Konstantinopel*, Nachrichten der Akademie der Wissenschaften in Göttingen, 5 (Göttingen, 1950), pp. 65–107; R. Janin, *Constantinople byzantine. Développement urbain et répertoire topographique*, 2nd edn (Paris, 1964), pp. 247–9. Cf. Heyd, *Commerce*, I, pp. 247–52, 260–1; F. Thiriet, *La Romanie vénitienne au Moyen Age. Le développement et l'exploitation du domaine colonial vénitien (XIIe–XVe siècles)*, Ecoles Françaises d'Athènes et de Rome, 193 (Paris, 1959), p. 46.

[2] Maltézou, 'Il quartiere veneziano', 34–5.

[3] Kinnamos, p. 282. Heyd, *Commerce*, I, pp. 200–2; S. Borsari, 'Il commercio veneziano nell' impero bizantino nel XII secolo', *RSI*, LXXVI (1964), 982–1011, especially 997–9; Schreiner, 'Untersuchungen', 188–9; Lilie, *Handel und Politik*, pp. 297–300.

ships 'in the service of the emperor' in the year 1150.[1] But the Venetians in Constantinople continued to make themselves unpopular by their behaviour. Kinnamos describes them as morally dissolute, vulgar and untrustworthy, with all the gross characteristics of seafaring people. Their wealth fed their cupidity and insolence. They abused and assaulted many of the Greek nobility, among them relatives of the emperor. Some of them cohabited with Greek women and set up house with them beyond the limits of the Venetian quarter. It remained to be seen how effective would be the emperor's efforts to corral them into one district.[2]

It was in Constantinople that the Venetian presence was most felt and most resented. But there were smaller Venetian colonies and trading stations in many of the provinces. Alexios I had given them the right to trade freely in Byzantine ports in Greece and Asia Minor. John II had extended that right to the islands of Crete and Cyprus. The former concession facilitated trade with Egypt; the latter gave Venice a new stepping-stone on the route to and from its already secured markets in Syria and Palestine. John II had perhaps unwittingly opened the door to a vision of almost unlimited and highly privileged trade and profit for Venice in the eastern Mediterranean. In addition, by abolishing the *kommerkion* payable by Byzantine merchants on their transactions with Venetians he had made trade with Venice a much more attractive proposition for his own people. His son Manuel had to contend with the consequences of a vastly increased volume of trade and the traffic and people that went with it. In the early years of the twelfth century Venetian trade with Constantinople and other ports in the Byzantine world had been irregular, in the form of pioneering enterprises sponsored by small investments of private capital. By the middle of the century, in the reign of Manuel, it had become better organised and supported by larger investments in Venetian companies and Byzantine property; and the normal means of currency was the Byzantine gold coin, the *hyperpyron*. The Byzantine economy was clearly affected by this development, but not entirely for the worse. In the twelfth century the empire was almost self-sufficient. Constantinople had little need of imports from foreign parts, though Italian ships might bring from the west such commodities as woollen stuffs, metal and Dalmatian timber, as well as luxuries like spices which they acquired in the east. The wealthy aristocracy of Byzantium affected to despise trade and commerce. They preferred to invest their money in land. Rather than going out to look for foreign trade they expected traders to come to them and add to the wealth of their city. The Venetians in the twelfth century certainly fulfilled this expec-

[1] *San Giorgio Maggiore*, II, no. 240, pp. 479–82 (October 1151).
[2] Kinnamos, pp. 280–2; Niketas Choniates, p. 171.

tation; and it was partly because they were so enterprising and so ostentatiously successful that they aroused jealousy and suspicion among the Greeks.

Outside Constantinople the Venetian trading posts were relatively small and more experimental. Yet in the twelfth century Venetian entrepreneurs invested quite large capital sums in expanding them and in buying property. The pattern of their settlement was similar to that which they had learnt in the Kingdom of Jerusalem: a street, a church, a hospice and perhaps a bakery would constitute a Venetian quarter. Most of the settlements were on or near the sea since the Venetians were less concerned with overland trade. The chrysobull of 1082 had named twenty-nine places where it was expected that Venetians would do most business. It was an impressive list, stretching from Laodikeia and Antioch in the east to Durazzo and Valona in Albania and the island of Corfu in the west. On the Greek peninsula mention was made of Vonitsa in Aitolia, of Modon and Coron (Methoni and Koroni) on the south-western tip of the Peloponnese, of Nauplion, Corinth, Thebes, Athens, Euboia, Demetrias and Thessalonica. In Thrace, nearer to Constantinople, it was anticipated that the Venetians would frequent the ports of Abydos, Raidestos, Apros, Herakleia and Selymbria, as well as the inland city of Adrianople. At Raidestos (Rodosto) there was a Venetian church with a hospice and a garden which was made over to the monastery of San Giorgio Maggiore in Venice in 1157, as well as a monastery which housed the merchants' weights and measures. Many of the other places, however, were rarely visited by Venetian ships and only a few contained Venetian residents or agents in the twelfth century. The Byzantine ports of Asia Minor, apart from Smyrna and Adramyttion, attracted little attention in this period. Italian merchants did more business in the markets of Greece and the Balkan peninsula.[1]

Durazzo on the Adriatic coast was of great importance as a halfway house between Venice and the Aegean Sea, and there the Venetians had a settlement with their own church granted to them by Alexios I. Thessalonica was curiously neglected by their merchants. Corinth and Thebes, however, are known to have had Venetian colonies in the twelfth century. Thebes lay inland but it was the capital of the Byzantine theme or province of Hellas and not too far from the sea at Corinth. It was a flourishing commercial town and also the centre of a silk industry, as the Normans discovered to their great benefit when they raided it in 1147. Venetian

---

[1] Raidestos: *TTh*, I, no. XLVII, pp. 103–5 (1145); no. XLIX, pp. 107–9 (1147); no. LVIII, pp. 137–9 (1157). *San Giorgio Maggiore*, II, no. 276, pp. 533–4 (1157). Venetian traffic with Smyrna: Morozzo della Rocca and Lombardo, *Documenti*, I, nos. 122, 131 (1156 and 1158) (cited hereafter as Morozzo–Lombardo).

merchants sometimes carried silk to the west. But as a rule they dealt in humbler and heavier commodities such as oil and wine, grain, linen and cotton. Theirs was a freight trade carrying bulk rather than luxury goods. In this respect Demetrias on the Gulf of Volos in Thessaly, mentioned in the charter of 1082, was of special importance. It was known to the Venetians by the name of Halmyros, the nearby port which seems to have superseded Demetrias. By the twelfth century there was a Venetian quarter in Halmyros with more than one church. The Pisans also had a quarter there; the Genoese did business there; and there was a thriving Jewish colony. Halmyros prospered through being the main export centre for all the produce of the plain of Thessaly, with two spacious and well-protected harbours. The Venetians regarded it as one of their most valuable markets, after Constantinople, Durazzo and perhaps Corinth.[1]

Though they might own properties within the empire, the Venetians were subject to Byzantine law. Not even in Constantinople were they permitted to have a governor or a magistrate of their own. They were answerable to the local Byzantine authorities for the preservation of law and order in their quarters, enjoying no more and no less autonomy than the native Greek inhabitants. They were also deemed to be the emperor's loyal servants, ever conscious of the fact that they were where they were because of his gracious favour, and prepared if required to do military service for him. No such restrictions or obligations were imposed upon Venetian residents and traders in the crusader states, where they were allowed to manage their own affairs; and though the restrictions applied equally to all the Latins in the empire, they must have seemed increasingly irksome to the large and prosperous Venetian community in Constantinople. Despising the Greeks as they did, some Venetians saw no reason why they should be bound by their laws and judged by their magistrates. Most of them, however, were content to act out the fiction of servitude to the emperor and his officials. It was a tolerable price to pay for the rich pickings that came their way as a consequence of their right to trade freely within his city and his empire.[2]

The Emperor Manuel's plans for a coalition of eastern and western powers to invade the Norman kingdom in Italy made little progress after the affair at Corfu. He himself was preoccupied with the suppression of Serbia and Hungary. His ally, the German Emperor Conrad III, died

---

[1] Heyd, *Commerce*, I, pp. 242–7. On Halmyros, see J. Koder and F. Hild, *Hellas und Thessalia*, Tabula Imperii Byzantini, I (Vienna, 1976), pp. 170–1.

[2] Niketas Choniates, p. 173 l. 16, describes the Venetians as being 'equal citizens' (*isopolitai*) with the Byzantines. Cf. Heyd, *Commerce*, I, pp. 255–8; Thiriet, *Romanie vénitienne*, pp. 45–6.

in 1152; and his successor, Frederick I Barbarossa, quickly showed that he was no friend of Byzantium and no supporter of Byzantine interests in Italy. Nevertheless, when Roger II of Sicily died in 1154, Manuel decided that the time was ripe to put his plan into action, with or without the co-operation of the German Emperor. In 1155 he sent a fleet to Ancona and from there the Byzantine offensive against the Normans was launched. At first it was a success. Bari was recaptured before the end of the year, and much of Apulia was occupied by the Byzantine army. But when the new Norman king, William I, rallied his forces and struck back, the success was proved to be ephemeral. In 1156 he defeated the Byzantines at Brindisi. In the following year Frederick Barbarossa's troops laid siege to Ancona. Manuel's attempt to restore Byzantine authority in Italy, if that was what he had in mind, was thwarted. In 1158 he signed a treaty with William I, recognising his royal title and his claim to the Norman kingdom in south Italy and Sicily. Byzantine troops, of which there had never been enough to ensure a victory, were withdrawn from Italy.[1]

The scene had changed. A new pattern of alliances was emerging. The treaty between Manuel and William was directed against Frederick Barbarossa, whose father had been the ally of Byzantium against the Normans. Frederick had an exalted conception of his own exclusive status as Emperor of the Romans. It irked him that Manuel, whom he contemptuously addressed as King of the Greeks, should intervene in the affairs of Italy which was so obviously a part of the Western Empire. The Venetians too were out of sympathy with Manuel's action. They had seen it coming and had made their own arrangements with the Normans and with Barbarossa. In 1154, after long negotiations, the Doge, Domenico Morosini, came to an agreement with William I. Venetian merchants were to be granted concessions in south Italy and Sicily; while the Normans declared the Adriatic Sea, above a line drawn westward from Ragusa (Dubrovnik), to be a Venetian preserve guaranteed against attack or interference. At the same time the Doge secured a renewal of the Venetian treaty with the German Emperor.[2] Venice thus advertised its neutrality. The Emperor Manuel felt cheated by this unfriendly behaviour. He had thought that he could rely on the Venetians to perform their customary service by sending help to his troops in Italy. When it was clear that they were in no mood to do so, Manuel approached their rivals Pisa

[1] Kinnamos, pp. 170–2; Niketas Choniates, pp. 91–9; DR, II, nos. 1396, 1417, 1420. Chalandon, Les Comnènes, II, pp. 377–81; Lilie, Handel und Politik, pp. 444–5. Niketas (p. 91) says that the emperor's commander recruited mercenaries for the campaign in Venice.

[2] Dandolo, pp. 245–6. The Venetian–Norman treaty of 1154 is cited in the similar treaty of 1175. TTh, I, no. LXVI, p. 174. Kretschmayr, I, pp. 236–41, 432.

and Genoa, the two other major maritime republics in Italy. In 1149 he had sent ambassadors to Pisa to ask for support in his projected campaign against the Normans. The Pisans were not very responsive. The Genoese, however, were more interested. In autumn 1155 a treaty of friendship was drawn up between Byzantium and Genoa. It was the first time that the Genoese had been favoured with the promise of trading privileges in Constantinople. But they too proved to be unreliable allies; for in the following year they made a commercial arrangement of their own with William of Sicily.[1] Manuel seemed powerless to influence events in the west as he would have wished. His failures there were, however, offset by his triumph in the east. It fell to Manuel to solve the long-standing problem of the principality of Antioch. In 1159 he received the submission of its Latin prince, Renauld of Chatillon, and made a ceremonial entry into the city. The drama of the occasion symbolised the fact that the Byzantine Emperor was now suzerain not only of Antioch but also of the Kingdom of Jerusalem, the acknowledged friend and protector of what was left of the crusader states in the east. The changed nature of relationships between Byzantium and the crusaders was shown when Manuel, after the death of his first wife in 1160, married Maria of Antioch, daughter of the late Raymond of Poitiers.[2]

Throughout the comings and goings of embassies and the shifts of diplomacy, the Venetians continued to ply their trade in Constantinople. In 1158 a call had gone out from Venice for all citizens to pack their bags and come home from the east. All hands were needed for war against Hungary. Not many answered the call. Business was booming in Constantinople.[3] It must not be interrupted for fear that it fall into other hands. The Venetians no longer had it all their own way. The emperor's overtures to Pisa and Genoa had encouraged other Italian merchants to move in. The Pisans had been legally established in Constantinople for some fifty years. The Genoese, however, had no formal arrangement with the authorities. The emperor had signed a treaty with them in 1155 but he had not issued a chrysobull officially defining their rights and their quarter in the city. None the less, five years later, there were about 300 Genoese merchants in Constantinople. Their presence was resented

---

[1] DR, II, nos. 1376 (1149), 1401, 1402 (1155). Heyd, Commerce, I, pp. 202–4. The supposed chrysobull of Manuel for Pisa dated July 1155, listed in DR, II, no. 1400, rests on a misapprehension. Cf. Lilie, Handel und Politik, p. 420 n. 89.

[2] Chalandon, Les Comnènes, II, pp. 219, 224, 522–3; Runciman, Crusades, II, pp. 345–61; Angold, Byzantine Empire, pp. 184–6.

[3] Morozzo–Lombardo, I, no. 143.

especially by the Pisans. In 1162 about 1000 of them attacked the Genoese colony. They were beaten back but they returned to the attack a few days later, supported by a crowd of Venetians and Greeks. Much damage was done to Genoese property and one man was killed. This was the first but by no means the last recorded instance of street fighting in Constantinople among the rival Italian traders. No emperor could allow such breaches of law and order in his city. Genoese and Pisans alike were turned out. The Venetians had played a minor part in the affray and were no doubt glad to see their rivals punished. Their turn for punishment was soon to come. Until it did they made the most of their opportunity to monopolise the foreign trade of Constantinople.[1]

To preserve the neutrality and independence of Venice the Doge had to steer a difficult course between the shoals of the empires of east and west and the Norman kingdom in the south. There was also the continuing threat to the Dalmatian coast from the King of Hungary. But it was Frederick Barbarossa's activities in the north of Italy that most alarmed the Venetians, for they had had the temerity to support the rival to his claimant to the papacy. The Doge was so concerned that he asked the Emperor Manuel to take action. Byzantine influence was still strong in Ancona, whose people, secretly subsidised, were loyal to the emperor. The Doge undertook, or so Kinnamos relates, to bring about the submission to Manuel of all the other towns of northern Italy if he would protect them. Manuel's agents were already at work in several of those towns. He responded by sending a secret mission to Venice in the spring of 1165. Its leader, Nikephoros Chalouphes, went prepared to subsidise a pro-Byzantine party in Venice, though he prudently left most of the money entrusted to him in Durazzo. Such was the feeling against Barbarossa that the Venetians declared themselves ready to co-operate with the emperor and promised to supply a fleet of 100 ships for the cause. This was the germ of the League of Lombard towns which was in the end to break the power of Frederick Barbarossa in northern Italy.[2]

The Venetian tune abruptly changed two years later. For five years and more Venice had been at war with Hungary over the possession of the towns on the Dalmatian coast. The Emperor Manuel had counted on Venetian support in his own campaign against Hungary. In 1167 he won a decisive victory. The Hungarian King Stephen III was forced

---

[1] Caffaro, *Annali genovesi*, ed. L. T. Belgrano, I (Genoa, 1890), pp. 67–8. Heyd, *Commerce*, I, p. 204; Lilie, *Handel und Politik*, pp. 456–9.

[2] Kinnamos, p. 228, 229–31, 237; *DR*, II, no. 1464. Chalandon, *Les Comnènes*, II, pp. 481, 572–3.

to abandon all his territorial claims and to accept the fact that Dalmatia and Croatia were restored to Byzantine authority. The Byzantine Empire had suddenly become a next-door neighbour of Venice. The northern Adriatic, which the Normans had agreed to respect as a Venetian preserve, was now hemmed in by the Byzantines. In December of the same year another mission arrived in Venice from Constantinople. The three ambassadors asked for what they described as the 'customary help' of a fleet. They were given short shrift. A few days later the Doge showed his displeasure and his independence by offering the hand of friendship to his old enemies in Hungary. His two sons were to marry Hungarian princesses. His clear intention was to undo the emperor's work and to help the Hungarian king to drive the Byzantines out of Dalmatia. Relations between Byzantium and Venice had seldom been less cordial.[1]

Dandolo reports that the Doge, Vitale Michiel, placed an embargo on trade with Byzantium. If he did so, it had no more effect than the recall of all Venetians from the east ten years earlier. The documentary evidence suggests that Venetian business in the Byzantine world had never been so brisk as it was between 1167 and 1170. These were the years when the Venetians had no competitors since the emperor had not yet forgiven the Pisans and the Genoese for their misconduct in 1162. It was in 1170 that the storm broke. In May the emperor relented and signed a chrysobull granting the Genoese trading rights and a quarter of their own in Constantinople. In July he gave the same privileges to the Pisans. If he was looking for a pretext to humble the pride and curb the independence of the Venetians it was they who provided it for him. Furious at the challenge to their monopoly they attacked and plundered the newly established Genoese quarter in Constantinople, tore down its houses and left it in ruins. The emperor ordered them to pay for the damage they had done, to rebuild the houses of the Genoese and to restore all the property they had stolen. They refused to obey and threatened him with a punitive raid on the empire such as they had visited on his father John II.[2]

---

[1] *Annales Venetici breves*, p. 71; Dandolo, p. 249; *DR*, II, nos. 1475, 1479. Kretschmayr, I, pp. 253–4; Chalandon, *Les Comnènes*, II, pp. 488–90, 585–6; Ferluga, *L'amministrazione bizantina in Dalmazia*, pp. 257–60; Lilie, *Handel und Politik*, pp. 468–74.

[2] Kinnamos, p. 282; *Historia Ducum Veneticorum*, p. 78; Dandolo, pp. 249, 250; *DR*, II, nos. 1488 (October 1169), 1495, 1497, 1498, 1499 (May and October 1170). Heyd, *Commerce*, I, pp. 205–14; Chalandon, *Les Comnènes*, II, pp. 586–8; Borsari, 'Il commercio veneziano', 1003; Angold, *Byzantine Empire*, pp. 200–1.

The sources are at variance as to what happened next. The Italian chroniclers have it that the emperor froze the Venetian assets in Constantinople and sequestered their money, whereupon the Doge forbade his subjects to trade there any more and most of them went home. Byzantium was thus greatly impoverished. The emperor realised his mistake and sent envoys to Venice to invite them back, tempting them with the promise of a secure monopoly of Byzantine trade. The Doge was persuaded, commercial relations were resumed, and very soon more than 20,000 Venetians returned to Byzantine territory bringing with them vast quantities of merchandise. Sebastiano Ziani and Orio Mastropiero were sent out as the Doge's representatives to supervise the revived Venetian quarter in Constantinople. The emperor's change of heart, however, was no more than a clever ruse to lure the innocent Venetians back to his city in large numbers so that he could take his revenge on them with greater effect. There are several improbabilities in this story. It would not have been possible for the Doge to order the evacuation of all Venetians from the empire and then to send 20,000 of them back again within the few months between May 1170, when the Genoese quarter was set up, and March 1171 when Manuel took action against them. Nor is the round figure of 20,000 very convincing.

The Greek version of events is more direct and, as one would expect, more sympathetic to the emperor. It does not, however, conceal the evidence that he had a plan carefully and secretly laid for the punishment of the insolent Venetians. His agents in Constantinople and throughout the provinces were privy to the plan; and it says much for Byzantine administrative efficiency and security that the secret was kept. On the appointed day, 12 March 1171, the plan was put into action in every corner of the empire. All Venetians were arrested at precisely the same moment in Constantinople and elsewhere. The prisons could not hold them all. There were more than 10,000 in the capital alone. Some had to be confined in monasteries. But the overcrowding was so acute that some had to be set free on parole after a few days. One of them was a well-known businessman, Romano Mairano, who used his wealth and influence to commandeer a large ship on which he and a few refugees slipped out of the Golden Horn by night. A Byzantine patrol spotted them, caught up with them near Abydos and tried to set fire to their ship. But the Venetians contrived to fend off the incendiaries, outstripped their pursuers and got away to Acre. They were lucky. Other Venetian ships were arrested by the imperial navy on the high sea. In the provinces all Venetian residents and merchants were rounded up and their goods were impounded. Only at Halmyros did the emperor's men bungle their task. Twenty Venetian ships managed to escape; and it was the refugees from Halmyros who brought the full story of their compatriots' misfortunes home to Venice.[1]

Revenge upon the wily Greeks who had outwitted them at once became the cry in the streets of Venice. No other consideration of state or foreign policy must stand in the way of war for the liberation of their countrymen and the recovery of their goods and property. The shipwrights in the Arsenal laboured for a hundred days to prepare a fleet; and at the end of September a hundred galleys and twenty smaller vessels sailed from Venice under the personal command of the Doge, Vitale Michiel. His objective seems not to have been very clear. Perhaps he proposed to terrorise the Emperor Manuel into repentance, as Domenico Michiel was supposed to have terrorised Manuel's father half a century before. He could hardly have hoped to storm his way into Constantinople. For a start he healed some of the hurt pride of his people by showing the flag of St Mark along the coast of Dalmatia which had so recently reverted to the Byzantine Empire. Zara and other towns declared for Venice. Ragusa had to be bullied into submission. The fleet then moved on to Euboia and attacked Chalkis, the capital of the island. The Byzantine commander there was surprised by the tenacity of the Venetians and offered to use his good offices with the emperor to effect an amnesty. The Doge accordingly sent two of his men to Constantinople to negotiate, and in the meantime he took his fleet to the island of Chios where, after some skirmishing with Byzantine troops, the Venetians settled for the winter.

It was a good centre for awaiting developments and for conducting piratical raids on Byzantine territory. When the two ambassadors rejoined the fleet at Chios they brought with them a Byzantine official, probably sent to spy and report back on the size and condition of the Venetian forces. The ambassadors had not been granted an audience by the emperor, who wanted to play for time. But his official proposed that another embassy should be sent which might be more successful. This was agreed and the two Venetian ambassadors went back to Constantinople together with one Filippo Greco, who presumably knew

[1] Kinnamos, pp. 282–3; Niketas Choniates, pp. 171–2; *Annales Venetici breves*, p. 72; *Historia Ducum Veneticorum*, p. 78; Dandolo, p. 250; Martin da Canal, *Les Estoires de Venise*, ed. A. Limentani, Civiltà Veneziana, Fonti e Testi, XII, serie terza (Florence, 1972), pp. 39–40; *Cronaca di Marco*, in *ASI*, VIII (1845), 260; *TTh*, I, p. 168; *DR*, II, no. 1500. E. Besta, 'La cattura dei Veneziani in oriente per ordine dell' imperatore Emanuele Comneno e le sue conseguenze nella politica interna ed esterna del commune di Venezia', in *Antologia Veneta*, I, 1–2 (1900), pp. 35–46, 111–23; J. Danstrup, 'Manuel I's coup against Genoa and Venice in the light of Byzantine commercial policy', *Classica et Mediaevalia*, X (1948), 195–219; Heyd, *Commerce*, I, pp. 214–18; Chalandon, *Les Comnènes*, II, pp. 587–8; Thiriet, *Romanie vénitienne*, pp. 51–2. On Romano Mairano, see below pp. 104–6.

Greek. The winter on Chios did not go well. Illness swept through the Venetian camp. It was rumoured that the emperor's agents had poisoned the local wine and water. More than 1000 soldiers and sailors are said to have died within a few days. In the spring the Doge decided to leave Chios and make for the island of Panagia. A Greek traitor had alerted them to the approach of a Byzantine fleet and army. They got out in time; but they took their plague with them to Panagia. There the second embassy returning from Constantinople reported that they had had no more success than before. A Byzantine officer who came with them suggested that they should try again, and a third legation set out. One of its two members was Enrico Dandolo, later to become Doge. The emperor was now well informed about the state of the Venetian army and navy, decimated and crippled by disease. He had nothing to fear and much to gain from further delaying tactics. From Panagia the Doge led his ships first to Lesbos and then to Skyros, as if trying to shake off the plague. He had meant to make for Lemnos which would have been nearer to Constantinople. But his men had had enough and he was forced to head for home, chased and harried by the emperor's fleet, with what was left of his great armada.

The Emperor Manuel had won the first round. He was determined to make the Venetians suffer for their arrogance. He was no doubt pleased that they had been providentially struck down by the plague; though he bitterly resented their imputation that he had ordered them to be poisoned. It was unfortunate that Enrico Dandolo was wounded and partially blinded in a brawl while on his mission to Constantinople. For that accident too was blamed on the emperor and Dandolo never forgot it. Manuel is said to have sent a message to the Doge. It is eloquent of Byzantine animus against the Venetians:

Your nation [he wrote] has for a long time behaved with great stupidity. Once you were vagabonds sunk in abject poverty. Then you sidled into the Roman Empire. You have treated it with the utmost disdain and have done your best to deliver it to its worst enemies, as you yourselves are well aware. Now, legitimately condemned and justly expelled from the empire, you have in your insolence declared war on it – you who were once a people not even worthy to be named, you who owe what prestige you have to the Romans; and for having supposed that you could match their strength you have made yourselves a general laughing-stock. For no one, not even the greatest powers on earth, makes war on the Romans with impunity.[1]

Vitale Michiel was not well received when he brought his battered fleet home in May 1172. The people of Venice had been thirsting for blood and for revenge against the Greeks. He had let them down. His ships

[1] Kinnamos, p. 285.

had also brought the plague with them. He was assassinated in the streets of his own city and his memory was condemned. He might have done better with patient diplomacy than with impulsive aggression. But it had been what his people wanted and it was one of them who killed him when it failed.[1]

The new Doge, Sebastiano Ziani (1172–8), was elected before the month of May was out. He had the sense not to prepare a second armada. He could hardly afford to. Venice was losing a great source of income in the east and its assets in Constantinople remained frozen. There were also thousands of Venetians still held in captivity. Trade was not interrupted with the Christian cities in Syria and Palestine and with the Muslims in Alexandria. But nothing could offset the loss of business in Constantinople and the Byzantine world in which so much capital had been invested. Furthermore, the longer the emperor procrastinated, the more time he had to prepare the defences of his empire against another attack. The Doge adopted more insidious and less aggressive tactics. His agents incited the Serbians to rebel against Byzantine rule. In 1173 he sent ships to help Barbarossa lay siege to Ancona, which remained faithful to the Byzantine cause.[2] He did not despair of a diplomatic solution, but it was hard to come to terms with an emperor who always had an excuse for not receiving ambassadors from Venice. After two more embassies to Constantinople had come back empty-handed, the Doge lost his patience. He opened negotiations with William II of Sicily with a view to renewing the treaty between Venice and the Normans. The negotiations were designed to alarm the Byzantine Emperor; and yet another embassy was sent to Constantinople to make sure that the emperor knew what was happening. It too came back with nothing achieved. The Venetians were then able to contrast the icy silence of the Greeks with the warm welcome offered them by the Normans. King William of Sicily saw their ambassadors without delay. In 1175 he signed a treaty of peace with the Doge which was to last for a minimum of twenty years; and he guaranteed concessions to Venetian merchants trading in his kingdom. The Doge then bade farewell to the emperor's envoys who were waiting in Venice and sent them back to their master.[3]

The treaty between Venice and the Normans was in effect little more

---

[1] Kinnamos, pp. 283–6; Niketas Choniates, pp. 172–3; *Historia Ducum Veneticorum*, p. 80; Dandolo, pp. 250–3; *Cronaca di Marco*, 260–1; *DR*, II, nos. 1509, 1510. Kretschmayr, I, p. 256; Heyd, *Commerce*, I, pp. 218–19; Chalandon, *Les Comnènes*, II, pp. 589–91; Cessi, *Storia*, I, pp. 162–4; Lilie, *Handel und Politik*, pp. 493–6.

[2] A. Carile, 'Federico Barbarossa, i Veneziani e l'assedio di Ancona del 1173. Contributo alla storia politica e sociale della città nel secolo XII', *Studi veneziani*, XVI (1974), 3–31.

[3] Niketas Choniates, p. 173; Dandolo, pp. 260–1; *TTh*, I, nos. LXIV, LXV, LXVI, pp. 171–5; *DR*, II, nos. 1511, 1512. Kretschmayr, I, pp. 260–1, 465.

than a reaffirmation of that which they had concluded in 1154. Yet it was calculated to impress upon the emperors of east and west the fact that Venice was an independent power with a mind and a foreign policy of its own. Manuel's grand design of manipulating affairs in Italy to his own advantage and so humiliating the German Emperor as well as the Normans had not been realised. He had succeeded only in isolating his empire. The western powers no longer took him seriously. The Venetians had shown that they were ready to support either of his rivals in Italy to suit their own interests. Meanwhile the Genoese were clamouring for a review of the concessions that he had granted them, for an enlargement of their colony in Constantinople and for settlement of the damage done to their property by the Pisans and the Venetians. In 1172 and again in 1174 envoys from Genoa put their demands to the emperor. The combined sum which they claimed in compensation against Pisa and Venice amounted to 84,360 *nomismata*.[1] Little by little Manuel was led to the conclusion that he must come to some arrangement with the Venetians. He could not go on much longer holding thousands of them in prison. Niketas Choniates suggests that the emperor was persuaded to change his mind when he heard of the new treaty between Venice and the Normans in 1175. Dandolo on the other hand has it that Manuel never relented and that the Venetians were not restored to favour in Byzantium until after he was dead. Independent Venetian evidence shows this to be false. The truth of the matter probably is that the emperor began to reconsider the position in the light of the Venetian treaty with the Normans; and that long and difficult negotiations took place, particularly about compensation for the destruction of Venetian property, before agreement was reached in 1179. Several commercial documents in the archives of Venice testify to the fact that Venetian merchants imprisoned in Byzantium had been set free in that year.[2]

The emperor was still, however, inclined to move with caution. All that he seemed prepared to do was to reopen the door a little way to the return of Venetian traders to his empire. Not all of them were at once released from prison. There appears to have been no commitment in writing in the shape of a formal treaty or of a chrysobull reinstating all their former privileges. The matter of the payment of compensation must have taxed the emperor's patience. The Venetians reckoned that they had lost ships and property in 1171 to a total value of 15 *kentenaria*

---

[1] Chalandon, *Les Comnènes*, II, pp. 582–4; Lilie, *Handel und Politik*, pp. 497–504.

[2] Niketas Choniates, pp. 173–4; *Historia Ducum Veneticorum, Supplementum*, pp. 90,92; Dandolo, p. 266; Morozzo–Lombardo, I, nos. 303, 305, 308, 311, 313, 314 (dating between March and November 1179); *DR*, II, no. 1532. Thiriet, *Romanie vénitienne*, pp. 52–3; Lilie, *Handel und Politik*, p. 516.

or 1500 pounds of full-weight gold *hyperpyra*, equivalent to 108,000 *nomismata*. This was well over twice the damages claimed by the Genoese, and it gives some indication of the extent of Venetian property in the empire. There is no evidence that Manuel agreed to pay it. It was left to his successors to work out the practical details of mending the fences between Byzantium and Venice. But the relationship between them was no longer one between allies, between partners, or even between friends. Venetian behaviour at Corfu in 1149 and at Constantinople in 1170, followed by the Byzantine reaction in 1171, had created an atmosphere of mutual suspicion and mistrust which nothing could dispel.[1]

The Emperor Manuel died on 24 September 1180. Sometimes he had given the impression of posing as a second Justinian intent on restoring a universal empire stretching from the Pillars of Hercules to the waters of the Euphrates.[2] His diplomatic tentacles had reached as far afield as England and France. He had subjected the Hungarians and imposed peace on the Balkans. He had worked to win the friendship or to curb the ambition of the Holy Roman Empire, the Norman kingdom, the Republics of Venice, Genoa and Pisa in Italy. But at the end he was left with almost no friends in the west. He had had more success with the crusader states in the east, especially since his show of imperial power at Antioch in 1159. The Seljuq Turks too had, for a time, been obliged to recognise his superiority. In 1162, after a series of defeats along his frontier in Anatolia, the Sultan Kilidj Arslan had gone to Constantinople cap in hand as the emperor's vassal. But Manuel wanted nothing less than the total surrender of the Sultanate and the conquest of its capital at Konya; for this would give him command of the road to Antioch and Jerusalem.

It was this ambition that led Manuel into his humiliating encounter with the Turks at Myriokephalon in 1176. His army was trapped in a mountain pass and he was forced to submit. It was not too costly a defeat. The casualties, though high, were bearable. The Sultan allowed the survivors to withdraw in peace and his terms were generous. The worst was the blow to the emperor's pride and prestige. It seemed to him, as it has since seemed to others, that the Byzantine defeat at Myriokephalon in 1176 complemented the similar defeat at Manzikert a century before. But at Manzikert the whole army had been wiped out and the emperor had been taken prisoner. Myriokephalon saw no such catastrophe. Yet it appeared to show up the weaknesses and the pretensions of an emperor who had made his name known in all the councils of the great in Christendom. In western opinion it cut Manuel down to

---

[1] Heyd, *Commerce*, 1, p. 220; Lilie, *Handel und Politik*, pp. 515-18.
[1] Cf. Niketas Choniates, p. 160.

his proper and humbler size, not that of Emperor of the Romans but that of King of the Greeks, as Frederick Barbarossa so rudely called him. It made no difference that Barbarossa too was crushingly defeated at Legnano in the very same year 1176 by the towns of the Lombard League which Manuel had subsidised. The German Emperor could make triumph out of disaster. The Byzantine Emperor could not.[1]

The Doge of Venice came out of it all very well. For his city on the lagoons was chosen as the peace conference centre of all the warring parties in Italy; and it was there in July 1177 that Frederick Barbarossa made his truce with the Lombard towns and was reconciled with the pope, Alexander III, whom he had refused to recognise for seventeen years. The Kingdom of Sicily too was party to the Treaty of Venice; and the Venetians made sure of their own arrangements with Barbarossa by signing a new pact with him in August of the same year. For the Doge Sebastiano Ziani it was his finest hour. Never had Venice played host to so great a throng of world leaders. No one thought it odd that the only interested party who had not been invited was the Emperor in Constantinople, the King of the Greeks, Manuel Komnenos.[2]

---

[1] Chalandon, Les Comnènes, II, pp. 493–515; Lamma, Comneni e Staufer, II, pp. 269–83; Ostrogorsky, History, pp. 390–1; Angold, Byzantine Empire, pp. 192–4.

[2] Kretschmayr, I, pp. 262–8, 432, 478–9; Lamma, Comneni e Staufer, II, pp. 283–92; Cessi, Storia, I, pp. 167–9.

7

THE CALM BEFORE THE STORM

THE year 1171 marks a turning-point in relations between Byzantium and Venice. The Venetians could never forgive the Emperor Manuel for his high-handed action in arresting and imprisoning thousands of their citizens. Nor could they tolerate his deliberate favouritism of their commercial rivals, the Pisans and the Genoese. They felt embittered and betrayed. The attack on the Genoese quarter in Constantinople in 1170 had been the work of local mobsters. It had not been inspired by the Doge and people of Venice; and the emperor had gone too far in punishing all Venetians throughout his empire. By no means all of them were guilty of the crime. Yet many of those who were innocent, who had by their own profitable enterprise been contributing to the wealth of Byzantium, were ruined and bankrupted as a consequence.

The career of one such Venetian entrepreneur in the Levant is exceptionally well documented. He was that Romano Mairano who contrived the escape of some of his countrymen from Constantinople in March 1171.[1] Romano was one of the nouveaux riches of Venice in the middle of the twelfth century. He married well and invested his wife's substantial dowry in his business ventures overseas. From 1153 he was engaged in trade between Venice and the ports of the Byzantine Empire, at Halmyros and Sparta. In 1155 he took a cargo of timber from Venice to Constantinople and set up a business in the capital which he made his headquarters for the next ten years. It was a family concern. Romano ran the business in partnership with his brother Samuel and at first acted as an agent or factor for his brother-in-law in Venice. He built up an efficient network of local agencies in the provinces, at Smyrna and Adramyttion on the coast of Asia Minor and at Halmyros in Greece. He

---

[1] The commercial activities of the Mairano brothers are documented in Morozzo–Lombardo, 1. The fullest study of them is that of R. Heynen, *Zur Entstehung des Kapitalismus in Venedig*, Münchner Volkswirtschaftliche Studien, 71 (Stuttgart–Berlin, 1905), pp. 86–120. See also Y. Renouard, *Les Hommes d'affaires italiens au moyen âge*, 2nd edn. revised by B. Guillemain (Paris, 1968), pp. 76–80; Thiriet, *Romanie vénitienne*, pp. 46–8.

visited Smyrna several times in 1157–8 and from 1161 he extended his interests to Acre and to Alexandria. Not until 1164 did he go back to Venice.

At the start of his career Romano conducted his business affairs according to the form of contract known as a *colleganza*, an association and a pooling of capital between the itinerant entrepreneur and the resident merchant. Romano or his agents would make such an arrangement at each of the ports they visited. The pooling of resources between the roving businessman and the Venetian merchant resident on the spot made it possible to buy local merchandise for export and resale. The local resident generally put up two-thirds of the capital and the profits were shared equally between the partners in the *colleganza*. The names and activities of other such partners in Venetian enterprises in the Byzantine Empire in the twelfth century are on record. Domenico Mastrocoli and a Slav trader from Dalmatia called Dobromir Stagnario operated from Corinth and Sparta, exporting vast quantities of oil to Alexandria and to Venice. Vitale Voltani almost monopolised the export of oil from Corinth, Sparta and Thebes between 1165 and 1171.[1] The careers of some of the resident merchants who acted as local agents are also documented, such as the brothers Natale and Marco Betani who owned properties at Halmyros. Their knowledge of local affairs and local produce and markets was invaluable to the itinerant businessmen. But the name and the credit of Romano and Samuel Mairano were known and respected from Constantinople to Syria, from Egypt to Greece.

After a spell in Venice, Romano went back to Constantinople in 1166. The fortune that he had by then accumulated enabled him to conduct his operations on a different basis. He raised his capital not by partnership in a *colleganza* but by means of loans. They cost him dearly in interest but he no longer had to share the profits of his enterprises. These he reinvested in merchant ships which he sailed out from Constantinople to Acre and Alexandria and back. In 1168 he was once more home in Venice, perhaps in response to the Doge's embargo on trade with Constantinople. His first wife had died and he now remarried, again to a lady of means, whose wealth he exploited to expand his business and to build a huge new three-masted ship. Clearly Romano did not anticipate the abrupt collapse of Venetian interests in Byzantium. In 1169, for a high price, the Patriarch of Grado farmed out to him all his revenues from the Venetian quarter in Constantinople. The deal included a six-year lease on a wharf on the Golden Horn; and on the strength of a number of loans Romano amassed the sum of 3075 *hyperpyra* which he invested

[1] Thiriet, *Romanie vénitienne*, pp. 48–9; Borsari, 'Il commercio veneziano', 989–94.

in merchandise. The event of 1171 seems to have taken him by surprise; but he managed to make his escape with a boatload of refugees, first to Acre and then to Venice, where he arrived almost destitute and without the means to pay his creditors.

The Mairano brothers were outstandingly successful in their business affairs. They therefore had more to lose than the smaller Venetian traders in Byzantium. But the overall losses in capital, in property and in profit over a number of years did great harm to Byzantium as well as to Venice. Romano found other outlets for his talents. Basing himself on Venice instead of Constantinople, he co-operated with his brother Samuel in making the most of the markets in Alexandria and Acre. By 1177 he was rich enough to build a new boat and six years later he was at last able to pay off all the debts that he had incurred as a result of his losses in 1171. By 1190 he was back in Constantinople after an absence of nearly twenty years. He died in Venice as a wealthy man in 1201. There was a materialistic streak in the Venetian character which Byzantines of the upper class affected to despise. The xenophobic mob of Constantinople had no such lofty feelings of moral superiority. Their hatred of the Latins or Italians was the instinctive loathing of one race for another, compounded by envy and jealousy; though their priests and monks willingly provided them with many good and pious reasons for condemning all westerners as misguided Christians. The Emperor Manuel had not won the hearts of his people by his Latinophile policies. They observed with disgust that too many Latins had found favour and riches at his court. Some even held high office in the army and the administration. Manuel left a legacy of resentment against the Christians of the west when he died in 1180. The terms of his will and the arrangements that he made for the succession to the throne made matters worse.

Manuel's son Alexios II was barely twelve years old, though already married to Agnes of France, the eight-year old daughter of Louis VII. He was the son of Manuel's second wife, Maria of Antioch. The daughter of his first wife, Maria the Prophyrogenita, was married to Rainier of the north Italian family of Montferrat, whose alliance Manuel had sought against the German Emperor. In his will he named Maria of Antioch, his widow, as guardian and regent for his son. The whole empire seemed to have been consigned to Latin management, supported by western mercenary soldiers and by Italian business interests. The reaction was not long in coming. There were other members of the imperial family of Komnenos who objected to living under the regency of a crusader princess. Prominent among them was Andronikos, the late Manuel's cousin and implacable rival, who had led an adventurous and colourful career of treason and plot, imprisonment and exile. Andronikos was already over sixty. But he was known to be anti-Latin; and on that ticket alone he could win much popular support in a bid for the throne. In 1182 he left his estate in Paphlagonia and marched on Constantinople at the head of his army. The imperial fleet at first prevented him from crossing the Bosporos. But when its admiral went over to him the way into Constantinople was open. The regent Maria of Antioch was delivered to him by her western bodyguard. Before making his formal entry into the city, however, Andronikos sent in his Paphlagonian troops to incite the people against the Latins. The people needed no encouragement. With an enthusiasm fired by years of resentment they set about the massacre of all the foreigners that they could find. They directed their fury mainly against the merchants' quarters along the Golden Horn. Many had sensed what was coming with the arrival of Andronikos Komnenos and had already made their escape by sea. Of those who remained the Pisans and the Genoese were the main victims. The slaughter was appalling. The Byzantine clergy shamelessly encouraged the mob to seek out the Latin monks and priests. The pope's legate to Constantinople, the Cardinal John, was decapitated and his severed head was dragged through the streets tied to the tail of a dog. At the end some 4000 westerners who had survived the massacre were rounded up and sold as slaves to the Turks. Those who had escaped by ship took their revenge by burning and looting the Byzantine monasteries on the coasts and islands of the Aegean Sea.

The massacre of April 1182 is most fully described by William of Tyre, who reported what he had heard from refugees. There are two Greek accounts of it. The Italian sources, however, are strangely reticent. One Pisan chronicle mentions the event; and the Genoese were later to claim substantial damages from the Byzantine authorities. No contemporary Venetian chronicler alludes to it. There is but one document of 1182 reporting an encounter between Venetian ships off Cape Malea in the Peloponnese. Those on their eastward journey were warned to proceed no further since the Venetians and all other Latins had been expelled from Constantinople.[1] The conclusion must be that very few if any Venetians were affected by the massacre and that therefore their colony in Constantinople had not been fully re-established by 1182; for its inhabitants would hardly have been spared because of their Venetian blood.

---

[1] Morozzo–Lombardo, I, no. 331, pp. 326–7 (June 1182). The sources for the massacre of 1182 are: William of Tyre, *Historia*, pp. 1082–4; Eustathios of Thessalonica, *De capta Thessalonica narratio*, ed. I. Bekker, in *Leonis Grammatici Chronographia*, pp. 365–512, *CSHB* (1842), pp. 34–6; Niketas Choniates, pp. 250–1; Bernardo Maragone, *Annales pisani*, ed. M. L. Gentile, *RIS*, VI/2 (Bologna, 1936), p. 73. Kretschmayr, I, pp. 269–71; Thiriet, *Romanie vénitienne*, pp. 53–4; C. M. Brand, *Byzantium Confronts the West, 1180–1204* (Cambridge, Mass., 1968), pp. 41–3, 195–6; Lilie, *Handel und Politik*, pp. 532–7.

The slaughter of foreigners which he had deliberately incited brought Andronikos Komnenos the loyalty of the people. He posed as the alternative regent for the young heir to the throne, Alexios II. Manuel's widow, Maria of Antioch, was soon convicted of conspiring against the state and murdered. Maria the Prophyrogenita and her husband came to a mysterious end, probably by poison. In September 1183 the patriarch was induced to crown Andronikos as emperor. The young prince Alexios was strangled soon afterwards; and Andronikos completed his triumph by marrying his widow, Agnes of France. She was the last of the Latins in high places in Byzantium. But she was only eleven years old.[1]

Andronikos Komnenos came to the throne through a welter of bloodshed and over the dead bodies of the family and relatives of his late cousin Manuel. He advertised himself as the champion of the people in Constantinople and the provinces; and he manipulated the mob for his own political purposes. He had traded on their fear of foreigners. Yet he was aware that Constantinople needed the support of western allies. The merchants of Pisa and Genoa were not likely to hurry back after what they had suffered. The Venetians, however, had suffered not from Andronikos but from his predecessor Manuel; and they might be persuaded that the new emperor was their friend. The first step was to order the release of those still held as prisoners in Constantinople and elsewhere. Some of them were safe home in Venice in 1183. No doubt they brought with them the glad news that the dark days were over and that Venetian traders were again welcome in Byzantium. No official exchange of embassies seems yet to have occurred, but by the end of 1183 some Venetians had evidently drifted back to Constantinople to resettle their quarter on the Golden Horn. The risks were great but so was the temptation to corner a monopoly of Byzantine trade now that the Pisans and the Genoese had left.

The Doge, Orio Mastropiero (1178–92), was keen to seize the opportunity, but not without an assurance that a new and formal agreement would be drafted and that the outstanding Venetian claim for damages would be settled. In the spring of 1184 he sent an embassy to Constantinople. Among its leaders were Enrico Dandolo, who could be relied upon to be firm with the Greeks, and Pietro Ziani, son of the late Doge Sebastiano. There is no record of their negotiations, but it is clear that Venetians had by then moved back into their quarter in Constantinople and that their merchants were enjoying at least some of their former privileges. There were minor disputes about property, especially about a wharf with twelve houses on it which the Venetians claimed as their

[1] On Andronikos Komnenos, see O. Jurewicz, *Andronikos I. Komnenos* (Amsterdam, 1970); Brand, *Byzantium*, pp. 31–75; Angold, *Byzantine Empire*, pp. 263–71.

own. But the Emperor Andronikos was surprisingly ready to compensate them for the losses that they had sustained in 1171. He agreed to pay the full sum of 1500 pounds of *hyperpyra* which they had demanded from Manuel. It would be up to them to divide the money among the numerous claimants according to their estimate of their losses. The total was to be paid in six annual instalments of 250 pounds; and Andronikos sent to Venice a first payment of 100 pounds. This was a promising gesture. A series of documents dated in February and March 1184 confirms the presence in Constantinople of Venetian traders and property speculators who evidently had confidence in the future. As late as February 1185, however, there was still some doubt among the Venetians in Thebes as to whether or not a new agreement had been signed between the Doge and the emperor.[1]

They were right to feel uncertain. No such agreement was ever signed. Before that year was out the Emperor Andronikos had met a violent death. By pretending to be the friend of the people he had alienated the Byzantine aristocracy. He had ignored the interests of the great families and surrounded himself with obscure upstarts as cruel and ruthless as himself in suppressing any attempts at opposition or revolt. The end of his reign of terror was precipitated by events in the west. Some of the disaffected nobility had made their escape to the Norman Kingdom of Sicily. It was even alleged that the young Alexios II was among them. King William II was pleased to take up their cause for it gave him a noble pretext for invading the Byzantine Empire. He followed the time-honoured route of Norman invaders. In June 1185 his army stormed and occupied Durazzo and marched overland towards Thessalonica, while his fleet captured Corfu and the Ionian islands of Cephalonia and Zakynthos and sailed up the Aegean Sea. No Norman invasion had ever got so far. The Byzantine army and navy were sadly disorganised and their commanders out of sympathy with their emperor. Thessalonica fell to the Normans in August after a siege by land and sea. Its Archbishop Eustathios, who stayed with his flock, wrote an eye-witness account

[1] *Historia Ducum Veneticorum*, p. 92; Dandolo, p. 266; *DR*, II, no. 1556; Morozzo–Lombardo, I, nos. 336, 338, pp. 332–3, 334–5 (return of Venetian prisoners); nos. 344–5, 347–9, pp. 340–5 (Venetian trade in Byzantium in the reign of Andronikos); nos. 358, 360–1, 365, 369, 378–80, pp. 352–6, 359–60, 362–3, 371–4 (payment of money by Andronikos); Maltézou, 'Quartiere veneziano', 42–4, nos. 3–8 (Venetians in Constantinople in 1184); Morozzo–Lombardo, I, no. 353, pp. 347–9 (Venetians at Thebes); R. Morozzo della Rocca and A. Lombardo, *Nuovi documenti del commercio veneto nei secoli XI–XIII*, Deputazione di Storia Patria per le Venezie: Monumenti Storici. Nuova Serie, VII (Venice, 1953), pp. 36–40 (disputed wharf in Constantinople). Heyd, *Commerce*, I, pp. 223–4; Brand, *Byzantium*, pp. 196–7; Lilie, *Handel und Politik*, pp. 547–50.

of the siege and of the savage violence of the conquerors.[1] It was as
if the western world had taken its revenge for what the Greeks had done
to the Latins in Constantinople three years before. It may have been
in anticipation of such vengeance that Andronikos had chosen to be so
generous to the Venetians, reminding them of their ancient pledge to
protect his empire by sea. The Venetians were unmoved by his reminder.
They were still bound by the treaty which they had made with the Normans in 1175. They would accept the emperor's goodwill and his money
but they would not help him out of his troubles. Part of the Norman
army advanced on Constantinople. It was the news of their approach,
following on the dreadful tidings of the sack of Thessalonica, that brought
about the downfall of the tyrant Andronikos. Panic seized the city. The
mob on whose shoulders he had risen to power turned against him.
They proclaimed as their emperor one Isaac Angelos, a last surviving
ringleader of the aristocratic opposition. Andronikos was caught trying
to escape. He was brought back to Constantinople in chains, tortured,
maimed, mutilated and finally put to death in the Hippodrome with
a frenzied and horrible bestiality unparallelled even by Byzantine standards.[2]

Andronikos was the last of the dynasty of Komnenos which had begun
so bravely with Alexios I in 1081 and brought such prestige and prosperity
to Byzantium. Isaac II Angelos was the first of a dynasty which sapped
the roots of the empire until, like a dying tree, it fell before the wind
of the Fourth Crusade. The threat from the Normans which had caused
panic in Constantinople in 1185 was soon dispelled. In November their
army was twice defeated in Thrace. They abandoned Thessalonica and
retreated to Durazzo, from where the Emperor Isaac dislodged them
in the spring of 1186 and sent them back across the water with heavy
casualties. They held on to the islands of Cephalonia and Zakynthos,
though they were forced to evacuate Corfu.[3] The occupation of
Corfu by Norman troops had brought Byzantium and Venice together
in times past. It lay at the end of the Adriatic Sea and was a point of
common concern. Isaac II needed the support of the Venetian fleet. He
must tempt the Doge into an alliance by reopening diplomatic relations
and offering terms of trade and profit which would persuade him to
overlook his treaty with the Norman king. He invited Mastropiero to
send an embassy to Constantinople. The three envoys who arrived were

---

[1] Eustathios of Thessalonica, *De Capta Thessalonica*; S. Kyriakides, ed., *La espugnazione di Tessalonica*, trans. V. Rotolo, Istituto Siciliano di Studi Bizantini e Neoellenici. Testi, 5 (Palermo, 1961). Niketas Choniates, pp. 297–308.
[2] Brand, *Byzantium*, pp. 68–75, 160–9; Angold, *Byzantine Empire*, pp. 268–9.
[3] Brand, *Byzantium*, pp. 169–75.

empowered to negotiate a treaty along the lines of the chrysobull for Venice which had last been signed by Manuel I in 1148. But they were also instructed to be firm about payment of the instalments still due by way of damages.[1] The Emperor Manuel had prevaricated. The Emperor Andronikos had made generous gestures. But the Emperor Isaac demonstrated that he meant to bring Venice and Byzantium together again in a new and stable partnership. The Doge's ambassadors got all that they could have hoped for, signed and sealed in three separate chryso-bulls in February 1187.

The first of the three confirms and renews all the commercial privileges granted to Venice by Alexios I, John II and Manuel I, the Latin texts of whose charters are quoted at length. Alexios had described the Vene-tians as true and faithful servants of his empire. Isaac extols them as 'long-standing allies, friends and supporters'. He reminds them, poin-tedly in the circumstances, of the service which they so valiantly rendered to his ancestor Alexios against Robert Guiscard and his Norman ships at Durazzo. The reward or the bait which was theirs on that occasion, enriched as it was by the Emperor Manuel, is now theirs again, word for word, item for item, with no alteration or diminution.[2] The second chrysobull reaffirms the extent and the properties of the Venetian quarter in Constantinople precisely as they were determined by Manuel in 1148.[3] These documents are little more than restatements of the rights and privi-leges that the Venetians had formerly enjoyed in Constantinople and other parts of the empire. The third document is also presented and phrased as an imperial chrysobull, but the tone and the contents are new. This is not a privilege granted from on high to an inferior power. It is more in the nature of a contract between equal partners, a pact or treaty of alliance between Byzantium and Venice which emperors of an earlier age would not have countenanced. Its preamble plays on the theme of the union which had once existed between the two and calls on the angel of peace to tear down the wall of enmity which has divided them. The emperor was careful not to apportion blame for the building of that wall. There had been faults on both sides.[4]

The many clauses of the document are almost all concerned with war and peace. The Venetians agreed to the following terms: They would make no alliance with any rulers, crowned or uncrowned, nor with any nation, Christian or pagan, inimical to the Emperor Isaac or his heirs, male or female. If and when such a ruler or nation should attack the

[1] Dandolo, p. 271; *TTh*, I, no. LXIX, pp. 178–9.
[2] *TTh*, I, no. LXX, pp. 179–89; *DR*, II, no. 1576.
[3] *TTh*, I, no. LXXI, pp. 189–95; *DR*, II, no. 1577.
[4] *TTh*, I, no. LXXII, pp. 195–203; *DR*, II, no. 1578.

empire with a fleet of over forty and up to 100 ships, the Doge was to supply a corresponding number of ships within six months of being notified; the ships would be built and equipped at Venice with funds supplied for the most part by the Emperor and each would be manned by a crew of 140; the shipwrights would be paid at the rate of sixty *hyperpyra* a man from the imperial treasury. The captains of the ships were to swear that their vessels were fully manned, to make up any deficiencies caused by deserters or absentees, and to account for any discrepancies in the pay of their crews, which would be provided by the emperor. The captains were also to swear that they would command their ships in a manner conducive to the honour of the empire and the fleet; their crews would be paid at the same rate as that paid to the Venetians at the siege of Corfu in 1148–9. To make up a ship's crew the emperor could conscript up to three-quarters of its complement from among Venetians resident in his empire between the ages of twenty and sixty. The Venetian fleet must be commanded by Venetian captains who would take the same oath of loyalty; and if they encountered a common enemy before they had joined forces with the imperial navy they must act at their own discretion. When the fleets had joined up, however, there must be a roll-call and any deficiencies in numbers made up as soon as possible. The captains and officers of the Venetian ships must swear to obey and abide by the orders of the captain of the imperial fleet and fight together with him against their common enemies, Christian or pagan. In any territory taken from an enemy the Venetians would be granted a church, a commercial quarter and a landing stage which they could use without payment of any tax.

The imperial fleet should always be of the same size or larger than that of the Venetians. Having done its duty, the Venetian fleet, or as many of its ships as seemed necessary, might return to Venice; though it must always be on call to come back should the emperor require it. Any refitting of the fleet or recruiting of its crews could take place in Venice, though at Byzantine expense. If for some reason the fleet was prevented from arriving from Venice within the appointed time, the emperor was at liberty to conscript to the service of his own fleet up to three-quarters of the number of Venetians resident in his empire. Likewise, if the empire was attacked by a fleet of between forty and 100 ships and there was no time to summon help from Venice, the emperor might conscript as mercenaries up to three-quarters of the Venetians living in an area stretching from Adrianople to Abydos and south to Philadelphia; and he could commandeer as many of their ships as possible. Such were the terms on which the Venetians were bound to assist in the defence of Byzantium against any attack by a hostile power. Two exceptions were, however, made; one was the 'King of Germany', so long as Venice remained at peace with him; the other was King William II of Sicily, whose twenty-year treaty with Venice had seven years and nine months still to run (from 1 January 1187). If, however, the King of Sicily could be shown to be the aggressor, Venice should provide a squadron of fifteen ships within four months of being notified, for which service they would be remunerated at the same rate.

Byzantine officials coming to Venice to recruit soldiers from Lombardy or for any other necessary and honourable purpose should be accommodated and protected so long as their business was not against Venetian interests. But they must not lead ships or men out of Venice against any friend or ally of the Venetians. Similar safeguards were laid down concerning the passage of Byzantine troops through Venice to the empire, and concerning the proven inability of the Venetians to fulfil their obligations to Byzantium due to their being involved in war with another power. All future Doges of Venice were to swear an oath of loyalty to the Byzantine Emperor and his heirs, male or female, on the same terms as those now agreed with the Doge Orio Mastropiero. Venetians who were in debt either to the Byzantine treasury or to private persons must discharge their debts. If they were unable to do so their creditors could bring the law upon them or their heirs. Finally, if any part of the empire were attacked by enemies, any Venetians living there must co-operate in its defence.

The Venetians were to observe the terms of this agreement and their oath of loyalty notwithstanding the hostility shown to them by the late Emperor Manuel. Nor were they to break their oath either under pressure from any crowned or uncrowned ruler or because they were offered absolution from it or excommunication on account of it by any bishop of the church, even by the Pope of Rome himself. They would remain faithful to its conditions so long as the Emperor Isaac and future emperors kept their part of the agreement. Thus, in the emperor's words, the Venetians were brought back to their former unity with the empire. The chrysobull continues with a statement of their reward: the renewal of the privileges granted them by Alexios I, John II and Manuel I; an assurance of their right to live and hold property in security and without fear in all the places which they had formerly frequented. All the losses which they had suffered as a result of the Emperor Manuel's action would be made good. All items of Venetian property which had found their way into palaces, monasteries, the treasury or anywhere else would be restored to their owners, whether or not they were listed in writing. The whereabouts of any items that could not at first be traced were to be carefully investigated by a specially appointed commission, whose members would have powers of repossession and of repurchase. The treasury would provide the funds. The obligations of Byzantium to Venice were then summarised: in the event of an attack on Venice by a hostile power Byzantium would come to its defence as though the attack had been made against its own territory. This would not, however, apply in the case of King William of Sicily; for if William fell out with the Venetians because they had agreed to furnish fifteen ships for Byzantium, the emperor would act as he thought best. The Venetians would be party to any peace treaty or truce that the emperor might conclude with any enemy against whom they had assisted him. In any territory conquered with the help of the Venetian fleet, Venice would be entitled to a church, a quarter and a landing stage free of tax. Byzantines who were in debt to Venetians must pay their creditors on the same terms and conditions as those laid down for Venetian debtors.[1]

The three chrysobulls of February 1187 were designed to bring Venice back within the orbit of Byzantium, to restore the amicable and mutually profitable relationship that had existed before the disaster of 1171. Their elaborately worded provisions seemed to be weighted in favour of the Venetians. They were again free to come and go in the Byzantine Empire to pick up the broken threads of their commercial ventures in its towns and harbours; and they were assured of their former privileges and properties in Constantinople. The obligations laid upon them were unlikely to be put to the test. There was little chance, in the circumstances of the time, that the Byzantines would exercise their right to use Venice as their port of entry into Italy and the west. The emperor no longer had any influence in the west. Even in central Europe his authority was challenged. The King of Hungary had taken advantage of Manuel's death to march into Dalmatia. The Serbians, whom Manuel had subdued, rebelled and founded a kingdom of their own; and in 1185 the Bulgarians also raised their standard of revolt. The Emperor Isaac did what he could to stop the rot from spreading. Having driven the Normans out of Greece, he led his army into Bulgaria and temporarily tamed the rebel leaders. But he was soon forced to acknowledge that a new Bulgarian Empire was being born on his northern borders. The spirit of separatism was infectious. In 1184 the island of Cyprus was seized by Isaac Komnenos, a nephew of the late Manuel, who adopted the imperial title; and in

---

[1] Kretschmayr, I, pp. 271, 470; Heyd, *Commerce*, I, pp. 225–6; Brand, *Byzantium*, pp. 197–9; Lilie, *Handel und Politik*, pp. 24–35, 564–8.

Asia Minor a number of cities, such as Philadelphia, proclaimed their independence under their own local archons.[1]

The emperor's problems were compounded by the announcement of a new crusade from the west. It was to be led by the German Emperor Frederick Barbarossa, Philip Augustus of France and Richard Coeur de Lion of England. Saladin of Egypt had overwhelmed the forces of the Latin Kingdom of Jerusalem and entered the Holy City in October 1187. The French and English contingents went by sea; and though they failed to recover Jerusalem their exploits were of little concern to the Byzantines. Barbarossa, however, chose to march to the east overland. He was an inveterate and devoted enemy of Byzantium and his passage through the Balkans was enthusiastically welcomed by the Serbians and the Bulgarians. The Emperor Isaac, who had no desire to see the German Emperor in Constantinople, came to an agreement with Saladin to delay the march of the crusade. Barbarossa and the whole of the western Christian world took this act to be the final and conclusive proof of Byzantine treachery. Memories of the massacre of 1182 were still vivid. In the event Isaac's diplomacy or treachery had little effect, for Barbarossa bullied him into providing ships, escorts and provisions for his crossing into Asia Minor and on to Jerusalem. He was destined never to reach it, for he died on his way there. But the Byzantine alliance with the infidel conqueror of the Holy City had done irreparable harm to relations between eastern and western Christians. It had hardened the suspicion in the west that the cause of the crusade would never be won so long as the Byzantines stood in the way. Barbarossa himself had proposed a crusade of another kind, to be directed against Constantinople, whose people were the enemies of God.[2]

The commitment of Venice to the Third Crusade was, as usual, dictated by self interest. In a show of piety the Doge Mastropiero summoned all Venetians living abroad to come home by Easter 1189 to join in the expedition to win back the Holy Land.[3] His piety was practical. There were Venetian trading colonies in most of the cities of the Holy Land, not least in Acre, which had surrendered to Saladin. The Doge provided ships to transport some of the crusaders to the east; and when Acre was recaptured after a two-year siege, Venetian merchants quickly re-established their quarter in the city.[4] Otherwise the part played by

---

[1] Ostrogorsky, *History*, pp. 403–6; Angold, *Byzantine Empire*, pp. 272–8. J. Hoffmann, *Rudimente von Territorialstaaten im byzantinischen Reich*, Miscellanea Byzantina Monacensia, 17 (Munich, 1974).

[2] Ostrogorsky, *History*, pp. 406–7; Brand, *Byzantium*, pp. 176–88.

[3] *Jussio* of November 1188 in *TTh*, I, no. LXXIII, pp. 204–6; Morozzo–Lombardo, I, no. 402, pp. 394–5.

[4] Kretschmayr, I, p. 274.

the Venetians in the crusade was limited. Nor did they join in the general condemnation of the part played by the Byzantine Emperor. They were not much concerned with the charge that he was an enemy of God and a traitor to the cause, though there might be something to be said for putting Constantinople under western control. They had their own reasons for suspecting Byzantine motives. The emperor had committed himself to restoring their lost property in Constantinople and to settling their large bill for damages. Over a year had passed and little had been done. They suspected him of the kind of procrastination to which Manuel had treated them. Perhaps their suspicions were unjust. The promised commission had been set up to conduct a thorough search for missing Venetian property. But it proved impossible to trace all of it after a lapse of sixteen years. In 1189 the Doge sent two ambassadors, Pietro Cornario and Domenico Memo, to remind the emperor of his promises; and in June of that year Isaac was persuaded to sign yet another agreement with Venice. Frederick Barbarossa was almost at the gates of Constantinople. Byzantium was badly in need of friends and allies.[1]

The chrysobull of June 1189 was the fourth which the Emperor Isaac signed in favour of Venice. He acknowledged that it had proved impracticable to restore to the Venetians all the goods that they had lost in 1171. He had therefore hit upon another way of settling their just claims in this respect. They had asked for an enlargement of their colony in Constantinople and for more landing stages. Bearing in mind that the men of Venice were not men of another race but Romans by origin and singularly devoted to the Roman Empire, their requests would be granted. There were French and German quarters in Constantinople which had been allotted by chrysobulls in times past. They had been little used and seldom visited by the merchants of those nations. Indeed it could be argued that they had been awarded not to France and Germany but simply for the convenience of occasional French and German traders.[2] They lay alongside the Venetian quarter on the Golden Horn. They would now be added to that quarter with their landing stages. This, it was estimated, would bring the Venetians an extra annual revenue of fifty pounds of gold, which would recompense them for their lost property. On the larger issue of the compensation for damages which the Emperor Andronikos had promised, Isaac agreed that 1400 pounds of gold remained outstanding. Andronikos had paid 100 pounds on account. Isaac would not let his hated predecessor steal his glory. He undertook to settle the bill for the entire sum of 1500 pounds and made

---

[1] *Historia Ducum Veneticorum*, p. 90; Dandolo, p. 271. Chrysobull of June 1189: *TTh*, I, no. LXXIV, pp. 206–11; *DR*, II, nos. 1589, 1590.
[2] This statement is confirmed by the lack of other documentary evidence for their existence.

over to the Doge's ambassadors a first instalment of 250 pounds. The remaining 1250 pounds would be paid in annual instalments over a period of six years until the debt was fully honoured. These were reckless promises which the emperor could hardly fulfil. Venetian documents tell of the receipt of the first 250 pounds and of further payments from the imperial treasury in 1191 and 1193. These were distributed *pro rata* to the merchants who had submitted claims for compensation. But the six years were up in 1195 when Isaac lost his throne and the debt was still far from being cleared.[1]

The carefully worded clauses and conditions of Isaac's four agreements with Venice are mainly of academic interest, for they were never implemented. No Venetian fleet of between forty and 100 ships was ever called upon to defend Byzantine interests. Venetian residents in the empire were never conscripted into service. No Byzantine fleet ever sailed to Venice. Indeed, for all his fine words, it is doubtful whether the emperor could muster more than a handful of warships by 1187.[2] Once the Third Crusade had passed him by, Isaac resumed his military campaigns in the Balkans with the object of stifling revolt in Serbia and Bulgaria, where the Venetians could be of no real help to him. It was in the course of his campaign in Bulgaria in April 1195 that he became the victim of a conspiracy led by his elder brother Alexios and a band of disgruntled aristocrats. He was deposed and blinded. His son Alexios, then aged about thirteen, was imprisoned, and his brother was proclaimed Emperor in his place as Alexios III. It is generally agreed that the decline of Byzantium, which had begun after the death of Manuel I, reached the point of no return under Alexios III Angelos. The new emperor had no talent for administration and no head for heroism. He was a hypochondriac of weak character; he earned a reputation for generosity to his aristocratic friends in the capital which was paid for by ruthless taxation of the provinces; and he tolerated if he did not encourage nepotism and corruption in the bureaucracy. The decentralisation and separatism which had already undermined the structure of the empire became uncontrollable. Serbia and Bulgaria both broke away and their rulers looked to Rome to provide them with the regal or imperial status which Constantinople refused to grant them.[3]

Further west new problems arose which were far beyond the competence of an emperor such as Alexios III. Frederick Barbarossa had died on his crusade. His son and heir, Henry VI, had married Constance,

[1] Morozzo–Lombardo, I, nos. 378–80, 403, 418, pp. 371–4, 395–6, 409–10. Heyd, *Commerce*, I, p. 226; Brand, *Byzantium*, pp. 199–200; Lilie, *Handel und Politik*, pp. 35–41.
[2] Lilie, *Handel und Politik*, p. 563.
[3] Ostrogorsky, *History*, pp. 408–11; Brand, *Byzantium*, pp. 110–16.

aunt of William II of Sicily; and when William died childless in 1189, Henry claimed the inheritance to his kingdom. In 1194 he was crowned at Palermo. For years the Byzantine Emperors had tried to play off the Norman Kingdom of Sicily against the German Empire of the West. The two were now united and the hostility towards Byzantium which they had severally shared was now concentrated. Henry VI inherited his father's dream of a universal Empire of the Romans and the ambition of the Normans of Sicily to conquer Byzantium. This new concentration of power in Italy alarmed the Venetians. Their arrangement with the Normans which had lasted for twenty years was now over. The Byzantines were even more dismayed. Henry VI was planning another crusade. At the same time he declared himself to be the champion and avenger of the dethroned and blinded Emperor Isaac II. The honour of his own family was at stake since his brother, Philip of Swabia, was betrothed to a daughter of Isaac. He demanded that the usurper Alexios III should surrender to him all the land between Durazzo and Thessalonica which the Normans had briefly held in 1185 and pay him enormous sums of gold by way of tribute. Alexios was driven to imposing what was known as the 'German tax' to satisfy Henry's demands. But his people were already overtaxed; the money was not there; and the demands could not be met. Two factors are said to have saved Byzantium. The first was the intervention of the pope, who refused to bless Henry's plan to turn his crusade on Constantinople. The second was Henry's death in September 1197. This was the view of Niketas Choniates, who was a minister of state at the time; though one may doubt whether Henry ever really intended to divert his crusade from Jerusalem to Constantinople.[1]

Alexios III had meekly submitted to Henry's demand for tribute. He was always inclined to take the easy way out of his difficulties, though to find even a portion of the required sum of money he was reduced to inventing a special levy and to plundering the tombs of his ancestors. The Byzantines were much relieved when Henry VI died and the German tax was abolished. So too were the Venetians. They suspected that Alexios would sooner pay tribute to the German Emperor than settle his accounts with Venice. He refused to pay any further instalments of the debt which Isaac had agreed to honour. He instructed his agents to collect taxes from Venetian property and shipping in flagrant breach of existing guarantees. Worse still he made no secret of the favours that he granted to their commercial rivals from Pisa, from Genoa and even from Ragusa. Isaac II had reopened the door to the Pisans and the Genoese partly

---

[1] Niketas Choniates, pp. 475–80. Ostrogorsky, *History*, pp. 411–13; Brand, *Byzantium*, pp. 189–94; Angold, *Byzantine Empire*, pp. 280–1.

to divert them from the piracy in Byzantine waters which many of them had taken to since being expelled from Constantinople in 1182. He had issued chrysobulls to the Republics of Pisa and Genoa in 1192–3 restoring their privileges and their trading quarters in the capital. Alexios III went further in his favouritism until the Venetians began to think that he was deliberately slighting them and encouraging their competitors.[1] The emperor was thought to be behind a number of Pisan attacks on Venetian ships in the Sea of Marmora and raids on Venetian premises in Constantinople. So much was at stake that Venice and Pisa went to war. The Emperor Henry VI put a stop to their fighting in Italy. But in the Byzantine world tension between them ran high. In 1196 a Venetian fleet stationed itself at Abydos at the entrance to the Hellespont and its captains refused to obey the Doge's order to return. It may have been there to protect Venetian merchant ships from attack by Pisan vessels.[2] But it could also be seen as a warning or a threat to Constantinople.

It is remarkable that fighting did not break out again in the streets of Constantinople, between Venetians and Pisans or between Latins and Greeks. There was always the fear that the Greeks would vent their hatred and envy of the foreigners in another murderous attack on their quarters. It had happened in 1187 when a drunken mob had tried to break in to plunder and kill. The Venetians had learnt to defend themselves against such onslaughts by erecting barricades in the surrounding streets and fighting back.[3] But they were also restrained from taking reprisals by their new Doge, Enrico Dandolo, who thought that the presence of a Venetian fleet at Abydos was unnecessarily provocative. Dandolo had been elected when Orio Mastropiero died at the end of 1192. He was over seventy years old and he had spent most of his life in the service of his country. He was shrewd and experienced. He was equal to the devious ploys of Byzantine diplomacy. His dislike and distrust of the Greeks was shared by many westerners. But Dandolo, it is said, held a personal grudge against them. He had taken part in the expedition led by Vitale Michiel to avenge the wrong done to Venice by the Emperor Manuel in 1171. He had gone to Constantinople on one of the many abortive missions to Manuel's court, and there he had been wounded and almost lost his eyesight. So at least it was believed

---

[1] *DR*, II, nos. 1606, 1607, 1609, 1610, 1611, 1612, 1616. Lilie, *Handel und Politik*, pp. 79–83, 100–2.
[2] *TTh*, I, no. LXXVIII, pp. 216–25. Brand, *Byzantium*, p. 200; Angold, *Byzantine Empire*, p. 290.
[3] The incident is recorded by Niketas Choniates, pp. 392–3, who speaks only of 'Latins'. In 1187, however, the Latins in Constantinople must have been mainly Venetians. Cf. Brand, *Byzantium*, pp. 82–3.

in later years.[1] As his eyesight faded so his wits sharpened and his
hatred of the Greeks became obsessive. He came to know them better
when he was sent on another embassy to Constantinople in 1184. He
and his fellow envoys learnt the lesson that negotiations with the Greeks
required patience. The emperors, secure in their sacred palace in the
Queen of Cities, still received foreign ambassadors with a patronising
air of superiority and, to the western mind, a childish desire to impress.
The Doges of Venice were perhaps better able to understand this than
other Latins, since they themselves had over the centuries acquired a
Byzantine love of pomp and splendour. But they had also come to understand that procrastination was a weapon of Byzantine diplomacy. Enrico
Dandolo was getting on in years. He believed, however, that time was
on his side, time to settle his accounts with the Byzantines. For, as
Niketas Choniates puts it, 'he boasted that so long as he failed to take
his revenge on them for what they had done to his people he was living
under sentence of death'.[2]

In the early years of his reign Dandolo's main concern was the protection of Venetian interests in the Adriatic, against the claims of Hungary
and the rivalry of Pisa. So long as Isaac II was on the throne in Constantinople Venetian interests there were protected. Alexios III, however,
seemed determined to be awkward. Dandolo protested and negotiations
began. They were long and difficult. Three embassies went from Venice
to Constantinople and back and two in the other direction. The Doge
instructed his envoys to be particularly firm with the emperor about
the payment of damages which he had refused to continue. They must
demand the arrears of 400 pounds of gold outstanding for two years,
or at the least 200 pounds. He also warned them to walk warily through

[1] His namesake, Andrea Dandolo (p. 260), connects the Doge's partial blindness with an
injury that he received at the court of Manuel I in 1172. See above, p. 99. On the other
hand, the much older *Historia Ducum Veneticorum*, p. 81, makes a point of observing that
the two envoys whom the Doge sent to Manuel on that occasion came back 'in good health'.
Niketas Choniates (p. 538), a nearer contemorary than Andrea Dandolo, says only that
the Doge was 'disabled in his eyesight'. Geoffrey of Villehardouin, another contemporary,
has it that the Doge's eyesight had been impaired by a wound in the head. (Geoffrey of
Villehardouin, *La Conquête de Constantinople*, ed. E. Faral, I–II, Les Classiques de l'Histoire
de France au Moyen Age, 18–19, Paris, 1938, c. 67. I, p. 69.) Another, though often fanciful,
account relates that Dandolo appeared to be able to see although his eyes had been gouged
out on the orders of the Emperor Manuel: *Chronicle of Novgorod, 1016–1471*, translated
by R. Michell and N. Forbes, Camden Society, 3rd series, xxv (London, 1914), p. 48.
See Kretschmayr, I, pp. 466–7.
[2] Niketas Choniates, p. 538. On Venetian adaptation of Byzantine court ceremonial and insignia, see A. Pertusi, 'Quedam regalia insignia. Ricerche sulle insegne del potere ducale a
Venezia durante il medioevo', *Studi veneziani*, VII (1965), 3–123, especially 96–121; Pertusi,
'Bisanzio e le insegne regali dei Dogi di Venezia', *RSBN*, n. s. II–III (1965–6), 277–84;
Pertusi, 'Venezia e Bisanzio', 12–13, 21.

the diplomatic minefield of Venetian and Byzantine relations with the German Emperor and the King of Sicily, which had been carefully regulated in the treaty of 1187.[1] The warning was perhaps unnecessary since at the time Henry VI was emperor of one and king of the other. But it was assumed that the basis of any new agreement between Venice and Byzantium must be the text of the chrysobull of Isaac II. Agreement became possible when Henry VI died in September 1197. After more long discussions the Doge's latest envoys, Pietro Michiel and Ottavio Quirino, in conference with the emperor's Logothete of the Dromos, Demetrios Tornikes, produced a draft treaty, initialled on 27 September 1198. Its content was incorporated in a chrysobull signed by the Emperor Alexios III in November of the same year, which was taken to Venice by an imperial protonotary.[2]

The new agreement was in large measure a restatement of the Venetian–Byzantine treaty of 1187, with certain amendments to bring it up to date with the changed political circumstances. The clause relating to the King of Sicily was omitted. But the Venetians were induced to commit themselves to coming to the defence of Byzantium in the event of its territory being attacked by the German Emperor. The defensive alliance was thus reaffirmed. In return for this commitment the Venetians were assured of all the rights granted to them by the Emperors Alexios I, John II, Manuel I and Isaac II. No mention was made of Andronikos. Their merchants were to be exempt from all commercial taxes on their goods whether home-produced or imported and whether conveyed by land or by sea. So that there would be no doubt or misunderstanding about the towns and districts in which they were to enjoy their freedom of trade, the chrysobull provides a comprehensive list of their names. In the past Venetian businessmen had been subjected to arbitrary taxation by some provincial governors and factors of church and monastic lands or crown estates on the ground that their privileges were invalid in such areas. In the future they could point to the official list of 1198, drawn up no doubt by the emperor's Logothete. Never before had the extent of Venetian privileges been spelt out in such detail. The list comprised almost every important town, port, province, estate and island in the Byzantine Empire of the time from Durazzo to the east, and even some, such as Antioch and Laodikeia in Syria, which were no longer within the empire. Only the provinces of the Black Sea were excluded. Six years later, in 1204, this remarkable gazetteer of Byzantine possessions was

---

[1] Dandolo, pp. 274–5; *DR*, II, nos. 1632, 1639. Enrico Dandolo's instructions to his envoys in 1197 are printed in Kretschmayr, I, p. 473; cf. Brand, *Byzantium*, pp. 200–2. Heyd, *Commerce*, I, pp. 226–7.

[2] Chrysobull of November 1198: *TTh*, I, no. LXXXV, pp. 246–80; *DR*, II, no. 1647.

to have its uses when the Venetians and the leaders of the Fourth Crusade came to divide the empire among themselves.

A special clause was added to the chrysobull at the request of Venice defining more clearly the legal status of Venetians trading and residing in Constantinople. Their envoys had complained that when one of their citizens had been brought to trial before their own authorities and found innocent, he was often tried again in a Byzantine court which reversed the verdict and condemned him to imprisonment. This was an anomaly created by that clause of the treaty of 1187 in which Venice had agreed that defaulting creditors could be tried in a Byzantine court. It was now laid down that in all disputes about money plaintiffs against Venetians should be heard before the Venetian authorities, while Venetian complaints against Greeks should be tried before the Logothete of the Dromos or, in his absence, the *megas logariastes*. In either case the plaintiff must present his charge in writing witnessed by a priest, a judge, or a notary. In the event of violent quarrels or riots between Greeks and Venetians leading to murder or serious injury, the case should be heard and tried before the Logothete or, if he were not available, the captain of the guard of the Blachernai palace. Minor cases of violence involving only one or two people and causing only minor injuries should be tried by the Logothete or the *megas logariastes*. Private Greek citizens bringing a case for injury against a Venetian should be tried by the legate and judges of the Venetians, unless they were of senatorial rank or of the nobility of the court, when they should be tried by the Logothete. The Logothete or his deputy was also responsible for the swearing in of all Venetian authorities on their arrival. The ceremony took place in the Venetian church in Constantinople after they had presented their credentials; and in the presence of the leading Venetian residents they swore to act without favour or prejudice in all cases. Judgment after trial was to be given within fifteen days, according to a decree of Manuel I. Lastly, it was agreed that the property of a Venetian who died in Byzantium should pass to the beneficiaries named in his will. If he died intestate his goods were not to be seized by any official, lay or ecclesiastical, nor by any of the emperor's family. They would remain Venetian property.[1]

These provisions clarified the legal and juridical position of Venetians living in Constantinople and brought nearer than ever before a practical definition of their colony as a foreign community with its own rights

---

[1] Heyd, *Commerce*, I pp. 227–8; Brand, *Byzantium*, pp. 202–3; Lilie, *Handel und Politik*, pp. 41–9. The Logothete of the Dromos had been made responsible for collection of dues from Venetian ships in 992. See above, p. 41. On his functions in the twelfth century and later, see Stein, *Untersuchungen*, pp. 34–9. The office of *megas logariastes* seems not to have existed before the eleventh century.

and responsibilities for its own affairs. Manuel I had designated the Latin residents in his empire as *burgenses*. Alexios III describes the Venetians as 'foreign citizens' (*cives extranei*) or resident aliens with equal rights of citizenship. All that was lacking was the recognition by the emperor of a properly constituted head or consul of the community in Constantinople who would be answerable to the Byzantine authorities. No such official seems to have existed in the twelfth century. The chrysobull of 1198 speaks only of legates, who may or may not have been the Doge's ambassadors, and of *judices* or judges. The Venetian clergy continued to play an influential part in the life of the community, acting as notaries and executors, supervising weights and measures and exercising the right which they had enjoyed since 1107 to hold or lease much real estate. But the church with all its holdings was nominally dependent on the Bishop of Castello or Venice. It had no bishop of its own. By 1198 the days were long past when the emperor could truthfully call the Venetians his 'servants'. Isaac II had praised them as his 'allies, friends and supporters'. Truth had little to do with it; but the myth persisted that the Venetians were bound to the emperor by ties of loyalty and service as old as the empire itself. For, as Isaac had said, they were Romans by origin and singularly devoted to the Roman Empire. Even Alexios III pretended that the Venetians longed for the embraces of Byzantium as a child longs for his mother. The fiction was also maintained that the Doge was still proud to bear the Byzantine title of *protosebastos* and to be called 'most loyal to the emperor'. Yet it was not suggested that he should appoint his deputy or consul in the capital, nor that the Venetian church should have its own bishop. These anomalies were soon to be rectified, when the Doge Enrico Dandolo established himself as lord of three-eighths of the whole Empire of Constantinople and secured the appointment of a Venetian as patriarch of its church.[1]

---

[1] Heyd, *Commerce*, I, pp. 255–8; Antoniadis-Bibicou, 'Notes sur les relations', 176–7; Pertusi, 'Venezia e Bizanzio', p. 124; Lilie, *Handel und Politik*, pp. 47–8.

8

THE FOURTH CRUSADE

THE chrysobull that Alexios III issued to Venice in November 1198 was the last of its kind. In January of the same year Innocent III had been elected pope. High on the list of his priorities was the mounting of a new crusade to achieve what Frederick Barbarossa had not lived to achieve, the liberation of Jerusalem from the infidel. The Venetians had never been enthusiastic crusaders. The Holy War was bad for business. In the first months of his pontificate the new pope had to remind the Doge and people of Venice that those who supplied the Saracens with arms, iron and timber for their ships were in danger of being excommunicated. The Byzantine emperors had protested about this treacherous traffic by Venice as long ago as the tenth century. The Venetian excuse was that, since they were not a race of farmers, they must make a living by sea and the trade that went by sea.[1] It was a strong argument against making war on their customers. Pope Innocent III had reservations about involving the Venetians in his new venture, the Fourth Crusade.

The modern literature on the subject of the Fourth Crusade is more abundant than the original sources.[2] Yet many problems remain unsolved, for the very reason that the sources are reticent where they might have been more explicit, or lacking where they are most needed. There is, in particular, no contemporary Venetian account of the enterprise in which the Doge Enrico Dandolo played a leading part. Posterity has therefore been left to infer or to guess at what his motives were.

---

[1] *TTh*, I, no. LXXXIII, pp. 234–8 (3 December 1198).

[2] The most recent of the many works on the subject are: D. E. Queller, *The Fourth Crusade. The Conquest of Constantinople, 1201–1204* (Philadelphia, 1977), in whose Bibliography (pp. 219–41) the primary sources and the modern literature are conveniently listed; J. Godfrey, *1204. The Unholy Crusade* (Oxford, 1980). Shorter accounts are: E. H. McNeal and R. L. Wolff, 'The Fourth Crusade', in K. M. Setton, ed., *A History of the Crusades*, II pp. 153–85; D. M. Nicol, 'The Fourth Crusade and the Greek and Latin Empires', in *CMH*, IV (1966), pp. 275–330. See also Angold, *Byzantine Empire*, pp. 284–96; Brand, *Byzantium*, pp. 222–69.

The Venetian chronicler nearest to the event is Martin da Canal, writing about the year 1275. He indulged in a blatant rewriting of history to prove the points that the participation of Venice in the crusade was blameless, had the blessing of the pope and brought nothing but glory to the most Christian Republic of Venice. This version of events was adopted as their own by later Venetian chroniclers.[1] The main eye-witness accounts are those of Geoffrey of Villehardouin, Robert of Clari and Niketas Choniates. Villehardouin was one of the leaders of the crusade and his history of the conquest of Constantinople is a literary and historical monument of the first rank. Robert of Clari, a simple knight from Picardy, tells the story from a lowlier though sometimes a livelier standpoint. Niketas Choniates was a sophisticated elder statesman of the Byzantine court who was at the receiving end of the crusade and, as a result, forced to escape from Constantinople as a refugee. All three writers are biased in their accounts. It could hardly be otherwise. Robert of Clari was a naive reporter of facts as he saw them. Niketas had no intimate knowledge of the way in which the crusade was planned and directed. Villehardouin was the only one who could have known all the facts, and yet there are crucial points in his narrative where he seems reluctant to tell all that he knows. Finally, there are the letters and acts of Pope Innocent III, whose crusade it was. Innocent tried hard to keep control of the holy war that he had set in motion and he was a most prolific correspondent. But it is evident that he was often poorly informed about the decisions taken by its leaders; and some of his letters to them were oddly mistimed or misdirected.[2]

In assessing what went wrong and why the crusade went to Constantinople and not to its proper destination, the modern historian has to work with sources that are full in detail but deficient in analysis of how the details came together. He may therefore be driven to conclude that the event of 1204 came about simply by a concatenation of circumstances, a series of mishaps and human errors whose predestined conclusion neither the pope nor any other power could prevent. Such is the manner in which Villehardouin presents the tale, a tale in which ulterior motives

[1] Martin da Canal, Les Estoires de Venise. Cf. K. M. Setton, The Papacy and the Levant (1204–1571), I: The Thirteenth and Fourteenth Centuries, Memoirs of the American Philosophical Society (Philadelphia, 1976), pp. 9–10.
[2] Villehardouin, La Conquête de Constantinople; Robert of Clari, La Conquête de Constantinople, ed. P. Lauer (Paris, 1924); Italian translation and commentary by Anna Maria Nada Patrone, Roberto di Clari, La conquista di Costantinopoli (1198–1216), Collana storica di Fonti e Studi, 13 (Genoa, 1972). Niketas Choniates, Historia. Letters and Acts of Innocent III, in MPL, CCXIV–CCXVII; Acta Innocentii PP. III (1198–1216), ed. P. T. Haluščynskyj, Pontificia Commissio ad Redigendum Codicem Iuris Canonici Orientalis: Fontes, Series III, Vol. II (Vatican City, 1944).

of greed or gain are discounted. Alternatively, the historian, eager to apportion blame for one of the greatest crimes in the annals of human affairs, may try to read between the bland lines of Villehardouin's text, the simple narrative of Robert of Clari, the tragic and bitter account of Niketas, and the public pronouncements of the pope, to find a culprit. One retains, however, the uneasy suspicion that the blame for the affair falls mainly on those who covered their tracks by committing nothing to paper at the time. Niketas Choniates had no doubt who was the villain of the piece. He was the Doge of Venice, Enrico Dandolo.[1]

When the crusade was first preached the response was disappointing. The King of Hungary was the only one of the crowned heads of western Europe who answered the call. Philip Augustus of France and Richard I of England had done their crusading. They were now committed to fighting nearer home; and early in 1199 Richard died. The successors of the late Henry VI of Germany, Philip of Swabia and Otto of Brunswick, were also engaged in their own domestic squabble. The leaders of the crusade had therefore to be sought elsewhere. Most of them came from northern France, from Normandy, Flanders and Champagne. They were inspired by an itinerant preacher, Fulk of Neuilly, and by the pope's legate, Peter Capuano. The first to take the Cross were Tibald, Count of Champagne, and Louis, Count of Blois, both nephews of Richard of England. Prominent among the many who followed their lead were Geoffrey of Villehardouin, Walter of Brienne, Baldwin, Count of Flanders, and his brother Henry. No previous crusade had been so methodically planned. Pope Innocent III was still young and untried, but the organisation of the Fourth Crusade was the first test and proof of his authority.

Perhaps it was as well that no crowned heads responded to his call. One lesson of the Third Crusade had been that monarchs in command of their own armies found it hard to co-operate. There was one monarch, however, whom the pope was keen to enlist. The Byzantine Emperor Alexios III had written to congratulate him shortly after his election. It was the start of a correspondence between pope and emperor. Innocent III had a refined and exalted concept of the divinely ordained universal authority of his office. It was grand and simple. But it could never be reconciled with the corresponding grandeur and simplicity of Byzantine political theory. For Innocent the issues were clear: the emperor must bring the Byzantine Church to admit the error of its ways in faith and practice and restore it to the communion of the church universal under the supremacy of the Holy See. It would then be possible and desirable

---

[1] Niketas Choniates, *Historia*, pp. 538–9, 616–17.

for the repentant Christians of the east to play their rightful part in the common cause of Christendom against Islam. The pope also corresponded with the Patriarch of Constantinople, chastising him for rejecting the universal authority of the Church of Rome as the mother and head of all churches, a proposition which distressed the patriarch since he could find no basis for it either in scripture or in tradition. The Byzantines had heard it all before from earlier Bishops of Rome and their apologists, but never in such confident and forceful terms.[1]

Alexios III had hoped to find a political ally in Innocent, for they had a common enemy in the person of Philip of Swabia. Philip's wife was a daughter of the Emperor Isaac II whom Alexios had blinded and deposed and who now lay incarcerated in Constantinople along with his own young son Alexios. Philip made much of the fact that his wife's honour had been slighted and that her father must be restored to his rightful throne. Alexios III was pleased to know that the new pope supported Philip's rival, Otto of Brunswick; though it was a pity that so powerful an ally seemed to be obsessed with the irrelevant issue of the union of the churches. Meanwhile, the pope's agents were raising funds for the crusade which was gathering its strength in France. It was decided that the expedition should make for Egypt with the object of outflanking the infidels in Palestine before marching on Jerusalem. The overland route through eastern Europe was considered too hazardous. The army would have to be ferried by sea. None of its leaders could provide the number of ships required. They agreed unanimously that an approach should be made to the Doge of Venice to ask him to supply warships and transport vessels. In the spring of 1201 a small delegation crossed the Alps and went to Venice empowered to make the best arrangement that they could. Geoffrey of Villehardouin was among them.[2]

The Venetians were at first reluctant to underwrite a venture that might lose them a lot of business, especially if it were true that the crusade was destined for Egypt. The Doge kept the delegates waiting for two weeks while he pondered the proposal and conferred with his Council. It was not a matter that could be hurriedly decided. By Venetian standards the crusaders were naive. They estimated that their army would number well over 30,000 men, a figure which the Doge probably knew to be unrealistic. To transport so large a force would need a fleet bigger than any that Venice had ever assembled. It would be necessary to suspend

[1] On Innocent III's correspondence with the emperor and patriarch and their replies, see Brand, *Byzantium*, pp. 224–9; J. Gill, *Byzantium and the Papacy 1198–1400* (New Brunswick, N.J., 1979), pp. 11–13; D. M. Nicol, 'The Papal scandal', in *Studies in Church History*, XIII: *The Orthodox Churches and the West*, ed. D. Baker (Oxford, 1976), pp. 145–7.
[2] Queller, *Fourth Crusade*, pp. 6–8; Godfrey, *1204*, pp. 39–48.

many other profitable operations and to divert labour from other projects until the job was completed. The deal must therefore be made only in the guaranteed certainty that the Venetians would gain and not lose from its making. They might not be very enthusiastic about crusades in general, but they could weigh the pros and cons of committing themselves to an enterprise which might bring them considerable profit in prestige as well as in real terms.

After his deliberations, the Doge presented the crusaders with a most businesslike proposition. The Venetians would build and equip a fleet to carry a total of 4500 horses and 9000 squires, 4500 knights and 20,000 foot-soldiers; and they would furnish provisions for the army and fodder for the horses for a period of twelve months. The cost was assessed at 85,000 silver marks. The Doge promised to send with the fleet fifty armed warships of his own: and this he would do 'for the love of God'. The armada would be ready to sail from Venice by 29 June 1202. There were two conditions to the agreement: the costs must be covered in advance; and the Venetians must have the right to one-half of any conquests that the crusade might achieve. The crusaders were in more of a hurry than the Doge. After a discussion that was all too brief they accepted the proposal, undertaking to pay the 85,000 marks in four instalments within the year. The Doge then put the matter before his Great Council and the assembly of the people, whose consent had to be obtained. Their consent was loudly unanimous, and on the following day the treaty between Venice and the crusaders was signed and sealed.[1]

Both parties had now made solemn commitments. The Venetians had the will and the resources to fulfil their part of the bargain. The crusaders, however, had overreached themselves. The only way in which they could find the agreed sum of 85,000 marks was by recruiting within twelve months an army of 33,500 men. This never seemed likely and it never happened. From the moment when Geoffrey of Villehardouin put his signature to the treaty the crusade was dominated by Venice. As many Byzantine Emperors had learnt, the Venetians were not prone to writing off debts. As a sign of good intent Villehardouin paid them 2000 marks on account before leaving for France. He had to borrow the money from a Venetian bank. The treaty had to be approved by the pope since it concerned the crusade that he had instigated. The pope was none too pleased. The leaders of the crusade should perhaps have consulted him

---

[1] Texts of the agreement in *TTh*, I, nos. XCII, XCIII, pp. 362–8, 369–73. Villehardouin, cc. 21–2: I, pp. 22–4, has it that the Venetians undertook to supply provisions only for nine months, and that the total cost was 94,000 rather than 85,000 marks. On the discrepancies, see Villehardouin, II, Appendix I, pp. 215–20; Queller, *Fourth Crusade*, pp. 10–11 and notes 12 and 13 (pp. 163–4).

before they made such expensive arrangements. He was also uneasy about the motives of the Venetians who were not usually noted for their crusading zeal. He may have begun to feel that the management of the crusade was passing out of his hands. He gave his approval on one condition: the crusaders must refrain from attacking Christians except for a just and essential cause, the morality of which would be determined by the papal legate going with them. This showed remarkable prescience on the part of Innocent III.[1]

In May 1201 Tibald of Champagne, who had been the accepted leader of the crusade, died. A new leader had to be found. There was much discussion, but on the proposal of Geoffrey of Villehardouin it was decided to invite Boniface, Marquis of Montferrat, to come to France and be invested as commander of the army. He accepted so readily that it seemed that he had been waiting for the invitation. Boniface was well connected in crusading circles. But he also had family connections with Byzantium. His brother Rainier had married a daughter of the Emperor Manuel I and had received the title of Caesar and an estate in Thessalonica which he referred to as his 'kingdom'. Rainier had later fallen foul of the tyrant Andronikos Komnenos and, with his wife, met a mysterious death. His other brother, Conrad of Montferrat, had served the Emperor Isaac II as a loyal officer and married the emperor's sister. He too had been made Caesar but having smelt the whiff of anti-Latin feeling in Constantinople he left for a career of greater glory in the Holy Land.[2] Boniface had cause to dislike the Byzantines and he may have thought that one day he would claim his brother's estate in Thessalonica. It is unlikely that the thought was in his mind when Fulk of Neuilly fixed the Cross upon his shoulder as commander of the Fourth Crusade at Soissons in September 1201. But on his way home to Montferrat he made a detour to pay his respects to his friend and suzerain Philip of Swabia in Alsace. He had much business to discuss with Philip and he stayed at his palace at Hagenau for Christmas. Both men had grievances against the Byzantines and in the course of their meetings over a period of weeks they must surely have aired them. Their minds were indeed concentrated on the question by the arrival of an unexpected but welcome visitor.

The young prince Alexios Angelos, son of the blinded Emperor Isaac II, had contrived to escape from Constantinople on a Pisan ship. In September or October he landed at Ancona and went at once to Alsace to seek the friendship and comfort of his sister and her husband Philip

[1] Queller, Fourth Crusade, pp. 9–18; Godfrey, 1204, pp. 49–55.
[2] Brand, Byzantium, pp. 18–20, 80–4; Queller, Fourth Crusade, pp. 25–7; and see above, pp. 106, 108.

of Swabia. He stayed at Philip's court as an honoured guest for some four months. Alexios was young and rather foolish. But he had a grievance against the reigning Byzantine Emperor which was more real and more immediate than those felt by Philip or by Boniface. He had come to the west to drum up support for the restoration of his father Isaac II and the recognition of his own right to the Byzantine throne. He may or may not have heard that a new crusade was being organised. But there at Philip's court was its appointed leader Boniface. It is hard to believe that the conversation over Christmas at Hagenau did not come round to the possibility of using the crusade to right the wrong done to Alexios's father. Previous crusades had passed through Constantinople. Alexios confidently assured his new friends that if they escorted him there the people would greet him with open arms and expel the usurper. It was an attractive proposition. It need not involve violence; though if an attack on Constantinople had to be made to effect the change of ruler it would not be the first time that such a plan had been suggested. Frederick Barbarossa and Henry VI, Philip's brother, had both thought of using a crusade for the conquest of Constantinople. The pope had indeed specifically forbidden Henry to do so.

The plan, if plan there was, would have to be laid before Pope Innocent III. He was not likely to sanction it. He had excommunicated Philip of Swabia and he disapproved of the appointment of Boniface as leader of his crusade. None the less the young Alexios was sent on to Rome in February 1202 to put his case. He poured out his troubles and asked for sympathy and help to drive out the usurper in Constantinople. The pope was not impressed. In his view, the young man's claim to the throne was not justified since his father, Isaac II, had not gained it by right of inheritance; and the incumbent of that throne, Alexios III, had shown some willingness to talk about the union of the churches. In any case the pope could not approve of the use of his crusade for so doubtful and risky a purpose. He dismissed the young Alexios and sent him on his way. A few weeks later Boniface of Montferrat arrived in Rome to discuss with the pope the arrangements for the crusade which he was about to lead. The pope made it quite plain to him that the scheme for taking the crusade by way of Constantinople, which he had already heard about, was out of the question. He repeated his admonition that the crusaders must avoid attacking Christians and must go straight to the Holy Land or at least to Egypt. Boniface consented and there, for a time, the matter rested.[1]

It had been agreed that the crusading host should assemble at Venice

---

[1] Queller, *Fourth Crusade*, pp. 19–35; Godfrey, *1204*, pp. 67–70.

for embarkation and departure by the end of June 1202. After Easter they began to converge on the assembly point assigned to them on the Lido. The Venetians had worked hard to fulfil their part of the agreement. The transports and warships were ready and waiting. But it was sadly evident that not more than a third of the estimated throng of 33,500 crusaders had arrived; and some had broken ranks by leaving for the Holy Land from other ports. The fleet which they had contracted to pay for was far too big. But the cost of it had to be found. The leaders of the crusade set a good example by turning in all their gold and silver plate. Those who had the money paid their fares in full as agreed. Others paid what they could afford. But when all was counted the total was 34,000 marks short of the agreed sum. The Doge knew well enough that the crusaders were honourable men. They would in due course pay their debt. But in the meanwhile and since they had put him and his people to so much trouble he proposed that they should perform a service for him. He invited them to embark and sail down the Dalmatian coast to attack and capture the port of Zara. If they consented he would postpone settlement of their debt and the crusade could then take its course. Zara was one of the cities claimed by the Doge in his capacity as Duke of Dalmatia. It had rebelled against Venice and placed itself under the protection of the King of Hungary, who had refortified it. Some of the crusaders deplored this proposed misuse of their army. Not only would it mean Christians fighting each other; they would also be fighting against the one Christian monarch who had sworn to take the Cross. The papal legate, Peter Capuano, who arrived in Venice in July, added his authoritative objections to the proposal. The Doge told him not to mix politics with religion and he went back to Rome to report his misgivings to the pope. In September he was back in Venice. He had convinced himself if not the pope that the capture of Zara was a 'just and necessary' cause, if only to prevent the collapse of the crusade. He gave it his blessing, which he was empowered to do. Some were still doubtful about .the morality or the wisdom of this underhand scheme. But they had been cooped up in the lagoons in the heat of summer and most of them were ready for a move in any direction.

The Doge Dandolo was delighted. One Sunday early in September 1202 he announced to the congregation of Venetians and crusaders gathered in St Mark's that he himself would now take the Cross and go with the crusade on its sacred mission, leaving his city in the care of his son. Weeping, he knelt at the high altar while the Cross of a pilgrim soldier of Christ was sewn not on his shoulder but on his hat, so that everyone could see it. It was a moment of high drama and emotion. Many Venetians present were moved to follow their Doge's example and join the crusade. Some of the vacant berths in the ships would now be filled and the expedition had gained a new leader, a man of great wisdom, courage and experience. When addressing the crowd in St Mark's he had confessed that he was old and frail and in need of rest. But he believed that no one could command and lead the crusade as well as he. It was the truth; for the Doge Dandolo knew the waters, the ports and the riches of the Adriatic, the Mediterranean and the Aegean seas better than any of the pilgrims, and he could lead them where he wished.[1]

Early in October the armada at length set sail from Venice. It was a magnificent sight. Robert of Clari, who was there, describes it vividly:

Each of the great knights had his own ship for himself and his men and his own transports for his horses; and the Doge of Venice had with him fifty galleys, all at his own cost. His own was all vermilion-coloured and it had an awning stretched above it of vermilion samite; and there were four silver trumpets at the prow and timbrels that made a most joyful noise. ... Never before had such rejoicing and such an armada been heard or seen. And the priests and clerks climbed up the masts of the ships to chant the *Veni Creator Spiritus*; and all, both great and small, wept for fullness of heart and for the great gladness that was in them. And when the fleet set forth from the harbour of Venice ... it was the goodliest thing to behold that ever hath been seen since the beginning of the world. ... But when they came to the open sea and spread their sails and hoisted their banners upon the castles of their ships, then verily did it seem that the whole sea was aswarm and ablaze ...[2]

They made a leisurely progress down the Adriatic. The Doge had business to attend to in a number of ports along the way and the Dalmatian cities could not fail to be impressed by so imposing a show of the naval might of Venice. There was in any case no great hurry. They could not sail across the Mediterranean in winter and the crusaders had already been told that they would have to stay at Zara until the spring. They reached there on 10 November 1202. The ships forced their way into the harbour. The soldiers disembarked and laid siege to the fortress. The inhabitants were prepared to surrender, but the chance was lost; and on 24 November after a siege of five days Zara was captured and sacked. The city was divided between Venetians and crusaders, the former occupying the harbour area. There they settled for the winter.[3]

The pope was furious when he heard the news. His first reaction was

[1] Villehardouin, cc. 62–9: I, pp. 64–70. Queller, *Fourth Crusade*, pp. 36–57; Godrey, *1204*, pp. 71–7.

[2] Robert of Clari, c. XIII: pp. 12–13.

[3] Villehardouin, cc. 80–90: I, pp. 80–90; Robert of Clari, cc. XIII–XVI: pp. 12–15. Queller, *Fourth Crusade*, pp. 58–65; Godfrey, *1204*, pp. 77–80.

to excommunicate all those responsible, even though his legate and the bishops there present had declared the attack on Zara to be a just cause. The crusaders, fearful for the state of their souls, sent a delegation to Rome. They explained that they had acted under duress; they spoke with humility; they begged for forgiveness. The pope was moved to absolve them from their sins on condition that they would be obedient to his orders in future and vow once again never to attack fellow Christians. Innocent knew where the real blame lay and who had put the crusaders under duress and made them commit their sin. The delegates pleaded with him to grant absolution to the Venetians as well. But on this he was firm. When they went back to Zara they took with them a bull of excommunication damning the Doge and all his men. Boniface of Montferrat was so upset that he suppressed the document. The papal legate too was convinced that its publication would mean the end of the crusade. The situation was beyond him. He consulted the pope and sailed off to Palestine.[1]

As leader of the crusade, Boniface should have taken his share of the blame. But he had an alibi. He was not at the scene of the crime. He did not reach Zara until two weeks after the event. Some business had detained him.[2] Where or what his business was is not revealed. But only a few days after his arrival messengers came to Zara from the court of Philip of Swabia. They brought with them a firm proposal from the young Alexios Angelos, backed by the recommendation of his brother-in-law Philip. If the crusaders would go by way of Constantinople and restore Alexios and his father Isaac to their inheritance they would be generously rewarded. Alexios would pay them 200,000 marks, supply provisions for their onward journey to Egypt, send an army of 10,000 Byzantine troops with them, and maintain a permanent force of 500 men in the Holy Land. In addition, he promised that his whole empire would recognise the supremacy of the See of Rome, from which it had long been separated. These, as Niketas says, were the wild promises of a witless youth.[3] Some of the crusaders were taken in, for Philip's messengers had played on their chivalrous feelings by emphasising that it would be a work of charity and justice to assist those who had been unlawfully dethroned. But only the Venetians understood the true state of affairs in Constantinople. Dandolo had been there twice in the past. His agents kept him well informed. He distrusted the Emperor Alexios III, who had just granted more privileges to his commercial enemies,

---

[1] Queller, *Fourth Crusade*, pp. 67–9; Godfrey, *1204*, pp. 80–2; Gill, *Byzantium and the Papacy*, pp. 15–17.
[2] Villehardouin, c. 79: I, p. 80.   [3] Niketas Choniates, p. 539.

the Pisans and the Genoese.[1] He had reasons of his own for disliking the Byzantines; and they already owed him a lot of money. He must have known that no Byzantine Emperor could fulfil the promises that Alexios Angelos was making.

It is hard to be sure how far the Doge had been a party to the scheme that had first been outlined at Hagenau the previous Christmas. But when it was submitted to the other leaders of the crusade at Zara, he strongly supported Boniface in urging its acceptance. There was much to be said for seizing the chance to put an emperor on the Byzantine throne who would be indebted to Venice, for the Venetian quarter in Constantinople and its affairs would be secure for the future; and even if that emperor could find no more than a fraction of the sums of money that he promised it would cover the debt owed to Venice by the crusaders. The same argument weighed heavily with their leaders, though there was much unease and dissension among the lower ranks and many defected and made their own plans for going directly to Syria. Most, however, favoured the idea of making for Egypt by way of Constantinople; and the bishops, who were mainly in agreement, were influential in persuading the waverers. A formal agreement was drawn up and sent to the court of Philip of Swabia with two knights who would escort the young Alexios to Zara. He was expected to arrive by Easter 1203.[2]

The decision had now been taken. The crusade was to go first to Constantinople to perform an act of charity for which it would be richly rewarded. When spring came round the ships were got ready and loaded for the voyage. On 20 April most of them put out for Corfu, their first port of call. Alexios reached Zara five days later and Dandolo and Boniface, who had been waiting for him, at once set sail. They went by way of Durazzo, which was still a Byzantine possession; and there the Greek citizens obligingly hailed Alexios as their emperor. When they reached Corfu, however, the inhabitants were not so obliging and staged a noisy demonstration against him. The crusaders must have wondered whether their act of charity was worth the trouble; and when Alexios personally confirmed the agreement and the promises that he had made there was further argument and dissension in their camp. The matter had now been brought into the open and many of the crusaders felt that they had been cheated and deceived. The pope was of the same

---

[1] In 1199: *DR*, II, nos. 1649, 1650, 1651.

[2] Queller, *Fourth Crusade*, pp. 69–71; Godfrey, *1204*, pp. 82–5. The Venetians later spread the myth that the crusaders and the pope were in favour of helping Alexios because he was 'of French lineage', Alexios II having married Agnes, daughter of Louis VII of France. But Alexios Komnenos and Alexios Angelos were not related. Martin da Canal, pp. 49–50; Dandolo, p. 277.

mind. He had been kept in the dark. He had not been properly informed of the change of plan. He wrote to Boniface and his colleagues, probably in May 1203; but the letter seems never to have reached them. In it he repeated his condemnation of the scheme as it had been outlined to him by Alexios and Boniface the year before. It was not the business of his crusade to go to Constantinople on what was a political errand of mercy or to meddle in the affairs of the church by accepting spurious offers of reunion from the Greeks; and he remained adamant about the excommunication of the Venetians. He was not to know, or so it appears, that the crusade was already on its way to Constantinople. Matters had passed beyond the pope's control.[1]

On 24 May 1203 the fleet left Corfu. It was a fine clear day with a favourable breeze. Rounding the Peloponnese, they sailed by way of the islands of Euboia and Andros to Abydos on the Hellespont, where those who had gone ahead waited for the rest to catch them up. On 23 June they anchored off the monastery of St Stephen within sight of Constantinople and marvelled at the splendour of the city with its great walls, towers, palaces and churches. Next morning they coasted along the walls and sailed first to Chalcedon and then to Skutari on the Asian side of the Bosporos. There they disembarked, pitched camp and went foraging for food. On 1 July there was some skirmishing between a reconnaissance party and a company of 500 Byzantine cavalry. The crusaders scored their first victory, capturing much booty and a number of horses which they badly needed. Next day an embassy from the Emperor Alexios III came to their camp, vainly promising them provisions and money if they would go on their way. The emperor had had ample time to prepare for the approach of the crusade, but he had done little to defend his city. There was indeed little that he could do. The Byzantine fleet was reduced to a few antiquated hulks. The army was Byzantine only in name, being largely composed of foreign mercenaries, of whom the bravest and most loyal were the Anglo-Saxons of the imperial Varangian guard. But the huge walls of the city had held off all comers in the past. There was no reason to fear that the crusaders would succeed where so many before them had failed. The young Alexios had boasted that his return to Constantinople would be greeted with joy by the citizens. But no one came out to welcome him; and the truth of the matter was brought home to the crusaders when they paraded him in the Doge's ship before the walls under a flag of truce. Far from hailing him as their liberator, the people crowding the battlements shouted abuse at him

[1] Letters of Innocent III to Boniface and the crusaders, in *TTh*, I, nos. CIV, CV, pp. 415–17, 417–19; *MPL*, CCXV, cols. 106–7, 107–9. Gill, *Byzantium and the Papacy*, pp. 18–19; Queller, *Fourth Crusade*, p. 85.

and hurled stones at his ship. Alexios III may have been unpopular, but the Byzantines would sooner live with him than with a puppet emperor foisted upon them by the Latins.[1]

It would be interesting to know how the thousands of Venetians then living in Constantinople felt about the arrival of their Doge and the largest Venetian fleet that had ever been seen. The wily old Dandolo must have been better informed by his agents in the city than to believe that the Greeks would rally round a young pretender who had vowed to lay them and their church under permanent obligation to the Latin west. The parading of Alexios under the sea walls may have been little more than a charade, stage-managed by the Doge, to prove the point that now the crusade would have to fight to achieve what it had come to do. On 5 July the fleet crossed the Bosporos and forced a landing on the European side. On the following day a Venetian ship rammed and broke the iron chain which closed the mouth of the harbour, and the fleet sailed into the Golden Horn. The army meanwhile marched unopposed to encamp by the land walls on the north side of the city, near enough to the Blachernai palace to be able to shoot their arrows through its windows. The final assault was to be a combined operation. The Venetians prepared scaling ladders and erected platforms on the masts of their ships, from which the soldiers could fire over the walls. They were greatly outnumbered but they were inspired by a righteous enthusiasm, and also by a sense of desperation. For their rations were short and their survival depended on their success.

On 17 July, when all was ready, the attack was launched. On the land side a party of soldiers who had mounted a ladder near the palace were beaten off in hand-to-hand fighting with the Varangian guards. But by sea the Venetians managed to bring their ships in a long line close under the walls. Dandolo directed the assault and his great flagship, flying the banner of St Mark, was the first to be run aground on the narrow strip of beach beneath the sea walls. His men swarmed ashore under his command. Others followed them and put ladders against the walls. The resistance, which had at first been strong, weakened as the attackers became more confident. Suddenly the Venetians found themselves scaling the walls and mastering twenty-five of the towers. To cover their movements they created a smoke screen by setting fire to some houses. The wind fanned the flames away from the walls and made the conflagration worse than had been intended. But it served its purpose.

Alexios III was finally induced to lead his troops out against the army encamped beyond the land walls. But when he saw that the crusaders

---

[1] Queller, *Fourth Crusade*, pp. 85–94; Godfrey, *1204*, pp. 101–4.

were drawn up in battle formation, he lost heart and withdrew. That night he packed together as many of his jewels as he could carry and fled from the city with his daughter Eirene. The Venetians, who had left their positions on the walls when they heard of the impending attack on the crusaders' camp, knew nothing of what was happening in the city. But in the morning they found to their surprise that the Greeks, bereft of their emperor, had brought Isaac II out of prison and set him on the throne, blind and senile though he was. They were thus presented with a *fait accompli*. Messengers came to them before dawn to announce that the object for which they had diverted their crusade had been accomplished. The young Alexios was no less bewildered than the crusaders. According to Byzantine tradition blindness unfitted a man to be emperor. Alexios had not expected that his prospective subjects would ignore tradition. The crusaders too felt that they had come so far out of their way on behalf of their protégé and not on behalf of his aged father, whom they had never seen. Some of them may have recalled that Isaac was the emperor who had so treacherously treated with the infidel Saladin and betrayed the cause of the Third Crusade. The Venetians, however, will have remembered how exceptionally generous Isaac had been to them in 1187. But the crusaders suspected a plot. They insisted on sending envoys into the city to make sure that, if they recognised Isaac as emperor, he in his turn would recognise Alexios as co-emperor, and also honour all the terms of the agreement that Alexios had made with them. Isaac hesitated, but consented; and Alexios was escorted into the city by his benefactors. On 1 August 1203 he was crowned co-emperor as Alexios IV.[1]

It now remained for him to honour all the pledges that he had so recklessly made when far from home. The people of Constantinople, however, who had chosen to reinstate his father and felt no indebtedness to the Latins, were in no mood to help him. The atmosphere was so tense that he had to ask the crusaders to keep to their camp on the opposite side of the Golden Horn. They were allowed to come across only as visitors and tourists. Some friendships were formed. The more devout of them, such as Robert of Clari, enjoyed seeing and venerating the vast collection of holy relics. Villehardouin declared that Constantinople had as many relics as there were in all the rest of Christendom.[2]

[1] Queller, *Fourth Crusade*, pp. 95–111; Godfrey, *1204*, pp. 104–9. To the sources there cited for the first conquest of Constantinople in 1203 must now be added the newly discovered letter of Hugh of St Pol to his friend R. de Balues, in R. Pokorny, 'Zwei unedierte Briefe aus der Frühzeit des lateinischen Kaiserreichs von Konstantinopel', *B*, LV (1985), 180–209 (text: 203–9).

[2] Robert of Clari, cc. LXXXII–XCII: pp. 81–90; Villehardouin, c. 192: I, p. 194. Queller, *Fourth Crusade*, pp. 113–15.

But the mere sight of the arrogant westerners strutting through the streets and poking into the churches was enough to provoke many of the Greeks. Isaac II had long known what his son Alexios soon discovered, that the imperial treasury could never provide the enormous sums of money that he had guaranteed. Between them they raised about half of the promised 200,000 marks, from which the Venetians were at last paid what the crusaders owed them. The Doge made certain that he got his dues. The crusaders were thankful for what was left, but they could go no further until the emperor found the balance as well as the reinforcements and provisions which he had promised.[1]

Alexios played for time, begging his creditors to be patient and to bear with him until the following spring. He raised money by expropriating the private wealth of aristocratic families, especially those loyal to his predecessor, and by melting down gold and silver plate from the churches. To the Byzantines this was sacrilege; but it was of small account compared to the sin of selling their church to Rome. Alexios had rashly undertaken to promote the union of the churches. The leaders of the crusade had written to the pope justifying their temporary presence in Constantinople on these grounds. But neither the emperor nor his patriarch seemed very willing to fulfil his undertaking. The pope exercised what he thought to be his right by summoning the patriarch to Rome to receive his pallium; and later, in February 1204, he wrote to the crusaders ordering them to expiate their various sins by working harder for the return of the daughter church of the Greeks to the mother church of Rome and, having done so, to press on with their real purpose, the recovery of the Holy Land.[2]

Time was not on the emperor's side. He knew that his own people were out of sympathy with him because he had come to his throne on the shoulders of the crusaders. If they abandoned him he would almost certainly be evicted from that throne. He went to their camp to tell them as much and appealed to them to delay their departure at least until the following March. Many of the crusaders were by now discontented and wanted to be on their way to Syria. But Dandolo calmed them down and won them over. He offered to prolong his treaty with them for another year, keeping his fleet at Constantinople through the winter and if necessary until Michaelmas at the end of September 1204. The emperor agreed to pay the extra money that this arrangement would involve and also to supply the crusaders with their needs. The Doge

---

[1] Robert of Clari, c. LVI: p. 56; Villehardouin, c. 193: I, p. 196. Queller, *Fourth Crusade*, p. 113 and n. 11 (p. 203); Godfrey, *1204*, p. 112.

[2] *TTh*, I, nos. CXI–CXIV, pp. 428–36; *MPL*, CCXV, cols. 237–40, 259–62. Gill, *Byzantium and the Papacy*, p. 20.

knew that Venetian interests in Byzantium could now be served only
by one of two alternatives: either Alexios IV must be propped up and
kept in power; or the crusade must be used to take the place over and
exact its own reward. The latter option might be preferable, if it could
be done. For the longer the crusaders stayed the more likely it was that
some incident would lead to open war.

In August, while Alexios and Boniface were in Thrace campaigning
against the Bulgarians and hunting the fugitive Alexios III, a Greek mob
attacked the Latin quarters in Constantinople, setting fire to the shops,
warehouses and churches of the Genoese, the Pisans and the Venetians.
Many of the residents fled in terror to join their countrymen across
the water. Some days later, a band of Flemings, Venetians and Pisans
came the other way. Animated by religious bigotry they attacked and
pillaged the Muslim quarter in the city and burnt the mosque. The native
Greeks came to the rescue of the Muslims and, to cover their retreat,
the Latins set fire to some buildings. There was a high wind that fanned
the flames and the fire was soon out of control. It lasted for a week;
and when the emperor got back in November he found that a whole
district of the city had been devastated. About 15,000 of the Latin residents, fearful of further mob violence and destruction, had crossed the
Golden Horn to seek refuge with the crusaders. They were a welcome
influx of manpower for the coming conflict between Greeks and Latins
which now seemed ever more inevitable.[1]

As the winter drew on, Alexios began to resign himself to the fact
that he would never be able to honour his agreement. The crusaders
repeatedly demanded their money and from time to time they were given
small amounts. But the full sum of their dues was not to be found, and
Alexios became more and more offhand with them, hoping that they
would simply go without bothering him further. There were those among
them who wished that they could so simply leave. But once again they
could do nothing without the consent of the Venetians; and the Doge
was determined to exploit the situation by adding to the emperor's embar-
rassments. Towards the end of 1203 the crusaders sent a deputation to
the emperor with an ultimatum. It was phrased in terms of the code
of chivalry which they understood as men of honour. If the emperor
would not fulfil his promises after all that they had done for him, they
would no longer regard him as their lord and protégé and, after due
warning had been given, they would be justified in going to war against
him to settle their accounts by force. Such blunt statements of fact were
not normal at the Byzantine court where the truth was usually veiled

[1] Niketas Choniates, pp. 553–6; Villehardouin, cc. 203–5: 1, pp. 206–10. Queller, *Fourth Crusade*, pp. 116–21; Godfrey, *1204*, pp. 112–14.

in clouds of rhetoric. The courtiers were shocked. The emperor was
stung to reply that he would not pay a penny more to such insolent
persons; and the messengers were lucky to escape with their lives.[1]

The way was open not only for war between Greeks and Latins, but
also for a rebellion of the Greeks against the emperor who had brought
them to this pass. Skirmishes took place in the harbour. The Greeks
tried unsuccessfully to set fire to the Venetian fleet; and a conspiracy
was formed for the election of another emperor who would redeem the
betrayal of the Byzantine church and people. The ringleader of the plot
was the *protobestiarios* Alexios Doukas Mourtzouphlos, a son-in-law
of Alexios III. In January 1204, however, a rioting mob in St Sophia
took the law into their own hands and proclaimed as their emperor a
young and reluctant nobleman called Nicholas Kannabos. Some of them
then tore down the great statue of Athena, which had once graced the
Acropolis at Athens, because the goddess appeared to be beckoning the
crusaders into the city. Seeing that the situation was out of control,
Alexios sought the protection of his western friends, offering to hand
over to them the Blachernai palace. His message was intercepted by Alexios Mourtzouphlos, who at once revealed its contents, took over the
palace himself and arrested the unfortunate Kannabos. Alexios IV, the
cause of all the trouble, was thrown into prison and strangled. His father
Isaac, who had withdrawn into a sad world of his own, died a few days
later, either of fright or of old age. Mourtzouphlos came to the throne
as Alexios V.[2]

It was the declared intention of the new emperor to disclaim every
item of the agreement which his predecessor had signed with the Latins,
and to clear them from the scene as soon as possible. In one way this
made things simpler for the crusaders. With Alexios and his father gone
they were free of moral obligations towards the Greeks. They had delivered their ultimatum; they had given due warning; they need have no
further scruples about adopting the second of Dandolo's options by helping themselves to Byzantium and all its wealth and appointing an emperor
of their own. The capture of Constantinople and the conquest of the
Byzantine Empire had become the professed object of the Fourth Crusade. The realism and cool calculation of the Venetians was mixed with
the righteous indignation and moral fervour of the crusaders. Their clergy
assured them that a war against the Greeks would be a just war, since
its aim would be to avenge the murder of Alexios IV and to place the
Byzantine Church and Empire under obedience to Rome. The Greeks

[1] Villehardouin, cc. 211–16: II, pp. 10–14.
[2] Niketas Choniates, pp. 557–64. Queller, *Fourth Crusade*, pp. 122–32; Godfrey, *1204*, pp. 115–17.

were wilfully in schism. Those who died in battle against them would die fortified by the same indulgences as crusaders against the infidel. Justice was on their side. These were grand and reassuring motives. But the scheme was also born of desperation. For the crusaders could expect no supplies and no protection from the new regime in Constantinople. Even to escape might be difficult. Once again they must fight or perish.[1]

Having made their decision they turned to anticipating its outcome. In March 1204 they drew up a new treaty concerning the management of the city and the empire which they planned to conquer. It was made between the Doge Dandolo on behalf of the Venetians, and Boniface of Montferrat, Baldwin of Flanders and two other French knights on behalf of the crusaders; and it provided for the division of the booty, the election of an emperor and the distribution of the provinces. The Venetians must first be reimbursed in full. The Doge was therefore to be allowed to have first pick of the spoils, up to three-quarters of the amount taken. The election of a Latin Emperor of Constantinople was to rest with a committee of six Franks and six Venetians. The successful candidate, whether Frank or Venetian, would have possession of the imperial palaces and of one-quarter of the city and empire; the disappointed party would have possession of St Sophia and the right to elect a Latin patriarch. The remaining three-quarters of the empire would be divided equally between Venetians and the rest. The crusaders would hold their acquisitions as fiefs from the emperor, whom all parties must agree to serve until March 1205; but the Doge himself would not be obliged to render military or other service to the emperor for his portion of empire. Whatever eventualities this treaty may have failed to envisage, whatever defects it may have had, it was above all designed to protect and expand the interests of Venice. The interests of the Greeks, who were to be ruled by a foreign emperor, were not considered; and in the excitement of the moment all but the most conscientious of the crusaders forgot about the Holy Land.[2]

The treaty is an instructive document. No one at the time seems to have commented on the way in which it reflects the changed attitude of those who composed it. The professed object of their long detour had been to assist a wronged but well-connected prince to regain his inheritance and to reap the reward for their act of mercy. None of the crusaders had been to Constantinople before. Only the Venetians, and particularly the Doge, knew the way there and knew what the city and its people were like. The crusaders, who were at first overawed by its

[1] Villehardouin, c. 225: II, p. 24.
[2] The two texts of the treaty are in *TTh*, I, nos. CXIX, CXX, pp. 444–52; *MPL*, CCXV, cols. 517–19. Villehardouin, c. 234: II, pp. 34, 36; Robert of Clari, c. LXVIII: pp. 68–9.

magnificence, came to be contemptuous of its Greek inhabitants. They were impressed by the wealth of its churches and monasteries and by the number of its holy relics. Their own clergy, however, encouraged them to think it a shame that so many relics of the saints and martyrs should be in the hands of misguided and deviationist Christians. The Venetians had for long maintained their own quarter in the city. But its stability and security had too often been threatened by the whims or the policies of the emperors. There were many good reasons for thinking that Constantinople would be a better place morally and materially if it were brought under western control and under the Roman Church. The reasons had been propounded and rehearsed for some fifty years. But when the decision was taken and when the moment seemed ripe for the conquest of the city, in March 1204, the scope of the enterprise was suddenly broadened. The westerners had now, without due warning, determined to right their wrongs by conquering not only Constantinople but also the whole Byzantine Empire, or the Empire of Romania as they called it. Again it is tempting to say that only the Venetians can have known what this broadened vision of conquest entailed. The treaty of partition, agreed in advance of the conquest, though later modified in detail, lists numerous towns, ports, islands and provinces which were nothing but names to the crusaders. The Venetians, however, were well acquainted with most of them; and they had a ready-made gazetteer of the empire in the text of the chrysobull granted them by Alexios III only six years before.

By the end of March all was ready for the attack. It was agreed that the main assault should again be directed against the sea walls along the line of the Golden Horn. The first attempt was made at dawn on 9 April. Alexios V, who fought with more spirit than his predecessor, had set up his headquarters on a hill from which he could look down on the fleet; and by midday, after fierce fighting all along the walls, the crusaders were forced to retire with heavy losses. Three days later they returned to the attack, doubling the line of their ships to accommodate a greater number of assault troops. Towards noon, when things were going badly, a wind got up which blew their ships closer to the shore. Some of the bolder knights clambered on to the walls, and four of the towers were soon taken. The first to enter the city was Aleaume, brother of Robert of Clari, who, under heavy fire, fought his way in through a postern gate. Before long three more gates had been forced, and the knights were pouring in on horseback. The emperor retreated to the Boukoleon palace; and Boniface with Baldwin and Henry of Flanders took up their stations in different parts of the city, to continue the struggle on the following day. Some of their soldiers, afraid of being surprised in the darkness, lit a fire which got out of hand and destroyed still more buildings. In the night Alexios V slipped away, to take refuge with his father-in-law in Thrace. A young nobleman called Constantine Laskaris was hurriedly proclaimed emperor in St Sophia. But it was too late to reorganise the defences. Not even the Varangian guard could be inspired to prolong the fight. Constantine Laskaris and his brother Theodore joined the crowd of refugees at the palace harbour and sailed to the Asian side of the Bosporos.[1]

When dawn broke on Tuesday, 13 April, the crusading army prepared for battle. They were unaware of what had happened during the night, that the emperor had gone and that the resistance was broken. They were surprised and delighted when a deputation of Byzantine priests escorted by Varangian guards waited on Boniface to tell him that the city was his. Those who could afford or contrive to do so had already fled with their belongings. But the common people are said to have lined the streets and hailed the Marquis of Montferrat as their new emperor. While their leaders moved in to the imperial palaces, the soldiers of the crusade were given leave to pillage the city. Regulations had been made about the collection and disposal of the booty and forbidding excesses. But in the event there was neither order nor discipline. The city of Constantinople, like the empire of which it was the capital, never fully recovered from the treatment that it received at the hands of the crusaders. Three disastrous fires, one of which was still smouldering on 13 April, had already swept away 'more houses than stood in the three largest towns of France'.[2] The western knights and soldiers, however, did more deliberate and lasting damage while unleashing their inhibited bitterness against the perfidious Greeks. Open murder was incidental to the more profitable activities of plunder and robbery. Perhaps no more than 2000 of the inhabitants were slaughtered. But lust and avarice raged through the streets.

The treasured monuments of antiquity, which Constantinople had sheltered for nine centuries, were overthrown, carried off, or melted down. Private houses, monasteries and churches were emptied of their wealth. Chalices, stripped of their jewels, became drinking cups; icons became gaming-boards and tables; and nuns in their convents were raped and robbed. The church of the Holy Apostles, the prototype of St Mark's in Venice and the burial place of Constantine the Great and many of his successors, was ransacked. The imperial tombs, already stripped by Alexios III to find the means to defend his city, were despoiled of their remaining riches. Even the corpse of Justinian was desecrated. In the

[1] Queller, *Fourth Crusade*, pp. 138–48; Godfrey, *1204*, pp. 121–5.
[2] Villehardouin, c. 247: II, p. 50.

cathedral of St Sophia the soldiers smashed the altar and stripped the sanctuary of its gold and silver. They piled their trophies on to mules and horses which slipped and fell on the marble pavement leaving it running with their blood; and a prostitute danced on the patriarch's throne singing lewd songs. Niketas Choniates contrasts the savagery of these 'forerunners of the Antichrist' in Constantinople with the restraint of the Saracens in Jerusalem, who had respected the church of the Holy Sepulchre and done no harm to the persons or the property of the conquered Christians. Greek witnesses of the horror may well have been driven to exaggerate and to paint the picture of the sack of Constantinople in too lurid colours. Yet Niketas gives a sober and sometimes verifiable list of the ancient statues and works of art destroyed in those terrible days; and one of the most horrifying accounts of all comes from the pen not of a Greek but of Pope Innocent III, who was quick to condemn what he might have foreseen but had been powerless to prevent.[1]

After three days a halt was called to the looting and destruction and the proceeds were collected in three of the churches. Never, says Villehardouin, since the world was created had so much booty been seen in any city. Although no one could assess its true value, and although much was withheld, it was estimated to be worth at least 400,000 silver marks, more than four times what the Venetians had demanded for the transport of the Fourth Crusade. When the Doge had been paid the sum of 50,000 marks, the rest of the spoil was divided according to the treaty. It remained to elect an emperor from among themselves and to divide and conquer the empire. For the position of emperor there were really only two candidates, Boniface of Montferrat and Baldwin of Flanders. The Doge was prepared to forgo the doubtful honour of becoming a feudal monarch on the throne of Constantinople; but he was determined to have his say in the election. For the future of the Latin Empire which was about to be created the appointment of Boniface might have been the more promising. The Greeks might have co-operated more willingly

[1] The sack of Constantinople is described by the following contemporaries of the event: Niketas Choniates, pp. 568–77; Nicholas Mesarites, *Epitaphios*, ed. A. Heisenberg, *Neue Quellen zur Geschichte des lateinischen Kaisertums und der Kirchenunion*, I, Sitzungsberichte der Bayerischen Akademie der Wissenschaften, Philosophisch-philologische und historische Klasse, V (1922). Villehardouin, cc. 237–51: II, pp. 38–55; Robert of Clari, cc. LXIX–LXXX: pp. 69–80; Innocent III, in *MPL*, CCXV, cols. 699–702, especially col. 701. On the destruction of ancient works of art and the despoiling of imperial tombs: Niketas Choniates, pp. 647–55. On the expropriation of holy relics: P. E. D. Riant, *Des Dépouilles religieuses enlevées à Constantinople au XIIIᵉ siècle*, Mémoires de la Société Nationale des Antiquaires de France, ser. 4, VI (1875), 1–214; P. E. D. Riant, ed., *Exuviae Sacrae Constantinopolitanae*, I–III (Paris, 1877–1904). Cf. Brand, *Byzantium*, pp. 264–6.

with a ruler whose family was already connected with Byzantium. The crowds in the streets had hailed him as emperor. Boniface himself had high hopes of being chosen, and he improved his prospects by marrying the widow of the Emperor Isaac II and installing himself in the Boukoleon palace. The Doge, however, favoured Baldwin. Feelings ran so high among the crusaders when it came to appointing the electors that they decided to nominate six churchmen. It was agreed that the unsuccessful candidate should be allotted the provinces of Asia Minor and the Peloponnese. In the end Baldwin, Count of Flanders and Hainault, was elected emperor; and eight days later, on 16 May 1204, he was crowned in St Sophia. Boniface, who had been obliged to move out of the palace, nobly assisted at the coronation and did homage to his rival.[1]

But his pride had been wounded and his supporters encouraged him to make things difficult for the new emperor. He called upon Baldwin to make a deal. Boniface would prefer to take the city of Thessalonica instead of the provinces allotted to him as disappointed candidate for the throne. It was there that his brother Rainier had had his Byzantine estate. Thessalonica, however, had still to be taken from the Greeks and, as it happened, Baldwin was the first to get there and to receive the submission of the city. Boniface took to arms; and a civil war, which might have split the Latin Empire at its outset, was averted only by the intervention of the Doge. Baldwin admitted his mistake and conferred on Boniface the title to the lordship of Thessalonica.[2]

It had fallen to Baldwin, now 'by the grace of God, Emperor of the Romans', to notify the western world of the achievement of the Fourth Crusade. In a letter addressed to the pope and to the whole of Christendom he related the events that had led to the capture of Constantinople and his own coronation. Innocent III, who had remained sceptical about the first attack on the city, now expressed his overwhelming joy at what must surely be accounted a miracle wrought by God and took the new empire and its pious ruler under his protection. His joy turned sour, however, when he heard the full details of the plunder of the city, and of the arrangements that the Venetians had made for the administration of its church. But for the moment, once peace had been restored between Baldwin and Boniface, the crusaders were happy to have their adventure blessed, and looked forward with excitement to plucking and enjoying its fruits.[3]

---

[1] Niketas Choniates, pp. 596–7; Villehardouin, cc. 256–63: II, pp. 60–70; Robert of Clari, cc. XCIII–XCVII: pp. 91–5. Godfrey, *1204*, pp. 129–30, 134–5.

[2] Villehardouin, cc. 264–5; II, pp. 70–2; cc. 272–30: II, pp. 80–108.

[3] *TTh*, I, nos. CXXII, CXXIV, CXXV, CXXVII, pp. 501–11, 516–21; *MPL*, CCXV, cols. 447–54, 454–5, 455–61, 510–11. Cf. Gill, *Byzantium and the Papacy*, pp. 26–9.

Before the conquest it had been agreed that, if the crusaders elected an emperor, the Venetians should appoint the Patriarch of Constantinople. The Greek patriarch had already fled and the Greek clergy had been evicted from St Sophia. Their place was taken by fifteen newly appointed Latin canons of the cathedral who took it upon themselves to elect as patriarch the Venetian Thomas Morosini, who was then in Italy. They further decreed that for the future only Venetians would be eligible for election to the cathedral chapter. This was presumptuous if not scandalous behaviour, for the Venetians were still under the papal ban of excommunication. The Doge had written to the pope in the summer of 1204 protesting the innocence of his people and asking that the ban be lifted in recognition of the great services that they had performed for the glory of God and of the Roman Church. Innocent III took his time. In November he wrote to the Latin clergy in Constantinople ordering them to appoint priests of their own rite to churches whose Greek priests had fled and also to see to the election of a rector or overseer to preside over them. It was as if the election of Thomas Morosini had not taken place.[1]

The capture of Constantinople had taken the pope by surprise. He still believed, however, that those who had accomplished it were all soldiers of Christ who had not yet fulfilled their vows to go to the Holy Land. He was incensed to learn that his legate, Peter Capuano, who had gone to Constantinople in January 1204, had presumed not only to release the Venetians from their crusading vows but also to absolve them from the ban of excommunication. Capuano was commanded to return to Palestine forthwith. His place in Constantinople would be taken by Benedict, Cardinal of Santa Susanna. In the end, however, Innocent had to admit that events had once more overtaken him and that he had been outwitted by the Venetians. In January 1205 he wrote to the clergy of Constantinople and to the Doge. He explained that his consistory had at first declared the election of Thomas Morosini to be invalid, since the so-called Venetian canons who elected him had no authority to do so. On reflection, however, and because of his concern for the cause of the crusade, for establishing order in the new Latin Empire and for the union of the churches, he himself now confirmed Morosini's appointment as Patriarch of Constantinople. To the Doge he wrote in guarded and diplomatic terms. He had never trusted Dandolo; but he was prepared to concede that the Doge had done great service for Christendom and that God would release him from his crusading vows. He was also pre-

---

[1] *TTh*, I, nos. CXXVI, CXXVIII, pp. 519–20, 521–3; *MPL*, CCXV, cols. 471–2, 511–12.

pared to believe, at least after he had verified the facts, that his legate had absolved all the Venetians from excommunication.[1]

It was a penalty under which the Doge had been labouring ever since the attack on Zara two years before. He seems to have carried it lightly. Nor did the other leaders of the crusade shun him like an untouchable. On the day before the final assault on Constantinople the clergy had summoned all the host, including the Venetians, to church to hear rousing sermons from their bishops and to take communion.[2] By the time it was all over Enrico Dandolo was about ninety years old. The state of his immortal soul had troubled him less than the settlement of his accounts with the Byzantines. He rendered that soul to God within the year. But at least for the last months of his life he was no longer under his private sentence of death for not having taken his revenge upon the Greeks. The fact that he was also at the end relieved of excommunication by his own church may have been an added, but a secondary, comfort.

[1] *TTh*, I, nos. CXXIX–CXXXIII, pp. 524–8, 529, 529–32, 532–4; *MPL*, CCXV, cols. 512–17, 517, 519–21, 521–3. Cf. R. L. Wolff, 'Politics in the Latin Patriarchate of Constantinople, 1204–1261', *DOP*, VIII (1954), 225–303, especially 227–46; Setton, *Papacy and the Levant*, I, pp. 14–15.
[2] Robert of Clari, c. LXXIII: p. 71.

9

VENICE IN BYZANTIUM:
THE EMPIRE OF ROMANIA

LATER generations of Venetians proudly boasted that Enrico Dandolo had, with God's help, made the Greeks pay the penalty for the wicked crime committed against them, and against him personally, by the Emperor Manuel.[1] At the time too the people of Venice were no doubt proud of what had been achieved in their name. But they may also have been apprehensive. The situation was without precedent in their political history. Their Doge showed no sign of coming home, though he sent back a large part of his fleet. His son Reniero continued to act as his regent in Venice while Dandolo plunged wholeheartedly into his new role as leader, defender and promoter of the Venetian cause in Byzantium. Constitutional reforms and developments in Venice in the twelfth century had tended further to control and curb the autocratic authority of the Doge. The *consilium sapientium* instituted in 1143 had been replaced by two advisory bodies, the Maggior Consiglio of thirty-five members and the Minor Consiglio of three with six councillors. Venice had become a Commune whose Doge's powers were hedged about with restrictions from the moment when he took his oath of office and pronounced his pledge or *promissio* to the people who had elected him. Enrico Dandolo behaved like a Doge of an earlier age.[2]

The Venetians in 'Romania', however, were glad to have him in their midst. At last they had their own temporal and spiritual leaders of their colony. The Latin Empire envisaged in the treaty of March 1204 and established by the conquest of Constantinople was in theory a condominium between Venetians and crusaders. The role of emperor had been given to Baldwin of Flanders; but he was quick to confer the Byzantine title of Despot on Dandolo, under whose guidance the Venetians had

---

[1] Dandolo, p. 279. Cf. Martin da Canal, c. LV: p. 62. On the use of the term 'Romania', see R. L. Wolff, 'Romania: The Latin Empire of Constantinople', *Speculum*, XXIII (1948), 1–34; Thiriet, *Romanie vénitienne*, pp. 1–7.

[2] Kretschmayr, I, pp. 324ff.

been equally quick to appoint one of their own as patriarch.[1] The Doge had much influence and much freedom of action. Unlike the crusaders, he was not obliged to do homage to the emperor as his lord. Furthermore, he knew better than they where he was; he was among friends; and he knew what he wanted. It was he who had intervened to settle the dangerous quarrel between Baldwin and Boniface over the possession of Thessalonica; and it was he who had seized the chance of doing a deal with Boniface over the title to Crete. The island is said to have been granted to Boniface by the Emperor Alexios IV. It was of little interest to him but of great interest to his friends in Genoa. The news that Boniface was negotiating the sale of Crete to the Genoese roused the Doge of Venice to action. In August 1204 he outbid his rivals and bought the island from Boniface by terms of a treaty which guaranteed that the Republic of Venice and the new realm of Thessalonica would assist each other against their mutual enemies.[2]

Dandolo paid Boniface 1000 marks for Crete. He was of course paying only for the title to the island, for Crete, like most of the rest of the Byzantine Empire, had still to be conquered. In September 1204 the interested parties addressed themselves to the distribution of the provinces of the empire. A commission of twelve Venetians and twelve crusaders drew up a new treaty of partition. It was based on that concluded between them in the previous March. Here again the influence of the Doge and his advisors was paramount. For only the Venetians had direct knowledge and experience of the geography of the Byzantine world; and indeed the terms of the partition treaty were much indebted to the text of the last imperial chrysobull granted to Venice in 1198.[3] The capital was divided between the emperor and the Doge, Baldwin taking five-eighths and Dandolo three-eighths of the city. In the surrounding country the emperor was to have the territory between Agathopolis on the Black Sea and Tzurulon on the Sea of Marmora, the Venetians the lands from Adrianople to the Sea of Marmora and west to Gallipoli, and the crusaders what remained. The eastern limit of Boniface's domain of Thessalonica

---

[1] George Akropolites, *Historia*, ed. A. Heisenberg, *Georgii Acropolitae Opera*, I (Leipzig, 1903), p. 13. V. Lazzarini, 'I titoli dei dogi di Venezia', 294–5; B. Ferjančić, *Despoti u Vizantiji i južnoslovenskim zemljama* (Belgrade, 1960), p. 33. For all his contempt of the Byzantines Dandolo kept his Greek title of *protosebastos*. Kretschmayr, I, p. 339.

[2] J. K. Fotheringham, *Marco Sanudo Conqueror of the Archipelago* (Oxford, 1915), pp. 32–5; J. Longnon, *L'Empire latin de Constantinople et la principauté de Morée* (Paris, 1949), pp. 55–61; Thiriet, *Romanie vénitienne*, pp. 74–6.

[3] The test of the *Partitio Romaniae* (or *Regni Graeci*) is in *TTh*, I, no. CXXI, pp. 452–501. There is an improved edition with full commentary by A. Carile, 'Partitio terrarum imperii Romanie', *Studi veneziani*, VII (1965), 125–305. Cf. Longnon, *L'Empire latin*, pp. 49–50, 60–2; Setton, *Papacy and the Levant*, I, pp. 18–19.

was taken to be at Mosynopolis in Thrace. Further afield, Asia Minor and the offshore Aegean islands, including Lesbos, Chios and Samos, were allotted to the emperor. The continent of Greece was to be shared between Venice and the crusaders. In the north the division followed the natural line of the Pindos mountains. To the west of that line the Venetians claimed everything from Durazzo south to Naupaktos on the Gulf of Corinth as well as the Ionian islands of Corfu, Leukas, Ithaka, Cephalonia and Zakynthos, and the western part of the Peloponnese down to the ports of Methoni and Koroni, or Modon and Coron as they came to be called. To the east of the Pindos range mainland Greece was to belong to the crusaders; though the Venetians claimed parts of the island of Euboia or Negroponte as well as the islands of Salamis, Aigina and Andros. The title of Crete they had already acquired from Boniface; and before long enterprising Venetian adventurers were to use their own initiative in acquiring other islands in the Aegean Sea.

The Venetians did well out of it. They had staked their claim to the whole of the Adriatic coastline south of Durazzo, the west coast of Greece and the islands that would be most useful to them as stepping-stones on the trade route between Venice and Constantinople. They were content to leave to the emperor and the crusaders the task of conquering the rest of the Byzantine Empire in Asia and in Europe. The conquest began before the year was out. At the end of 1204 Baldwin and his brother Henry set out from Constantinople to invade Asia Minor, while Boniface assumed command of an army to descend upon Greece from Thessalonica. The conquest of Greece was not too difficult. Such resistance as there was came mainly from self-interested local dynasts, the most troublesome of whom was Leo Sgouros of Nauplion, who had made himself lord of Argos and Corinth. In the north, in Thessaly and Boiotia, there was little opposition. Westerners in the form of Italian and Jewish merchants were already familiar figures in Halmyros; at Thebes the citizens welcomed Boniface as a friend; and Athens submitted without a fight. The former Empress Maria whom Boniface had married had many friends in Greece, among them being one Michael Komnenos Doukas, a cousin of her first husband Isaac II. Michael accompanied Boniface and his army on their march from Thessalonica; but somewhere along the line he deserted and slipped across the Pindos mountains to join his relative, the Byzantine governor of Epiros. There he stayed; and there, based on the city of Arta, he laid the foundations of an independent state poised between the Venetians on one side and the crusaders on the other. The Latin conquest of the Peloponnese in the south was largely the work of Geoffrey of Villehardouin, a nephew of the chronicler. A chance adventure landed him on the coast at Modon. From there,

with the consent of Boniface, he set about establishing a crusader principality in what came to be called the Morea. One last stand was made
by the Greeks in Messenia. They were defeated and before the end of
1205 the crusaders could congratulate themselves that they had conquered
most of the Greek mainland. They were not concerned with Epiros and
the north-west of the country since that region had been allotted to
Venice; yet Michael Doukas, its self-appointed ruler, was soon to become
their most persistent and perfidious enemy.[1]

In Asia Minor the Emperor Baldwin found the going harder. The
resistance was not united or concentrated. Several local Greek magnates
simply exploited the confusion to transform their estates into autonomous
units; and at Trebizond a Byzantine Empire in microcosm had already
been founded by two grandsons of Andronikos I, David and Alexios
Komnenos. The most determined adversary of the Latins in Asia Minor,
however, was Theodore Laskaris, brother of that Constantine who had
been offered the crown in Constantinople on the night before its fall.
He was a son-in-law of Alexios III and, with his brother and his family,
he had escaped across the water. Theodore Laskaris, like Michael Doukas
in Epiros, was in due course to fashion a resistance movement into an
empire in exile; although his first encounter with the crusaders, in
December 1204, ended in his defeat. Baldwin and his men might then
have followed up their victory had they not been diverted by events
nearer their base. To the north of Thrace lay the emerging Kingdom
of Bulgaria, whose defiance of Byzantium the emperors of the Angelos
dynasty had been powerless to check. In 1204 its ruler Kalojan had just
succeeded in having himself recognised by the pope as King of the Bulgarians and the Vlachs; and he was confident that the Latin Emperor in
Constantinople would receive him at least as an equal ally. Baldwin rudely
rejected his overtures. Kalojan went to war and invaded Thrace. Baldwin
had to abandon his campaign in the east and rush to the defence of Constantinople against the Bulgarians. His army suffered heavy casualties
and he himself was captured at Adrianople in April 1205. His brother
Henry brought up reinforcements but he came too late to save the day.
The Doge Dandolo, who had been at the head of his own troops, helped

[1] W. Miller, *The Latins in the Levant. A History of Frankish Greece (1204–1566)* (London,
1908), pp. 30–40; Longnon, *L'Empire latin*, pp. 69–76; A. Bon, *La Morée franque. Recherches
historiques, topographiques et archéologiques sur la principauté d'Achaïe (1205–1430)* (Paris,
1969), pp. 51–64; Setton, *Papacy and the Levant*, 1, pp. 21–6. The career of Michael Doukas
in Epiros is outlined in D. M. Nicol, *The Despotate of Epiros [1204–1267]* (Oxford, 1957)
(cited hereafter as Nicol, *Despotate*, 1); though it has now been shown that Michael never
held the title of Despot and was therefore not the founder of what came to be called the
Despotate of Epiros.

to extricate the remnants of the army and bring them to safety on the coast.[1]

It was a catastrophic defeat. Thousands of the crusaders, now hopelessly demoralised, concluded that their venture had been a failure. The crusade had been in vain. The Latin Empire was still-born. They crowded on to Venetian ships in the Golden Horn and left for home.[2] The stouter hearts that remained did not despair, though they had little confidence in the immediate future. They had no emperor, for Baldwin was taken off to the Bulgarian capital at Trnovo and never seen again; while the Doge Dandolo, who had tested his strength to exhaustion, succumbed to the infirmity of his advanced years. He died on 1 June 1205 and was buried in St Sophia. This was the first great crisis of the Latin Empire. It was now deprived of two of the leaders who had created it. When it became clear that Baldwin had died in captivity, his brother, Henry of Flanders, who had been acting as regent, was the obvious choice as his successor. He was crowned as emperor by the Venetian Patriarch Thomas Morosini on 20 August 1206. His crown lay heavy on his head, for he was called to rule an empire that seemed to be crumbling before its foundations had been laid. Kalojan of Bulgaria had proved its weakness and he scented victory in the air, victory which would bring to him the prize of Constantinople. In campaign after campaign he pressed his advantage in Thrace, making a desert of the countryside; and the Latins had to put every man in the field to defend Constantinople. They had to endure one further disaster before the tide turned in their favour. In the summer of 1207 Boniface of Montferrat, who had paid his homage to the new emperor, joined him in Thrace. In September he was ambushed by the Bulgarians and killed. Kalojan had done his work well. Within three years he had accounted for the deaths of Baldwin, Dandolo and Boniface. A few weeks later, however, while he was preparing an attack on Thessalonica, he himself was struck down. It was the feast of St Demetrios, patron of the city, who had so often thwarted its enemies in the past. Kalojan's Bulgarian empire dissolved in chaos after his death, bringing a welcome relief to those whom he had hoped to conquer.[3]

The death of Enrico Dandolo had left both Venice and the Venetian

[1] Longnon, L'Empire latin, pp. 77–80; Godfrey, 1204, pp. 140–2. A new source for the disaster of 1205 is the letter of the Emperor Henry to the Christians of the west edited by R. Pokorny, 'Zwei unedierte Briefe'. On Theodore Laskaris and the Empire of Nicaea, see Alice Gardner, The Lascarids of Nicaea. The Story of an Empire in Exile (London, 1912); M. Angold, A Byzantine Government in Exile. Government and Society under the Laskarids of Nicaea (1204–1261) (Oxford, 1975).
[2] Villehardouin, c. 376: II, p. 184.
[3] Niketas Choniates, pp. 615–24; Villehardouin, cc. 388, 441, 499: II, pp. 198, 254–6, 312–14. Longnon, L'Empire latin, pp. 81–9, 96–101.

community in Constantinople without a head. The old Doge had not relinquished either office, nor had he given any advice for the future. Those in Constantinople at once took their own initiative and elected a new leader for themselves. He was Marino Zeno and he adopted the title of Podestà (*potestas*) and Lord of three-eighths of the Empire of Romania (*quartae partis et dimidiae totius imperii Romaniae Dominator*). He took office without delay and his first edict, dated 29 June 1205, was witnessed by his officials.[1] They held the same titles as those held by the officials of the commune of Venice. It seemed that the Venetian colony in Constantinople was brazenly assuming an independent status equivalent to if not greater than that of Venice itself. It was later put about that there were those who now favoured the idea of transferring their capital from Venice to Constantinople. They can hardly have been a majority; but the very suggestion was enough to make the Venetians at home yet more apprehensive about the child that they had spawned in Byzantium. Messengers took the news of Dandolo's death to Venice in July 1205. They also reported that the Venetians in Constantinople had elected their own Podestà and *dominator* in Romania. Reniero Dandolo, who was still acting Doge, asked for a report in writing; and in September Marino Zeno, as Podestà, sent him a full account. He emphasised that his own election posed no threat or challenge to the authority of the Doge and people of Venice. Those in Constantinople would indeed be ready to accept as their Podestà anyone whom the Doge might send out.[2]

On 5 August 1205 a new Doge was at last elected. He was Pietro Ziani, son of the former Doge Sebastiano Ziani. He was anxious about the balance of power between his own government and that of his countrymen in Romania. He accepted the fact that they had elected Zeno as their Podestà. But he made sure that his own supremacy over them would be respected. In October Zeno was obliged to sign a document ceding to the direct control of Venice all the territories in the north-west of Greece which had been assigned to the Venetians in the partition treaty, including Durazzo and the island of Corfu. This cession nipped in the bud the growing assumption that all lands allotted to Venice in that treaty would come under the jurisdiction of the Podestà in Constantinople. The assumption was further challenged by a second edict of the

[1] *TTh*, I, NO. CLIV, pp. 558–61.

[2] *TTh*, I, no. CLVII, pp. 566–9; Dandolo, p. 282; *Historia Ducum Veneticorum*, pp. 94–5. R. L. Wolff, 'A new document from the period of the Latin Empire of Constantinople: the Oath of the Venetian Podestà', *Pankarpeia. Mélanges Henri Grégoire*, IV (*Annuaire de l'Institut de Philologie et d'Histoire Orientales et Slaves*, XII, Brussels, 1953), 539–73, especially 544–7.

new Doge: any citizens of Venice were at liberty to appropriate such Greek lands and islands as they could without reference to the authorities in Constantinople and to hold them as hereditary properties. It was finally laid to rest by the requirement that, for the future, the Podestà must take an oath of loyalty to the Doge and commune of Venice; and it soon became the rule that each new Podestà was sent out from Venice instead of being elected by his friends in Constantinople; he had to swear obedience to the Doge as his faithful agent; and even the title of *dominator* passed to the Doge of Venice. The oath may first have been sworn by Ottaviano Quirino, who was sent from Venice to replace Marino Zeno in 1207. Its text reveals that the new constitution of the Venetian colony in Constantinople was modelled on that of Venice. The Podestà was, like the Doge, dependent on the majority vote of his council which was the counterpart of the Minor Consiglio of Venice. The colony was taken to be a commune in miniature, with its own judges, court and treasury. It was also made quite clear, however, that the Podestà and his councillors were subordinate to the Doge and his council in Venice. They had to obey all commands emanating from this higher authority in accordance with the oath of the Podestà to uphold the profit and honour of Venice and the interests of Romania.[1]

The Podestà was primarily responsible for the government and administration of the Venetian quarter in Constantinople, indeed for the three-eighths of the city allotted to Venice by the partition treaty. It was no longer a restricted area graciously granted to them by the emperor; and it covered much more ground, extending probably right along the Golden Horn as far as the Blachernai district where stood the imperial palace. The first Podestà, Marino Zeno, built a new wall separating it from the rest of the city and its defence seems to have been assured by a fortress (*castrum*). Giacomo Tiepolo was later to build a grand new commercial centre to accommodate the growing volume of traffic and number of businessmen. The extended area brought several other churches and monasteries under Venetian control. The monastery of Christ Pantokrator, built by John II Komnenos, was the most important. There the Venetians housed the famous icon of the Virgin Hodegetria painted by St Luke, which they had forcibly removed from St Sophia in 1206 in defiance of their patriarch.[2] The monasteries of the Virgin Peribleptos

---

[1] *TTh*, I, no. CLIX, pp. 569–71; *ActAlb*, I (Vienna, 1913), nos. 129, 130, pp. 41–2 (October 1205). The text of the oath is published by Wolff, 'A new document', 547–57. Thiriet, *Romanie vénitienne*, pp. 91–3.

[2] *TTh*, II, no. CLXXVIII, pp. 45–7. R. Janin, 'Les sanctuaires de Byzance sous la domination latine (1204–1261)', *Etudes Byzantines*, II (1944), 134–84, especially 174–5; Janin, *Géographie ecclésiastique*, I, 3, p. 531; R. L. Wolff, 'Footnote to an incident of the Latin occupation of Constantinople: the Church and the Icon of the Hodegetria', *Traditio*, VI (1948), 319–28.

and of Christ Pantepoptes also passed into Venetian hands. Both seem to have housed Benedictine monks and the latter was made over to the Benedictine monastery of San Giorgio Maggiore in Venice in 1206. The church of St Mark *de Embulo*, or of the market, which had been Venetian before the conquest, was also attached to San Giorgio Maggiore; while that of St Akindynos, which had been Venetian since the eleventh century, remained under the jurisdiction of the Patriarch of Grado.[1] The first Podestà followed the example set by the Doge Ordelafo Falier in 1107 by consigning to the Patriarch of Grado the freehold of all the land and landing stages in the Venetian quarter of Constantinople. The patriarch did well out of the rents of his leaseholders.[2]

The rival Italian colonies in the city, notably those of Pisa and Genoa, were not deliberately driven out by the Venetians, but their operations were much reduced in scale. The Pisan quarter had suffered almost irreparable damage as a consequence of the fire and the pillage in 1204. Bit by bit, however, it was reconstituted and Pisan colonies elsewhere in Romania, particularly at Halmyros in Thessaly, continued to flourish. The Genoese on the other hand were openly at war with the Venetians for years after the Fourth Crusade and their presence could not be tolerated. When the war ended, however, Venice could afford to be more tolerant. In the peace treaty of 1218 the Genoese were granted all the concessions and all the properties in Constantinople and in the empire which they had received from Alexios III; though they were obliged to pay the same taxes and dues that they had then paid. The Venetians seem to have had no fear that either of their former rivals would prosper to the extent of challenging their own commercial supremacy.[3]

The Doge had made sure that the provinces and islands of the Byzantine Empire lying nearest to Venice should come under his direct control. This seemed sensible for the protection of Venetian shipping in the Adriatic. But his claim had to be enforced. In the summer of 1205 the fleet from Venice which was escorting the new Latin Patriarch to Constantinople attacked first Durazzo and then Corfu. The crusade had visited Durazzo on its way east two years before. There were many Venetian residents there who probably welcomed the thought of direct rule from home. It would certainly be preferable to the anarchy prevailing in the city after the collapse of the Byzantine administration; and it would forestall the plans of others, notably the Genoese, to capture Durazzo. At all events there was little opposition and in July one of the captains

---

[1] Janin, 'Les sanctuaires', 175–6; Janin, *Géographie ecclésiastique*, pp. 218, 514, 515–23.
[2] Heyd, *Commerce*, I, pp. 285–6; Maltézou, 'Il quartiere veneziano', 47–50, especially 48–9 (no. 24: February 1207).
[3] Heyd, *Commerce*, I, pp. 289–92.

of the fleet, Marino Valaresso, was installed as the first Venetian governor of Durazzo. The city was thought to be such a prize that he was given the title of Duke.[1] The fleet sailed on to Corfu. Here it was not so well received. Part of the island had already been seized by a Genoese pirate called Leone Vetrano whose ships also used the ports of Modon and Coron for their rapacious activities. After much resistance Vetrano was evicted; but almost as soon as the Venetian fleet had left he reappeared. In 1206 another expedition had to be sent from Venice under the command of Reniero Dandolo to make certain of the conquest of Corfu. Again there was strong opposition before the citadel was finally taken by assault. Vetrano escaped but he was arrested at Modon. He was brought back to Corfu and there hanged with sixty of his accomplices as a warning to others. The citadel was refortified and a Venetian governor was appointed. The Republic soon realised, however, that direct rule over so troublesome a colony would be expensive and difficult to maintain. In 1207 Corfu and the nearby islands were leased to ten Venetian nobles and their heirs, on condition that they kept up its defences and paid to the Republic a yearly sum of 500 *hyperpyra*. Venetian traders in the island would enjoy special privileges and care was to be taken to protect the rights of the Greeks and of the Greek Church so long as they were loyal to Venice.[2]

The islands to the south of Corfu, Cephalonia, Ithaka and Zakynthos, had also been allotted to Venice in the partition treaty. But they had not belonged to the Byzantine Empire since the Norman invasion of 1185, in the course of which they had been appropriated by a Sicilian admiral, Magaritone of Brindisi. When he fell foul of the Emperor Henry VI, they had passed to his son-in-law, Count Maio (or Matthew) Orsini, who still held them at the time of the Fourth Crusade. Orsini had actively supported the Genoese pirate Vetrano; but when the Venetians occupied Corfu he repented of his life of buccaneering and sought the protection of the pope for his island county of Cephalonia. Two years later, however, he thought it prudent to seek recogition from Venice as well. He swore

---

[1] Dandolo, p. 282. The fullest account of these events is in the unedited *Historia veneta* of Daniele Barbaro written in the sixteenth century, extracts from which are printed in Fotheringham, *Marco Sanudo*, pp. 105–9. See Ducellier, *La Façade maritime de l'Albanie*, pp. 121–31.

[2] Dandolo, pp. 282–4; Marino Sanudo, *Le vite dei Dogi di Venezia*, cols. 534–5; Lorenzo (Laurentius) de Monacis, *Chronicon de rebus venetis ... ab u. c. usque ad annum MCCCCLIV*, ed. F. Cornelius, *RIS*, Appendix to Vol. VIII (Venice, 1758), Book VIII, p. 143; Martin da Canal, cc. LXV–LXIX: pp. 68–72; *TTh*, II, no. CLXXXII, pp. 54–9 (July 1207). Miller, *Latins in the Levant*, pp. 46–7.

an oath of perpetual fidelity to the Republic and declared himself to be a vassal of the Doge.[1]

The cases of Durazzo, Corfu and Cephalonia illustrate the various stages by which the government of Venice experimentally groped its way to the establishment of a colonial empire on the ruins of Byzantium. Possession of Durazzo was to be assured by the maintenance there of a governor and a garrison directly answerable to the Doge and commune of Venice. Corfu was entrusted as a hereditary fief to the heads of ten families who would defend and manage it in the interest of Venice. This arrangement was in line with the edict of Pietro Ziani encouraging Venetian citizens to help themselves to Greek islands. The edict was most successfully implemented by Marco Sanudo, nephew of the Doge Dandolo, who on his own initiative seized the island of Naxos in 1207 and built up around it his island Duchy of the Egeo Pelago or Archipelago in the Cyclades. To allow such private enterprise was in a sense an admission of weakness, an acknowledgment that the Doge of Venice could not hope to acquire or control such a multitude of scattered colonies. Marco Sanudo and his companions were all Venetian citizens. They were committed to the principle that lands conquered by Venetians could never be alienated to men of another race. But they were also committed to recognising the suzerainty over them of the Latin Emperor and the Venetian Podestà in Constantinople. The case of Cephalonia exemplified yet another method of colonisation, for there the island's non-Venetian ruler pledged allegiance to the Doge.[2]

The partition treaty had assigned to the Venetians the western portion of the Peloponnese or Morea. The fleet that went to Corfu in 1206 had gone on to capture and occupy the ports of Modon and Coron at the south-western tip of the peninsula. Venice had not the means, and perhaps not the will, to invade and settle the land behind the two harbours. It had in any case been occupied by Geoffrey of Villehardouin and was being transformed into the French Principality of Achaia. The simplest solution was to remind Villehardouin that the Venetians had a prior right to a large part of his principality and to make him sign a document of vassalage to them. In June 1209 the deed was done. Villehardouin acknowledged that he had received as a fief from Venice all the land of the Peloponnese from Pylos north to Corinth. He and his heirs were granted Venetian citizenship. Modon and Coron, however, remained directly under Venetian rule; and it was agreed that Venetian merchants should be exempt from payment of taxes throughout the French princi-

---

[1] Letters of Innocent III, *MPL*, ccxv, cols. 1129, 1224–5; Dandolo, p. 284. Nicol, *Despotate*, I, pp. 10, 19–20.

[2] Fotheringham, *Marco Sanudo*, pp. 56–80.

pality. Geoffrey of Villehardouin therefore, like Marco Sanudo, was a citizen of Venice whose primary allegiance, however, was to the Latin emperor in Constantinople.[1]

In Euboia or Negroponte on the other side of Greece a somewhat similar arrangement was made. Three of the companions of Boniface of Montferrat, all of them from Verona, had conquered the island and divided it into three large fiefs, taking the title of *terzieri* or triarchs of Negroponte. The Venetians were quick to point out that the partition treaty had allotted to them the important towns of Oreos in the north, not far from their well-established colony at Halmyros, and of Karystos in the south. In March 1209 the triarchs were constrained to make a treaty by terms of which they were designated as vassals and tributaries of Venice along with all the Greek and Latin inhabitants of their island.[2] Of far greater significance, however, was the island of Crete, which the Venetians had bought from Boniface. It was the largest of all the Greek islands and it lay at the crossroads of trade with Egypt and Syria as well as with Constantinople. Venice spent more time, effort and resources on the conquest of Crete than on any other of its acquisitions from the Fourth Crusade. It became a battle ground in the war with Genoa. The Genoese, led by Enrico Pescatore, Count of Malta, had set up house in the centre and east of the island and they easily fought off the first Venetian attack in the summer of 1207. For two more years Pescatore remained master of the island despite the presence of a few Venetian garrisons. He even tried to persuade the pope to proclaim him King of Crete. In the end the Venetians wore him down, though it was a costly business. Pescatore, poorly supported by his own government in Genoa, surrendered in 1212. Fighting between Venetians and Genoese went on for another five years; but the treaty of peace between them, signed in 1218, ceded victory to the Venetians in Crete. Crete was a special case and treated with special care. Its administration was entrusted to a Duke carefully selected and appointed by the Doge and his council in Venice. It was a valuable but an unruly province of the Venetian empire. The native Cretans had helped the Genoese. They did not take kindly to the form of heavy-handed government which the Venetians imposed upon them. Crete had to be well controlled and guarded. It

[1] *TTh*, II, no. CCVI, pp. 97–100. Longnon, *L'Empire latin*, pp. 112–13; Bon, *Morée franque*, pp. 66–7.
[2] *TTh*, II, no. CCV, pp. 93–6. J. Koder, *Negroponte. Untersuchungen zur Topographie und Siedlungsgeschichte der Insel Euboia während der Zeit der Venezianerherrschaft* (Vienna, 1973).

could not be entrusted to the administration of a mere agent of the Republic.[1]

This was a lesson that they learnt too late in the territories that lay nearest to Venice. They had taken over Durazzo and Corfu but they had done little to substantiate their claim to the coast and mainland south of the one and opposite the other, in Albania and Epiros, though these had been itemised and written into the cession of lands which they had forced upon their Podestà in 1205. The longer they delayed the harder it became. For Michael Doukas, who had assumed the role of defender of Epiros against both Venetians and crusaders, was fast developing his resistance movement into a political and military power in its own right. His terrain comprised the regions known to the Byzantines as Old Epiros in the south and New Epiros in the north. It ran from the limits of the Duchy of Durazzo down to Naupaktos on the Gulf of Corinth. Surrounded as it was by mountains on the east and by sea on the west it was naturally fitted for the establishment of an independent state. Michael Doukas preserved and strengthened its autonomy by playing a skilful if often unscrupulous diplomatic game with the crusaders on one side and the Venetians on the other. When Boniface of Montferrat died in 1207 a dispute arose over the succession to his title to Thessalonica. It was settled by the personal intervention of the Latin Emperor Henry who came to Greece for the purpose. Michael of Epiros took the opportunity to negotiate with him, offering his daughter in marriage to Henry's brother and one-third of his territory as her dowry. The offer was accepted and Michael was reassured that the crusaders would leave him alone. A year later he made a no less reassuring agreement with Venice.[2]

The Venetians had already had some dealings with Michael through their governor of Durazzo. It may have been through him that the Doge Pietro Ziani suggested a way in which the Venetian claim to Epiros might be settled to the benefit of all concerned. He cannot have been pleased to hear that Michael had signed away to the Latin Emperor one-third of his territory, since this was in breach of the terms of the partition treaty. The Doge therefore proposed that Michael should rule the lands that he held as the agent and the vassal of Venice. It was an attractive proposal. By pretending to hold his domain as a fief from Venice Michael could secure it against invasion and also compromise the claims of the Emperor Henry. Venetian merchants had for long done business in Arta

[1] *TTh*, II, no. CCLI, pp. 197–205. Fotheringham, *Marco Sanudo*, pp. 81–99; Thiriet, *Romanie vénitienne*, pp. 87–8, 95.
[2] Longnon, *L'Empire latin*, pp. 106–11, 122; Nicol, *Despotate*, I, pp. 27–9.

and other ports of Epiros.[1] It was on a small scale compared to their markets elsewhere. But if they were tempted to expand it by favourable concessions the economy would benefit. Michael accepted the proposal and on 20 June 1210 a formal treaty was signed between himself and the Doge.

The Latin text of this document survives. It is described as a 'concession' on the part of the Doge Pietro Ziani and a 'promise' on the part of 'Michael Comnanus Dux'. The Doge ceded to Michael as a fief all the country lying to the south of the Duchy of Durazzo as far as Naupaktos. As a loyal vassal of Venice Michael promised to ensure the safety of all Venetians and citizens of Durazzo and their right to trade tax free by land or sea throughout his domain. The export of corn from Epiros to Venice was to be encouraged; the Venetians would have their own commercial quarters, churches and courts; and they would have all the privileges formerly granted to them by the Emperor Manuel I. In addition, Michael promised to assist in suppressing any symptoms of rebellion against Venetian rule shown by the people of Corfu or of Albania and to pay an annual tribute of forty-two pounds of *hyperpyra*. He was liberal with his oaths of present and future fidelity to the Doge and to St Mark, to both of whom he sent gifts by the hand of one of his bishops.[2]

This arrangement was in some ways similar to that reached between Venice and Geoffrey of Villehardouin a year earlier. Villehardouin too had agreed to hold part of his territory in the Morea as a fief from Venice. The difference was that he was a westerner committed to the conquest and subjugation of Greece. Michael Doukas was a Byzantine and, though not native to the soil on which he ruled, he was committed to the defeat and eviction of the foreigners who had invaded Greece. Had the Doge listened to the advice of the Emperor Henry he would have learnt that Michael of Epiros was not one whose word could be trusted. Confident that he had now covered himself on both fronts, he at once broke all the pledges that he had made to the Latin Emperor and went to war. His troops, many of them Latin mercenaries, invaded Thessaly and captured the town of Larissa, thus severing the land route between Thessalonica and the French duchy that had been created in Athens and Thebes. The Emperor Henry was scandalised by Michael's treachery. The pope was horrified to learn that there were so many Latins in his army, lured by the promise of high pay and often shipped to Epiros by way of Venice.

[1] Venetian merchants were visiting Arta at least as early as 1131. Morozzo–Lombardo, I, no. 61, pp. 64–5.

[2] *TTh*, II, nos. CCXXIII, CCXXIV, pp. 119–23; *ActAlb*, I, no. 140, p. 44; Dandolo, p. 284. Nicol, *Despotate*, I, pp. 29–31.

Michael was also in league with the Albanians in the mountains behind Durazzo. He relied on them to help him capture it. The Venetians prized Durazzo. They had given it the special status of a Duchy. They had offended the pope by insisting that its archbishop would be appointed from Venice. It was, as the Normans had long ago discovered, one of the main ports of entry to the Via Egnatia, the road across the mountains to Thessalonica and Constantinople. Reinforcements for the Latin Empire could be sent that way so long as Durazzo was in western hands. But the Doge had not reckoned either with the treachery or with the military strength and resources of Michael Doukas. Barely three years after declaring himself the lifelong vassal of Venice, Michael attacked Durazzo and forced the Venetian garrison to withdraw. No details of his victory are recorded; but he was certainly in control of the city by 1213, for a Greek archbishop was appointed to Durazzo in that year. Having thus driven the Venetians out of the northern limits of his domain, Michael turned to the conquest from them of the island of Corfu, the acquisition of which had cost them so much in 1207. Once again, the details of the conquest have all been forgotten. The ten Venetian nobles to whom the island had been leased cannot have manned the defences very efficiently. But no chronicler, either Greek or Italian, reports the event; and the fact that Corfu changed hands can be deduced only from the evidence that its Greek bishop had been reinstated by 1214, and from a later document attesting that Michael Doukas issued a charter renewing the privileges granted to its people by the Emperor Isaac II. He died in the following year, leaving to the care of his half-brother Theodore Komnenos Doukas a principality which he had built into a power to be reckoned with by Venetians and crusaders alike.[1]

The Byzantine empire in exile in Asia Minor had also gone from strength to strength. Its founder, Theodore Laskaris, had made the most of the disasters that had befallen the crusaders, of the deaths of the first Latin Emperor Baldwin and of the Doge Dandolo. While they were fighting for survival against the Bulgarians in Europe, Laskaris was given time to consolidate his position in Asia Minor. He made the city of Nicaea his capital and in 1208 he had himself proclaimed and crowned as emperor. Nicaea was much better placed than faraway Arta in Epiros for the reconquest of Constantinople from the Latins. But it was beset by the Seljuq Turks as well as by the crusaders. By heroic efforts Theodore

---

[1] Nicol, *Despotate*, I, pp. 37–43; Ducellier, *Albanie*, pp. 149–51.

Laskaris successfully imposed treaties on both the enemies of his infant empire, on the Sultan of the Turks and the Emperor of the Latins. In 1214 the Emperor Henry was obliged to cut his losses in the east and to recognise the existence of a rival empire with an agreed frontier whose capital was at Nicaea. Two years later he died. He had no heir and his appointed successor as Latin Emperor was his brother-in-law, Peter of Courtenay, who was then in France. Peter was crowned by the pope in Rome and set out for Constantinople from Brindisi in April 1217. Travelling with him was the pope's legate, the Cardinal John Colonna. Venice supplied some of the ships to transport his army of over 5000 men. They were to go by way of Durazzo, to recapture it from the Greeks.[1] There are many and various accounts of this adventure, for it became a *cause célèbre*. Some say that Peter of Courtenay vainly laid siege to Durazzo before continuing his journey overland. Others imply that Theodore Doukas, the new ruler of Epiros, was intimidated by the arrival of so large an army and surrendered the city to the emperor. All the sources agree, however, that Peter elected to take the overland route along the Via Egnatia through Albania and Macedonia. It was a rash decision. He and his men had not got far into the mountains when they were ambushed by Theodore and his men. Peter of Courtenay and the pope's legate were captured; their troops were disarmed and dispersed; and Theodore had no difficulty in keeping or regaining possession of Durazzo.

The fate of the third Latin Emperor was as mysterious as that of the first. Peter of Courtenay was never seen again. The cardinal legate, John Colonna, was, however, eventually released and sent back to Italy after the pope, Honorius III, had threatened Theodore Doukas with a crusade of retribution. The Doge of Venice was among those whom the pope called to arms; and a number of aspiring crusaders began to assemble at Venice and Ancona towards the end of 1217. The threat of a crusade persuaded Theodore to set the cardinal free in March 1218. The pope was delighted. But the Venetians felt cheated. They had rather hoped that a crusade against Epiros would result in the permanent recovery of Durazzo. Theodore Doukas had outwitted them. He had expressed

---

[1] The agreement between Peter of Courtenay and the Doge Pietro Ziani is in *TTh*, II, no. CCIL, pp. 193–5. That Peter undertook, if successful, to restore Durazzo to the Venetians is emphasised by the continuator of Robert of Auxerre, in *Recueil des historiens des Gaules et de la France*, ed. M.-J.-J. Brial (Bouquet) and L. Delisle, XVIII (Paris, 1879), pp. 284–5.

his apologies to the pope and his loyalty to the Holy See. Pope Honorius therefore forbade the Venetians to attack the territory of such a devoted son of the church whom he had taken under his special protection. It was an odd turn of events.[1]

Since the day in April 1204 when their great Doge Enrico Dandolo had led them into the city of Constantinople the Venetians had been bemused by the dreams of acquisition and conquest which he bequeathed them. The Venice in Italy and the Venice in Byzantium did not always see eye to eye about how the fruits of empire could best be plucked and exploited. Clearly the Genoese could not be allowed to keep their footholds in Corfu, in Modon and in Crete. The conquest of these places, directed from Venice and not from Constantinople, had been expensive but necessary. The maritime routes were not safe so long as Genoese pirates roamed the seas. The war with Genoa had been won by 1218; and though the Venetians had been outwitted by the rulers of Epiros at Durazzo and at Corfu, they had acquired and conquered enough. They could join with their compatriots in Romania in making the most of the commercial opportunities now within their grasp. Being realists they could see that the Byzantine Empire at Nicaea had come to stay and seemed indeed to have a greater expectation of life than the already enfeebled Latin Empire in Constantinople. It was the Podestà, Giacomo Tiepolo, who took the initiative. In August 1219 he elicited from the Emperor of Nicaea, Theodore Laskaris, a chrysobull giving Venetian merchants the right to trade freely and without payment of dues in all his dominions. The arrangement was somewhat one-sided since the emperor's subjects were not granted the same privileges in the Latin Empire. This information is, however, interesting in itself, for it reveals that the Venetians in Constantinople were imposing customs duties on all foreign traders. No less interesting is the clause in the chrysobull in which each party agreed not to copy or to counterfeit the coinage

---

[1] Akropolites, pp. 25–6; Dandolo, p. 287. On the other French and Italian sources for this episode, see Longnon, *L'Empire latin*, pp. 153–7; Nicol, *Despotate*, I, pp. 50–3; Ducellier, *Albanie*, pp. 161–4. None of the sources records an alleged five-year truce between Venice and Theodore, as indicated by myself and by Ducellier. The earliest mention of it seems to be in Marco Antonio Sabellico, *Historia Vinitiana* (Venice, 1544), p. 65; (Venice, 1558), p. 102. Sabellico concocted it from Dandolo (pp. 287, 288), who confuses Theodore of Epiros with Theodore Laskaris of Nicaea by calling them both 'Theodoro Coniano Lascaro'. Sabellico clearly refers to the five-year truce made by the Podestà Giacomo Tiepolo with Theodore Laskaris, even though he calls him 'Theodoro Epirota'.

of the other; while the emperor undertook not to export gold coins from Constantinople without the approval of the Podestà.[1]

The extent of territory within the Empire of Nicaea in 1219 was not great but it seemed likely to grow at the expense of the Latins. The Venetians in Constantinople were aware of this. There is no documentary evidence to show that their merchants availed themselves of the privileges granted to them by Theodore Laskaris. The significance of the treaty for them as well as for him was that his existence had been recognised. It had been initiated by the Podestà of Constantinople and not by the Doge of Venice. The same Podestà, Giacomo Tiepolo, made treaties with Egypt in 1217 and with the Seljuq Sultan in October 1219. There was no effective Latin Emperor of Romania in those years. The Podestà, who claimed the title of Despot of the empire, took it upon himself to act as foreign minister if not as regent. None the less he realised that the Latin Empire was built on fragile foundations. It could not survive without continuing support from the west. The Venice in Byzantium must put itself unreservedly under the protection of its mother city. In December 1219, when his term of office was drawing to an end, Tiepolo wrote to the Doge expressing his anxieties and humbly begging for help and support. Specifically he asked the Doge to send out at least ten warships to protect Venetian citizens and their interests. The French barons of the empire had just elected a regent, Conon of Béthune, who had ratified the existing treaties between Venetians and crusaders. The time seemed to have come for the Podestà to renounce the role that he had adopted, to submit to the authority of his master the Doge, and to make the Commune of Venice aware of its obligation to maintain and defend its loyal citizens in foreign parts. No one knew better than Giacomo Tiepolo the strengths and weaknesses of the colonial empire that he had helped to found. He had been the first Venetian Duke of Crete. He was to return to Constantinople in 1224 for another term

---

[1] Dandolo, p. 288; *TTh*, II, no. CCLII, pp. 205–07; *DR*, III, no. 1703. Heyd, *Commerce*, I, pp. 304–5; Kretschmayr, II, pp. 15, 560; Angold, *Nicaea*, p. 114. S. Brezeanu, 'Le premier traité économique entre Venise et Nicée', *RHSEE*, XII (1974), 143–6, argues that the treaty of 1219 was a renewal of a treaty signed between Venice and Nicaea five years earlier. On the clause about the minting of coinage, see M. Hendy, *Studies in the Byzantine Monetary Economy c. 300–1450* (Cambridge, 1985), p. 521. In 1319 the Emperor Andronikos II was to claim that Theodore's successors at Nicaea, John III Vatatzes and Theodore II Laskaris, had a similar commercial arrangement with Venice. But there is no documentary evidence of the fact. See below, p. 238.

as Podestà; and in 1229 he was to be elected Doge of Venice. His words and his warnings carried weight. The mother city was henceforth to take more seriously its responsibilities for the upkeep and defence of its colonies in Romania.[1]

[1] Tiepolo's letter to the Doge Ziani is in *TTh*, ii, no. CCLVII, pp. 215–21 (10 December 1219). Thiriet, *Romanie vénitienne*, pp. 90–2.

10

VENICE:
CHAMPION OF A LOST CAUSE

THE chrysobull that Theodore Laskaris granted to Venice in 1219 was evidently no more than a gesture. It was never revoked, but it was never renewed. The greatest of the emperors at Nicaea, John III Vatatzes, who succeeded Laskaris in 1222, aimed to make his empire self-sufficient, not dependent for its economic survival on trade with the Italians. Nor was he keen to do business with them in Constantinople. If and when his ships sailed into the Golden Horn it would be to take the city from them, to overthrow the Latin regime and restore the Byzantine Empire. The regime was already tottering. Its new emperor, Robert of Courtenay (1221–8), was a self-indulgent youth with none of the adventurous spirit which had fired the leaders of the Fourth Crusade. The French principality in the Morea and the French Duchy of Athens and Thebes which they had founded seemed to have a future. But the Latin Empire of Constantinople, of which they were fiefs, could not survive without a new influx of manpower and resources. The first of its outposts to fall was the so-called Kingdom of Thessalonica. Theodore of Epiros had dealt a memorable blow to the Latin regime by capturing its emperor in 1217. In the next few years he capitalised on his success by expanding his dominions at the expense not only of the Latins in Thessaly but also of the Bulgarians in Macedonia. His supporters confidently predicted that Thessalonica would soon fall to him and that, once master of the second city of Byzantium, he would have a better claim to the imperial title than any emperor in Nicaea.

The Latins too were anxious about the fate of Thessalonica. The widow of Boniface and her young son Demetrios of Montferrat fled to Italy in 1222. Pope Honorius III was induced to preach a crusade for the defence of the city against Theodore Doukas whom he could no longer regard as a 'devoted son of the church'. Its leader was the half-brother of Demetrios, William of Montferrat. It evoked little enthusiasm in the west. The Venetians were invited to take part and may have supplied some ships. Thessalonica was not one of their principal markets. But they had come to see themselves as defenders of the Latin regime wherever it was to be found for fear that it might collapse entirely. Their help came too late, for at the end of 1224 Thessalonica, for long besieged and isolated, surrendered to Theodore Doukas. The crusade reached Greece some months later but it got no further than Halmyros in Thessaly, where William of Montferrat and many of his men perished miserably in an epidemic of dysentery.[1]

There were now two Byzantine Emperors in exile to contest the prize of Constantinople. Theodore complemented his triumph by having himself crowned as emperor at Thessalonica. There is no record that Venice recognised him as such; indeed in 1228, after the seizure of the cargo of a Venetian ship wrecked at Corfu, they forbade their merchants to put in at any of the ports in his territory.[2] The regents of the Latin Empire in Constantinople, however, once more bereft of an emperor, thought it prudent to flatter Theodore as his troops advanced nearer to their city. In December 1228 they made a truce of one year with the 'emperor' of Thessalonica. The walls of Constantinople would doubtless have held him off and he had no navy to match that of its Venetian defenders. But Theodore brought his ruin upon himself by turning aside to make war on the ruler of Bulgaria, John Asen. In April 1230 he was defeated in a battle at Klokotnica on the Marica river and taken prisoner by the Bulgarians. John Asen followed up his victory by invading and occupying Thrace and Macedonia. In an inscription recording his achievements he claims to have conquered all the land as far as Durazzo and the Adriatic Sea, though there is no evidence for a Bulgarian occupation of Durazzo.[3] He allowed the Empire of Thessalonica to survive, at least in name, with Theodore's brother Manuel as its emperor. The emperor in Nicaea was glad to see his rival brought low. Theirs was a world in which there could be only one true Emperor of the Romans. John Vatatzes was an abler and a wiser statesman than Theodore Doukas. The institution that he had inherited was built on more secure and realistic foundations. Within a few years he transformed it from a little enclave in Asia Minor into an empire that extended into Europe as well. The Latins were increasingly at his mercy. They too were glad to have

---

[1] Nicol, *Despotate*, I, pp. 57–64.

[2] R. Predelli, ed., *Il Liber Communis detto anche Plegiorum del Reale Archivio generale di Venezia: Regesti* (Venice, 1872), nos. 616, 642, pp. 147–8, 153 (10 June and 19 August 1228). Nicol, *Despotate*, I, p. 106. It is not known how long the embargo lasted; but trade with Ragusa, then subject to Venice, was guaranteed by the Greek rulers of Thessalonica and Epiros in 1234 and again in 1237. B. Krekić, *Dubrovnik (Raguse) et le Levant au moyen âge*, Documents et Recherches, V (Paris–The Hague, 1961), nos. 3, 5, pp. 167, 168; Nicol, *Despotate*, I, pp. 123,133.

[3] Ducellier, *Albanie*, pp. 166–7; Nicol, *Despotate*, I, pp. 107–14.

weathered the storm of an emperor in Thessalonica. But without the devoted support of Venice, Constantinople would surely have fallen to the emperor in Nicaea.

The Doge of Venice for most of the reign of John Vatatzes was Giacomo Tiepolo (1229–49), the former Podestà of Constantinople. Tiepolo saw the protection of the Latin Empire and of Venetian interests in it as a priority. It was he who supplied the ships to transport the army of its new emperor, John of Brienne, to Constantinople in 1231 with an escort of fourteen galleys. It was he who persuaded that emperor to renew all the privileges of Venetian traders throughout Romania.[1] In 1234–5, when the forces of Nicaea and Bulgaria united to attack Constantinople by land and sea, Tiepolo sent out a fleet of twenty-five ships to help fend them off. When they returned to the attack in 1236 the Prince of Achaia brought his own army and navy over from Greece; and the Pisans and the Genoese joined the Venetians in the city's defence.[2] Its emperor, John of Brienne, was a valiant if elderly warrior, but without substantial reinforcements from the west he was fighting a losing battle. Only Venice supplied such reinforcements. In 1236 the Young Baldwin II, the heir to the throne and the ward of John of Brienne, was sent to see the pope and King Louis IX of France, to whom he was related. His mission was to stir the conscience of the western world to save his Christian empire in the east. While he was away, John of Brienne died, in 1237. It was a critical time for the Latin Empire. Constantinople was cut off by land. John Vatatzes controlled both sides of the Hellespont and his troops were raiding the suburbs right up to the walls of the city. Food was scarce. Many escaped by night; and the population was so reduced that it was doubtful whether, in the event of a siege, there would be enough men to guard the walls.[3]

Money too was in short supply. The acting baillie of the empire, Anseau of Cayeux, and his barons arranged a loan from the Podestà and certain other Venetians and Genoese in Constantinople. It was raised on the security of one of the city's most holy relics, the Crown of Thorns. The sum subscribed amounted to 13,134 *hyperpyra* and the relic was transferred from the Boukoleon palace to the care of the Podestà, Albertino Morosini. By September 1238 the money had been spent and there was no sign of financial or military help coming from the west. Another loan was underwritten by a Venetian banker, Nicolò Quirino, though

---

[1] *TTh*, II, nos. CCLXXVII, CCLXXIX, CCLXXX, pp. 277–99 (29 May 1231, not '3 May'); Dandolo, p. 292. Cf. Thiriet, *Romanie vénitienne*, p. 96.

[2] Akropolites, pp. 46–8; Martin da Canal, pt i, cc. LXXX–LXXXIV, pp. 80–4. Longnon, *L'Empire latin*, p. 173.

[3] Longnon, *L'Empire latin*, pp. 174–5.

on much more stringent terms. The Crown of Thorns was again pledged as security; but it was now to be deposited in the monastery of the Pantokrator in the care of the chamberlain of the Venetian community in Constantinople. If it were not redeemed within the month of October or at latest by 10 November it would become the property of Quirino and could be taken by him or his deputy to Venice. There he could break the seals of its casket and exhibit the relic to the Doge and other good men of Venice in the presence of the Franciscans and Dominicans there residing before sealing it up again. It was understood that within a period of four months thereafter Quirino would receive from the Emperor Baldwin or his agent the equivalent in Venetian currency of the 13,134 *hyperpyra* which he had lent, at the rate of 8¼ *hyperpyra* to each *miliarium*, a total of 1592 *miliaria*. On receipt of this sum in full, the Crown of Thorns would be handed back to the emperor and barons of Constantinople. If the four months passed with no payment having been made, Quirino would have the right to keep the Crown or to sell it or to dispose of it as he saw fit.[1]

The four months did not run their course and neither Quirino nor the Doge and people of Venice were allowed to keep the relic. The news that it had been pawned reached Baldwin while he was in Paris. The Crown of Thorns was already well known in France. Baldwin I had given one of its thorns to King Philip II in 1205.[2] Baldwin II played on the religious and patriotic susceptibilities of Philip's grandson, the saintly King Louis IX. It would be a splendid thing, he suggested, for the honour and glory of his lord and relative, if this precious jewel of Christendom could be brought to France. To make the transaction sound less materialistic, he begged Louis to accept it as a gift from himself. The offer seemed to be inspired by divine providence. The king, we are told, was glad that God had selected France as the place to which His Son would return to claim his Crown at the last trump and to judge

---

[1] The document concerning the Venetian loan on the security of the Crown of Thorns, dated 4 September 1238, is in *TTh*, II, no. CCXCVI, pp. 346–9; A. Teulet, *Layette du Trésor des Chartes*, II (Paris, 1866), no. 2744, pp. 391–2; Riant, *Exuviae sacrae Constantinopolitanae*, II (Geneva, 1878), pp. 119–21 (cf. also p. 118). The Podestà subscribed 4175 *hyperpyra*; 4300 were subscribed by the abbey of Percheio ('Perceul') in Constantinople; 2200 by the Venetians Nicolò Corner and Pietro Ziani; and 2459 by certain gentlemen of Genoa; making a total of 13,134 *hyperpyra*. The *miliaria* were 'thousandweights' of lead, each equivalent to 8¼ *hyperpyra*. I am indebted for this information to Professor Philip Grierson. On the Cistercian abbey of Santa Maria de Percheio, see Janin, *Géographie ecclésiastique*, pp. 581–2. Dandolo, p. 295, states that a piece of the Cross, the Holy Lance and the Sponge were also put in pawn.

[2] Nivelet, Bishop of Soissons, had given another to his cathedral in 1205; and the Emperor Henry gave some more to Philip of Namur in 1206. Riant, *Exuviae sacrae*, II, pp. 33, 60, 64, 74, 81, 107, 190, 191.

the quick and the dead. Without delay he dispatched two Dominicans to Constantinople with a royal messenger bearing letters patent to the barons of the Latin Empire. They arrived to find that the relic had already been pawned and was about to be shipped to Venice; but it was arranged that they should go with it on its voyage. They set sail at Christmas 1238. The Emperor John Vatatzes had got wind of the business through his spies in Constantinople and tried to intercept their ship and its precious cargo on the high seas. But they got safely to Venice and the Crown was placed in the treasury of St Mark's. One of the two Dominicans was posted to guard it while the other hurried back to France to announce the good news to King Louis who at once sent ambassadors to Venice armed with the money to redeem the sacred relic. Some French merchants who were there on business effected the necessary exchange of currency; and the holy Crown of Thorns, still sealed in its casket, was carried in triumph to Paris where, in due course, St Louis built the Sainte Chapelle to house it.[1]

The Venetians were sorry to lose so potentially profitable a pilgrim and tourist attraction. It would have been a unique addition to their well-known collection of relics. But they could not go back on their word. Nicolò Quirino may even have been out of pocket as a result of the transaction since the sole record of payment to him by Louis IX refers to a sum of 10,000 *hyperpyra*, over 3000 short of the original loan.[2] None of the interested parties had given a thought to the fact that the Crown of Thorns properly belonged to the Byzantine Church and the people of Constantinople; and it is far from clear how its translation to Paris helped the cause of the penurious Latin Empire except by the settlement of a debt to the Venetians. The main beneficiary was the Kingdom of France whose monarch was, after all, the sovereign lord of all the French knights and barons of Romania. They could at least take comfort from the thought that so holy a relic was housed in their own country, where it would be safer than in Constantinople and out of the hands of the perfidious and schismatic Greeks. The grateful King Louis and the pope, Gregory IX, between them succeeded in raising some interest in the dying cause of the Latin Empire of Romania. A crusading army began to assemble. Many of those who joined it, however, were once again more of a mind to make for Syria and they set out on their own by sea. Those in Constantinople impatiently awaited the

---

[1] The history of the translation of the Crown to Paris was written in 1239 or 1240 by Gautier de Cornut (Gualterius Cornutus), Archbishop of Sens, and is published in Riant, *Exuviae sacrae*, I, pp. 43–53. F. de Mély, *Les Reliques de Constantinople au XIIIᵉ siècle*, II: *La Sainte Couronne* (Lille, 1901) (from *Revue de l'Art Chrétien*, 1899, 35–133).

[2] Teulet, *Layette du Trésor*, II, no. 2753, p. 395; Riant, *Exuviae sacrae*, II, p. 123 (cf. pp. 122–3).

long overdue return of their emperor with men and money for their salvation. But it was not until the end of 1239 that Baldwin finally arrived, having brought an army of 700 knights, with numerous soldiers and horses, overland through Germany, Hungary and Bulgaria. They were very welcome and for a while the Latin Empire enjoyed a respite.[1]

It was destined to survive for another twenty years. It could hardly have done so without Venetian protection by sea. But its existence was prolonged mainly by the fact that its natural enemies could not bring themselves to join forces. The ephemeral empire set up in Greece by Theodore Doukas was soon added to the Empire of Nicaea. In 1246 John Vatatzes incorporated Thessalonica into his dominions. The mantle of emperor in exile on the Greek mainland was assumed, however, by Theodore's nephew, Michael II Doukas of Epiros, who based himself on his father's capital at Arta. He was not an emperor by right or title, though he held the imperial title of Despot. But his ambition was to repair that deficiency by resurrecting his uncle's Empire of Thessalonica. The Latin Empire of Constantinople would surely have been brought to an earlier end but for the implacable rivalry and open warfare between John Vatatzes of Nicaea and Michael II of Epiros. So far as is known, the Venetians had no direct dealings with either of them. Venice seems not to have disputed the possession of Corfu and Durazzo by Michael, nor that of the islands of Lesbos, Chios and Samos which had been taken over by Vatatzes. Michael of Epiros had no fleet to challenge Venetian control of the sea passage along his coast; while the navy of the Empire of Nicaea, as one of its admirals complained, was no match for the Italians. The point had been proved in 1235 when a reputed 100 warships from Nicaea had been driven away from Abydos by a mere twenty-five Venetian galleys. It was proved again in 1241 when twenty-five ships from Nicaea on their way to blockade Constantinople were captured or routed in the Sea of Marmora by a squadron of thirteen Venetian warships sent out by the Podestà, Giovanni Michiel.[2]

Apart from the defence of Constantinople, vital to the structure of its colonial empire, Venice was most concerned with the pacification and settlement of Crete.. The importance of the island was perhaps at first more strategic than commercial, for it lay on the route to Egypt and also to Syria and Palestine where there were still thriving Venetian establishments. The men of Crete had never deen disposed to settle down under Venetian rule and their propensity to rebel was eagerly fostered by the Emperor of Nicaea whom they regarded as their natural ally

[1] Longnon, L'Empire latin, pp. 180–2.
[2] Akropolites, pp. 59–60; Martin da Canal, pt i, cc. LXXX–LXXXIV: pp. 80–4; Dandolo, pp. 295, 298.

and potential liberator. The Venetian Duke of Naxos, though called upon to help subdue the island, was strangely reluctant to commit himself; and for some years John Vatatzes was able to maintain Byzantine garrisons in parts of Crete. The Greek ruler of Rhodes, Leo Gabalas, proved to be a more useful ally of Venice than their own Marco Sanudo; and it was with his assistance, by terms of a treaty that he made with the Doge in 1234, that Venice was able to impose its will on Crete. Two years later the last of the Greek troops from Nicaea were permitted to evacuate the island.[1] Next in importance to the Venetians among their colonies were Negroponte or Euboia. Building on the treaty that they had signed with the Lombard conquerors of the island in 1209, they quickly established a dominating influence. A Venetian baillie or governor was installed in the capital city of Chalkis, and it was he who apportioned the land among the quarrelsome heirs of the first triarchs. Characteristically, the Venetians were not eager to go to the trouble of conquering the place. But their baillie became in effect governor and arbiter not only of Chalkis but of the whole island of Negroponte; and the Lombard triarchs as well as the local Greek magnates took an oath of loyalty to him and to the Republic of Venice. They paid him a yearly tribute; Venetian weights and measures were in use in all the towns; and Venetian merchants as well as fortune hunters from Lombardy came to live in the island. Negroponte was at first a less troublesome colony than Crete, for the Lombards and Venetians got on well together and the native inhabitants were less rebellious by nature. There was much trade to be done there in grain and timber, and it was conveniently close to the much older Venetian trading station on the mainland at Halmyros.[2]

The smaller Greek islands of the Aegean had their uses as ports in a storm or stepping-stones on the sea route to and from Constantinople; and some produced valuable and exportable commodities such as honey and wax. In the Morea or Peloponnese the Venetians were content to reap the fruits of the comparatively stable and prosperous government imposed by the French Princes of Achaia, using the ports of Modon and Coron in the south-west as their commercial and naval bases. The greatest of those princes was William of Villehardouin (1246–78). It was he who completed the French occupation of the Morea by conquering the rock of Monemvasia on the eastern tip of the peninsula, a task for which the Venetians lent him ships. It was he also who, in 1255, provoked a war over the succession to what he claimed as his portion of the island

[1] *TTh*, II, nos. CCLXXXIX, CCXCIIII, pp. 319–22, 333–5. Fotheringham, *Marco Sanudo*, pp. 100–2; Thiriet, *Romanie vénitienne*, pp. 97–100.

[2] Miller, *Latins in the Levant*, pp. 77–9; Thiriet, *Romanie vénitienne*, pp. 93–5.

of Negroponte. The war spread over most of continental Greece and
brought in the Genoese as William's allies to fight on the opposing side
to the Venetians. The victory went to William and in 1259 the Doge
of Venice authorised the baillies of Negroponte to make peace with him.
Trade was more important than honour in such cases. Warfare was bad
for business.[1]

William of Achaia was without doubt the ablest of the Latin rulers
of Romania. He would have done better to collaborate with the Venetians
in defending Constantinople than to come to blows with them. By 1259
the Venetians were acutely aware of the mortal weakness of the regime
of Baldwin II and of the gathering strength of his enemies. Some years
earlier they had again acted as brokers to help the emperor out of his
financial difficulties. Two of their merchants in Constantinople, Giovanni
and Angelo Ferro, had taken custody of Baldwin's son and heir, Philip
of Courtenay, as security for a loan. Philip was shipped off and lodged
in Venice, a pawn in a losing game. It was the last that he saw of Constantinople, for his redemption was effected from another quarter.[2] His
unhappy father and his barons were none the less reduced to selling
almost all that they had and to stripping the lead from the roofs of the
palace to make ends meet.[3] Reports reaching Venice persuaded the
Doge, Reniero Zeno, to sound the alarm and to propose an emergency
plan for the rescue of Constantinople. Using the baillie of Negroponte
as his agent and plenipotentiary, the Doge called upon all the French
and Italian lords of Greece and the Greek islands to contribute to a
permanent standing garrison of 1000 men to hold the city. The cost
would be shared among them. It was a brave idea, but it was too late.
It seems to have been proposed in 1260. By then the strongest of the
lords of Greece, William of Villehardouin, had been removed from the
scene.[4]

The rivalry between the contending Greek claimants for the liberation
of Constantinople reached its climax in 1259. John Vatatzes, Emperor
at Nicaea, had died five years before. His son and successor, Theodore

[1] *TTh*, III, nos. CCCXXXIX, CCCXL, pp. 25–8. Miller, *Latins in the Levant*, pp. 102–8; Longnon, *L'Empire latin*, pp. 220–3; Bon, *Morée franque*, pp. 118–20; Setton, *Papacy and the Levant*, I, pp. 77–80.
[2] The full story of the pawning of Philip of Courtenay is told by R. L. Wolff, 'Mortgage and redemption of an Emperor's son: Castile and the Latin Empire of Constantinople', *Speculum*, XXIX (1954), 45–84.
[3] *Fragmentum Marini Sanuti Torselli*, ed. C. Hopf, *Chroniques gréco-romanes inédites ou peu connues* (Berlin, 1873), p. 171; ed. R. L. Wolff, 'Hopf's so-called "Fragmentum" of Marino Sanudo Torsello', *The Joshua Starr Memorial Volume* (New York, 1953), 150–1.
[4] Document printed in W. Norden, *Das Papsttum und Byzanz* (Berlin, 1903), Appendix N. XIII, pp. 759–60. Thiriet, *Romanie vénitienne*, pp. 144–5; Setton, *Papacy and the Levant*, I, p. 91.

II Laskaris, cut less of a figure; and Michael II, the Despot in Epiros, saw his chance to advance towards Thessalonica. The rulers of the Byzantine states in exile had seldom counted the Venetians among their friends or allies. They had, however, cultivated the friendship of other western powers. John Vatatzes had negotiated with the popes as a means of winning Constantinople by diplomacy. Both he and the rulers of Epiros had gained the ear of Frederick II of Sicily, the declared enemy of the papacy. Vatatzes had taken Frederick's daughter to wife. Most kings of Sicily were drawn to Constantinople as by a magnet. Frederick II would have preferred it to be in Greek hands. His son Manfred, however, who took over the kingdom in 1250, was not so altruistic. Following the example of his Norman predecessors, Manfred invaded Corfu and Durazzo in 1257 and placed garrisons along the coast of Epiros preparatory to an overland march to the east. The Despot Michael was taken unawares. He too was planning to march east, first to Thessalonica and then to Constantinople. But he calculated that his best course would be to try to draw Manfred of Sicily to his side. He offered him the hand in marriage of his daughter Helena. Her dowry would consist of Corfu and many of the places on the mainland of Epiros which Manfred had already occupied. The arrangement suited both parties and the wedding of Manfred to Helena took place in Apulia in June 1259. Michael made a similar arrangement with William of Villehardouin. William too had his reasons for joining forces with the Despot of Epiros. Marino Sanudo later explained that the Prince of Achaia was motivated by his desire to turn the Venetians out of Constantinople by way of revenge for their support of the revolt in Negroponte. He accepted the offer in marriage of Michael's other daughter Anna. He married her in the summer of 1258.[1]

The Emperor Theodore II of Nicaea feared that the prize of Constantinople, which was almost within his grasp, might well be snatched from him by this coalition so cleverly forged by his enemy in Greece. The rivalry between the Greeks in exile was now to be resolved in battle. Theodore II died in August 1258. His place was usurped by a leading light of the aristocracy of Nicaea, Michael Palaiologos. Michael posed as regent for the lawful heir to the throne, the infant son of Theodore II, John Laskaris. His ambition was stronger than his honesty. He knew what he wanted and before the year was out he was proclaimed and crowned co-emperor, as Michael VIII. He was an experienced soldier

[1] Marino Sanudo Torsello, *Istoria del Regno di Romania*, ed. Hopf, *Chroniques gréco-romanes*, p. 107. Nicol, *Despotate*, i, pp. 169–73; D. J. Geanakoplos, *Emperor Michael Palaeologus and the West 1258–1282* (Cambridge, Mass., 1959), pp. 47–59 (cited hereafter as Geanakoplos, *Emperor Michael*).

and he understood the danger that confronted his empire. He posted
reinforcements to Thessalonica under the command of his brother John
Palaiologos and began to assemble an army large enough to beat back
the presumptuous Despot of Epiros and his foreign allies. The issue was
finally decided in an encounter at Pelagonia in Macedonia in 1259.
Manfred of Sicily sent a contingent of cavalry. William of Villehardouin
brought his own knights and soldiers. The army from Nicaea was united
in purpose and in leadership. Michael of Epiros and his French and German allies fought under separate command and were suspicious of each
other's motives. The coalition collapsed even before the fighting began.
Michael and his army decamped in the night and what battle there was
at Pelagonia was fought between John Palaiologos and the French and
German horsemen. It was an easy victory for the army of Nicaea and
John followed it up by invading Thessaly and Epiros. It was a disaster
for the Despot Michael, though one from which he was quickly to
recover. For the Latin Empire of Constantinople, however, it was the
death knell. William of Villehardouin, the empire's most competent soldier, was taken prisoner near the field of battle and carried away to
Nicaea. The Latins now knew that their days were numbered. They
had often been heartened by the thought that their Greek enemies were
divided. It was no longer the case. They were now at the mercy of the
nearer and the stronger of those enemies, the new Emperor in Nicaea,
who had been crowned as such on 1 January 1259. In desperation they
begged him for a truce of one year. Perhaps if they kept bargaining and
playing for time more help might come from the west.[1]

At the end the only western powers still concerned to save the wreck
of the Latin Empire were the papacy and Venice. Pope Alexander IV
had no help to offer. Even the Venetians were beginning to lose heart.
Business in Constantinople seems to have declined in the prevailing uncer-
tainty about the future. Sanudo records that the Venetians were burdened
with intolerably heavy expenses for the upkeep of the city. Further loans
were negotiated. In 1259 the Doge authorised Marco Gradenigo, the
Podestà, to raise the sum of 3000 *hyperpyra* for the city's defence. In
1260 the Podestà and his councillors borrowed 200 *hyperpyra* from a
Venetian merchant for the same purpose.[2] But the Doge's brave idea

[1] The truce, made in January 1259, is mentioned by George Pachymeres, *Relations historiques*,
ed. A. Failler, trans. V. Laurent, *CFHB*, XXIV/1 (Paris, 1984), ii. 10: 1, pp. 148–9; *DR*,
III, no. 1858. On the battle of Pelagonia, see Nicol, *Despotate*, I, pp. 173–7; Geanakoplos,
Emperor Michael, pp. 59–74; Setton, *Papacy and the Levant*, I, pp. 85–90.

[2] (Sanudo), *Fragmentum*, ed. Hopf, p. 171; ed. Wolff, p. 150; *TTh*, III, no. CCCXXXVIII, pp. 24–
5; document of August 1260 published by Geanakoplos, *Emperor Michael*, Appendix B,
no. 1, pp. 378–9. The merchant, Giovanni Gustoni, was still trying to get his money back
from Venice thirty years later.

of recruiting a permanent garrison of 1000 men to hold Constantinople seems never to have been realised. The Venetian fleet, however, was still a powerful deterrent to any attacker. So long as Venetian ships patrolled the Hellespont and the Bosporos, Michael VIII could hardly fight his way into the city by sea. There were traitors within its walls. But they were not reliable, as Michael discovered when he led an army from Thrace up to the gates in the spring of 1260. The traitor who had promised to let him in failed to appear. The attempt ended in a futile attack on Galata across the Golden Horn; and the Emperor Baldwin seized the occasion to prolong his truce for twelve more months.[1]

About the end of 1260 some messengers from Genoa arrived at the court of Michael VIII. He listened to them with growing interest. In 1258, after bitter warfare in Syria, the Venetians had expelled the Genoese from their commercial quarter in Acre. To have their revenge, the Genoese were prepared to give the emperor the services of their ships to run the Venetians out of Constantinople. If the deal were well done they might hope to be rewarded by inheriting the Venetian monopoly of Byzantine trade. Michael welcomed the offer. It seemed providential. The details were discussed in secret and in March 1261 a draft treaty was drawn up at Nymphaion in Asia Minor.[2] The emperor sent envoys of his own to Genoa; and on 10 July 1261 the treaty was ratified by the Genoese assembly. Its prime purpose was stated to be the making of war on Venice. The Genoese were to put up to fifty ships at the emperor's disposal, though the cost of manning them would be borne by him. In return they would enjoy the privilege of free trade in all parts of his empire as well as self-governing quarters in several towns and islands. They were also to have free access to the ports of the Black Sea which had always been declared out of bounds to Italian ships by earlier emperors and which the Venetians had scarcely begun to explore since 1204. In Constantinople their merchants would be granted all that they had owned before and a large part of the Venetian quarter and its buildings, provided that Genoa rendered immediate and effective support in recovering the city.[3]

Many more concessions were promised in the text of the treaty and its general tone was one of unprecedented generosity on the emperor's part. He needed, or he thought that he needed, the co-operation of a

[1] Akropolites, p. 175; *DR*, III, no. 1885. Geanakoplos, *Emperor Michael*, pp. 75–9.
[2] That the Treaty of Nymphaion was made on the initiative of Genoa and not of the emperor was established by Geanakoplos, *Emperor Michael*, pp. 81–7. On the war between Venice and Genoa that preceded it, see Prawer, *Royaume latin de Jérusalem*, II, pp. 359–73.
[3] *DR*, III, no. 1890. Geanakoplos, *Emperor Michael*, pp. 87–91. On Venetian interest in the Black Sea, see below p. 181 n. 1.

naval power hostile to Venice to achieve his aim. Once master of Constantinople he could reconsider the matter. The Genoese were eager to meet
the provision that they should send immediate support. As soon as the
treaty had been approved they sent out a fleet of sixteen warships. Perhaps
more were to follow. But in the event neither the ships nor the treaty
were necessary. For the city of Constantinople fell to Michael VIII Palaiologos, as some say that it fell to the crusaders fifty-seven years before,
by a concatenation of coincidences. While waiting for his truce with
the Emperor Baldwin to expire in August 1261, Michael sent his general
Alexios Strategopoulos with a small company of men to inspect the
defences of Constantinople. The Latins had long since abandoned their
land outside the walls and made it over to Greek farmers who had free
access to the city. It was from them that Strategopoulos learnt that almost
all of the Latin garrison was at that moment absent. The Podestà, Marco
Gradenigo, had persuaded Baldwin to allow him to take them away
in thirty ships to attack the island of Daphnusia off the Bithynian coast
in the Black Sea. The island belonged to the Empire of Nicaea and it
was the Podestà's view that it would be good for the flagging morale
of the Latins to take some direct action against their Greek enemies,
on however humble a scale. It was a reckless act, for it left the city
almost bereft of able-bodied men, in charge of the feeble Baldwin II,
and open to the plans and plots of any traitors within its walls. It is
tempting to believe that the Emperor Michael or his agents arranged
that the Venetian fleet should be away at the appropriate moment. But
there is no evidence that it was any more than a stroke of good fortune
for his cause. Strategopoulos made the most of it.

The Greeks knew of an underground passage into the city and of a
spot where scaling ladders could safely be erected. Strategopoulos was
cautious by nature; but the opportunity seemed too good to miss. In
the dead of night some of his troops made their way under or over the
land walls, surprised the guard at the Gate of the Fountain, and hacked
it open from inside before the alarm could be sounded. On 25 July 1261
a Greek army marched once more into Constantinople. There was some
fighting in the streets, but by the break of day it was seen that the Greeks
had taken possession of the land walls. As they advanced on the imperial
palace, the Emperor Baldwin escaped to the harbour where he boarded
a Venetian merchant ship and fled to Negroponte. His crown and imperial
regalia were found abandoned in the palace. To forestall the return of
the Venetian fleet and the army from Daphnusia, Strategopoulos was
advised to set fire to the Venetian quarter of the city; and when its owners,
hearing of the disaster, sailed back with the soldiers, they found their
homes and properties in flames and their families crowded on the quays,

like bees smoked out of their hives. All that they could do was to salvage what remained, swarm aboard their ships and sail away. Among them was the Podestà, Gradenigo. His thirty ships made the evacuation possible, though there were other ships in harbour including a huge Sicilian vessel. One account has it that there were 3000 refugees. Some of them lined the decks as they left the Golden Horn in the morning, shouting farewell to the land that they had come to call their own. They made for the Venetian island of Negroponte. But they were short of food and water; the boats were overcrowded; and many died of hunger and thirst before they reached safety.

The Emperor Michael VIII, who was encamped many miles away, at first refused to believe the news. But when a courier arrived bringing the abandoned regalia of Baldwin II he knew it was true. He rejoiced and gave thanks that God had seen fit to deliver Constantinople to him. Three weeks later, on 15 August 1261, Michael entered the city by the Golden Gate and walked in solemn procession, with the icon of the Hodegetria held aloft, along the ancient triumphal way to the cathedral of St Sophia. There, after a service of thanksgiving, he was crowned as emperor for a second time. His infant son Andronikos was proclaimed to be his heir. The legitimate heir, the young John Laskaris, whom Michael had sworn to protect, had been left behind in Nicaea. Within the year he had been blinded and immured in a castle on the Black Sea. Michael VIII Palaiologos, the 'new Constantine' as he liked to be called, hoped that the glory of winning the prize of Constantinople would outshine the darkness of the crime by which he established his power and founded his dynasty. He was wrong. He had many political enemies; and the church never wholly forgave him.[1]

One of his first acts as Emperor of Constantinople was to reward the Genoese for the services which they had promised but never rendered. In accordance with his treaty he made over to them the monastery of Christ Pantokrator which the Venetians had used as their headquarters. They were so thrilled by this token of the humiliation of Venice that they demolished much of the building and sent the stones home to Genoa.[2] The sixteen Genoese ships had presumably reached Constantinople after the event and after the Venetians had fled. But there were Genoese residents in the city on their own account; and there were also

[1] Longnon, L'Empire latin, pp. 226–8; Geanakoplos, Emperor Michael, pp. 92–122; Setton, Papacy and the Levant, I, pp. 92–4.
[2] Annales Ianuenses, ed. C. Imperiale, Fonti per la Storia d'Italia. Scrittori, secoli XII e XIII, IV (Rome, 1926), p. 45. The monastery is described as 'palacium latum et amplum ad formam castri'.

still a few Venetians as well as merchants from Pisa.[1] The loss of Constantinople was a deadly blow to Venice, the end of all that the Doge and the Podestà had laboured to preserve. The shock was aggravated by the new emperor's manifest determination to favour the Genoese. 'The Doge and the commune,' writes Sanudo, 'examined every way and means of recovering the city and the empire.'[2] The Treaty of Nymphaion had assigned to the Genoese quarters and properties not only in Constantinople but also in Thessalonica, Adramyttion, Smyrna and the islands of Crete, Negroponte, Chios, Lesbos and other places. The prime concern of the Doge of Venice was to make certain that his own colonies, particularly Crete and Negroponte, were well prepared against Genoese attack or infiltration. He knew that Genoa had incurred the anger and the anathema of the pope by making friends with Michael Palaiologos and directly or indirectly contributing to the loss of Constantinople. The pope lamented the downfall of the Latin Empire. It had shattered the ideal or the illusion of the unity of Christendom, which the great Innocent III had seen as the good that came out of the evil of the Fourth Crusade. He excommunicated the Genoese for taking the side of the schismatic Greeks who had caused it. The Doge for once saw the pope as his ally in the just and holy war to win back the jewel that had been lost. But first he must see to the protection of what was left of Venetian Romania. As soon as the disastrous news reached him, he sent out a fleet of eighteen warships. Their commander, Marco Michiel, was instructed not to attack Constantinople but merely to defend Venetian possessions elsewhere. The recovery of Constantinople would require more than eighteen ships and it would have to be carefully and patiently planned.[3]

The Genoese seemed reluctant or unable to exploit to the full the opportunities offered to them. There is no proof that they were deterred by the pope's disapproval of them. They may well, however, have been hampered by political troubles and changes of government in their mother city. Large numbers of Genoese ships are said to have been sent to the east but they achieved little. In the summer of 1262 the Doge of Venice ordered another fleet of thirty-seven ships to go and hunt them out. They found sixty of them off Thessalonica; but they were well armed and protected and their captain declined to come out and fight.[4] Not

[1] Pachymeres, ii. 35: 1, pp. 224–7 (*CFHB*); *DR*, III, no. 1898. Geanakoplos, *Emperor Michael*, pp. 131–5.
[2] (Sanudo), *Fragmentum*, ed. Hopf, p. 173; ed. Wolff, p. 152.
[3] Martin da Canal, pt ii, c. xxv: p. 180.
[4] Martin da Canal, pt ii, c. xxvi: pp. 180–2; Dandolo, p. 311. Geanakoplos, *Emperor Michael*, pp. 147–9.

all of the sixty were Genoese. The new Byzantine Emperor had thought
it vital to rebuild an imperial fleet of his own. He was convinced that
he could never securely hold Constantinople unless he had complete
control of the sea. It was not enough to depend on the Genoese to keep
the Venetians at bay. A number of skirmishes in Byzantine waters are
reported in the years immediately after 1261, some not far from Constantinople. But the first real naval battle was not fought until the summer
of 1263, when a Venetian fleet of thirty-two ships commanded by Giberto
Dandolo intercepted thirty-eight Byzantine and Genoese warships making south for the Morea. The battle took place off the island of Spetsai
(Settepozzi) near Hydra. The Genoese suffered many casualties before
they made their escape.[1]

It was a minor engagement but it had important consequences. For
it undermined the emperor's confidence in his friends from Genoa, the
wages of whose sailors he was committed to paying. Shortly after the
battle at Spetsai he discharged about sixty Genoese ships and ordered
them to go home. The pope was delighted at the news and withdrew
the interdict that he had imposed on the city of Genoa. But it was not
the pope who caused the final rupture between the emperor and his
allies. Capitalising on the generous terms of the Treaty of Nymphaion,
Genoese merchants and adventurers had come to settle in Constantinople
in growing numbers. As in the twelfth century, they made themselves
unpopular by their arrogance and avarice. They had begun to explore
and exploit the markets of the Black Sea where no Italian merchants
had been allowed to penetrate before. They enjoyed trade concessions
which made it impossible for the Greeks to compete with them. They
were becoming an embarrassment to the emperor. His trust in them
was finally shattered when he found that their Podestà in Constantinople
was alleged to be organising a conspiracy to hand the city over to the
Latins and that he was in negotiation with King Manfred of Sicily. When
summoned to the palace the Podestà made a full confession of his guilt.
The emperor now felt free to rid himself of the allies on whom he had
pinned such hopes. He commanded that all Genoese citizens were to
leave Constantinople at once and to move their goods and chattels to
Herakleia on the Thracian side of the Sea of Marmora. His alliance with
them was not formally renounced. But he was firm. He refused to listen
to the requests of ambassadors sent posthaste from Genoa proposing
that their colony might move instead to Galata across the Golden Horn
from Constantinople.[2]

---

[1] Matin da Canal, pt ii, cc. xxx–xxxv: pp. 186–92; *Annales Ianuenses*, iv, pp. 51–2; Dandolo,
pp. 311–12. Geanakoplos, *Emperor Michael*, pp. 149–54.
[2] Geanakoplos, *Emperor Michael*, pp. 161–71.

Michael VIII was an accomplished diplomat even by Byzantine imperial standards. For one brought up in the microcosm of the empire in
exile, he had an astonishing grasp of the power structure of the wider
world. In the very first year of his reign in Constantinople he made
his presence known by embassies and letters to the pope, to the Genoese,
to the French prince and barons of Achaia, to the Mongol Khan of the
Golden Horde and to the Sultan of Egypt. Four years went by, however,
before he made contact with Venice. The Genoese seemed to have failed
him. He would therefore try on his own account to come to some arrangement with their enemies, at least to propose an end to the state of war
prevailing between Byzantium and Venice. It proved harder than he
expected. In 1265 he released a noble Venetian, Enrico Trevisano, from
prison and sent him to Venice with a secret message for the Doge. The
Doge, Reniero Zeno, sent him back to Constantinople with another
envoy. They were soon followed by a more formal delegation led by
Jacopo Dolfin and Jacopo Contarini; and on 18 June 1265 the draft
of a treaty was drawn up for ratification by the Doge and his council.
The emperor may have thought that its terms were generous. He offered
new quarters and new concessions to Venetian settlers in Constantinople
and elsewhere, including Thessalonica, Adramyttion and Smyrna. In the
capital they would have the right to be administered by their own baillie
(bajulus) or rector. They were also encouraged to settle where they
pleased in the Black Sea, a privilege first formally accorded to the
Genoese.[1] The emperor promised to order the Genoese to leave his
empire altogether and to make no further treaty with them without the
consent of Venice. In return the Venetians would undertake not to participate in any western attack on Constantinople and to help defend the
city, if necessary, against such an attack if made by a power friendly
to Venice. The Venetians would keep possession of Crete and of the
ports of Modon and Coron in the Morea, as well as their properties
in Negroponte; though here the emperor reserved the right to make
war on the Lombard barons and to retain access to the Venetian colony
at Halmyros for that purpose. The islands in the Aegean Sea and the
Archipelago, however, which were not directly administered from

---

[1] The Venetians had made some tentative forays into the Black Sea, especially in the Crimea,
between 1204 and 1261. Morozzo–Lombardo, II, nos. 478–9 (May 1206), 662 (March 1232).
See Marie Nystazopoulou-Pélékides, 'Venise et la Mer Noire du xiᵉ au xvᵉ siècle', *Thesaurismata*, VII (1970), 15–51, especially 22–3; F. Thiriet, 'Les Vénitiens en Mer Noire: organisation
et trafics (xiiiᵉ–xvᵉ siècles)', *Archeion Pontou*, XXXV (1979), 38–53; M. E. Martin, 'The first
Venetians in the Black Sea', *Archeion Pontou*, XXXV (1979), 111–22. Dandolo (pp. 33, 308)
records the capture of Mesembria on the Black Sea coast by a fleet of ten Venetian ships
in 1257.

Venice, must revert to Byzantine rule along with all the other places acquired by citizens of Venice as a result of the Fourth Crusade.[1]

The draft was duly taken to Venice for approval and ratification. The Doge and his councillors rejected it. They felt that their ambassadors had either exceeded their orders or been hoodwinked by the crafty emperor. The Doge wanted all or nothing. It must have been a painful decision to make when faced with the prospect of an open door to the market of Constantinople and of building afresh the greatest commercial colony that Venice had ever had. But Reniero Zeno was ambitious. He was proud still to style himself Lord of one-quarter and one-eighth of the Empire of Romania.[2] He would not bow to a Greek emperor who addressed him as Doge of Venice and Lord of Croatia, Dalmatia 'and the other places and islands subject to his authority'. He would not accept that emperor's charity and put his signature to a document that was all too reminiscent of the treaties imposed upon Venice by Byzantium in an earlier age. There were other ways of making the Venetian presence felt, of recreating the Venetian Empire of Romania in all its unfettered glory. For already plans were being made in the western world to repair the damage done in 1261 and to put the Latin Emperor Baldwin II back on his throne in Constantinople. The Doge could afford to wait to see how those plans matured and, if the moment came, to ride to Byzantium on the wave of another Fourth Crusade.

Reniero Zeno was Doge at a particularly proud moment in the history of Venice. It was during his reign that the Piazza San Marco and the façade of the church overlooking it took on their present form. The work of enlarging the piazza and of reconstructing and embellishing the church had begun almost a century before, under Sebastiano Ziani. But the Fourth Crusade had provided the impetus and much of the wealth to bring it to its brilliant conclusion. The Venetians lost their hold on Constantinople in 1261; but by then they had carried off much of its moveable property with them to Venice. In Reniero Zeno's time no Venetian walking in the centre of his city could fail to be aware of Byzantium. It was like a museum of Byzantine artefacts and souvenirs. The Piazza had been paved with red bricks set in herring-bone pattern. Dominating the façade of St Mark's were the four gilded bronze horses, the first and the grandest of the secular trophies brought from Constantinople

---

[1] Martin da Canal, pt II, cc. XXXVII, CV–CVI: pp. 194, 266–8; Dandolo, p. 313. The Greek and Latin texts of the treaty are in *TTh*, III, no. CCCV, pp. 62–89; Greek text only in *MM*, III, pp. 76–84; *DR*, III, no. 1934. Thiriet, *Romanie vénitienne*, pp. 147–9; Geanakoplos, *Emperor Michael*, pp. 182–5.

[2] In his letter to Pope Urban IV in September 1264 he styles himself: 'Raynerius Zeno, Venetiarum, Dalmatiae atque Croatiae Dux, dominus quartae partis et dimidiae totius Imperii Romaniae'. *TTh*, III, no. CCCL, p. 56.

by the Doge Enrico Dandolo, or rather transported at his command
on a Venetian ship commanded by Domenico Morosini. The story was
told that a foot was detached from one of the horses and that it remained
in the possession of the Morosini family. No one knew quite what to
do with them since the great Dandolo never came home to tell them.
For about fifty years they were stored, not very securely, in the Arsenal,
until Reniero Zeno had them placed on the newly built loggia above
the entrance to St Mark's like trophies on a triumphal arch.[1]

Many other spoils and trophies of the just war of the Fourth Crusade
were displayed on or around St Mark's. Quantities of marble of different
colours and of columns, especially of porphyry, imported from Constantinople added to the grandeur of the reconstructed church. Such was
their influence on Venetian art and taste at the time that it is now difficult
to tell which of the column capitals came from Constantinople and which
were local work.[2] The two granite columns of St Mark and St Theodore
overlooking the quay, which may have come from Alexandria, were
earlier acquisitions, placed where they now stand in 1172; though the
statue of St Theodore with his dragon was not put on its column until
1329. But the two ornamental pillars called after St John of Acre, which
stand outside the Porta della Carta, were shipped from Constantinople
after 1204. They were part of a huge haul of architectural bits and pieces
from the ruined church of St Polyeuktos near the Holy Apostles. The
porphyry monument of the tetrarchs saluting each other, fitted on to
a corner of St Mark's, was another of the spoils of war recycled. The
church was transformed inside and out. It became a monument to Venetian taste for Byzantine art, for the trophies brought from Constantinople
were not a random collection. About one-third of the loot amassed in
1204 went to the Venetians. But they were selective, not indiscriminately
greedy or destructive like the crusaders. The interior of St Mark's displayed their selectivity. The Pala d'Oro, the altar piece, was enlarged
and enriched by command of Dandolo's successor, the Doge Pietro Ziani,
with precious stones and enamels from churches in Constantinople. The
work was supervised by the procurator of the cathedral in 1209, Angelo
Falier, who seems to have taken the occasion to remove an imperial
portrait and replace it by a picture of his own distinguished ancestor,
Ordelafo Falier, dressed up like an emperor.[3] Many years later, in 1438,

---

[1] Marino Sanudo, *Vitae Ducum Venetorum*, col. 534. The fullest account in English is: *The
Horses of San Marco Venice*, translated by John and Valerie Wilton-Ely, Procuratorio di
San Marco, and Olivetti (Milan and London, 1979).

[2] F. W. Deichmann, *Corpus der Kapitelle der Kirche von San Marco zu Venedig* (Wiesbaden,
1981).

[3] On the Pala d'Oro, see above pp. 65–7 and references.

the Greek Patriarch of Constantinople visited Venice with the Emperor John VIII. He claimed to recognise that some of the enamel icons in the Pala d'Oro had come not from St Sophia, as had been supposed, but from the monastery church of Christ Pantokrator in Constantinople, which the Venetians had used as their headquarters during the Latin regime.[1] Many of the treasures of that church came to Venice at the end of that regime in 1261. The Latin Patriarch Pantaleone Giustiniani before he fled gathered up what he could in the way of jewels and valuables, some of which were added to the riches of the Pala d'Oro.[2]

The smaller items of loot were housed in the Treasury of St Mark's, among them what might be called the spiritual spoils of a holy war. The Venetians had always been devoted collectors of holy relics. The capture of Constantinople enabled them to add some very substantial and particularly sacred and efficacious pieces to their collection. St Mark's, and with it the city of Venice, became as a consequence more than ever a centre of pilgrimage.[3] The Doge Dandolo had chosen the four horses as his own. He also took first pick of the holiest relics. He and his officials from Venice had the advantage of being able to read the Greek inscriptions on reliquaries that they found in Byzantine churches. They were thus able to pick and choose with more perception than the crusaders. They were also more familiar with Byzantine saints and martyrologies.[4] Dandolo chose for himself and his city a phial containing drops of the blood of the Saviour; the cross encased in gold which Constantine the Great had taken into battle with him; a part of the head of St John the Baptist; and an arm of St George. These he ordered to be placed in St Mark's. One of the nails from the Cross, taken from

---

[1] Sylvester Syropoulos, ed. V. Laurent, Les 'Mémoires' du Grand Ecclésiarque de l'Eglise de Constantinople Sylvestre Syropoulos sur le Concile de Florence (1438–1439) (Paris, 1971), pp. 222–4, 628.

[2] Sanudo, Vitae Ducum Venetorum, col. 560.

[3] On the Treasury, see A. Pasini, Il Tesoro di San Marco a Venezia (Venice, 1885–6); R. Gallo, Il Tesoro di San Marco e la sua storia, Civiltà Veneziana, Saggi, 16 (Venice–Florence, 1967) (which contains, pp. 273–402, all the known inventories of the Treasury's contents from 1283 to 1845); The Treasury of San Marco, (cited above, p. 67 n. 1). The standard works on the relics removed from Constantinople in and after 1204 are: P. E. D. Riant, Des Dépouilles religieuses, and Riant, Exuviae Sacrae, I–II, of which Vol. II gives the fullest lists of relics taken to Venice, mainly derived from Dandolo, pp. 261–74. Sanudo, Vite dei Dogi, pp. 76–85, lists all the corpi santi and the churches in which they were to be found in Venice in his day. On the Byzantine relics in St Mark's, not all of which were acquired in 1204, see A. Frolow, 'Notes sur les reliques et les reliquaires byzantins de Saint-Marc de Venise', Deltion of the Christian Archaeological Society of Athens, IV/4 (1964–5), 205–26. The problem of the provenance of the icon of the Virgin Nikopoia in St Mark's, apparently first identified as such in the seventeenth century, is discussed by Gallo, Il Tesoro, pp. 133–55. On the collecting of relics from Constantinople in general, see Godfrey, 1204, pp. 149–54.

[4] Riant, Des Dépouilles religieuses, p. 52.

the monastery of Christ Pantepoptes, was also removed to St Mark's. The body of St Lucia was taken to the Monastery of San Giorgio Maggiore. That of St Agatha was generously given to some pilgrims from Sicily who happened to be in Constantinople. The church of the Holy Apostles, the Byzantine prototype of St Mark's, was especially productive of treasures, if one can believe a seventeenth-century account of the depredation of 1204.[1] The Venetians took from it a fragment of the pillar of the Flagellation of Christ, icons and statues and jewels for the Pala d'Oro, as well as secular objects such as imperial crowns and breastplates, jasper cups and vases.[2]

These were all counted as part of the official spoils that were taken to Venice in or just after 1204. But in the course of the Latin occupation many more relics were removed from Constantinople through the private enterprise of individuals. Some of them seem to have been rendered gullible by their credulous piety. One Aicardo, for example, is said to have secretly purloined the body of St Helena from the monastery of that name in 1211. There is, however, no Byzantine evidence for the existence of this monastery; and the tomb if not the body of St Helena, mother of Constantine, was still to be seen in the church of the Holy Apostles in the fifteenth century. The body of St Anastasios, which Heraclius had brought from Persia, was taken by one Valaresso about 1204 and enshrined in the church of the Holy Trinity in Venice.[3] Two Venetian citizens, Andrea Balduino and Angelo Drusiaco, managed 'with some difficulty' to carry away the body of St Symeon the Prophet from the church of the Virgin near St Sophia. In 1214 Roaldo, prior of the abbey of St Daniel in Venice, collected the body of a third-century martyr, John. In 1222 Paul, abbot of San Giorgio Maggiore, obtained permission from the Podestà, Marino Storlato, to take away from the monastery of Christ Pantepoptes the body of St Paul who had been martyred under the iconoclast Emperor Constantine V. The monastery had been made over to the Benedictines of San Giorgio and Paul had been its first Latin prior.[4]

A few years later one Giovanni de Bora acquired the body of the Blessed Marina the Virgin by bribing and entreating the monks of a

---

[1] Paulus Rhamnusius, *De Bello Constantinopolitano*, Editio altera (Venice, 1634), pp. 129–34.
[2] Part of the Flagellation pillar had found its way to Venice in 1123, according to Pasini, *Il Tesoro*, p. 31. But this may be a confusion with the stone on which Christ sat. Dandolo, p. 234; and see above, p. 80 n. 1. The columns said to have been taken to Venice from the church of the Anastasis or Resurrection in Constantinople (Riant, *Des Dépouilles religieuses*, p. 178) seem in fact to have been removed to adorn the altar of St Sophia. Letters of Innocent III, xi. 76: *MPL*, ccxv, col. 1392.
[3] Dandolo, p. 285. Cf. Janin, *Géographie ecclésiastique*, p. 109.
[4] Dandolo, pp. 287, 289. Janin, *Géographie ecclésiastique*, p. 514.

monastery outside Constantinople. In 1239 Jacopo Lanzolo obtained the body of St Paul the first hermit from the then Latin abbot and monks of the monastery of the Peribleptos. The hermit's head had already gone to Rome; but his body was laid in the church of San Giuliano in Venice.[1] In 1246 the monastery of San Giorgio Maggiore was further enriched when the body of St Eutychios was brought from Constantinople. In 1257 Jacopo Dauro with ten galleys raided the town of Mesembria on the Black Sea coast and stole from its church of St Sophia the headless body of St Theodore the Martyr. Theodore, having killed a dragon, had been decapitated by the pagan Emperor Licinius. Dauro's relative Marco later took the body to Venice and placed it in the church of the Saviour.[2] Later still Theodore and his dragon were commemorated by the statue placed on top of his column in Venice. Lastly, an early four-teenth-century writer tells of the translation to Venice by one Rafaele Basilio in 1258 of the body of St Barbara – though which St Barbara it is hard to know; for the relics of one St Barbara had been given as a wedding present to Giovanni Orseolo by the Emperor Basil II in 1004.[3]

The Venetians were by no means alone in the business of disseminating the holy relics of Constantinople. The French did very well out of it, and almost every cathedral and abbey in western Europe gained some-thing. The Crown of Thorns was a great prize for Paris. But the other instruments of Christ's Passion were spirited away to other places in less sordid circumstances. Several sources testify to the fact that the Trea-sury of St Mark was gutted by fire in 1231. It is impossible to know what or how much was lost. The earliest known inventory was not made until 1283. The sources agree that the most holy of the relics, the wood of the Cross, the phial of the Saviour's blood and the head of St John the Baptist, were miraculously spared by the flames.[4] None of them seems to suggest, however, that this miracle was wrought because of God's special care for the city of Venice. The Venetians combined realism with their religiosity to a remarkable degree, just as they combined the practical with the ideal in their art and architecture. Reniero Zeno, who was Doge thirty years after the fire, at the time when the Greeks recap-tured Constantinople, thought more about the future than about the past. God had spared the most sacred relics in the Treasury. But God

---

[1] Dandolo, pp. 292, 297. Riant, *Exuviae sacrae*, I, pp. 147–8. Janin, *Géographie ecclésiastique*, p. 218.

[2] Dandolo, pp. 33, 308.

[3] The account of the translation of St Barbara in 1258, written by Pietro Calo (died 1310), is printed in Riant, *Exuviae sacrae*, I, pp. 182–3. For the other St Barbara, see above, p. 46.

[4] Dandolo, p. 292.

helps those who help themselves. There were plenty more treasures, both real and religious, to be acquired from Byzantium. Reniero Zeno mourned the loss of trade and profit more than he mourned the loss of relics. He looked for the best way of getting them back.

11

BYZANTIUM, VENICE AND
THE ANGEVIN THREAT

WHEN turned out of Constantinople in 1261, the Latin Emperor Baldwin
II with the Venetian Podestà had sailed to Negroponte. In Greece he
rewarded the homage and sympathy of the French lords of Thebes and
Athens by investing them with empty titles. The French Prince of Achaia,
William of Villehardouin, could not receive his emperor, for he was
a prisoner in Constantinople. From Greece Baldwin sailed on to Italy
and landed in Apulia, where he was warmly greeted by King Manfred
of Sicily. Manfred persuaded him to go to see the pope at his palace
at Viterbo. Pope Urban IV, elected in August 1261, had been stunned
by the news from Constantinople. It was a fearful blow to Christendom.
He seems first to have heard it from a Venetian delegation that had come
to congratulate him on his appointment.[1] His immediate reaction had
been to authorise a crusade against the usurper and schismatic Michael
Palaiologos 'who calls himself Emperor of the Greeks'. The Venetians
were at first fully in accord with this plan. They promised to provide
a fleet. The crusade was preached and funds were collected in France,
Castile and England. But the pope's hands were tied by events in Italy.
The man who saw himself as leader of a crusade to Constantinople was
Manfred of Sicily, who had sent Baldwin to see the pope. Manfred's
kingdom was well situated for an invasion of Byzantine territory. He
already owned bases on the coast of Albania and northern Greece. He
was also a son-in-law of the Despot of Epiros who still had his own
designs on Constantinople and who, like the pope, regarded Michael
VIII as a usurper. But the pope could never bring himself to nominate
Manfred, the rebellious and excommunicated bastard son of the loath-
some Hohenstaufen Frederick II, as the man to right the wrongs done
to Christendom. It was in vain that Baldwin tried to mediate between
Manfred and the pope. Urban IV could not and would not commit himself

---

[1] Dandolo, p. 311.

to a crusade for the recovery of Constantinople until he had disposed of the enemy at his doorstep.[1]

He found the champion of his cause in Charles, Count of Anjou, brother of Louis IX of France. Charles was ready and willing to fight a just and holy war against Manfred and, with God's help, to make himself King of Naples and Sicily. Pope Urban IV did not live to see the outcome. It was his successor, Clement IV, who received the glad tidings that Manfred had been killed in battle at Benevento in 1266 and that the very last of the Hohenstaufen 'brood of vipers' had been defeated at Tagliacozzo two years later. Charles of Anjou had done what was asked of him. He at once inherited Manfred's kingdom and with it the ambition to conquer Byzantium which had spurred so many of the rulers of southern Italy in the past. His agents quickly occupied the ports and islands across the water in Greece, which Manfred had acquired. By January 1267 Corfu was in Angevin hands. In May of that year, at the pope's palace at Viterbo, plans were formally drawn up for the restoration of the Latin Empire of Constantinople. The principal contracting parties were Charles of Anjou and the Latin Emperor Baldwin II. Baldwin's son Philip was to marry Charles's daughter. One of Charles's sons was to marry the daughter of William of Villehardouin, Prince of Achaia, who had ransomed himself from Byzantine captivity in 1261. William would acknowledge Charles as suzerain of his principality; and Charles promised to prepare an army of 2000 knights within six or seven years for the 'sacred task' of wresting Constantinople from the schismatic Greeks and restoring it to the Holy Roman Church. The professed and immediate object of the treaty of Viterbo in May 1267 was the reinstatement of Baldwin II on his throne in Constantinople. But it was plain to see that the objective in the longer term was to secure the inheritance to that throne and to the Latin Empire for the heirs of Charles of Anjou.[2]

Two years earlier, in his proposed truce with Venice, the Emperor Michael VIII had listed by name those western powers who were manifestly hostile to him. They were: the pope, the King of France, the King of Sicily (Manfred), the King of Castile, the King of England, the King of Aragon, the brother of the King of France, the Count Charles (of Anjou), and the Communes of Genoa, Pisa and Ancona. Against all or any of these he had solicited the alliance of Venice.[3] At the time, the Doge Reniero Zeno may have hoped that he would be invited to

---

[1] Geanakoplos, *Emperor Michael*, pp. 139–43; Setton, *Papacy and the Levant*, I, pp. 94–7.

[2] S. Runciman, *The Sicilian Vespers* (Cambridge, 1958), pp. 65–138; Geanakoplos, *Emperor Michael*, pp. 192–200; D. M. Nicol, *The Last Centuries of Byzantium, 1261–1453* (London, 1972), pp. 53–5; Setton, *The Papacy and the Levant*, I, pp. 103–5.

[3] *TTh*, III, pp. 67, 79.

play a major part in any scheme being hatched to restore the Latin Empire. He was disappointed. The treaties of Viterbo made only one mention of Venice. It was to the effect that, if all went well, the Venetians would be guaranteed all their former privileges in Constantinople. The Doge was alarmed also by the rapid annexation of Corfu and the Albanian coastline by the new French King of Sicily. For centuries the Venetians had dreaded the prospect of their access to the Mediterranean being blocked by a hostile power across the Adriatic. Things were not turning out the way the Doge had hoped. Then in the summer of 1267 the Emperor Michael sent an embassy to Genoa. Since the Venetians appeared reluctant to accept his terms, he would offer a new deal to their enemies, the Genoese. It was not long since he had ordered them all to leave Constantinople and move to Herakleia. He had refused to entertain their suggestion that they would be happier to settle in Galata or Pera across the Golden Horn. In 1267 he changed his mind. The Genoese were now to be granted the district of Galata as their place of residence and their commercial quarter. There were certain restrictions on the offer. Galata had been a fortified suburb of Constantinople. The crusaders had used it as such in 1203. Its fortification walls must be dismantled. In addition, the Genoese permitted to settle there must consider themselves as the emperor's vassals. Their Podestà must make humble obeisance when summoned to court. Their ships must salute when sailing past the imperial palace at Blachernai.[1] No such humiliating conditions had ever been imposed on other Italian communities. But the arrangement ensured that the Genoese would no longer reside in Constantinople. They were in a special category of resident aliens. They had proved provocative and even seditious. They were now relegated to a suburb across the water where their behaviour would not offend the peace-loving Byzantines of the capital city or annoy the smaller Italian colonies of Venetians and Pisans who continued to live there.

The Genoese did not hesitate to accept the offer. However humiliating its terms it gave them legal possession of a plot of land to call their own within the harbour of Constantinople. The Doge of Venice, however, must have reflected that the wily Emperor Michael had indeed hoodwinked and outwitted him. It was time for Reniero Zeno to sink his pride. On 1 November 1267, shortly after Michael's negotiations with Genoa, he sent two envoys, Marco Bembo and Pietro Zeno, to Constantinople to reopen discussions. This time he was more careful

---

[1] *Annales Ianuenses*, IV, pp. 107–8; Pachymeres, ii. 35; v. 30: I, pp. 224–7; II, p. 537 (*CFHB*); Nikephoros Gregoras, *Byzantina Historia*, ed. L. Schopen, *CSHB* (1829–55), iv. 5: I, p. 97. Pseudo-Kodinos, *De Officiis*, ed. J. Verpeaux, *Traité des Offices* (Paris, 1966), pp. 234–6, describes the prescribed obeisance of the Genoese. Geanakoplos, *Emperor Michael*, pp. 206–9.

about his etiquette. In 1265 he had addressed Michael VIII as 'Emperor of the Greeks'. In 1267 he addressed him as 'Emperor of the Romans' and 'The New Constantine', a title which Michael was very fond of.[1] Flattery has its uses; but the emperor was not to be hurried. He knew that he could now play off the Genoese against the Venetians and that he need not be so generous to them as he had been two years before. A treaty was in due course agreed and signed in Constantinople on 4 April 1268.

The proposed treaty of 1265, whose terms the Doge had rejected, had been technically a truce in the war between Byzantium and Venice. But it had stipulated no time limit. The truce or treaty of 1268 was limited to a period of five years. Each party swore not to make alliance with the enemies of the other; and the Venetians had to promise that they would not transport the troops of any other power against the empire. All Greeks held prisoners during the state of war between the two parties must be released and allowed to stay where they were or to go with their families wherever they wished on Byzantine territory. The emperor undertook to leave the Venetians in undisturbed possession of Crete, Coron and Modon and to respect their treaty with the Prince of Achaia over the island of Negroponte. The same would apply to the islands of the Archipelago, at least to those from which the Doge and Commune of Venice derived revenue. The emperor would not be bound to grant the Venetians permanent quarters in Constantinople or elsewhere. Those coming to his empire would, however, be able to rent houses, bakeries and baths wherever it suited them on fixed terms. In such places they could employ their own weights and measures, have their own churches and priests and baptise their offspring according to their own rite.

The obligation to pay rent for their establishments must have seemed irksome, even though Venetian merchants were to retain their privilege of trading without payment of taxes. The obligations laid on them with respect to the Genoese must have been still more annoying. In 1265 the emperor had offered to expel the Genoese. Now they were to remain installed in their new quarters in Galata, on the understanding that they and the Venetians would refrain from fighting out their rivalry in Byzantine waters, between Abydos at the entrance to the Hellespont and the Black Sea. If this rule were broken by either side, the emperor would act as arbiter in the dispute. Other clauses in the treaty dealt with legal, judicial and commercial matters. A Venetian accused of a crime against a Greek was to be judged by his own baillie or rector in Constantinople.

---

[1] *TTh*, III, no. CCCLVI, pp. 89–90; cf. pp. 88, 93.

Cases of homicide, however, would be brought before the emperor. The baillie would also, in most cases, be empowered to dispose of the property of Venetians who died on Byzantine territory. Those suffering shipwreck would receive every assistance from the emperor's men. Venetian ships were permitted freely to purchase grain in the empire and to export it wherever they wished, except to lands hostile to the emperor, so long as its price held at fifty *hyperpyra* per 100 *modioi* (bushels). If the price increased they could export it only under licence. The emperor promised to set free all Venetians imprisoned or detained anywhere in his empire and to prohibit the manufacture of weapons for use against the Venetians. Finally, the baillie was to be held responsible for the nefarious activities of any Venetian pirates, to bring them to trial and to compensate their victims; though this ruling would not apply to the Venetians in the islands who were not subject to the authority of the Doge and Commune of Venice. Nothing was said about the far more nefarious activities of Greek pirates in the Aegean and Ionian Seas, of which Venice had cause to complain not many years later.[1]

The text of the treaty was ratified and adopted by the Doge Reniero Zeno in Venice on 30 June 1268. He died a few days later. His grateful people gave him a sumptuous funeral. He had done much to glorify and adorn their city. He had done his best to revive their commercial empire in Romania; and perhaps the treaty that he signed before his death, though superficially less favourable to Venice than that proposed three years before, was set down in a contractual form that would be more legally binding and harder to evade or circumvent. Time was to prove that this document, ostensibly no more than a truce for a period of five years, was to be the basis of the new and the most long-lasting chapter in relations between Byzantium and Venice. The Emperor Michael made sure that it would not die with the death of Reniero Zeno. He sent ambassadors to Venice in July to ask the new Doge, Lorenzo Tiepolo, to confirm it without delay.[2] Michael had indeed reason to think that he had gained the advantage in his diplomatic dealings with the warring Italian republics. The Venetians were henceforth precluded, at least for five years, from giving aid to those in Italy who had pledged themselves to restoring the Latin Empire. They were forbidden even to transport troops. They had solemnly agreed to these restrictions, even though the Genoese, far from being expelled, were to be their neighbours in Constantinople. The emperor had wisely insisted that they must not

---

[1] Latin text in *TTh*, III, no. CCCLVIII, pp. 92–100; *DR*, III, no. 1960. Heyd, *Commerce*, I, pp. 432–3; Geanakoplos, *Emperor Michael*, pp. 214–16.

[2] Confirmation by Lorenzo Tiepolo on 30 July 1268: *TTh*, III, no. CCCLIX, pp. 101–2.

fight out their battle with Genoa in Byzantine waters. One salutary effect of his diplomacy was the abatement of that battle. In August 1270 Venice and Genoa signed a truce of five years. Twenty years were in fact to elapse before they went to war again.[1]

None the less, it was hard for the Venetians to face the new realities of the situation in Romania. Martin da Canal has left a long and vivid eye-witness account of the festivities and ceremonies that attended the election of the new Doge, Lorenzo Tiepolo, son of the famous Giacomo, in July 1268. He was the first to be elected according to a new and highly intricate procedure devised to ensure that the Doge should be above suspicion. When the voting had taken its tortuous course and the successful candidate's name had been announced the ceremonies began. The fleet sailed past the palace followed by ships from all the islands in the lagoons. A long and colourful procession of the guilds of the city's craftsmen then came on foot to salute the new Doge and his wife. First came the locksmiths, then the furriers and skinners, the weavers, the tailors, the cobblers, the haberdashers, and the barbers led by two armed knights on horseback, the glassblowers and the master goldsmiths glittering in their finery of gold brocade and jewels. It was a glorious affirmation of the prosperity and confidence of Venice. Constantinople, the source of much of the wealth on display, had fallen into the hands of the Greeks. The Doge's people were confident that this was a temporary misfortune. One way or another they would be back in the Queen of Cities. They hailed Lorenzo Tiepolo not merely as Doge of Venice, of Dalmatia and Croatia, but also as Lord of one-quarter and one-half of a quarter of the whole Empire of Romania.[2]

For the time being the Venetians cautiously decided that the surest hope of giving substance to the Doge's title lay in observing their treaty with the Byzantine Emperor. They politely declined to be associated with the more direct method of conquest being ever more loudly advocated by Charles of Anjou. In September 1269 Charles sent two envoys to the Doge appealing to him to join in the holy war to right the wrongs that the Greeks had done to the Church and to Baldwin, Emperor of Romania, and William, Prince of Achaia. Pointed reference was made to the rights and privileges which Venice had enjoyed and ought still to have in the empire. The Doge was not impressed. He sent the envoys away with the excuse that he could not commit himself to war with

[1] Thiriet, *Romanie vénitienne*, p. 150.
[2] Martin da Canal, pt ii, cc. CVIII–CXXXIV: pp. 270–304. The Doge's full title is given twice: cc. CXII, CXV: pp. 280, 284.

the Byzantine Emperor until their five-year truce had expired.[1] The truth was that Charles's activities in the Adriatic and in northern Italy were causing much concern in Venice. Charles could not wait, however. At Viterbo in 1267 he had declared that he would mount his invasion of Byzantium within seven years at most. The Emperor Michael employed all his diplomatic ingenuity to avert the threat of this catastrophe. He concentrated particularly on the papacy, rightly assuming that only the pope could translate an act of aggression into a holy war or a crusade. He wrote to Pope Clement IV urging him to restrain the King of Sicily from attacking fellow Christians. Clement had grave doubts as to whether the Greeks were truly Christians. He suggested that they should give some proof of this by returning to the fold of the Church of Rome. He spelt out to the emperor in great detail the terms on which this most desirable union of Christendom could be effected. If the terms were not acceptable to the Greeks, then the unity of Christendom, so pleasing in the sight of God, would have to be accomplished by force. It was not by chance that the treaty of Viterbo was arranged and signed in the pope's palace. It was clear that the restoration of Baldwin II to his lost throne was also pleasing in the sight of God and that God's agents for this purpose were Charles, King of Sicily, and William, Prince of Achaia.[2]

For a few years Charles's attention was diverted by other adventures. His saintly brother, Louis IX of France, persuaded him to postpone his plans in Europe and to join him in a crusade against the infidel in North Africa. It was there, at Carthage, that Louis died in August 1270. Six months later Charles was back in Italy, ready to resume preparations for his crusade against Byzantium. In 1271 he added the strategic port of Durazzo to his possessions across the water. The city had been devastated by earthquake and its Byzantine garrison had perished or fled. The local Albanians proclaimed Charles as their king.[3] He was able to ship greater and greater quantities of arms and men over the sea to establish the bridgehead for his march across the mountains to Thessalonica and Constantinople. In the same year 1271, after a long interregnum, Gregory X was elected pope. The Emperor Michael, now seriously alarmed at the build up of enemy forces on his western frontier, at once reopened negotiations on the union of the churches. He could see no

[1] G. del Giudice, *Codice diplomatico del regno di Carlo I.° e II.° d'Angiò*, 1 (Naples, 1863), pp. 300–1. D. A. Zakythenos, *Le Despotat grec de Morée*, édition revue et augmentée par Chrysa Maltézou, 1 (London, 1975), pp. 47–8; Geanakoplos, *Emperor Michael*, pp. 221–2.
[2] Geanakoplos, *Emperor Michael*, pp. 200–6.
[3] Nicol, *The Despotate of Epiros 1267–1479* (Cambridge, 1984) (hereafter *Despotate of Epiros*, II), pp. 14–15.

other way to prevent the invasion of his empire being sanctioned as a crusade. Gregory X was more sympathetic than Clement IV, but his terms were the same. The emperor and his church and people must humbly confess the error of their ways and return to the fold of Rome, outside of which there was no salvation. He invited Michael to come or to send representatives to a council which he was planning to convene at Lyons in 1274. There they could make their submission, abjure their errors and be received back into the family of Christendom. They would then be assured of the pope's protection against their enemies, among them Charles of Anjou.[1]

By 1272 Charles was already lord of the French colonies in Greece; he was King of Albania; and he had made alliances with the rulers of Serbia and Bulgaria. He was keenly aware that the Byzantine Emperor was playing on the sympathy of the pope and that if the Greek Church submitted to Rome the just cause for his expedition to Constantinople would be called in question. Time was running out. If he could win the Venetians to his side he might achieve his aim more quickly. Their truce with Byzantium was due to expire in 1273. The pope repeatedly warned them against renewing or extending it; the Byzantine Emperor was still in schism. The Doge, however, preferred to make his own decisions. His help was much sought after. At the end of 1272 he found himself playing host to ambassadors from Charles of Anjou, from the Latin Emperor Baldwin and from Constantinople. The Byzantine envoys had brought with them 500 Venetian prisoners of war who had been taken at Negroponte. The Doge was not yet disposed to throw in his lot with Charles and Baldwin. But there is no clear evidence that he was persuaded to renew his truce with Michael VIII. The only contemporary source for this gathering of suitors for the hand of Venice, Martin da Canal, is lamentably vague; though he records that the envoys from Constantinople were escorted home on Venetian ships. The Doge was doubtless waiting to see which way the wind would blow in all the comings and goings between Byzantium, the papacy and the Kingdom of Sicily. He already had a foot in the door in Constantinople. It would be safer not to commit himself too far to any of the interested parties. It appears that he let it be known that his truce with the Byzantine Emperor would remain in force, though without being formally renewed.[2]

The Byzantines could therefore for a little longer count on the neutrality

[1] Runciman, *Sicilian Vespers*, pp. 139–47; Geanakoplos, *Emperor Michael*, pp. 237–41; Setton, *Papacy and the Levant*, I, pp. 106–12.
[2] Martin da Canal, pt ii, c. CL: p. 322; Dandolo, p. 320; *DR*, III, no. 1985a. Geanakoplos, *Emperor Michael*, pp. 254–6.

if not the active support of Venice. The Emperor Michael, however, found it even harder than he had expected to convince his church and people that they could only thwart the intentions of their enemies in the west by submitting to the will and the primacy of the pope. The experience of the Fourth Crusade had bred in the Byzantines a deep distrust and hatred of the Roman Church. Most of them believed that their salvation depended on preserving the purity of their Orthodox faith. God would surely abandon them to their fate if they compromised that faith by accepting the pope's terms for the union of the churches. The emperor was driven to persecuting and imprisoning large numbers of those who opposed his policy. In the end, however, he was able to assemble a small delegation of bishops and laymen to represent him at the pope's council at Lyons; and there, in July 1274, the reunion of the Churches of Rome and Constantinople was proclaimed and celebrated.[1] The emperor had his reward; for Pope Gregory at once instructed Charles of Anjou to lay down his arms and declare a truce of one year. Charles was so cross at being thus thwarted that he bit the top off his sceptre.[2] Only a few months before, he had given his daughter Beatrice in marriage to Baldwin's son Philip, as arranged at Viterbo. Baldwin had died in December 1273, so that Charles had become father-in-law of the new Latin Emperor of Constantinople. It might well be inexcusable for Christians to make war on fellow Christians, now that the Byzantine Emperor seemed to have been identified as such by the pope. But a case for a just war against the Emperor Michael could still be argued, on the grounds that he had usurped the throne that properly belonged to Baldwin's son and heir, Philip, now Charles's son-in-law. There were those who felt that the pope had gone too far by recognising Michael VIII as the legitimate Emperor of Constantinople.

The union of Lyons was a diplomatic triumph for Michael. He made the most of it by launching an offensive against his enemies Greek and Latin, against the rebel Byzantine princes in Epiros and Thessaly who still refused to obey him as emperor, against the bases that Charles of Anjou had established in Albania, and against the French and Italian rulers in Greece and the Greek islands. For a time he was lucky to have the services of an adventurer from Verona called Licario, who had fallen out with the Venetian and Lombard governors of Negroponte. Licario was a talented buccaneer. He achieved some remarkable successes, not

[1] Geanakoplos, *Emperor Michael*, pp. 237–45, 265–76; Setton, *Papacy and the Levant*, I, pp. 112–20.

[2] D. M. Nicol, 'The Byzantine reaction to the Second Council of Lyons, 1274', *Studies in Church History*, VII, ed. G. J. Cuming and D. Baker (Cambridge, 1971), p. 116 n. 2 (reprinted in Nicol, *Byzantium: Its Ecclesiastical History and Relations with the Western World*, London, 1972, no. VI).

only in Negroponte, where he made himself master of almost the whole of the island, but also against the Venetian lords of the islands of the Archipelago. Several Venetian families whose forebears had acquired island domains under cover of the Fourth Crusade lost them as a result of Licario's subsidised piracy, some for ever. The island of Lemnos reverted to Byzantine rule. Filippo Ghisi, self-appointed lord of the northern Sporades, was carried off in chains to Constantinople.[1] The Venetians preserved their neutrality during Licario's campaigns in Negroponte, according to the terms of their truce with the emperor. But they recognised Licario for what he was – a successful pirate operating under orders from Constantinople and in the pay of the emperor, who honoured him with the title of Grand Duke and bestowed Negroponte on him as an imperial fief. There were others like him, buccaneers and corsairs of varied origins, some of them freebooters, others in the service of the emperor, causing serious damage and disruption to the peaceful traffic of trade in the Aegean Sea. It is not impossible that much of their disruptive activity was sponsored by the emperor in order to bring the Venetians back to the conference table, to discuss a more formal agreement.

The union of the churches proclaimed at Lyons in 1274 changed the scene. It seemed that, after all, there was going to be no crusade for the re-establishment of the Latin Empire of Romania. The Doge of Venice had preferred not to commit himself. His representatives at the Council of Lyons had publicly protested that Venice would never relinquish its claims in Romania.[2] But Lorenzo Tiepolo had always suspected the motives of Charles of Anjou. Tiepolo died in August 1275; and it was his octogenarian successor as Doge, Jacopo Contarini (1275–1280), who took the initiative in proposing a new agreement with the Byzantine Emperor. He must have known that the Genoese had just succeeded in renewing their treaty with Michael VIII. They were now well entrenched in their colony at Galata.[3] After some preliminary discussions, Contarini sent as his plenipotentiaries to Constantinople Marco Bembo and Matteo Gradenigo. They were empowered to negotiate a formal revision of the truce signed between Byzantium and Venice in 1268, perhaps on more favourable terms. In his letters of credit the Doge tactfully omitted his title to three-eighths of Romania, styling himself simply as Doge of Venice, Dalmatia and Croatia and 'lord of the lands

[1] Sanudo, *Istoria*, ed. Hopf, pp. 122–7; Gregoras, iv. 5: 1, pp. 96–8. Miller, *Latins in the Levant*, pp. 136–41; Geanakoplos, *Emperor Michael*, pp. 235–7, 295–9.

[2] Martin da Canal, pt ii, c. CLXVIII: pp. 338–9; Dandolo, p. 321. Geanakoplos, *Emperor Michael*, p. 278.

[3] Byzantine–Genoese treaty of October 1275: *DR*, III, no. 2019. A Venetian embassy led by Marino Valaresso is known to have been in Constantinople in 1275. *TTh*, III, pp. 184, 237, 249.

and islands subject to his authority'. He was also careful to address Michael VIII as Emperor of the Romans and the New Constantine. His envoys arrived in Constantinople in September 1276. Gradenigo died in the course of the deliberations, and the deal was finally concluded by Marco Bembo alone on 19 March 1277. The document that emerged was not in the form of a truce or a treaty between equal partners. It was a chrysobull, signed and sealed with the golden bull of the emperor in the presence of witnesses in the imperial palace of Blachernai. This was a reversion, surely deliberate, to an older mode of diplomacy in which the Emperor of the Romans graciously dispensed privileges to favoured nations. The Genoese had not been treated in this fashion. The last emperor to issue a chrysobull to Venice, and then in very different circumstances, had been Theodore Laskaris in 1219. The 'New Constantine' was standing on his dignity.[1]

So much was clear from the opening sentence of the document. The emperor, desirous of keeping the peace with all Christians, condescended to conclude a truce and a convention with the Doge's emissary, Marco Bembo. It was to run for a period of two years and longer if both parties were in agreement. If at the end of two years one or the other party wished to terminate it, six months' notice should be given. The convention that followed was long and detailed. Concerning the remaining Venetian colonies in Romania, the emperor agreed not to dispute the possession of Crete, of Coron and Modon. In the island of Negroponte, however, both he and the Doge would retain the right to conquer it if the opportunity arose. At the Doge's request the status of the Venetian-occupied islands of the Archipelago was at last clarified. Marco II Sanudo, Lord of Naxos, and Bartolomaeo Ghisi of Santorini, with their dependencies in the Aegean Sea, were held to be bound by the truce, on condition that they did not support the emperor's enemies or give asylum to pirates hostile to him. The Venetians in the islands had suffered much from the emperor's own licensed pirate, Licario. They must have been grateful to have been included in their Doge's agreement.

Marco Bembo deserved the thanks of his people for one particular item in the chrysobull. The Venetians were to be granted a new and permanent residential and commercial quarter in Constantinople. Its limits were well defined. They ran within the sea wall along the Golden Horn, from the Gate of the Droungarios or Vigla along by the churches of St Akindynos and of the Virgin to the street of the Zonarai and down

---

[1] Greek text of chrysobull in *MM*, III, pp. 84–96; Latin text in *TTh*, no. CCCLXVIII, pp. 133–49; Dandolo, p. 324; *DR*, III, no. 2026. The existence of an earlier treaty made in 1275, postulated by Norden, *Papsttum und Byzanz*, p. 540 n. 1, and Ostrogorsky, *History*, p. 410 n. 1, seems to be dubious. Geanakoplos, *Emperor Michael*, p. 301 n. 100.

to the Gate of Perama. Within this area three houses were to be provided, one for the Venetian baillie, one for his councillors, and another for use as a warehouse. Venetian merchants coming from abroad would have the use of a further twenty-five houses without payment of rent. The number could be increased if it proved inadequate for their accommodation, or decreased if it proved too great. They would also have the use of two churches, that of the Virgin and that of St Mark. A similar quarter was to be assigned to the Venetians in Thessalonica. There they were to have the church formerly used by the Armenians and three houses, one for their consul, one for his councillors and one as a warehouse, with extra accommodation of up to twenty-five houses or more for merchants in transit, all to be held rent free. In other parts of the empire Venetians would be at liberty to rent houses, baths and bakeries according to their needs.[1] An unprecedented clause in the chrysobull refers to the fruits of Venetian liberty in the past, the offspring of mixed marriages or cohabitations, half-castes or *gasmouloi*, born during the Latin occupation. They and their heirs were to be considered as Venetian citizens, with corresponding rights and freedoms.[2] The Venetians in Constantinople and Romania would be allowed to use their own weights and measures and freely to practise their own religion, with their own churches, priests and forms of baptism. Since it had been decreed that the Genoese were not to be expelled, care must be taken to ensure that there should be no disagreements between them and the Venetians. They must live peacefully together, especially in the district between Abydos and the Black Sea. Any differences between them in that area would be referred to the arbitration of the emperor, who would expect the injured party to be satisfied within six months. If compensation were not forthcoming the emperor would undertake to provide it from his treasury.

Venetians were to be free to come and go about their business and to buy and sell to Latins or Greeks throughout the empire whether on land or sea without payment of any duties or taxes, provided that they were dealing in Venetian goods. Foreign goods would have to be declared. If it were proved that imperial customs officers had taken anything from a Venetian merchant, compensation would be paid from the treasury. Ultimate responsibility for the conduct of Venetians rested with the baillie

---

[1] Heyd, *Commerce*, I, pp. 465–6. On the churches of St Mark and the Virgin 'de Embulo', see Janin, *Géographie ecclésiastique*, pp. 571–3.

[2] There was much reference to those 'who class themselves as Venetians'. The problem of entitlement to Venetian citizenship was to recur. See Julian Chrysostomides, 'Venetian commercial privileges under the Palaeologi', *Studi veneziani*, XII (1970), 267–356, especially 276ff.; and see below Chapter 12, pp. 232–4.

or rector of their community; and it was expected that the Doge of Venice would cause such officials, before they came to Constantinople, to swear an oath to be nothing but truthful and honestly impartial about their countrymen. One curious clause affirms the absolute inviolability of the privileges of Venetians in the empire. No one, from the emperor downwards, is to impose any duty or burden on any Greek or Latin which might conflict with the free enterprise of the Venetians. There were to be no restrictions within the empire on the necessary purchase of any equipment for Venetian ships. The emperor pledged to indemnify Venetians who had suffered losses at the hands of his subjects since the time of his treaty in 1268; likewise, Venetians would compensate Greeks whom they had wronged. The remaining clauses of this lengthy document for the most part reiterate or amplify statements made in the earlier treaty concerning, for example, the disposal of the property of deceased Venetians; assistance to those shipwrecked; and their right to buy and export grain, though its price had now doubled from fifty to 100 *hyperpyra* per 100 *modioi*, and Venetians were now to be allowed to transport it from the Black Sea. Also restated were the clauses referring to the responsibility of the baillie or rector to bring Venetian malefactors or pirates to justice; the liberation of all Venetians held in imperial custody; and the liberation of all Greeks held as prisoners in Crete, Coron, Modon and Negroponte.[1]

By far the most important and potentially advantageous new concession to Venice was the grant of a residential and business quarter in Constantinople. The emperor had not felt so bountiful nine years before. It was evidently not as extensive as the Venetian quarter that had existed before 1204, though occupying the same site. But its buildings were to be freehold and maintained at the emperor's expense; and the community there would continue to be administered by its own baillie appointed by the Doge, as proposed in 1268. The cession of a similar quarter in Thessalonica with its own consul was another innovation which might have been of value to Venice, if its lodgings had been more attractive and the inhabitants more welcoming.[2] There was, however, a note of caution on both sides. The truce and the arrangement so carefully itemised were to be in force for only two years; though if either party infringed the terms

[1] The rise in the price of grain was due in part to the debasement of the *hyperpyron* by Michael VIII. Pachymeres, *De Andronico Palaeologo*, vi. 7: II, pp. 493–4 (*CSHB*). D. A. Zakythenos, 'Crise monétaire et crise économique à Byzance du xiiie au xve siècle', *L'Hellénisme contemporain* (Athens, 1947–8), 8–9 (reprinted in Zakythenos, *Byzance: Etat–Société–Economie*, London, 1973, no. xi); M. F. Hendy, *Studies in the Byzantine Monetary Economy*, pp. 526–30.
[2] See O. Tafrali, *Thessalonique au quatorzième siècle* (Paris, 1913), pp. 126–9; and below, pp. 239–40.

agreed, the other would not at once go to war. It was for this reason that the Venetian baillie was not accorded the same privileges at the Byzantine court as the Genoese Podestà, with whose government the emperor had made a more lasting treaty.[1] There was mistrust as well as caution. The people of Constantinople had long memories. They did not welcome the Venetians back in their midst. Furthermore, the Emperor Michael was still engaged in his battle of wits with the papacy and Charles of Anjou. If he lost that battle there remained a strong chance that the Venetians would join the winning side and help themselves to more than he was offering in the treaty of 1277.

They had ample cause to distrust him. He had offered to compensate any Venetians who had suffered loss or damage at the hands of his subjects during the previous ten years. In March 1278 the Doge submitted to him a list of over 300 case histories of damage done during those years to Venetian merchants, their goods and their ships. The culprits were mainly pirates, most of whom were clearly in the emperor's pay; though some were customs officials acting in contravention of the terms of the truce. The cases had been referred, on the sworn testimony of the plaintiffs, by the baillies of Negroponte and Constantinople to a panel of judges in Venice, who had considered the evidence and assessed the damages. Some of the tales of woe may have been exaggerated. But the whole document constitutes a vivid record of lawlessness and an indictment of the emperor who claimed to be the dispenser of privileges to Venice.[2] The pirates operated from Negroponte, from Monemvasia, from Thessalonica, from Rhodes, and from Anaia on the coast of Asia Minor facing Samos. Those most active and dangerous were Giovanni Senzaraxon, Andrea Gafforo, Giovanni de lo Cavo, and one Rolando of Thessalonica. They worked mainly in the Aegean islands and round the shores of Greece, though Giovanni de lo Cavo and his friends scoured the seas as far north as Valona and Spinaritza on the Albanian coast; and Rolando ran a family business of piracy based on Thessalonica. Others to be feared were Daimonoioannes of Monemvasia and Niketas and Kryvitziotes of

---

[1] Pseudo-Kodinos, pp. 235-7. Marco Bembo himself had acted as the first baillie in 1268. On the institution and duties of the Venetian baillie, see Chrysa Maltézou, *O Thesmos tou en Konstantinoupolei Venetou Bailou (1268–1453)* (Athens, 1970) (cited hereafter as Maltézou, *Thesmos*).

[2] *TTh*, III, no. CCCLXX, pp. 159–281: the document is entitled *Judicum Venetorum in causis piraticis contra Graecos decisiones*, and dated March 1278. The only serious study of it appears to be by G. Morgan, 'The Venetian claims commission of 1278', *BZ*, LXIX (1976), 411–38. See also P. Charanis, 'Piracy in the Aegean during the reign of Michael VIII Palaeologus', *Mélanges Henri Grégoire*, II (Brussels, 1950) (*Annuaire de l'Institut de Philologie et d'Histoire Orientales et Slaves*, x, 1950), 127–36. The most senior of the three judges, Giberto Dandolo, had commanded the Venetian fleet at the battle at Spetsai in 1263.

Rhodes. Their names reveal that most of them were not Greeks. Gafforo
was Genoese; Rolando came from Pisa. But they are described as being
'the emperor's men' (*homines domini imperatoris*). Kryvitziotes, who
must have been Greek, is designated as 'captain' of Rhodes; while Giovanni de lo Cavo from Genoa was, like Licario before him, honoured
with the imperial title of Grand Duke or High Admiral.[1]

It must suffice to cite only a few instances of the flagrant breach of
the truce and of maritime law to illustrate the hazards facing Venetian
merchants in the 1270s. Giovanni Bembo and others from Negroponte,
making for Makri in Asia Minor with one shipload of grain and wine,
were seized by Kryvitziotes of Rhodes who had one warship and three
smaller vessels. They were robbed of all they had, taken to Rhodes,
beaten and thrown into gaol where they were made to do forced labour
for eight months. When set free, Bembo went to the emperor in Constantinople and obtained letters ordering the said Kryvitziotes to return his
goods, valued at 990 *hyperpyra*. The emperor's letters had no effect.
Bembo never saw his property again.[2] Another merchant, Alberto
Stella, being on his return voyage from Anaia to Negroponte with one
cargo ship belonging to Giovanni Sanudo, was plundered at Ephesos
by the local governor's men. He lost all his goods and merchandise to
the value of 370 *hyperpyra* and was imprisoned at Ephesos for four and
a half months, until liberated through the unexplained intervention of
Kyra Martha, the emperor's sister. He then went to the governor and
asked for the restitution of his goods, but to no avail.[3] In April 1277
one Giovanni Michiel, sailing from Nauplion with one ship loaded with
salt, had obtained clearance to go by way of the harbour of Monemvasia.
But two warships of the emperor's men led by Giovanni de lo Cavo
from Monemvasia and Marchetus from Anaia apprehended him when

---

[1] Sanudo, *Istoria*, pp. 146–7, describes the varied nationality of the pirates, 'from all parts
of the world', though most of their captains were Genoese. In 1260 one Theodore Kryvitziotes
was Dux of the Thrakesion theme, whose capital was Ephesos. *PLP*, vi, no. 13838. Niketas
is also described as 'captain of Rhodes'. *TTh*, iii, pp. 167, 170. Sanudo, *Istoria*, p. 132,
reports the seizure of two cargo ships by the emperor's admiral Giovanni de lo Cavo. This
incident, in which Sanudo's father was involved, cost his family dear. The loss of the same
two ships is specifically mentioned in the Byzantine–Venetian treaty of 1285. *TTh*, iii, pp. 337,
351.

[2] *TTh*, iii, pp. 196–7.

[3] *TTh*, iii, pp. 193–4. On Anaia, see P. Lemerle, *L'Emirat d'Aydin. Byzance et l'Occident*
(Paris, 1957), p. 16 and n. 5; C. Foss, *Ephesus after Antiquity* (Cambridge, 1979), pp. 124–5.
The document calls Ephesos 'Alter Locus', a latinisation of Alto Luogo, as the Italians called
it. See Foss, p. 121. The local governor is described as the *megas dux* 'de Lonatuli . . . nomine
Megaduriniti', perhaps the Dux of the Anatolikon theme, by name Dorianites. The emperor's
widowed sister Maria had become a nun with the name of Martha and founded the convent
known as Kyra Martha in Constantinople. See Janin, *Géographie ecclésiastique*, pp. 324–6.

he had got into the harbour. The deed was done in sight of and with the full co-operation of the people of Monemvasia; and Michiel was robbed of goods worth 762 *hyperpyra*.[1] One Salo from Negroponte with some others, sailing to Gallipoli 'when the truce was in force between the emperor and Venice', sought reassurances as Venetian citizens from the local castellan before entering his territory. They were captured just the same and relieved of their ship and their goods to the value of 400 *hyperpyra*.[2] Giorgio Sardo of Negroponte, sailing down the Hellespont with his wife and others, despite bearing letters of safe conduct from the acting baillie of Constantinople, was arrested at Lampsakos and robbed of all that he had, including his ship.[3]

Some of the culprits were higher in the social scale than mere pirates. An official of the emperor, named only as the *sebastokrator*, was held responsible for one particularly shocking crime. His men seized a Venetian ship sailing up the west coast of Greece from Modon to Clarentza in the Morea. On board were the Latin archdeacon and the Bishop of Modon. The archdeacon protested that he was a Venetian. He was murdered and despoiled of all his property, his money and his horses, to the value of 450 *hyperpyra*. A complaint was made to the emperor's governor in the Morea, but he dismissed it with contempt.[4] If the *sebastokrator* in the case was the emperor's brother, Constantine Palaiologos, who is referred to in other cases as imperial governor of the Morea, the offence was even more outrageous.[5] Another merchant claimed to have been robbed of goods worth thirty-two *hyperpyra* by the emperor's other brother, the Despot, while sailing from Constantinople to Durazzo; he was captured and held in prison for four months.[6] Complaints were made of robbery on land as well as by sea. One Giovanni Pellipario, travelling by horse-drawn wagon from Patras to Lepanto on business, was set upon and robbed of goods to the value of seventy-five *hyperpyra* by thirteen of the emperor's men armed with bows and arrows. He was thrown into prison in the castle of 'Licolourato', where he was

[1] *TTh*, III, pp. 225–6. A third ship sailing with the pirates was commanded by one Saladino.
[2] *TTh*, III, pp. 202–3.
[3] *TTh*. III, p. 211. His losses amounted to eighty *hyperpyra*.
[4] *TTh*, III, pp. 170–1. The emperor's 'capitaneus' in the Morea is named as 'domino pro Theoratoni (?)'.
[5] The *sebastokrator* 'fratrem domini Imperatoris' is mentioned in *TTh*, III, p. 255; cf. pp. 231, 232.
[6] *TTh*, III, p. 174. The Despot, brother of the emperor, must be John Palaiologos, who died in 1273–4. See P. Magdalino, 'Notes on the last years of John Palaiologos, brother of Michael VIII', *REB*, XXXIV (1976), 143–9. The same merchant had earlier been robbed of 500 *hyperpyra* in goods by 'Calogianum, Ducam de la Patra', i.e. the rebel John Doukas (Kaloioannes) of Neopatras in Thessaly, against whom John Palaiologos had waged unsuccessful war.

guarded by two Greeks in the emperor's service, George Kalokyris and Sgouros.[1] Two more Venetians complained of having been robbed during a brawl between Greeks and Latins in Constantinople. Some others were robbed and imprisoned at Thessalonica by the infamous Rolando when they went ashore to change their currency.[2]

There were many complaints about the demands made on Venetian merchants to pay customs dues, which were in direct contravention of the truce of 1268, as the plaintiffs regularly pointed out. One poor wretch, who had already been stripped of goods worth 500 *hyperpyra*, was then illegally charged seventeen *hyperpyra* in duty at Lepanto.[3] Several other cases are cited of Venetians being made to pay *kommerkia* or taxes on their cargoes, at Mesembria and Pontoherakleia in the Black Sea, and at Anaia and Thessalonica.[4] Especially disturbing also, in view of the stated conditions of the truce, was the arbitrary fixing of the price of grain, apparently according to the whim of the emperor. One Pietro Grisuni brought six *centenaria* (600 *modioi*) of grain from Varna to Constantinople. He was hoping to sell it at between 160 and 170 *hyperpyra* per *centenarium*; but the emperor or his officials would give him no more than 133. Pietro would not accept so low a price. He was therefore forbidden to sell his grain and it was impounded under bond on the emperor's orders. After six weeks of waiting, he went to the imperial court with Pietro Badoer, then baillie of Constantinople, to ask the emperor either to let him sell it or to raise the price. The emperor would not relent. He claimed to have made a proclamation that no one was to buy grain from any Venetian on any terms. At the end of three months the merchant had to let his cargo be bought for a mere 116 *hyperpyra* and was thus defrauded and impoverished by the emperor's delays and prohibitions.[5]

Another similar case reported during the time when Pietro Badoer was baillie concerned a merchant who had loaded grain that he had bought in Constantinople. The emperor's men boarded his ship and took it with its load to Blachernai at the head of the Golden Horn. The merchant

---

[1] *TTh*, III, p. 175. 'Patras' here probably stands for Neopatras. 'Georgium Calocuriti et Loscuro' may be transcribed as Kalokyris and Sgouros. 'Licolourato' may be the island of Salamis which was known as Colori or Coulouris. See O. Markl, *Ortsnamen Griechenlands in "fränkischer" Zeit*, Byzantina Vindobonensia, I (Graz–Köln, 1966), p. 55.

[2] *TTh*, III, pp. 231, 268–9.

[3] *TTh*, III, p. 174: 'comerclatum de XVII hyperperis a Lupatho per comerclarios, quod non debeat fieri Venetis'.

[4] *TTh*, III, pp. 238–40, 244, 254, 278–81.

[5] *TTh*, III, pp. 179–80. The emperor's alleged proclamation forbidding the purchase of grain from Venetians is repeated at p. 276. A similar case is at pp. 189–90.

went with the baillie and others to see the emperor, to ask him why this had been done. He received no satisfaction. He went again in company with Marino Valaresso, then ambassador of Venice in Constantinople, to ask that the emperor should at least pay him the market price for his cargo if he would not release the vessel. In the end the emperor paid him at the rate of fifty *hyperpyra* per 100 *modioi* (*centenarium*), whereas the going rate was between 160 and 170. The merchant thus lost about 300 *hyperpyra*, taking into account the cost of his ship and its crew held at Blachernai for six weeks.[1] Another case concerned a cargo of salt, which Buffone Paulino brought from Negroponte to sell in Constantinople. The emperor put guards on his ship and forbade him to sell his salt. The ambassadors from Venice who were in town, Marino Valaresso, Marco Giustiniani and Angelo Marcello, together with the baillie Giovanni Zeno, took the case up with the emperor. Buffone was kept waiting for three months, losing money all the time through having to pay his crew. He was finally allowed to unload his cargo on payment of forty *hyperpyra* to the emperor's officials. He lost in all some 500 *hyperpyra*.[2] It was also while Valaresso was in Constantinople as the Doge's ambassador that one Marco Signolo bought 500 *modioi* of grain from a Genoese merchant, making a down payment of 100 *hyperpyra*. The emperor intervened and forbade the transaction. A delegation of Venetians, led by Valaresso and the baillie, went to see the emperor. They complained that this was a serious wrong, 'for Venetians in Constantinople and in all places where the emperor's word was law, were supposed to be safe, free and protected whether carrying merchandise or not'.[3]

These were indeed all serious wrongs and serious and flagrant violations of the pledges which Michael VIII had made to Venice in 1268. Some of the incidents reveal mere malice against the Venetians. One of the plaintiffs tells how, when approached by a pirate ship from Anaia, he and his colleagues produced papers to prove that they were Venetians. The pirate replied that they were just the men he was looking for, tore up their papers and stole everything that they had.[4] It may well be that some Venetians were profiteering. The emperor had stipulated that they were free to purchase and export grain so long as its price did not exceed fifty *hyperpyra* per *centenarium*. If the price went up they could export it only under licence. By 1277 the rate had doubled. Those trying to sell their grain at 160 to 170 *hyperpyra*, which they said was the market price, should perhaps not have been surprised when the emperor's officials

---

[1] *TTh*, III, p. 249; cf. p. 274.   [2] *TTh*, III, pp. 183–4.
[3] *TTh*, III, pp. 237–8.   [4] *TTh*, III, p. 219.

intervened. The sum total of damages came to about 35,000 *hyperpyra*. The settlement of these and other claims was to be a recurrent theme in negotiations between Byzantium and Venice for many years to come. In 1285, after much haggling, Michael's successor, Andronikos II, agreed to pay the sum of 24,000 *hyperpyra* in compensation to the Venetians. It was less than they had demanded. But it is interesting to note that, when the money reached them, their Maggior Consiglio gave instructions to the mint that the Byzantine coins should be converted into gold ducats, the new currency of Venice.[1]

The union of the churches proclaimed at Lyons in 1274 had its desired effect for a few years. Pope Gregory X, who had arranged it, was grieved and disappointed that the emperor continued to make war on the Latin Christians in Romania. But he still refused to give his blessing to the crusade which Charles of Anjou was so eager to lead to Constantinople. Gregory died in January 1276. His successor became increasingly sceptical about the nature of the union. The emperor strove to convince him that everything possible was being done to persuade or coerce the Byzantines into accepting it. But the pope knew through his agents in Constantinople that the majority of the Greeks would sooner suffer and die for the cause of Orthodoxy. The opposition was loud and strong and the emperor had to use the tactics of terror to stifle it; while the rebel Greek Despot of Epiros, whose domain lay closest to Italy and next to the Angevin Kingdom of Albania, made friends with Charles of Anjou and encouraged him to strengthen his military bases on the coast. In 1279 Charles appointed as commander of all his lands and armies in Albania and Epiros a Burgundian knight called Hugues de Sully. He was to make the final preparations for the invasion when the moment came. In August 1280 Pope Nicholas III died. He had made it plain that he was out of patience with the Byzantine Emperor's prevarication over the matter of the union of the churches. But he had forbidden Charles of Anjou to attack the empire. After his death, however, Charles was given a free hand, for six months were to pass before a new pope was elected. In the autumn of 1280 Hugues de Sully received orders to lead the advance inland from Durazzo to lay siege to the fortress of Berat, the key to the road from Albania through to Macedonia. The Byzantine garrison was ready for him, however, and the Emperor Michael rushed reinforcements to the scene. Berat was under siege throughout the winter.

[1] R. Cessi, *Deliberazioni del Maggior Consiglio di Venezia*, III, Reale Accademia dei Lincei, Commissione per gli atti delle assemblee costituzionali italiane (Bologna, 1950), pp. 98–9, 160–1; F. Thiriet, *Délibérations des Assemblées Vénitiennes concernant la Romanie*, I (Paris–The Hague, 1966), p. 49 (10–13 March 1285), p. 53 (28 November, 5 December 1286) (cited hereafter as Thiriet, *Assemblées*).

But in the spring of 1281 the great Sully was ambushed and captured. Bereft of their leader, his men turned and fled back to the coast, with the Byzantine army in hot pursuit.[1]

It was a famous victory for the Emperor Michael, confirming his conviction that God was on his side. The French prisoners taken at Berat, among them the towering figure of Hugues de Sully, were paraded in chains through the streets of Constantinople, to the great delight of the people. But the danger was not over. Charles of Anjou was not one to give in at the first defeat. He licked his wounds and reconsidered his strategy. He would make his second attempt by a different route and with the added confidence of papal blessing. For in February 1281 he had helped to secure the election of a French pope, Martin IV, who was ready to identify the interests of the church with the interests of the house of Anjou. Pope Martin, perhaps rightly, considered the union of Lyons to be a sham. He reverted to the view that the Greeks could be cured of their religious errors only by force; and he announced that Charles of Anjou was the man to lead a crusade for that purpose. Charles was pleased that his patience had been rewarded. The defeat of his army at Berat had convinced him that his crusade must go by sea. His own kingdom could hardly muster enough ships for so great an undertaking. Only the Venetians could help him.

Their truce with Byzantium, so elaborately enshrined in the emperor's chrysobull of 1277, had run its two-year course. Neither party had rejected it. Neither party had asked for its extension. It had not brought to Venice the many advantages that it promised. The emperor had done little or nothing to satisfy the many Venetian claims for damages against him. Pirates continued to plunder Venetian ships in the Aegean. The profit from commerce in Constantinople and the Black Sea which should have been going to Venice was being taken by Genoa. There was something to be said for a change of policy with regard to Byzantium. But the Doge and his advisers would not be hurried. Their agents are reported to have been in consultation with Charles of Anjou for about four years before a decision was reached. On three occasions Charles sent ships of his own to help defend Negroponte against the Greeks. They achieved nothing, partly because their crews fell out with the Venetians. In February 1281 the Venetian consul in Apulia was instructed to report on Charles's activities and to await further orders.[2] Charles was then busily sending reinforcements to his army which was laying siege to Berat in Albania. Before long the Venetian consul was able to report that that

[1] Geanakoplos, *Emperor Michael*, pp. 329–34; Nicol, *Last Centuries of Byzantium*, pp. 68–71; Setton, *Papacy and the Levant*, I, pp. 132–7.
[2] Sanudo, *Istoria*, pp. 129–31; Cessi, *Deliberazioni*, II, p. 134.

army had been defeated and driven to the coast. The news was received
with some relief in Venice, where the prospect of an Angevin kingdom
stretching across the Adriatic had always been a source of anxiety. Two
other factors cleared the air and made the Venetians more responsive
to an alliance with the Kingdom of Sicily. One was the election of Pope
Martin IV, who had no doubts about the morality of a crusade against
Byzantium. The other was the election of a new Doge. The aged Contarini
had abdicated in March 1280, to be succeeded by Giovanni Dandolo
(1280–9). It may not be irrelevant that Dandolo, a former baillie of Acre,
had been one of the victims of piracy in the Aegean four years earlier.[1]

On 3 July 1281, in the city of Orvieto which Pope Martin IV had
chosen for his residence, an alliance was formed between Charles of
Anjou, ambassadors from Venice, and Charles's son-in-law Philip
of Courtenay, the titular Latin Emperor of Constantinople. The object
of the alliance was expressly stated to be the recovery of the empire
usurped by Michael Palaiologos and the installation of Philip on the
throne once occupied by his father Baldwin. The project was dressed
up in pious phrases about the reunion of Christendom, the reintegration
of the Apostolic See and the recall of the dissident Greeks to obedience
within the mystical body of the church. Its real purpose was not so
otherworldly. The Doge of Venice was honoured with his full title of
dominator of one-quarter and one-eighth of the whole Empire of Romania; and he was promised repossession of all the rights and properties
that his people had held in Constantinople in the years of the Latin
occupation. It was agreed that the Doge, Philip and Charles of Anjou,
or his eldest son Charles, should all personally take part in the expedition.
Charles and Philip would provide some 8000 men and horses and the
ships to transport them. The Venetians were to supply a convoy of at
least forty warships for protection on the high seas. The date of their
departure was fixed at not later than April 1283. The combined forces
would assemble at Brindisi by the middle of that month.[2]

On the same day, also at Orvieto, another agreement was made
between the three parties concerned. It envisaged an advance guard to
prepare the ground for the main expedition. The Doge was to provide
a fleet of fifteen warships for seven months of the year. Charles and
Philip would also contribute fifteen ships and ten cargo boats carrying
about 300 horses and 300 men. The Venetian and Angevin fleets were
to meet at Corfu not later than 1 May 1282. Their object was to make
war on the Emperor Michael and others who were illegally occupying
the Empire of Romania. The 'others' were presumably the Genoese.

[1] *TTh*, III, p. 277. Morgan, 'The Venetian claims commission', 420.
[2] *TTh*, III, no. CCCLXXIII, pp. 287–95.

Both agreements were approved and ratified by the Doge in Venice on 2 August 1281.[1]

The treaty of Orvieto, like that of Viterbo fourteen years earlier, was drawn up in the palace of the pope. The *dramatis personae* had changed. William of Villehardouin, Prince of Achaia, had died in 1278 and his principality had passed under the direct suzerainty of Charles of Anjou. Baldwin too had died, but his title had passed to his son, who had married Charles's daughter. Venice had played no part at Viterbo; but the treaty of Orvieto offered the Venetians a major role in the drama, whose leading protagonists were, as before, the pope and his champion Charles. While Venice supplied the warships, Pope Martin IV supplied the moral sanction to justify the campaign as a crusade (*passagium*) for the glory of the faith, the healing of the schism and the recovery of the lost Latin Empire of Romania. A few weeks after the treaty had been signed the pope excommunicated Michael VIII. All the work of the Council of Lyons and all the emperor's efforts during the previous twenty years to prevent another Fourth Crusade were undone. The union of the churches was at an end. The Byzantine emperor was no longer to be regarded in any sense as a Catholic prince obedient to Rome.[2]

Charles of Anjou seemed to have united not only Venice and the papacy but also almost all the Balkan powers against Byzantium. The rulers of Serbia and Bulgaria declared their support. The Despot of Epiros, Nikephoros, ever ready to strike at the Emperor Michael, joined the coalition and signed a treaty with Charles, Philip and the Doge in September 1281.[3] The whole of Latin-occupied Greece was on Charles's side. But Michael's diplomacy was equal to the occasion. There were other allies on whom he could call. The Genoese were naturally eager to prevent a new Venetian takeover of Constantinople. They kept the emperor aware of what was afoot in Italy and the west. The King of Hungary was Michael's son-in-law; the Mamluk Sultan of Egypt would lend him ships; and the Tatars of the Golden Horde in south Russia, whose khan had married one of Michael's daughters, could keep an eye on the Bulgarians. But there was one Catholic ruler in the west who was known to have personal reasons for hating Charles of Anjou. King Peter III of Aragon had married a daughter of the late Manfred of Sicily whom Charles had dispossessed. He had a fleet and his agents were busy stirring up rebellion against Angevin rule in Sicily. The native Sicilians, forced to pay for Charles's ambitious projects, were in a mood

---

[1] *TTh*, III, nos. CCCLXXIV, CCCLXXV, pp. 296–8, 298–308. Geanakoplos, *Emperor Michael*, pp. 335–44.

[2] *Les Registres de Martin IV (1281–1285)*, ed. F. Olivier-Martin (Paris, 1935), p. 112.

[3] Nicol, *Despotate of Epiros*, II, p. 29.

to rebel. Peter of Aragon was poised to help them. The Byzantine Emperor had the means to underwrite a revolt in Sicily and an invasion of the island by the Aragonese fleet.[1]

It had been agreed at Orvieto that the crusade against Constantinople would assemble in April 1283. Preparations were well in hand when, without warning, in March 1282, the citizens of Palermo in Sicily rose up in arms and massacred all the French in the city. The uprising, known as the Sicilian Vespers, spread throughout the island. The fleet that Charles was preparing was destroyed. In August Peter of Aragon arrived in Sicily at the head of his own fleet and the French were driven out. The Sicilian Vespers, as a rebellion against French tyranny, would probably have broken out sooner or later. But the timing of it was all-important to the Byzantine Emperor. Michael VIII's involvement in it has been matter for debate among historians. But he himself claimed soon afterwards that he had been God's agent in effecting the liberation of the Sicilians.[2] By so acting he had at last removed the long-standing threat of an invasion or a crusade against his empire from Italy. The empire and the dreams of Charles of Anjou were shattered. Pope Martin IV, who had longed for those dreams to come true, solaced himself by excommunicating Peter III and preaching a crusade against the Aragonese. The Venetians felt cheated. For once they had backed the wrong horse. Charles of Anjou tried to involve them in his own bid to reconquer Sicily. In November 1282 he sent messengers to the Doge asking him to send the promised fleet. But the Doge did not consider that the terms of the treaty of Orvieto applied to a domestic conflict between the French and the Aragonese. Far from becoming involved he ordered all Venetians to leave Sicily within one month; and when in 1284 the Doge declined to join the pope's crusade against Aragon and forbade his bishops to preach it, the city of Venice was laid under an interdict by Martin IV.[3]

Michael VIII did not live to enjoy the fruits of his triumph over his western enemies. He died in December 1282. His passing was not mourned. He had no hero's funeral. His policy of appeasement towards the papacy as the means of saving his empire from destruction had made

[1] Sanudo, *Istoria*, says that the emperor promised to subsidise Peter of Aragon's invasion of Sicily by 60,000 *hyperpyra* annually. Runciman, *Sicilian Vespers*, pp. 194–5; Geanakoplos, *Emperor Michael*, pp. 335–44, 363–4.

[2] Michael VIII Palaiologos, *De Vita sua*, ed. H. Grégoire, *B*, XXIX–XXX (1959–60), 461, 462. Runciman, *Sicilian Vespers*, pp. 201ff., 214ff.; Geanakoplos, *Emperor Michael*, pp. 344–58, 364–7.

[3] C. Minieri-Riccio, 'Memorie della Guerra di Sicilia negli anni 1282, 1283, 1284', *Archivio storico per le provincie Napoletane*, I (1876), 96; Cessi, *Deliberazioni*, II, p. 139; III, pp. 27, 28; Thiriet, *Assemblées*, I, pp. 43–4 (May 1283); Sanudo, *Vitae Ducum*, cols. 574–5; *Registres de Martin IV*, pp. 221, 226, 280.

him more foes than friends. The New Constantine died as an outcast, excommunicated by the pope, condemned as a heretic by his own church and detested as a traitor and a tyrant by most of his people. The first act of his son and successor Andronikos II was to disown the union of Lyons and proclaim the restoration of Orthodoxy. To the Byzantines it seemed that a new age was dawning. The spectres that had haunted them for so long were dissolving. Philip of Courtenay, who might have sat on his father's throne in Constantinople, died almost exactly a year after Michael VIII, in December 1283. His champion and protector, Charles of Anjou, and the master spirit behind the enterprise, Pope Martin IV, died within three months of each other in 1285. Of those who had signed the treaty of Orvieto only the Doge of Venice, Giovanni Dandolo, was left. There would now be no crusade, no wave of righteous indignation and pious fervour to carry the Venetians to Byzantium. They would have to work out their own arrangements with the new Byzantine Emperor.

12

BYZANTIUM, VENICE AND GENOA

BY terms of the treaty of Orvieto signed in July 1281 Venice had declared
war on Byzantium. The Doge had miscalculated. The chance of riding
to Byzantium on a wave of moral fervour had passed. Yet so long as
a state of war existed it was not safe for Venetian merchants to sail to
Constantinople and the empire. They were specifically forbidden to do
so by several decrees of their government between 1282 and 1285.[1]
There were still Venetians living in Constantinople. Many of them had
been born there. But the commercial quarter which Michael VIII had
granted them in 1277 lay dormant or closed down. The Genoese across
the water in Galata reaped the benefit of the Doge's miscalculation. It
was an expensive mistake and its effects were aggravated by events nearer
home. The interdict imposed on Venice was not lifted until a new pope
was elected in 1285. There was rebellion in Istria and Trieste, vigorously
supported by the Patriarch of Aquileia. A series of natural disasters had
left hundreds of citizens homeless and hungry. The food shortage could
have been alleviated if Venetian convoys had been able to resume their
shipments of corn from Constantinople and the Black Sea. The major
Venetian colonies in Romania, especially Modon, Coron, Negroponte
and Crete, had not changed hands, and repeated orders went out for
the strengthening of their fortifications and defences in the war against
the emperor.[2] Crete provided welcome supplies of corn, though rebellion was constantly being subsidised by Byzantine agents in the island;
and in Negroponte the Venetians had to fight the Byzantine army to
retain possession. But without their link with Constantinople the colonies
were like members without a head. There were many reasons for recreating that link on the best terms possible.

The initiative came from Venice. The new emperor in Constantinople,
Andronikos II, was only twenty-four years old when he came to the

---

[1] Cessi, *Deliberazioni*, III, pp. 25–6, 62–3, 69, 103–4; Thiriet, *Assemblées*, I, pp. 41, 43,
50.

[2] Thiriet, *Assemblées*, I, pp. 40–2.

throne in December 1282. His father had made elaborate arrangements to ensure the succession of the dynasty of Palaiologos. But Andronikos knew that the arrangements could be subverted by those who had opposed his father on political and religious grounds. Michael VIII's grandiose schemes and diplomatic manoeuvres, however necessary for the preservation of his empire, had been ruinously expensive; and he had left a legacy of bitterness, not wholly dispelled by his son's prompt renunciation of the union of the churches and his declaration of the purest Orthodoxy. Byzantium could do with the economic benefits that might accrue from a resumption of Venetian trade. But popular opinion, which Michael VIII had overriden, would not take kindly to the resettlement of crowds of Latins in the heart of Constantinople. The Latins of Genoa were not so offensive because they lived beyond the city walls. It was therefore up to the Venetians to make the first move. They did so in September 1283. Two ambassadors came to Constantinople to explore the possibilities of a reconciliation with the new emperor. The last treaty between Byzantium and Venice, signed in 1277, had run longer than its prescribed term of two years; but its spirit had been violated when Venice joined the Angevin alliance at Orvieto in 1281. The ambassadors to Constantinople in 1283, Andrea Zeno and Marino Morosini, were empowered to propose a treaty lasting for seven to ten years; and one of their priorities was the matter of the outstanding compensation for damage done to Venetian persons and property by Greek malefactors, which they estimated at between 66,600 and 100,000 *hyperpyra*.[1]

It was not until the spring of 1284 that Zeno and Morosini reached Constantinople. In June of the same year the emperor sent two representatives to Venice to continue the discussions. They were authorised to protest that the Venetian claim for damages was excessive. A month later they sailed back to Constantinople with a second Venetian embassy; and with them went two Venetian merchants who felt so strongly about their losses that they wanted to put their own case to the emperor. The Doge was very proper about procedure. All on board were strictly forbidden to carry any goods for sale or to conduct any business transactions in Byzantium except for the purchase of foodstuffs and provisions.[2] No agreement was reached, however. In February 1285 another Byzantine embassy arrived in Venice; and the Doge was prompted to try again.

---

[1] Cessi, *Deliberazioni*, III, p. 49, nos. 157, 160, 163; p. 50, nos. 164, 165, 167; p. 52, no. 184; p. 96, no. 214. Angeliki E. Laiou, *Constantinople and the Latins. The Foreign Policy of Andronicus II, 1282–1328* (Cambridge, Mass., 1972), pp. 57–8 (cited hereafter as Laiou, *Andronicus II*).

[2] Cessi, *Deliberazioni*, III, p. 70, nos. 56, 59; p. 71, nos. 60–2, 65–6; p. 73, nos. 74, 76, 77; p. 74, no. 81; p. 75, nos. 88–9. Thiriet, *Assemblées*, I, pp. 45, 47–8.

In March a third Venetian delegation left for Constantinople. It was led by Angelo Marcello and Marco Zeno. Their instructions contained a curious item. Rumours had reached Venice that the Emperor Andronikos might at any moment be overthrown by revolution. If they found another emperor on the throne when they arrived, they should carry on the negotiations with him. Andronikos had his enemies; but no Byzantine source confirms that he was about to lose his throne in 1285. The tale that reached Venice seems to have gathered strength in its telling.[1]

There had been some hard bargaining. There was much mutual suspicion. But a treaty was agreed on 15 June 1285. It was signed by the Emperor Andronikos in the Blachernai palace in the presence of eminent witnesses; and although the emperor's gold seal was appended to the document, it was not a chrysobull in the older Byzantine sense of a privilege bestowed as a charity.[2] Its terms were substantially the same as those set down in the treaty of Michael VIII with Venice in 1277. There were, however, two important modifications. It was to run for a period of ten years or longer if both parties agreed; and neither party was to be free during those years to ally with any Christian or pagan power hostile to the other. A clause of this nature might have made the Venetians think twice before taking sides with Charles of Anjou. On the other hand, it could well make things difficult for the emperor when it came to reviewing his arrangements with the Genoese. The clauses concerning the existing Venetian possessions in Crete, Coron, Modon and Negroponte and to Byzantine recognition of Venetian control of the islands of the Archipelago are taken almost verbatim from the treaty of 1277. So also are the terms and conditions relating to the Venetian quarters in Constantinople and Thessalonica, the freedom of their merchants to trade throughout the empire and their peaceful relations with the Genoese. There was no question of the Genoese being expelled. Certain items are resurrected from the treaty of 1268, notably those referring to the wreck of Venetian ships; the right of Venetians to buy and export grain within the empire and from the Black Sea at a price of 100 *hyperpyra* per *centenarium* or less; the right of Venetians to be tried by their own baillie except in cases of homicide; the mutual undertaking to release all prisoners; the manufacture of weapons and the activities of pirates. The document ends with the agreed compromise over the compensation payable to Venetian citizens for the damage done to them by those pirates and their imperial paymasters between 1277 and 1281. The emperor promised to settle the account with an immediate and final payment of 24,000

---

[1] Cessi, *Deliberazioni*, III, p. 96, no. 214; p. 98, no. 9; pp. 100–1, nos. 30, 33. Thiriet, *Assemblées*, I, pp. 49–50. Laiou, *Andronicus II*, pp. 59–60.

[2] Latin text in *TTh*, III, no. CCCLXXVIII, pp. 322–39; *DR*, IV, no. 2104.

hyperpyra. The ambassadors from Venice had hoped to get about three times that amount. They had to be thankful for smaller mercies. The treaty was confirmed item by item by the Doge Giovanni Dandolo in Venice on 28 July 1285.[1]

The document confined itself to the facts. Neither in its preamble nor in its text are there any of the flowery phrases about past friendship and co-operation between Byzantium and Venice which had adorned their earlier treaties. The emperor did not admit that he had forgiven the Venetians for their treachery to his father. The Venetians admitted nothing. The treaty was a licence for their merchants to resume their activities in the Byzantine Empire and the Black Sea in the hope if not the certainty that they would be legally protected for at least ten years. The day after the treaty had been confirmed the Maggior Consiglio decreed that Venetian ships were free to return to Romania, to the emperor's territory and to the Black Sea, and proceeded to the appointment of a baillie and two councillors to be sent to Constantinople.[2] The Doge and his council had had to swallow some of their pride. In particular they had had to settle for a much reduced amount in compensation.[3] The emperor had won certain substantial points. What he had failed to win was a true understanding with Venice. He was naive enough to suppose that the Venetians and the Genoese would now settle down together as his friends and allies, assisting him in the defence of an institution in which they had such valuable interests. It was partly this illusion that induced him to economise by disbanding his own navy. In 1283 he had been able to put a fleet of about eighty ships to sea. By 1285 there were almost none. The emperor's advisers are said to have argued that a fleet was an unnecessary expense. The threat from Italy was over; the Venetians and the Genoese, bound to the empire by treaty, could look to its defence by sea; and in any case God would protect it from all its enemies now that the pious Emperor Andronikos had condemned his father's heresies and restored the true faith of the Orthodox church. Andronikos was undoubtedly pious, but he was not at first swayed by these arguments, for he felt that the possession of a navy was vital to the prestige as well as to the security of an empire. In the end, however, he gave in and the deed was done. The Byzantine fleet was allowed to run down or was deliberately dismantled. The crews of its derelict

---

[1] *TTh*, no. CCCLXXIX, pp. 339–53; Cessi, *Deliberazioni*, III, p. 113, no. 103; p. 115, no. 115; p. 116, no. 123. A useful summary of the diplomatic exchanges that led to the treaty of 1285 is in Setton, *Papacy and the Levant*, I, pp. 144–6.

[2] Cessi, *Deliberazioni*, III, pp. 116–17, nos. 124, 128–33. Thiriet, *Assemblées*, I, p. 51.

[3] The money reached Venice in November 1286. Cessi, *Deliberazioni*, III, pp. 160–1, nos. 145, 147. Thiriet, *Assemblées*, I, p. 53.

warships, with little hope of alternative employment, took service with
the Genoese, the Venetians and the Turks, or joined the international
bands of pirates in the Aegean Sea. Some immediate economies were
probably achieved by this act but it was quickly proved to have been
shortsighted and ultimately disastrous. Little by little Constantinople
was to become wholly dependent upon the Italians for its livelihood
as well as its defence.[1]

The Venetians meanwhile returned in growing numbers. The Genoese,
who had enjoyed a monopoly of Byzantine markets as well as the benefi-
cence of two emperors, resented the competition, especially in the Black
Sea. They had set up a thriving commercial colony at Caffa in the Crimea
and they were not pleased when in 1288 the Venetians established a
rival settlement with its own consul at nearby Soldaia (Sougdea).[2] For
some years after 1285 the Venetians behaved with studied correctness,
keeping to the letter of the treaty for fear of losing the gains that it
had brought. But there were incidents that led to disagreements; and
the seeds of conflict between Venice and Genoa were being sown in
the Crimea and elsewhere. In 1287 the Doge had cause to complain
about unspecified damage done to his people by some Greeks.[3] Some
Venetians too evidently found the terms of the treaty too restricting on
their movements. In 1291 one Pancrazio Malipiero attacked the island
of Kos among other places. In 1292 Giacopo Tiepolo followed his example. Byzantine officials confiscated the property of some Venetian citizens, probably by way of reprisal; and the Doge sent an envoy to
Constantinople to protest. Further complaints about Byzantine treatment
of Venetians were lodged in June and September 1293.[4] The new relationship between Byzantium and Venice was turning sour. The emperor
could neither sweeten it nor bring it to an end. The Venetians and the
Genoese were about to resolve their commercial rivalry in open war.

In May 1291 the Mamluk Sultan of Egypt captured the city of Acre,
the last bastion of the Kingdom of Jerusalem and the crusader states
in Syria. The Venetians fought valiantly in its defence. They were lucky
to have ships on which to escape the general massacre of its inhabitants
by the Muslims. They and their ancestors had done good business in
Acre for almost 200 years. It had been their main outlet for trade with

[1] Pachymeres, *De Andronico Palaeologo*, i. 26: II, pp. 69–71; Gregoras, vi. 3: I, pp. 174–6.
Hélène Ahrweiler, *Byzance et la mer* (Paris, 1966), pp. 374–81; Laiou, *Andronicus II*, pp.
74–6.
[2] Cessi, *Deliberazioni*, III, pp. 201–2, nos. 14, 16; Thiriet, *Assemblées*, I, p. 55.
[3] Cessi, *Deliberazioni*, III, pp. 170, 171, nos. 25, 28.
[4] Cessi, *Deliberazioni*, III, p. 320, no. 45; p. 326, no. 46; p. 344, no. 69; p. 348, no. 98;
pp. 358–9, no. 18; p. 368, no. 71. Thiriet, *Assemblées*, I, pp. 66, 68–9. Laiou, *Andronicus
II*, p. 68.

central Asia and the Orient and they had kept it to themselves. They had contrived to expel the Genoese from Acre in 1258 and its traders from Pisa and Amalfi were not dangerous competitors. It was said later that the Genoese had taken their revenge by helping the Sultan to capture the city.[1] But in truth the Genoese had already sensed the changing wind of trade. They had seen that the future lay not in the dying cause of the crusader states in Syria but in the ports of the Black Sea. The new outlets for the trade of the Orient would be at Trebizond on the southern shore and at Caffa in the Crimea. The Venetians had already gained a foothold there. When they lost their market in Acre their merchants were driven to look for business further north. Conflict between Venice and Genoa was nothing new, but it might have been confined to Italy and the Adriatic Sea. They had been at war from 1256 to 1269. The truce that they had signed in 1270 had been extended, but it expired for the second time in 1291, the year that Acre fell. It was not formally renewed. Both sides prepared for the eventuality of war, for a commercial war for predominance in Byzantine waters. The situation was so grave that in May 1294 a new assembly, the Council of Thirty, was created in Venice solely to supervise relations with Genoa.[2] The Genoese were the first off the mark. They defeated their rivals in a sea battle at Lajazzo (Ayas) on the Gulf of Alexandretta in Cilicia, went on to attack and destroy Canea in Crete and sank a Venetian merchant fleet in the harbour at Modon in the Peloponnese.[3]

The Emperor Andronikos was a neutral party bound by mutual obligations to both sides. He would have liked to keep out of it. But in 1296 about seventy-five Venetian ships sailed up the Hellespont without warning. They were led by Ruggiero Morosini, known as Malabranca, the Evil Claw. The emperor sent a Venetian nobleman to ask him the purpose of his visit. Morosini refused to say. But it was soon clear that he had come in pursuit of some Genoese ships and, having come thus far, he would not go until he had attacked their colony at Galata. Galata had not then been fortified. Its Greek and Genoese inhabitants asked for asylum within the walls of Constantinople. The emperor took pity on them; and as a precaution he ordered the arrest of all Venetians in the city, including their baillie Marco Bembo. Morosini's men then set fire to some Greek houses outside the walls and destroyed all the abandoned Genoese warehouses and other buildings in Galata as well as all

[1] Sanudo, *Vitae Ducum*, col. 578. Heyd, *Commerce*, I, pp. 347–50.
[2] Cessi, *Deliberazioni*, III, p. 368, no. 71. Thiriet, *Assemblées*, I, p. 70. On Genoese exploitation of the Black Sea, see G. I. Brătianu, *Recherches sur le commerce génois dans la Mer Noire au XIIIe siècle* (Paris, 1929).
[3] Dandolo, in Muratori, *RIS*, XII (Milan, 1728), col. 404. Laiou, *Andronicus II*, pp. 102–3.

the ships lying in the harbour. This was a flagrant violation of the treaty
of 1285 by which the Venetians had agreed not to pursue their vendetta
with the Genoese in the district between Abydos and the Black Sea.
The treaty had run its allotted ten years but neither side had revoked
it. The emperor was furious. He ordered his own troops to fight alongside
the Genoese, and the Venetians withdrew after one of their commanders
had been killed. Their breach of the peace had been so shameless that
the chronicler Andrea Dandolo later felt bound to invent a pretext for
it. His version was that the emperor had been persuaded by the Genoese
to arrest the Venetians in Constantinople before their fleet arrived.
Nothing seems less probable.[1]

When the Venetians left they took with them an official note of protest
to their government. It was carried by the Orthodox Bishop of Crete,
Nikephoros, who might be thought to have some influence with the
Venetians. At the same time the emperor reasserted his own dignity
by confiscating Venetian property in Constantinople to the value of
80,000 *hyperpyra* to pay for the damage done at Galata. By so doing
he himself may have overstretched the letter of his treaty with Venice.
It mattered little. The Venetians were now again at war with Byzantium;
and the Genoese could not wait for reparations that might not come.
In December some of them took the law into their own hands and murdered the baillie Marco Bembo and as many other Venetians as they
could find in Constantinople. It was a brutal attack directed mainly
against the aristocracy. The humbler Venetians managed to hide and
later to escape. It seemed that the emperor had lost control of order
in his city. He was afraid too that he would be accused of being an
accomplice in the Genoese brutality. He sent two messengers to Venice
to apologise and to explain that he had had no hand in it. One of them
was the monk Maximos Planoudes, more celebrated for his literary activities. By his own account he was not well treated in Venice.[2] The Venetians were angry. They refused to consider renewing the treaty of 1285
until the emperor paid them the full value of their property in Constantinople which he had confiscated. The emperor was not to be bullied
or intimidated; but he had been pushed into the position of a reluctant
ally of the Genoese in their war with Venice.[3]

The Venetians had it their own way for a while. In 1296 Giovanni

---

[1] Dandolo, col. 406; Pachymeres, *De Andronico Palaeologo*, iii. 18: II, pp. 237–41. Heyd,
Commerce, I, pp. 445–6; Laiou, *Andronicus II*, pp. 104–5.

[2] Maximos Planoudes, *Letters*, ed. M. Treu, *Maximi monachi Planudis epistulae* (Breslau,
1890), no. V, p. 11.

[3] Pachymeres, iii. 19: II, pp. 241–4; *TTh*, III, no. CCCLXXXVII, pp. 373–4. Laiou, *Andronicus
II*, pp. 105–6.

Soranzo took twenty-five ships up the Black Sea and set fire to the
Genoese colony at Caffa. They also seized a Byzantine vessel near Chios,
for which the emperor was to claim a large sum in compensation.[1]
There were skirmishes elsewhere in the Aegean and the Black Sea from
which the Genoese suffered most. But in 1298 they had their revenge.
Off Korčula (Curzola) on the Dalmatian coast their admiral Lamba d'Oria
overwhelmed a Venetian fleet of ninety-five ships. All but ten were destroyed; at least 7000 Venetians were killed and 5000 taken prisoner.
Among the captives was Marco Polo, who passed his days in a Genoese
prison by composing his celebrated report on his travels in the east.
The battle of Korcula was a notable triumph for Genoa but it exhausted
the belligerents. Venice had greater resources and greater powers of recovery; but neither side wanted to fight to the death. Both looked for
ways of reaching a settlement without losing face. A solution was offered
by Matteo Visconti, Lord of Milan. Through the good offices of Charles
II of Naples and with the blessing of the pope, Visconti brought the
Venetians and the Genoese to make a treaty on 25 May 1299. The treaty
of Milan did not suggest that either party had won the war. But it seemed
to take for granted that the Genoese were still, if only in theory, the
allies of the Byzantine Emperor, while the Venetians were still at war
with him. What had begun as a commercial quarrel between Venice and
Genoa had developed into a war between Venice and Byzantium. The
unhappy Emperor Andronikos, now denied the active help of those
whom he had befriended, was left to face the wrath of Venice on his
own. Just before the treaty of Milan, while the emperor was in Thessalonica, Venetian agents had approached him to propose a new settlement
of their differences. They were even ready to be reasonable about the
property that he had confiscated three years before. It was a fair offer
and the emperor was minded to accept it. But he was advised to keep
the Venetians waiting a little longer. It was not the first time that Andronikos had been misled by his counsellors.[2]

It took the Venetians some time to recover from their disaster at Korcula. They had to replace the lost ships and find crews to man them;
and as usual the government's first concern was the defence of its existing
colonies in the Aegean, especially Modon, Coron and Crete. In September 1300 an attempt was made to effect an exchange of prisoners
of war with Byzantium. The Venetians badly needed the manpower.

[1] Dandolo, cols. 406–7; *DR*, IV, no. 2231.
[2] Dandolo, cols. 407–9; Jacopo da Varagine, ed. C. Monleone, *Iacopo da Varagine e la sua
Cronaca di Genova dalle origini al MCCXCVII*, Fonti per la Storia d'Italia. Scrittori, Secolo
XIII (Rome, 1941), II, pp. 97–9; Pachymeres, *De Andronico Palaeologo*, iv. 6: II, pp. 286–7;
TTh, III, no. CCCXC, p. 391. Laiou, *Andronicus II*, pp. 106–8.

In April 1301 a Byzantine embassy went to Venice in the hope of negotiating a renewal of the treaty of 1285, perhaps for a period of twenty years. The ambassadors also asked for 29,000 *hyperpyra* in payment for the ship seized off Chios. The Venetians were not in generous mood. They would consider a truce for ten years and no more than 18,000 *hyperpyra* in compensation. Nothing came of the discussions.[1] Another Byzantine embassy is known to have been in Venice in May 1302; but in the summer of that year the Venetians decided to frighten the emperor into submission by a show of force. On Saturday 21 July 1302 at midday thirteen ships commanded by Belletto Giustinian sailed into the Golden Horn accompanied by seven pirate ships which they had picked up in Crete and Negroponte. They anchored opposite the Blachernai palace and their men went ashore to do as much damage as they could. They set fire to some bales of straw that they found on the strand. The flames could be seen from the city walls and from the palace. Too late the emperor realised that without ships he was powerless to retaliate. It was suggested that a bridge of boats might be built across the Horn from which his troops could attack the Venetians. He thought that this might do more harm than good.

When night fell the pirate ships attacked the Princes Island in the Sea of Marmora. It was crowded with refugees from the Turks in Asia Minor. Such of them as could not afford a ransom were murdered. Others were brought within sight of Constantinople and tortured before the emperor's eyes with the connivance of the Venetians. The emperor protested to their commander Giustinian, sending him 4000 *hyperpyra* as ransom money for the surviving refugees. Giustinian, realising that his pirate accomplices had gone too far, apologised and declared that he was now ready to negotiate a truce provided that the question of reparations could be resolved. He sailed for Italy with his ships, taking two Byzantine ambassadors with him. Discussions began in Venice in September; and on 4 October 1302 a new treaty was agreed and signed by the Doge Pietro Gradenigo. It was ratified by the Emperor Andronikos in Constantinople on 7 March 1303.[2]

Byzantium and Venice were at peace again. But the emperor had to pay the price. The treaty of 1302 was for the most part simply a renewal

---

[1] R. Cessi and P. Sambin, *Le deliberazioni del Consiglio dei Rogati (Senato) serie Mixtorum*, Deputazione di Storia Patria per le Venezie: Monumenti Storici. Nuova serie, xv, vol. 1 (Venice, 1960), no. 35, p. 6; no. 95, pp. 26–7; no. 100, pp. 28–9; nos. 107–9, 112, pp. 30–2 (cited herafter as Cessi–Sambin). Laiou, *Andronicus II*, pp. 109–10.

[2] Pachymeres, *De Andronico Palaeologo*, iv. 23: II, pp. 322–7; Gregoras, vi. 11: I, pp. 207–10; Sanudo, *Vitae Ducum*, col. 579. The texts of the treaty are in *DVL*, nos. 7, 8, pp. 12–16, 16–19; *DR*, IV, nos. 2231, 2243, 2247, 2250. Cf. R.-J. Loenertz, 'Notes d'histoire et de chronologie byzantines', *REB*, XVII (1959), 158–62. Laiou, *Andronicus II*, pp. 109–11.

of that of 1285. There were, however, some important additions and amendments to meet the changed circumstances. In the course of the hostilities the Venetians had laid hold of a number of islands in the Aegean Sea. Some were to be handed back to the emperor, to whom they belonged; but the four islands of Keos, Seriphos, Santorini and Amorgos were henceforth to remain in Venetian control. On the other hand, the Doge agreed to a new limitation on exports from the empire. For the future Venetian merchants would be forbidden to trade in salt and mastic, the former being an imperial monopoly, the latter soon to become a Genoese preserve. Most of the rest of the treaty concerned the problem of compensation for damages inflicted on each side during the fighting. The emperor claimed nothing for the destruction that Ruggiero Morosini had caused six years before; and he agreed to make reparation for the Venetian property that he had seized, to the value of 79,000 *hyperpyra*. The Doge generously conceded that the emperor could subtract from this sum the amount of 24,000 *hyperpyra* in payment for the ship captured off Chios. This was less than the emperor had originally demanded but more than Venice had been prepared to pay in 1301. The emperor was still, however, required to find 14,000 *hyperpyra* which he had earlier agreed to pay in settlement of damage done by his troops to Venetian property. The scores between Venice and Genoa had been settled in the treaty of Milan in 1299. Neither sought any further compensation from Byzantium; though an inquiry would be made into a claim by some Venetians for 7000 *hyperpyra* allegedly stolen from them when they and their baillie were detained in Constantinople.

The treaty was meant to last for ten years, with the possibility of renewal by common consent. A new baillie, Jacopo Trevisan, was sent out from Venice in October 1302 and with him went an ambassador to see that the emperor paid his debts as promised.[1] Venetian merchants returned to pick up the threads of their business in Constantinople and elsewhere in the empire. The war with Genoa and then with Byzantium had indeed been bad for business. The trade and the economy of Venice had suffered greatly and to no great purpose or advantage. Four islands in the Aegean Sea had come their way but the Genoese still held effective control of the Black Sea; and it was they who seemed to have won most out of the whole sorry confusion. The emperor still believed that he needed the help of their ships, for all that they had landed him in a war with their rivals; and sometimes they answered his call. In 1292 they had come to his aid with a fleet of at least forty ships against the

---

[1] Cessi–Sambin, I, nos. 256–62, pp. 71–2; nos. 273–82, pp. 75–8; nos. 290–2, p. 81. Thiriet, *Assemblées*, I, pp. 97–101. Maltézou, *Thesmos*, p. 106.

rebel Despot in Epiros.[1] They were well rewarded. In May 1303 he gave them a new and bigger site on which to rebuild their colony at Galata destroyed by the Venetians. In March 1304 they requested and received permission to fortify it with a circuit wall.[2] It seemed that the Genoese had only to ask and they would be given. They were assured of the emperor's favour. One Genoese family did particularly well as a result. In 1275 the brothers Benedetto and Manuele Zaccaria had been granted the right to exploit the alum mines at Phokaia near Smyrna on the coast of Asia Minor. They had amassed a fortune from the proceeds by marketing the alum to the textile industry of Genoa. In 1305 Benedetto occupied the island of Chios to the west of Phokaia and persuaded the Emperor Andronikos to cede it to him as a freehold property for ten years. Chios was famous for its wine and oil, but it was the sole producer of the aromatic resin known as mastic; and the Zaccaria family diversified their business interests by combining their heavy trade in alum with a luxury trade in mastic, a trade which had been specifically forbidden to the Venetians.[3] Another Genoese adventurer, Andrea Morisco, offered his services to the emperor in 1304. He was rewarded with a title; and a year later he attacked and occupied the island of Tenedos at the entrance to the Hellespont.[4]

Those who lost most from the war were the Byzantines; and the emperor must take some share of the blame. Andronikos II was never a forceful or decisive ruler. There were indeed those who said that he was ruled by his patriarch, for his piety was exemplary and he took care not to offend his clergy, who could remember how his father had persecuted them. He had won the support of most of them by renouncing the hated union with Rome. But not until the twenty-seventh year of his reign was he able to end the schism in his church and heal the last of the wounds that Michael VIII had inflicted on it. The Arsenites, who had challenged the legitimacy of the house of Palaiologos since its inception, were at length reconciled in 1310.[5] In foreign no less than in domestic affairs Andronikos had to face the consequences of his father's policy. Michael VIII had perforce concentrated his military resources on defending the western approaches to his empire against the threat of invasion from Italy. The eastern frontiers had been left too thinly protected. They began to crack and then to crumble irremediably in

[1] Nicol, Despotate of Epiros, II, pp. 38, 41–2.
[2] DR, IV, nos. 2256, 2261. Laiou, Andronicus II, pp. 112–13.
[3] John Cantacuzenus, Historiae, ed. L. Schopen, CSHB, 1828–32, ii. 10: I, p. 370; DR, IV, no. 2259. Geanakoplos, Emperor Michael, pp. 210–13; Laiou, Andronicus II, pp. 152–3.
[4] Pachymeres, De Andronico Palaeologo, vi. 9, 34: II, pp. 494–6, 556–8: DR, IV, nos. 2276, 2287.
[5] Laiou, Andronicus II, pp. 245–6; Nicol, Last Centuries of Byzantium, pp. 110–11.

the last decades of the thirteenth century, as wave upon wave of Turkoman raiders streamed westwards following the upheaval of the Mongol conquest of the Seljuq Sultanate. The raiders had little sense of common purpose but their livelihood depended on plunder and, as fanatical Muslims, they were fired with the zeal of holy warriors or *ghazis* against the Christians. By 1300 only a few of the ancient Greek cities of Asia Minor held out against them. The emperor's response to this new crisis was erratic and seldom effectual. He had personally commanded armies in Asia Minor, particularly in the vital province of Bithynia in the north west, the nearest to Constantinople. But many of the Greek inhabitants felt that they had been neglected for too long. There were local rebellions and mutinies. Some went over to the Turks as their only hope of security. Others, in ever larger numbers, fled to the coast or to Constantinople to add to the crowds of homeless and destitute refugees. Those whom the Venetians rounded up on the Princes Island had gone there to escape the Turks.

In July 1302 a Byzantine army fought and lost a battle at Bapheus in Bithynia. The Turks were there led by a *ghazi* chieftain called Osman, later to be celebrated as the founder of the Osmanli or Ottoman people. He followed up his victory by ravaging the land around the cites of Nikomedia, Nicaea and Prousa. More refugees fled across the water to Constantinople or to the islands. Contemporaries rightly regarded the Byzantine defeat at Bapheus as a turning-point in their history. Yet at the time Osman was only one among a number of *ghazi* leaders carving out little principalities or emirates in western and southern Asia Minor. The Italians in the Greek islands had more to fear from the emirs of Aydin and of Menteshe in the south. For they were the first of the new Turks to take to the sea and to raid the coastline and islands. The emir of Aydin was to capture Ephesos in 1304 and then Smyrna; and his corsairs roamed the Aegean as far as the Venetian island of Negroponte and the Greek mainland. There was no Byzantine navy to challenge them; the Byzantine army, mainly made up of mercenaries, was defeated and demoralised. The emperor was more relieved than cross when the Genoese looked to the defence of their own interests against the Turks at Phokaia and then occupied the island of Chios in 1305.[1]

After the catastrophe of 1302 Andronikos clutched at every straw. Asia Minor seemed to be lost. But suddenly a new ray of hope appeared in the west. A band of professional mercenaries known as the Catalan

---

[1] On the early conquest of the Turks in Asia Minor and the battle at Bapheus, see G. G. Arnakis, 'The Early Osmanlis' (in Greek) (Athens, 1947); P. Lemerle, *L'Emirat d'Aydin*; S. Vryonis, *The Decline of Medieval Hellenism in Asia Minor* (Los Angeles, 1971); Nicol, *Last Centuries of Byzantium*, pp. 130–6.

Company offered him their services. They had been fighting in the cause
of the Aragonese against the Angevins in Sicily. That conflict came to
an end in August 1302. The Catalans were paid off and in search of
new employment. Their leader, Roger de Flor, demanded a high price
for the hire of his Company. But the emperor thanked heaven that some
good could come out of the west and signed a contract with them. It
proved to be the most expensive of all the mistakes that he had yet made.
The Catalans were a private army responsible only to their own commander. They ignored the emperor's orders. He had engaged them to
fight the Turks and in 1304 they rampaged through Asia Minor terrorising
Greeks and Turks alike. But when their commander was killed they
ran amok, seized the peninsula of Gallipoli, massacred or enslaved the
inhabitants and proclaimed it to be Spanish territory. For two years
they devastated the countryside, creating what the Byzantines called 'a
Scythian desert', and invited bands of Turks to come over the water
to join them. Then they moved west, plundered Mount Athos and
attacked Thessalonica, before being driven south into Thessaly. They
finally came to rest in Athens in 1311, having beaten the French Duke
of Athens in a pitched battle; and there they raised the Spanish flag which
they had so brazenly planted at Gallipoli. The French Duchy of Athens
and Thebes, founded by knights of the Fourth Crusade, passed under
Catalan rule.[1]

The tornado of the Catalans sweeping through the Byzantine Empire
had widespread effects. It did little lasting harm to the Turks in Asia
Minor, though it had introduced many of them to European soil for
the first time. It further ruined the Byzantine economy, necessitating
another devaluation of the currency. It destroyed the agricultural land
to the west of Constantinople and raised the price of food. It brought
new streams of starving refugees into the capital. In the western world,
however, it caused a new excitement, a recurrence of the dream that
the Latin Empire of Romania could be reconstituted. The Catalans might
be the forerunners of a crusade to conquer the Byzantine Empire and
hand it over to those in France who still claimed title to it. The title
had passed to Catherine of Courtenay, granddaughter of the last Latin
Emperor, Baldwin II. In 1301 Catherine had married Charles of Valois,
brother of Philip IV of France. Her new husband became obsessed with
the idea of reclaiming his wife's inheritance and realising the project that
Charles of Anjou had envisaged. He created a network of alliances with

[1] On the Catalans, see K. M. Setton, *Catalan Domination of Athens 1311–1388*, 2nd edn
(London, 1975); Setton, *Papacy and the Levant*, I, pp. 441–68; Laiou, *Andronicus II*, pp.
92, 134–99.

those who might be helpful. It included Frederick II of Sicily, the King of Serbia and, he hoped, both Genoa and Venice.

The new Turkish threat to Asia Minor and the Aegean islands had alarmed both republics. The Genoese had perhaps less to fear and less to lose since their main interests were in Constantinople and the Black Sea. When Charles of Valois approached them they hesitated and then declined to help his cause. The Venetians found the prospect much more tempting. It was almost exactly a hundred years since their ancestors had brought Byzantium to its knees. To be in at the kill again would be exciting. It would also eliminate their Genoese rivals. In December 1306 the Doge Pietro Gradenigo signed a treaty with the envoys sent to him by Charles of Valois. With an eye to what might come of it he signed himself 'by the grace of God, Lord of one-quarter and one-eighth of the whole Empire of Romania'.[1] The sanction of God for the enterprise was provided by the pope, Clement V, who blessed it as a crusade and in June 1307 excommunicated the Emperor Andronikos II and all who sided with him. The fact that the last treaty between Venice and Byzantium had still six years to run was of small account. The pope had overruled it by excommunicating the emperor and by promising the Doge and his people the indulgences offered to crusaders.[2]

The basis of their arrangement with Charles of Valois was the text of the treaty that they had made with Charles of Anjou in 1281 with certain modifications. The crusade was to sail from Brindisi before March 1308. Its announcement was welcomed even by some influential men in Byzantium who were alarmed by the advance of the Turks and disenchanted with their emperor. They saw Charles of Valois as a potential deliverer from the former and as a substitute for the latter. Three of them wrote to him and his wife promising their support. One of them was the military commander of Thessalonica. He addressed Charles as his lord and emperor and offered to surrender his city.[3] There was certainly much dissatisfaction with the Emperor Andronikos. One Venetian chronicler tells the strange tale that a Venetian fleet attacked Constantinople in 1307. They had come on the invitation of the emperor's son, Demetrios Palaiologos, who had paid them to help him depose his father and seize the throne. This is an improbable story which would surely have been recorded by the Byzantine historians if it were true.[4] The crusade of Charles of Valois, at all events, never came near Constantinople. He had hopes that the Catalans in Greece would serve as his allies

---

[1] *DVL*, I, no. 27, pp. 48-53.
[2] *DVL*, I, no. 21, p. 38; no. 28, pp. 53-5; nos. 33, 34, pp. 61-2.
[3] Laiou, *Andronicus II*, pp. 212-17, 341-3.
[4] Cited by Maltézou, *Thesmos*, pp. 225-6.

and agents on the way there. But they were not much interested. It slowly became clear that the French had neither the money nor the resources to translate their imperialist dream into reality within the allotted time. The Venetians became impatient and began to withdraw their support.[1]

By 1310 they could wait no longer. Their interests in Romania were suffering. Genoese pirates were attacking their ships off the Peloponnese. Some, like Andrea Morisco, were in the pay of the Byzantine Emperor. The Catalans too were proving to be a menace. It had become too dangerous for ships to sail on their own. An order went out from Venice that they must travel in convoy. Between 1307 and 1309 special measures were taken for the protection of Venetian property in Romania and further repairs were made to the fortifications at Modon, Coron and Negroponte. Two captains were appointed to take special charge of the defence of Romania and to patrol the coast of Asia Minor.[2] In May 1309 a first attempt was made to restore formal relationships with Byzantium by the dispatch of an embassy from Venice. Negotiations continued into the following year.[3] The Emperor Andronikos must have suspected that the Venetians would abruptly change their tune if and when Charles of Valois launched his crusade. This possibility grew ever more remote. The emperor was patient. It was in his interest to keep the discussions going. As the year wore on the Venetian senate became increasingly anxious to bring them to a conclusion. They were even ready to accept a compromise over the matter of reparations. It would not have been their style to express any remorse for their behaviour. They knew that they had made a mistake, but it was to be judged in diplomatic and not in moral terms.

A treaty was finally drawn up and signed in the Blachernai palace in Constantinople on 11 November 1310. It contained little that was new, for it was substantially a confirmation of the two agreements that Venice had made with the emperor in 1285 and 1302.[4] The presence of the Catalan Company in Greece, however, presented a new problem and one that was of concern to both parties. The Venetians agreed to forbid their merchants to traffic in any part of the empire occupied by the Catalans. Business could be resumed when they had gone. In 1310 the Catalans were in Thessaly and had not then moved down to Athens.

---

[1] DVL, I, no. 32, pp. 59–60 (May 1307); nos. 41, 42, pp. 75–8 (July and September 1309). Laiou, Andronicus II, pp. 200–20; Setton, Papacy and the Levant, I, pp. 163–70.

[2] Cessi–Sambin, I, no. 70, p. 108; nos. 231, 235, p. 122; Thiriet, Assemblées, I, no. 138, p. 115; nos. 168, 169, p. 124. Laiou, Andronicus II, p. 235. The course of the war between Venice and Byzantium from 1306 to 1309 is documented by Maltézou, Thesmos, pp. 222–8.

[3] Thiriet, Assemblées, I, nos. 174, 207, 214, 216, 228, pp. 125, 133, 135, 138.

[4] Latin text in DVL, I, nos. 45, 46, pp. 82–5; DR, IV, no. 2325.

The prohibition must therefore have affected the Venetian market at Halmyros; though the extent of the damage that they had done to Venetian ships was so great that the senate decided to take the matter up with the King of Aragon.[1] Another new item in the treaty dealt with the payment to Venice of reparations for damage inflicted on their property and ships by Greeks since 1285. The sum amounted to 40,000 *hyperpyra* in the newly devalued currency. The emperor promised to pay it in four annual instalments of 10,000 *hyperpyra* and declared that he would make no corresponding claim for damage done to Byzantine property by Venetian citizens. He was generous as well as patient with his troublesome allies. They had even had the effrontery to ask if they could keep some of the smaller Aegean islands which had come their way in the course of the recent fighting. No doubt they kept them, though the matter was not formally mentioned in the treaty.[2]

The treaty was supposed to last for twelve years. Given the history of earlier agreements between Byzantium and Venice this might have seemed optimistic. But the emperor was grateful for it and the Venetians wanted it to last. They did not entirely abandon the hope that an alliance of western powers might one day reconstitute the Latin Empire of Constantinople. But their prime concern after the Catalan occupation of Athens in 1311 was the protection of their colonies in Greece, especially in Negroponte. It was with this more limited object in mind that they made friends with Philip of Taranto, who had acquired the title of Latin Emperor through his marriage to Catherine of Valois.[3] Their treaty with Andronikos in 1310 came as a relief to both parties; for it opened the way to a more stable and enduring settlement between Byzantium and Venice for the first time since the restoration of the empire in 1261. Many disagreements and misunderstandings remained, and they were to be aired if not resolved in succeeding years. But it seemed to have been accepted that differences between the two governments should henceforth be discussed in a new spirit of détente. A common distrust of the Catalans and a common anxiety about the Turks had much to do with bringing them together.

---

[1] Thiriet, *Assemblées*, I, no. 227, p. 138 (October 1310).
[2] Cessi–Sambin, I, no. 86, p. 134 (August 1310). Maltézou, *Thesmos*, pp. 227–8; Laiou, *Andronicus II*, pp. 236–7.
[3] Thiriet, *Romanie vénitienne*, pp. 158–9.

13

CONFLICTING INTERESTS AND
COMPETING CLAIMS

IN the decade before the signing of their new treaty in 1310 both Constantinople and Venice had suffered harrowing experiences. The Emperor Andronikos had been unnerved by the depredations of the Catalans in Thrace. He seemed to have no plan for the rescue of Asia Minor from the Turks. Constantinople was packed with thousands of refugees. They were homeless and they were hungry. There had once been a central system of control over the wholesale and retail trade in food in the city. It had long since broken down. The emperor had not the time or the talent to revive it. He was too feeble and confused to overrule his civil servants or to punish them for their dishonesty and inefficiency. The people starved while the rich businessmen in Constantinople, not all of them Italians, piled their granaries with grain to sell at high prices when the market was low. Byzantine writers of the time condemned the bribery and corruption of imperial officials and the anti-social greed of wealthy entrepreneurs.[1] What the emperor seemed powerless to remedy, the patriarch roundly and loudly denounced.

The Patriarch Athanasios (1289–93; 1303–09) was moved by a social conscience rare even among Byzantine monks. He was a hermit by inclination and his standards of mortification and puritanism were higher than many of his clergy could tolerate. He was forced to resign in 1293. Ten years later he was recalled in a wave of popular frenzy, for the poor and the hungry of Constantinople looked on him as a man of God who put God's precepts into practice by caring for them. The letters that Athanasios addressed to the emperor and his officials are full of denunciations of the prevailing dishonesty and depravity in Byzantine society and of calls to action by the government to alleviate the hardships of the poor.[2] He threatened to excommunicate those who were making

---

[1] Pachymeres, *De Andronico Palaeologo*, iii. 8, 25: II, pp. 208, 258; vi. 1: II, p. 461.

[2] The Letters of Athanasios are edited with translation and commentary by Alice-Mary Maffry Talbot, *The Correspondence of Athanasius I Patriarch of Constantinople*, Dumbarton Oaks Texts, III (*CFHB*, VII) (Washington, D.C., 1975).

a profit out of stockpiling corn and wine for sale at inflated prices. He painted a dreadful picture of the beggars in the streets calling out not for money but for food. The famine was at its worst in the winter of 1306–7 when Venice was at war with Byzantium. In order to drive the Catalans out of Thrace by starvation, the emperor had forbidden the local Greek farmers to sow their crops. This was either a bold or a desperate policy. It added to the influx of refugees into Constantinople and it made the city more than ever dependent on imports of food from the Black Sea. The Patriarch Athanasios thought it very shortsighted and told his emperor so. The famine was made worse by the refusal of the Bulgarians to allow any supplies to be exported to Constantinople until the emperor agreed to relinquish his claims to the ports on the Black Sea coast which they considered to be theirs. Andronikos had to give a little granddaughter in marriage to the Bulgarian king before supplies of corn were resumed. Most of the carrying trade from those ports in 1306 was in the hands of the Genoese who no doubt continued to make a profit out of the stocks that they had stored at Galata before the famine.[1]

The patriarch detested all foreigners and made no distinction between Genoese and Venetians. For him they were all despicable Latins or Italians, denizens of 'a foreign land peopled by barbarians of the utmost insolence and stupidity'. All the empire's wealth and riches in gold and silver had fallen into their hands; and in their arrogance and scorn they boasted of selling their corn in exchange for the favours of Greek wives.[2] The patriarch proposed that the emperor should introduce new regulations and appoint a special commissioner to supervise the sale of corn and the baking of bread in Constantinople. It would be one of the commissioner's duties to ensure that cargoes of grain were promptly distributed to the bakers and not diverted to the warehouses of the profiteers. He would also keep strict watch on correct weights and measures in the markets. Until these regulations were fully in force, the patriarch earned the gratitude of the hungry by setting up soup kitchens in various parts of the city.[3] Such measures might save the bodies of the people but they could not save the souls of their masters. It was the often-expressed opinion of the Patriarch Athanasios that the sorry state of the Byzantine Empire at the beginning of the fourteenth century was caused by the

---

[1] Letters of Athanasios, no. 67, pp. 158–61; no. 72, pp. 178–83. Pachymeres, *De Andronico Palaeologo*, vii. 27: II, pp. 628–9; Gregoras, vi. 5: I, pp. 181–4. Cf. Angeliki E. Laiou, 'The provisioning of Constantinople during the winter of 1306–1307', *B*, xxxvii (1967), 91–113; Laiou, *Andronicus II*, pp. 125–6, 193–9.

[2] Letters of Athanasios, no. 84, p. 222; no. 93, pp. 242–5.

[3] Letters of Athanasios, no. 78, pp. 194–7.

immorality and unchristian behaviour of its inhabitants. Only repentance and a return to the highest standards of the Orthodox faith could make them worthy of the help of divine providence. It was no good appealing for help to the western world, for the westerners were themselves immoral and offensive in the sight of God. Do not delude yourself, he warned his emperor, that we shall prevail by force of arms, not even if the whole of the west were to fight on our side. Our only hope is to turn back to God in that spirit of repentance for which He is patiently waiting.[1] Athanasios had a simplistic view of the relationship between God and man. It was shared by many of the monks, though some of the higher clergy found it embarrassing and uncomfortable. In 1309 he despaired of converting them to a proper sense of sin and for a second time retired to end his days in monastic seclusion.

He had cast a spell on the Emperor Andronikos, who was given to bouts of piety. His successor as patriarch was a less bewitching but a more worldly and sophisticated person. The emperor felt less burdened by his guilt and more free to pursue his own policies. One result of his emancipation was his treaty with Venice in 1310, of which Athanasios would surely have disapproved. The treaty was a sign of the emperor's new approach to the western world against which the patriarch had warned him. In 1311 he had even proposed an alliance with Philip IV of France and his brother Charles of Valois, suggesting that one of his sons should marry Charles's daughter Catherine, the heiress to the Latin Empire; and, if western sources are to be believed, his emissaries to Pope Clement V on this matter had promised that the marriage would heal the schism and reunite the Churches of Rome and Constantinople. The idea was never put to the test, for Charles of Valois had other plans for his daughter's marriage. But it illustrates the emperor's changing policy. If anything of his empire was to be saved from the Turks and the Catalans he must overcome the kind of xenophobia and isolationism preached by the Patriarch Athanasios.[2]

The Venetians were pleased by this new attitude. They too had been through bad years before 1310. A dispute over the possession of the city of Ferrara had led to war with the troops of Pope Clement V who claimed it as his own. The Doge Pietro Gradenigo refused to submit. In March 1309 the pope retaliated by placing Venice and its people under interdict. Venetian trade with the mainland of western Europe came to a halt. No one would do business with an excommunicated people. Ferrara fell to the pope's forces after a siege that was eagerly supported by the European enemies and rivals of Venice. The crisis revived the

[1] Letters of Athanasios, no. 37, p. 78.
[2] Laiou, *Andronicus II*, pp. 241–2.

spirit of faction which had often bedevilled Venetian society in the past. The Doge Gradenigo had been obstinate and vain. The older ruling families conspired to unseat him and replace him by a hero of their own persuasion, Bajamonte Tiepolo. The conspiracy was put down; its organisers were given exemplary punishment; and Bajamonte was exiled to Dalmatia. But the crisis had threatened the stability and shaken the confidence of the Commune. One of its constitutional consequences was the formation by the Maggior Consiglio of a new security force, the Council of Ten, whose business it was to keep the peace and forestall any uprisings in the city. Instituted as a temporary measure to meet an emergency, the Council of Ten soon became an indispensable organ of government, partly as a secret service, partly as an advisory body to the Doge and his councillors. The affair at Ferrara had shown that the machinery of government was too unwieldy to take quick decisions in matters of peace and war. The rules for membership of the Maggior Consiglio had been changed in 1296 and by 1311 it had over 1000 councillors. The crisis had also shown that the Doge could make mistakes. The Council of Ten would help to correct these deficiencies in the future. It became a permanent privy council to the Doge and the Maggior Consiglio in 1344.[1]

Pietro Gradenigo, the Doge who had made the mistake over Ferrara, died in August 1311. His passing was greeted with relief. The Doge who replaced him was chosen because he was by comparison a harmless and pious nonentity. He died less than a year later. His elected successor was Giovanni Soranzo (1312–28). He was elderly but he had a distinguished military career behind him. It was he who, through his envoy, persuaded the reluctant pope to lift the ban of excommunication on Venice. Trade with western Europe could be resumed. Soranzo also acted quickly to suppress a revolt in the Dalmatian city of Zara, which did much to repair the battered prestige of Venice. In the years after 1310, therefore, when Venice and Byzantium were at peace, there began a new era of stability and prosperity under the guidance of an enlightened and respected Doge who was receptive to the new sense of goodwill towards the west emanating from the emperor in Constantinople. The Genoese had made the most of the crisis in Venice. The papal interdict had had little effect on trade with Byzantium, since the pope held the Greeks and their emperor to be in schism. But Venetian ships making their way to and from Constantinople had been constantly liable to attack by the Genoese. In 1313 Giovanni Soranzo took his revenge. Forty galleys led by Giustiniano Giustinian sailed into the Golden Horn and

---

[1] Sanudo, *Vitae Ducum*, cols. 584–92. Kretschmayr, II, pp. 179–84.

threatened Galata. The emperor must have feared that he was about to be drawn into another round of the war between Venice and Genoa. But the Genoese surrendered and paid the Venetians what they wanted in reparations. The Doge made sure that his merchants and their profits would henceforth be protected by sending warships to patrol the Aegean Sea and to keep the Catalans out of Negroponte.[1]

Soranzo was much concerned with the protection of Venetian rights and privileges in Byzantium and of Venetian possessions in Romania. He was keen to preserve the spirit of the treaty that his predecessor had made with the emperor in 1310, however much the letter of that treaty might need revision. He would be courteous but firm with the Greeks. In 1315 he received an embassy from Constantinople concerning the status of the Greeks in Crete and listened sympathetically to their complaint.[2] In 1318, at the emperor's request, the Commune of Venice offered to send two well-equipped galleys to transport his son Theodore to Italy, which they would gladly do out of their respect for and devotion to the emperor.[3] There were signs of polite goodwill on both sides. Yet the question of damages still to be paid by the emperor was not resolved; and there is ample evidence to show that Venetian merchants on the spot in Constantinople and other Byzantine cities had good reasons for not feeling so courteous to the Greeks.[4]

In 1317 the outgoing baillie of Constantinople, Marco Minotto, addressed a report to the Doge and Commune of Venice.[5] Minotto was perhaps not an impartial witness. Some ten years before, when Venice was at war with Byzantium, he had attacked and plundered the island of Lemnos and, in the tradition of earlier adventurers, he had purloined the relics of St Alexander which he found there and sent them home to Venice.[6] His report to the Doge, however, is a precious document. It is one of the very few of its kind to have survived; and it highlights some of the problems of day-to-day co-existence between Greeks and Italians in Constantinople. One of them was the question of Venetian citizenship. All agreements between Byzantium and Venice had stipulated that Venetians would be exempt from the payment of taxes on their

---

[1] Sanudo, *Vitae Ducum*, cols. 598–9; Dandolo, cols. 411–12.

[2] *DVL*, I, no. 54, p. 98; *DR*, IV, no. 2408.

[3] *DVL*, I, nos. 68, 69, pp. 117–20; Cessi–Sambin, I, nos. 256, 257, pp. 198–9; Thiriet, *Assemblées*, I, no. 408, pp. 178, 306; *DR*, IV, nos. 2405, 2417.

[4] The question of reparations owed by the emperor had dragged on under Soranzo's predecessors. Cessi–Sambin, I, nos. 73, 78, p. 133 (1309–10); no. 84, p. 134 (1310); no. 101, p. 135 (1311); no. 102, p. 136 (1311).

[5] *DVL*, I, no. 59, pp. 103–5. J. Chrysostomides, 'Venetian commercial privileges', 267–356, especially 277–9.

[6] Sanudo, *Vitae Ducum*, cols. 579–80. Maltézou, *Thesmos*, pp. 224–5.

trade. To be a Venetian citizen in the empire was thus a special and a valuable privilege. It was one coveted by many Greeks, not because they admired the Venetians but because they would like to share the privilege of tax-free trade. The problem had been noted in earlier treaties by the phrase 'those who are or class themselves as Venetians'. But it had been compounded by a clause in the treaty of 1277 which had declared that the children of mixed marriages between Venetian men and Greek women, the *gasmouloi*, and their descendants should be deemed to be full Venetian citizens with corresponding rights and liberties. Doubtful claims to citizenship had to be decided by the Venetian authorities in Constantinople.[1]

In 1317 Marco Minotto reported that the authorities were enforcing this requirement so rigorously that the interests of Venice were at risk. Witnesses testifying on behalf of a claimant were being obliged to state the nationality not only of his father but also of his grandfather and his great-grandfather. This was not always possible, even though the claimant had thought of himself as being Venetian for generations. As a consequence many who could not provide the facts were driven to opt for Genoese citizenship, since the Genoese would accept anyone for naturalisation without question. The number of Venetian citizens in Constantinople was thus falling while the Genoese population was growing. Some Greeks also were taking Genoese citizenship as a way of avoiding the extra taxes imposed by their emperor. An added complication was that the fathers of some of the half-caste *gasmouloi* in Constantinople had found it prudent to declare themselves to be Greeks in the years when Byzantium and Venice were at war. Now that the war was over, their children protested that they would much rather be Venetians like their ancestors. Minotto warned that these were matters for urgent consideration by the Doge, since it was to the advantage of the Commune and its merchants in Romania to be supported by as large a Venetian population as possible.

In 1319 Minotto was sent back to Constantinople for a second term as baillie, and in 1320 he wrote a much more bitter report to the Doge.[2] He complained that the emperor was forcing Venetians of mixed parentage to adopt Greek citizenship. It was natural that the Venetians should want to maintain or increase their numbers. It was no less natural that

---

[1] See above, p. 199. On the three categories of Venetians in Constantinople and the empire – citizens, subjects and those of protected status – see D. Jacoby, 'Les Vénitiens naturalisés dans l'empire byzantin: un aspect de l'expansion de Venise en Romanie du xiiie au milieu du xve siècle', *TM*, viii (1981), 207–35. Chrysa A. Maltézou, 'Paratirisis ston thesmo tis Venetikis hypikootitas', *Symmeikta*, iv (1981), 1–16.

[2] *DVL*, i, no. 80, pp. 164–8 (3 March 1320).

the emperor should want to ensure that the number of his own subjects should not fall, for they were the taxpayers; and his treasury was sorely in need of revenue. But Minotto had harsher things to say. In his experience, the emperor and his officials always discriminated against the Venetians. The Genoese could do no wrong. But the poor Venetians were beaten, robbed and hounded everywhere from Thessalonica to Constantinople. There were, for example, Genoese and Anconitans who lived in huts or cabins along the shore outside the walls of the capital and ran taverns for the sailors. The authorities winked at this impropriety, which would certainly not be the case if the culprits were Venetians. Minotto itemised a long list of instances in which Byzantine officials in Constantinople, Thessalonica and elsewhere were violating the spirit or the letter of the treaty. He protested that, though all Venetians were supposed to have the freedom of the empire, it was almost impossible for them to settle anywhere because the Greeks and the *gasmouloi* abused and assaulted them at every turn. The emperor did nothing to punish the criminals. If a Venetian lodged a complaint against a Greek he was subjected both to the law's delays and to the insolence of office. His only hope of obtaining justice was by buying it, for the judges would always take their cut and the official interpreters expected to be bribed. Unfair discrimination against Venetian traders was commonplace. In the market in Constantinople they could not sell the corn that they brought from the Black Sea unless the buyer paid a tax on each measure. Byzantine officials justified this by observing that the tax was payable by their own people and not by the Venetians. But it was contrary to the treaty between Byzantium and Venice; and, if Minotto is to be believed, it did not apply to Greeks buying goods from Genoese, Pisan or Anconitan merchants. Likewise, Venetian fishmongers, butchers and other retailers were at a disadvantage because their Greek customers had to pay a tax on their purchases and so went elsewhere. Venetian cobblers, leather-workers and tanners were bullied, beaten and thrown into gaol by government officials when they plied their trade within the city, despite the emperor's promise that they were free to do so. All in all, Marco Minotto believed that the Venetians living in Constantinople had never been so badly treated as they were in 1320; and reports reaching him from consuls in Thessalonica and other places indicated that things were no better in the provinces.[1] The emperor had been informed time and time again but he did nothing. Nor did he respond to repeated requests for payment of the 14,000 *hyperpyra* and other smaller amounts of damages which

---

[1] The Venetian consul in Thessalonica had to be transferred to Ainos in 1315 after he had been robbed. Thiriet, *Assemblées*, I, no. 326, p. 158.

he still owed to Venice and Venetian citizens, many of whom were living in poverty in Constantinople.

Other Venetians had their own tales of woe about their treatment by the emperor. In 1313 Giacomo Orsilio reported how his father had been arrested along with many other loyal subjects of Venice at the time of the Venetian alliance with Charles of Valois. The emperor had confiscated his father's house and goods to the value of 2100 *hyperpyra* and then put him in prison, where he died. His son had suffered further losses when Belletto Giustinian came to attack the Genoese. The emperor had ignored his claims for redress. The authorities in Venice were sorry for Orsilio. They voted that he should be granted a house in the street of the furriers in Constantinople to be held rent free until such time as the Byzantine government might make amends to him.[1] A similar case was that of Jacopo Beth, a Venetian resident who had formerly lived in Acre. About 1317 the emperor had ordered that his house and property should be seized and that he should be arrested. He died in prison. Representations to the emperor had no effect. The Venetian Senate therefore ruled that the victim's homeless son should be given a house near that of the baillie in Constantinople.[2]

Neither the Venetians nor the Greeks always behaved in the ways that their governments would have liked. But the Doge and the emperor were both concerned to maintain cordial relations at the highest level. There was much diplomatic exchange. Fantino Dandolo went to Constantinople as Venetian ambassador in November 1313 and stayed there as baillie for two years until Marco Minotto took over. Another embassy went to Constantinople in February 1315. Dandolo's talks with the emperor elicited a written assurance from him about the status of Byzantine subjects in Crete, to the effect that they would never become the serfs of Venetians. The Senate in Venice had in any case already voted that all Byzantine citizens were free to leave Crete if they so wished. The Doge sent another ambassador to the emperor in November 1316 to strengthen their ties of friendship; and Byzantine envoys known to have been in Venice in May 1317 were probably returning the compliment.[3] By 1319 the superficial courtesies had reached the point at which the Emperor Andronikos could address the Doge Soranzo as his sincere, special and most dear friend.[4]

The courtesies underlined the fact that Byzantium and Venice now

[1] Thiriet, *Assemblées*, I, no. 283, pp. 150, 298.
[2] Thiriet, *Assemblées*, I, no. 391, p. 175.
[3] Cessi–Sambin, I, no. 152, p. 140; no. 2, p. 145; no. 262, p. 168. Thiriet, *Assemblées*, I, no. 372, p. 170; *DVL*, I, no. 54, p. 98; *DR*, IV, no. 2358. Maltézou, *Thesmos*, pp. 108–9.
[4] *DVL*, I, no. 69, p. 119: 'carissimo amico imperii sui . . . amico sincero et speciali'.

needed each other, however much their citizens might find it hard to live at peace together. For in the wider world the security and prosperity of the Venetian colonial empire in Romania and of the much-truncated universal empire of Byzantium were being menaced by enemies dangerous to both; and in 1317, after a poor harvest, there was a serious shortage of wheat and other cereals in Coron, Modon, Negroponte and even Crete.[1] Negroponte remained particularly vulnerable, for the Catalans in Athens and Thebes were aggressive neighbours. Their troops fought the Venetians on the island while their pirate ships added to the hazards of trade in the Aegean and happily co-operated with the Turks of the new emirates on the coast of Asia Minor. The Turks attacked the Venetian islands of Karpathos and Santorini in 1318. Crete and Negroponte daily expected similar attacks. The Catalans had shown the Turks the way on to the mainland of Europe at Gallipoli. They were now doing them the same service by sea. Once again the Venetians protested to their supposed suzerain, Frederick II of Aragon and Sicily, claiming damages for the losses they had suffered and asking for a truce. In June 1319 an agreement was reached at a conference in Negroponte. The Catalans promised to end their attacks on Venetian property, to disarm their merchant ships and to dismantle the rest of their fleet. They would confine their maritime activities to the Gulf of Corinth, well away from Negroponte and out of reach of their Turkish accomplices. The agreement was for six months. But the Venetians held them to it. It was renewed in 1321 and again in 1331. As a result the Catalan threat to merchant shipping in the Aegean Sea was almost extinguished.[2]

Reasons of state required that there should be at least a show of peace and goodwill between Byzantium and Venice. But the reports of Marco Minotto on the realities of life in Constantinople and the shortcomings of the emperor and his agents prompted a spate of complaints from Venice. The embassies exchanged in 1319 and 1320 were concerned not with courtesies and mutual compliments but with hard facts: with the interpretation of the terms of the treaties between them, with specific grievances and with matters of principle affecting the sovereign rights of the Doge and the emperor over their subjects. The details are contained in eight long documents of petitions and counter petitions, accusations and justifications, taken back and forth between Constantinople and Venice in those years. First in the series comes a list of thirty-one complaints taken to Venice by the emperor's ambassadors, the lawyer (*dikaiophylax*) Gregory Kleidas and the interpreter Andronikos Ierakites.[3] Most of them

---

[1] Thiriet, *Assemblées*, I, nos. 379, 389, pp. 171, 174.
[2] Setton, *Catalan Domination of Athens*, pp. 26–7, 34–5; Laiou, *Andronicus II*, pp. 272–3.
[3] *DVL*, I, no. 72, pp. 124–7; *DR*, IV, no. 2423.

relate to injuries or losses inflicted by Venetians on Greek ships in the Aegean in the years between 1312 and 1319. Byzantine merchants were evidently back in business, undeterred by their obligation to pay the *kommerkion* or 10% tax from which the Venetians were exempted. They can hardly have been serious competitors with the big business of Venice. Many of their operations were based on Monemvasia; though mention is made of one Sophonias of Athens who was robbed of his goods by a Venetian on his arrival at Crete from Alexandria in December 1313.[1] Crete was the base of most Venetian pirates; and they did not confine themselves to plunder. There are several reports of Greeks being captured by Venetians and sold into slavery in Crete, Rhodes and Cyprus. An imperial envoy on his way back to Constantinople in August 1317 was captured and robbed of all his belongings by three Venetians who then sold him. His ransom had cost the emperor the price of 'a fine castle'. The emperor's ambassadors presented the Doge with a bill for about 10,000 *hyperpyra* on behalf of Greek merchants from Thessalonica, Constantinople and elsewhere. They also emphasised his continuing concern on two other points. He sought some ruling on the status and the liberty of his subjects living in Crete in confirmation of the earlier Venetian pledge that those who wished to leave the island would be free to do so; and he wished to enforce his own ruling that Venetian ships were free to export corn from the Black Sea by way of Constantinople but not to sell it in the city except under special licence and on payment of the appropriate tax by the purchaser.

The Venetian reply to these requests was long, ponderous and indignant.[2] On the matter of Greek subjects in Crete they protested that they had behaved in full accordance with the letter of the two previous treaties. Those who had wanted to leave the island while Venice was at war with Byzantium had been allowed and indeed encouraged to do so. They pointedly reminded the emperor that they were still waiting for the 14,000 *hyperpyra* which he had promised in compensation so long ago. They would soon have to take special measures for the relief of those who had claims on the money; for many of them were reduced to poverty and even to begging on the streets. What annoyed the Venetians most was the emperor's interference in the Black Sea corn trade. They had been willing to accept restrictions on their exporting corn grown

---

[1] On the revival of Byzantine merchant shipping, see N. Oikonomides, *Hommes d'affaires grecs et latins à Constantinople (XIIIe–XVe siècles)*, Conférence Albert-le-Grand (Montreal, 1979), especially pp. 120ff.; Angeliki E. Laiou-Thomadakis, 'The Byzantine economy and the medieval trade system: thirteenth–fifteenth centuries', *DOP*, XXXIV–XXXV (1982), 177–222.

[2] *DVL*, I, no. 73, pp. 128–32; *DR*, IV, no. 2427. Cessi–Sambin, I, nos. 413, 414, p. 212 (September 1319).

on Byzantine soil, especially in time of crisis. The Genoese too had been prohibited from exporting Byzantine corn in 1304. But they objected to limitations being imposed on the export and the price of corn grown in other parts of the world. They contended that their earlier treaties with the emperor had entitled them to buy and sell in all parts of the empire without payment of any tax all commodities except salt and mastic, and Byzantine corn if its price exceeded an agreed sum. Corn brought from the Black Sea ports of Bulgaria or the Crimea was not grown on the emperor's territory; and corn was not salt or mastic. He therefore had no right to impose duty either on its export or on its sale by those who imported it to Constantinople. They were also cross about the emperor's insistence that even if they tried to sell such corn under his special licence, the Greek buyers of it must pay a pro rata tax to the treasury. This 'purchase tax' caused great offence. It put Venetian traders at a disadvantage; and it could be construed as a violation of the privileges that they were supposed to enjoy.[1]

The emperor was not in a strong legal position when arguing the contrary. Almost two hundred years earlier, in 1126, his predecessor John II had specifically declared that the tax (*kommerkion*) imposed on Byzantines doing business with Venetians was a misunderstanding and must cease.[2] The Emperor Andronikos claimed that his more recent predecessors, John III Vatatzes, Theodore II Laskaris and his own father Michael VIII, had levied a similar tax. But there is no documentary proof of this and the Venetians did not believe him.[3] The treaty which he had signed in 1285 had in fact reiterated in some detail that Venetians could buy and sell all commodities free of tax whether on the vendor or the purchaser, be he Greek or Latin. The problem had much wider significance than the mere buying and selling of corn. It was akin to the matter of those who claimed to be Venetian citizens in the empire. For by giving in on either point the emperor would be diluting the principle of his authority over his own subjects and losing a substantial source of revenue. The Venetian demands pointed the way to the complete takeover of Byzantine trade by Venice.

As to the list of complaints from Greek merchants who had been wronged by Venetians, the Doge rather testily replied that the ambassadors must surely know that the correct forms and procedures for investigating and dealing with such cases were laid down in the treaties agreed

---

[1] See G. I. Brătianu, 'La question de l'approvisionnement de Constantinople à l'époque byzantine et ottomane', in *Etudes byzantines d'histoire économique et sociale* (Paris, 1938), pp. 157–68; Chrysostomides, 'Venetian commercial privileges', 316–20.

[2] See above, p. 164 n. 1.

[3] *DVL*, I, p. 141.

between Byzantium and Venice. All his rectors in Romania would be reminded of their duty to observe and implement these procedures; and he himself would take the appropriate action with respect to the accused who lived in Venice. At the same time he forwarded a list of Venetian subjects who had been similarly victimised on the high seas by Greeks, with the amount of damages that each claimed. It was comparatively short; but it was accompanied by three much more comprehensive lists of complaints and grievances against the emperor and his agents. The first itemises a great number of alleged infringements of the treaty in day-to-day business affairs and property holdings.[1] The emperor's tax officials forbade Venetians to sell cloth, sails and other such goods in Constantinople without levying a tax on those buying them. They contrived by indirect means to demand customs dues from the patrons of Venetian ships coming in to Constantinople. Those who tried to recover the tax in accordance with the treaty were sent from pillar to post in their quest, whereas it was the emperor's duty to order immediate repayment from his treasury. The officials insisted on taxing the wages of Greek sailors who took service as crews on Venetian ships. Venetians holding land or property in Constantinople and the empire were forbidden to sell them to anyone else. All these actions made a mockery of the freedom and security which the Venetians were supposed to enjoy in Byzantium. A final grievance illustrated the obfuscations and delays of Byzantine bureaucracy, of which Marco Minotto complained. A Venetian who had been robbed on Byzantine territory would report to the baillie and his councillors who would then notify the emperor, since the emperor was committed by treaty to make restitution from his treasury. The emperor would give the plaintiff a form to take to a certain office. If he succeeded in finding the place after much trouble and expense he would as like as not get no satisfaction. He would then go back to the baillie empty-handed and out of pocket. This was a regular occurrence and it seemed that Venetians could never get satisfaction for the injuries they suffered.

The second list of grievances submitted to the emperor itemises the wrongs done to Venetians by Byzantine officials in Thessalonica.[2] The Venetian colony there had been provided for by Michael VIII in 1277. It seems to have grown since 1310 but it was never a great success. The Venetians were even less popular there than they were in Constantinople. Their consul complained that the local customs men frequently held up the unloading of cargoes for three or four days until they had

[1] DVL, I, no. 74, pp. 132–3.
[2] DVL, I, no. 75, p. 134. F. Thiriet, 'Les Vénitiens à Thessalonique dans la première moitié du xive siècle', B, xxii (1952), 323–32.

been satisfactorily bribed. Venetian residents were forbidden to buy vege-
tables and if they protested they were beaten. The houses allotted to
them were so small as to be uninhabitable, fit only for fishmongers and
the like. Any altercation over deals done between a Venetian and a Greek
was settled in favour of the latter, without reference to the Venetian
consul. If the Venetian complained he was thrashed. There was also evidence of pro-Genoese feeling in Thessalonica. In 1319 a Venetian selling
corn had it taken from him by the emperor's officials, who gave it to
a Genoese friend of theirs to the great distress of its owner. The third
document submitted lists the petitions and claims for compensation made
by individual Venetian citizens for damage done to their persons and
property in Greece between 1314 and 1319.[1] Many of the incidents
had taken place off the coast or in the ports of Epiros in the north west,
where at the time the emperor had been trying to reassert his authority
over the rebel Despot Thomas; and much of the damage was done, acci-
dentally or deliberately, by the Byzantine army. The document reveals
the presence of Venetian merchants and residents with their own consul
in the Despot's capital city of Arta on the Ambracian Gulf, at Valona
on the Albanian coast and in other parts of Epiros.[2] The sum total
of these and other claims submitted by Venetians in the Morea and the
islands exceeded the estimate of 14,000 *hyperpyra*, some of which, it
appears, had at length been lodged with the baillie in Constantinople.
The baillie was Marco Minotto; and it was to him that these documents
were sent from Venice in September 1319 to be presented to the emperor.
They must have confirmed him in his worst suspicions of the Greeks.

It was just after the end of Minotto's first term of office as baillie
that an incident occurred which was to have greater consequences. The
Genoese from Galata sailed across the Golden Horn and attacked the
Venetians in 1318.[3] Hostility between Genoese and Venetians was never
far below the surface; and the Byzantines were generally blamed when
it erupted. The Doge demanded restitution from the emperor for what
the Genoese had done. The emperor thought it was no business of his.
The Venetians quoted at him the text of the treaty of 1285: injuries inflicted
upon Venetians by a force armed and equipped in his empire would
be paid for from his treasury. This clause had certainly appeared in that
treaty, taken over from the treaty of 1268. But the emperor rightly
observed that it had been repealed in the treaty of 1302, which had deliberately absolved him from having to pay for damages occasioned on either
side during hostilities between Genoese and Venetians anywhere in his

---

[1] *DVL*, I, no. 76, pp. 135–9.   [2] Nicol, *Despotate of Epiros*, II, pp. 77–9.
[3] *DVL*, I, pp. 137–8.

empire.[1] The emperor reinforced the legality of his own position by trying to clarify the exact meaning of the treaty of 1285. A 'force equipped in his empire' meant a Greek or Byzantine force, not a Genoese one. The Venetians would not accept this interpretation. They maintained that the emperor had undertaken to recompense them for injuries inflicted by any force equipped within his empire, and that this was an ancient treaty obligation agreed before there was any mention of the Genoese. These were nice legal points which gave employment to the lawyers on both sides. But one feels sorry for the emperor.[2]

His detailed reply was taken to the Doge by the same two ambassadors, Gregory Kleidas and Andronikos Ierakites.[3] Its tone is in striking contrast to the querulous demands of the Venetians. It is as if the pious emperor was shocked and hurt by their graceless materialism. They were inclined to think of the Greeks as tiresome children not yet schooled in the ways of the world. They spoke only of damages and sums of money. The Byzantines did not care to be so brutally realistic. They preferred to raise the tone of the debate by veiling the realities in rhetoric. The emperor's reply is larded with references to the will of God and the hope of lasting reconciliation. He urges the Doge not to spoil their new friendship by dwelling on the things that divided them. In a remarkable outburst of self-pity he complains that almost everyone seems to be out to do him down, he who has harmed no one, sought no territorial expansion, seized or usurped nothing from anyone. But for the clemency of God and the intercession of His immaculate Mother his empire would not have been able to sustain the onslaughts of its numerous enemies; and it is indeed still possible that his house will fall upon him and that he will perish in the ruins.[4] He did his best to answer all the charges made against him. With regard to his subjects in Crete he observed that many of them were refugees from the Turks in Asia Minor. They too should be free to leave the island and not be held against their will as vassals of Venice. On the matter of payment of indemnities to Venetians wronged in the Morea, in Thessalonica and in Epiros, he pointed out that there was documentary evidence to prove how much had already been paid; and he added that the Doge's case would be stronger if he could show similar evidence of compensation paid to Greeks who had suffered from Venetians. The treaties imposed mutual obligations in this respect. The damage done to Venetian property by his troops in Epiros was admittedly unfortunate. But it had been done in time of war, when

---

[1] TTh, III, pp. 99, 333; DVL, I, p. 14.   [2] DVL, I, pp. 148–9, 162–3.
[3] DVL, I, no. 77, pp. 139–50; DR, IV, no. 2423.
[4] DVL, I, p. 140.

his troops were fighting against the rebellious Despot Thomas, whose cause some Venetians had supported. The rebel had now been struck down by the justice of God. Finally, the emperor was dismayed by the Doge's remarks about the tax payable by Greeks on purchases from Venetians and on Greeks who served on Venetians ships. He had agreed that Venetians should be able to buy and sell goods throughout his empire tax free; but he had not undertaken to grant the same exemption to the Greeks. To do so would be to abdicate his authority and sovereignty over his own subjects. This was an important point which should have been obvious to the Venetians.

Another challenge to the emperor's authority seemed to be presented by the Venetian Jews living in Constantinople. By the end of the thirteenth century if not before, Jews who counted as Byzantine subjects lived in the district of the city known as Vlanga.[1] Jews who claimed to be subjects of Venice had also come to settle in Constantinople, most of them probably from the Venetian colonies in Romania. The Doge complained that the emperor had discriminated against them by forbidding them to carry on their business as leather-workers and tanners. He had assigned three houses to the baillie and his officers and twenty-five to Venetian merchants; and he had agreed that Venetians could reside anywhere else in his empire on payment of rent and could ply their trade freely. Venetian Jews, however, did not enjoy these privileges.[2] The emperor replied that Byzantine Jews came under his jurisdiction and had their own quarter in Constantinople, where they carried on their own trade and rendered to his treasury the dues required of them. In the course of time they had been joined by many Venetian Jews who preferred to live with those of their own faith and to work together with them. They agreed among themselves that the Venetian Jews would provide the leather and hides while the Byzantine Jews did the tanning and curing. This arrangement worked well until the emperor ordered the Byzantine Jews to abandon the leather business and to find some other occupation. The Venetian Jews then turned to the tanner's trade, which they had never practised before, in defiance of their own agreement and of the emperor's orders. They were therefore punished and evicted from the Byzantine Jewish quarter.[3]

It seems probable that the Venetian Jews were evicted because, as

[1] See D. Jacoby, 'Les quartiers juifs de Constantinople a l'époque byzantine', B, xxxvii (1967), 167–227, especially 189–205; Jacoby, 'Les Juifs vénitiens de Constantinople et leur communauté du xiiie au milieu du xve siècle', Revue des Etudes Juives, cxxxi (1972), 397–410; Jacoby, 'Les Vénitiens naturalisés', 227–8; S. B. Bowman, The Jews of Byzantium 1204–1453 (Alabama, 1985), pp. 20–4, 50–60.

[2] DVL, I, p. 129.

[3] DVL, I, pp. 142–3.

10

9

8

6

Venetians, they were exempt from taxation and had thus found a way of making a Jewish monopoly of the tanning industry. There was, however, nothing to prevent them from settling in the Venetian quarter, where they could do what they liked, or from renting accommodation elsewhere, as stipulated in the treaty. The Venetians were not satisfied with this explanation, for they claimed that those of their Jews who had taken houses on payment of rent had been persecuted and forbidden to work as tanners. They begged the emperor to leave them alone and to allow them to practise their traditional crafts. They knew what was happening in Constantinople. They knew that quite recently the emperor had sent his men with interpreters into the Jewish quarter to ransack the houses. They had forcibly removed all the hides that they found, burning some, throwing some into the sea and carrying the rest away. This represented a loss of more than 70,000 *hyperpyra* to the Venetian Jewish community, a loss which the emperor must make good.[1] The value set upon the hides gives an idea of the tax-free profits being made by the Jews in Constantinople and also of the consequent loss of revenue to the imperial treasury. The Venetians had a way of forcing the emperor into a corner.

Among a number of specific cases mentioned in these exchanges between Doge and emperor two stand out. The first was that of Lodovico Morisco, the brother of the Genoese captain Andrea Morisco, whom the emperor had honoured as a loyal servant. Lodovico had been captured in 1309 by Andrea Cornaro of Venice after he had attacked the island of Karpathos and incited its inhabitants to rebellion. Cornaro had already occupied Karpathos. He sent Morisco to be imprisoned in Crete on a charge of piracy. The fact that he was Genoese did not endear him to the Venetians. The fact that he was no better than a pirate excluded him from the general amnesty granted to Greek and Venetian prisoners by the treaty. The emperor protested that Lodovico Morisco was no pirate. He was a vassal of the empire and counted as a Greek subject; and he had been appointed to command the islands near to Rhodes, which the emperor had assigned as a fief to his late brother Andrea Morisco. The Venetians therefore had no right to detain him as a prisoner any longer, whatever he may have done at Karpathos. The emperor was tactful enough not to enquire how Andrea Cornaro had come into possession of Karpathos. But the Venetians rejected his request.[2]

The second case which recurs in all the documents was that of the

[1] DVL, I, p. 153.
[2] DVL, I, pp. 125, 131–2, 143–4, 156. K. Hopf, 'Die Cornaro von Skarpanto', in *Veneto-Byzantinische Analekten*, Sitzungsberichte der k. Akademie der Wissenschaften, phil.-hist. Classe, xxxII/3 (Vienna, 1859), pp. 116–33.

Genoese captain Napoleone Del Mar. In November 1318 the Doge had
kindly offered to put two galleys at the disposal of the emperor's son
Theodore to bring him to Italy. In the event Andronikos sent his son
on one of his own ships in a convoy led by a warship belonging to
its captain, Napoleone, who also carried the ambassador, Stephen Syropoulos. The Doge sent out an escort to greet Theodore and bring him
safely into Venice. The ambassador also reached Venice safely. But Napoleone alleged that four Venetian galleys had intercepted him off Valona
in the Adriatic and relieved his convoy of a cargo ship with all its valuable
contents. The Doge disclaimed any knowledge of this incident and declared Napoleone to be a liar. The fact was that Napoleone, having left
Venice, took to piracy in the Adriatic, attacking and robbing Venetian
ships in their own waters and almost in sight of Venice. The cost of
the damage that he did must be met by the emperor. Andronikos could
not and did not claim that the culprit in this instance was his vassal
or his subject. He was relieved to be able to declare that Napoleone
Del Mar was of pure Genoese stock. Any complaints against him should
therefore be addressed not to Constantinople but to Genoa. The Venetians were not impressed by this argument.[1]

Indeed they were not impressed by any of his arguments and protestations. The last of the series of documents, composed in 1320, is also
the longest.[2] It contains a detailed refutation of all the emperor's replies
to the charges levelled against him and his officials. Only in one case
does the Doge express any satisfaction or gratitude to the emperor for
having made the required restitution. It is perhaps unfortunate that the
emperor's replies have been transmitted only in Latin translation. The
well-kept archives of Venice have survived. Those of the Byzantine chancery in Constantinople have for the most part perished. None the less,
it cannot be said that the Latin documents present only one side of the
story, since the Venetian refutations of the Byzantine defence nearly
always cite the text of that defence at the outset. What is abundantly
clear is that the Doge and his legal advisers were determined to hold
the Greeks closely to the letter of a treaty which had been none too
clearly drafted in the first place. In the final exchange of charges and
counter charges the Venetian lawyers revealed several instances of slip-
shod reading of the treaty's text by the Byzantines, making it possible
for the Doge to reprove the emperor for not looking more carefully

---

[1] *DVL*, I, pp. 125, 130–1, 143, 154–5; Cessi–Sambin, I, no. 274, p. 200. Laiou, *Andronicus
II*, pp. 264–6.
[2] *DVL*, I, no. 79, pp. 158–64.

at the text before trying to wriggle out of its implications or misinterpret-
ing its clauses.[1]

No doubt the exchange of embassies would have continued until some
of the misunderstandings had been resolved or until a new and more
satisfactory treaty had been agreed. Yet another list of damages done
to Venetians by Byzantines in the Aegean Sea was lodged in 1321. It
amounted to 14,135 *hyperpyra*.[2] In 1322 the *sapientes ordinum* of
Venice, the select committee of the Senate for maritime trade and colonial
affairs, applied their wise old minds to the proper briefing of an embassy
to be sent to Constantinople to draw up a new treaty which would
clarify the anomalies in the existing convention. They examined closely
the texts of the treaties of 1285 and 1302. The question of outstanding
reparations loomed large in their deliberations. But they had no thought
of going to war or of pulling out of Constantinople. On the contrary,
they advised that their ambassador should make representations to the
emperor about the status and the security of the Venetian quarter in
the city. They maintained that its residents lived in constant dread of
attack or of fire. There were fires in 1316 and again in 1319 which had
destroyed some of their property.[3] Their ambassador should ask the
emperor to grant them an enclosed area surrounded by a wall behind
which their people could live in greater safety. The baillie and his councillors should decide where a new quarter could best be situated. It is
clear that the Venetians in Constantinople, for all their dissatisfaction
and complaints, were digging in rather than pulling out.[4]

The decision to send a new ambassador to Constantinople was taken
in July 1321.[5] It was a bad moment. The news coming to Venice from
Byzantium must have been bewildering. Civil war had broken out.

---

[1] *DVL*, I, pp. 158, 162, 163.   [2]*DVL*, I, no. 88, pp. 181–6.
[3] Thiriet, *Assemblées*, I, no. 340, pp. 162, 301; *DVL*, I, p. 166.
[4] *DVL*, I, nos. 90–2, pp. 187–91.
[5] Cessi–Sambin, I, nos. 158, 164, 171, pp. 234–5; Thiriet, *Assemblées*, I, no. 431, p. 183.

14

BYZANTIUM,
VENICE AND THE TURKS

ABOUT 1320 the Emperor Andronikos II imposed a further round of taxes on his subjects. The taxgatherers did their work thoroughly. The failing economy of the empire showed signs of reviving. The emperor proposed to spend some of the proceeds on building a fleet of twenty warships and on maintaining a standing army of 1000 cavalry in Bithynia in Asia Minor and 2000 in Thrace and Macedonia. He needed the rest for administration, for embassies and for satisfying his creditors in Venice and other places. His subjects were already overtaxed. They knew that much of what they were asked to pay went into the pockets of the emperor's officials and not into the treasury. This was one of the causes of the general discontent with the government and the policies of Andronikos II. But there were also particular discontents within the ruling family; and it was these that precipitated a war for the possession of the throne. By 1321 Andronikos had reigned for nearly forty years, years during which things seemed to have gone from bad to worse. There were many in high places who felt that the time had come for him to go and to hand over to a younger generation with new ideas. He had planned that his dynasty should be perpetuated through his son Michael IX and his grandson Andronikos III. But Michael died in 1320. It was said that his death had been hastened by the behaviour of his son, the young Andronikos, who had once been his grandfather's favourite. He had been crowned as a co-emperor in 1316. In 1321 his title was taken from him and he was disinherited. The old emperor reigned alone with no heir apparent and no desire to abdicate. This was the moment for which the younger generation had been waiting.

Andronikos III was about twenty-five years old when he was disinherited. His cause was at once taken up by a number of his friends who encouraged him to fight for his right to the succession. They were mostly of an age with him, ambitious young men of aristocratic breeding and inherited wealth. Prominent among them was John Cantacuzene, whose family owned vast estates in Thrace, Macedonia and Thessaly. His career as a soldier and statesman, which began effectively with his support for his friend Andronikos III, was ultimately to lead him to the throne. Much of Byzantine history in the fourteenth century was to be shaped by his policies and narrated by his pen in the memoirs which he composed in later life. The ground for rebellion was prepared in Thrace. At Easter 1321 the young Andronikos escaped from the clutches of his grandfather and joined his friends at Adrianople. There he was hailed as emperor. There he assured himself of a loyal following by announcing an end to taxation. The people of Thrace took to arms to fight for the young pretender who had relieved them of their burden. The struggle for power was decided in three stages. The old emperor had his own loyal supporters and he had the advantage of being in possession of Constantinople. He proposed compromises which proved to be unacceptable or unworkable. In July 1322 he reluctantly conceded that his grandson should reign as his colleague, though junior in authority. In February 1325 Andronikos III was crowned as co-emperor; and in October 1326 he obeyed his grandfather's wishes by marrying an Italian, Giovanna or Anne, daughter of Count Amadeo V of Savoy. For about five years, from 1322 to 1327, there was an uneasy partnership between the two emperors. But there was no real trust or confidence.[1]

It was during those years that the long negotiations between Byzantium and Venice which had begun in 1319 resulted in a new agreement between them. The embassy from Venice that was to have gone to Constantinople in July 1321 seems to have been postponed, doubtless because of the uncertain situation. Not until June 1322 was there talk of sending another, and the Senate advised its leader to do no more than demand from the emperor the 14,000 *hyperpyra* that he owed in damages. No serious discussions could be held until that debt had been settled. In November the *sapientes* heard evidence from Marco Minotto and from Fantino Dandolo, who had been baillie in Constantinople before him; and before the end of the year 1322 ambassadors had been fully briefed and were ready to set out.[2] Fantino Dandolo was one of them. The emperor was none too securely on his throne and he was keen to win the favour of his friends from Venice. He presented Dandolo with a cloth of gold which was later handed over to the procurators of St Mark's in honour

---

[1] Ursula V. Bosch, *Kaiser Andronikos III. Palaiologos* (Amsterdam, 1965); Nicol, *Last Centuries of Byzantium*, pp. 159–66.

[2] Cessi–Sambin, nos. 93, 102, pp. 254–5; no. 185, p. 261; nos. 211, 212, 219, 220, p. 263; no. 336, p. 273.

of the patron saint.[1] After some further exchanges, a delegation from Constantinople went to Venice in 1324 empowered to sign a preliminary treaty. It was led by Stephen Syropoulos, who was an experienced diplomat; and he took with him the required 14,000 *hyperpyra*. The Doge was pleased to acknowledge receipt of the money. For once the Greeks had got their priorities right. The preliminary treaty was signed in Venice on 11 June 1324 in the presence of the Doge, Giovanni Soranzo.[2] In October the fuller and more comprehensive text of the new agreement between Byzantium and Venice was signed by the emperor in Constantinople and handed to the baillie, Tommaso Soranzo. It was sealed by his golden bull. The ceremony was witnessed by a number of the emperor's relatives, but not by his grandson and supposed co-emperor Andronikos III. The excuse may have been that the young man had still to be crowned. But it can hardly have been by accident that he was not present on so formal an occasion.

The text of the treaty of 1324 survives in its Greek original and in a Latin translation.[3] Its term was to be five years beginning from 11 June. It enshrined all the conditions and clauses of the treaties of 1285 and 1302, 'with the amendment of certain items which needed to be more clearly expressed'. The clarifications were almost all in the interests of Venice. All that they had protested and argued about for years was now granted them. The emperor had given in. Venetian merchants were henceforth to be free to buy and sell Black Sea corn anywhere in the Byzantine Empire without any restrictions or impediments. In other words, the much-disputed purchase tax levied on their customers was to be waived if not explicitly abolished. The restriction on their export of corn grown on Byzantine territory remained the same as before. But they were now at liberty to buy, sell, or export any other kind of agricultural produce in the empire. The emperor also capitulated on the contentious issue of Genoese or other attacks on Venetian persons and property. He undertook to pay compensation from his treasury if anyone, Greek, Latin or of other race, did violence to Venetians in his empire; though he would ask for no corresponding reparation from Venice for injuries inflicted on his own subjects by Venetian merchants or officials. Finally, he agreed to pay debts and damages to Venice amounting to 12,000 *hyperpyra*, part of which was a loan that had been made to his own nephew Andronikos Palaiologos. The first instalment of 4000 *hyperpyra*

[1] Thiriet, *Assemblées*, I, pp. 185, 307 (8 January 1323).
[2] Cessi–Sambin, no. 282, p. 269 (April 1323); nos. 393, 394, 400, 413, pp. 277–9 (January–February 1324); nos. 21, 22, p. 284 (June 1324); *DVL*, I, nos. 94, 95, pp. 194–6 (11 and 28 June 1324). *DR*, IV, no. 2510.
[3] Greek text in *MM*, III, pp. 100–5; Latin text in *DVL*, I, no. 98, pp. 200–3. *DR*, IV, no. 2515.

was duly lodged with the baillie, Tommaso Soranzo, before the end of July 1325.[1] The treaty was confirmed by the Doge in Venice on 30 April of that year in the presence of a Byzantine ambassador.[2]

The treaty of 1310 had lasted rather longer than its allotted twelve years; but it had never been wholly satisfactory. The Doge, the successive baillies of Constantinople, the senate and the *sapientes* had disputed nearly every clause of it. They had preferred to build a new agreement on the earlier treaties of 1285 and 1302. They achieved their aim after months of protest and legal wrangling. Their envoys and their lawyers wore the emperor down until they broke his resistance. Some points were not raised in 1324: the Venetian request for a new and safer quarter in Constantinople; the matter of Venetian Jews; and the tax payable by Greek sailors serving on Venetian ships. But it seemed that Venice had won on every major point affecting its trade and profits. The rest could be discussed at a later date. One wonders why the emperor surrendered so much. He had claimed that by relieving his subjects of the payment of purchase tax he would be weakening his authority over them as well as losing revenue. In 1324 he seemed willing to do both without asking for anything in return. It has been argued that his surrender to the demands of Venice was a sign of his new policy of making friends with the powers of western Europe.[3] This is no doubt true. But it was still more a sign of his own sense of insecurity. He knew that there were those who wanted him to abdicate. He was elderly and tired and he could not compete with the new vitality of Venice. The Serenissima had found fresh strength and confidence under the leadership of Giovanni Soranzo. The leadership of Byzantium was split by a family feud between grandfather and grandson. Andronikos III was formally crowned as coemperor in February 1325; and for a few months the fiction was enacted that there were two emperors reigning in harness in Constantinople. It was about this time that the house of Palaiologos adopted the device of the double-headed eagle. It symbolised not, as is often supposed, a great empire that looked at once to east and west, but a sordid division of imperial authority between two disputatious emperors of the same family. The future history of that family was to show how apt a device it was.[4]

There was, however, one other factor that brought Byzantium and

---

[1] Thiriet, *Assemblées*, I, pp. 187–8. The abolition of the purchase tax payable by Greeks was noted by the Venetian Senate in August 1324 and instructions were accordingly sent to all rectors in Romania. Cessi–Sambin, no. 46, p. 286.

[2] *DVL*, I, no. 99, pp. 203–4; Cessi–Sambin, no. 172, p. 296.

[3] Laiou, *Andronicus II*, pp. 311–12.

[4] B. Hemmerdinger, 'Deux notes d'héraldique', *BZ*, LXI (1968), 304–9.

Venice together. The Doge had forced his will upon the Catalans in Greece. The Turks were not so easy to manage, for they were not united among themselves and had no single leader. Turkish pirates and raiders from the emirates that had been established in Asia Minor became bolder and more adventurous. The Knights of St John, who had made their headquarters in Rhodes in 1308, policed the seas round about their island. But the most successful of the Turkish emirates was that of Aydin which lay further to the north. About 1317 Mehmed, emir of Aydin, captured the upper citadel of Smyrna; and for some years his warships fought running battles off the coast against the navies of the Genoese family of Zaccaria in Chios and the Knights of Rhodes, while his pirate ships preyed on Venetian merchantmen in the Aegean and plundered Venetian islands. The Byzantines were more nearly affected by the advance of the Osmanli or Ottoman Turks in Bithynia. While they were engaged in their own civil war the emirate of Osman expanded up to the Bosporos and the shore of the Black Sea. In April 1326 Osman's son Orchan captured the city of Prousa (Bursa). It became the first capital of the new Osmanli emirate; and there Osman, its founder, was buried when he died in 1326. Orchan was left to complete the conquest of the remaining Greek cities in Bithynia.[1]

The growing threat from the Turks was a matter of common concern to Greeks and Latins. The Venetians began to consider how they could co-operate with the Byzantine government in driving them back. In March 1325 the Senate commissioned the *sapientes* to examine the possibility of forming an anti-Turkish alliance or league. The Byzantine Emperor would be asked to join it. The idea developed slowly. In July 1327 the Senate proposed that membership of the league should be extended to include the Grand Master of the Knights of Rhodes and the Genoese lord of Chios, Martino Zaccaria. The baillies of Constantinople and Negroponte and the Duke of Crete were to discuss the plan with the emperor before the end of the year.[2] The emperor must have welcomed the idea. But in the winter of 1327–8 he was not free to pursue it. The final round of his struggle for power in Constantinople had begun. Half an empire and half a crown were not enough for the young Andronikos and his friends. They persuaded him that the time had come to end the business by force. In January 1328 the city of Thessalonica surrendered to him. He was ready to fight his way into Constantinople to make himself sole master of the empire. The citizens were ready to have him as their emperor, for they were tired of the fighting and short of

---

[1] Lemerle, *L'Emirat d'Aydin*, pp. 19–62; Nicol, *Last Centuries of Byzantium*, pp. 150–6.

[2] Cessi–Sambin, no. 175, p. 296 (March 1325); nos. 194, 202, pp. 341–2 (July 1327). Laiou, *Andronicus II*, pp. 312–14.

food. At this critical moment in the history of Byzantium the Venetians and the Genoese had come to blows again. A Venetian fleet of forty ships was blockading Galata and the mouth of the Golden Horn by way of reprisal after a local dispute. Genoese food ships from the Black Sea could not get through to the harbour. The people were hungry as well as angry with the senior emperor who had brought them to this state. It was a graphic illustration of the control that the Italians could exercise over the daily life of Constantinople. Andronikos III tried to turn the affair to his advantage by secretly bribing the Venetians to withdraw. But they were interested only in getting their pound of flesh from the Genoese. The Byzantines might be starving. Their emperor might be about to lose his throne. The first concern of the Venetians was the settlement of their own private quarrel with their commercial rivals.[1]

In May 1328 Andronikos III, accompanied by his friend John Cantacuzene, at length marched into Constantinople. His grandfather, now forced to abdicate, expected the worst and begged for mercy. He was treated with courtesy and humanity. A few months later he became a monk and in February 1332 he died, perishing, as he had foretold, in the ruins of his empire. The war against him had been won at a ruinous cost; and it had set a precedent. There would be other civil wars in Byzantium. For in the struggle between Andronikos III and his grandfather other rivalries and jealousies had found expression; and neighbouring states had found that there was profit to be made by fostering those rivalries. In the years between 1321 and 1328 the rulers of Serbia and of Bulgaria had happily accepted invitations to take sides; while the Italians and still more the Turks had taken advantage of the empire's malaise. The new emperor, Andronikos, had a vigour and energy which his grandfather had lost. He could manage his European enemies. He was able to counter the presumption of the Bulgarians and force them to come to terms in 1329. But things had been allowed to go too far in Asia Minor. In May of the same year he and his commander-in-chief John Cantacuzene led an improvised army against Orchan, the son of Osman, in Bithynia. It was the first military encounter between a Byzantine emperor and an Osmanli emir. Victory went to the Turks. The Emperor was wounded. His troops panicked and fled to the coast. The collapse of Byzantine resistance was thereafter swift and complete. The city of Nicaea, once the capital of the empire, surrendered to Orchan in 1331. Two years later the emperor admitted defeat. He invited Orchan to meet him in Bithynia and the first treaty between Greeks and Turks was signed in August 1333. A military solution to the problem was no longer

---

[1] Gregoras, ix. 5: 1, p. 416. Cessi–Sambin, no. 315, p. 351 (February 1328).

practicable. It was better to accept a compromise, better to have the Osmanlis as allies than as enemies, even if it meant abandoning a province to them and paying tribute to their ruler.[1]

Andronikos III pursued, or hoped to pursue, a similar policy towards the other Turkish emirates in Asia Minor. In the autumn of 1329 he had seized the chance of a revolt of the Greeks on Chios to dispossess the Genoese lord of the island, Martino Zaccaria, and instal a Greek governor. The Genoese had made large profits out of Chios. It was a valuable asset for the Byzantine treasury. The Genoese at Phokaia on the mainland opposite swore allegiance to the emperor; and from there he invited Umur of Aydin and one of the other emirs to meet him and discuss a settlement along the lines of that agreed with Orchan. This tentative new policy of co-existence with the Turks was not to the taste of the western powers, who had interests of their own in the Aegean Sea. The popes saw it as treachery to the Christian cause. The Venetians and the Genoese were also displeased. For in 1329 Umur of Aydin had completed his father's work at Smyrna by capturing the lower town and harbour of the city. His Turkish ships then had a safe haven from which to conduct their piratical raids on Greece and the islands.[2]

The Venetians were still toying with their idea of a league of Christian powers against the Turks. They had an influential propagandist in the person of Marino Sanudo Torsello. Sanudo was related to the Venetian Dukes of Naxos and he was something of an expert on Byzantine affairs. His history of Romania (*Istoria del Regno di Romania*) is an invaluable narrative of events in Latin-occupied Greece and the Venetian colonies up to the year 1310. He is better known, however, for his *Secreta fidelium Crucis* in which he explained to the western Christian world the necessity for a crusade against the Turks. Sanudo saw the Levant as a whole, from Alexandria to Constantinople, and he understood the complexities and the seriousness of the Turkish problem in Asia Minor and the Aegean. He did not confine himself to theorising. He broadcast his knowledge and his warnings in letters to the pope, to the Kings of France and of Naples and to the Byzantine Emperor, whom he came to regard as a valuable potential ally in the crusade. He presented a copy of his *Secreta* to Pope John XXII.[3] Not all of his own countrymen shared Sanudo's enthusiasm for a crusade, however disturbed they might be about Turkish

---

[1] Bosch, *Andronikos III*, pp. 146–9, 152–8; Nicol, *Last Centuries of Byzantium*, pp. 172–6.
[2] Lemerle, *L'Emirat d'Aydin*, pp. 56–68.
[3] On Marino Sanudo, see: A. S. Atiya, *The Crusade in the Later Middle Ages*, 2nd edn (New York, 1965), pp. 114–27; Angeliki E. Laiou, 'Marino Sanudo Torsello, Byzantium and the Turks: the background to the Anti-Turkish League of 1332–1334', *Speculum*, XLV (1970), 374–92; Laiou, *Andronicus II*, pp. 312–14, 354–5.

pirates and raiders on their shipping routes and in their islands. A defensive league against the Turks was one thing. A crusade meant all-out war; and as the Venetians had often said before, war was bad for business. In his communications with Andronikos II in 1319–20, the Doge had made two important generalisations about Venetian policy. He repeated what many of his predecessors had said, that Venice could not survive without imports from the sea; and he emphasised that his people were merchants whose trade went better in conditions of peace than in time of war.[1]

Whether the proposed league against the Turks took on the character of a crusade depended on the pope at Avignon, John XXII, and his fervent admirer, Philip VI of France. Neither of them was as well-briefed or as realistic as the Doge of Venice. The King of France tried to get the Doge to commit himself to joining a crusade. But the idea of a defensive alliance seemed more attractive to Venice. In July 1332 the new baillie being sent to Constantinople was instructed to enrol the Emperor Andronikos III as a member. Discussions had been taking place for some months to get him to pay the final instalment of 4000 *hyperpyra* owed by his grandfather and also to renew the treaty of 1324, which had expired the year after he came to power.[2] The Venetians may have been cautious in their approach to the new emperor; but it was they who took the first step towards renewing their treaty. In June 1331 and again in June 1332 the emperor authorised the dispatch of embassies to Venice for the same purpose.[3] The negotiations were still in progress when the anti-Turkish league was formally constituted. Its three leading members were Venice, the Byzantine Emperor and the Grand Master of the Knights of Rhodes. The Doge, Francesco Dandolo (1328–39), and his senators had been hard at work whipping up support. The key figures in the formation of the league were Pietro Zeno, baillie of Negroponte, and Pietro da Canale, captain of the Gulf. It was described as 'a union, society and league for the discomfiture of the Turks and the defence of the true faith'. The emperor was pleased to be a member for all that he had made his own arrangements with some of the Turkish emirs; and on 26 August 1332 he authorised Pietro da Canale to express his willingness to join forces with the Knights of Rhodes. The Doge had already drawn up a similar authorisation and in September Canale, representing Byzantium as well as Venice, met the Grand Master at Rhodes and concluded the

---

[1] *DVL*, I, pp. 131, 161, 208.

[2] F. Thiriet, *Régestes des Délibérations du Sénat de Venise concernant la Romanie*, I, Documents et Recherches, I, II, IV (Paris–The Hague 1958) (cited hereafter as Thiriet, *Sénat*), no. 6 (15 March 1330); cf. no. 3 (3 July 1329), no. 20 (7 July 1332).

[3] *DVL*, I, no. 112, pp. 223–4; *DR*, IV, nos. 2773, 2784. Cf. Thiriet, *Sénat*, I, nos. 16, 18.

formalities. The emperor described the document that he had signed as a chrysobull, though he had to apologise for not having his golden bull to hand since he was away from Constantinople. The Doge on the other hand drew up his document in the comfort of his palace; and though it was sealed only with a lead seal it may be significant that he styled himself 'lord of one-quarter and one-eighth of the whole Empire of Romania'. The league's stated purpose would be to maintain a fleet of twenty fully-armed warships for a period of five years. They would be based on Negroponte and be ready to set out to do battle against the Turks by 15 April 1333.[1]

There was plenty for the league to do. Umur of Aydin, operating from Smyrna, had become the scourge of the Aegean Sea. His ships attacked and plundered Crete, Coron, Modon, Negroponte and the Greek mainland. The members of the league were slow in organising themselves, however. The Venetians were hampered by a rebellion in Crete. The Byzantine Emperor was anxious not to upset his own arrangement with Umur. The other interested parties who had been so keen on a crusade, the pope and the Kings of France and Naples, continued to express approval, interest and concern. But it was not until March 1334 that Pope John XXII gave the league its stamp of holiness. At his palace at Avignon it was agreed that forty galleys should be assembled at Negroponte in May. The Knights would provide ten, Venice ten, the King of Cyprus six, the Byzantine Emperor six and the King of France eight. The King of Naples, who had talked so much about it, was notably absent from the membership, as was the Republic of Genoa. The greatest achievement of this first anti-Turkish crusade was a naval battle fought in September 1334 off Adramyttion on the Asia Minor coast. It silenced the activities of one of the lesser Turkish emirs and it was hailed as a great Christian victory. But the Christian fleet failed to recover Smyrna and at the end of the year they dispersed, leaving Umur in possession of his harbour and free to carry on his deadly work. In December Pope John XXII died. King Philip of France had problems nearer home. Venice tried to keep the interest alive. But as a holy war it had lost its impetus.[2]

The creation of the league had brought Byzantium and Venice closer

[1] DVL, I, nos. 116–17, pp. 225–30; Thiriet, Sénat, I, nos. 20, 22; DR, IV, nos. 2784–5. Dandolo, col. 413; Sanudo, Vitae Ducum, col. 601.
[2] Bosch, Andronikos III, pp. 119–28; Lemerle, L'Emirat d'Aydin, pp. 89–101; Setton, Papacy and the Levant, I, pp. 179–82; N. J. Housley, 'Angevin Naples and the defence of the Latin East. Robert the Wise and the Naval League of 1334', B, LI (1981), 549–56; Elizabeth A. Zachariadou, Trade and Crusade. Venetian Crete and the Emirates of Menteshe and Aydin (1300–1415), Library of the Hellenic Institute of Byzantine and Post-Byzantine Studies, II (Venice, 1983), pp. 21–40.

together. The renewal of their treaty, which had been so much discussed, had taken place in November 1332. It had been arranged by the ever-useful Gregory Kleidas and Stephen Syropoulos, who had gone to Venice as the emperor's plenipotentiaries. The Venetian senate had debated whether it should be signed for a period of seven years or not more than four. They had also proposed that neither party should be free to contract a separate truce with the Turks.[1] In the event it was signed for six years and nothing was said about the Turks. It was to run from 4 July 1332. There are Greek and Latin texts of the emperor's sworn testimony.[2] The terms were precisely those of the treaty of 1324. No new clauses or clarifications were added. The major part of the document deals yet again with the recurrent theme of damages demanded by the Doge and Commune for maltreatment of Venetian subjects by Greeks. In particular the Venetian consul in Thessalonica was to be recompensed for houses that had been promised to his community but never handed over. The emperor agreed to pay a total of 15,800 *hyperpyra* in annual instalments over three years. All other state claims for reparations submitted before July 1332 were to be dropped or regarded as settled. Given the Venetian obsession with such claims this was a triumph for the emperor. But he did not escape scot free. For he was faced with another list of itemised Venetian claims for compensation from private individuals. Among them were the creditors of his uncle, Andronikos Palaiologos, who seems to have been constantly in debt to Venetian moneylenders and to have arbitrarily appropriated some Venetian houses in Constantinople. One case concerns the wrongful appropriation by the emperor himself of some houses belonging to a Venetian for the use of some merchants from Provence.[3] Not all the plaintiffs were in Constantinople. Nine of them were in business in Arta in Epiros and at Valona in Albania, where conditions were far from settled at the time.[4] The emperor promised that their claims would be met by those responsible within two years; otherwise his own treasury would pay them in full. The document ends with the customary clause about the renewal of the treaty after its allotted six years and the possibility of its termination by either side after six months' notice. It was signed and sealed with the emperor's golden bull in the presence of a crowd of witnesses, the most distinguished

[1] Thiriet, *Sénat*, I, nos. 16, 22; R. Cessi and M. Brunetti, *Le Deliberazioni del Consiglio dei Rogati (Senato) Serie Mixtorum*, Deputazione di Storia Patria per le Venezie: Monumenti Storici. Nuova serie, XVI (Venice, 1961) (cited hereafter as Cessi–Brunetti), no. 138, p. 142 (18 June 1332).

[2] Greek text in *MM*, II, pp. 105–11; Latin text in *DVL*, I, no. 118, pp. 230–4. *DR*, IV, no. 2787.

[3] In 1340 Andronikos III was to grant privileges in Constantinople to merchants from Narbonne. *DR*, IV, no. 2843. Heyd, *Commerce*, I, pp. 479–81.

[4] Nicol, *Despotate of Epiros*, II, pp. 99–101.

of whom was the Grand Domestic, John Cantacuzene. It was then delivered to the baillie of Constantinople, Giacomo Soranzo.

In later years the same John Cantacuzene, looking back on the history of relations between Byzantium and Venice, observed that the conventions between them had always been more in the nature of truces than of treaties. Since the days of Michael VIII neither had felt inclined to conclude a lasting peace, only arrangements for stated numbers of years which could be extended or terminated by mutual agreement.[1] He wrote from experience as one who had had many dealings with the Italians. In 1332 his friend Andronikos III had committed himself to paying Venice the sum of 15,800 *hyperpyra* in three annual instalments. In June and July 1334 the baillie of Constantinople was instructed to remind the emperor of his obligation. In January 1335 he was told to threaten the emperor that all Venetians would have to leave his empire within six months if no money was forthcoming.[2] It was an idle threat. The loss to Venice would have been immeasurably greater than the paltry sum that they were demanding; and they could not seriously have contemplated leaving the Genoese a free hand in Constantinople. They had indeed comforting evidence that Byzantine patience with the Genoese was running out. In 1335 Benedetto Zaccaria, brother of Martino who had been dispossessed of Chios six years before, borrowed some ships from his countrymen in Galata and tried to recapture the island. He failed; but later in the same year the Genoese lord of Phokaia on the mainland hired some ships from Genoa and the Knights of Rhodes and attacked and occupied the island of Lesbos. The Genoese in Galata had encouraged both of these enterprises. The emperor retaliated by ordering that the defences built around their settlement, which they had just reinforced, be demolished.

The incident strengthened his belief that the Turks were more reliable allies than the Italians. At the end of 1335, leaving some ships to blockade Lesbos, he sailed over to the mainland to lay siege to Phokaia. His Turkish friends answered his call for help. The Genoese were evicted first from Phokaia and then from Lesbos. The most significant outcome, however, was a new treaty between Greeks and Turks. Umur of Aydin came to meet the emperor at Kara Burun between Chios and Smyrna. It was a festive occasion in the course of which Umur struck up a lasting friendship with the Grand Domestic John Cantacuzene. The treaty was in the nature of a defensive alliance between Byzantium and the emirate of Aydin against the Osmanlis as well as the Italians. It implied Byzantine

---

[1] Cantacuzenus, iv. 25: III, p. 188. Cf. Pseudo-Kodinos, pp. 235-7.

[2] Cessi–Brunetti, no. 496, pp. 318-19 (7 June 1334); no. 541, p. 333 (11 July 1334); no. 727, pp. 389-91 (19 January 1335). Thiriet, *Sénat*, I, nos. 54, 57.

recognition of the emirate as a permanent institution, a sovereign state to whose ruler the emperor had to pay tribute. But it brought peace; and it also brought the promise of large numbers of Turkish ships and troops to fight alongside the Byzantine army.[1]

In the next few years that promise was usefully fulfilled. Umur of Aydin gladly provided troops to support the emperor in Europe. Without them he might not have been able to complete the reconquest of northern Greece, which contemporaries regarded as his greatest achievement. Between the years 1333 and 1340 the provinces of Thessaly and of Epiros were reincorporated into the Byzantine Empire. The last of the rebellious Despots of Epiros, who had preserved their independence since the Fourth Crusade, was carried off to Constantinople.[2] An imperial governor was installed in his place. It appeared that the emperor had been right to cut his losses in Asia Minor and to concentrate on the revival of Byzantium as a great power in Europe. The Venetians were impressed by these new signs of Byzantine vitality. They must have enjoyed seeing their Genoese rivals humiliated and the fortress harbour of Galata rendered defenceless. They issued no more threats of pulling out. In June 1338 they ordered their baillie in Constantinople to remind the emperor that his treaty with Venice was about to expire and that they could not contemplate extending it until he had paid his outstanding debts. These had now risen to 19,000 *hyperpyra*, as a result of troubles in Thessalonica and elsewhere which had caused losses to Venetian citizens. In February 1340 an ambassador to Constantinople, Giovanni Gradenigo, was instructed to look into these matters and to make quite certain that the Byzantines were held to payment of the full sum claimed when the treaty was renewed. By July 1340 it had still not been signed; but nine months later news reached Venice that the emperor had reaffirmed the treaty of his own accord. The baillie was commanded to send an urgent report to the Senate by special courier.[3]

The news changed rapidly. The Emperor Andronikos III returned to Constantinople after his long campaigns in northern Greece in the spring of 1341. A few months later, on the night of 14–15 June, he died after a short illness. The Venetian ambassador, Pietro da Canale, was quick to offer his condolences to the heir apparent, John V, and to remind him of his father's debts. Privately, however, the Senate advised

[1] Gregoras, xi. 1: I, pp. 525–9; Cantacuzenus, ii. 29: I, pp. 476–95. Heyd, *Commerce*, I, pp. 487–9; Lemerle, *L'Emirat d'Aydin*, pp. 102–15; Zachariadou, *Trade and Crusade*, pp. 38–40.
[2] Nicol, *Despotate of Epiros*, II, pp. 102–22.
[3] Thiriet, *Sénat*, I, no. 54 (July 1334); no. 57 (January 1335); no. 77 (June 1338); no. 84 (January 1339); no. 86 (February 1339); no. 98 (February 1340); no. 112 (July 1340); no. 124 (March 1341); Thiriet, *Assemblées*, I, no. 477, p. 194 (March 1340).

Canale that he should in any event proceed with the renewing of the treaty.[1] Canale must have been better informed than the Doge or the Senate in Venice. It was not easy for him to negotiate with an emperor who was still a child. John V was barely nine years old when his father died; and there was much dispute as to who should act as regent of the empire until he came of age. His father's lifelong friend, John Cantacuzene, assumed that it was his privilege and duty so to act. But his mother, the dowager empress Anne of Savoy, who had always distrusted Cantacuzene's influence over her husband, favoured the claim of the patriarch to be regent. The dispute over the regency uncovered and released many deeper tensions in Byzantine society. It was one of the causes of a second and still more disastrous civil war that was to last for nearly six years, until Cantacuzene asserted what he thought to be his rights by fighting his way back to Constantinople. Throughout those long and bitter years the government of Venice behaved with strict constitutional propriety, acknowledging the empress–mother and the patriarch as the lawful regents for her son John V. They had no truck with the pretender in exile. It was perhaps a comfort to them that the empress, Anne of Savoy, was herself an Italian. It was certainly a comfort to her to find in her hour of need that she could turn to the bankers of Venice to bail her out.[2]

The Genoese were the first to benefit from the new regime in Constantinople. In September 1341 Anne and her son John were induced to sign a new agreement with the Republic of Genoa.[3] It went far to restoring the confidence of the Genoese in Galata whom Andronikos III had punished. The patient efforts of the Venetian ambassadors to Constantinople were similarly rewarded in March 1342 when the treaty or the truce between Byzantium and Venice was at last renewed for seven years. Its text contained nothing that was new. Even the Venetian demands for settlement of old and new debts had a familiar ring.[4] It seems that 4000 of the 19,000 *hyperpyra* claimed had been paid. The rest would follow in equal instalments over the next five years. One or two cases of damages payable to individuals were recorded; and the document was signed by the hand of the ten-year-old emperor in the Blachernai palace on 25 March. It was no doubt little more than a formality. The Doge and the Senate must have been increasingly aware that the emperor's

[1] Thiriet, *Sénat*, I, no. 132 (July 1341).
[2] Bosch, *Andronikos III*, pp. 176–93; Nicol, *Last Centuries of Byzantium*, pp. 191–6.
[3] *DR*, v, no. 2864.
[4] It was signed on 25 March 1342. Greek text in *MM*, III, pp. 111–14; Latin text in *DVL*, I, no. 132, pp. 257–9. F. Dölger, *Facsimiles byzantinischer Kaiserurkunden* (Munich, 1931), n. 11, pp. 16–18; *DR*, v, no. 2876.

mother and regent, Anne of Savoy, was caught up in the crippling expense of war and that she would probably never be able to pay them. The war was fought mainly on land, in Macedonia and Thrace where John Cantacuzene's partisans had proclaimed him as emperor in 1341. Venetian interests were therefore not much in danger. But it was important to have their position in Constantinople regularised by treaty.

The empress's financial difficulties were revealed less than two years after the war had begun. In the spring of 1343 she begged a loan of 30,000 ducats from Venice. She made her request through Pietro da Canale; and on 5 April the Senate resolved that it should be met on certain strict conditions. She must lodge securities for the loan and she must undertake to pay to the baillie in Constantinople the sum of 10,000 ducats a year with interest at 5%, the money to be found from the revenue of the imperial customs duties. If the loan were not repaid within three years, the securities would be at the disposal of Venice.[1] It was a substantial sum. The gold ducat of Venice was worth about two of the debased *hyperpyra* of Byzantium in the middle of the fourteenth century.[2] The empress would find it hard to lay her hands on the equivalent of 20,000 *hyperpyra* a year. As early as June 1343 the Doge was having doubts about the wisdom of lending her so much money. The baillie, Giovanni Gradenigo, failed to reassure him by reporting that she could not possibly repay any of it for the present and that she appeared to be trying to augment her revenue from customs by levying a tax on corn imported from Turkish-occupied territory, which was surely in violation of the treaty.[3] But in August of the same year the deed was done. The baillie made over to the empress 30,000 ducats as a loan repayable over three years. The money was subscribed by a consortium of Venetian merchants in Constantinople, who were to be reimbursed with interest by a similar consortium in Venice before the end of the year. More than a hundred years earlier the Venetians had propped up another tottering regime in Constantinople by floating a loan to its Latin ruler. On that occasion the security offered had been the holy Crown of Thorns. In 1343 the Venetians were offered something more easily valued in material terms— the Byzantine crown jewels, or a large part of them. The promissory note completing the transaction was signed by the young John V. He can hardly have known what he was being asked to do. The pawning

---

[1] Thiriet, *Sénat*, I, no. 153.

[2] G. I. Brătianu, 'L'hyperpère byzantin et la monnaie d'or des républiques italiennes au XIIIᵉ siècle', reprint in *Etudes byzantines d'histoire économique et sociale* (Paris, 1938), pp. 217–39; T. Bertelè, 'L'iperpero bizantino dal 1261 al 1453', *Rivista italiana di numismatica*, v, serie 5, LIX (1957), 78–89; Thiriet, *Sénat*, I, pp. 226–7; Thiriet, *Romanie vénitienne*, pp. 306–7.

[3] Letter of Gradenigo to the Doge Andrea Dandolo, ed. Maltézou, *Thesmos*, pp. 229–31 (13 June 1343). Cf. Thiriet, *Sénat*, I, nos. 157, 164.

of the crown jewels was his mother's work. She was recklessly optimistic. Her son had been properly crowned as emperor in November 1341. If things went well the jewels would not be needed again for another generation, by which time the money would have been found to buy them back and pay the interest on the loan. She was wrong. The jewels were never redeemed. They were still in the treasury of St Mark's when Constantinople fell to the Turks in 1453; and demands for the repayment of the loan with the accumulating interest on it figured in almost every treaty between Byzantium and Venice until that date.[1]

Fortified by her new-found wealth, the Empress Anne and her regents held the whip hand in the civil war for a while longer. The principal supporters and allies of John Cantacuzene were his friend Umur, the Turkish emir of Aydin, and the ambitious ruler of Serbia, Stephen Dušan, who had come to his throne ten years before the struggle began. Umur eagerly supplied Cantacuzene with ships and men. Dušan gave him hospitality and refuge in Serbia when his cause seemed all but lost. Neither was a disinterested ally. Both, but especially Dušan, saw profit to be made from intervening in Byzantine politics. The empress hoped for support from the west. It was known in Constantinople that Pope Clement VI was anxious to assemble a new anti-Turkish league of Christian powers. In the summer of 1343 she sent one of her own Savoyard knights to Avignon to announce that she and her son were devoted servants of the Holy See. They were in grave danger from the Turks. Only ships and soldiers from the west could save them. Earlier in the year she had sent another of her knights to Venice with the same plea; and she had asked the Doge to use his influence with the King of Serbia to dissuade him from comforting her enemy John Cantacuzene.[2] Venice was to be deeply involved in the new league against the Turks, though again for reasons different from those that inspired the pope. Pope Clement VI thought in terms of a crusade. The Venetians, and the Byzantines, had a more limited objective: to put a stop to the activities of Umur of Aydin, whether as a pirate or as an ally of John Cantacuzene. His

---

[1] DR, v, no. 2891. Sanudo, Vitae Ducum, cols. 617–18 (he provides an inventory). The documents concerning the pawning of the crown jewels to Venice are collected in T. Bertelè, 'I gioielli della corona bizantina dati in pegno alla Repubblica veneta nel sec. xiv e Mastino II della Scala', Studi in onore di Amintore Fanfani, ii: Medioevo (Milan, 1962), pp. 90–177. Mastino della Scala of Verona, moved by love for John V and his mother, vainly offered to repay the whole sum. Venetian demands for repayment began as early as April 1344. Bertelè, 'Gioielli', Documents 8 (22 April 1344), 9 (24 January 1345), 10 (4 February 1347), pp. 154–5; Thiriet, Sénat, i, nos. 168, 174 (= DVL, i, no. 151, p. 287), 195, 199, 200; Thiriet, Assemblées, i, no. 506 and p. 310.

[2] DR, v, nos. 2888, 2890. Thiriet, Sénat, i, no. 155.

ships were said to number as many as 250 to 300. The pope's league was set up in August 1343. Venice contributed ten of the twenty galleys; the pope, the King of Cyprus and the Knights of Rhodes provided the rest. Martino Zaccaria, former lord of Chios, commanded the pope's contingent; and the combined fleets assembled at Negroponte. They had contracted to stay together for three years. It was a remarkable instance of co-operative action against the common enemy of the faith; but it was hardly a crusade. Zaccaria had to be prevented from using it to help him recover Chios; though in the course of events a Genoese squadron led by Simone Vignosi independently captured the island.[1] Its greatest success, if not its raison d'être, was the destruction of Umur's fleet and the occupation of the harbour and lower town of Smyrna in October 1344. The victory was greeted with joy in the western Christian world and rekindled some of the old fire of crusading zeal. Humbert, the French Dauphin of Viennois, felt moved to pose as the pope's champion and leader of a crusade which, it seemed, would approach Jerusalem by way of Smyrna. He assumed command of the league. But he was back in France by the summer of 1347.[2]

In all the excitement of the 'crusade' the Byzantines had been left out of account. By the time that it died down their domestic conflict had been resolved. The people of Constantinople had suffered more than they had gained from the operations of the league. Once again they had gone hungry. The Venetian and Genoese food ships from the Crimea were coming in empty, for the local Khan of the Tatars had suddenly expelled all Italian merchants from his territory. There was famine in Constantinople and, as usual, prices rose. The Venetians had been able to import grain from Turkish-held lands in Asia Minor, though they complained about the customs dues that they had to pay. But the anti-Turkish league effectively closed those markets too. The famine spread to the Venetian colonies and to Italy, where it was the worst that anyone could remember. In desperation the Venetian government made a treaty of its own with the Tatars so that grain ships could again sail to the Crimea. The Genoese were furious and did all that they could to stifle

---

[1] Gregoras, xv. 6: ɪɪ, pp. 765–7; Cantacuzenus, iii. 95: ɪɪ, pp. 583–4. Chios remained in Genoese hands from 1346 until its conquest by the Turks in 1566. P. Argenti, *The Occupation of Chios by the Genoese and their Administration of the Island*, ɪɪ (Cambridge, 1958), pp. 26–32. The emperor sent an embassy to Genoa to protest in 1347. Bertelè, 'Gioielli', pp. 102–3.

[2] Smyrna remained in Christian hands until 1402. Atiya, *Crusade in the Later Middle Ages*, pp. 290–318; Lemerle, *L'Emirat d'Aydin*, pp. 180–203; Setton, *Papacy and the Levant*, ɪ, pp. 182–223; Zachariadou, *Trade and Crusade*, pp. 49–54.

this Venetian initiative in the Black Sea. Everything pointed to another round in the trade war between Venice and Genoa.[1]

Meanwhile the civil war in Byzantium was drawing to its close. When Umur of Aydin could no longer help him, John Cantacuzene found another Turkish ally in the person of Orchan, son of Osman, whose emirate was closer to Constantinople. In 1346 he gave his daughter Theodora as wife to Orchan, who was glad to send soldiers to fight in Thrace; for it was from Thrace that he proposed to advance on Constantinople. Meanwhile, his former friend and protector, Stephen Dušan of Serbia, had embarked on the conquest of Byzantine Macedonia and the encirclement of the city of Thessalonica. His sights too were set upon the greater prize of Constantinople. Dušan conceived the idea of a new form of universal empire in which Slavs would predominate over Greeks. In April 1346 he adopted the crown and the title of Emperor of the Serbs and Romans. He looked to Venice for assistance in the conquest of Constantinople, since he had no navy of his own. The Venetians were embarrassed by the request. They congratulated Dušan on his proclamation as emperor, for he was their friend. But they could not help him in the matter of Constantinople because they were bound by treaty to the Byzantine Empire.[2]

John Cantacuzene was even more embarrassed by the presumption of the Serbian king. He too hastened to have himself crowned as emperor. The ceremony took place at Adrianople in Thrace on 21 May 1346. There were now three Emperors of the Romans in a world where God had ordained that one was enough. But only one of the three, the young John V, was in possession of Constantinople; and he alone had been crowned with the regalia of his ancestors which now lay in pawn in Venice. His mother, Anne of Savoy, had not the means to pay the interest on the loan let alone redeem the crown jewels. The regency was bankrupt. Cantacuzene's friends in the capital prepared the ground for his arrival. On the night of 2 February 1347 he contrived a way into the city with a small body of men. There was almost no resistance. Cantacuzene was far from being a popular hero. He was an unrepentant aristocrat. But the people had endured enough. Turkish mercenaries had blighted their land. Hunger and misery had worn them down. They would accept peace at any price. The dowager empress and the patriarch had to admit defeat. The empress reluctantly conceded that Cantacuzene should reign as senior colleague with her son, the Emperor John V, for a period

[1] DVL, I, no. 141, pp. 273–4; no. 167, pp. 311–13; no. 170, pp. 334–8. Sanudo, *Vitae Ducum*, cols. 614–15. Thiriet, *Sénat*, I, nos. 162, 164, 175, 180, 196, 201, 203. Zachariadou, *Trade and Crusade*, pp. 45–9.
[2] Thiriet, *Sénat*, I, no. 189.

of ten years. The two families would be united by John's marriage to Cantacuzene's daughter Helena. There were to be no reprisals; all political prisoners would be released; the past was to be forgotten.[1]

It would be interesting to read what the baillie of Constantinople may have written to the Doge in February 1347. The Venetians in the city must have followed events with some concern. Reports from their consul in Thessalonica were not reassuring; for there the feeling against John Cantacuzene had caused a social and political revolution without precedent in Byzantine history. A faction calling themselves the Zealots had seized power and set up a form of government by commune that was to last until 1350. The Venetians in both cities must have watched these developments closely. But their reports on them have not survived. The first intimation that they knew of the change of government in Constantinople dates from July 1347. The Senate instructed its ambassadors who were on their way to the Crimea to confer with the baillie and his councillors while passing through the capital. They might also, if they saw fit, pay their respects to the Emperor John Cantacuzene to assure him of the goodwill of Venice and to remind him of 'the great love and benevolence which had always flourished between his empire and the commune of Venice and which would, with the will of God, continue to flourish'. They might also call on the young emperor and his mother.[2] By then Cantacuzene had been crowned as emperor for a second time. The new patriarch performed the coronation in the church of the Virgin at Blachernai. The date was 21 May 1347, a year to the day after his first coronation at Adrianople. If the Venetian baillie had been present as a guest he would have noticed, as did Greek observers at the ceremony, that the crown jewels were made of glass and that the plate for the banquets was made of pewter and clay. The Empress Anne had sold most of the gold and silver plate from the palace to make ends meet during the civil war. The Venetian baillie would have known where the real crown jewels lay, safely stored in the treasury of St Mark's[3].

---

[1] Nicol, *Last Centuries of Byzantium*, pp. 208–14.

[2] *DVL*, I, no. 165, p. 310; Thiriet, *Sénat*, I, no. 203 (14 July 1347).

[3] There may in fact have been no Venetian baillie residing in Constantinople at the time. Marco Foscarini left in 1346 and his successor, Nicolò Querini, was not appointed until Feburary 1348. Maltézou, *Thesmos*, p. 112. Gregoras, xv. 11: 11, p. 788, comments on the evident poverty of the coronation ceremony.

15

BYZANTIUM:
THE VICTIM OF COMMERCIAL RIVALRY

IN the last year of the Byzantine war for possession of the throne the Genoese stopped supplying corn to Constantinople, partly as a reprisal for the sinking of two of their ships. They boasted that they alone could determine whether the city's inhabitants survived or starved, since they could get corn from no other source.[1] The boast was not strictly true so long as Venetian ships came in from the Black Sea. But the new emperor, John Cantacuzene, knew well enough what they meant. He knew too that, while the Genoese had taken no active part in the fighting that had brought him to his throne, their sympathies were with his opponents, the Empress Anne of Savoy and her family. They had also turned the confusion of the war to their own advantage by reoccupying the island of Chios and the mainland ports of Phokaia which Andronikos III had reclaimed in 1329.[2] Cantacuzene had more to fear from the Genoese than from the Venetians. The activities of the Venetian residents in Constantinople could be watched and to some extent controlled. The Genoese colony of Galata across the Golden Horn was an autonomous enclave beyond the control of the emperor and his officials, setting its own tariffs and collecting its own dues. In 1348 it was estimated that the annual revenue of Galata was nearly seven times that of Constantinople. When, as a matter of form, the Genoese asked permission to enlarge and refortify their settlement the emperor refused. They took no notice and did as they wished.[3]

The Venetians were jealous. They had never acquired the kind of independent status which the Genoese enjoyed at Galata. Before they could take any action, however, a catastrophe of global dimensions struck the

---

[1] Gregoras, xv. 6: II, pp. 766–7.

[2] Gregoras, xv. 6: II, pp. 765–6; Cantacuzenus, iii. 95: II, pp. 583–4. *Chronica Byzantina Breviora*, ed. P. Schreiner, *Die byzantinischen Kleinchroniken*, CFHB, xii/1–3 (Vienna, 1975–9), II, p. 266 (cited hereafter as *Chron. brev.*). Atiya, *Crusade in the Later Middle Ages*, pp. 311–14; P. Argenti, *The Occupation of Chios*, I, pp. 86–105.

[3] Gregoras, xvii. 1: II, pp. 841–2.

just and the unjust alike. Bubonic plague, known as the Black Death, swept the world from east to west. This too had its origins in the Crimea. Tradition links it with the Tatar siege of Caffa in 1346. From there the plague was carried by the rats on Italian ships. It reached Constantinople and then Trebizond in the summer of 1347. By the end of the year it had reached Marseille; and by March 1348 it had spread to Venice. Demographically the Black Death was one of the greatest disasters in human history. Statistics are hard to come by. The fullest and most literary account of its effects in Constantinople and the Byzantine world is that given by the Emperor John Cantacuzene in the memoirs that he wrote later in his long life. His youngest son was a victim. But he gives no figures, no roll-call of the dead; and his description of the symptoms and the suffering is derived sometimes word for word from the celebrated account written by Thucydides of the plague at Athens in the time of Pericles. His contemporary Gregoras rightly records that the infection was brought to Constantinople from the Scythian or Tatar country of Lake Maiotis or the Sea of Azov. A western chronicler declares that eight-ninths of the population of Constantinople died. This is doubtless an exaggeration. But no figures whatever are to be found for its effects in other cities of the empire or in the Turkish emirates in Asia Minor; and there is little evidence for its consequences in Romania, though it is known to have reached the Peloponnese and Crete by February 1348.[1]

It must be presumed that many of the Venetian residents in Constantinople and of the Genoese in Galata died in the epidemic. But the numbers are not recorded. The case of Venice itself is a little better documented. Ten years before it reached the lagoons the total population may have been about 100,000. Five years afterwards it had been reduced to about 40,000. In the summer of 1348 people in Venice were said to be dying at the rate of 600 a day. Fifty noble families died out completely. Andrea Dandolo, the historian, who was Doge at the time, unfortunately laid down his pen at the year 1339; and his continuator, Caresini, has disappointingly little to say about the Black Death. Sanudo, however, reckoned that one-third of the population died and that the membership of the Maggior Consiglio was reduced from 1250 to 380. Lorenzo de Monacis, writing in 1428, sets the death rate as high as seven out of ten. Venice was so alarmingly empty of people that the government voted to extend tax immunity and other incentives to all foreigners who would come to live in the territory of the commune. The statistics are little

[1] Gregoras, xvi. 1: II, pp. 797–81; Cantacuzenus, iv. 8: III, pp. 49–53; *Chron. brev.*, II, pp. 271–2; *Chronicon Estense Marchionum Estensium*, *RIS*, xv (Milan, 1729), col. 448. For the plague in Crete: Thiriet, *Assemblées*, I, nos. 545, 546, 553. See in general, P. Ziegler, *The Black Death* (London, 1969).

more than estimates. The consequences of the plague in depopulation and loss of manpower can, however, be observed. It was no longer possible for Venice to send out large fleets manned exclusively by Venetian citizens. Crews had to be recruited from Dalmatia or from the colonies in Romania. The fleet became more heterogeneous, less disciplined, less reliable; and there was an acute shortage of ship's caulkers and carpenters.[1]

The Black Death left its survivors, in the east and in the west, in a state of shock, of nervous apprehension that it would return, as it did, though in less virulent form, on several occasions in the next hundred years. In Constantinople and the few remaining provinces of the Byzantine Empire it came at the end of a civil war which had already made normal life impossible. The treasury was empty; the fields and vineyards in Thrace had been devastated in the fighting, not least by the Turkish troops that both sides had engaged to fight their battles. The capital city was falling into ruins and the money could not be found for its upkeep. The cathedral of St Sophia had been badly damaged by earthquake in 1346. Funds for its repair were subscribed not by the citizens of Constantinople but by the Grand Duke of Moscow, who fancied himself as the protector of Orthodoxy. Yet most of his generous donation went on paying for the hire of Turkish mercenaries. As if to compound the misfortunes of Byzantium, the self-styled Serbian Emperor Stephen Dušan chose this moment to invade the provinces of northern Greece, which Andronikos III had triumphantly restored to his empire only eight years before. Dušan had befriended the Emperor John Cantacuzene so long as it suited his purpose. But his territorial and imperialist ambitions had grown in the course of the civil war. He had come to see himself as emperor in Constantinople. In 1348 the Byzantine governor of Thessaly died of the plague. Serbian armies marched into Thessaly and Epiros and were soon in control of most of mainland Greece as far south as the Gulf of Corinth. The Catalans still held Athens and Thebes. But further north only Thessalonica remained Greek and many of its rebellious citizens would rather surrender to Stephen Dušan than acknowledge Cantacuzene as their emperor.[2]

The odds seemed stacked against him. Cantacuzene was not beloved by his people. They saw him as the leader of the oppressive aristocracy

[1] *Raphayni de Caresinis Cancellarii Venetiarum, Cronica AA. 1343–1388*, ed. E. Pastorello, *RIS*, xii/2 (Bologna, 1923), pp. 4–5; Sanudo, *Vitae Ducum*, cols. 614–15; Lorenzo (Laurentius) de Monacis, pp. 313–15. Thiriet, *Assemblées*, i, no. 547 (22 June 1348); Lane, *Venice*, pp. 18–21.
[2] Nicol, *Last Centuries of Byzantium*, pp. 225–6; Nicol, *Despotate of Epiros*, ii, pp. 128–31.

who had aggravated their miseries by his selfish struggle for power. The ravages of the Black Death sapped what little optimism they had left and reduced them to a fatalistic despondency. Yet the new emperor had powerful supporters among the rich and, for all his faults, he had plans for stimulating an economic and military recovery. He saw clearly that Byzantium had been allowed to fall into the grip of a mercantile stranglehold. The Genoese had boasted that they could hold Constantinople to ransom by cutting off its food supplies. The Venetian empire in Romania and the Aegean islands was draining away the resources of the provinces. Foremost among the emperor's plans for recovery was the construction of a native Byzantine navy of warships and merchant ships. It was not easy to raise the money; and it proved even harder to raise enthusiasm among the apathetic people of Constantinople. The Genoese were none the less alarmed. They began to fear that their lucrative monopoly might be challenged if a Byzantine fleet were recreated. Their alarm turned to fury when they learnt that the emperor proposed to divert merchant traffic from Galata by lowering the tariffs payable by ships unloading at Constantinople. In August 1348, while the emperor was away, they sailed over and attacked the Byzantine shipyards, burning all the cargo ships that were lying at anchor and the few warships that were on the stocks. They met with fierce resistance and when they returned to the attack they were beaten back in confusion. It was this incident that cured the apathy of the Byzantines. When the emperor came back in October he had no further difficulty in persuading his people that they must build more ships. New taxes were levied and the money was found; though the timber for the ships had to be hauled by oxen from the mountains of Thrace, since the Genoese controlled the sea routes. They realised with some regret that they had brought a war with Byzantium on themselves. They approached the emperor with proposals for peace. He would have none of it unless they first dismantled their fortifications at Galata.

In the spring of 1349 the new Byzantine fleet was ready. There were nine large warships and about a hundred smaller vessels. The plan was for them to lure the Genoese into a sea battle while an army marched round to lay siege to Galata from behind. The ships may have been seaworthy but their captains and crews, hastily mustered, had little knowledge of how to handle them. The chance capture of a Genoese ship off the Princes Island gave them false hope. But when they launched their main attack the inexperience of their commanders was quickly demonstrated. A gale or a gust of wind blew up. Some of the sailors were blown overboard. The rest panicked and jumped into the sea, leaving their ships empty. The soldiers on land also took fright when they saw

what was happening and ran all the way back to the safety of Constantinople. The Genoese could hardly believe their eyes. They towed the
empty ships over to Galata. The next day they cruised in triumph along
the sea walls of Constantinople, insolently trailing the Byzantine standards behind them. Fortunately for the emperor, ambassadors from
Genoa arrived a few days later empowered to make peace. They realised
that their countrymen at Galata had behaved with shameless impropriety.
They agreed that Genoa would pay the emperor an indemnity of more
than 100,000 *hyperpyra* and pledged that their people would never again
attack Constantinople. They even consented, after further representations, to pay rent for possession of the islands of Chios which they
had illegally occupied, at least for a period of ten years, after which
the island would revert to Byzantine rule.[1]

The Genoese may well have laughed in scorn at the antics of the new
Byzantine navy. But they were impressed by the emperor's show of
confidence. There is no evidence that the Venetians in Constantinople
played any part other than that of interested and doubtless incredulous
spectators in the Byzantine–Genoese skirmish of 1348–9. They may have
been tempted to join in; and their intervention might have turned humiliation into victory for the emperor. In March 1349, at his request, the
Senate in Venice authorised the dispatch to Constantinople of arms and
equipment for the Byzantine fleet; and in April they considered the merits
of making an alliance with the emperor against the Genoese. The idea
did not, for the time being, find favour. But the situation was so tense
that all Venetian merchant ships were ordered to return to the safer waters
of the Adriatic.[2] By then the treaty with Venice which the Empress
Anne and her son John V had signed in March 1342 had run its course
of seven years. The time had come to renew it, lending substance to
the expressions of goodwill which the Venetian ambassadors had conveyed to the new emperor in July 1347. It was awkward, for Venice
held the new emperor responsible for repayment of the loan of 30,000
ducats made to the empress in 1343. In February 1348 the baillie in
Constantinople, Nicolò Querini, received instructions to demand the
full sum, with the threat that the crown jewels, the security for the loan,
would be sold if they were not soon redeemed. In July of the same

---

[1] Gregoras, xvii. 1–7: II, pp. 841–67; Cantacuzenus, iv. 11–12: III, pp. 68–84; Alexios Makrembolites, *Logos Istorikos* (*Historical Discourse on the Genoese*), ed. A. Papadopoulos-Kera-
meus, *Analekta Hierosolymitikes Stachyologias*, I (St Petersburg, 1891), pp. 144–59; *Chron.
brev.*, II, pp. 273–5; *DR*, v, nos. 2944, 2946–9. P. Schreiner, 'La chronique brève de 1352,
IVme partie' (1348–1352), *OCP*, xxxiv (1968), 40–6. D. M. Nicol, *The Byzantine Family
of Kantakouzenos* (*Cantacuzenus*) *ca. 1100–1460*, Dumbarton Oaks Studies, xi (Washington,
D.C., 1968), pp. 69–70; Ahrweiler, *Byzance et la mer*, pp. 385–7.

[2] Thiriet, *Sénat*, I, nos. 222, 224.

year the senators wrote to John Cantacuzene, giving him four months
to repay the capital sum with interest or to send a representative to
Venice to assist in the sale of the jewels. There was no response.[1]

The Senate resolved none the less to pursue the matter of renewing
their treaty with Byzantium. In January 1349 they voted to send an
ambassador to Constantinople to talk to the emperor and particularly
to press for repayment of the loan in full or, failing that, of the interest
on it. Alternatively the emperor might consider adding further securities.
As a last resort the crown jewels would be sold. The ambassador was
also to make it clear that all Venetian claims for damages must be settled
forthwith according to the just evaluation of their cost made by the baillie
in Constantinople and his councillors. Given these assurances, the
ambassador could renew the treaty for five years. If he succeeded in
this mission he should remain in Constantinople as baillie. If he failed
he should leave at once, giving the emperor the option of sending an
envoy of his own to Venice. The ambassador, appointed by the Doge
Andrea Dandolo as his plenipotentiary, was Zaccaria Contarini. He
seems to have left Venice in April 1349 and his final instructions were
to be firm about the settlement of damages and the repayment of the
loan of 30,000 ducats.[2] With strict attention to protocol, Contarini
was accredited to both emperors, John VI Cantacuzene and his son-in-
law John V Palaiologos, since they were officially colleagues in authority.
There was much bargaining and discussion before the treaty was signed
by both emperors in the Blachernai palace on 9 September 1349.[3]

It was expressly a repetition and confirmation of that signed in 1342.
It was to last for five years. Most of its text has to do with the settlement
of earlier and outstanding Venetian claims for compensation. Cantacuzene must have felt that the sins of his late adversary, Anne of Savoy,
were being visited upon him and her son. In 1342 she had agreed to
pay to Venice the remainder of the 19,000 *hyperpyra* which were owed
by her late husband. She had not done so. 12,000 were still owing, and
the Venetians estimated that damage done to their citizens and subjects
since 1342 amounted to 22,000 *hyperpyra*. Cantacuzene and his co-
emperor were thus faced with a bill for 34,000 *hyperpyra*. It could not
be written off. The Venetians needed the money. The emperors were
made to promise that they would at once make over to Zaccaria Contarini

[1] Bertelè, 'Gioielli', Document no. 14, p. 159; Thiriet, *Sénat*, I, nos. 210, 213.

[2] Thiriet, *Sénat*, I, nos. 218, 221, 224. On Zaccaria Contarini as baillie (1349–50), see Maltézou, *Thesmos*, pp. 113–14.

[3] Greek text in *MM*, III, pp. 114–20; Latin text in *DVL*, I, no. 171, pp. 341–5. The end of the document is published in Dölger, *Facsimiles byzantinischer Kaiserurkunden*, n. 13, pp. 18–19. *DR*, V, no. 2952.

5,667 *hyperpyra*, or one-sixth of the total sum. The remaining 28,333 would be paid to the Doge and Commune of Venice within five years in equal annual instalments. It was, however, agreed by both parties that other claims for damages outstanding from the treaties signed before 1342 should now be cancelled, at least up to 5 July 1349. This remission would not, on the other hand, apply to settlements between private citizens; and there remained of course the problem of the capital and interest on the 30,000 ducats loaned to the empress seven years before. The treaty seems to have been ratified in Venice in November 1349, despite the reservations expressed by some senators about the payment of debts. The Byzantine ambassador who delivered it to the Doge announced that it was the wish of his emperors that the crown jewels be returned to Constantinople on the next Venetian convoy going that way. This could only be done when they had been redeemed from pawn. The senators listened sympathetically to his plea for help against the Turks. They replied that they would prefer to wait for the next move on the part of the league of Christian powers, the pope, the King of Cyprus and the Grand Master of the Knights of St John.[1]

The treaty of 1349 was no more than a renewal of a working arrangement and an attempt to tie up loose ends between Byzantium and Venice. It was in no sense an alliance. The hateful subject of the Genoese was not raised, though it was one of common concern to both parties. Early in 1350 another Byzantine ambassador was in Venice with various requests from the emperor. He asked that Venetian ships might be allowed to import corn to Thessalonica. The city was encircled by the Serbian armies of Stephen Dušan. Supplies by land could not get through. The request was turned down.[2] Dušan was something of an embarrassment to Venice. His dominions extended to the Adriatic coast. To fulfil his ambition of making Constantinople his capital he needed the support of a maritime power. He hoped that the Venetians would understand his needs. He coveted the title of Venetian citizen. If they would grant him that and help him to become emperor in Constantinople he would reward them by giving them possession of the Genoese colony of Galata and of the whole of Epiros. These were tempting baits. But the Venetians wisely declined to rise to them. When Dušan invited the Doge to meet him at Ragusa or some other city on the Dalmatian coast the senators turned him down declaring, with manifest disregard for historical truth, that their laws forbade the Doge to leave Venice. They were happy to

---

[1] Sanudo, *Vitae Ducum*, col. 620. Thiriet, *Sénat*, I, no. 231 (17 November 1349); *DR*, v, no. 2955.

[2] The full text of the Senate's reply is printed in Chrysostomides, 'Venetian commercial privileges', Document no. 4, p. 333. Thiriet, *Sénat*, I, no. 237; *DR*, v, no. 2959.

flatter him with honorary membership of their company as a citizen of Venice. But they could offer him no help in the fulfilment of his other dreams, for they were bound to Byzantium by treaty.[1]

In the autumn of 1350 Cantacuzene succeeded in winning control of Thessalonica after its rebel leaders, the Zealots, fell out among themselves. He was there from October to December, restoring order and clearing the neighbourhood of Serbian troops. During his stay four ships from Venice put in to the harbour. They were taking the new baillie, Jacopo Bragadino, to Constantinople. He brought with him a plea from his government that the emperor would enter into alliance against the Genoese on whom Venice had just declared war. It was the emperor's turn to be embarrassed. He told the Venetians that he would rather not become involved. His first concern was to deal with Stephen Dušan. Bragadino offered to intercede with Dušan on his behalf. He was after all a Venetian citizen. The emperor rejected the offer. Bragadino had been authorised to win him over by proposing to return the crown jewels. The proposal was not very tempting. The loan would still have to be repaid and the Venetians now demanded not merely simple interest on it but compound interest. The emperor had no intention of paying what he called 'the interest on the interest'. It would have amounted to 10,500 ducats on top of the capital sum of 30,000. Bragadino went on his way to Constantinople empty-handed.[2]

Venice had declared war on Genoa on 6 August 1350.[3] The Genoese

[1] Cantacuzenus, iv. 21: III, pp. 152–3. Thiriet, Sénat, I, no. 222 (March 1349), no. 237 (March 1350), no. 241 (April 1350). N. Jorga, 'Latins et Grecs d'Orient et l'établissement des Turcs en Europe, 1342–62', BZ, xv (1906), 179–222, especially pp. 206–7.

[2] Cantacuzenus, iv. 18: III, p. 118. Bertelè, 'Gioielli', Document no. 19, p. 163; Thiriet, Sénat, I, no. 243. Bragadino was appointed as baillie on 14 March 1349. Maltézou, Thesmos, p. 114.

[3] The war between Venice and Genoa in 1350–5 is well documented by Byzantine, Venetian, Genoese and other sources: 1. Byzantine: Gregoras, xxv. 20–6, xxvi. 12–23: III, pp. 46–51, 77–92, 106–7; Cantacuzenus, iv. 25–31: III, pp. 185–200, 209–37; Alexios Makrembolites, pp. 144–59; Chron. brev., II, pp. 277, 279–81. 2. Venetian: Caresini, pp. 6–7; Sanudo, Vitae Ducum, cols. 621–7; Lorenzo de Monacis, pp. 207–23. 3. Genoese: Stella, Annales Genuenses, ed. Balbi, RIS, xvII/2 (1975), pp. 151–4. 4. Aragonese: G. Zurita, Los cinco libros postreros de la primera parte de los Anales de la Corona de Aragón (Saragossa, 1562–80), II, pp. 184–8. 5. Florentine: Matteo Villani, Cronica, ed. A. Racheli, II (Trieste, 1858), pp. 68, 84–5. The causes and details of the war have been studied by: Jorga, 'Latins et Grecs d'Orient', 207–13; Kretschmayr, II, pp. 205–11, 604–5; A. Sorbelli, La lotta tra Genova e Venezia per il predominio del Mediterraneo, Memorie della Reale Accademia delle Scienze dell' Istituto di Bologna, Cl. di Scienze Morali, sez. I, vol. 5 (Bologna, 1911); M. Brunetti, Contributo alla storia delle relazioni veneti–genovese dal 1348 al 1350, Miscellanea di storia veneta, serie III, IX/2 (Venice, 1916); C. P. Kyrris, 'John Cantacuzenus, the Genoese, the Venetians and the Catalans (1348–1354)' Byzantina, IV (1972), 331–56; M. Balard, 'A propos de la bataille du Bosphore. L'expédition génoise de Paganino Doria à Constantinople (1351–1352)' TM, IV (1970), 431–69.

had goaded them into action by their behaviour at Caffa. They had forbidden Venetian ships to go to Tana, an act which brought indignant protests from Venice about the freedom of the seas. They had occupied Chios, an act which, though sanctioned by Byzantium, seemed to imperil Venetian interests in the Aegean as well. The Doge regretfully informed the pope that his commune could no longer afford to subscribe to the league of Christian powers against the Turks. He had other more pressing concerns.[1] The Emperor John Cantacuzene, in his own account of affairs, stresses how reluctant he was to be drawn in to the conflict between the Italians. But it was hard to remain neutral when the subject of their dispute was the trade route through the Bosporos to the Black Sea and when the Genoese were so firmly entrenched at Galata in full view of Constantinople. The war began with a series of local incidents. In September 1350 a Venetian fleet led by Marco Ruzzini surprised fourteen Genoese merchantmen near Aulis on the east coast of Negroponte and captured ten of them. The rest fled to Chios. In October the Genoese retaliated by sending Simone Vignosi with sixty ships over from Chios to attack Negroponte. They did very serious damage to Venetian houses, installations and ships in the harbour and went back to Chios in triumph with many prisoners, much loot and the keys of the city of Chalkis. Meanwhile, Ruzzini had sailed on to Constantinople. There he had less success and after about a month spent vainly assaulting the fortifications at Galata, he took his fleet up into the Black Sea.

Both sides now prepared for war in earnest and on a wider field. Both looked for allies. The destruction at Negroponte was a particularly deadly blow to the Venetians. They saw that they must concentrate their strength on defending their possessions in Romania and the Aegean Sea. They could protect their homeland in Italy by finding a friend who would make life difficult for the Republic of Genoa. They found him in King Peter IV of Aragon. In January 1351 Peter became the ally of Venice and the scourge of Genoa. Not only did he harass the Genoese in Italy. He offered to contribute eighteen galleys to the war against them in Romania and to appeal to the Catalans in Athens and elsewhere to support the Venetians. Venice still needed more ships and more men, however. The obvious source of both was Byzantium. In times past the Venetians had gone to the aid of the Byzantines as their allies in Italy against the Normans. Now it was the turn of the Byzantines to come to the help of Venice against the Genoese. This could be achieved only if Venice paid for the equipment and maintenance of Byzantine ships and their

---

[1] Thiriet, *Sénat*, I, nos. 244–6, 250.

crews, and if the Byzantine Emperor could be made to see the folly of his neutrality.[1]

Peter of Aragon was so enthusiastic to humiliate the Genoese that he sent a messenger to the emperor in Constantinople to persuade him to throw in his lot with Venice. The emperor still hoped to keep out of the conflict.[2] But he was under increasing pressure to take one side or the other. The Genoese sent several embassies to him, offering bribes and promises of undying friendship. In March 1351 a Venetian fleet of fourteen ships commanded by Nicolò Pisani made another vain attack on the walls of Galata, assisted by Byzantine troops.[3] Pisani had brought with him a new ambassador from Venice, Giovanni Dolfin, whose task it was to break down the emperor's reluctance to come in on the Venetian side. Many incentives and rewards were proposed. Still the emperor refused to commit himself. The Venetians were so annoyed that they recalled their baillie from Constantinople and sailed off. No sooner had they left than the Genoese from Galata, probably suspecting that the emperor had done a deal with their enemies, catapulted a rock over the walls of Constantinople in broad daylight. The emperor made a formal protest. The next day another rock was hurled into the middle of the city. It was this that finally changed the emperor's mind. Evidently neutrality was no longer possible. He recalled the Venetian ambassador and signed a treaty with him on the spot. Byzantium was now at war with Genoa. The commercial privileges first granted to the Genoese by Michael VIII ninety years before were abruptly terminated and their merchants were given eight days to evacuate their settlement at Galata.[4]

The agreement between Byzantium and Venice so hastily drawn up in May 1351 was of a very different nature from that signed in 1349.[5] It purports to be a chrysobull granted as a privilege. It is in fact a treaty of alliance between the Emperor John Cantacuzene alone and the Doge and Commune of Venice as equal partners. The alliance is expressly directed against the Genoese, whose past and recent ingratitude and perfidy the emperor sadly recapitulates. War is to be waged against them and their subjects wherever they are to be found, on land and sea, but especially in Pera (Galata), Chios and their other settlements in Romania.

---

[1] Heyd, *Commerce*, I, pp. 503–4. Schreiner, 'Chronique brève de 1352', 49–51. The numbers of Ruzzini's fleet are variously given as between nineteen and forty galleys.

[2] Cantacuzenus, iv. 25: III, p. 186, calls Peter of Aragon the 'King of Ravenna'.

[3] Cantacuzenus and the *Chron. brev.* speak of fourteen ships, others of twenty-two or twenty-five. Heyd, *Commerce*, I, p. 504.

[4] Gregoras, xviii. 2: II, p. 880; xxv. 20: III, pp. 45–6; Cantacuzenus, iv. 26: III, pp. 186–91. Schreiner, 'Chronique brève de 1352', 51–3. *Chron. brev.*, II, p. 279.

[5] Only the Latin text survives: *DVL*, II, no. 5, pp. 4–12; *DR*, v, no. 2975. Argenti, *Occupation of Chios*, I, pp. 121–2.

The contract is to be in force up to 29 September and thereafter for four years. During that time neither party will enter into agreement with the Genoese without the consent of the other. The emperor will provide twelve galleys summer and winter alike to maintain a continuous offensive against the enemy, to blockade Galata and to prevent the Genoese from entering or leaving the Black Sea. The galleys are to be armed by the emperor, but the pay of their crews and the cost of their upkeep will be divided. The Venetians will pay for eight of them, at the rate of 10,776 *hyperpyra* a month or 1347 for each galley. The document sets out precise details of the equipment, arms and manning of each of the warships and of the appointment of their captains. Regulations are laid down for the fair division of any booty or territory that may be gained. If, with God's help, the allies acquire Galata, they agree in advance that it will be totally demolished and annihilated, though its proceeds in the way of property and plunder will be equally divided. If they acquire the island of Chios and the town of Phokaia, these will revert to the empire, to which they belong.

The emperor undertook to maintain a continuous blockade of Galata by land with 300 armed cavalry, the expense to be equally shared between the allies, each contributing 1500 *hyperpyra* a month, allowing seven *hyperpyra* a month as the pay for each man. At the end he wrung from Venice what was to him an important concession. It was agreed that, if his forces contributed to the capture and destruction of Galata, Venice would reward him by returning the crown jewels without any further talk of capital or interest. Finally, in the event of a successful counter offensive by the Genoese, the allied fleet could take refuge in the imperial arsenal at Kosmidion. The crews of the ships would not lose their pay so long as they stayed on board. If they jumped ashore they would get no further remuneration. Memories of the disaster of 1349 and the indiscipline of the Byzantine sailors were obviously still fresh.

One of Cantacuzene's reasons for not committing himself to an alliance earlier had been that he was more concerned to settle his accounts with Stephen Dušan of Serbia. By May 1351 he was ready to postpone that settlement if the Venetians would act for him by inducing Dušan to negotiate. The grand designs envisaged in the new treaty of alliance were never executed. For a few weeks the Byzantine army carried out the plan to besiege Galata from the landward side while the allied fleet blockaded it from the sea. The Venetian admiral, Nicolò Pisani, at first thought in terms of a war of attrition instead of a direct assault on the fortress of Galata, and the emperor bowed to his wishes. The total number of their warships was thirty-two. Pisani's strategy was soon seen to be ineffective and an assault was planned for 28 July. But on the night before word reached Pisani from Venice that sixty or seventy Genoese warships were on their way to the relief of Galata. The Doge commanded him to withdraw from Constantinople for fear of being hemmed in and out-numbered. Much to the emperor's disgust, his Venetian allies at once sailed off and made for Negroponte. The Byzantines were left on their own to fight out a war which they had neither planned nor wanted. They fought bravely but without much hope before being driven away from the walls of Galata.[1]

A Genoese fleet had indeed set out in July. It was under the command of Paganino Doria and its first destination was Negroponte. Pisani was lucky to get there before it arrived. From 15 August to 20 September Doria laid siege to Negroponte, until the news that a combined fleet of Venetians and Catalans was making for the island caused him to with-draw to the shelter of Chios. A few weeks later he continued his voyage to Constantinople. On the way his ships put in at the island of Tenedos and then at the Thracian port of Herakleia, ostensibly to collect supplies. Fighting broke out between the Italian sailors and the inhabitants of the port and on 23 October the Genoese stormed and pillaged the city, taking over 700 prisoners, an event vividly described by the local Greek bishop.[2] Herakleia had been caught unawares. But Constantinople was well prepared. The emperor had ordered that the sea walls be strengthened and all his own ships be brought into harbour. The people had gathered behind the walls and the army which had been sent to the relief of Herak-leia had been recalled. Orders had also gone out to the Greek cities on the Black Sea coast to look to their own defences. Paganino Doria was thwarted. From Galata he took his ships up to the Bosporos to the Black Sea on a plundering expedition and captured the city of Sozopo-lis, the only Greek city that had ignored the emperor's orders.

By then it was November. The Venetian admiral, Pisani, had been back to Italy and had picked up twenty-six Aragonese vessels at Messina. The emperor impatiently awaited the arrival of his allies; but they were held up by the necessity of collecting provisions on their way and by storms. Annoyed by the long delay, the emperor made a last effort to disentangle himself from the war, to pursue his own policy by persuading the Genoese in Galata to dismantle their fortifications and come to terms. When that failed, he sent messages to Pisani to stop cruising around

[1] Gregoras, xxvi. 40: III, p. 106; Cantacuzenus, iv. 26: III, pp. 193–200; *Chron. brev.*, II, p. 279. Lorenzo de Monacis, pp. 209–11, says nothing about the withdrawal of the Venetian fleet.

[2] Philotheos (Kokkinos), 'Logos istorikos (Historical Discourse on the Siege and Capture by the Latins of Herakleia, 1352)', ed. C. Triantafillis and A. Grapputo, Anecdota Graeca e Codicibus Manu Scriptis Bibliothecae S. Marci, I (Venice, 1874), pp. 1–33; ed. B. S. Psevton-gas, *Philotheou Kokkinou Logoi kai Omilies*, II (Thessaloniki, 1981), pp. 235–64.

the Aegean islands and to make straight for Constantinople.[1] The long lull before the action was giving the Genoese time to consolidate their position. They had asked the Turkish emir Orchan of Bithynia to help them. Orchan was the personal friend and ally of John Cantacuzene, who had given him a daughter in marriage. But he had grievances against the Venetians. Cantacuzene was shocked to think that his son-in-law could be so treacherous and told him so. Orchan was unmoved. He saw no harm in helping the Genoese to the extent of supplying them with information about the movements of their enemies. The Turkish emir of Aydin also assisted them by supplying them with provisions through the port of Ephesos.[2]

In the first days of February 1352 the long-expected Venetian and Aragonese fleet came in sight of Constantinople. The Genoese were waiting for them under the walls of Galata and on the morning of 13 February battle was joined near the mouth of the Bosporos. The Byzantine ships fought alongside their allies, giving them a slight numerical superiority. But the Venetian admiral, Nicolò Pisani, was not adventurous and the Aragonese commander, Ponce de Santa-Pau, had never sailed these seas before and knew nothing of the local reefs and currents. There was fierce fighting until nightfall. In the morning the sea was strewn with wrecks and corpses. Neither side, however, could claim a decisive victory. The Aragonese suffered most casualties. The final outcome was determined by the attitude of Nicolò Pisani, who was either a coward, as Cantacuzene and the Aragonese believed, or an unusually cautious and circumspect admiral. Pisani declined to listen to the emperor, who was all for finishing the job by launching an immediate attack on Galata. He preferred to lie up in the harbour of Therapeia on the Bosporos to await further orders from Venice. The Aragonese commander died on 9 March. The alliance, which had been so much sought by the Venetians and so carefully spelt out with the emperor, broke up; and early in April Pisani withdrew with what ships he had left, abandoning the emperor to fight alone or to make what terms he could with the common enemy. Pressure was put upon him when the Genoese, joined by a contingent of troops from the Turks, surrounded Constantinople. The emperor had no option but to make a treaty of his own with the Genoese, on 6 May 1352.[3]

He had cause to feel that the Venetians had let him down. His treaty

[1] DR, v, nos. 2984, 2986.
[2] DR, v, no. 2987. Balard, 'A propos de la bataille du Bosphore,' 443–4, shows that there was no formal alliance between Orchan and the Genoese until after February 1352.
[3] Gregoras, xxvi. 18–25: III, pp. 84–92; Cantacuzenus, iv. 30–2; III, pp. 218–34; Matteo Villani, Cronica, pp. 84–5. Text of treaty with Genoa (6 May 1352) in Liber iurium reipublicae Genuensis, ed. E. Ricotti, Monumenta Historiae Patriae, vii–ix, II (Turin, 1854), pp. 601–6: DR, v, no. 2991.

with Genoa was weighted against him. It assumed that the Genoese were still at war with the Venetians and that Byzantium was on the wrong side. For this error of judgment the Byzantine Emperor must be made to pay. He had to confirm and in some cases extend all the concessions and privileges that his predecessors had made to Genoa. He could no longer pretend to set limits to the size or the strength of the fortified colony of Galata, whose annihilation he had sworn to achieve. He could no longer complain about the Genoese occupation of Chios and Phokaia. The battle in the Bosporos in February 1352 was only an incident in a chapter of the larger conflict between Venice and Genoa. Nicolò Pisani made one more appearance before the walls of Galata at the end of the year, but again he withdrew when challenged by the Genoese. The larger conflict was enacted elsewhere. There were skirmishes in Romania, at Modon and in the Gulf of Patras. But the real battles took place in the western Mediterranean.[1]

What the Italians could not achieve by warfare, however, they soon learnt to attempt by political intrigue among the Byzantines. The race was on to put an emperor on the throne in Constantinople who was favourable or indebted to one side or the other, to Venice or to Genoa. That this was bound to provoke further civil war among the Byzantines themselves was of small account when the stakes were so high. For the winner would gain complete control of the Hellespont, the Bosporos and the markets of Constantinople and the Black Sea. The Venetians knew that there was growing tension between the young John V Palaiologos and the emperor's son Matthew Cantacuzene, who felt that he should be heir to his father's throne. They offered to subsidise John V to rebel against his father-in-law the emperor. They tendered him a loan of 20,000 ducats if he would grant them the island of Tenedos and let them keep it until their war with Genoa was over. Tenedos was well placed to police the entrance to the Hellespont. John V had been granted an appanage in Thrace; and it was at Ainos on the Thracian coast that the Venetians made their proposal to him on 10 October 1352. They made the offer more tempting by advancing him the sum of 5000 ducats, for which he gave them security in the shape of yet another precious stone. But another twenty years were to pass before the island of Tenedos changed hands.[2]

The Venetians were not alone in fishing in the troubled waters of the rivalry between the ruling families of Byzantium. John V had many

---

[1] Gregoras, xxvii. 55: III, pp. 171–2; Sanudo, *Vitae Ducum*, col. 625. Heyd, *Commerce*, I, pp. 509–10.

[2] Text in *DVL*, II, no. 8, pp. 17–18; *DR*, v, no. 3005. Cf. *DVL*, II, no. 21, p. 42, and below, p. 312. One of the Venetian negotiators was the admiral Nicolò Pisani.

other supporters. Stephen Dušan of Serbia saw him as a pawn in his
own game of power politics. His mother Anne of Savoy, who had taken
up residence as empress in Thessalonica, was approached by the Genoese.
The senior emperor tried to keep the peace. But in the summer of 1352
fighting broke out in Thrace. Stephen Dušan as well as the Bulgarian
Tsar John Alexander sent troops to fight for John V. Orchan of Bithynia
kindly supplied a large force of Turkish cavalry to assist Matthew Cantacuzene. It was they who carried him to victory in a battle on the Marica
river. At the end of 1352 John V was captured and deported to the
island of Tenedos, which he had so recently offered to Venice. In March
of the following year he sailed up the Hellespont and made a desperate
but futile bid to fight his way into Constantinople. He went back to
his island exile. In April Matthew Cantacuzene was proclaimed co-
emperor by his father in place of his brother-in-law. The dynasty of
Cantacuzene seemed to be taking over from that of Palaiologos.[1]

Public opinion, however, was against the change. The patriarch
resigned rather than crown Matthew as emperor. The Cantacuzene family
had never won the hearts of the people. John VI had antagonised them
by hiring the Turks to fight his battles. His personal and family relationships with Orchan and earlier with Umur of Aydin had shown his willingness to live at peace with the Turks. It was a risky and unpopular policy.
Orchan had sided with the Genoese against the Venetians at a critical
moment. His son Suleiman did not feel bound by any gentleman's agreement with the emperor. Suleiman had brought an army over to Thrace
in 1352 to fight for Matthew Cantacuzene. When the battle was won
he refused to go home and claimed that a fortress close to Gallipoli was
his by right of conquest. It was the first permanent settlement of the
Osmanlis on European soil. Two years later, in March 1354, Gallipoli
itself was destroyed by earthquake and Suleiman moved in to occupy
the ruins and repopulate the city with Turks. Gallipoli was the key point
dominating the passage over the Hellespont from Asia into Europe. Its
capture was a triumph for the Turks. Half a century earlier the Catalans
had used it as a base for their mindless brigandage. For the Turks it
became a base for the systematic conquest of eastern Europe.[2]

The Venetians were well informed about the crisis in Byzantium. In
August 1354 their baillie in Constantinople, Maffeo Venier, reported
that the Emperor John V was in alliance with the Genoese and the
Emperor John VI with the Turks. Their subjects were so alarmed and

---

[1] Gregoras, xxviii. 8, 18: III, pp. 182, 187–8; Cantacuzenus, iv. 34–7: III, pp. 253–70; *Chron.
brev.*, II, pp. 281–3.

[2] Gregoras, xxviii. 67–8: III, pp. 220–2; Cantacuzenus, iv. 38: III, pp. 277–8; *Chron. brev.*,
II, pp. 283–4.

distressed that they would gladly put themselves under foreign protection, either of Serbia or of Hungary, though they would prefer to be governed and defended by Venice.[1] The Venetians could do nothing. They were wholly immersed in their war with Genoa. Since the battle in the Bosporos in 1352 the major engagements in that war had been fought in western waters, off Sardinia and in the Adriatic. The last and in some ways the most serious episode, however, took place at Zonklon (Old Navarino) near Modon in the Peloponnese in November 1354. The Genoese admiral Paganino Doria, having frightened the wits out of his enemies by sailing up the Adriatic almost to Venice, turned about to take his fleet into the Aegean Sea. At Zonklon he surprised a squadron of thirty-five Venetian galleys led by Nicolò Pisani. All of them were captured. Thousands of their men were taken prisoner. Hundreds were slaughtered. Pisani escaped to Venice. It was his last disgrace; he was cashiered and never given a command again. It was this disaster that finally brought the Venetians to the negotiating table in January 1355 and to sign a peace treaty with Genoa in June. Its most revealing clause was a reciprocal agreement that neither party would send a merchant ship to Tana for three years.[2]

At almost the same time, in November 1354, the crisis in Byzantium was reaching its climax. In the summer the Emperor John VI had gone to Tenedos to try to settle his differences with his son-in-law John V. Nothing came of his gesture. The younger emperor knew by then that circumstances had worked in his favour. He would be certain of support if he could make his way undetected into Constantinople. On 28 November he slipped out from Tenedos with a few ships. It was a dark, stormy night and he reached harbour without being seen. Later accounts tell that he was accompanied by a Genoese buccaneer called Francesco Gattilusio who had offered him his services. Gattilusio pretended to be master of an innocent cargo vessel in danger of shipwreck. He was allowed within the gates and once inside the city he raised the cry that the young emperor was back. The word spread quickly. By dawn the streets were thronged with his supporters, many of them expressing their joy by looting the house of Cantacuzene's relatives and friends. They urged him to take up arms. He preferred to negotiate; and after a few days

---

[1] S. Ljubić, *Monumenta spectantia historiam Slavorum Meridionalium*, III (Zagreb, 1872), no. cccc, pp. 265–7. Thiriet, *Romanie vénitienne*, pp. 171–2; Jorga, 'Latins et Grecs d'Orient', 217; Maltézou, *Thesmos*, p. 114.

[2] V. Lazzarini, 'La battaglia di Porto Lungo nell'isola di Sapienza', *Nuovo archivio veneto*, VIII (1894), 5–45. On the site of Zonklon, Zonchio (Old Navarino or Porto Lungo), see Bon, *Morée franque*, pp. 668–9 and index, under 'Port de Jonc'. Sanudo, *Vitae Ducum*, cols. 630–2. The text of the Genoese–Venetian treaty of 1355 is in *Liber iurium reipublicae Genuensis*, II, pp. 617ff.

a settlement was agreed. The two emperors were to share the government. Matthew Cantacuzene would reign as an independent emperor in Thrace until he died. It was an impracticable plan and the senior emperor knew it. On 9 December he faced the facts and abdicated. He entered a monastery in Constantinople and for the last twenty-nine years of his long life he was known by his monastic name of Joasaph or, as a mark of deference to an elder statesman, as 'the emperor and monk Joasaph Cantacuzene'.[1]

Andrea Dandolo, the Doge of Venice since 1343, died in September 1354, three months before the abdication of John Cantacuzene. The two men had never met. But they had shared and lived through many of the same experiences, not least that of the Black Death. It is instructive to compare their careers and their characters, as representatives of their two different cultures. Dandolo was only thirty-six when he was elected Doge; Cantacuzene was over fifty when he was crowned emperor in Constantinople. Both were wealthy members of a gilded aristocracy. Both were men of letters as well as men of action, though neither seemed able to master the political and military events which he set in motion, Dandolo with the Genoese, Cantacuzene with the Turks. Both wrote works of history, the one in the form of a Chronicle, the other in a more polished literary style modelled on Thucydides. Dandolo begins his Chronicle with what he believed to be the election of the first Doge and the tale of how the relics of St Mark were brought to Venice – the two most significant events in the foundation of the Republic. Cantacuzene, in the manner of Thucydides, concentrates on one relatively short period of history, from his own rise to power in 1321 until his abdication in 1354.[2] His work is part memoirs, part apologia; and in this he is perhaps closer to the style of Julius Caesar than to that of his ancient Greek model. Dandolo's Chronicle is naive and uncritical by comparison. But it is not an apologia, either for himself or for Venice. The prejudices that Dandolo betrays are in favour of his own state and his own people, not of his own merits. His propaganda for the past and present glories of Venice may not all be true. But at least it is sincerely felt. It is not always easy to respect the truth and the sincerity of the history of John Cantacuzene. Nevertheless, he was the last of the

[1] D. M. Nicol, 'The abdication of John VI Cantacuzene', *BF*, II (1976) (*Polychordia. Festschrift F. Dölger*) (Amsterdam, 1967), 269–83; chronology revised by A. Failler, *REB*, XXIX (1971), 293–302; *REB*, XXXIV (1976), 119–24. *Chron. brev.*, II, pp. 284–5. Nicol, *The Byzantine Family of Kantakouzenos (Cantacuzenus) ca. 1100–1460*, Dumbarton Oaks Studies, XI (Washington D.C., 1968), pp. 83–6.

[2] See H. Hunger, 'Thukydides bei Johannes Kantakuzenos. Beobachtungen zur Mimesis', *JÖB*, XXV (1976), 181–93; T. S. Miller, 'The plague in John VI Cantacuzenus and Thucydides', *GRBS*, XVIII (1976), 385–95.

Byzantine historians to record the events of his own time. Those who took over where he left off all lived in the fifteenth century, after the Turkish conquest of Constantinople.

Both men were religious, though their faith and their feelings took different forms. Both left their mark on the churches of their cities. It was in Dandolo's day and on his orders that the Pala d'Oro in St Mark's in Venice acquired its final form. Cantacuzene supervised the repair of the marble and mosaic decoration of St Sophia in Constantinople after the church had been damaged by earthquake.[1] Dandolo was careful to record the translation of holy relics to his city in the past. He had a religious view of history. It coloured his account of relations between Byzantium and Venice. He believed that the schism between the Churches of Rome and Constantinople had soured that relationship. He believed that his ancestor, Enrico Dandolo, had been fired as a crusader against the Greeks by a justifiable religious zeal, to right the wrongs done to Venice and to himself by the scheming and schismatical Emperor Manuel I.[2] Cantacuzene was convinced that God was on his side and sad that others did not share his conviction. He claimed that he had always longed to become a monk, once he had set the world to rights. Like so many Byzantines he was obsessed with theology, particularly the abstruse and mystical theology of the Hesychasts, as it was formulated by Gregory Palamas. Palamas was his personal friend and constant protégé. Cantacuzene presided over the council of the Byzantine church in 1351 which finally declared the formulations of Palamas to be in accord with Orthodox tradition; and he spent much of his retirement composing theological and polemical tracts in support of Palamite doctrine. Dandolo, by contrast, was a humanist who numbered Petrarch among his friends. It would be hard to pin the label of humanist on John Cantacuzene.

It was in the lifetime of both men that two exquisite and lasting expressions of their different cultures were accomplished. Giotto was painting the walls of the Arena chapel at Padua at precisely the same moment that the church of the Chora (Kariye Djami) in Constantinople was being adorned with mosaics and wall-paintings by its anonymous artists. If Dandolo had seen the one and Cantacuzene had seen the other, they might have appreciated that their differences were not all to do with broken treaties, unpaid debts and damages for past wrongs.

Dandolo was precluded by the constitution of his Commune from founding a dynasty. He was the fourth and last member of his family to be made Doge. Cantacuzene on the other hand tried to oust the ruling

---

[1] Cantacuzenus, iv. 4: III, pp. 29–30.
[2] See F. Thiriet, 'Byzance et les byzantins vus par le Vénitien Andrea Dandolo', *Revue des Etudes Sud-Est Européennes*, X (1972), 5–15.

dynasty of Palaiologos in favour of his own family. He failed. His son
Matthew was the last of the Cantacuzenes to bear the title of Emperor.
Sanudo rounds off his epitaph on Andrea Dandolo with the words: 'In
his time there was almost continual war, plague and famine.' The same
words could be used to describe the reign of John Cantacuzene.[1]

---

[1] Sanudo, *Vitae Ducum*, col. 628: 'In questo suo tempo sempre quasi fu guerra, peste, e
carestia.'

16

THE PROFIT AND HONOUR OF VENICE

THE year 1354 was the point of no return for the Byzantine Empire. In that year the Ottoman Turks put down their roots on European soil at Gallipoli. In that year John Cantacuzene, who had tried to contain the enmity of the Turks and to loosen the stranglehold of the Italians, was forced to abdicate. His policies had failed. The Venetians no less than the Genoese opposed his efforts to reconstitute a Byzantine fleet. They had too much to lose. Andrea Dandolo, who died in 1354, had faithfully recorded his view of the changing nature of the relationship between Byzantium and Venice. From being a province of Byzantium, Venice had graduated to being a protectorate, an ally and a partner. By the time of Dandolo's death Byzantium had long ceased to be the senior partner in the relationship. It was scarcely a partnership at all. Neither could live without it. But the profit and the honour went all to Venice. It was to uphold these two principles that the Venetians went to war with Genoa and browbeat the Byzantine Emperors into regular renewals of the commercial privileges on which their profits depended.[1]

Dandolo had lived to see the colonial empire of Venice, the empire within an empire, firmly established. Before the Fourth Crusade the Venetian quarter in Constantinople and the trading stations in the Byzantine world had led a precarious existence, dependent on the goodwill of the emperors, the good behaviour of their inhabitants and the caprice of the Greeks among whom they lived. The foundation of the Latin Empire had changed all that. It had made it possible for Venetians to see themselves as permanent residents in Byzantium and in 'Romania' and to make plans and investments accordingly. The volume of their trade and traffic grew in spectacular fashion. Before 1204 Venetian docu-

---

[1] Care for the 'profit and honour of Venice' ('proficuum et honorem Venetiarum') was constantly impressed upon Venetian ambassadors and agents in Romania. See, e.g., N. Jorga, 'Veneţia in Mare neagră', *Analele Academiei Române, Memoriile secţiunii istorice*, ser. 2, XXXVI (1913–14), 1059: 'pro honore et bono nostro et nostrorum mercatorum'; 1060: 'pro honore nostro et bono nostrorum'. See above, p. 154.

ments relating to trade in Byzantium and the Levant are for the most part records of the enterprise of private individuals and companies, such as those of the Mairano family. From the thirteenth century onwards the whole machinery of the Venetian state was involved in the administration, defence and exploitation of its colonies and the promotion of their trade, not only with Byzantium but also with Egypt and the Black Sea. The state archives of Venice concerned with overseas affairs become embarrassingly numerous and abundant in detail. Diplomatic exchanges with emperors and sultans, commercial and military records and negotiations for the purchase or disposal of property, movable and immovable, lie side by side with regulations for the salaries and households of consuls, ambassadors, interpreters and doctors in the colonies. Above all, the records tell of trade, of the regular convoys of cargo ships that plied back and forth on well-organised voyages between Venice and Byzantium, Venice and Romania, Venice and Alexandria, Venice and the Levant. Without overseas trade Venice could never maintain the prestige and wealth, the profit and honour, that it acquired in the time of the Doge Enrico Dandolo. When the popes or the emperors taxed the Venetians with trafficking with the infidel, they often retorted that they had to live by imports from the sea since they had no fields or vineyards of their own. Venice was a maritime republic. Its people lived on the sea and by the traffic of the sea.[1]

In an earlier age, before the year 1000, the Venetians had made their living by trade with the mainland in salt and fish and, on a larger scale overseas, in slaves and timber. There was a ready market for these commodities in the Muslim world where the Arabs were eager to buy slaves for their armies and wood for shipbuilding. They paid in gold and silver currency which could then be exchanged for luxury goods in the markets of Constantinople. The Venetians had access to plentiful supplies of shipbuilding material from the forests at the head of the Adriatic; and they were not much troubled by the ethics of selling timber to the infidel rulers of North Africa. The line between trade and piracy was not clearly drawn. The Venetians indulged in piracy of their own on the high seas. But they knew that the security of their sea route up and down the Adriatic and so the growth of their overseas trade depended on their control and suppression of rival pirates; and for this purpose they were glad to act as the agents if not the subjects of the Byzantine Emperors. The Narentan pirates of Dalmatia had been a dangerous nuisance in the ninth century. But they had also provided a steady supply of Slav recruits for the slave market which the Venetians were keen to steal or to buy.

[1] See, e.g., the Doge's letter to Pope John XXII in 1327, *DVL*, I, no. 105, p. 208.

The conversion to Christianity of the Slavs and of the Narentani had its effects on the pattern of trade in the Adriatic. Christians could not be sold as slaves. They must be found further afield. When in the year 1000 the Doge Pietro Orseolo led his great fleet out of Venice to show the flag of St Mark along the Dalmatian coast, he was expressing the new confidence and the new orientation of Venetian enterprise. When, eighty years later, the Byzantine Emperor Alexios I called on the help of Venice against the Normans at Durazzo, the Doge did not hesitate to lead his own ships to the scene of action. For what was at stake was the command of the Adriatic Sea, the Gulf, which the Venetians had come to regard as their lifeline to the trade of the east.

The population of Venice was never large, perhaps no more than 100,000 souls. They could never aspire, nor did they ever wish, to conquer and annex great tracts of territory. Their strength lay in command of the sea, secured by the foundation of naval bases along its shores and in its islands. In pursuit of this end they showed remarkable flexibility and potential for adapting to political and other circumstances. Their part in the Fourth Crusade proved their adaptability at its most striking. It was a gamble. Enrico Dandolo committed himself to providing fifty armed galleys for a year. They would need a complement of 6000 men, or about half of all able-bodied Venetians. For the galleys were manned by free citizens of Venice and not by slaves. The gamble brought handsome rewards. The Venetian empire of Romania, inaugurated by the commercial privileges granted by Alexios I in 1082, came to maturity as a result of the Fourth Crusade. Yet its success and its future still depended on the initiative and enterprise of private individuals. The Byzantines, who were accustomed to a centralised bureaucracy which aimed to restrict their movements at every turn, were bewildered by the freedom of Venetian society and the flexibility of its ways. Merchant ships and warships were frequently interchangeable. Their crews, who were armed, could provide either service. The government of Venice could intervene to requisition large merchantmen for war service, as in the Fourth Crusade; and ships generally travelled in convoy commanded by an admiral appointed by the Doge. They were required to conform to certain specifications with regard to their rigging, loading, manning and arms before leaving the port of Venice. But most merchant vessels were privately built and privately financed through family businesses or *colleganze*, such as those of the Mairano brothers in the twelfth century. Many of the richest patrician families of Venice made their fortunes from shares and investments in such seafaring partnerships. In 1255 the Doge Reniero Zeno published a new codification of maritime law. It was designed more to protect than to curb private enterprise, though it laid greater emphasis on the responsibilities of the owners of the ships, one of whom, designated as the *patronus*, was supposed to sail on each voyage and to act effectively as captain.[1]

The law also regulated the times of year at which the convoys were expected to sail from Venice along the main trade routes, either to Romania and Constantinople or to the Levant, to Cyprus, Syria and Palestine. The sailing seasons were known as *mude* and the term was also used to describe the convoys or caravans. Sailing time from Venice to Constantinople was usually about eight weeks. Caravans set out from Venice to trade in Romania twice a year, one in the spring, the other in August. The first *muda* would come back in the autumn. The second would winter in Romania and return the following Easter or even later. Many of the ships would load and unload wares on the mainland or island ports of the Aegean on their way to and from Constantinople. But they would try to avoid sailing in the winter months. Negroponte was a normal assembly point for such convoys. Modon and Coron on the south-west tip of the Morea were the harbours from which they would collect cargoes from local agents on their return trip. They were also the vital look-out stations, 'the chief eyes of the Republic', which guarded the waters of Romania. No foreign ship could get round the Morea without being sighted and challenged by the coastguards of Modon and Coron.[2]

The *mude* operated between Venice and Constantinople. But the creation of the Latin Empire encouraged Venetian merchants to expand their activities by doing business in Romania, carrying cargoes from one Greek port to another or from the islands to Egypt. In 1218 the Genoese admitted defeat in their running battle with Venice for the possession of Crete. The consequent peace between the two republics enabled the Venetians further to develop their trade in the Aegean and the eastern Mediterranean. Their treaty was renewed in 1251. By then, however, the Latin Empire of Constantinople, within whose framework the Venetian colonial empire was built, was already doomed to die. When, ten years later, the Greeks recovered their capital city, it seemed that the Genoese were to inherit the wealth that Venice had lost. The new emperor, Michael VIII, treated Genoa as the most favoured nation among the Italians. The Venetians were made to pay the price for their part in the Fourth Crusade. Yet the Genoese proved to be unsatisfactory allies of Byzan-

[1] F. C. Lane, 'Maritime Law and Administration', in *Venice and History. The Collected Papers of Frederic C. Lane* (Baltimore, 1966); Lane, *Venice. A Maritime Republic*, pp. 36, 45–54.
[2] On Modon and Coron as the 'oculi communis capitales', see Bon, *La Morée franque*, I, p. 444. Modon was described as the 'pupillam oculi': Sathas, K. N., *Mnemeia Hellenikes Historias. Monumenta Hellenicae Historiae. Documents inédits relatifs à l'histoire de la Grèce au moyen âge* (Venice–Paris, 1880–96), II, no. 412, p. 178. (Hereafter Sathas, *Documents*.) A. Momferratos, 'Methoni and Koroni under Venetian rule' (in Greek) (Athens, 1914).

tium; and they never built up a colonial empire to match that which
Venice still held in Romania. The Genoese settlement at Galata profited
from the emperor's favour. But its people lived under a government of
their own and were often at variance with the mother city in Italy.

The collapse of the Latin Empire in 1261 was a disaster for Venice.
It came at a time, however, when new developments in sailing technique
were beginning to have their effect. The invention of the compass soon
after the middle of the thirteenth century and improvements in the steering
mechanism of ships revolutionised the art and scope of navigation. Venetian sailors and shipbuilders eagerly adopted these innovations. Navigation by compass made it possible for ships to sail in cloudy or overcast
weather, without being afraid of losing sight of land. Convoys from
Venice could set out in the winter months, in January or February.
The earlier pattern of *mude* leaving twice a year was changed. The first
convoy to Romania and Constantinople did not have to wait in Venice
until the spring. The second convoy could leave in the summer and
come back in the autumn or at the beginning of winter without having
to winter abroad as had formerly been the rule. The introduction of
the stern-post rudder meant that bigger ships could be built and held
on course when at sea. The invention of compass bearings led to improvements in map-making. Charts or portolans could be drawn showing
the position of the main harbours and islands of the Mediterranean and
Aegean Seas. The earliest were drawn on vellum in Venice and Genoa.
Such portolan charts, or compass charts, were a great advance on the
earlier *portolani* or guides for sailors, since they gave much more accurate
and reliable information on the coastlines and staging posts. Maps of
the coasts of the numerous islands in the Aegean and Ionian Seas, known
as *isolarii*, with directions for navigation and sometimes descriptions of
the history and geographical features of each island, were also a great
help to sailors plying between Venice and Constantinople. The earliest
known are those compiled by the Florentine Cristoforo Buondelmonti
about 1420 and by Bartolomeo dalli Sonetti of Venice about 1485, which
was the first such *isolario* to be printed.[1]

These improvements, though they took many years to perfect, lowered
the cost of long-distance transport and made sailing a full-time profession.
Ships thus equipped could sail the seas all year round. Large galleys
with two or three lateen sails were developed for commercial purposes
as cargo ships, with as many as 200 crew and oarsmen aboard; and after

---

[1] D. Howse and M. Sanderson, *The Sea Chart* (Newton Abbot, 1973), pp. 19–21. On navigation in the early fourteenth century, see F. C. Lane, 'Manuali di mercatura e prontuari
di informazioni pratiche', in A. Stussi, ed., *Zibaldone da Canal, manoscritto mercantile
del secolo XIV* (Venice, 1967).

1300 round bottoms known as *coche* or cogs came into use. The round ships had square sails but no oars and they were built with 'castles' at prow and stern for defence and protection against the elements. In addition light galleys or triremes with only one lateen sail were employed for defence and patrol duties. The resulting increase in Venetian trade and traffic in the fourteenth century was carefully controlled by the Senate in Venice. The round ships might have a certain freedom in the timing and planning of their voyages to find grain, salt and other bulk cargoes. But the voyages of the great galleys were organised on regular schedules by the government, for they carried the more precious cargoes; and those sailing between Venice and Constantinople and the Black Sea routes went in convoy, armed and equipped as state-owned war fleets whose commanders and captains or *patroni* were paid servants of the Commune. The profit and honour of Venice was their business.[1]

The Byzantines were unable to compete with the Venetians and the Genoese in maritime affairs. The 'nautical revolution' of the fourteenth century seems to have passed them by. The imperial navy, which Andronikos II had disbanded and which John Cantacuzene failed to revive, was never again a force to be reckoned with. There was something of a revival of Byzantine trade by sea, though the operations of Greek merchants are mainly recorded in Italian sources. After the middle of the fourteenth century, when most of the mainland of eastern Europe had been overrun first by the Serbians and then by the Turks, wealthy Byzantines who had capital to invest turned to commercial ventures by sea, among them many members of the traditionally conservative landed aristocracy. Some of their names figure in the detailed account books of the enterprising Venetian merchant banker Giacomo Badoer, who was active in and around Constantinople from 1436 to 1440.[2] But their ships were small and old-fashioned and there is no evidence that their captains enjoyed the benefits of the western innovations in navigational techniques. There was never any prospect of Byzantine convoys of cargo ships making voyages as far afield as Venice. Greek mathematicians knew about the astrolabe but not about the compass; and the earliest Greek

---

[1] F. C. Lane, 'Venetian merchant galleys 1300–1334: private and commercial operation', *Speculum*, XXXVIII (1963), 179–205; Lane, *Venice. A Maritime Republic*, pp. 119–34; W. H. McNeill, *Venice the Hinge of Europe 1081–1797* (Chicago–London, 1974), pp. 46–64.

[2] *Il Libro dei Conti di Giacomo Badoer (Costantinopoli 1436–1440)*, ed. V. Dorini and T. Bertelè, Il Nuovo Ramusio, Raccolta di Viaggi, Testi e Documenti relativi ai Rapporti fra l'Europa e l'Oriente a cura dell' Istituto Italiano per il Medio e Estremo Oriente, III (Rome, 1956). See Oikonomides, *Hommes d'affaires grecs et latins à Constantinople*; A. E. Laiou-Thomadakis, 'The Byzantine Economy in the Medieval Trade System', 177–22; and 'The Greek merchant of the Palaeologan period: a collective portrait', *Praktika* of the Academy of Athens, LVII (1982), 96–132.

sea charts or portolans date from the sixteenth century. If the Byzantines had studied, instead of simply copying, the manuscripts of Ptolemy's *Geography* which lay in their libraries things might have been different. Ptolemy was not 'discovered' by a wider world until manuscripts of his work were taken to the west by Greek refugees after the fall of Constantinople in 1453.[1]

Many years were to pass after the restoration of the Byzantine Empire in 1261 before the Venetians were encouraged to feel at home again in Constantinople. Michael VIII's treaty with the Doge in 1277 opened up new doors for them; and it was to the letter of that treaty that the Doges and their lawyers referred whenever they thought that their privileges were being eroded. The treaty of 1324 helped still further to clear the air. Yet right to the end the Venetian community in Constantinople was at a disadvantage compared to the Genoese in Galata. The emperors repeatedly refused to allow them to fortify their residential quarter. The fortress of Galata, built in defiance of their wishes, lay beyond the city limits. Obviously the emperors could not countenance a walled citadel of foreigners inside their capital. The Genoese may have been unsatisfactory friends but they were treated with greater diplomatic respect than the Venetians. Their relationship with Byzantium was regulated on the basis of their treaty with Michael VIII signed at Nymphaion in 1261. That had been a treaty of a new kind in the long history of Byzantine diplomatic relations. It was an arrangement made between two heads of state as almost equal partners and with no limit of time. When the same emperor Michael dealt with the Venetians in 1268 and again in 1277 he did so as the superior partner in what was technically only a truce in the continuing state of war between Byzantium and Venice. This pattern never changed in all subsequent 'treaties' between the two. They were, as Cantacuzene observed, more in the nature of truces, never alleged to be permanent and never supposed to last for more than an expressly limited number of years.[2]

The treaty of 1277 granted the Venetians a well-defined residential and commercial quarter in Constantinople to be administered by their own baillie or rector. Thereafter the office of baillie was to become a position of great power and influence. The Byzantines could hardly fail to notice this. Yet they continued to show their mistrust and suspicion

[1] A. Delatte, *Les Portulans grecs*, I (Liège–Paris, 1947), II (Brussels, 1958); Anna Avrameas, 'The cartography of the Greek coastlands', in *The Greek Merchant Marine* (National Bank of Greece: Athens, 1972), pp. 175–80; Anna Avramea, 'Maps of the Aegean', in *Maps and Mapmakers of the Aegean*, ed. V. Sphyroeras, Anna Avramea, S. Asdrachas (Athens, 1985), pp. 22–32; Howse and Sanderson, *The Sea Chart*, pp. 9–21.
[2] Cantacuzenus, iv. 25: III, p. 188.

in ways that the Venetians must have found aggravating. In matters of ceremonial and etiquette the Byzantine court was conservative in the extreme. Even in the middle of the fourteenth century and probably beyond, the Venetians were made to feel their inferior status. Every Sunday it was the custom for the leading Latin residents in Constantinople, the Genoese, Venetians, Anconitans and Pisans, to visit the palace to pay homage to the emperor and acclaim him as their sovereign. The Podestà of the Genoese and the consuls of the Anconitans and Pisans were honoured to join the emperor and his courtiers at dinner. The Venetians, however, had to leave hungry and go back to their quarter. The Podestà of the Genoese, when calling on the emperor, was permitted to kiss his hand, his foot and his cheek. The Venetian baillie was denied this privilege; nor was he allowed to join the others in wishing the emperor long life. When a new Genoese Podestà first called at the palace he was required to make obeisance by bending the knee twice and then kissing the emperor's hand and foot. His ships had to salute the emperor. A new Venetian baillie on the other hand had to make only one genuflexion without kissing the emperor; and on subsequent audiences he had only to raise his hat. Venetian ships were not bound to salute the emperor. The author of the Byzantine handbook of offices and ceremonies written about 1350 emphasises that these niceties of discrimination arose because the Genoese were allied to Byzantium by an everlasting treaty of peace, while the Venetians were in a state of war punctuated by truces of limited duration.[1]

These petty humiliations dated from the time of Michael VIII. They could not disguise the fact that, as time went on, the Venetian baillie in Constantinople became probably the second most powerful man in the city. The baillie was nominated and commissioned by the Doge and the Senate, usually for a term of two years. He was paid a salary ranging from 800 to 1000 ducats in the later period. Earlier in his career he might have served as baillie of Negroponte, Trebizond, or Corfu; and he liked to claim superiority over them all by sporting the title of *Baiulus Constantinopolis et totius Imperii Romaniae*.[2] He was surrounded by his own suite of four sergeants, eight pages or servants, a chef, two grooms for his eight horses and a priest who acted as notary. He lived and held court in great style in a mansion in the city with his own stables and livestock. He was assisted in his many duties by two councillors and

---

[1] Cantacuzenus, i. 12: 1, p. 61; Pseudo-Kodinos, pp. 208–9, 234–7. On the office of baillie in general and in detail, see Maltézou, *Thesmos*, *passim*; C. Diehl, 'La colonie vénitienne à Constantinople à la fin du xive siècle', *Mélanges de l'Ecole Française de Rome*, iii (1883), 90–131.

[2] Maltézou, *Thesmos*, p. 28.

often by a vice-baillie. His councillors were allowed to engage in trade to supplement their stipends, which the baillie himself was strictly forbidden to do.[1] The baillie's duties and responsibilities are clearly set out in several documents of the fourteenth century. One is the so-called *Capitularium* of Venetian weights and measures drawn up in January 1361 by the ambassador and baillie Nicolò Falier. Others are the texts of the Senate's instructions or commissions to their ambassadors to Constantinople, who frequently stayed on as baillies. The *Capitularium* is much more than its title suggests, for it contains also the statutes of civil and criminal law for the baillie's guidance. It was added to in later years and, as the manuscript now exists, it represents the minutes of the baillie's chancery in Constantinople almost to the end of the Byzantine Empire in the 1450s. It thus covers most aspects of the conduct of the life of the Venetian community there, the administration, the supervision of commerce, taxation, the maintenance of property, the sale of goods by Venetian shopkeepers or taverners, even the ringing of church bells.[2]

The baillie had to sit in judgment with his councillors three times a week in the trial of all civil and criminal cases involving Venetian citizens. Their only appeal against his sentence, usually a fine, was to the proper authorities in Venice. The baillie was responsible for the finances and revenues of the community and had to present a full account to Venice. He was expected to supervise every detail of the daily life of his community while at the same time acting as the representative of the Doge in negotiations with the emperor or the sultan in larger matters of state and foreign policy. Above all and in all matters large or small he was commissioned to uphold 'the profit and honour of Venice'. The baillies took special care to see that successive Byzantine Emperors honoured the terms of their agreements with Venice, or at least what the Venetians construed those terms to be. They made sure that they were legally protected in every detail, so that no one could accuse them of malpractice or corruption. They were a tight-knit and well-ordered community. But they were not liked. It was partly their efficiency that made them unpopular. The Byzantines called it greed.

The emperors were particularly dismayed at the expansion of the Venetian population in Constantinople and at the new ways which they found to turn their ancient privileges to their own profit. John Cantacuzene

---

[1] Thiriet, *Sénat*, I, nos. 401, 406 (1363), 444, 449 (1367–8).

[2] The *Capitularium* is published by Maltézou, *Thesmos*, pp. 133–221. Diehl, 'La colonie vénitienne', made much of the *Commissio* to Andrea Gradenigo in February 1375 (not '1374') on the mistaken assumption that it was unique, and published parts of its text in *Mélanges*, 128–31. Gradenigo was never in fact baillie of Constantinople despite the title of the manuscript of his commission. There was no baillie between 1372 and 1376. See Maltézou, *Thesmos*, pp. 116–17.

expressed his concern about the continual extension of Venetian property in the city. In 1350 he asked that the baillie be forbidden to acquire any more. The Senate dismissed his request. In their opinion the emperor should be glad not sorry that the Venetians owned so much property in his dominions, since the more they had the more they would be content and so well disposed to his empire.[1] Cantacuzene was also concerned about the growing number of taverns in Constantinople run by Venetians and about the readiness with which the baillie issued naturalisation papers to Greeks who could as a result evade taxes by claiming to be Venetian citizens. It seemed that he was on the way to turning all Greeks into Venetians. The problem of citizenship was an old one; and the Venetian response was the same as it had always been. Careful reading of the texts of past treaties would clarify any misunderstandings.[2] The emperor was probably aware, however, of the extraordinary measures which the Venetians had taken to swell the numbers in their smaller colony at Tana in the Crimea. There the Senate had authorised its resident consul to 'create Venetians' by granting citizenship to up to fifty ethnic 'Latins'.[3]

Cantacuzene had cause to be annoyed about the loss of revenue at a time when he was labouring to find the money to build up his fleet and to break the dependence of Constantinople on the Italians. His concern about the spread of Venetian-owned taverns in the city was prompted by much the same considerations. The matter had first been aired in 1344 when the then government in Byzantium declared its intention of prohibiting all foreign traders from selling wine retail. The Venetians at once protested and again appealed to the letter of past treaties, which gave them the right to buy and sell whatever they pleased tax free.[4] Cantacuzene's protest six years later shows that the threat to outlaw foreign publicans had never been carried out. The number of retail wine merchants had if anything increased. Venetian taverners were popular because they could undercut their Greek rivals by selling wine more cheaply, thus cheating the Byzantine treasury. The Venetians were importing vast quantities of foreign wine free of duty and selling it at prices far below that of the local produce. Most of it came from Crete. The obvious answer to Venetian objections was to draw a distinction between wholesale and retail trade in wine, to point out that their tax immunities covered buying and selling at wholesale prices but did not

---

[1] Thiriet, *Sénat*, I, no. 237; full text in Chrysostomides, 'Venetian commercial privileges', 333-4, Document no. 4.

[2] Chrysostomides, 'Venetian commercial privileges', 280, 334.

[3] *DVL*, I, p. 251.

[4] *DVL*, I, p. 274; Thiriet, *Sénat*, I, no. 164.

extend to the sale of goods in shops or taverns. It was left to John V to make this point in 1359. The Venetians pretended to be hurt and surprised by such an unfriendly suggestion, not least because the emperor complained that many of the Venetian publicans in Constantinople were really Greeks who had illegally acquired Venetian citizenship to avoid taxation. A compromise was reached in 1361 when the Venetians agreed to impose a tax on wine sold in taverns run by their own citizens. The proceeds would of course go to Venice and not to the imperial treasury. But at least it would help to make things fairer for Greek taverners.

The problem remained, however. The only way to save the livelihood of Greek wine merchants and also of the owners of Greek vineyards was to restrict the quantity of wine being imported by the Venetians either for a period of years or for ever. This would have been too damaging to Venetian interests. In 1363 Venice therefore agreed instead to restrict the number of Venetian taverns in Constantinople to fifteen. This led to the imposition of licensing laws almost as absurd as those obtaining in England in the twentieth century; and perhaps the emperor did well to place an embargo on all wine imported by Venetians. Only if this were agreed would he ratify his treaty with Venice. The estimated loss of revenue must have been great for the emperor to go to such lengths over so simple a matter as the retail wine trade. But his successors right up to the last of them, Constantine XI, were adamant about the restriction on the number of Venetian taverns and on the payment of tax on Venetian-imported wine. By the fifteenth century Venetian wine sellers had been taxed out of existence. Their taverns were deserted; and the financial loss to the Venetian community in Constantinople was so great that they could no longer afford to pay their baillie his annual salary of 1000 ducats.[1]

The story was much the same in the matter of the sale of corn by the Venetians in Constantinople. The treaty of 1324 permitted them to sell imported, foreign corn duty free anywhere in the empire, except in the corn market in Constantinople. In succeeding redactions of the treaty it became clear that there was room for doubt about the location or the number of the city's corn markets which were reserved for Greek traders. The protection of the Greek corn markets from competition was vital for the empire's flagging economy, for only in them could the necessary purchase tax be levied. The Venetians claimed that there were only two such markets while the Emperor John V insisted that there were more. In 1375 he went so far as to suggest that foreign corn, imported from the Black Sea or from Turkish-occupied territories and

---

[1] Chrysostomides, 'Venetian commercial privileges', 298–311. Thiriet, *Romanie vénitienne*, p. 320.

stored in Venetian granaries in Constantinople, was subject to tax or
storage duty. Venetian protests led him to abandon this idea. No objections were raised to the limitation set in 1277 on the export or sale of
corn grown and harvested on Byzantine territory. But the matter of
Venetian trade in foreign or imported corn was never really settled. The
Venetians repeatedly justified their actions by appealing to the treaties
of the past which had granted them so many privileges and immunities,
regardless of the fact that their insistence on what they thought to be
their rights worked against the economic recovery of Byzantium.[1]

It was again the Byzantine–Venetian treaty of 1277 that gave the merchants of Venice the freedom to compete with the Genoese in the markets
of the Black Sea. This privilege, denied to them in an earlier age, transformed the pattern of their trade coming to or passing through Constantinople. The documents relating to Venetian claims for damages in 1278
reveal the varied nature of the cargoes being carried by their ships at
that time, from nuts to pitch to sardines. The commonest load by far,
however, was wheat or grain, followed by barley, oil, salt, wine and
cloth of different kinds.[2] There is little mention of the luxury goods,
silks and spices which one supposes Venetian merchantmen carried from
east to west. The opening up of the Black Sea made for a greater diversity
of trade. The most profitable markets were at Trebizond in the south
and at Caffa and Tana in the Crimea in the north. The Genoese had
set up their counters at all three before the Venetians moved in. It was
not until 1319 that Venice made its own arrangements with the independent Greek emperor at Trebizond. He granted them a residential and
commercial quarter in his city.[3] Trebizond was the principal outlet
for trade coming from Persia, in minerals, silks, spices and luxury goods.
On the western shore of the Black Sea the Bulgarian ports of Mesembria
and Varna, and of Mavrokastro at the mouth of the Dniester river, were
important sources of cereals, wheat, barley and millet. In the Crimea
in the north Venetian merchants were doing business at Soldaia in the
thirteenth century, loading and exporting grain, salt, fish, furs and slaves.
But it was the Genoese, operating from their nearby base at Caffa, who
had pioneered exploration of the Sea of Azov and set up an emporium
at Tana at its north-eastern extremity.

Tana lay at the estuary of the river Don, at the receiving end of regular
caravans bringing slaves and furs from Russia and silk, spices and jewels
from central Asia and India. It stood more firmly than Caffa within
the confines of the Tatar Empire of the Golden Horde, whose khan

---

[1] Chrysostomides, 'Venetian commercial privileges', 312–27.
[2] Morgan, 'The Venetian Claims Commission', 436–7.
[3] Thiriet, *Assemblées*, I, nos. 420, 427, 435. Thiriet, *Romanie vénitienne*, pp. 347–8.

confirmed the right of Venetians to trade there in 1333. They maintained a consul at Tana and a baillie in Trebizond, though neither constituted a colony such as the settlements in Romania which were under Venetian rule. Each was leased from the local ruler, who never forfeited his rights over the territory involved.[1] Their trading stations at Tana and at Trebizond increased the volume of Venetian business in luxury items. But still the bulk of their export trade was made up of cereals, wheat and barley, as well as salt and dried fish. When in 1343 the Khan of the Tatars expelled both Venetians and Genoese from Tana there was famine, not only in Constantinople but in the west and in Venice itself. The Byzantines had come to rely on the annual supplies brought to them from the Black Sea on Italian ships. The Venetians had come to rely on the immense profits that they made as the leading corn market in the north of Italy.[2]

The Genoese, however, had been the first to discover and exploit the rich markets of the Black Sea and the Crimea and they felt that they had a right to monopolise them. They made it plain to their Venetian competitors that they were not welcome to share the profits. The emperors at Trebizond were content to encourage foreign trade from any quarter. In the Crimea the ruling Khans of the Golden Horde were less predictable hosts and on occasion their hostility worked the miracle of uniting Venetians and Genoese against them. In 1344, after he had turned them both out of Tana, the Genoese allowed Venetian merchants to carry on their business through the port of Caffa. The arrangement did not work well. The Venetians found it irksome and opened negotiations of their own with the khan. The Genoese were righteously indignant and took to seizing Venetian ships. The seeds of the war between Venice and Genoa that ended in 1355 were sown not in Italy, not in Constantinople, not in Romania, but in the Crimea.[3]

---

[1] The known Venetian consuls at Tana and baillies at Trebizond are listed in Nystazopoulou-Pélékides, 'Venise et la Mer Noire', 44–51.

[2] Gregoras, xiii. 12: II, pp. 684–7. The Florentine merchant Pegolotti records the rates of exchange and the goods for sale and purchase at Tana and Caffa in the first half of the fourteenth century. Francesco Balducci Pegolotti, *La pratica della mercatura*, ed. A. Evans (Cambridge, Mass., 1936), pp. 22–6.

[3] Thiriet, *Romanie vénitienne*, pp. 341–3; Nystazopoulou-Pélékides, 'Venise et la Mer Noire', 17–51; Lane, *Venice. A Maritime Republic*, pp. 128–33.

17

JEWELS FOR AN ISLAND

ᴏɴ 16 March 1355 the Venetian baillie in Constantinople wrote to his colleague in Negroponte deploring the pitiful state of the Byzantine Empire which was almost at its last extremity. He hinted that the best course would be for Venice to take it over before the Turks conquered it.[1] The Doge and his advisers had grave misgivings about the new Emperor, John V. He was barely twenty-three years of age and he had had little experience of government. He was also, or so it seemed, too partial to the Genoese. In June 1355 he confirmed them in possession of Chios for a peppercorn rent of 500 *hyperpyra* a year. In July he rewarded the adventurer Francesco Gattilusio, who had helped him enter Constantinople, by making him his brother-in-law and granting him the island of Lesbos as an imperial fief.[2] Just before the outbreak of their war with Genoa, in 1350, the Venetians had thought to offset the Genoese occupation of Chios by obtaining for themselves the Ionian islands of Corfu, Cephalonia and Zante, which then belonged to the Angevin rulers of Naples. They offered to buy them for the sum of 50,000 ducats. In January 1351 the Senate went so far as to nominate a Venetian captain and rector for Corfu, a castellan for Butrinto on the Albanian coast, a count for Cephalonia and a castellan for Zante. The matter went no further at that time, though the island of Leukas or Santa Mavra passed into Venetian hands a few years later.[3] Corfu would have been a most valuable acquisition for Venice, standing as it does at the entrance to the Gulf or the Adriatic. It would have to wait. In 1355 the challenge to Venetian supremacy in the Aegean Sea was more urgent, once Lesbos

---

[1] Lazzarini, 'La battaglia di Porto Lungo', Document no. ɪᴠ, pp. 35–6. In April 1355 the baillie of Negroponte, Michele Falier, reported to his government on the tragic events in Constantinople. Jorga, 'Latins et Grecs d'Orient', 217; Thiriet, *Romanie vénitienne*, p. 172.

[2] Argenti, *Occupation of Chios*, ɪ, p. 135; ɪɪ, pp. 173–5. *Chron. brev.*, ɪɪ, p. 285; *DR*, ᴠ, nos. 3042, 3043.

[3] Thiriet, *Sénat*, ɪ, nos. 249, 251 (23 September 1350; 30 January 1351). F. Thiriet, 'Les interventions vénitiennes dans les Iles Ioniennes au xɪᴠᵉ siècle', *Actes du 3ème Congrès Panionien 1965* (Athens, 1967), 374–85; Nicol, *Despotate of Epiros* ɪɪ, pp. 133–4.

had been added to Chios as an insular possession of Genoa. The challenge could be met if the emperor could be persuaded to hand over the island of Tenedos, as he had promised three years before. The acquisition of Tenedos took priority over that of Corfu. It would serve as a garrison island to prevent the passage of Genoese ships through the Hellespont.

The matter must be carefully handled. To begin with, the Byzantines must not be allowed to forget that they were heavily in debt to Venice. In August 1355 the Senate resolved to send an ambassador to Constantinople to pay the customary respects to a new emperor. He was to be as businesslike as possible. He should not discuss an extension of the treaty last signed in 1349 unless certain demands and conditions were at least partially fulfilled. The 28,333 *hyperpyra* which had then been promised to Zaccaria Contarini had still to be paid. The Byzantines still owed 30,000 ducats with interest now amounting to 25,000 on the security of the crown jewels. Again the threat was made that the jewels would have to be sold, unless the emperor paid a minimum of 5000 ducats. If the emperor complained about injuries inflicted on him and his subjects by the Genoese, the ambassador would offer sympathy but no redress, since the emperor had broken the terms of his alliance by making a separate treaty with Genoa.[1] The ambassador seems to have reached Constantinople in September 1355. Early in the following year he reported that he had made no progress. The emperor had not even paid the minimum of 5000 ducats; and Venetian merchants in the city were being subjected to many hardships and illegal extortions on the excuse that they were no longer protected by the treaty of 1349. In July 1356 there was still no sign of the emperor fulfilling all his obligations, though he appears to have made a down payment of 3000 *hyperpyra*.[2]

It is hard to understand why the Venetians failed to carry out their repeated threat to reimburse themselves by putting the crown jewels up for sale on the open market. They were near losing their patience with the young emperor. But they kept the door open for further negotiations as a matter of self interest. They were anxious about his dealings with the Genoese; they hoped to secure the island of Tenedos; and they wanted the privileges of their merchants in Constantinople to be confirmed in writing. Their perseverance was rewarded in October 1357. The new Doge, Giovanni Dolfin (1356–61), through his ambassador Giovanni Gradenigo, at last induced the emperor to sign another treaty for five years on the terms and conditions that Venice demanded. John V contracted to pay the remainder of the 28,333 *hyperpyra* outstanding,

---

[1] Thiriet, *Sénat*, I, no. 275 (13 August 1355).
[2] Thiriet, *Sénat*, I, no. 285 (30 January 1356), no. 291 (11 April 1356), no. 303 (31 July 1356).

in five annual instalments to a total of 25,333 *hyperpyra*. He also acknowledged that he still owed 30,000 ducats, the price of the crown jewels,
as well as the 5000 ducats which had been loaned to him on other security
in 1352.[1] The Venetians were hard-headed and practical men. They
had had long experience of emperors who promised to pay their debts
in annual instalments and never met their commitments. But at least
they could now refer to the letter of a treaty which confirmed the special
status of their citizens in Romania; and when that status was abused,
as it was in 1358, the Byzantines could no longer shelter behind the
excuse of a lapsed agreement.[2]

The Venetian baillie had rightly reported in 1354 that many Byzantines
were looking to western Christendom for protection against the Turks.
The strongest power in the eastern Christian world and the only one
capable of stemming the Turkish tide was Serbia. Its ruler Stephen Dušan,
however, was not disposed to protect Constantinople until he had made
it his own. He came very close to realising his dream. But in December
1355 he died; and his vast empire, like that of Alexander the Great,
at once disintegrated into a number of successor states. In the same month
the Emperor John V launched his appeal to the west. He addressed
himself not to Venice nor to Genoa but to the pope, as keeper of the
conscience of the western Christian world. He no doubt knew that Pope
Innocent VI was planning to reconstitute the league of Christian powers
against the Turks. What the emperor had in mind was more in the nature
of a crusade for the relief of Constantinople. He wrote to the pope asking
him to send a fleet and an army for this purpose. In return he promised
to effect the conversion of all his people to the Roman faith and to send
his infant son Manuel as a hostage to the papal court at Avignon. Pope
Innocent VI was shrewd enough to see that these were the reckless proposals of a desperate young man. He did not take them very seriously.
He instructed his legate, Peter Thomas, who was then in Serbia, to go
and interview the emperor; and there the matter rested. The pope saw
more future in recreating his own league of Christians against the Turks,
as he did in 1357. He died five years later; and for some time there
was no more talk of a papal armada sailing to the relief of Constantinople.[3]

The pope had been right in suspecting that John V was desperate
as well as being naive. The Turks were advancing rapidly into Thrace

[1] Treaty of 8 October 1357: Greek text in *MM*, ii, pp. 121–6; Latin text in *DVL*, ii, no.
21, pp. 39–43; *DR*, v, no. 3070. O. Halecki, *Un Empereur de Byzance à Rome* (Warsaw,
1930), p. 66.
[2] Thiriet, *Sénat*, i, no. 335 (20 July 1358).
[3] Halecki, *Un Empereur*, pp. 31–59, 64; Nicol, *Last Centuries of Byzantium*, pp. 269–72.

from their base at Gallipoli. The Florentine chronicler Matteo Villani records that they had reached the walls of Constantinople in 1359. Didymoteichon and Adrianople had fallen by 1361.[1] Only a fleet of ships patrolling the Hellespont could prevent the Turks from ferrying more and more soldiers and settlers across the Thrace. Since the pope was reluctant to sponsor such a fleet, the emperor must turn to the Venetians or to the Genoese. The Genoese were inclined to regard the Turks as friends. In 1356 the pope had exhorted them to have no more truck with the infidel. The Venetians seemed more likely to help, though doubtless on their own terms. In June 1361 therefore the emperor wrote to the Doge Giovanni Dolfin to say how pleased he was that two envoys from Venice had come to see him and that he would shortly return the compliment with a view to strengthening the bond of friendship that had always existed between Byzantium and Venice.[2] Early in 1362 Andronikos Oinaiotes presented his credentials to Dolfin's successor, Lorenzo Celsi (1361–5). He began by asking if the Doge could supply him with copies of the treaties of 1342, 1349 and 1357. The originals appeared to have been lost or mislaid in the recent turbulent events in Constantinople. Without them it was difficult to establish the truth of the many allegations being made by the baillie about the infringement of Venetian rights and privileges in the city. These the emperor did his best to answer and refute. With regard to the matter of the crown jewels, he declared through his ambassador that he would be quite content if the Doge were to make arrangements to sell them or to keep them. If they sold for more than the sum required, the surplus money could be transferred to Constantinople. If they sold at a loss, the emperor would make up the deficit. The Venetians, like the pope, knew that they were dealing with a young man of limited experience. But they must have been astonished that his chancery had mislaid three important documents of state and surprised that he set so little store by his crown jewels.[3]

They persevered, however, for they too were alarmed by the advance of the Turks. Venetian merchants had recently resumed business in the Black Sea and the Doge had sent several embassies to Tana. If the Turks were allowed to close the straits or even to capture Constantinople the

---

[1] Matteo Villani, *Cronica*, p. 300. The date of the Turkish conquest of Adrianople has been much disputed. See *Chron. brev.*, II, pp. 289–90.

[2] *DVL*, II, no. 45, pp. 76–7; *DR*; v, no. 3079. The Doge's ambassadors were Francesco Bembo and Niccolo Giustiniani. Thiriet, *Sénat*, I, nos. 369, 370, 372. Letter of Innocent VI to the Genoese in Halecki, *Un Empereur*, Document no. 2, pp. 359–60.

[3] *DVL*, II, no. 49, pp. 82–5; *DR* v, no. 3081. In 1359 the Senate had offered to return the crown jewels to Constantinople on payment by the emperor of the interest due on the loan. The offer was repeated in 1362. Thiriet, *Sénat*, I, no. 342 (19 March 1359), no. 372 (16 March 1361).

Black Sea trade might well come to an end. More than ever it was vital that Venice should have control of the island of Tenedos. With this in mind the Doge sent Francesco Bembo and Domenico Michiel to Constantinople in March 1362. It was time to renew the five-year treaty. It was long past time to take up the question of damages still unsettled. When these matters had been agreed, the Doge's ambassadors were empowered to propose the creation of an anti-Turkish league of a new kind. Its members would be Byzantium, Venice and Genoa. It would consist of a fleet of eight galleys, four being provided by the emperor, and two each by the Venetians and the Genoese. The fleet would be based on Tenedos. The number of ships was not great but it seemed enough to cope with the small number of Turkish vessels engaged in carrying troops across the Hellespont to Thrace. The Venetian ambassadors were authorised to invite others to join the league, the Emperor of Trebizond, the King of Cyprus, the Grand Master of the Knights and even the Tsar of Bulgaria. It would operate for a period of two years in the first instance.[1]

It was never more than a plan. The Venetians insisted that the emperor must first give them Tenedos, as he had agreed ten years before. They offered him 20,000 ducats as well as the crown jewels in exchange. The emperor refused. He had cause to cherish the loyalty of the island's inhabitants to his cause in 1354 and he was not prepared to sell them and their homeland to Venice. Nor was there much hope that the Genoese, who were on good terms with the Turks, would join the league as partners with their rivals. Venice had recently lodged a number of formal protests with the Doge of Genoa, Simone Boccanegra, about the hostility of the people of Galata and about Genoese attacks on Venetian ships in the Black Sea.[2] The Genoese in Galata paid little heed to their government in Italy. They were more concerned to keep the Venetians out of Tenedos. Finally, the Venetians themselves would soon have had to withdraw from the league whose formation they had proposed. For they were about to become embroiled in suppressing a rebellion in Crete which broke out in 1363 and which commanded the undivided attention of their government for some three years.

The league was thus never constituted. The Venetians succeeded, however, in persuading the emperor to confirm 'the customary treaty'

---

[1] *DVL*, II, no. 48, 81–2; Thiriet, *Assemblées*, I, no. 684; Thiriet, *Sénat*, I, nos. 355, 358. Halecki, *Un Empereur*, pp. 75–7; F. Thiriet, 'Una proposta di lega antiturca tra Venezia, Genova e Bisanzio nel 1362', *ASI*, CXIII (1955), 321–34; Thiriet, *Romanie vénitienne*, pp. 172–3. Domenico Michiel had served as baillie in Constantinople from 1359–61. His successor Nicolò Falier took part in the proceedings. Maltézou, Thesmos, p. 115.

[2] *DVL*, II, nos. 31–3, 50–1, pp. 57–60, 85–6 (1359–62).

between Byzantium and Venice for another five years. Two Byzantine envoys to Venice were charged with completing the formalities in October 1362; and the document was signed by the Doge Lorenzo Celsi on 13 March 1363.[1] The emperor's offer to permit the sale of his crown jewels was simply ignored. He was reminded that he still owed not only 30,000 ducats on this account but also the 5000 advanced to him in 1352. The fact is that the Doge was disappointed in him. The jewels had been sent to the baillie of Negroponte in 1362, to be shipped on to Constantinople if and when the emperor agreed to hand over the island of Tenedos. When he refused to do so, the baillie was ordered to put the jewels on a galley bound back for Venice. The emperor was being tiresomely obstinate about the possession of Tenedos. He could expect little sympathy from the Venetians. In the summer of 1363 they instructed their baillie in Constantinople to chivvy him about payment of his debts and to threaten that all their merchants would have to leave his empire if he persisted in ignoring or infringing their treaty rights.[2]

The rebellion in Crete which broke out in August 1363 was an embarrassment to Venice, for it was not simply a revolt of the Greeks against alien rule. Many of the leading Venetian families in the island shared the grievances of the natives against a regime which, though their own, levied more and more taxes on them to satisfy the needs of the Commune in Italy. They were particularly aggrieved that all positions of authority in Crete were held by men appointed and sent out from Venice. The uprising of the Venetians was soon suppressed. The Greeks, however, went on fighting for three years; and the measures taken to bring them to heel further strained relationships between Byzantium and Venice.[3] Meanwhile, the Emperor John V once more turned for comfort to the papacy. He had heard that Pope Urban V, who had been elected in 1362, was planning a new crusade. Its leaders were to be the Catholic rulers of Cyprus and Hungary; and one of its most enthusiastic supporters was Amadeo, Count of Savoy, who was a cousin of the emperor. The news encouraged the emperor to write to the pope at Avignon, offering

[1] *MM*, III, pp. 129–30 (1 October 1362); Latin text of treaty of March 1363 in *DVL*, II, no. 53, pp. 87–92; *DR*, v, no. 3089. The Byzantine envoys were Theophylaktos Dermokaites and Constantine Kaballaropoulos.
[2] Thiriet, *Assemblées*, I, no. 695 (27 June 1363), no. 698 and pp. 323–4 (24 July 1363); Thiriet, *Sénat*, I, nos. 402, 403 (12 and 28 March 1363), no. 414 (23 July 1363). Bertelè, 'Gioielli', pp. 120–1, 170–3; Thiriet, 'Una proposta di lega', 328–9.
[3] Heyd, *Commerce*, I, pp. 513–14; J. Jegerlehnen, 'Der Aufstand der kandiotischen Ritterschaft gegen das Mutterland Venedig', *BZ*, XII (1903), 78–125; S. Xanthoudides, 'The Venetian occupation in Crete and the struggles of the Cretans against the Venetians' (in Greek), Texte und Forschungen zur byzantinisch-neugriechischen Jahrbücher, no. 34 (Athens, 1939), pp. 81–110. In 1364 it was rumoured in Venice that a Byzantine fleet was being armed to help the insurgents in Crete. Thiriet, *Assemblées*, II, no. 751.

to co-operate in whatever way he could. He made none of the extravagant promises that he had made to Pope Urban's predecessor in 1355. His letter was diplomatic and realistic and the pope was impressed. But the crusade never took the road to Constantinople and it ended in a raid on Alexandria led by Peter I of Cyprus in October 1365.[1]

King Louis of Hungary played no part in it after all. But the fact that he had taken the Cross to fight the infidel gave John V hope that, as the nearest Catholic ruler in Europe, he might be induced to come to the relief of Constantinople and drive the Turks out of Thrace. Pope Urban nourished this hope in a letter to the emperor in January 1366, in which he outlined plans for yet another crusade. He also announced the glad news that Count Amadeo of Savoy was preparing to set out for Constantinople with an army of his own. The emperor felt prompted to travel to Hungary to plead his own cause before King Louis the Great. Never before had a Byzantine Emperor sunk his pride and his dignity by visiting a foreign monarch. It had always been assumed that it was the part of lesser princes to pay court to the one true emperor in Constantinople. John V could not afford to stand on his dignity. Times had changed, and once the precedent had been set it was to be much followed. The result was doubly humiliating. King Louis was not minded to help him; and on his return journey John was detained at the frontier with Bulgaria. The Bulgarians, who were at odds with Hungary, would not allow the emperor to pass through their territory.

While he was being held captive in Bulgaria, his cousin Amadeo of Savoy reached Constantinople at the head of his crusade. He had found it difficult to muster enough ships for his enterprise. The Venetians were, as usual, wary of crusades, and they had been preoccupied by the rebellion in Crete. They had opted out of the pope's plans in 1365, leaving it to the Genoese to provide naval support for the crusade against Alexandria; and as soon as that was over they entered into a new trade agreement with the Sultan of Egypt. Amadeo's expedition to Constantinople was more to their taste. But they were cautious. They leased him eight galleys. The rest of his fleet of twenty or twenty-two ships, carrying up to 4000 men, came from Genoa and Marseille. The Venetians regarded the whole business as suspicious because of the Genoese involvement. Special security measures were enforced during Amadeo's brief stay in Venice in June;

---

[1] DR, v, no. 3097. Halecki, Un Empereur, pp. 86–8; Setton, Papacy and the Levant, i, pp. 258–72. Amadeo VI was the son of Aimon, a half-brother of John V's mother Anne of Savoy.

and the baillies of Negroponte and Constantinople were ordered to be on their guard and to keep close watch on his movements in Romania.[1]

The pope had given his blessing to Amadeo's initiative on the understanding that he would do all he could to bring the Byzantine Emperor and his people over to the Roman Church. There was a small but influential band of Greeks who were already convinced that the healing of the schism in the church, even on Rome's terms, was the empire's only hope of survival. Amadeo did his best. In August 1366 his little armada attacked and captured Gallipoli, driving out the Turks. He probably knew by then that his cousin John V was stranded in Bulgaria. He wasted no time in Constantinople but sailed on at once up the Black Sea coast and bullied the Bulgarians into releasing their imperial captive and escorting him through their country. By then Amadeo had spent all the money that he had. But he did not forget that the pope had charged him with a sacred mission. Back in Constantinople in 1367 discussions took place about the union of the churches. Before he left for Italy, Amadeo had persuaded the emperor that the only way to elicit more substantial help from western Christendom was to make his personal submission to the pope, to beg forgiveness for his errors and to accept the faith and doctrine of the Roman Church. To make sure that he would not forget, Amadeo required his cousin to hand over some jewels and other securities in cash. These would be deposited with Genoese bankers either in Italy or in Galata to be held as pledges until such time as the emperor redeemed them by fulfilling his promise to make obeisance to the pope.[2]

The greatest service that Amadeo rendered to Byzantium was his recovery of Gallipoli. For about ten years the Turks were deprived of their only harbour in Europe. His moral blackmail of the emperor bore fruit in 1369, when John V decided that the moment had come to make his promised visit to the pope. He left his eldest son Andronikos as regent in Constantinople and his second son Manuel in charge of Thessalonica. In October, in a brilliant ceremony on the steps of St Peter's in Rome, the Emperor John V solemnly abjured the errors of his Orthodox faith and kissed the pope's feet in the presence of all the cardinals. It was a private and personal submission publicly performed. Not even the pope pretended that the emperor's conversion symbolised a union of the Churches of Rome and Constantinople. The best that could be said was that, like Constantine the Great, he had set an example for his people

[1] Thiriet, *Assemblées*, II, no. 791 (March 1366); Thiriet, *Sénat*, I, nos. 435, 436 (July and August 1366). Halecki, *Un Empereur*, pp. 138–41.

[2] The most recent and fullest account of Amadeo's crusade and his relations with John V is by Setton, *Papacy and the Levant*, I, pp. 284–326, where the sources and the older literature are cited. See also Atiya, *The Crusade in the Later Middle Ages*, pp. 379–97.

to follow. Now that he was fully accepted by western Christendom as a Catholic ruler he might expect long-term rewards in the form of military and economic aid. He had his immediate reward when the pope commanded Amadeo of Savoy and the Genoese to release the financial and other securities which the emperor had lodged with them. He needed them to help pay the cost of his journey.[1]

John V stayed in Rome for about five months. He had gone there by way of Naples. He had been uncertain of his welcome at Venice. Before he left, in 1368, a Venetian ambassador had arrived in Constantinople to discuss the renewal of the treaty of 1363, but not before reminding the emperor of his mounting debts to Venice. There were 25,663 *hyperpyra* outstanding in damages; 30,000 ducats with accumulated interest amounting to 37,500; and 5000 ducats on other security. It had been suggested that, if the emperor could not manage to settle all his debts, he should at least pay the interest on them or an agreed fraction of the total sum. The Venetians, with unwonted charity, were now demanding only simple and not compound interest on the loan. The suggestion had been repeated in February 1369.[2] It was therefore fresh in his mind when he reached Italy. He was also probably aware that the Venetians had been negotiating with the new emir of the Ottoman Turks, Murad, who had offered to lease them an entrepot at Skutari on the Bosporos opposite Constantinople, which might become their equivalent of the Genoese colony at Galata.[3]

Soon after his arrival at Naples, the emperor wrote to the Doge Andrea Contarini (1368–82), in August 1369. He declared his wish to continue talks about renewing his treaty with Venice. This was a tactful move and it was well received by the Doge and the Senate. Their reply reached the emperor in Rome, and they appointed two ambassadors, Tomà Sanudo and Marco Giustiniani, to conclude the business. Their instructions covered most of the familiar points of contention but in somewhat less aggressive style, 'having respect to the goodwill and disposition of the emperor towards the Venetians as expressed in his letter'.[4] His goodwill did not, however, dispose him to give in on every point. There were long weeks of argument in Rome before agreement was reached. No doubt the pope and his cardinals helped to foster a spirit of compromise and tolerance. The final version of the new five-year treaty between Byzantium and Venice was signed and sealed by the emperor on 1 Febru-

[1] Halecki, *Un Empereur*, pp. 188–212.
[2] Thiriet, *Sénat*, I, nos. 459, 470. Bertelè, 'Gioielli', 174–5, Documents nos. 30, 31.
[3] Thiriet, *Sénat*, I, no. 461 (April 1368).
[4] Deliberations of the Senate between 6 and 29 October 1369 in Halecki, *Un Empereur*, Document no. 13, pp. 371–8. Cf. Thiriet, *Sénat*, I, nos. 480, 482, 483; *DR*, v, no. 3121.

ary 1370.[1] In view of the desperate plight of the Byzantine Empire
and the reasons for John V's visit to Italy, it is a strangely irrelevant
document. Most of its clauses concern the status and the rights of the
Venetians in Constantinople, their entitlement to own or rent real estate,
the number of their drinking shops in the city, and the perennial problems
of the selling of corn and claims to Venetian citizenship. Of his outstanding debts it appears that the emperor had paid 4500 *hyperpyra*, leaving
a balance of 21,163. This he contracted to pay in five annual instalments
beginning from 1 January 1371. The crown jewels were to remain in
Venice, as were the securities given in 1352 on the loan to the emperor
of 5000 ducats. Nowhere, however, does the treaty of 1370 allude to
the island of Tenedos, on account of which the 5000 ducats had been
advanced. Nor are the bitter truths of the Turkish threat to Byzantium
considered. The Venetians boasted that they had made some concessions
in view of the unhappy condition of the empire; and the emperor was
pleased to feel that he had won some points and some stays of execution.
A misguided optimism inspired him to press his luck still further and
to go to Venice to put his case in person.

He left Rome in March 1370 and, after another stay at Naples, sailed
up the Adriatic by way of Ancona. It might have been a splendid occasion
of pomp and ceremony. No Byzantine Emperor had ever visited Venice
before; and the Venetians loved putting on a gorgeous show for visiting
princes and potentates. But the Doge did not feel inclined to lavish money
on celebrating the arrival of a visitor who was heavily in his debt and
who might well be looking only for more money to get him home to
Constantinople. He received his guest courteously and with the honours
befitting his rank but he staged no great show of welcome. John V was
certainly always looking for more money. But there were various ways
of getting his creditors to part with it. On his arrival at Venice he
announced, with an air of mystery, that he had a proposition to make
which his hosts would find singularly attractive. A committee of five
was appointed to hear it. What the emperor offered was the island of
Tenedos, which the Venetians had been angling to acquire for nearly
twenty years. The offer was certainly attractive. The prospect of obtaining
a market at Skutari, which they were still negotiating with the Turks,
made the possession of Tenedos still more desirable. They would see
that the emperor was given a fair recompense. They would give him
back his crown jewels; they would give him six empty ships which he
could arm at his own expense; and they would give him a lump sum
of 25,000 ducats. The deal was agreed on these terms on 21 July and

---

[1] Latin text in *DVL*, II, no. 89, pp. 151–6; *DR*, v, no. 3127. Halecki, *Un Empereur*, pp.
222–7.

the grateful Senate voted to pay the emperor an advance of 4000 ducats. Full payment could not of course be made until the island had been formally handed over. This part of the transaction was to be performed by the emperor's son Andronikos, who was acting as regent in Constantinople during his father's absence. It was at this point that the deal began to founder. Andronikos refused to obey the order that his father sent him. His refusal was very probably prompted by the Genoese, who had no wish to see their rivals occupying Tenedos at the mouth of the Hellespont. John V was placed in a most embarrassing and humiliating position. He had neither money nor credit. He could not even repay the advance which he had been given. He was to all intents and purposes detained in Venice at the Doge's pleasure as an insolvent debtor. He appealed to Andronikos to raise money for his rescue by selling some of the church treasures in Constantinople, a suggestion which his son piously rejected. In the end John V was saved by his second son Manuel, who hurried to Venice from Thessalonica bringing with him the means to bail his father out and to provide security for a further loan.

Such, in part, is the substance of the only Greek account of John V's problems in Venice. It was written long after the event by the historian Laonikos Chalkokondyles, who is notoriously inaccurate and fanciful about fourteenth-century affairs. It was taken up and embellished by the sixteenth-century forger, Makarios Melissenos, author of the so-called *Chronicon maius* of Pseudo-Phrantzes. Chalkokondyles in fact says nothing of the offer of Tenedos to the Venetians. In his version, John V was detained in Venice simply because he could not pay his debts.[1] There is, however, an independent witness to the facts in the Venetian Chronicle of Gian Giacomo Caroldo. He too wrote in the sixteenth century but he had access to Venetian documents now lost. Caroldo alone describes the deal over Tenedos, the Venetian offer in exchange of the crown jewels, six ships and 25,000 ducats as well as the advance to the emperor of 4000 ducats on account. He also records, however, that, for reasons unexplained, the emperor had second thoughts about the terms of the deal and turned the offer down. It is difficult to understand why he should have done so. It is probably true that John's son Andronikos declined to hand over Tenedos. It is equally probable that he was

---

[1] Laonikos Chalkokondyles, *Historiarum Demonstrationes*, ed. E. Darkó, 1 (Budapest, 1922), pp. 46–7; Pseudo-Phrantzes, in *Georgios Sphrantzes, Memorii 1401–1477: în anexă Pseudo-Phrantzes: Macarie Melissenos Cronica 1258–1481*, ed. V. Grecu (Bucharest, 1966), p. 194.

influenced by the Genoese. The Genoese lord of Lesbos, Francesco Gatti-lusio, John's brother-in-law, had gone with him to Rome. He may have been privy to the fact that the emperor intended to produce the sale of Tenedos as his trump card in Venice.

There were other grounds for the emperor's reluctance to accept the Venetian offer. Having had time to do his sums, he may well have suspected that it was not as generous as it seemed. The Venetians had always been sticklers for full payment of the interest due on the loan of 30,000 ducats, which had been made in 1343. They had waived their insistence on compound interest. But even at simple interest the total sum had risen to 67,500 ducats by 1368. John V, it seems, considered himself bound to the payment of interest only for the three years after the original loan was advanced, from 1344 to 1347. This amounted to 4500 ducats; and in the course of the haggling at Venice in 1370 he persuaded the Venetians that this was acceptable. He would still, however, have to repay the principal of 30,000 ducats on which the interest was assessed. Thus, even accounting for the 25,000 ducats which he would receive as part of the bargain over Tenedos, he would be out of pocket. He would get his crown jewels back but he would have to find 9500 ducats, the balance between the principal and interest of 34,500 and the 25,000 ducats advanced to him for Tenedos. What he probably hoped was that the Venetians would agree to cancel the original debt of 30,000 ducats, whatever about the interest on it, and to accept Tenedos in exchange for the jewels and 25,000 ducats. This would have been tantamount to their paying 55,000 ducats for the island, which they were not prepared to consider.

Time was on their side. They regretted the emperor's change of mind. But the door had not been closed on the deal over Tenedos; and the Doge bore him no ill will. He stayed on in Venice through the winter together with his son Manuel, who had come to join him, until the weather became more favourable for sailing home. On 2 March 1371, about a month before he left, the Senate resolved that he should be allowed to keep the 4000 ducats advanced to him as a loan, despite the fact that the rest of the transaction had not gone through. They also gave him provisions for the crews of his ships. His son Manuel received a personal gift of 300 ducats, though he was required to stay in Italy for some time as a security or a hostage of Venice. The emperor did not hurry home. Not until October 1371 did he reach Constantinople. He had been away for almost two years. He had set out with great expectations of the rewards that would follow his conversion to the Roman faith. He came back weary and disenchanted. The pope, Urban V, whose feet he had kissed, had died in December 1370. The emperor had found little to cheer him in Venice. His long and tiring journey seemed to have brought no tangible benefit to his empire.[1]

The news that greeted him when he reached Constantinople was grave. A few weeks before, on 26 September 1371, the Turks had fought and won the first really decisive battle in their conquest of eastern Europe. At Črnomen on the Marica river they had annihilated the combined Christian armies of two of the Serbian successors of Stephen Dušan. Amadeo of Savoy had expelled the Turks from Gallipoli. It was still in Christian hands. But the battle at the Marica proved the point that there were already Turkish forces in Europe in overwhelming numbers. They did not have to wait for reinforcements to come across from Asia Minor. Their victory had lasting consequences. It opened to them the gateway to Macedonia, to Serbia and to Greece. The remaining Serbian princes were bound as vassals to the Turks, forced to pay tribute to them and to fight alongside them when summoned.[2] It would not be long before the Byzantine Emperor was in the same plight. Even if the reward for his conversion to Rome were now to come in the form of a crusade for the relief of Constantinople, it would have to fight its way through miles of enemy territory. Constantinople was cut off from western Europe by land. In March 1372 the Venetian Senate grudgingly agreed to deliver some arms and armour to the Emperor John V, but only in the interest of their merchants in his empire and only upon immediate cash payment. With 400 breastplates and 300 javelins one could hardly save the empire from the Turks. A few months later the new baillie of Constantinople was instructed to demand that the emperor put a stop to the continuing violations of the treaty protecting the rights and liberty of Venetian citizens. This was a matter of greater concern to Venice than the plight of the emperor himself.[3]

By the end of 1372 John V had despaired of any help coming from the west, for all the sacrifices that he had made. The only alternative

---

[1] The Chronicle of Caroldo is still mainly in manuscript. The passages relevant to these events have, however, been published by R.-J. Loenertz, 'Jean V Paleologue à Venise (1370–1371)', *REB*, XVI (1958) (*Mélanges S. Salaville*), 217–32 (especially 229), and, more fully and accurately, by Julian Chrysostomides, 'Studies on the Chronicle of Caroldo, with special reference to the history of Byzantium from 1370 to 1377', *OCP*, XXV (1969), 123–82 (especially 160–1). See also Julian Chrysostomides, 'John V Palaeologus in Venice (1370–1371) and the Chronicle of Caroldo: a reinterpretation', *OCP*, XXXI (1965), 76–84. The account given by Halecki, *Un Empereur*, pp. 227–34, can no longer be considered reliable. Cf. Setton, *Papacy and the Levant*, I, pp. 315–20. On the importance of Caroldo's Chronicle, see F. Thiriet, 'Les chroniques vénitiennes de la Marcienne et leur importance pour l'histoire de la Romanie greco-vénitienne', *Mélanges de l'Ecole Française de Rome*, LXVI (Paris, 1954), 241–92 (especially 266–72).

[2] Nicol, *Last Centuries of Byzantium*, pp. 285–6.

[3] Thiriet, *Sénat*, I, nos. 507, 510.

was to make his peace with the enemy. He did so on the same terms as the princes of Serbia. He became a vassal of the Ottoman leader Murad, who now liked to be known as Sultan. By early 1373 the emperor was to be found at Murad's camp in Asia Minor, fighting for a lord and master to whom he was bound to pay tribute.[1] The full significance of the emperor's humiliation was not at first understood in the western world. At Venice it was supposed that he had simply joined forces with Murad for a combined naval operation. Since this would present a serious danger to Venetian ships in Romania, precautions must be taken.[2] While he was away performing his duties to his lord the Sultan, John V had again left his son Andronikos in charge of Constantinople. Andronikos had not been the most obedient of sons. He had friends among the Genoese and friends among the Turks. In May 1373 he abandoned his charge as regent and expressed his disobedience in open rebellion. The Sultan Murad also had a disgruntled son. He joined forces with Andronikos. It is hard to know what this combined revolt of sons against fathers was expected to achieve. It was soon put down. Murad arrested and blinded his son and commanded John V to do the same. Andronikos was put in prison, though not irremediably blinded. He was, however, disinherited. His imperial title was given to his more loyal brother Manuel, who was summoned from Thessalonica and crowned as co-emperor in September 1373. The consequences of this extraordinary affair gave new scope for the enemies of Byzantium to achieve their ends by fostering the feuds among members of the imperial family.[3]

John V had tried to tell the Venetians the truth. In April 1373 he had asked them to send him a reliable representative to whom he could talk without having to rely on an interpreter. Maybe the talk was to be about the cession of Tenedos; for soon afterwards the Senate ordered that the emperor's crown jewels should again be placed on a vessel going to Romania. A year later Venetian ships were using Tenedos as a base for observing the movements of the Genoese and the Turks, evidently with the emperor's permission.[4] Yet when the time came to consider renewing the five-year treaty of 1370, the Venetians behaved as if nothing had changed, as if the emperor had never been to Venice, and as if the only crisis in world affairs was his financial indebtedness and the infringement of Venetian rights in Constantinople. In February 1375 Andrea

---

[1] G. Ostrogorsky, 'Byzance, état tributaire de l'empire turc', ZRVI, v (1958), 49–58.

[2] Thiriet, Sénat, I, no. 541 (14 July 1374).

[3] J. W. Barker, Manuel II Palaeologus (1391–1425). (New Brunswick, N.J., 1968), pp. 19–23; Nicol, Last Centuries of Byzantium, pp. 288–9.

[4] Thiriet, Sénat, I, nos. 521, 523 (April and June 1373), nos. 541, 545 (July 1374); DR, v, no. 3137. Halecki, Un Empereur, p. 271.

Gradenigo, when about to go to Constantinople as ambassador, received his instructions from the Senate. He was to remind the emperor that he still owed 21,163 *hyperpyra* in damages. If, because of the dire condition of his empire, he could not find the whole sum, at least he should pay the greater part of it. Other questions that Gradenigo should raise were: the import of foreign wine into Constantinople, which the emperor was trying to prohibit; the storage of corn; the restriction on taverns and on Venetian real estate; and the ill-treatment of Venetian citizens in Constantinople, Thessalonica and Mesembria. Should the matter of the crown jewels be raised, Gradenigo would say nothing. He was, however, authorised to approach the emperor's son Manuel if he thought this would be helpful to his mission. In July Gradenigo reported back that the emperor was not at all co-operative and seemed in no mood to renew the treaty.[1]

By November Gradenigo, having made one last vain effort to bring the emperor round, had returned to Venice with nothing achieved. The Senate then appointed a commission of five to review the whole situation 'in Romania, the Black Sea, Turkey and Trebizond'. Gradenigo was one of the five. There was much to consider. It was vital to maintain the Venetian colony in Constantinople. The screws must be turned on the emperor. He must if necessary be frightened into accepting his obligations. Trade in the Black Sea must also be protected against the machinations of the Genoese. Trade with Trebizond had been resumed at its emperor's request in 1363. A baillie of the Venetian community there had been appointed in 1366 and two years later their colony was fortified for greater security and permanence; and the Doge had gratified or mollified the Emperor of Trebizond by sending him a clock as a present. Protests had to be lodged with him from time to time about the treatment of Venetians in his city and the violation of their rights. In 1374 the baillie had to threaten to evacuate the Venetian quarter unless conditions improved and agreements were respected.[2] So far as concerned 'Turkey', nothing had come of the negotiations with the Sultan Murad, who had offered Venice a market at Skutari; and Murad's plans for enlarging the

[1] Chrysostomides, 'Venetian commercial privileges', 345–8, Document no. 13; Thiriet, *Sénat*, I, nos. 550–3, 566; Caroldo, ed. Chrysostomides, *OCP*, xxxv (1969), 162–4. C. Diehl, 'La colonie vénitienne à Constantinople à la fin du xive siècle', in Diehl, *Etudes byzantines* (Paris, 1905), pp. 241–75.

[2] Thiriet, *Sénat*, I, nos. 413 (1363), 427 (1365), 434–5 (1366), 441–2 (1367), 450, 465 (1368), 499 (1371), 510 (1372), 535 (1374), 565 (1375). By 1375 Venice was so displeased by the Emperor of Trebizond, Alexios III Komnenos, that the commission of five recommended that either he should be replaced by a pretender whom they would support or they should mount a punitive raid on his city and collect their own reparations. Thiriet, *Sénat*, I, no. 576 (12 March 1376).

Turkish fleet were causing concern. But the key to the whole situation was Constantinople.[1]

These were the matters to which the commission of five in Venice applied their minds in the winter of 1375–6. On 12 March 1376 the Doge Andrea Contarini signed a detailed list of instructions for a delegation to be sent to Constantinople. Its leader was Marco Giustiniani, who had dealt with the Emperor John V in Rome in 1370.[2] Giustiniani was 'Captain General of the Sea' and it was in this capacity that he was to lead his delegation. He was not an ambassador but an admiral; and his orders were to proceed by way of Modon and Negroponte to pick up an armada of ten galleys from Crete with which to sail to Constantinople. On arrival there he would not go ashore. The leaders of the Venetian community would come aboard to report. They would convey the admiral's request for an immediate audience with John V, or with his son Manuel, to discover why he had refused to discuss the treaty with Gradenigo. Giustiniani would then send his junior colleagues to the palace, if the emperor agreed to meet them. If he played for time, 'as is the custom of the Greeks', matters would go no further. If, however, he seemed chastened, then he would be asked to confirm his treaty with Venice for five years on the terms proposed by Gradenigo, with firm assurances on all points, not least concerning the immediate payment of at least a portion of his debts. His crown jewels would meanwhile stay in Venice. The Senate had so little faith in John V that they authorised Giustiniani's delegation to pay a call on the former emperor, John Cantacuzene, who was then living as a monk in Constantinople. He had an older and a wiser head. But the most ominous note in the instructions given to Giustiniani was that, if his mission failed, and if he could get no satisfaction from any of the Byzantine Emperors, he should visit the Sultan Murad to make him a gift of 400 *hyperpyra* and to remind him of his proposal to grant Venice a commercial colony on his territory.[3]

The patience of Venice had often been tried near to exhaustion by the Byzantines. The message that Marco Giustiniani brought to Constantinople was that the Doge and Senate would stand no more. They knew that John V could not afford to be so obstinate any more than he could afford to pay his debts. Giustiniani brought an ultimatum. It had the desired effect. The sight of ten Venetian galleys in the Golden Horn and the curt and officious nature of the message that they brought signalled to the emperor that he could hold out no longer. He agreed to all that

---

[1] Thiriet, *Sénat*, I, nos. 423, 461, 541, 546.

[2] He was accompanied by two Provedditori (*provisores*), Pietro Corner and Marino Memo.

[3] Caroldo, ed. Chrysostomides, 164–6; Thiriet, *Sénat*, I, no. 575. Halecki, *Un Empereur*, pp. 320–1.

the Venetians demanded. He would renew his treaty with them for five years precisely on the conditions prescribed by Gradenigo; and he would do his best to pay his debts and settle his accounts for damages. He would go even further. In what may have been a fit of remorse he put forward a proposal of his own which had not been on the agenda. Neither Gradenigo nor Giustiniani had been empowered to discuss the fate of the emperor's jewels. Neither had been authorised to talk about the island of Tenedos. The return of the jewels and the cession of the island had been sides of the same coin for twenty years and more. Giustiniani was not an ambassador; and he was too correct an officer to raise matters which he had not been commissioned to discuss. It was the emperor who made the suggestion. He would now part with Tenedos for 30,000 ducats and the return of his jewels. The only conditions were that the people and clergy of Tenedos should remain under the jurisdiction of the Patriarch of Constantinople and that the Byzantine flag should fly alongside the banner of St Mark on the island, implying a form of condominium. This apparently happy solution to a long-standing problem had to be referred to Venice and a special commissioner was sent to Constantinople without delay to confirm it. The renewal of the treaty and with it the new deal over Tenedos were agreed late in May or early in June 1376.[1]

There were those in Venice who applauded the takeover of Tenedos. But there were others who opposed it, on the grounds that it was bound to provoke the Genoese.[2] They were right. The agreement had not been ratified in Venice before its first consequences were felt. The Genoese at Galata were well aware of what was afoot. They took their own measures to prevent it. In July 1376 they engineered the escape from prison of John V's son Andronikos and whisked him over to Galata. From there he made contact with the Sultan Murad who gladly lent him troops. With their help he besieged Constantinople for thirty-two days until, on 12 August, he fought his way in through one of the gates. His father and his brothers Manuel and Theodore did not give in easily. But in October Andronikos arrested them and threw them all into prison. He appointed his own patriarch to crown him as emperor. Those who had befriended him had already had their rewards. On 23 August he assigned Tenedos to the Genoese. On 3 September he surrendered Gallipoli to the Sultan. The Genoese at once sent a force to take possession of Tenedos. The inhabitants would have none of them. They and their Greek governor remained loyal to the father of Andronikos. They fought back and the

---

[1] Caroldo, ed. Chrysostomides, 167–8, 150–3; *DR*, v, no. 3150. Halecki, *Un Empereur*, pp. 321–2.

[2] Caroldo, ed. Chrysostomides, 172.

Genoese had to withdraw. Not long afterwards, in October 1376, the Venetians sailed in to occupy the island. The formalities of its cession to them had still to be completed; but Giustiniani, who commanded the fleet, rightly saw that he must act quickly if Tenedos was not to be lost to the Genoese. The people and the governor of the island welcomed the Venetians as their saviours and protectors, coming out to meet them with crosses in their hands. They knew that it was their friend, the Emperor John V, who had put them under the protection of Venice. Giustiniani nominated as the island's first Venetian governor Donato Tron, who had been much involved in the negotiations with the Emperor John, and went back to Venice taking the treaty documents that John had signed.[1]

In a letter that he wrote at the time, Demetrios Kydones, the prime minister and confidant of the unhappy Emperor John V, gives a vivid description of these events. He writes:

The emperor [Andronikos] promised Tenedos to the Genoese when he was with them, after his escape from prison. But the Venetians have forestalled them by seizing the island; and now, having fortified it and its citadel with walls, provisions, men, arms and everything that makes a fortress impregnable, they have left a garrison there and gone home. They expect to come back in the spring with a great number of ships. But the Genoese cannot rest while their rivals occupy the island of Tenedos, for they feel that they will be deprived of access to the sea and of their maritime trading profits ... Wherefore they are planning to blockade the island with ships and engines of war of all kinds; and they are obliging the emperor to co-operate with them, for otherwise, so they say, he would connive at the robbery of the Venetians and take their side. To clear himself of this suspicion the emperor has agreed to be their ally and now, for all our poverty, he is making ready weapons, munitions and ships and is compelled to hire soldiers, a thing which is for him more difficult than flying. But even these evils, grave though they are, can be accounted tolerable compared to our domestic ills. For the emperor's father and brothers are still held in prison from which there is no escape...[2]

The battle lines were now drawn. The usurper in Constantinople, Andronikos IV, was indebted to the Genoese whether he liked it or not. His father, John V, whom he had imprisoned, was the ally of the Venetians. Each was in fact a pawn in the great war of commercial rivalry between Venice and Genoa which was about to break out. The squabble

[1] *Chron. brev.*, II, pp. 311–17; Caroldo, ed. Chrystostomides, 170–1. F. Thiriet, 'Venise et l'occupation de Ténédos au XIVe siècle', *Mélanges de l'Ecole Française de Rome*, LXV (Paris, 1953), 219–45; R.-J. Loenertz, 'Notes d'histoire et de chronologie byzantines', 166–7; G. T. Dennis, *The Reign of Manuel II Palaeologus in Thessalonica, 1382–1387*, OCA, 159 (Rome, 1960), pp. 27–9, 37–40; Chrysostomides, 'Studies on the Chronicle of Caroldo', 152–5; Barker, *Manuel II*, pp. 23–30.

[2] Demetrios Kydones, Letters, ed. R.-J. Loenertz, *Démétrius Cydonès, Correspondance*, I, Studi e Testi, 186 (Vatican City, 1956), no. 167, pp. 38–9.

over Tenedos precipitated the first engagement in that war. As soon as it was known that the island was in Venetian control, Andronikos gratified his Genoese friends by attacking the Venetians in Constantinople, confiscating their property and arresting their baillie and his councillors. Two Venetian ships coming in from Tana were seized in sight of the city; and the Genoese of Chios joined in the retaliation by attacking a number of Venetian ships on the high seas. Meanwhile, Marco Giustiniani had got back to Venice. The treaty that he had taken with him was ratified. The Venetian occupation of Tenedos was confirmed. In January 1377 Antonio Venier was appointed as its baillie and captain. Some months passed before he reached the island, but it was strongly held and garrisoned.

In the spring of 1377 a Genoese embassy arrived in Venice to demand that Tenedos be surrendered to the Emperor Andronikos. The reply was predictable. In Venetian eyes Andronikos was a usurper and worse still a protégé of Genoa. The Venetian occupation of Tenedos had been legally confirmed by the true Emperor, John V. As word came back to Venice of the damage inflicted on their citizens in Constantinople and of the arrest of their baillie, the Senate resolved to take more direct action. In May 1377 the new Captain General, Pietro Mocenigo, was ordered to take ten galleys to Constantinople to threaten the 'emperor' Andronikos. If he refused to set free the baillie and make reparations for the damage that he had caused, Mocenigo was authorised to call on the Greeks to rise up and depose him and put on the throne either his father John or his brother Manuel, or even Matthew, son of the former Emperor John Cantacuzene. If this ploy did not succeed, he was to approach the Sultan Murad for assistance in restoring order in Constantinople and then to sign a treaty confirming the Venetian control of Tenedos with whichever emperor happened to emerge from the muddle. An alternative plan was to land a force of 400 men in Constantinople to overthrow Andronikos. This the Senate wisely rejected. At the same time an ambassador from Venice went to Genoa to make formal complaints about Genoese behaviour in Constantinople and to issue a warning that Venice was well prepared if it should come to open war. Both sides dressed their naked ambition in pious assertions of loyalty to one or other of the Byzantine Emperors. But neither of the emperors could act as a free agent. John V was in prison. Andronikos IV was a captive of Genoese policy.

Later in May 1377 the Venetians changed their plans when it became known that Genoa was equipping a fleet of twelve galleys to go to Constantinople as reinforcements for Andronikos. Mocenigo's mission was cancelled. Instead two more warships were sent from Venice, first to

Crete and then on to Constantinople. They were commanded by Michiel
Sten and Carlo Zeno. Donato Tron joined them with two more ships.
They reached Constantinople on 16 July, before the Genoese had arrived;
and 'for the honour of Venice' they attacked the ships and installations
in the harbour and burnt villages and fields of corn around the city.
On 26 July they sailed to Tenedos, where they left Carlo Zeno to take
charge of the defences with a garrison of 300 men and two galleys. The
Genoese reinforcements reached Constantinople after the Venetians had
left. They joined forces with what ships their ally Andronikos had and
then captured the island of Lemnos in his name. It was the nearest inha-
bited island to Tenedos. Andronikos and the Genoese between them
had over twenty warships; and in November they made for Tenedos.
But the Venetians, led by Carlo Zeno, put up strong resistance; and
after three or four days of fierce fighting, Andronikos and his allies had
to retire with heavy losses.[1]

No amount of diplomacy could now resolve the dispute between
Venice and Genoa. It appeared to be over the possession of one of the
smaller islands of the Aegean Sea. In truth it was over the control and
the profits of the trade routes between Italy, Constantinople and the
Black Sea. After the Venetian victory at Tenedos in November 1377
war was formally declared. The Venetians were well entrenched in Tenedos and they had the full support of its Greek inhabitants. In 1378 they
sent out a raiding party to plunder the Genoese colony of Chios. But
the theatre of war then shifted west to Italian waters; and it was there
that the rival republics fought each other to exhaustion in 1381. All that
the Byzantines gained from it was a deeper sense of their inability to
shape their own destiny. Their emperors had degenerated into puppets
whose strings were manipulated by foreigners, Italians or Turks. Andronikos IV was the creature of the Genoese and of the Turks, to whom
he had freely and feebly surrendered the prize of Gallipoli. John V had
courted the favour of the King of Hungary, of the pope and of the Doge
of Venice. They had all lost patience with him. But only the Venetians
knew how to use him for their own purposes, how to exploit his weaknesses and his misfortunes. They had worn him down by calling in the
debts that he could not pay. After years of talk and indecision, they
had won from him the island of Tenedos which they considered vital

[1] Caroldo, ed. Chrysostomides, 172–80; Daniele di Chinazzo, *Cronica de la guerra da Vene-
ciani a Zenovesi*, ed. V. Lazzarini, Deputazione di Storia Patria per le Venezie; Monumenti
Storici. Nuova serie, XI (Venice, 1958), pp. 18–19; Caresini, *Cronica*, pp. 18–20; Sanudo,
Vitae Ducum, col. 679; Stella, *Annales Genuenses*, pp. 169–70; Jacobus Zeno, *Vita Caroli
Zeni*, ed. G. Zonta, *RIS*, XIX/6 (Bologna, 1940), pp. 14–15; Letter of Donato Tron to the
Doge, 29 August 1377, ed. V. Lazzarini, 'Due documenti sulla guerra di Chioggia', *Nuovo
Archivio Veneto*, XII (1896), 140–2.

to their needs. In return they had promised him that the Byzantine crown jewels would be sent back where they belonged. That promise was never kept. Perhaps it was on the point of being fulfilled in June 1376. But a month later the Emperor John was deposed and then cast into prison. The Venetians were very correct when it came to keeping their promises in such matters. But they could not send the crown jewels to a usurper who was also in league with their enemies. The jewels remained locked in the Treasury of St Mark's to be a bargaining point between Byzantium and Venice until there were no Byzantine Emperors to wear them.[1]

---

[1] The matter of the crown jewels and the money owed to Venice for their redemption was raised every time the treaty with Byzantium was renewed, in 1390, 1406, 1418, 1423, 1442 and 1448. The relevant documents are collected in Bertelè, 'Gioielli', 163–77. See also J. W. Barker, *Manuel II*, Appendix 1, pp. 443–5. Thiriet, *Romanie vénitienne*, p. 177 n. 1, and in 'Venise et l'occupation de Ténédos', 225, and again in *Sénat*, 1, no. 523, states that the jewels were restored to John V in 1373. But the document of the Senate which he cites in support says only that 'it is *possible* for the emperor's jewels to be sent to Constantinople' ('Quod jocalia domini Imperatoris Constantinopolis *possint* mitti Constantinopolim cum galeis viagii Romanie').

18

BYZANTIUM IN THRALL TO
THE TURKS AND IN DEBT TO VENICE

THE war between Venice and Genoa that had begun at Tenedos in 1376 ended at Chioggia in 1381. It was the most destructive of all the wars between the two republics. Among its heroes on the Venetian side were Vettore Pisani, nephew of the Nicolò Pisani who had disgraced himself at Porto Lungo in 1354, and Carlo Zeno, who had distinguished himself at Tenedos. Among those who worked for a Genoese victory were King Louis the Great of Hungary and Francesco da Carrara of Padua. Venice could count on at least the moral support of King Peter II of Cyprus, whose island had been seized by the Genoese in 1373, and on the more active help of Bernabo Visconti of Milan. Neither side sought or expected the Byzantine Emperors to take part. The battles were fought too far away from Constantinople. Chioggia lies at the south-western tip of the lagoons of Venice. It was there that the last phase of the war was fought. The Genoese occupied the town in August 1379. Venice was encircled. Through the heroic efforts of its Doge and people what looked like certain defeat and destruction was turned into triumph. In December the Doge Andrea Contarini and Vettore Pisani, at the head of a hastily rebuilt fleet, sailed down to Chioggia and closed its harbour. The Genoese were hemmed in with no means of escape. On 1 January Carlo Zeno arrived from the east with reinforcements. The blockade of Chioggia continued for six months until the 4000 Genoese, reduced to starvation and seeing no hope of rescue, surrendered in June 1380. The war dragged on for another year. Both sides, exhausted and impoverished, were relieved when Amadeo, Count of Savoy, offered his services as a mediator. In August 1381, at Amadeo's castle at Turin, a peace conference was held attended by representatives of all the participants in the war of Chioggia.[1]

---

[1] The text of the Treaty of Turin is in *Liber iurium reipublicae Genuensis*, II, cols. 858–906. Cf. L. A. Casati, *La guerra di Chioggia e la pace di Torino* (Florence, 1866); Kretschmayr, II, pp. 229–42, 608–11.

Neither Venice nor Genoa did very well out of the Treaty of Turin.
Neither had won the war. The Venetians regained the strongholds around
the lagoon which had been occupied by the troops of Francesco da Carrara. But they had to concede that their Doge was no longer Duke of
Dalmatia. The King of Hungary had annexed Dalmatia twenty years
before. The treaty confirmed that it was his in law. The war had had
its beginnings in the island of Tenedos. It might well break out again
if the possession of Tenedos remained in dispute. Amadeo of Savoy knew
the lie of the land in that part of the world better than the Carraresi
or the Hungarians. He believed that the only way to make the world
safe for trade without conflict up and down the Hellespont was to render
Tenedos neutral and useless to Venice and Genoa alike. The Treaty of
Turin therefore provided that the Venetians were to evacuate the island
and surrender it to Amadeo. His agents would then supervise the total
destruction of all its castles, walls, defences, houses and habitations from
top to bottom, 'in such fashion that the place can never be rebuilt or
reinhabited'. The Commune of Genoa was to foot the bill for the demolition. The Venetians gave pledges to Amadeo in money or jewels that
they would leave the island of Tenedos within fifty days. The Greek
inhabitants were not consulted. They must go where they were told,
leaving their homes in ruins and their island a desert. They would be
compensated.

In November 1381 the baillie of Tenedos, Zanachi Mudazzo, got orders
from his government in Venice. He was to consign his island to the
agent of the Count of Savoy when he arrived. A Genoese observer would
be there to see that the treaty terms were carried out. Mudazzo would
also have the delicate task of telling the inhabitants that they were to
be evicted. They were to be moved either to Crete or to Negroponte.
The pill was sweetened for them by the promise that they would for
ever after be treated with special respect and be exempt from all except
the ordinary taxes and duties payable to Venice. To prevent trouble,
however, they were to be transported and resettled in small groups and
not as a single community; and any who resisted being moved could
be offered small bribes. The evacuation did not go smoothly. The baillie
Mudazzo, convinced of the absurdity of the arrangement, refused to
obey his orders. He explained his disobedience in letters to his Doge.
He emphasised the arrogance of the Genoese, whose observer openly
boasted that the island which Venice was deserting would quickly be
refortified by Genoa. He reported that the garrison troops in the island,
whose pay was in arrears, were siding with the Greeks who were loth
to move. Mudazzo was a loyal and patriotic citizen of Venice. He claimed
that his hand was being forced to disobey his orders. The senators in

Venice had some sympathy for him. But they could not condone such indiscipline; and they put a price on his head.

Mudazzo was not alone in thinking that the evacuation and destruction of Tenedos was absurd. In the course of the debates in Venice in June 1383 the Doge, Antonio Venier (1382–1400), protested that such wanton vandalism was an offence against God and humanity. He had himself been baillie at Tenedos. He knew that as a deserted and unguarded island it could easily fall to the Turks. The Doge therefore proposed that it should be handed back to the Byzantine Emperor, on the understanding that he would preserve its neutrality. The Genoese would never have accepted such a solution. The senators voted against their Doge. Mudazzo had turned himself into a rebel against his own government and a hero among the Greeks. It took more than a year to break his resistance. In April 1383 he gave in and was allowed to leave Tenedos as a free man.

His successor as captain of the island, Giovanni Memo, was charged with implementing the Treaty of Turin within six months. The evacuation of the Greeks began towards the end of the year. There were more than 4000. Some were shipped to Negroponte, where they were not well received. The majority, the more fortunate ones, were taken to Crete. Scrupulous attention was paid to their welfare. A sum of 15,000 ducats was set aside for those who had no money and no possessions and it was distributed at the rate of 10 ducats to each head of family. The Duke of Candia was allotted 43,000 *hyperpyra* for distribution to the islanders settling in Crete. Work on the demolition of the houses, the walls and finally the fortress of Tenedos began as soon as the inhabitants had left. The Venetians were as good as their word. They left Tenedos deserted and unfortified. But they always thought of the island as their own property and from time to time used it as a haven or a depot for their warships, or as a look-out station to keep an eye on the movement of the Turks. Never again, however, did they suggest that it might revert to the Byzantine Emperor.[1]

At the start of the war over Tenedos in 1376 the Emperor John V, who had sold it to Venice, was in prison in Constantinople. The Venetians were anxious to get him out and to be rid of his unruly son Andronikos IV who was the friend of the Genoese. They tried more than once. The

---

[1] Thiriet, *Sénat*, I, nos. 610 (November 1381), 615–17 (March 1382), 620–3, 627, 629–32, 636–7, 640–1, 647, 649, 652, 657, 662, 666 (1382–4); Thiriet, *Assemblées*, II, no. 842 and pp. 289–93 (15 August 1382) no. 854 (4 June 1383), no. 857 (16 September 1383). The proposal of the Doge Antonio Venier is printed in N. Jorga, 'Veneţia in Mare neagră', 1066, no. XII; 1068, nos. X, XI, XV, XVI, cf. 1065; Thiriet, *Sénat*, I, no. 652. Thiriet, 'Venise et l'occupation de Ténédos', 228–43; Setton, *Papacy and the Levant*, I, pp. 323–5.

bold Carlo Zeno led a rescue operation which his admiring grandson Jacopo narrates in colourful detail in his biography. He tells how the Emperor John, who was an old friend of Zeno, sent him a letter by the hand of his gaoler's wife. She happened to be one of the emperor's lady friends, for he had a reputation as a philanderer. Zeno enjoyed adventure and answered the call. He sailed under the walls of the prison and climbed up to a window. John V was never a one for taking quick decisions. His liberator had come too soon. He would not leave without his sons and they were in another part of the prison. Zeno left without him. A while later the emperor sent him another message. This time he promised that, if he got his freedom, he would formally make Tenedos over to Venice. The gaoler's wife again obliged him by acting as a courier. But she was caught by the wife of Andronikos IV. Under torture she told all. Carlo Zeno escaped to Tenedos, bringing with him the emperor's written promise to surrender his right to the island. The details of this adventure story may be fanciful. But there is probably some substance in it; and it is certain that the Venetians would rather have John V at liberty and his son Andronikos behind bars.[1]

During the war of Chioggia, however, John V effected his own escape, taking his sons with him. The circumstances are obscure; but in June 1379, after nearly three years in captivity, they fled by boat across to Skutari and made their way straight to the court of the Sultan Murad. There was really nowhere else that they could go. The Sultan must have enjoyed being thus put in the position of king-maker. The story goes that he consulted the opinion of the people of Constantinople by messenger. It was hardly necessary. For John V promised, when restored to his throne, to pay a larger tribute to the Sultan than ever before. The Venetians, who had their own reasons for wanting him back as emperor, lent ships for an assault on Constantinople. The Turks supplied an army; and on 1 July 1379 John V and Manuel re-entered the city. Andronikos escaped across to Galata, taking with him as hostages his mother, her now elderly father John Cantacuzene, and her sisters.[2]

The feud was not yet settled, however. For more than a year there was a civil war of a new kind, fought across the Golden Horn between Constantinople and the Genoese of Galata. Andronikos had left a garrison of three hundred Genoese troops in the city. A few days after his escape some Venetian ships arrived on the scene and attacked them. The Greeks spurred them on with shouts of 'Viva San Marcho'. The ubiquitous Carlo Zeno is said to have been in the forefront of the attack, though in fact he was at Tenedos at the time. On 4 August the Genoese were forced

[1] Zeno, pp. 13–14. Barker, *Manuel II*, Appendix IV, pp. 458–9.
[2] Barker, *Manuel II*, pp. 31–5; Nicol, *Last Centuries of Byzantium*, p. 292.

to lay down their arms. John V was at last in full control of Constantinople, while his son Andronikos IV was entrenched across the water
with his friends at Galata. Both were the agents and the victims of an
offshoot of the conflict between Venice and Genoa. John besieged Galata
by land and sea, the Venetians supplying the ships, the Turks the soldiers.
The defenders were short of food; disease broke out. But the fighting
went on for a year and more. Many of the Venetian ships assisting John
V had been recalled to the defence of their motherland. Carlo Zeno had
left for Venice at the end of 1379. Finally, in May 1381, the rival emperors,
father and son, came to an agreement. Andronikos was to be forgiven
and reinstated as heir to the throne. The succession was to pass through
him to his son John VII. He was given a principality in Thrace. He
had won a moral victory, at the expense of his younger brother Manuel
who had been led to expect the imperial inheritance for some ten years.
Manuel felt that his father had deceived and cheated him. In 1382 he
left Constantinople to go back to Thessalonica. There he resolved to
reign as emperor in his own right, no longer as the loyal son and unques-
tioning servant of his father's policy towards the Turks. For almost five
years Manuel struggled to make Thessalonica a new rallying-point of
resistance and the capital of a restored Byzantine province in Macedonia
and Thessaly.[1]

The Treaty of Turin was signed in August 1381, a few months after
the fighting had stopped in Byzantium. Doubtless under the inspiration
of Amadeo of Savoy, the treaty solemnly advised the Emperor John
V to receive his son Andronikos back into favour as heir to the throne.
The news that this had already happened had evidently not reached Turin.
Again under the influence of Amadeo, the treaty urged both Venetians
and Genoese to remind the Emperor John of his devotion to the Roman
Church. His conversion seems to have lost some of its fervour over
the years. The rewards that he had expected had not come his way.
Venice and Genoa were not noted for their missionary activities, nor
much concerned with the state of the emperor's immortal soul. They
were more interested in repairing the damage done to their business and
their trade by a long war which had sapped the energy and the resources
of both contestants.[2]

It had been proved before that the Venetians were more resilient than
their rivals. They were quicker and more adaptable at picking up the

[1] Doukas, ed. V. Grecu, *Ducas, Istoria turco-bizantină (1341–1462)* (Bucharest, 1958), XII.
4: p. 73; Chalkokondyles, I, pp. 57–8; *Chron. brev.*, II, pp. 320–1, 323–4; *DR*, V, no. 3171.
Caresini, p. 36; Chinazzo, ed. Lazzarini, pp. 214–17; Zeno, pp. 23–6; Sanudo, *Vitae Ducum*,
col. 683; Stella, pp. 176–7. Dennis, *Manuel II*, pp. 41–6.
[2] Setton, *Papacy and the Levant*, I, pp. 322–3.

threads of their interrupted trade in the east. The Treaty of Turin had
stipulated that they must stay clear of the Black Sea for two years. This
did not prevent them from sending embassies to the Khan of the Tatars
in the Crimea and to the Emperor of Trebizond to explain the situation
and to hold the door open for further business.[1] They were also quick
to come to terms with the new regime in Byzantium. In September 1381
they sent Pantaleone Barbo as ambassador to Constantinople to begin
the process of renewing the treaty, which had run its five-year course.
He was commissioned to pay his respects to John V and, as usual, to
remind him of his debts to Venice. There remained 17,163 *hyperpyra*
to be paid on his earlier accounts and there were more recent claims
to be settled as well. The return of the crown jewels was not to be
discussed; and if the emperor said that he wanted Tenedos back, he
must be told that the Treaty of Turin forbade such a transfer. Barbo
was also authorised to send a polite message from Constantinople to
the Sultan Murad, addressing him as a 'friend of the Commune' and
mollifying him by some presents to the value of not more than 200 *hyperpyra*. John V was in no hurry to confirm his treaty with Venice and
in no position to pay his debts. By prevaricating he hoped to get everyone
to agree that the island of Tenedos still belonged to him; and he said
as much to the Venetians in January 1383. He had after all lost a piece
of his dwindling empire and got no recompense.[2]

The reviving energy and enterprise of the Venetians was also demonstrated in another quarter and another island. Corfu had been detached
from Constantinople since the Fourth Crusade. Its Greek inhabitants
thought of themselves as Romans or Byzantines. Yet their fate was not
bound up with that of the Byzantine Empire. Their island had been
briefly held by the Venetians from 1207 to 1214 when the independent
ruler of Epiros took it from them. His successor had allowed it to pass
to Manfred of Sicily; and when Charles of Anjou defeated Manfred in
1266, Corfu became a part of the Angevin empire of Naples and Sicily.
By the fourteenth century that empire was in decline. Venice first thought
of relieving its harassed rulers of Corfu in 1350. Some negotiations took
place but no deal was done.[3] For some years thereafter the weakness
of the Byzantine Empire, the westward drive of the Turks and the rebellion in Crete made Tenedos seem a more desirable and useful island.
Venice maintained a consul on Corfu, however, and Venetian ships regularly called in there on their way to and from Coron and Modon.

[1] Thiriet, *Sénat*, I, nos. 605, 607 (21 and 27 October 1381).
[2] Thiriet, *Sénat*, I, no. 606 (25 October 1381), no. 611 (15 November 1381), no. 619 (20 April 1382), no. 637 (26 January 1383); *DR*, v, no. 3178.
[3] Thiriet, 'Les interventions vénitiennes dans les Iles Ioniennes', 374–85; and see above, p. 296.

In 1350 its nominal ruler had been Robert, Prince of Taranto, a great-grandson of Charles of Anjou. When Robert died in 1364 his principality with its appurtenances passed to his brother, Philip II (1364–73). It was with Philip that the Venetians resumed talks about the lease or purchase of Corfu in 1366. On 7 December of that year an agreement was drafted and 'a certain sum of money' was offered to Philip as a pledge or a deposit.[1] Again the matter seems to have been dropped. After the Treaty of Turin, the Venetians regarded Corfu as an even more desirable property. Its chief commercial value lay in its saltpans. Its strategic value lay in its position at the end of the Gulf. A garrison stationed there could keep watch on the Dalmatian coast, which the treaty had assigned to the King of Hungary. They mounted a campaign of propaganda to lure the leading citizens of Corfu into believing that Venice was their best friend. The local consul, Giovanni Panemsaco, was instructed to flatter the Greeks who expressed a preference for Venetian rule. Their loyalty would never be forgotten. The consul was also to make a careful record of all the privileges and immunities accorded to the Corfiotes in times past and to send a full copy to Venice. The Senate was to send an ambassador in secret to Jacques des Baux, the new prince of Taranto, who succeeded his uncle Philip in 1373, to explain the terms being offered for Corfu. A few weeks later a proposition was put to the prince. Seeing that the leading men of Corfu were eager to accept Venetian rule and that Venice was happy to take them under its protection, the Senate would either put down a deposit on an agreed purchase price, or rent the island from Naples, or buy it outright.[2]

A Venetian delegation went to see Charles III of Anjou–Naples, the sovereign lord of the Princes of Taranto. A special committee was appointed, the *collegium Corphu*, to keep the pressure up, for the Genoese had expressed an interest in buying or seizing the island and they too were having meetings with Charles III.[3] In August 1384 a form of contract was drafted for the sale of Corfu to be presented to the King of Naples for his signature. In November one Angelo Condulmer was sent to Barletta to pursue the matter at Charles's court. The Venetians were anxious that the Genoese might have stolen a march on them by acquiring Corfu behind their backs. If this proved false, Condulmer was authorised to offer 60,000 ducats for the island. If the Genoese had already offered the equivalent he could raise the price to 70,000, 80,000, or even 100,000 ducats. He was empowered, if necessary,

[1] Thiriet, *Sénat*, I, no. 440.
[2] Thiriet, *Sénat*, I, nos. 625–6; Thiriet, *Assemblées*, II, nos. 840–1 (May and June 1382).
[3] *DVL*, II, no. 188, pp. 184–5 (19 November 1382). Thiriet, *Sénat*, I, nos. 634, 651; Thiriet, *Assemblées*, II, nos. 848–9.

to make an immediate down payment of 20,000, or better of 25,000 or 30,000 ducats, or to offer securities. He was also free to disburse 5000 ducats as bribes or favours to persons of influence. The King of Naples must be persuaded that the possession of Corfu was vital to Venice, lest it should fall into other hands. Condulmer must spare no effort to clinch the deal.[1]

Jacques des Baux, Prince of Taranto, died in 1383. Charles III of Anjou–Naples died in February 1386. Corfu was without a feudal lord. Some of its citizens swore loyalty to Charles's infant son, Ladislas; others turned to Venice or to Genoa for protection; and some offered their island to Francesco da Carrara of Padua, the bitterest enemy of Venice. Francesco was delighted and at once sent an agent to occupy the town. The Venetians then abandoned the diplomacy of the conference table and took direct action. Giovanni Miani, Captain of the Gulf, landed on the island and addressed an assembly of its people. He explained that Venice was eager to help and protect them. The Genoese would treat them like slaves. The lord of Padua had no ships. Only Venice knew all their ancient rights and privileges. Only Venice would respect and honour them. Venetian propaganda had prepared the ground. The Corfiotes accepted Miani's arguments without protest. Francesco's agent eventually escaped by night on a Genoese ship. The Angevin garrison came to terms; and Corfu was a Venetian protectorate or colony by May 1386. It proved to be the most enduring of all the Venetian possessions in Romania. The Turks never conquered it and it remained a Venetian island until the end of the Republic in 1797. It had in the end been appropriated and not purchased. The Venetians intended to pay for it. But they could force the price down by procrastinating. Not until 1402 did Ladislas of Naples ultimately settle for the sum of 30,000 ducats, half the lowest price offered to his father.[2]

The Treaty of Turin had obliged the Genoese to make their peace with the Emperor John V and to work for a reconciliation between him and his eldest son Andronikos. They did as they were told; and in November 1382 a treaty was signed in Constantinople between the two emperors, John and Andronikos, and the Genoese of Galata. It is an instructive document. The senior emperor undertook not to make war on Andronikos or his son, John VII, and to respect their rights over

[1] Thiriet, *Assemblées*, II, no. 867 and pp. 295–7, nos. 868–70 (5 and 7 November 1384); Thiriet, *Sénat*, I, no. 684.
[2] Thiriet, *Sénat*, I, nos. 698, 703–4, 712, 720–1, 729–31, 733 (1385–7); II, no. 1066 (August 1402); *DVL*, II, nos. 151–6, pp. 263–86 (June to November 1402); *Chron. brev.*, II, pp. 329–30 (the Short Chronicles seem to indicate that the Venetians took Corfu before August 1385). Cf. Miller, *Latins in the Levant*, pp. 525–9; Thiriet, *Romanie vénitienne*, pp. 357–8, 395–6.

their principality in Thrace; and he promised to come to their aid against all aggressors except the Sultan Murad and the Turks. The Genoese for their part agreed to support John V in case of attack by his son; and they promised to come to his aid against all aggressors except the Sultan Murad and the Turks.[1] The treaty thus expressed the evident truth that both sides had to make exception of the Turks because both were to a great extent dependent upon the Sultan for their survival. All the emperors were sworn vassals of Murad and had forfeited their freedom of action. By surrendering Gallipoli to the Sultan in 1376 Andronikos had ensured that the initiative lay with the Turks and not with any of the claimants to the Byzantine throne. Andronikos was a restless man. He soon broke the peace that he had made with his father and would doubtless have done so more than once, had he not been carried off by death in June 1385. John V mourned the passing of a son who had given him so much trouble. But there was more trouble to come; for Andronikos's son and heir inherited his father's restlessness and bitterness; and the Genoese, who had respected the Treaty of Turin so far as concerned their old friend Andronikos, concluded that it need not apply to his son. They were eager to promote the claim of the young John VII to the imperial throne.[2]

The reconciliation between John V and Andronikos in 1381 had been made at the expense of John's second son Manuel. Manuel was a stronger character than either of them. He was out of sympathy with his father's appeasement of the Turks and his brother's reliance on the Genoese. In 1382 he left Constantinople to set himself up as emperor in Thessalonica, with or without his father's blessing. He was in close touch with his youngest brother, Theodore Palaiologos, who in 1381 had been appointed Despot or governor of the comparatively thriving Byzantine province in the Morea, whose capital was at Mistra. Both Manuel and Theodore had more courage and enterprise than their ageing father or their scheming brother Andronikos. But in Thessalonica Manuel fought a losing battle. The Sultan Murad did not like his Christian vassals to take independent action; and he knew that Manuel's own father looked on him as something of a rebel. The Turks had made good use of the years of civil war in Constantinople. They had had time to consolidate and expand their conquests in eastern Europe. Manuel's little empire in Thessalonica was a thorn in the Sultan's side. In 1383 he ordered that it be conquered and that its 'emperor' be brought before him. From

---

[1] *DR*, v, no. 3177. Dennis, *Manuel II*, pp. 50–1.

[2] Doukas, xiv. 2–3: p. 83; *Chron. brev.*, ii, pp. 330–1. Dennis, *Manuel II*, pp. 108–13; R.-J. Loenertz, 'Fragment d'une lettre de Jean V Paléologue à la Commune de Gênes 1387–1391', *BZ*, li (1958), 37–40.

the end of that year until the spring of 1387 Thessalonica was under siege by the Turks.

Manuel knew that he could not hope to hold the city on his own. He conferred with his brother Theodore, who was also in need of help; and he decided to approach the Venetians. He was known in Venice, perhaps as a more honest and less devious man than his father. Early in 1385 therefore he sent a list of requests to the Doge. The Senate considered them on 18 April. Manuel asked for two large transport ships, 200 suits of armour, 20,000 arrows and seventy crossbowmen to serve as mercenaries for three months. Manuel understood his Venetians. They would want cash on account. This he would give them through their bankers at Negroponte. He also asked for a loan of 6000 ducats, or a lesser amount, for which he would pledge some of his lands and castles as security; and he suggested that a mutual agreement might be reached for the exchange of galleys between Thessalonica and Negroponte. His envoy to Venice also presented the case for his brother Theodore. He too promised to cede some of his territory if the Venetians sent him help.[1] Finally, Manuel hoped that the Doge would use his influence to arrange a truce with the Sultan Murad. The senators were not enthusiastic. They were still vainly trying to coax Manuel's father into confirming his treaty, a matter which was of far greater importance since it affected the profits of their citizens in Constantinople. Thessalonica was of secondary interest. There is no evidence that the Venetians were still maintaining a large colony there in 1385.[2] It was their turn to prevaricate. They replied that they were hesitant about sending arms and ships to Manuel's aid. They would be more ready to do so if he were to send the money for the hire of them in advance and direct to Venice. In any case, they could not spare the bowmen for at least a year. His request for a loan of 6000 ducats was turned down on a point of order. Manuel's envoy had no written instructions either to accept the money or to promise land as security for it. The suggestion that they might lend him their galley from Negroponte could not even be considered. It had to be on hand at all times to guard the island.[3]

Behind these replies lay various unspoken considerations. The risks in helping Manuel were too great. His empire in Thessalonica was probably doomed in any case. But above all, Venice could not afford to antago-

---

[1] Theodore had already presented the castle of Monemvasia to the Venetian castellan of Modon, Pietro Grimani, as a reward for his devotion to John V and his family in 1376. Thiriet, *Sénat*, I, no. 668 (29 March 1384); Maltézou, *Thesmos*, p. 118.

[2] There were some Venetian merchants in Thessalonica in 1393. Thiriet, *Sénat*, I, no. 838.

[3] Text of Manuel's request and the Senate's deliberations in Dennis, *Manuel II*, Appendix A, pp. 163–4. Thiriet, *Sénat*, I, no. 693; *DR*, v, no. 3181b.

nise the Sultan by going to the rescue of his rebellious vassal; and it
would be impolitic to offend Manuel's father by comforting his dis-
obedient son. On the very same day on which they discussed Manuel's
requests, the senators were faced with an offer from John V to give them
a fortress (*fortilicium*) in Constantinople. They wisely decided not to
accept it unless the emperor could be more explicit.[1] They wanted a
confirmation in writing of their privileges in Constantinople, not some
unspecified fortess. Their commercial interests must come first. The
greatest risk in sending aid to Manuel was that they might turn the Sultan
Murad against allowing their merchants to trade on his territory.[2] The
best that they could do for Manuel was to assure him that they would
work through diplomatic channels to bring the Sultan to make a truce
with him. Two years later almost to the day, on 9 April 1387, Thessalonica
fell to the Turks. Manuel's courageous leadership had not inspired its
people to fight on. He left them to their own devices and sailed away.
In the summer of the same year he was to be found at the camp of
the Sultan in Asia Minor. As with his father in 1379, there was really
nowhere else that he could go. Murad was kind to him considering the
circumstances. He knew that he was master of the situation. Even the
Venetians were beginning to dance to his tune. Having reminded Manuel
of his duties as a vassal, the Sultan sent him on to his father in Constantinople.[3]

In the last years of Manuel's reign in Thessalonica there had been
a lull in the Turkish advance elsewhere in eastern Europe. Murad was
preoccupied by events in Asia Minor. It might have been the moment
for an organised counter offensive by the Christians. The Byzantine
Emperors were powerless. Again it was the Serbians who took the initiative. Murad sensed a dangerous spirit of rebellion growing in his European
territories. He stifled it at birth by leading an army into Serbia. On
15 June 1389, at the famous battle of Kossovo, the Serbians and their
allies were massacred. In the heat of the battle Murad himself was killed;
but his place was immediately taken by his formidable son Bajezid. The
victory of the Turks at Kossovo complemented their triumph at the Marica eighteen years earlier. Now that they controlled Thessalonica and
had set their stamp of conquest on the Balkans, Constantinople was
more isolated than ever from western Christendom. The new Sultan Bajezid, known as Yildirim or the Thunderbolt, meant to keep it so and,

---

[1] Thiriet, *Sénat*, I, no. 694 (18 April 1385).
[2] Discussions with the Sultan were at a delicate stage. Thiriet, *Sénat*, I, nos. 667, 672 (March
and April 1384), nos. 677, 678 (22 July 1384). Full text of no. 678 in *DVL*, II, no. 116,
pp. 193–6; Jorga, 'Veneţia in Mare neagră', nos. I–V, 1093–5.
[3] On the fall of Thessalonica in 1387, see Dennis, *Manuel II*, pp. 151–9.

in due course, to make it his own. Until that moment came he could weaken its resistance still further by fostering the feuds among the imperial family. Bajezid regarded Manuel as less useful to his purposes than the young John VII, son of the late Andronikos IV. John had the devoted support of the Genoese. He went to Genoa in 1389 to advertise his claim to the throne in Constantinople. When he came back in 1390, Bajezid lent him some troops to force his way into the city. In April he seized the palace and for about four months he reigned as emperor. His grandfather John V, however, had barricaded himself in his castle at the Golden Gate of the city; and in August his son Manuel sailed to his rescue, as he had done before. John VII was thrown out and escaped to his protector, the Sultan Bajezid.[1]

The Venetians were not alone in being bewildered by the pace of events and the changes of rulers in Byzantium and the east. They had failed to come to a satisfactory arrangement either with the Emperor John V or with the Sultan Murad.[2] In 1390 Murad was dead and no one in Venice was quite sure who was in charge in Constantinople. Unlike the Genoese, the Venetians prudently refrained from taking sides in the Byzantine family feud. When the news of Murad's death had been confirmed in July 1389, they deliberated about sending a delegate to his son, to tender their condolences and to sound the ground about his intentions with regard to their merchants. At the same time they sent Andrea Bembo to Constantinople to remind the Emperor John V about his debts and his treaty with Venice.[3] Five years had passed since the last visitation of a Venetian ambassador, Lodovico Contarini. He had evidently tried to bully the emperor in a tactless manner; and John V had felt impelled to write twice to the Doge, Antonio Venier, to protest at Contarini's offensive and dishonest behaviour. It had been the ambassador's fault that the customary treaty had not been confirmed in 1384. The emperor had lost none of his love and friendship for Venice.[4] These fine words belied the fact that the Venetians in Constantinople com-

---

[1] Chron. brev., II, pp. 340–1, 342–3. J. W. Barker, 'John VII in Genoa: a problem in late Byzantine source confusion', OCP, XXVIII (1962), 213–38; Barker, Manuel II, pp. 68–78.

[2] Thiriet, Sénat, I, no. 735 (September 1387).

[3] Jorga, 'Veneţia in Mare neagră, no. XII, 1099–1110; Thiriet, Sénat, I, no. 760 (23 July 1389). If the emperor raised the matter of Tenedos and the crown jewels, Bembo was instructed to hide behind the letter of the Treaty of Turin. In March 1390 Francesco Querini was briefed to go as the first official Venetian ambassador to Bajezid. Jorga, 'Veneţia in Mare neagră', nos. XIII–XVI, 1101–3; Thiriet, Sénat, I, no. 768. M. Silberschmidt, Das orientalische Problem zur Zeit der Entstehung des Türkischen Reiches nach venezianischen Quellen, Beiträge zur Kulturgeschichte des Mittelalters und der Renaissance. Herausgegeben von Walter Goetz, 27 (Leipzig–Berlin, 1923), pp. 55–64.

[4] Thiriet, Sénat, I, no. 665 (20 January 1384); DVL, II, nos. 115, 117, pp. 192–3, 196–7 (12 June and 25 November 1384).

plained more and more about the injustices inflicted on them by the emperor's officials. Andrea Bembo returned to Venice with nothing achieved; and in April 1390 the Senate briefed a new ambassador, Francesco Foscolo. There was some doubt about what he would find when he got to Constantinople. He was instructed to seek audience either of John V or of his grandson John VII, depending on which of them was in power. In either case he was to issue an ultimatum to the effect that, if no satisfaction was given and if difficulties were made about renewing the treaty, the Venetian merchants in Constantinople would simply have to be evacuated for their own safety. Ships would be at hand to take them to Negroponte. If, however, Foscolo found that the Sultan Bajezid was already in charge of the city, he should temper his demands. Clearly the Venetians were expecting the Turks to march into Constantinople at any moment.[1]

Foscolo was lucky to reach Constantinople during the brief reign of John VII, for John gave him no trouble. Presumably on the grounds that he needed all the friends he could get, he lost no time in giving the Venetians all that they wanted without quibbling or prevaricating. The treaty which Venice had been trying to renew with John's grandfather for fourteen years was drawn up and signed in a matter of days on 2 June 1390.[2] Venice had never recognised John's father Andronikos IV as anything more than a usurper planted by the Genoese. John too was the friend of Genoa. But the political circumstances were so confused and the future so uncertain that the Venetians felt it was better to recognise him as emperor than to lose the chance of confirming in writing the status of their colony in Constantinople. The treaty is written in the solemn legal language required in such documents. It gives nothing away concerning the stirring events of the time. It deals mainly with the familiar problems and grievances of the Venetian residents and traders in Constantinople. The national debt to Venice for damages still stood at 17,163 *hyperpyra*, which the Emperor John, in true imperial style, promised to pay in five annual instalments. He acknowledged that 30,000 ducats with interest had still to be found to redeem the crown jewels pawned

---

[1] Jorga, 'Veneţia in Mare neagră', nos. XVII, XVIII, 1104. Thiriet, *Sénat*, I, no. 772 (9 April 1390). The identification of a mysterious 'Empress of the Romans' and 'mother of the emperor', who passed through Venice on her way home from Milan in 1390, is discussed by Barker, 'John VII in Genoa', 232–8, who published the relevant documents. Cf. Silberschmidt, *Das orientalische Problem*, p. 72. Barker believes that she was the mother of John VII, Maria Kyratza. She might more plausibly have been Helena Cantacuzene, wife of John V and mother of Manuel II, who was only 57 years of age in 1390 and thus not, as Barker claims, 'too old to be travelling'. Helena was still active in affairs of state in 1392. See Thiriet, *Sénat*, I, no. 820.

[2] Greek text in *MM*, III, pp. 135–44; Latin text in *DVL*, II, no. 135, pp. 224–9. *DR*, V, no. 3192.

to Venice forty-seven years before, and another 5000 ducats lent on other security. It is interesting that he refrains from recording the names of his forebears who had incurred these debts. Only in the case of damages more recently suffered by the Venetians in Constantinople does he refer to 'the Emperor of the Romans of most blessed and serene memory, the late Andronikos Palaiologos, my father'. The only reference to Tenedos is to the effect that the Byzantines seek no recompense for its loss or for injuries inflicted on them as a consequence of the war for its possession.

John VII's adventure as emperor ended in September 1390. In August, foreseeing the worst, he had asked the Venetians to intervene on his behalf. They had got what they wanted of him. They replied that it was not their custom to take sides in the internal disputes of others, least of all in disputes between members of the same tongue, flesh and blood.[1] By the time that their reply was formulated, John V was already back on his throne, reinstated by his son Manuel. Manuel had to pay a high price for his action. He had taken it without consulting the Sultan Bajezid. The Sultan peremptorily summoned him to his court as a hostage. John VII, whom he had dethroned, was already there. Towards the end of 1390 both were bound as vassals to join in the Turkish siege and capture of the last Byzantine stronghold in Asia Minor, the city of Philadelphia. Soon afterwards the Sultan demanded of the Emperor John V that he should demolish the fortifications which he had recently built at the Golden Gate. He too could only tremble and obey; for otherwise the Sultan threatened to imprison and blind his son Manuel. It was the last humiliation. John V was less than sixty years old. But his bitter experiences and disappointments had aged him before his time. He died on 16 February 1391. The Venetians did not lament his passing. He had played cat and mouse with them for too long. They had got more satisfaction from the Emperor John VII, who had reigned for only four months, than from his grandfather, who had tried their patience for nearly thirty-seven years. Now they would have to begin again with a new emperor, unless the Sultan decided to be done with them all and to take Constantinople for himself.[2]

Bajezid was not yet ready to do so. Nor was he ready for the next move made by his hostage Manuel Palaiologos. As soon as he heard of his father's death, Manuel slipped out of the Sultan's camp and hurried to Constantinople before his nephew John VII could forestall him. By

---

[1] Jorga, 'Veneţia in Mare neagră', no. xx, 1105 (4 October 1390); Thiriet, Sénat, I, no. 780: DR, v, no. 3192a.

[2] Doukas, xiii. 4–5: p. 77; Chron. Brev. II, pp. 345–6. Barker, Manuel II, pp. 74–80; Nicol, Last Centuries of Byzantium, pp. 302–5.

March 1391 he had moved into the palace. Bajezid disliked being outwitted. He was angry. He at once imposed yet more humiliations on the Byzantines; and he summoned Manuel back to serve him in Asia Minor. Manuel could perhaps have disobeyed the summons; but he felt it wise to appear subservient while the Sultan was in his present mood. He was not free to return to his capital until January 1392. In February he married Helena, a daughter of the Serbian prince Constantine Dragaš; and on the next day, 11 February 1392, he was crowned emperor by the patriarch. A Russian pilgrim who was in Constantinople attended the ceremony and has left a vivid account of the coronation. He observed that among those present were Venetians and Genoese decked out in all their finery. The Venetians may well have shown a proprietary interest in the crown jewels worn by the emperor. A delegation from their motherland was about to remind him that he owed them 30,000 ducats for the jewels which they still held in St Mark's.[1]

The government in Venice knew of Manuel's arrival in Constantinople by June 1391. In July they knew through their baillie that he had been summoned to join the Sultan. They ordered the baillie to get an assurance from Manuel as soon as he returned that he would respect the treaty with Venice.[2] In March 1392, after his coronation, the Senate sent Pantaleone Barbo to Constantinople to congratulate the new emperor on his accession and to point out that he was now responsible for remission of all the debts and other obligations incurred by his predecessors. A little later they were alarmed to hear that Bajezid was equipping a navy for purposes of war. Rumour had it that it was to be commanded by the Emperor Manuel and that it might be directed against the Venetian colonies in Romania. Three galleys were promptly detailed to observe the movements of Turkish ships around the Hellespont and to look to the defence of the Aegean islands. Another galley was to go to Constantinople to see what the emperor was up to. Failing that, two spies should be sent there, men who knew both Greek and Turkish, to collect intelligence. The Venetians had been alarmed before by rumours of naval alliances between Turks and Greeks. It was understandable that they should have been nervous. But their fears seem to have been groundless. In July 1392 their emissaries found the Emperor Manuel not on the high seas but in Constantinople, although he seemed to be in no mood

[1] *Chron. brev.*, II, pp. 345–6, 348. Barker, *Manuel II*, pp. 82–104; Nicol, *Last Centuries of Byzantium*, pp. 310–12.

[2] Jorga, 'Veneţia in Mare neagră', no. XXIV, 1106 (14 July 1301); Thiriet, *Sénat*, I, nos. 795, 797–8.

to confirm the treaty with Venice which his nephew had so impetuously signed.[1]

The Venetians had greater cause to be apprehensive about the plans of Bajezid. He was not a man to trifle with. In the winter of 1393 he summoned all his leading Christian vassals to his presence at Serres, to the east of Thessalonica. They included the Emperor Manuel, his brother Theodore, and their nephew, John VII. The Sultan's purpose was simply to frighten them, to demonstrate that he was the lord and master of them all. When he got back to Constantinople, Manuel concluded that the Sultan was neurotic. It would never be possible to have any rational relationship with him. The next time that Bajezid summoned him Manuel ignored the order and stayed behind the walls of his city. Better to sit it out patiently until help came from abroad. Bajezid would not tolerate such insubordination. In the spring of 1394 he sent a huge army to blockade the city and to make a desert of the surrounding countryside. The blockade was to last for about eight years. The Venetians were distressed, since some of their own citizens were suffering. They instructed their baillie in Constantinople to extend their sympathy to the emperor, to assure him of their goodwill and to advise him to stay where he was and hold out. They also urged him to make the facts as widely known as possible by writing to the pope, to the German Emperor and to the Kings of France and England. Help would then be organised for him on a large scale. Meanwhile, a plan to send two galleys to Constantinople to protect Venetian interests there was postponed pending further information about the intentions of the Turks.[2]

The Venetians, who pretended to observe a nominal neutrality between Greeks and Turks, could still beat the Turkish blockade of Constantinople by sea. It was unlikely that the Turks could breach the massive walls of the city on the landward side. The Sultan's best hope of forcing its emperor into submission was to starve his people to death or surrender. In other respects they were safe enough behind their walls. In July 1394 the Venetians again urged Manuel to stay at his post and not to lose courage. A report from the east had indicated that Bajezid might have to withdraw his troops from Constantinople to make war on 'the Emperor of the Tatars', the Mongol leader Timur Lenk. If, however, Manuel could bear it no longer, they were willing to provide his means of escape

<hr>

[1] Jorga, 'Veneţia in Mare neagră', nos. XXVIII, XXX, XXXIV, 1107–9; Thiriet, *Sénat*, I, nos. 808–9 (February and March 1392), 813–14 (April 1392), 820 (July 1392). The full texts of nos. 813 and 820 are printed in Loenertz, *Démétrius Cydonès, Correspondance*, II, pp. 446–8, 449–50. Silberschmidt, *Das orientalische Problem*, p. 73–82; Barker, *Manuel II*, pp. 104–5.

[2] Text in Jorga, 'Veneţia in Mare neagră', no. XL, 1111–13. Thiriet, *Sénat*, I, no. 851 (21 May 1394).

by sea and asylum in Venice. Alternatively, they might take him to the island of Lemnos which, it seems, he had offered to sell them. It might have been a substitute for Tenedos; but the Senate could not see its way to considering it at such a critical moment. The emperor would do better to write again to the pope and to the Christian princes of the west. Then, if he stood firm, help would surely come to him.[1] He was glad of their advice. He asked if they could show their concern by sending some food for his hungry people. Supplies were running dangerously low, as the Venetians must have been aware. At the end of 1394 they sent a shipment of grain to the city; and they reassured the emperor and his family that a Venetian ship was standing by to take them aboard if they were in immediate danger. In his letter to Venice Manuel had asked if it were true that a new league of Christians against the Turks was in process of being formed in the west. Something like it was certainly true; and the Venetians knew about it. But, with typical caution, they declined to commit themselves to supporting it until they knew more about the number and the nature of its participants.[2]

Once again it was the King of Hungary who sounded the alarm in Europe. In 1393 the Turks had overrun the neighbouring Kingdom of Bulgaria, captured its capital city of Trnovo and executed its ruler. King Sigismund of Hungary had allied with his other neighbours in Wallachia, north of the Danube. But they too went down before the Turkish wave in 1395. Sigismund appealed to all the crowned heads of Europe to save his own kingdom from conquest by the infidel. The time had come to fight a crusade for the survival of western Christendom. What the Byzantine Emperor had termed a league was transformed into a holy war, sanctified by the pope in Rome and the pope in Avignon. It was planned on a grand scale. The armies, numbering thousands, were drawn mainly from France and Hungary, Wallachia and Germany, with smaller contingents coming from England, Poland, Bohemia, Italy and Spain. They were to assemble in Hungary and march down the Danube valley. When they reached the Black Sea they would need ships. The Hungarians reck-

[1] Text in Ljubić, Monumenta, IV, no. CCCCLXXIII, pp. 332–4. Thiriet, Sénat, I, no. 860 (24 July 1394); DR, V, nos. 3246a, 3249–51. The confidence of Venice in its naval superiority over the Turks was expressed several times. Jorga, 'Veneţia in Mare neagră', no. XXXII, 1109 (20 July 1392): 'ostendendum quod simus potentes in mari et quod habeamus cordi velle sustinere franchisias nostras et conservare nostrum honorem'; no. XLVI, 1114 (3 December 1395): 'ostendamus nos potentes et fortes in illis partibus de magno numero galearum'.
[2] Partial text in Ljubić, Monumenta, IV, no. CCCCLXXXII, p. 338; Thiriet, Sénat, I, no. 868 (23 December 1394); DR, V, no. 3248. Doukas, xiii. 7: p. 79. Barker, Manuel II, pp. 123–6. In his extremity, the emperor told the Venetians that he was now ready to confirm his treaty with them, provided that the clause about Tenedos were modified. The Senate would have none of it. Thiriet, Sénat, I, no. 871 (March 1395); DR, V, no. 3252.

oned that twenty-five warships would be enough to guard the Hellespont and Bosporos, at a cost of up to 40,000 ducats a month. They hoped that the Venetians would co-operate generously. The Venetians, how-ever, had serious misgivings about the enterprise. Only out of their devotion to the Catholic faith and their respect for the King of Hungary did they agree to arm one-quarter of the required number of ships, on condition that other Christians provided the rest. They were loth to become too deeply involved. They pointed out to King Sigismund's envoys that they were at peace with the Turks. They had many merchants on Turkish territory whose lives and properties would be at risk if they displeased the Sultan.[1] War, as they had often observed in the past, was bad for business. Later in the year 1395 they explained to the Emperor Manuel that their neutrality in the war against the Turks, though more apparent than real, was to the benefit of Constantinople; for it made it possible for them to bring food supplies to the city. None the less, the emperor felt that the Venetians could have done more after all their talk about help coming to him from the west. At least they could lend him some more money so that he could play his own part in the rescue of Europe and his empire. He played on their vaunted devotion to the faith by offering them a number of holy relics as security for a further loan. They were not tempted. They were more interested in getting him to settle his existing debts and renew his treaty with them.[2]

The emperor also sent his own ambassador to Hungary. He returned to Constantinople by way of Venice, where he reported on the result of his mission in March 1396. King Sigismund was planning to lead his crusade down the Danube to be within reach of the Black Sea by June. He had arranged for the Byzantine ambassador to collect 30,000 ducats in Venice, which the emperor would use to equip ten warships for a month. The Venetians changed tack. They had been about to send a delegation to the Sultan Bajezid. They decided to cancel it now that Byzantium and Hungary were in alliance and Sigismund was assembling his crusading army. Instead they sent an envoy to the Emperor Manuel to say how delighted they were that the help which they had long pre-dicted was on its way and to announce that another shipment of grain would follow.[3] They were still in two minds, however, about the wis-dom of the venture. They sent no more than four ships in support of

[1] Thiriet, *Sénat*, I, no. 870 (10 March 1395). Silberschmidt, *Das orientalische Problem*, pp. 104–10; Setton, *Papacy and the Levant*, I, pp. 343–4.

[2] *DR*, v, no. 3256; Thiriet, *Sénat*, I, nos. 892, 896 (9 December 1395, 17 February 1396). The most sacred of the relics on offer was the tunic of Christ. G. T. Dennis, 'Official documents of Manuel II Palaeologus', *B*, XLI (1971), 45–58 (46–7).

[3] The Byzantine ambassador to Hungary was Manuel Philanthropenos. *DR*, v, no. 3255; Thir-iet, *Sénat*, I, nos. 900, 901 (1 March 1396). Setton, *Papacy and the Levant*, I, p. 346.

the crusade. They expected that Sigismund would reach the Bosporos by the middle of August. He got no further than Nikopolis on the Danube. It was there that the main body of the Turkish army, led by the Sultan, met the crusaders. The French and the Hungarians had already disagreed about their tactics as well as their objective. Sigismund was cautious and prudent. The French were impetuous and aggressive. At Nikopolis their disagreement proved fatal. On 25 September 1396 they were routed by the Turks in a welter of bloodshed. The Sultan ordered that his Christian prisoners be massacred, with the exception of a few of their leaders who might fetch a ransom. Sigismund was lucky to escape on a ship belonging to the Knights of St John. When he reached the Black Sea he was transferred to a Venetian warship which took him by way of Constantinople to Venice. It was the only practical part that the Venetians had played in the crusade of Nikopolis.[1]

News of the disaster reached Venice about a month after the battle. To meet the emergency the Sultan had had to withdraw some of his troops from the blockade of Constantinople. It was the only practical benefit that the crusade brought to the Byzantines. They foresaw, however, that his victory at Nikopolis would inspire the Sultan to resume his siege of the city in force. The Venetians were desperately worried. The Senate took immediate measures for the security of their citizens and colonies in Romania and for the defence of Constantinople by sea. If it fell to the Turks, as seemed quite likely, the officers responsible must make certain that none of their galleys was captured before getting away to Negroponte. Some of the senators voiced regret that they had ever allowed themselves to become involved in the crusade. The fact that they had sent even four ships to Sigismund was bound to turn the Sultan against them. It would have been wiser to preserve their nominal neutrality.[2]

The danger was so great that the Senate voted that eight galleys should at once be armed to protect Venetian property in the Aegean. The absurdity of the destruction of Tenedos was more apparent than ever. The Turkish navy was based at Gallipoli. A Christian fleet stationed at Tenedos could keep watch on the Turks and hem them in. Early in 1397 Venice asked the Genoese if they would agree to refortifying the island in breach of the Treaty of Turin. They quoted the opinion of the King of Hungary and other Christian leaders that the destruction of Tenedos was the main cause of the growing naval power of the Turks in the

[1] On the crusade of Nikopolis, see A. S. Atiya, *The Crusade of Nicopolis* (London, 1934); Runciman, *Crusades*, III, pp. 455–62; Atiya, *The Crusade in the Later Middle Ages*, pp. 435–62; Setton, *Papacy and the Levant*, I, pp. 341–69.
[2] Thiriet, *Sénat*, I, no. 917 (29 October 1396). Setton, *Papacy and the Levant*, I, pp. 357–8.

area. The Genoese were not very co-operative. They proposed that the island should be made a protectorate of the papacy and that the cost of its defence should be shared between Venice and Genoa. The Venetians wanted nothing less than total control over Tenedos.[1] At the same time they sent repeated messages of sympathy and encouragement to the emperor in Constantinople and even to the Genoese in Galata, warning them against making a separate peace with the Sultan Bajezid. The Emperor Manuel was so shocked by the consequences of the crusade of Nikopolis that he thought of abandoning Constantinople and making it over to the Venetians. Alternatively, he would give them the island of Imbros, or Lemnos. They saw nothing but trouble in any of these propositions. The emperor must be patient. More help would come to him. If, however, he was obliged to make peace with the Sultan, Venice must be represented among the negotiators. Any truce or treaty must ensure that the Turkish fleet was confined to its base at Gallipoli and not allowed out into the Aegean Sea. It must also ensure that the rights of Venice over its recent acquisitions in Romania were respected, for they had been obtained not by violence but by the voluntary submission of their inhabitants.[2]

In the ten years before the disaster at Nikopolis, the Venetians had added many places to their empire in Romania. In 1386 they had appropriated Corfu. In 1388 they laid claim to Argos and the useful port of Nauplion in the Morea. Their claim was substantiated in 1394, though the Turks took their revenge by destroying Argos three years later. In 1394 they acquired Athens and, albeit with some hesitancy, the rock of Monemvasia. Nearer home, on the Albanian coast, Durazzo reverted to Venetian rule in 1392. What God abandoned Venice defended. This was not mere imperialism. Nor was it greed, like the descent of carrion crows on a dying body. It was part of a calculated policy of protectionism, to maintain and consolidate the trade routes by sea between Venice and the east on which the profit and honour of the Commune depended. They were not tempted by everything that came their way. In 1387 they had declined to take responsibility for Thessalonica. In 1395 they refused the offer of Corinth and Megara. Their most serious loss was the island of Tenedos. But they turned down the emperor's gift of the neighbouring islands of Imbros or Lemnos.[3]

---

[1] Thiriet, *Sénat*, I, nos. 924, 926, 928 (January to March 1397). Thiriet, 'Venise et l'occupation de Ténédos', 241–2.

[2] Thiriet, *Sénat*, I, no. 932 (7 April 1397). Dennis, 'Official documents of Manuel II', 47.

[3] Thiriet, *Sénat*, I, nos. 858, 872–4, 883. Zakythenos, *Despotat grec de Morée*, I, pp. 131–9; Silberschmidt, *Das orientalische Problem*, pp. 89–96; Miller, *Latins in the Levant*, pp. 339–42; Thiriet, *Romanie vénitienne*, pp. 355–63.

As the fourteenth century drew to its close the fate of Constantinople hung in the balance, and with it the fate of its Venetian community. The Sultan Bajezid was unpredictable. No one could be sure that, if he captured the city, the Venetian community would be allowed to stay. The only certainty was that he would take his revenge on the Emperor Manuel and that there would be no more question of the Byzantines paying their debts or renewing their treaty arrangements with Venice. The Venetians therefore continued to counsel the emperor not to leave his post and not to come to any settlement of his own with the Sultan. He did as they told him. Bajezid had scornfully bidden him to shut the gates of his city and play out his act as emperor within its walls. Everything outside those walls was already the Sultan's property.[1] After Nikopolis he had angrily demanded that the city should surrender. The emperor and his people refused to give in. Before long they could see in the distance that work had begun on the construction of a great castle on the Asiatic side of the Bosporos. It came to be called Anadolu-Hisar. From here the Sultan planned to direct the conquest of Constantinople. The inhabitants, penned behind their walls, short of food and the means to procure it, were living on their nerves. Many died of starvation; others fled. A few were driven to disloyalty and treachery by their emperor's policy of passive defiance. The emperor himself was near despair; and at every hour of every day that passed he offered up this prayer: 'Lord Jesus Christ, let it not come to pass that the great multitude of Christian peoples should hear it said that it was during the time of the Emperor Manuel that the City, with all its holy and venerable monuments of the faith, was delivered to the infidel.'[2]

---

[1] Doukas, xiii. 5: p. 77. [2] Doukas, xiv. 4: p. 85.

19

BYZANTINE OPTIMISM
AND VENETIAN VACILLATION

AMONG the prisoners of rank taken by the Turks at Nikopolis was a
French knight, Jean le Meingre, known as Marshal Boucicaut. The Sultan
had set him free on parole to raise the ransom money for the other distinguished prisoners-of-war. Like Amadeo of Savoy, Boucicaut was an
intrepid and adventurous soldier. He longed to take his revenge on the
infidel. When he returned to France he reported to his sovereign lord,
King Charles VI. Charles was well briefed on eastern affairs and still
mourning the loss of so many of his subjects at Nikopolis. The Emperor
Manuel had often written to him begging for his help; and he had an
extra interest in Constantinople since, in 1396, he became overlord of
Genoa and so of the Genoese at Galata and elsewhere in the Byzantine
world. It was even rumoured that Manuel's nephew, John VII, had
thought of selling his title to the Byzantine crown to the French king
in 1397.[1] Marshal Boucicaut had been to Constantinople and had probably met the emperor. He knew the situation at first hand. In June
1399 Charles VI asked him to lead a small expedition to the relief of
the city. He accepted with enthusiasm.[2]

Boucicaut's little crusade grew in numbers and in strength as it made
its way east, though it never amounted to more than 1200 men. The
Genoese were slow to provide the ships required of them; but Venice
surprisingly contributed eight galleys. They assembled at Tenedos and
fought their way through the Turkish blockade in the straits, disembark-
ing at Constantinople in late summer. The distraught citizens gave them
a rapturous welcome. They hailed the French marshal as 'an angel of
the Lord'. The emperor honoured him with the Byzantine title of Grand

---

[1] The middle man in the transaction was to be Francesco II Gattilusio, the Genoese Lord
of Lesbos. See P. Wirth, 'Zum Geschichtsbild Johannes' VII Palaiologos', *B*, xxxv (1965),
592–600; Barker, *Manuel II*, p. 164; Setton, *Papacy and the Levant*, I, pp. 363–4.

[2] The adventures of Marshal Boucicaut are narrated by his biographer in *Le Livre des faicts
du Bon Messire Jean le Meingre dit Boucicaut, Mareschal de France et Gouverneur de Gennes*,
in J. F. Michaud and J. J. F. Poujoulat, ed., *Nouvelle Collection des mémoires pour servir
à l'histoire de France*, VII–IX (Paris, 1825).

Constable and together they made a number of raids on the enemy's positions beyond the city walls and even across the water in Turkish territory. They showed that the Turks were not invulnerable. They showed what a much larger force might be able to achieve. Boucicaut soon concluded that the emperor had better go back with him to the west to act as his own ambassador. Manuel agreed. The only difficulty was to find someone to take charge of Constantinople while he was away. He was not on speaking terms with his nephew, John VII. Boucicaut saw the problem and turned diplomat. He worked the miracle of bringing together the two parties in a family feud that had lasted for a generation. The reconciliation between Manuel II and John VII eased the tension among their rival supporters and made it possible for Manuel to leave Constantinople under the regency of his nephew. The marshal detailed his lieutenant Jean de Chateaumorand to stay behind with a hundred men-at-arms.[1]

The emperor with the marshal sailed out of Constantinople on Venetian galleys on 10 December 1399. It was to be more than three years before he came back. On his way he stopped at Monemvasia, where he left his wife and two little sons to be cared for by his brother, the Despot Theodore. He had already written to the Venetians to make sure that, if the worst came to the worst in the Morea, they would give asylum to his wife and family and his brother Theodore at Modon or Coron.[2] From Greece he sailed on to Venice. He had stayed there before, though more as a hostage for his father's conduct than as an honoured guest. When his father visited Venice the authorities had treated him with proper respect but without the pomp and pageantry that the visit of an emperor might have dictated. Manuel's reception in 1400 was quite different. The Doge, Andrea Contarini, sailed out to meet him in the state launch. The Senate had voted that 200 ducats be set aside for the emperor's entertainment, and he was lodged in the palace of the Marquis of Ferrara on the Grand Canal. The Maggior Consiglio listened with patience and sympathy to his account of the desperate state of Constantinople and promised him help. There was also talk of forming another league of Christian powers, a matter which Manuel had been discussing with Genoa and the Knights of Rhodes. The Venetians, who were party to the plan, wrote to John VII in Constantinople in March 1400 to tell him about

---

[1] Barker, *Manuel II*, pp. 160–5 and Appendix XIV, pp. 490–3.
[2] N. Jorga, 'Notes et extraits pour servir à l'histoire des Croisades au xvᵉ siècle', *ROL*, IV (1896), 228 (cited hereafter as Jorga, 'Notes', IV). The Senate replied that they would prefer to give them refuge in Venice. Thiriet, *Sénat*, II, no. 978 (27 February 1400); *DR*, V, no. 3279. For the date of Manuel's departure from Constantinople, see *Chron. brev.*, II, pp. 365, 616.

it, urging him to hold on as an obedient nephew, to preserve Constantinople and the Venetian colony, and above all to turn a deaf ear to the
false promises of the Turks. He must always bear in mind the deep friendship of the Venetians for Byzantium and the huge sums of money which
they had spent on its defence.[1]

Manuel may not have expected so lavish a welcome and so sympathetic
an audience in Venice. The Venetians had failed to persuade him to sign
a new treaty. He had come cap in hand, though he was heavily in their
debt; and he was cross with them about the island of Tenedos. He was
to be no less pleasantly surprised by his reception in the other cities
of northern Italy. For when he left Venice on his journey to Paris he
went by way of Padua, Vicenza, Pavia and Milan. Much had changed
since his father John V had visited Italy thirty years before. The battles
of Kossovo and Nikopolis had brought the Turkish threat home to the
Christians of the west. People spoke with bated breath of the dreaded
Sultan Bajezid. The Emperor Manuel had been the Sultan's vassal, hostage
and victim. He had a tale to tell. But he did not cut a pitiful figure.
He had a more dignified bearing and a more commanding presence than
his father. No one hearing the tales he told could doubt his courage.
He was also an urbane and scholarly man; and he came to Italy at a
time when men of learning were becoming eager to rediscover the delights
and depths of ancient Greek literature and philosophy. It was fashionable
to cultivate Byzantine Greeks as the purveyors of the new scholarship.
In 1396 Manuel's friend, Manuel Chrysoloras, had been appointed to
teach Greek at Florence. By 1400 he had moved to Milan, where the
emperor was delighted to meet him on his travels.[2] Manuel and his
friends were excellent advertisements for many of the qualities which
the budding humanists of Italy expected to find in a Greek. The revival

---

[1] The fullest account of Manuel's visit to western Europe remains that by A. A. Vasiliev,
'Putešestvie vizantijskago imperatora Manuila II Paleologa na zapadnoj Evrope', 41–78, 260–
304. See also G. Schlumberger, *Un Empereur de Byzance à Paris et à Londres* (Paris, 1916);
D. M. Nicol, 'A Byzantine Emperor in England. Manuel II's visit to London in 1400–1401'
University of Birmingham Historical Journal, XII/2 (1971), 204–25; Barker, *Manuel II*,
pp. 167–99. His stay in Venice is recorded by Andrea Gataro, *Istoria Padovana*, RIS, XVII
(Milan, 1730), cols. 836–7; Andrea de Redusiis, *Chronicon Tarvisinum*, RIS, XIX (Milan,
1731), col. 794. Jorga, 'Notes', IV, 229 (4 April 1400). A detailed list of the wine, food
and accommodation for the emperor and his suite in Venice was drawn up on 27 January
1400. Thiriet, *Assemblées*, II, no. 962 and p. 303. Thiriet, *Sénat*, II, no. 981 (26 March 1400).
Manuel brought with him, in lieu of money, a sealed casket of jewels which he deposited
with the procurators of St Mark's and whose return he requested in March 1403. Thiriet,
Assemblées, II, no. 1009 and p. 306.

[2] On Manuel Chrysoloras, see G. Cammelli, *I dotti bizantini e le origini dell'umanesimo*,
I: *Manuele Crisolora* (Florence, 1941); J. Thomson, 'Manuel Chrysoloras and the early Italian
Renaissance', *GRBS*, VII (1966), 63–82.

of Greek learning had taken root in Florence and in Padua. The Venetians were more practical than academic. Many of their merchants in Romania had picked up enough colloquial Greek for business purposes. But the Greek of Plato and Aristotle would have been beyond them and perhaps not to their taste. In 1391 they had honoured Demetrios Kydones, the teacher of Chrysoloras and a leading scholar of fourteenth-century Byzantium, with the gift of Venetian citizenship. But Kydones had lived in Venice as an ambassador for several months, and the honour was bestowed on him more for his diplomacy than his scholarship.[1]

One wonders whether Manuel's entertainment in Venice included a tour of the Treasury of St Mark's, where he might have seen the crown jewels which his grandmother had pawned over fifty years earlier. The records of his visit are sparse; but it seems that the Venetians spared him the shame of bothering him about his debts. He reached Paris in June 1400. Marshal Boucicaut had gone ahead to prepare the ground. King Charles VI received him with the greatest honour and promised to send another army to Constantinople. In December the emperor crossed over to England, where King Henry IV gave him an equally courteous welcome. From London he wrote to his friend Chrysoloras extolling the magnanimity of Henry of England, who was going to raise an army and a fleet for the rescue of Constantinople. Back in Paris in February 1401, Manuel settled down as the guest of Charles VI. Only slowly did it dawn upon him that all the promises of help from England and from France were inflated and illusory. The crowned heads of western Europe had other things to do. Even Marshal Boucicaut's zeal seemed to have waned. He left to become governor of Genoa in 1401.

The Venetians kept track of the emperor's travels but refrained from interfering. They were in touch with his nephew John VII about the security of Constantinople and their interests there. They emphasised how important it was for him to keep the peace with them and with the Genoese.[2] They were always afraid that he would make a separate pact with the Sultan or indeed with his Genoese friends. The Turks thought that they could manipulate him. They were under the impression that it was Bajezid who had driven the Emperor Manuel out of Constantinople. He is said to have given John an ultimatum. 'If,' he announced, 'I have expelled Manuel from the city, I did it not for your sake but

---

[1] D. J. Geanakoplos, *Greek Scholars in Venice* (Cambridge, Mass., 1962), pp. 24–8; Barker, *Manuel II*, pp. 170–2.

[2] Jorga, 'Notes', IV, 237–8; Thiriet, *Sénat*, II, no. 1007 (22 March 1401). They also pressed him to release some Venetians captured during a Turkish raid on Coron and Modon. Their ambassador to John VII was Francesco Foscarini. Zakythenos, *Despotat grec de Morée*, I, pp. 162–3.

for my own. If therefore you want to have me as your friend, get out and I shall give you a province of your choice to govern. If not, may God and his great Prophet be my witnesses, I shall spare no one. I shall utterly destroy you all'.[1] John was not to be intimidated. He had the gallant Jean de Chateaumorand at his side; and the Venetians gave him much encouragement. In April and again in August 1401 the Senate passed a vote of special sympathy while deploring the general indifference of the rest of Europe. They would send two galleys for the defence of his city. If the Turkish fleet at Gallipoli seemed too menacing, the galleys would lie in at Tenedos and wait for the moment to strike when the September convoy arrived from Venice. Business went on despite the dangers. It was still possible for cargo ships to get through to Constantinople, to Trebizond and even to Tana in the Crimea.[2]

From the comfort of Paris Manuel wrote to the Kings of Portugal and of Aragon and to the pope at Avignon. He seemed to be in no hurry to go home to face the realities of beleaguered Constantinople. He whiled away his time by writing belles-lettres and theological treatises. The Venetians were not pleased with him. They thought it their duty to keep him abreast of the latest news from Romania. In May 1401 they sent a messenger to him in Paris with despatches from the east. By the end of the year they thought that he had been away from his post long enough. They sent him another messenger with reports from Constantinople and exhorted him to go back as soon as he had obtained whatever help he could get from his friends in the west. The help was slow in coming, however; and Manuel wrote asking the Venetians to use their diplomatic skills by interceding for him with the Kings of France and England. He suggested that they should provide six galleys for the defence of Constantinople, to be joined by six from Genoa. The Venetians were rather indignant. They replied that they had done what they could by diplomacy in 1399. The emperor was better placed than they to state his case in Paris; still more so if the Genoese were to be involved, since Genoa now belonged to the French. They could not possibly provide six galleys. They had already posted two to the vicinity and four were needed to protect Negroponte and the Aegean. With characteristic ambivalence, however, they intimated that if the French king and the Genoese made some great effort for the defence of Constantinople, they for their part would see what more they could do. But it was time the emperor

---

[1] Doukas, xv. 5: p. 89. Pseudo-Phrantzes, p. 204, records that John VII made a treaty with Bajezid. This is almost certainly untrue. *DR*, v, no. 3195.

[2] Jorga, 'Notes', IV, 241–2 (23 April 1401); Thiriet, *Sénat*, II, no. 1023 (August 1401), no. 1038 (January 1402).

went home. He should go by way of Corfu, not Modon, where plague was raging.[1]

Manuel was still in Paris in the autumn of 1402 when word reached him of a miraculous turn of events in the east. The Sultan Bajezid had been defeated and captured in a battle with the Mongol leader Timur Lenk. The name, and the legend, of Timur or Tamberlaine had been widely known for some years. In 1395 his troops had burnt and pillaged the Venetian establishment at Tana.[2] Charles VI of France had communicated with him. The Genoese of Galata had exchanged embassies with him; and in August 1401 John VII had proposed that, if he defeated Bajezid, the Byzantines would pay to him the tribute that they had formerly paid to the Turks. In 1400 Timur's army had destroyed Sivas (Sebaste) on the eastern border of Bajezid's territory. He then turned on Syria and on Baghdad, which fell to the Mongols in July 1401. The sack of Sivas had stung Bajezid into action. He boasted that an upstart like Timur could not so lightly tempt the vengeance of the lord of the universe. Timur was provoked to return to the attack in Asia Minor; and on 28 July 1402 the Ottoman and Mongol armies met near Ankara. 15,000 Turks and their Christian vassals are said to have perished in the battle. The Sultan Bajezid was caught trying to escape. He died of shame, perhaps by his own hand, a few months later. But four of his sons got away, to dispute the succession to his Sultanate among themselves.[3]

The facts were known in Venice by September 1402. In the excitement of the moment some of the senators declared that this was the time to buy Gallipoli from one or other of the Turkish leaders. A sum of 20,000 ducats was suggested. The majority felt that it would be better to see how things developed. But Gallipoli in Venetian hands would so benefit the Christian cause that the matter was carefully studied. Giovanni Cornaro, a Venetian commander who was at Constantinople in September 1402, reported that efforts were being made to close the Hellespont to Turkish ships. In October the senators confirmed the good news in a letter to the Emperor Manuel and urged him again to go home as soon

---

[1] Jorga, 'Notes', IV, 242, 250, 251; Thiriet, *Sénat*, II, no. 1016 (6 May 1401), no. 1039 (29 January 1402), nos. 1055, 1063 (8 May and 6 July 1402); *DR*, V, no. 3288, 3291. In June 1402 John VII wrote on his own account to King Henry of England. Barker, *Manuel II*, pp. 213–14, 500–1.

[2] Jorga, 'Veneţia in Mare neagră', no. LII, 1116–17 (22 February 1396); Thiriet, *Sénat*, I, no. 898; II, no. 981. Thiriet, *Assemblées*, II, no. 933. Silberschmidt, *Das orientalische Problem*, pp. 127–40.

[3] See Marie-Mathilde Alexandru-Dersca, *La Campagne de Timur en Anatolie (1402)* (Bucharest, 1942); K.-P. Matschke, *Die Schlacht bei Ankara und das Schicksal von Byzanz*, Forschungen zur mittelalterlichen Geschichte, 29 (Weimar, 1981).

as he could.[1] They were anxious to be in on the new settlement which would have to be made with the heirs of Bajezid; and they would rather the arrangements were made by Manuel than by John VII. Manuel had already received a first-hand account of Timur's victory from Jean de Chateaumorand, who had come back to France from Constantinople in September. The Turkish siege of the city had been lifted. His presence there was no longer required. No one was certain of what the great Timur might do next. He was determined, however, that the shattered fragments of the Ottoman Sultanate in Europe and Asia should not be reunited. For a while he acted the part of kingmaker among the disputatious sons of Bajezid. The eldest of them was Suleiman. He wisely based himself at Adrianople, in Europe, out of reach of his father's conqueror. From there he could make his own deal with the Byzantines and the Italians. He sent a messenger to Venice to announce that he wanted to live in peace with the Emperor Manuel, whose return he awaited.[2]

The Venetians were able to tell Suleiman that Manuel was at last on his way. He left Paris on 21 November 1402, having sent word ahead to Venice to say that he was coming. The Senate replied that he would be most welcome but that he must get back to Constantinople. He went by way of Genoa, where his old friend Boucicaut entertained him. From there he sent another message to Venice, asking for ships to be prepared for his voyage home. He also asked that the Venetian ambassador in Genoa be authorised to confer with him and with the Genoese to work out a policy in view of the changed situation in Constantinople. The Venetians were not keen on this idea. They would rather wait for more information from the east. They were deeply suspicious of the intentions of the Genoese and of Manuel's well-meaning proposal to devise a policy that would bring Venice and Genoa together.[3] Manuel left Genoa in February 1403 but he did not reach Venice until 21 March. No one knows why his journey took so long. He kept sending messages ahead about the ships required to transport him and his retinue. The Venetians wanted him back in Constantinople without delay. He annoyed them

---

[1] Sanudo, *Vitae Ducum*, cols. 794–5; Jorga, 'Notes', IV, 254, 255–6; Thiriet, *Sénat*, II, nos. 1070, 1071 (22 and 23 September 1402), 1074, 1078 (9 and 30 October 1402); Sathas, *Documents*, II, p. 102. Alexandru-Dersca, *La Campagne de Timur*, pp. 125–8.

[2] Suleiman expressed his belief that Venice had always been at one with the Byzantines and he promised commercial privileges to Venetians in his dominions. Jorga, 'Notes', IV, 257–8; Thiriet, *Sénat*, II, no. 1083 (7 December 1402).

[3] Jorga, 'Notes', IV, 258, 263; Thiriet, *Sénat*, II, nos. 1088, 1092 (29 December 1402; 31 January 1403). Barker, *Manuel II*, pp. 220–2. *DR*, v, no. 3293.

by announcing that he would not go straight there. He wanted to spend about a month in the Morea, where an ambassador from Suleiman was expected to call on him.[1]

Those on the spot in Constantinople could wait no longer for the senior emperor to return. They were under pressure from Suleiman to reach an amicable settlement. While Manuel was making his leisurely way to Venice, they made their own terms with the Turks. A conference took place at Gallipoli. It went on for more than three months. In January or early February 1403 a treaty was signed by John VII, by Suleiman and by representatives of Venice, Genoa and Rhodes. It was unbelievably favourable to the Christian powers. The Byzantines were relieved of the payment of tribute and the burden of vassalage to the Turks. The city of Thessalonica was restored to them, as well as a long stretch of the Black Sea coast north of Constantinople and the Aegean islands of Skiathos, Skopelos and Skyros. The Venetians were assured of their commercial privileges. Suleiman's ships would not enter the Hellespont or the Bosporos without the permission of the emperor and his allies; and he swore to serve the emperor as his vassal, like a son to his father.[2]

Suleiman had been in a hurry to make friends with his father's enemies in Constantinople for fear that Timur might cross over from Asia Minor into Europe. Timur, however, soon tired of playing kingmaker among the Turks and in the spring of 1403 he led his armies away to the east, to his capital at Samarkand. Two years later he died. The Mongols had come and gone like a plague of locusts. Neither Turks nor Christians need fear that they would come back. The treaty signed at Gallipoli in 1403 was undoubtedly the work of Suleiman and the emperor–regent John VII. John's uncle Manuel knew nothing of it until he reached Venice in March. The Venetians had made proper arrangements for his reception, but they hoped that he would not outstay his welcome. For it was more than ever imperative that he should return to Constantinople, to confirm the treaty with Suleiman by signing it with his own hand. The Senate had already appointed an ambassador, Giacomo Suriano, to give it the seal of their authority, since their representative at its drafting had been

[1] Jorga, 'Notes', IV, 263, 264–5 (12 and 26 February 1403); Thiriet, Sénat, II, no. 1097; DR, V, no. 3294.
[2] Doukas, xviii. 2: p. 111; DR, V, no. 3201. The text of the treaty exists only in an Italian translation. G. T. Dennis, 'The Byzantine–Turkish treaty of 1403', OCP, XXXIII (1967), 72–88; DVL, II, no. 159, pp. 290–3. Barker, Manuel II, pp. 225–7; Matschke, Die Schlacht bei Ankara, pp. 40–56.

no more exalted a person than the Lord of Andros, Pietro Zeno.[1] They were annoyed by Manuel's delay in reaching Venice. It meant that they had to change the plans made for his homeward voyage. In February he had told them that the Genoese had kindly promised to lend him three galleys. Not to be outdone, the Venetians at once agreed to provide warships to escort him to Modon, which was where he appeared to want to go. His friend Carlo Zeno was to accompany him. The plans had to be revised when it was reported that the Genoese had sent out a fleet, commanded by Marshal Boucicaut, bound for Cyprus. Carlo Zeno and his warships had to be sent ahead to keep an eye on them. When Manuel finally arrived in Venice, the Senate decided to send him to the Morea with the convoy that was taking their ambassador Suriano on to Gallipoli and Constantinople. Its commander was Leonardo Mocenigo, and he sailed out of Venice with the emperor and his retinue early in April 1403.[2]

The orders given to Suriano have a familiar ring. He was first to confirm the treaty with Suleiman at Gallipoli and then to proceed to Constantinople. There he would negotiate a renewal of the customary treaty with Venice last signed in 1390. He must demand at least an advance on the still outstanding debt of 17,163 hyperpyra. If the Emperor Manuel was not there, of if he had been kept out by his nephew John VII, Suriano would be polite to John but would not discuss the treaty with him.[3] Again the plans went awry. The convoy duly took Manuel to Modon to join his wife and family. But Suriano decided to wait there until they were ready to complete their voyage. On 2 May he received orders from Venice to wait no longer. He must get on with his mission to the Turks. Manuel was left high and dry in the Morea. He rescued himself by some clever diplomacy. He knew that Carlo Zeno had stationed his warships at Modon. He discovered that Marshal Boucicaut with his Genoese fleet en route for Cyprus was not far off. Boucicaut was ready, if necessary, for a fight with the Venetians. But Manuel prevailed upon his friend Zeno to permit his other friend, Boucicaut, to land at Modon. After a joyful reunion, Manuel announced that he would now like to be taken

[1] Jorga, 'Notes', IV, 265–6, 268–9; Thiriet, Sénat, II, nos. 1104, 1107 (March, April 1403); Sathas, Documents, I, no. 5, pp. 5–6. Pietro Zeno reported to his government between January and March 1403. He was recompensed by a grateful Senate and got his reward some years later. Documents in Dennis, 'The Byzantine–Turkish treaty of 1403', 82–5, 87–8. Jorga, 'Notes', IV, 271 (2 June 1403), 299 (10 January 1409); Thiriet, Sénat, II, nos. 1117, 1339. Barker, Manuel II, pp. 227–8.

[2] Jorga, 'Notes', IV, 264–6; Thiriet, Sénat, II, nos. 1097–1100, 1104, 1106. Barker, Manuel II, pp. 228–30.

[3] Jorga, 'Notes', IV, 268–9; Thiriet, Sénat, II, no. 1107 (9 April 1403). Suriano was also commissioned to negotiate with one of Suleiman's brothers in Asia Minor.

home. Boucicaut offered him the services of Jean de Chateaumorand, who was with him, and four galleys. The Venetians saw that they were being upstaged by the Genoese. Carlo Zeno, for the honour of his city, at once offered the emperor four galleys of his own. The final stage of Manuel's journey home was thus made with a joint escort of Genoese and Venetians, though Boucicaut left them at an early stage. The emperor must have been pleased to be the agent as well as the beneficiary of such an unlikely collaboration. He reached Gallipoli in May. John VII was there to meet him. Suleiman may also have been present; and there, or in Constantinople, Manuel at last put his signature to a revised version of the treaty with Suleiman which his nephew had signed earlier in the year.[1]

Manuel's travels had not brought him many substantial rewards. John VII, who had been a loyal caretaker of the empire's affairs during his uncle's long absence, also received less than his deserts. It seemed that, even after three years of separation, the two could not live together in the same city. Manuel obliged John to assume the governorship of Thessalonica, which the Turks had relinquished by terms of Suleiman's treaty. The Venetians were doubtless pleased. They had never trusted John. With him out of the way they could press on with the urgent business of renewing their treaty with Manuel for the protection of their merchants in Constantinople. It is hard to see why the business could not have been done while Manuel was in Venice or while he was with the ambassador Suriano on his voyage home. It may be that no one was sure whether John VII would step down when his uncle returned. John had achieved much. His initiative in negotiating with Suleiman after the death of Bajezid had changed the course of Byzantine policy and opened up new possibilities. From being the tribute-paying vassals of the Turks, the Byzantines had become their suzerains; and the chance was there for Manuel to take his turn at playing puppet-master among the sons of Bajezid. He needed time to explore how best he could exploit his advantages. The constant demands of the Venetians for confirmation of their privileges and payment of their debts were of comparatively small account. Manuel clearly understood that the respite granted to his empire could not last. If and when the Turks of Europe and Asia were reunited under a single Sultan they would almost certainly return to the attack. It was vital therefore to keep western Christendom alive to the danger that still threatened the east. The emperor appointed his friend Manuel Chrysoloras

---

[1] Jorga, 'Notes', IV, 270; Thiriet, Sénat, II, nos. 1111, 1122 (2 May and 10 July 1403). The part played by Boucicaut is narrated only by the Marshal's biographer. Le Livre des faicts, II, pp. 622–3. Dennis, 'The Byzantine–Turkish treaty of 1403', 76–80; Barker, Manuel II, pp. 231–8. Matschke, Die Schlacht bei Ankara, p. 47.

as his ambassador at large to travel round the courts of France, England and Spain. He did not spend long in Venice.[1]

The Venetians had come to terms with Suleiman. They were officially partners to the treaty of 1403. In other respects, however, their ambassador Suriano, who had accompanied Manuel to the Morea, had had little success. He had not convinced the emperor of the necessity of legalising the position of the Venetian community in Constantinople by signing another document. In May 1404 the Senate appointed Paolo Zeno as a new ambassador for this purpose. They gave him his orders in July. He was to congratulate Manuel on his safe return; to remind him of his debts (17,163 *hyperpyra*); and to get him to renew his treaty with Venice even if he refused to discuss the problem of the island of Tenedos. The problem of Tenedos would not go away, however. The emperor saw it as a major obstacle to be overcome before he would gratify the Venetians. Paolo Zeno was thus no more successful than Suriano, although, at the emperor's request, he stayed in Constantinople as baillie.[2] Towards the end of the year Manuel demanded that Venice should renounce all claim to the island. The demand was naturally rejected. He then modified it, resigning himself to the fact that Tenedos belonged to Venice but suggesting that it should be refortified at the expense of a consortium of Byzantines, Genoese and Venetians. The senators were caught off their guard. On 31 January 1405 they asked for time to think it over and to insert it in the text of their forthcoming treaty with Byzantium. On the same day they considered a number of other points which the emperor had raised. He had asked them to provide transport for him whenever he wanted to visit his province in the Morea or the Venetian colonies in Romania. This they would do, provided he paid his fare and his expenses. He could maintain an agent at Coron and Modon. With regard to his debts they would make no concessions until they had closely scrutinised all the documents. Manuel had complained about one or two cases in which he believed that he and his subjects had been wronged by Venetians. In particular he protested about the ill-treatment of Greek merchants in Crete. The senators produced their usual suave explanations or refutations of all these complaints.[3]

There were others who deplored the misuse of the island of Tenedos. In June 1405 the Grand Master of the Knights of Rhodes applied for

[1] Dennis, 'Official documents of Manuel II', 51. Barker, *Manuel II*, pp. 261–8.
[2] Jorga, 'Notes', IV, 274; Thiriet, *Sénat*, II, nos. 1158, 1165 (27 May and 19 July 1404). Maltézou, *Thesmos*, pp. 119–20.
[3] Jorga, 'Notes', IV, 276–8; Thiriet, *Sénat*, II, nos. 1175–6 (23 and 31 January 1405); *DR*, V, no. 3303. The Byzantine ambassador to Venice was John Moschopoulos, a cousin of Manuel II.

permission to build a fortress there at the expense of his Order. The Venetians were indignant. They told him that Tenedos belonged to them and referred him to the Treaty of Turin. No one had the right to construct any fortresses on the island. The Grand Master must also know that the presence of his Knights was not required in that part of the world. Venice, ceaselessly vigilant and heedless of the cost of defending the Christian east, could manage without them.[1] The Venetians jealously and selfishly guarded their exclusive right to Tenedos. They piously pointed out to all comers that they had never infringed the Treaty of Turin by rearming the island. They were determined that no one else should do so. Yet they continued to use it as a harbour and to regard it as their property. The Byzantine ambassadors to Venice, who regularly raised the question, were told that it could not be resolved until their emperor had renewed his lapsed treaty with the Doge. In March 1406 much alarm was caused in Venice by reports from Constantinople that the Emperor Manuel in concert with the Genoese of Galata had a scheme to fortify Tenedos. The panic was such that some of the senators were for sending the Captain of the Gulf with all his galleys to occupy the island. The emperor could be told that it was only for his own good and the protection of his empire. The motion was not carried and the reports seem to have been false. But the incident demonstrates how sensitive the Venetians were on the subject and how determined to bar Tenedos to all strangers, especially the Genoese.[2]

In the end, after much haggling, the Venetians had their way. The treaty between Byzantium and Venice, last signed by John VII in 1390, was confirmed for five years, signed and sealed with his golden bull by Manuel II on 22 May 1406.[3] It is almost word for word the same document, meticulously transcribed. The emperor's debts to Venice remain at precisely the same figures. His plans for paying them off in instalments are the same. The only significant alteration in the text refers to Tenedos. In 1390 John VII had tamely agreed that he would seek no recompense for its loss. In 1406 Manuel II got the Venetians to agree that, while the treaty would make no specific or immediate recommendation about Tenedos, the matter should remain 'in the air', or open to

[1] Sathas, *Documents*, I, no. 11, pp. 11–12; Thiriet, *Sénat*, II, no. 1194 (21 September 1405). Thiriet, 'Venise et l'occupation de Ténédos', 241–2.

[2] Jorga, 'Notes', IV, 282–3; Thiriet, *Sénat*, II, no. 1203 (11 February 1406), no. 1208 (30 March 1406). Thiriet, 'Venise et l'occupation de Ténédos', 242–3.

[3] Greek text in *MM*, III, pp. 144–53; partial Latin text in *DVL*, II, no. 163, pp. 301–2. Parts of the document are reproduced in facsimile in Dölger, *Facsimiles byzantinischer Kaiserurkunden*, N. 14, p. 20, and in Barker, *Manuel II*, fig. 18, pp. 258–9. *DR*, V, nos. 3310, 3311; Jorga, 'Notes', IV, 283–4; Thiriet, *Sénat*, II, no. 1216 (29 May 1406).

further discussion so long as the treaty was in force.[1] In all other respects
the Venetians were now content. The legal status of their community
in Constantinople had been reaffirmed along with the privileges of their
citizens in a document binding upon all the emperor's officials for another
five years. Much of the credit for overcoming Manuel's reluctance to
sign the document must go to Paolo Zeno, who had served his Doge,
Michele Steno, as ambassador to the emperor and then as baillie in Constantinople for two years. He asked to be relieved of his post and recalled
to Venice. His wish was granted in July 1406 and he went home taking
the text of the treaty with him. He also took a letter from the emperor
imploring the Venetians, as good Christians, to bury their differences
with the Genoese so that they could join forces in the fight against the
Turks. It was perhaps a naive request. But Manuel never gave up hope
that the Italian republics might rate the defence of their religion higher
than the protection of their profits.[2]

In 1408 Manuel felt that conditions were settled enough for him to
pay another visit to his province in Greece, the Despotate of the Morea.
His brother, the Despot Theodore, had died the year before. Manuel
had got on well with Theodore. He composed a long funeral oration
for him which he proposed to deliver at Mistra.[3] He was still there
when he heard of the death of his nephew John VII in Thessalonica
in September 1408. John had given him more trouble than joy. Manuel
mourned his passing as a matter of convention. Before going back to
Constantinople, he appointed his son Theodore (II) as Despot at Mistra
and his infant son Andronikos as Despot at Thessalonica. While he was
in Greece the struggle for power between the sons of Bajezid had become
more violent. It had broken out in 1404 when Musa, who was in Asia
Minor, had declared war on his brother Suleiman. In 1409, when it
seemed that Suleiman might be losing the battle, Manuel wrote to the
Venetians asking them to help keep the two brothers apart by sending
eight warships to reinforce two of his own in patrolling the Hellespont.
Their answer is eloquent of Venetian ambiguity. On 10 January 1410
the Senate declared that, while it was a sound idea to keep the warring
Turks apart and patrol the straits, Venice could do nothing on its own.
Other Christian nations must be induced to play their part. The emperor
had complained that Venetian ships were actually ferrying Turks back

[1] *MM*, III, p. 150.
[2] Jorga, 'Notes', IV, 288; Thiriet, *Sénat*, II, no. 1230; *DR*, v, no. 3315. In March 1407 Giovanni
Loredan, as ambassador to Suleiman, was instructed to go on to see Manuel to discuss
the situation in Romania. Jorga, 'Notes', IV, 287–8; Thiriet, *Sénat*, II, no. 1248.
[3] J. Chrysostomides, ed., *Manuel II Palaeologus, Funeral Oration on his Brother Theodore*,
CFHB, XXVI (Thessaloniki, 1985).

and forth across the Hellespont, to and from Gallipoli. The senators replied that they could not prevent this. It was up to the emperor to use his own resources to police the straits more efficiently. On the other hand, they would comply with his request to provide transport by sea for members of the imperial family who wanted to leave Constantinople, though only if the ships happened to be going the same way and the passengers paid their fares. The Venetians were seldom altruistic. They made themselves unpopular. One is not surprised to learn that some of them had been injured in brawls with the Greeks in Constantinople; or that their baillie reported various breaches of the peace and arrests of Venetians by the emperor's agents.[1]

The Turks resolved their own conflict without the intervention of Venice. In July 1410 Suleiman was encircled by his brother Musa at Adrianople. His Greek friends enabled him to hold out for a while. But in February 1411 he was captured and strangled. Musa then turned on all those who had taken Suleiman's side. He annulled the treaty of 1403, attacked Thessalonica and laid siege to Constantinople. Manuel had foreseen such a possibility. He had made sure that the city was well stocked and prepared for a siege. He also had diplomatic plans to meet the emergency. He called on Mehmed, the last of the sons of Bajezid, to come over from Asia Minor and make war on Musa. Mehmed failed at his first attempt. But in 1413, backed by Byzantine and Serbian troops, he drove his brother out of Adrianople and ran him to ground in Serbia. By proces of elimination Mehmed thus became the first of the heirs of Bajezid to establish himself as Sultan of Rumelia and of Rum, of Europe and Asia. The Venetians had been aware of what was happening but they would not come out openly on the emperor's side. What they most feared was the threat to their trade in the east. In 1409 they had sent an ambassador to Suleiman.[2] They had declined to help halt the traffic of Turks across the Hellespont. In July 1410 they suspended their tribute to Suleiman pending the outcome of his conflict with Musa; and in August they increased the armed escort of their ships between Tenedos and the Bosporos because of that conflict.[3] By April 1411 they had heard from their baillie that Suleiman was dead; they hastened to reassure his brother Musa of their goodwill towards him. The idea was floated in Venice that the Emperor Manuel should now occupy Gallipoli without delay. Alternatively, the Venetians should take it over for fear that it

---

[1] Jorga, 'Notes', IV, 311–12; Thiriet, *Sénat*, II, nos. 1362, 1364 (10 and 11 January 1410); *DR*, v, no. 3327.

[2] Jorga, 'Notes', IV, 299–303; Thiriet, *Sénat*, II, nos. 1343, 1347 (February and March 1409).

[3] Jorga, 'Notes', IV, 317, 318; Thiriet, *Sénat*, II, nos. 1384–5, 1387.

might fall into other hands. The idea did not find favour in the Senate.[1]
Between 1411 and 1413, when the Byzantines were staking all on the
triumph of Mehmed over his brother Musa, a number of envoys went
from Venice to Musa's camp. The emperor complained bitterly that the
Captain of the Gulf had taken it upon himself to sign a truce with 'the
Sultan' Musa under the walls of Selymbria not far from Constantinople.
Venice was even committed to paying tribute to him. By July 1413,
however, the baillie in Constantinople, Fantin Viaro, was instructed to
pay no more tribute to Musa if it was true that he had been defeated
by his brother Mehmed.[2]

Throughout the crisis of the war among the Turks and the opportunities
which it presented to the Christians, Venice acted solely in the interest
of its own people, property and profit. There is no record that the Venetians gave any encouragement to the Emperor Manuel in his bid to win
a friend among the Turks by backing Mehmed against his brother Musa.
They would no doubt have said, as they had said before, that it was
not their practice to take sides in the internal disputes of other peoples.
It might be more true to say that they were quick to pay their respects
to whichever side seemed to be winning at any given moment. They
had made a truce with Musa and paid tribute to him while he seemed
to be in the ascendant. They were not concerned that this might be
counter to the emperor's policy. They were far more anxious to prevail
upon him to renew his trade agreement with them which he had signed
in 1406. The negotiations were conducted by their baillie in Constantinople, Fantin Viaro, and concluded on 31 October 1412. The full text
of the treaty has not survived; but there was nothing new to say. Manuel
had evidently not paid any of his debts to Venice and he still refused
to recognise Venetian rights over Tenedos.[3] He had other things on
his mind. When he had helped secure the victory of the Sultan Mehmed,
he applied to Venice for some assistance. He received the now familiar
reply that Venice could only help him if other Christian princes contributed their portion.[4]

The Venetians had been represented at the making of the treaty with
Suleiman in 1403. They were not party to the settlement reached between

---

[1] Jorga, 'Notes', IV, 509–10; Thiriet, Sénat, II, no. 1415 (17 April 1411). It had been proposed
that Venice should occupy Gallipoli after the battle of Ankara in 1402. Jorga, 'Notes', IV,
254, 256.

[2] Jorga, 'Notes', IV, 510–14, 524, 529–30; Thiriet, Sénat, II, nos. 1419, 1422, 1424, 1431,
1444 (1411–12), 1452 (5 May 1412), 1463 (22 July 1412), 1496 (24 July 1413). The text
of the Venetian treaty with Musa is in Jorga, 'Notes', IV, 515–17.

[3] Jorga, 'Notes', IV, 524–6; Thiriet, Sénat, II, nos. 1454, 1463 (May and July 1412). DVL,
II, no. 165, p. 304; DR, v, no. 3333 (31 October 1412).

[4] Jorga, 'Notes', IV, 532; Thiriet, Sénat, II, no. 1514 (8 January 1414).

Manuel and Mehmed ten years later. They therefore gained none of the benefits with which Mehmed rewarded those who had helped him to victory. Manuel's reward was substantial. The new and grateful Sultan restored to him all the territories and privileges granted by Suleiman in 1403. He swore that as long as he lived he would be the emperor's faithful servant.[1] Mehmed was a man of his word; and, save for one blunder that Manuel committed two years later, peace and harmony reigned between Greeks and Turks until Mehmed died in 1421. It was the last period of peace that the Byzantines were ever to know. The Venetians had to make their own terms with the Sultan. In 1414 their baillie Francesco Foscarini was instructed to go and see him at Adrianople to propose an agreement similar to that made with his late brother Musa, though without payment of tribute. Foscarini was not very efficient. A year later his government reprimanded him when the Sultan Mehmed complained that no ambassador from Venice had yet called on him.[2]

The Emperor Manuel knew all too well that his hard-won peace with the Turks depended on his personal relationship with Mehmed. It might well end when Mehmed died or was replaced. If he were to make anything of it he must act quickly. In the summer of 1414 he appealed once again to Venice; and once again the answer came that Venice was always ready to help him but could offer nothing substantial unless the other Christian powers would make their contribution. Manuel had long hoped that this would be the case. Twice he had offered to act as a mediator in the continuing conflict between the Venetians and King Sigismund of Hungary. Twice they had declined his offer, as though they did not want the Byzantine Emperor to interfere in their affairs. They were, however, concerned about the new Sultan's concentration of naval forces in the Aegean and the consequent threat to Negroponte and the other Venetian islands.[3] Manuel was protected by his alliance with Mehmed. But he too was concerned about the future safety of Thessalonica and of the Despotate of the Morea. He spent the winter of 1414 with his young son Andronikos in Thessalonica and in the following spring went on to the Morea. He sailed there by way of Negroponte, where the Venetian governor received him courteously.[4] Manuel's plan was to build a wall spanning the six miles across the Isthmus of Corinth. It would turn the Morea into a Byzantine island safe from any future Turkish

---

[1] Doukas, xx. 1: p. 133; DR, v, no. 3334.

[2] Jorga, 'Notes', IV, 533–5, 548–9; Thiriet, Sénat, II, nos. 1526, 1538 (May and July 1414), 1584 (July 1415).

[3] Sathas, Documents, III, no. 624, pp. 72–3; no. 633, pp. 78–80 (11 October 1414); Thiriet, Sénat, II, nos. 1544 (24 July 1414), 1546, 1555; DR, v, no. 3338.

[4] Sathas, Documents, III, no. 660, p. 110 (30, not 24, April 1415); Jorga, 'Notes', IV, 542; Thiriet, Sénat, II, no. 1574.

invasions from the north. The work was done at speed and the wall, known as the Hexamilion, was completed in twenty-five days. The Venetians congratulated the emperor on his achievement. But when it came to meeting his request for a contribution to its cost they were less enthusiastic. The cost had been high. Money had been raised by levying special taxes on the Greeks of the Morea, many of whom had fled to Venetian territory to avoid paying them. The Venetians were willing to send at least some of them home. But they protested that their other commitments made it impossible for them to help pay for the Hexamilion wall.[1]

The Venetians were intent on keeping the wheels of commerce turning in a changing world. But they were sensitive to accusations that they were in league with the Turks. In August 1415 they proposed to send a circular to all Christians, refuting these charges. They wanted it to be known that Venice had always held a deep hatred of the infidels, especially the Turks. Venice had supplied the ships to effect the escape from Constantinople of Sigismund of Hungary, in defiance of a powerful Turkish navy. During subsequent negotiations Venice had consistently offered him assistance against the Turks. If in recent years they had attacked Hungary while he was there, what would they not have done if he had been absent?[2] It may have been as much for the sake of their reputation as their trade that the Venetians showed a new interest in the formation of another maritime league against the Turks. The plan seems to have been initiated by the Lord of Andros, Pietro Zeno, in 1415, before they had made their truce with Mehmed. The Knights of Rhodes and the Genoese of Chios and Lesbos were to join the alliance along with Venice. The Emperor Manuel was very receptive to the idea and suggested broadening its scope. But, in view of his personal relationships with Mehmed, he insisted that it be kept secret. He was surely right in this. But nothing came of it.[3]

The participants expected the alliance to achieve different things. The emperor thought of the protection of Constantinople. The Venetians thought of the defence of their colonies in Greece and the Aegean. The Genoese were never more than half-hearted about it. The danger from the Turks by sea was in any event soon to be much reduced. In the

---

[1] Jorga, 'Notes', IV, 547–8, 558, 584–5; Thiriet, Sénat, II, no. 1583 (23 July 1415), no. 1592 (23 September 1415), no. 1599 (8 February 1416); DR, v, no. 3352. Venice also agreed to send back other Greeks who had sought asylum in Venetian colonies during Musa's attacks on Constantinople and Thessalonica. Zakythenos, Despotat grec de Morée, I, pp. 167–72; Barker, Manuel II, pp. 301–17.

[2] Jorga, 'Notes', IV, 550.

[3] Sathas, Documents, III, no. 672, pp. 119–20 (31 August 1415); Jorga, 'Notes', IV, 554, 558, 573–4; Thiriet, Sénat, II, nos. 1589, 1592, 1599, 1635 (1415–17); DR, v, nos. 3352, 3354, 3367.

summer of 1416 the Captain of the Gulf, Pietro Loredan, sank most of Mehmed's navy in a battle off Gallipoli. The encounter had occurred almost by chance. The Venetians were justifiably proud of their victory and made sure that it was broadcast to the whole of Christendom. The Senate congratulated Loredan and gave thanks to God and St Mark.[1] Negotiations between Venice and the Sultan went on for months afterwards. The return of prisoners taken in the battle caused endless trouble; and a treaty of peace was not formally concluded until 6 November 1419. But the Sultan seems to have laid no blame for the affair on the Emperor Manuel.[2]

The baillie in Constantinople, Giovanni Diedo, who conducted many of the negotiations, was supposed to keep the emperor informed.[3] It fell to his successor, Bertuccio Diedo, to get the emperor to renew his treaty with Venice which he had last confirmed in 1412. The Venetians had many complaints to make about the treatment of their citizens in Constantinople and about the activities in the Morea of the Despots of Mistra, whom they accused of being worse neighbours than the Turks. The emperor complained about the fate of the Greeks who had been captured at Gallipoli in 1416 and about the fraudulent evasion of taxes by Venetian Christians and Jews.[4] On 30 October 1418, however, he appended his signature and his golden bull to the document that the baillie put before him.[5] It was word for word the text of that signed in 1390 and again in 1412. Only the date was changed. It legalised the status of the Venetians in Constantinople for another five years. It confirmed that the emperor had kept none of his pledges to pay his debts to Venice. The magic figure of 17,163 *hyperpyra* reappeared, as did the figures of 30,000 ducats with interest outstanding since 1343. The question of Tenedos remained 'in the air'. It was all a formality. The Venetians knew well enough that the emperor could never find the money to pay the instalments or the interest, let alone to clear his debts.

Their victory off Gallipoli made life easier for the Venetians. They were spared the expense of heavily armed convoys for their merchant

[1] Jorga, 'Notes', IV, 566–7; Thiriet, *Sénat*, II, no. 1622 (5 July 1416). Loredan had been briefed on 2 April 1416. Jorga, 'Notes', IV, 562–3; Thiriet, *Sénat*, II, no. 1610. The battle was fought on 29 May. Doukas, XXI. 8: pp. 147–9; Chalkokondyles, I, pp. 188–90; Sanudo, *Vitae Ducum*, cols. 901–9. Heyd, *Commerce*, II, pp. 277–8; Thiriet, *Romanie vénitienne*, p. 368; Barker, *Manuel II*, p. 337.

[2] Jorga, 'Notes', IV, 575–8, 608–10; Thiriet, *Sénat*, II, nos. 1641–2, 1645, 1647, 1649, 1707, 1746, 1750. The text of the treaty is in *DVL*, II, no. 172, pp. 318–19; Jorga, 'Notes', IV, 610–14.

[3] Jorga, 'Notes', IV, 577–8; Thiriet, *Sénat*, II, no. 1647 (May 1417).

[4] Jorga, 'Notes', IV, 591, 595–7; Sathas, *Documents*, III, no. 731, pp. 174–80; Thiriet, *Sénat*, II, nos. 1688, 1697, 1705 (March, June, July 1418).

[5] Greek text in *MM*, III, pp. 153–63; partial Latin text in *DVL*, II, nos. 170, 171, pp. 316–17; *DR*, V, no. 3373.

fleets sailing up and down the Hellespont. The Emperor Manuel no doubt secretly rejoiced at the destruction of the Turkish navy, though he was in close alliance with the Sultan Mehmed at the time. But it did not much help his cause. Manuel continued to think in terms of rousing the whole of western Christendom to a holy war against the Turks in general, not simply against Mehmed. It was with this in mind that he persisted in offering to resolve the dispute between Venice and Hungary. The Venetians always blamed Sigismund for being argumentative and obstructive; and for a long time they declined the emperor's offer.[1] But in January 1420 his ambassador to Venice, Manuel Philanthropenos, at last convinced them that peace with Hungary was the only way in which a concerted offensive against the infidel could be mounted, for only Sigismund, it seemed, could or would lead another crusade before it was too late. The Venetians allowed Philanthropenos to work together with their own envoy to Sigismund. He went on to Hungary and from there to Poland and Lithuania. He advertised to a wider world the fact that the Emperor Manuel was looking to the future, in the certain knowledge that the goodwill of the Turks was not likely to survive the death of the Sultan Mehmed.[2]

Their goodwill had been severely strained by an incident that occurred about 1415, when a pretender to the sultanate appeared to challenge Mehmed. His name was Mustafa and he claimed to be a long-lost son of Bajezid. Byzantium and Venice both became involved in Mustafa's rebellion. The Venetians arranged his crossing from Asia Minor to Europe, where he joined up with another Ottoman rebel. Manuel saw him as a valuable pawn in the game of Turkish power politics. When the Sultan seemed about to round up both of the rebels, they were given refuge in Thessalonica. Mehmed demanded that they should be handed over to him. Manuel politely refused. Instead he undertook to hold them in permanent confinement if the Sultan would pay him an annual pension for their maintenance. Mehmed agreed. Mustafa was put on the island of Lemnos. The affair illustrated the precarious nature of the relationship between emperor and Sultan. It rested on a gentleman's agreement which neither wanted to break. Mehmed realised that Manuel now had in his hands a pretender who might one day have his uses. It was a clever stroke, but a dangerous one.[3]

[1] DR, v, nos. 3354–5; Jorga, 'Notes', IV, 558; Thiriet, Sénat, II, no. 1599 (8 February 1416).
[2] DR, v, nos. 3378–82; Jorga, 'Notes', IV, 615–16; v, 151–2; Thiriet, Sénat, II, nos. 1758, 1802, 1915. Barker, Manuel II, pp. 337–9.
[3] Doukas, xxii. 3–5: pp. 155–61; Chalkokondyles, I, pp. 190–2; Sphrantzes, Chronicon minus, p. 6. Jorga, 'Notes', IV, 540–1, 558, 562–3; Thiriet, Sénat, II, nos. 1563–4 (15 and 18 January 1415), 1599 (8 February 1416), 1610 (2 April 1416); DR, v, nos. 3348, 3361–5. Barker, Manuel II, pp. 340–4.

In January 1421 Manuel caused his eldest son, John VIII, to be crowned as co-emperor in Constantinople. At the same time John's marriage to Sophia of Montferrat was celebrated. She had been brought from Italy on a Venetian ship.[1] John was not without experience of government. He had acted as regent while his father was away in Greece; and he had assisted his brother Theodore in the Despotate of the Morea for about two years.. His father Manuel was seventy-one years of age and in poor health. He felt that the time had come to retire and let his son take over. There were those of John's generation who welcomed Manuel's retirement. They longed for some more vigorous show of action against the Turks. Their chance to try it came four months after John's corona-tion. The Sultan Mehmed died on 21 May 1421. His legitimate son and successor was Murad II. The old emperor wanted to recognise him as such. But he was overruled. John VIII and his brothers elected to bring the pretender Mustafa out of his confinement and put him up as the Byzantine choice for Sultan. It was a rash and risky ploy and it was quickly frustrated by Murad. In January 1422 Mustafa was captured and hanged. Murad II was now undisputed Sultan of Europe and Asia. He too was of the younger generation. Even if he had believed that gentlemen's agreements with the Greeks were in order, as his father had done, their shabby attempt to deprive him of his patrimony would have disillusioned him. He was furious. He had no time for the Byzantine ambassadors who were sent to mollify him. He made immediate prepa-rations to lay siege to Constantinople and Thessalonica. The respite was over. The Byzantines were back where they had been before the Sultan Mehmed came to power in 1413. The old Emperor Manuel, who had advised his son against such trickery, resigned responsibility for its conse-quences as he had already resigned his authority.[2]

---

[1] Jorga, 'Notes', IV, 621–2; Thiriet, Sénat, II, nos. 1782, 1791. Travelling on the same ship was Cleope Malatesta, bride to be of John's brother Theodore II, Despot of the Morea.

[2] Doukas, xx. 5–6: pp. 137–9; xxii. 10 to xxiii. 2: pp. 165–71; xxvii. 1–7: pp. 223–31. Chalko-kondyles, I, p. 192; II, pp. 1, 6. Sphrantzes, Chronicon minus, pp. 8–14. Chron. brev., II, pp. 410–13. Barker, Manuel II, pp. 349–60.

20

BYZANTIUM THE SUPPLIANT OF VENICE

⟷————————————————————⟷

THE treaty which Venice signed with the Sultan Mehmed in November
1419 listed by name all the towns and islands in Romania which the
Sultan recognised as being Venetian possessions. There were thirty-
eight.[1] The number had grown in accordance with their policy of establishing a solid line of defence west and south of Tenedos and the straits.
The Turks might take Constantinople, but they would have to concede
that the Aegean islands and the harbours of the Morea and Greece
belonged to Venice. In the years before 1419 the valuable Greek ports
of Navarino, Clarentza, Patras and Lepanto (Naupaktos) had more or
less voluntarily accepted Venetian rule. On the other hand, the expansion
and prosperity of the Byzantine Despotate of the Morea was not always
to the liking of Venice. The Senate had applauded the construction of
the Hexamilion wall across the Isthmus of Corinth in 1415 but they
had declined to contribute to its cost. They had ferried the Emperor
Manuel back to Constantinople and brought his son John out to join
his brother, the Despot Theodore II. In the Despot's incessant warfare
against the last of the Latin Princes of Achaia, however, the Venetians
tried to remain neutral; and they had to lodge numerous complaints
about the damage being done to their property and their citizens.[2]

The new Ottoman Sultan Murad II began his siege of Constantinople
towards the end of June 1422. It was the worst that the Byzantines
had endured. The Sultan did everything that he could to break their
resistance. An eye-witness account describes the ferocity of the attack
and the heroism of the defenders led by the young Emperor John VIII.

---

[1] *DVL*, II, no. 172, p. 319. A special commission of five had been set up to supervise the
administration of the new territories in the first half of the fifteenth century, the *Sapientes
terrarum de novo acquisitarum*. Thiriet, *Sénat*, II, p. 230 n. 1.

[2] Sathas, *Documents*, I, no. 48, pp. 65–6 (25 July 1417), no. 75, pp. 109–12 (8 May 1421);
III, nos. 660, p. 110, 668, p. 116 (24 April and 23 July 1415), 764, pp. 207–8 (19 April
1420). Jorga, 'Notes', IV, 595–7 (21 July 1418); Thiriet, *Sénat*, II, nos. 1666, 1705, 1766,
1808. Zakythenos, *Despotat grec de Morée*, I, pp. 180–6; Thiriet, *Romanie vénitienne*, pp.
369–71.

The siege was lifted and the Turks withdrew on 6 September 1422, either because of the miraculous intervention of the Virgin Mary, or as the result of further Byzantine diplomacy. The old Emperor Manuel championed the claim to the Sultanate of yet another pretender in Asia Minor, thus forcing Murad to withdraw his troops to suppress a rebellion across the water.[1] It was the last time that the Byzantines were given a chance to play off one Ottoman ruler against another. As before, it brought them a momentary respite. But Murad quickly took his revenge. Once he had captured and eliminated his rival, he returned to the attack in Europe. The siege of Constantinople was not resumed. Instead he concentrated his forces on the blockade of Thessalonica; and in 1423 his armies invaded Albania and attacked the Despotate of the Morea from the north. The Hexamilion wall, of which Manuel had been so proud, proved no obstacle to his general Turahan, whose troops ravaged the peninsula.[2]

The events following the death of the Sultan Mehmed in 1421 seem to have taken the Venetians by surprise. In October they had told their baillie in Constantinople, Benedetto Emo, to pay their respects to Murad, taking him gifts worth 400 ducats, and to ask him to grant protection to Venetian merchants in his dominions. It was ominous that the true purpose of the baillie's mission was to be concealed from the emperor. The Venetians wanted to be sure of coming to terms of their own making with the new Sultan. Yet it is perhaps to their credit that they had no hand in his deception; and they were alarmed by his prompt revenge. In August 1422 they instructed their Vice-Captain of the Gulf, Stefano Contarini, to go to Constantinople to advise the emperor. If he found the city under siege he was to present letters of credit to empower the baillie to assure both the Emperor and the Sultan that Venice wanted nothing more than a peaceful settlement between them. The proposal that Contarini should stage a show of naval strength to impress the Turkish fleet at Constantinople was, perhaps wisely, rejected. But the Byzantines were to be told that Venice could send them no help before the spring of 1423.[3]

In September 1422 the pope, Martin V, sent a Franciscan, Antonio da Massa, as his legate to Constantinople. He brought great promises of western aid; though naturally, since the pope was to help provide

[1] John Kananos (Cananus), De Constantinopoli oppugnata (1422), ed. I. Bekker, in Georgius Phrantzes, CSHB (1838), pp. 457–79.

[2] Barker, Manuel II, pp. 361–71.

[3] Sathas, Documents, I, no. 79, pp. 119–23; III, no. 807, pp. 240–1. Jorga, 'Notes', ROL, v (1897), 124–5; Thiriet, Sénat, II, nos. 1854–5 (26 August 1422).

it, the prerequisite was the repentance of the Greeks and their reduction
to the Roman Church. It was hardly the moment to enter into theological
controversy. The Turkish siege of the city had been lifted only four
days earlier. The Emperor Manuel, who had come out of his retirement
to meet the apostolic legate, collapsed with a stroke after listening to
him. He never recovered. The pope had the best of intentions, however.
Antonio da Massa was to be found in Venice in March of the following
year, sounding the intentions of the Doge about the rescue of Constantinople. The Venetians estimated that ten well-armed galleys together with
those of the emperor would be enough to defend the city; and they
should set out as soon as they could. Venice would be prepared to furnish
three of them at its own expense, but only if other Christian states bore
their share of the burden. As usual, the Venetians would not act unilater-
ally.[1]

In the same year, however, they were given a chance to act independently which they found to be irresistible. In 1423 the Despot Andronikos, Manuel's youngest son, decided that he could no longer hold
Thessalonica against the Turks. He offered it to Venice, on condition
that the Venetians would assume responsibility for the defence of the
city, allow its people their own municipal government and respect their
property and their church. Andronikos was only twenty-three. He was
an invalid. He had been given a charge far beyond his competence. Even
an older and a healthier man might have despaired of saving Thessalonica
from the Turks with the resources at his disposal. It had been under
siege from the landward side for more than a year. Its walls were strong
and communications by sea with Constantinople were kept open. But
inside the walls conditions were becoming intolerable. Cut off from food
supplies from the surrounding countryside, the citizens began to go
hungry. The port, though precariously open, was idle. Commerce had
stopped. Many people packed up and fled and the population was reduced
to perhaps a mere 25,000. There was no prospect of relief coming from
any other quarter. Andronikos turned to the Venetians to save what
looked like a dying cause. Later Greek historians unkindly put it about
that he sold the city to Venice for 50,000 ducats. There is no truth in
this allegation. It was not a sale and it was not a surrender. It was a
businesslike transaction carried through with every regard for the welfare

[1] Jorga, 'Notes', v, 133–4; Thiriet, *Sénat*, II, no. 1883 (31 March 1423). J. Gill, *The Council
of Florence* (Cambridge, 1958), pp. 33–6; Barker, *Manuel II*, pp. 327–9; Setton, *Papacy
and the Levant*, II (Philadelphia, 1978), pp. 42–5.

of Thessalonica and its Greek inhabitants; and it was done with the full knowledge and assent of the Emperor Manuel II.[1]

Andronikos did not deal directly with Venice. He approached the Venetian authorities in Negroponte. They at once passed the proposal on to their government in Italy. At the beginning of July the Senate considered it. They had come to look on Thessalonica with greater favour, perhaps in view of the imminent fall of Constantinople to the Turks. In 1419 they had reprimanded their baillie in the capital, Bertuccio Diedo, for having imposed taxes on Venetian merchants and their goods coming from Thessalonica. They had decided to re-establish their consulate there and had appointed one George Philomati, who must have been a Greek by birth and whose brother Demetrios had been a victim of the arbitrary action of the baillie in Constantinople. Three years later Demetrios himself became consul after his brother had been drowned at sea.[2] A new and more adventurous Doge of Venice had been elected in April. He was Francesco Foscari (1423–57). He was not to know that he would be the last Doge of Venice to have dealings with a Byzantine Emperor in Constantinople. In 1423 he was intent on taking more vigorous action against the Turks; and for this purpose Thessalonica might provide a testing-ground and a base. Besieged as it was by land, it could hardly be much use as a commercial centre. But strategically it had great possibilities.

The matter none the less required careful deliberation. The senators interrogated a number of merchants who were well informed about affairs in Thessalonica. On 7 July they voted that the Captain of the Gulf should

[1] The tale that Andronikos sold the city to the Venetians derives from the much later account of Pseudo-Phrantzes, *Chronicon maius*, p. 260. Cf. Doukas, xxix. 4: p. 247; *Chron. brev.*, II, pp. 423–4. The truth of the transaction is contained in the Venetian documents published by K. D. Mertzios, *Mnemeia Makedonikis Historias*, Makedoniki Bibliothiki, 7 (Thessaloniki, 1947), pp. 18–99, and C. Manfroni, 'La marina veneziana alla difesa di Salonicco (1423–1430)', *Nuovo archivio veneto*, nuova serie, anno x (1910), xx/1, 5–68. Both of these make extensive use of the unpublished Chronicles of Antonio Morosini and Gasparo Zancaruolo, on which see Thiriet, 'Chroniques vénitiennes', 272–9. On the Venetian occupation of Thessalonica between 1423 and 1430, see also A. E. Vakalopoulos, 'Contribution to the history of Thessalonica under Venetian rule (1423–1430)' (in Greek), *Tomos Konstantinou Harmenopoulou* (Thessaloniki, 1952), 127–49; P. Lemerle, 'La domination vénitienne à Thessalonique', *Miscellanea Giovanni Galbiati*, III (*Fontes Ambrosiani*, xxvII) (Milan, 1951), 219–25; A. E. Vakalopoulos, *A History of Thessaloniki*, translated by T. F. Carney (Thessaloniki, 1963), pp. 65–75; 2nd Greek edition, in Greek (Thessaloniki, 1983), pp. 175–85; Setton, *Papacy and the Levant*, II, pp. 19–31. Much new evidence is supplied by Symeon, Archbishop of Thessalonica, in his *Discourse on the Miracles of St Demetrios*, ed. D. Balfour, *Politico-Historical Works of Symeon Archbishop of Thessalonica (1416/17 to 1429)*, Wiener byzantinische Studien, xIII (Vienna, 1979) (cited hereafter as Balfour, *Symeon*).

[2] Jorga, 'Notes', IV, 602; V, 128; Thiriet, *Sénat*, II, no. 1725 (15 January 1419), no. 1863 (10 December 1422).

at once dispatch a galley to Constantinople. The baillie there, having received his instructions by letter, would inform the emperor of the offer made by his son Andronikos and announce that, with his consent, Venice was willing to take Thessalonica under its protection. Transport would be available for any messenger that the emperor might wish to send for further discussion. For security against the Turks four warships were to be armed by Negroponte, by the Duke of the Archipelago, by the Podestà of Nauplion and by the governor of Tinos and Mykonos. They would assemble at Negroponte and await further orders. A week later two deputies (*provedditori*), Nicolò Giorgio and Santo Venier, were appointed to take possession of Thessalonica in the name of Venice and to advise on the measures to be taken for its defence. They would go with four galleys and troops, present their respects to the Despot Andronikos and congratulate him on his initiative. As representatives of their government, they would pledge to honour his wishes in respecting the traditions, the privileges and the institutions of the city and the rights and independence of its Orthodox Archbishop, Symeon, and his clergy. Any Greeks who wished to leave would be free to sell their property and go. The deputies must make it clear to the Despot or his representative that they had come to protect their city from the Turks. One of them was saddled with the unenviable task of going to see the Sultan Murad, to tell a different tale: the Doge wanted to live at peace with him and had accepted the burden of Thessalonica only for fear that it might fall into the hands of other Christians.[1]

The formal cession of the city took place on 14 September 1423, the Feast of the Exaltation of the Cross. The Venetian deputies brought stores and provisions for the starving inhabitants, who hailed them as saviours and applauded them as they planted the banner of St Mark in the square and on the walls. In October the Senate in Venice received with joy the announcement that Thessalonica was Venetian. A festival was held on 22 October to celebrate the event. The Senate then considered the report that they had received about reinforcements for the defence of the city. More help and more food would have to be sent there without delay.[2] Andronikos left as soon as he could and went with his infant son to the Morea, where he died four years afterwards. A later Venetian report hinted that he had allied himself with the Turks to try to get his city back, only to be captured by its Venetian governors and sent into exile. There is no truth in this slanderous story. The Turks were

[1] Sathas, *Documents*, I, nos. 86, 88–9, pp. 133–9, 140–50; Jorga, 'Notes', v, 141, 143; Mertzios, *Mnemeia*, pp. 32–40; Thiriet, *Sénat*, II, nos. 1891, 1892, 1894, 1896–8 (July 1423).
[2] Sanudo, *Vitae Ducum*, cols. 970, 974. Jorga, 'Notes', v, 147–9; Thiriet, *Sénat*, II, no. 1908 (20 October 1423).

not pleased, however, that Venice had taken Thessalonica from under their noses. They strengthened their blockade of the city and the Venetian governors sent out distress signals pleading for more men, more weapons and especially more food. Early in 1424 Nicolò Giorgio, to whom it had fallen to explain matters to the Sultan at Adrianople, was arrested and imprisoned. The report reached Venice by way of Corfu and caused uproar. The Senate ordered that more ships be sent to the area 'so that the said Turk and the whole world should be made aware that the arrest of the ambassador was and remained a serious and scandalous offence, that Venice prized the city of Thessalonica and had no intention of relinquishing it'.[1]

The Venetians had misjudged the Sultan Murad. They commissioned their most experienced admiral, Pietro Loredan, the victor at Gallipoli in 1416, to sail for Thessalonica, picking up other warships on the way. He would confer with the remaining governor, Santo Venier. Venier was authorised to negotiate with the Sultan over the release of his colleague and to suggest paying to the Turks a tribute of 1000 or 2000 ducats. It was hoped that the people of Thessalonica would be heartened by the sight of a large Venetian fleet offshore. If the city was still under siege, Loredan would leave one or two galleys there and make for the straits of Gallipoli to attack the Turks and prevent them from crossing. If their captain at Gallipoli required some explanation for this behaviour he would be told that it was a consequence of his Sultan's siege of Thessalonica and the arrest of a Venetian ambassador. The Venetians had legally acquired the city from its lord and they had done so not to provoke the Turks but to prevent it falling into the hands of 'other Christians', who would give the Sultan more trouble than Venice. There was some truth in this statement. The Genoese would have liked to have Thessalonica. It was also true that the Venetians had no desire to go to war with the Turks. A naval demonstration, however, would do no harm, especially one mounted by Pietro Loredan whom the Turks had cause to remember.[2]

Preoccupied as they were with the problems of Thessalonica, the Venetians did not forget that the time had come to renew their treaty with the emperor in Constantinople. In June 1423 they had sent Pietro Contarini to see him. His letters of credence were signed by the Doge, Francesco Foscari, on 25 July. The Emperor Manuel was too tired and his son John was too busy to raise any objections. The formalities were quickly concluded and on 30 September 1423 the treaty confirming the rights

---

[1] Sanudo, *Vitae Ducum*, col. 973. Jorga, 'Notes', v, 163–4; Thiriet, *Sénat*, II, no. 1929.

[2] Sathas, *Documents*, I, no. 101, pp. 163–4; Jorga, 'Notes', v, 164–6; Thiriet, *Sénat*, II, no. 1931 (17 April 1424). Manfroni, 'La marina veneziana', 15–21.

of Venetians in Constantinople was renewed for another five years. The
document incorporated the texts of the treaties formulated in 1390, 1406
and 1418 without alteration; the question of Tenedos remained 'in the
air'; and on the Byzantine side it was signed not by the senior Emperor
Manuel but by his son John VIII. Manuel had heard it all before and
was past caring. For his son it was the first occasion for him to append
his golden bull to a document of state, however irrelevant it might be
to the needs of his empire. John VIII had effectively taken over the government of Constantinople from his crippled and elderly father.[1]

Towards the end of the year he decided that the situation was so desperate that he must go again in person to alert the western world to the
danger. There was no point in going to France and England for they
were at war. He would concentrate on the diplomatic plan which his
father had worked on for so many years, to bring Hungary and Venice
together. The Venetians were alarmed by the Turkish invasion of Albania
and the consequent threat to their possessions and their traffic in the
Adriatic. King Sigismund of Hungary still seemed the most likely leader
of a crusade for the relief of Constantinople and the expulsion of the
Turks from eastern Europe. John left Constantinople by sea on 14
November 1423. He reached Venice on 15 December. He was received
like an honoured guest. The Senate set aside 200 ducats for his entertainment. The Doge sailed out to meet him at the Lido in the state launch;
and he was lodged at the Commune's expense in San Giorgio Maggiore.[2]
He stayed in Venice for more than a month. The answers to his appeal
for help and to his offer to mediate with Hungary were courteous but
familiar. The senators recalled their past exertions on behalf of his empire
and announced their intention to send an armada to Constantinople in
the spring. They would willingly co-operate in the defence of Byzantium
if, in the course of his travels, he could find anyone else with whom
to co-operate. But they would not bear the burden alone. With regard
to Hungary they could only repeat their complaint that the main obstacle
to an agreement was King Sigismund himself. His consistently hostile
attitude had forced them into an alliance with the Duke of Milan and,
since 1421, Lord of Genoa, Filippo-Maria Visconti, whose approval must
now be sought before any further overtures could be made to Hungary.[3]

John had hoped to float another substantial loan on the security of
two precious stones which he valued at 40,000 ducats. The senators were

---

[1] Greek text in *MM*, III, pp. 163–73; Sathas, *Documents*, I, no. 92, p. 153; partial Latin
text in *DVL*, II, nos. 177, 178, p. 341; *DR*, v, no. 3408. Jorga, 'Notes', v, 139; Thiriet,
Sénat, II, no. 1885.
[2] Sanudo, *Vitae Ducum*, cols. 971, 972; Jorga, 'Notes', v, 150–1 and 150 n. 1.
[3] Jorga, 'Notes', v, 151–2; Thiriet, *Sénat*, II, no. 1915 (30 December 1423).

not impressed by Greeks bearing gifts and declared that they could not accept his valuation. He had also brought a letter from his father about affairs in Constantinople which the senators construed as being detrimental to their interests. The best that they could do for him was to pay his expenses, at least to a maximum of eight ducats a day, and, at his request, to lend him 1500 ducats on a security which was deposited in the monastery of San Giorgio Maggiore. He was obliged to stay in Venice until the Duke of Milan gave permission for him to intervene in Hungary. On 17 January 1424 he was finally allowed to go, even though the awaited message from Milan required some clarification. John was impatient to be on his way; and he left Venice with the comforting assurance that the promised fleet for Constantinople would shortly set sail and that his mission to Hungary was important for the whole of Christendom.[1]

John's travels thereafter had in fact little influence either on Christendom or on the fate of the Byzantine Empire. He encountered obstructionism or lack of commitment at every turn. After a brief visit to Milan he wrote to Venice asking for news from the east and also for a Venetian ambassador who might go with him to Hungary. This the Senate would not sanction. He also visited Mantua, whose ruler was Sigismund's vicar-general in the north of Italy and who seems to have lent him some more money. Not until the summer of 1424 did he reach Hungary. Sigismund had little to offer him, apart from a lecture on the benefits which would come to the unhappy Greeks if they would accept union with the Church of Rome. John was back in Constantinople by 1 November. He had achieved nothing except to gain a clearer appreciation of the politics that kept the Christian west divided. It is possible, however, that he had helped to bring Venice and Hungary a little closer together. For in 1425 Sigismund put forward a number of proposals for co-operation.[2] It is also possible that John's travels in Italy and Hungary caused the Sultan Murad to suspect that the Christians of east and west might be uniting against him.

In March 1424 the Venetians had agreed to send news from Constantinople to John in Milan. They may or may not by then have known that the Byzantines had arranged a peace treaty with the Turks. Earlier in the year the Emperor Manuel or his son Constantine, who was acting

---

[1] Sathas, *Documents*, I, no. 97, pp. 158–60; Jorga, 'Notes', v, 152–4 (13 January 1424); Thiriet, *Sénat*, II, no. 1916; *DR*, v, nos. 3395–6, 3408a, 3409–11.

[2] See below, p. 367. On 3 May, when he was back in Milan, John wrote to the Doge, Francesco Foscari, asking him to transfer some securities which he had deposited in Venice to the Prince of Mantua, Gianfrancesco de Gonzaga. Latin text of John's letter in Sp. P. Lambros, *Palaiologeia kai Peloponnesiaka*, III (Athens, 1926), p. 353. *DR*, v, nos. 3416–17.

as regent, had sent two exploratory embassies to the Sultan. The second was led by Loukas Notaras and by the historian George Sphrantzes, who proudly reports its success in his memoirs. On 20 February 1424 terms of peace were agreed. The treaty was a success only in so far as it relieved the pressure on Constantinople. There was little else left of the Byzantine Empire. Its emperor was reduced to renting his throne from the Sultan for an annual tribute of 100,000 ducats. Almost all the towns and territories that had been restored to him by Suleiman and Mehmed I were now in Turkish hands, with the exception of Thessalonica.[1] At least the treaty made it possible for the Emperor Manuel to end his days in peace. He died on 21 July 1425. He was buried in the church of the Pantokrator in Constantinople; and Bessarion of Trebizond, the future Bishop of Nicaea, pronounced his funeral oration. We are told that the people mourned Manuel's death more deeply and more sincerely than that of any of his predecessors. He had appealed to their pride and to their natural xenophobia. For over thirty years he had preserved them from their enemies without making any unnecessary concessions to the Latins. He had championed the rights of Greek merchants and customs officials in Constantinople against the increasingly imperious demands of the Venetians. He had visited the west. But he had never sold his dignity for cheap rewards; and he had never, like his father, rejected his Orthodox faith to gratify a pope and win a crumb of comfort from the Latins. The papal legate to Constantinople in 1422, Antonio da Massa, had put forward a plan for reuniting the Greek and Latin Churches. It had been patiently explained to him, doubtless under Manuel's influence, that reunion could not be effected simply by the fiat of an emperor. The schism went too deep for such easy solutions. The Byzantines could not compromise the faith of their fathers without putting their immortal souls at risk. They would rather, if the worst came to the worst, submit their bodies to the Turks.[2]

The historian Sphrantzes records a conversation that he overheard in the palace between Manuel and his son John. On the subject of the union of the churches Manuel advised his son to be wary of the baits thrown out by the Latins:

The Turks [he said] are very worried that we might come to an agreement with the Christians of the west; for they sense that if this occurred it would be dangerous

---

[1] Sphrantzes, *Chronicon minus*, p. 16; Doukas, xxix. 1: p. 245; Chalkokondyles, II, p. 17. Doukas alone of the Greek historians records the terms of the treaty. For its date, see *Chron. brev.*, II, p. 426. Sanudo, *Vitae Ducum*, col. 975, records a version of the treaty according to a report from Coron dated 22 February 1424. Barker, *Manuel II*, pp. 379–81.

[2] Barker, *Manuel II*, pp. 381–5 and Appendix XIX, pp. 510–12 (on Manuel's alleged visit to the pope).

to them. Therefore it would be wise to go on studying and investigating the matter as long as possible, especially when you have need of something to frighten the Turks. But do not really try to put it into practice; for in my opinion our people are not in the frame of mind to discover a way of uniting with the Latins or to put themselves out to create an atmosphere of peace, concord and mutual understanding ... and I fear that if we are not careful a worse schism may come about and then we shall be left defenceless before the infidel.

John VIII is said to have retired pensive and in silence after hearing his father's advice.[1]

The Venetians were not troubled by such matters of conscience. Manuel would like to have known, however, that the coalition of Venice and Hungary, on which he had laboured so long, came into being three months after his death. In October 1425 the Venetians responded favourably to a plan put to them by Sigismund for an offensive anti-Turkish league. They had just succeeded in making a treaty with the Sultan Murad. None the less, they would assist the Hungarians if they attacked the Turks, particularly by cutting Turkish communications by sea and in the Danube. Sigismund could then make use of Thessalonica and other Venetian stations in the east. He could recruit soldiers and ships' carpenters on Venetian territory. The Venetians even consented to lend him 50,000 ducats for the duration of their truce and to receive him with pleasure in their city, if he came with a suitably modest retinue. The Duke of Milan would, of course, be party to the arrangement.[2] Maybe the Venetians would have welcomed Sigismund's presence with an army in Thessalonica in 1425. Things had not been going well in 'the second Venice'. The unfortunate Nicolò Giorgio remained a prisoner at Adrianople. in May 1424 the Senate had appointed two new governors for Thessalonica, Bernabo Loredan with the title of Duke and Giacomo Dandolo as Captain, for a period of two years. It was a dangerous assignment. The first two Venetians to be approached had in fact declined the honour. In June further military and naval reinforcements were sent to the city. But the senators were beginning to count the vast cost of the enterprise; and before long they were obliged to withdraw the greater part of their war fleet from the Levant to defend their territories in Italy and on the Adriatic coast against Visconti of Milan, with whom war had broken out. In November Santo Venier reported that the Turks were staking all on capturing the city; if, however, the defenders could hold out during the winter the Sultan might be ready to come to a settle-

---

[1] The conversation is recorded by Pseudo-Phrantzes, *Chronicon maius*, p. 320. Cf. Barker, *Manuel II*, pp. 329–30, 382–3.

[2] Jorga, 'Notes', v, 210–11; Thiriet, *Sénat*, ii, nos. 2006, 2039.

ment favourable to Venice.[1] It was a fond hope. Not until 1426, after several vain attempts, was any kind of settlement reached between Venice and the Sultan, and then on payment to him of a large annual tribute and the cession of a Turkish quarter in Thessalonica with its own magistrate. The tribute had to be raised in 1427 and trebled in 1428.[2]

The Venetians were dismayed by what they perceived to be the base ingratitude of the Greek inhabitants of Thessalonica. When they first assumed the government and defence of the city, they had confirmed the constitutional and commercial rights of its citizens and the inviolability of its bishop and church. But they were never liked or trusted. They were and remained foreigners, who failed to live up to the promises that they had made. They regarded the Archbishop, Symeon of Thessalonica, as spokesman for his people. Symeon was made in the same mould as the earlier Patriarch Athanasios of Constantinople. He saw the Venetians as misguided Latins, potential corrupters of the souls of his Orthodox flock. He had advised and campaigned against their takeover of his city, not because he would prefer to have the Turks for masters but because he feared the insidious influence of the Venetians. They imagined that they could win him round with gifts and bribes, which sometimes worked wonders with the Turks; and against all the evidence they persisted in describing him as 'a most loyal servant of the Republic'.[3] He considered the Venetian occupation of his city to be a form of divine chastisement for the multifarious sins of its inhabitants, the worst of which were their inability to live together in harmony and the expressed wish of many of them to save their lives and their property by surrendering to the Turks.

Manuel II in his younger days had found the Thessalonicans to be discouragingly apathetic and contentious. They had tasted the gall of Turkish occupation for fifteen years, from 1387 to 1402. They had expected that Venetian rule would be less irksome and more tolerable, as well as more tolerant. They were soon disenchanted. The Venetians had promised that they would have their own municipal government. This was not the only promise that they broke. They showed little respect for the traditions and institutions of the city which they had agreed to honour. They courted unpopularity by their arrogance. They bred bitter-

---

[1] Jorga, 'Notes', v, 168, 170, 180; Thiriet, Sénat, II, nos. 1933, 1942–4, 1960. Manfroni, 'La marina veneziana', 36.

[2] Sathas, Documents, I, nos. 103–8, 113, 116–17, pp. 163–86; Jorga, 'Notes', v, 316–18, 380–1; Thiriet, Sénat, II, nos. 2018 (20 April 1426), 2066 (24 July 1427), 2111 (31 August 1428). In 1428 the annual tribute had been increased from 100,000 to 300,000 aspra; the Venetian ducat was equivalent to 32–45 aspra.

[3] Jorga, 'Notes', v, 171 (16 July 1424); Thiriet, Sénat, II, no. 2149 (14 July 1429); Mertzios, Mnemeia, pp. 86, 88 ('fidelissimus noster'). Cf. Balfour, Symeon, pp. 150–2.

ness by imposing an authoritarian regime. At the end of June 1425 the people sent a delegation to Venice to complain and to make a number of requests to the Doge, Francesco Foscari. In particular they asked that the Duke of Thessalonica, Bernabo Loredan, and his Captain, Giacomo Dandolo, should allow them a greater measure of autonomy, as had been agreed; and that Venice should spend more on repairing the walls of the city and on bringing food to its starving inhabitants.[1] The city was under almost constant siege by the Turks. Stocks of food were perilously low. Venice encouraged privateers to transport corn and barley, especially from Crete, with promises of handsome rewards.[2] But there were never enough ships and never enough food to go round. Early in 1426 the Turks launched what they hoped was the decisive assault on the city, throwing in some 30,000 men. They were driven off; and the Venetians were able to say that it was thanks only to the presence of five well-armed galleys in the port. The Turks lost 1200 to 2000 men, though there were heavy losses on both sides. In July the Captain of the Gulf, Andrea Mocenigo, was sent to Thessalonica to exhort the citizens to persevere in their resistance and to see to the repairs of the fortifications. In September he was ordered to stay with his six warships in the area throughout the winter. It was the first time for many years that such an order had been given.[3]

The citizens had all but lost their will to resist. Many of them felt and said that they were being driven to extremities of famine and distress merely to satisfy the ambition of their Italian masters. The Venetians were alarmed by the growing spirit of defeatism. They took to arresting and deporting those who seemed to be spreading it. Four were sent as prisoners to Crete, where one of them died. The other three, however, were suspected of fomenting anti-Venetian prejudice there too and were taken in secret to Venice and then, for still greater security, to Padua.[4]

[1] The Venetian reply to these requests, dated 7 July 1425, is translated into Greek in Mertzios, *Mnemeia*, pp. 46–61. Cf. Thiriet, *Sénat*, II, no. 1995. Vakalopoulos, *History of Thessaloniki* (1963), pp. 66–7.
[2] Food supplies to Thessalonica: Sathas, *Documents*, III, no. 833, p. 259 (December 1423), no. 899, p. 315 (August 1426), no. 907, p. 322 (June 1427), no. 959, p. 371 (March 1430). Jorga, 'Notes', V, 178, 182 (October and December 1424); Thiriet, *Sénat*, II, nos. 1967 (February 1425), 2012 (December 1425); Jorga, 'Notes', V, 326, 336–41, 346–7, 350, 353–4 (July and December 1426, April 1427), 360–1 (June and July 1427); Thiriet, *Sénat*, II, nos. 2033, 2058, 2061–2, 2064, 2077–8, 2081 (December 1427, February and March 1428).
[3] On the date and the circumstances of the Turkish attack, see Balfour, *Symeon*, pp. 266–8. Jorga, 'Notes', V, 324–5; Thiriet, *Sénat*, II, no. 2027. Manfroni, 'La marina veneziana', 39–41.
[4] Jorga, 'Notes', V, 383–4; Thiriet, *Sénat*, II, nos. 2115, 2135. The two who survived were set free in May 1430 to save the cost of keeping them in prison. Thiriet, *Sénat*, II, no. 2197.

Many of the well-to-do among the Greeks were shipped with their families to the islands or to Venice on the specious excuse that there would be less risk of famine if there were fewer mouths to feed in Thessalonica. The Greeks knew that the Sultan Murad was playing for time and that the many ambassadors sent to him from Venice were wasting their breath. He was never going to be reconciled to the Venetian occupation of Thessalonica. More and more of the inhabitants came to think that there was no hope of peace and no end to their privations unless they gave in. Their city would fall to the Turks sooner or later. It would be better to surrender it of their own free will than have it sacked and plundered by a vengeful Ottoman army. But the Venetians would not hear of it. In 1427 and 1428 they sent more food and more troops; and they took strong measures against any Greeks who tried to exercise their free will. Those who wanted to escape were arrested. Those who talked of surrender were tortured or executed. Public order in the city broke down.

In 1429 a second Greek delegation went to see the Doge. They brought another list of thirty-one complaints and grievances. They painted a frightening picture of conditions in their city. The senators gave them a fair hearing on 14 July. They apologised for some of the evident shortcomings and the maladministration of the Venetian governors, especially in the matter of the distribution of food. But they refused to grant permission for Greeks to leave the city, even though many had already gone, abandoning their houses and belongings.[1] Perhaps the Venetians too were beginning to lose heart in the enterprise. Since 1426 they had been engaged in war against the Duke of Milan, which was expensive but seemed to offer a better investment than the occupation of Thessalonica. Unless they could reach a proper understanding with the Turks they could hardly afford to hold on to the city, let alone exploit its commercial advantages. Its defence and maintenance were putting them to 'endless expense' and costing them at least 60,000 ducats a year. Yet an understanding with the Turks seemed more remote than ever. Giacomo Dandolo, newly appointed Captain of Thessalonica, had been sent on yet another mission to the Sultan. In March it was reported that he had been arrested. He died in prison.[2] Venice had not wanted to declare war on the Turks. Now there was no alternative. The Sultan knew that the Venetians were sheltering yet another pretender to his throne in Thessalonica. The Venetians knew that the Genoese of Chios and Lesbos were actively assisting the Turks. It would really have been wiser to

[1] Mertzios, *Mnemeia*, pp. 72–86 (Greek translation); Jorga, 'Notes', *ROL*, VI (1898), 57–9; Thiriet, *Sénat*, II, no. 2149. Cf. Vakalopoulos, *History of Thessaloniki*, pp. 68–70.

[2] Sanudo, *Vitae Ducum*, cols. 1004–6; Jorga, 'Notes', V, 387; VI, 53, 63, 70. Thiriet, *Sénat*, II, nos. 2126–7, 2129, 2136, 2175. Manfroni, 'La marina veneziana', 46–7.

cut their losses and surrender Thessalonica. In July 1429 Andrea Mocenigo attempted a bold but foolhardy assault on the Turkish naval base at Gallipoli. His officers refused to support him and the Turks had the satisfaction of seeing the invincible Venetian fleet withdrawing in disarray.[1]

The end came in March 1430. The Sultan Murad decided that the affair at Thessalonica had gone on long enough. He marched on the city in person at the head of a huge army, improbably estimated by Venetian sources to number 190,000 men. On Sunday 26 March he came within sight of the city walls. He had been assured that the Greeks would rise up against the Venetians and hand over their city without a fight. But the Venetian governors made certain that this would not happen. The Turkish assault began at dawn on 29 March. It was led by Sinan Pasha, the Beglerbeg or governor-general of Rumelia. By midday his soldiers had scaled the walls and entered the city. The capture and sack of Thessalonica is vividly described by an eye-witness, John Anagnostes.[2] It is a terrible tale. He reckoned that 7000 citizens, perhaps about one-fifth of the population, were carried off to slavery. The law of Islam allowed for three days and nights of pillage for cities that resisted conquest. Thessalonica received the full force of that law. Those who had advocated voluntary surrender long before were vindicated; but they were not spared the horrors of the sack of their city. Its Archbishop, Symeon, would doubtless have interpreted the horrors as punishment for the sins of his people. He was lucky to die six months before the conquest. The Venetians had fought with courage. They lost 270 men, among them the son of Paolo Contarini, the last Duke of Thessalonica. But they too were lucky, for they had a means of escape denied to those penned inside the walls. They had three galleys waiting in the harbour. The governors and other officials scrambled aboard, some only half-dressed, and fled to Negroponte. They were later charged with dereliction of duty and put in prison for a while.[3]

The news reached Venice on 16 April 1430 and was confirmed by

[1] Genoese support for the Turks: Jorga, 'Notes', v, 197; Thiriet, Sénat, II, nos. 1979, 1983. On Mocenigo's exploits at Gallipoli, see Manfroni, 'La marina veneziana', 46–57.

[2] John Anagnostes, De Thessalonicensi excidio narratio, ed. I. Bekker in Georgius Phrantzes, CSHB (1838), pp. 481–528; ed. J. Tsaras (Thessaloniki, 1957). Other accounts are in Doukas, xxix. 5: pp. 249–51; Sphrantzes, Chronicon minus, p. 48; Chalkokondyles, II, p. 14. Cf. Chron. brev., II, pp. 440–1. Sanudo, Vitae Ducum, cols. 1007–8; Mertzios, Mnemeia, pp. 88–93. S. Vryonis, 'The Ottoman conquest of Thessaloniki in 1430', in A. Bryer and H. Lowry, eds., Continuity and Change in Late Byzantine and Early Ottoman Society (Birmingham and Dumbarton Oaks, Washington, D.C., 1986), pp. 281–321.

[3] Mertzios, Mnemeia, pp. 91–2. Sathas, Documents, III, no. 969, pp. 381–8. Balfour, Symeon, pp. 239–40.

more reliable reports later in the month. The details of the disaster were contained in a letter written at Negroponte by Antonio Diedo and received in Venice on 8 May.[1] The Venetians were not given to lamenting their losses or wasting time licking their wounds. They had held the second city of the Byzantine Empire for seven years. It had cost them huge sums of money. One Venetian chronicler put the total expense at 700,000 ducats.[2] But life must go on. They had lost face with the Turks. One lesson to be learnt from the whole sorry episode was that the survival of the Venetian commercial empire in Romania and the Black Sea now depended not on the goodwill of the Byzantine Emperors but on the favour of the Ottoman Sultan. Peace with the Turks was now more desirable than ever. On 29 April 1430, when the news from Thessalonica was still only imperfectly known, Silvestro Morosini, Captain-General of the Sea, was instructed to seek out the Sultan and present new terms to him. The Venetians would not try to recover Thessalonica if the Sultan would undertake not to attack their possessions in Albania, Greece and the Aegean islands, a list of which was again produced. It was hoped that the treaty could be signed by the end of August. Until that moment, however, Morosini was to do as much damage as he could to the Turks to bring the Sultan more quickly to the conference table.[3]

Earlier in the year and before the capture of Thessalonica some ambassadors from Constantinople on their way to Rome arrived in Venice. They brought a letter from the Emperor John VIII. He suggested that the best way to do damage to the Turks was to promote division among them and he asked Venice to co-operate to this end. He also deplored the action of the Venetian authorities in interfering with Byzantine ships trading with the Turks across the straits. The senators were not sympathetic. They asked for further enlightenment on the first point and replied on the second that it was their policy to inflict all possible harm on the Turks by closing the straits to their ships. It was regrettable that Byzantine trade had to suffer as a result.[4] The Sultan, however, was induced to sign the desired treaty with Venice in September 1430. He had got what he wanted. The Venetians too were pleased with the outcome. They had to pay a substantial tribute. But they had secured a freedom of the sea which the Turks would never have allowed them while they held Thessalonica. The Sultan agreed that his warships from

[1] Jorga, 'Notes', VI, 78–80; Thiriet, Sénat, II, nos. 2191–2 (27 and 29 April 1430).
[2] Antonio Morosini, cited by Thiriet, 'Les chroniques vénitiennes', 278. For other smaller estimates, see Jorga, 'Notes', VI, 73; Mertzios, Mnemeia, pp. 98–9; Setton, Papacy and the Levant, II, p. 30.
[3] Jorga, 'Notes', VI, 70–80; Thiriet, Sénat, II, no. 2192.
[4] Jorga, 'Notes', VI, 85–6; Thiriet, Sénat, II, no. 2209 (19 July 1430); DR, V, nos. 3425–6.

Gallipoli and elsewhere would not sail south or west of Tenedos. In October the Senate felt confident enough to order that the fleet be disarmed; and before long the Venetian consulate in Thessalonica was re-established.[1]

The Byzantine Emperor had been a passive and helpless spectator of events at Thessalonica. What had been the second city of his empire and the seat of government for his father Manuel was irretrievably lost in March 1430. He had had no hand in its defence and no say in its destiny. The Venetians had acquired it and lost it of their own accord. It had certainly brought them no profit, commercial or otherwise. All the more reason to make sure that their profits and their trade in the first city of the empire were protected. In May 1430 they turned to the emperor to grant them almost the only privilege left in his gift, a renewal of his treaty with them. It was three years overdue, since it had last been confirmed in 1423. The Doge entrusted the negotiations to the new baillie of Constantinople, Martino da Mosto; and on 26 May 1431 the necessary document was signed by the Emperor John VIII and sealed with his golden bull in the Blachernai palace.[2] It incorporated the texts of all the treaties between Byzantium and Venice since that of 1390. The litany of the emperor's debts and obligations had been rehearsed three times since then. Both sides knew it by heart. It required no changes or modifications. In 1390 the emperor's uncle Andronikos had bequeathed to his son John VII debts to Venice of 17,163 *hyperpyra* in addition to the 30,000 ducats loaned on the security of the crown jewels in 1343 and 5000 ducats on other security. The sums remained the same. Nothing had been paid. Even the problem of the ownership of the island of Tenedos was left 'in the air'. Not a word was said about Thessalonica or about the realities of the increasingly desperate plight of Constantinople. The Venetians, however, were content to have their commercial privileges solemnly confirmed. They had burnt their fingers at Thessalonica. Their policy after 1430 was, so far as possible, to live at peace with Greeks and Turks alike, to revert to a position of neutrality, so that the lucrative trade routes between Romania, Constantinople and the Black Sea would not be closed to them. They would go to war against the Turks, but only if the rest of the western Christian world went with them.

The Emperor John VIII too believed that only a concerted show of

---

[1] An Italian version of the text of the treaty is in *DVL*, II, no. 182, pp. 343–5; Jorga, 'Notes', VI, 88–91. Thiriet, *Sénat*, II, no. 2217 (9 October 1430). Demetrios Philomati, consul before 1423, was reinstated on 3 February 1431. Thiriet, *Sénat*, III, no. 2225.

[2] Greek text in *MM*, III, pp. 177–86. *DVL*, II, no. 183, p. 346; Thiriet, *Sénat*, II, no. 2194; Jorga, 'Notes', VI, 80. *DR*, V, no. 3433.

Christian strength could save his city from the infidel. His father Manuel had counselled him against proposing the union of the churches as a means of bringing this about. John could see no alternative. The year after his father's death he proposed to Pope Martin V that a council might be convened to unite Christendom. In 1430 he sent another embassy to the pope by way of Venice.[1] In times past the popes had been annoyed by the Byzantine insistence on holding a council. In the fifteenth century the idea found more favour. There was a growing faction in the Western Church which argued that the authority of a council was greater than that of the pope, an argument somewhat in line with Byzantine thought. In 1431 the conciliarists, as they were called, met at Basel. In the same year Martin V died and Eugenius IV, himself a Venetian, was elected pope. The emperor was quick to get in touch with him.[2] The conciliarists, hearing what was afoot, invited the emperor to send delegates to their assembly at Basel. Thereafter the matter developed into a race between the pope and the conciliarists to win the favour of the Greeks for reasons of prestige. Both parties sent ambassadors to Constantinople to put their case. The Byzantines had never been so flattered and courted by the western church.

The Venetians were, as often, in two minds. They were distracted by events nearer home, by the fear that the Genoese were again preparing for war and by the renewed hostility of Sigismund of Hungary, whom Pope Eugenius had crowned as emperor in 1431. They made their peace with Sigismund in June 1433; but they were doubtful about the plan for a council to heal the schism between the Eastern and Western Churches, for the outcome would probably be another crusade against the Turks. As they observed to the pope in 1433, they themselves had not been at war with the Turks since they lost Thessalonica and they had no intention of stirring up enmity against them.[3] Three years later, however, they were approached by the fathers at the council at Basel to provide four ships to bring a Greek delegation to Italy, at the emperor's request, and two warships and 300 bowmen to defend Constantinople while the emperor was away. The total cost would be 26,200 ducats. The senators replied that they had always fervently prayed for the reunion of the Greek Church, that they would supply the ships to bring the Byzantine delegates as far as Italy, but that they could not possibly contribute more than a fraction of the cost, impoverished as they were by their war in Italy. There was much coming and going of ambassadors between Constantinople and Basel. But the emperor made it clear that

---

[1] DR, v, nos. 3420, 3425.
[2] DR, v, nos. 3431–2. Gill, *Council of Florence*, pp. 51–2.
[3] Thiriet, *Sénat*, III, no. 2317 (2 April 1433).

neither he nor his patriarch, who was old and infirm, would go as far as Basel to attend a council.[1]

The Greeks who had been to Basel reported that the conciliarists were divided among themselves on the question of co-operation with the papacy. In May 1437 Pope Eugenius succeeded in winning over the minority faction among them and agreed to summon a council of his own in Italy. He at once asked Venice for a ship to take his envoys to Constantinople. The Venetians consented, though they expressed anxiety about the Sultan's reaction if he were to hear that the Byzantine Emperor was on Venetian territory; for it had been suggested that the pope's council might be held in Friuli or Udine or even Padua.[2] The pope had aleady decided, however, that it should assemble at Ferrara. He acted quickly to forestall the conciliarists. His envoys discussed the details with the emperor in Constantinople. He arranged with Venice to lease him four ships to bring the Byzantine delegation to Italy and appointed his Venetian nephew, the Captain-General Antonio Condulmer, to command them. They reached Constantinople in November 1437. A few days later messengers arrived from Basel bringing ships of their own to transport the Byzantines to an alternative council. They came too late. The emperor and his patriarch had made their decision; and on 24 November they embarked on the galleys sent by the pope. Four ships would hardly hold them all, for there were close on 700 delegates. The emperor had ordered four ships of his own to be armed for the voyage; and, since they were heading for Venice, it was arranged that they should sail with the Venetian merchant convoy returning from Tana.[3]

They made a leisurely journey. It was a bad time of year for sailing and they had to make frequent stops, since the patriarch and the more elderly prelates found it difficult to eat or sleep except on dry land. The Venetians had expected them to arrive about Christmas. But they spent Christmas at Modon. The council to which they were going held its first sessions at Ferrara while they were still at Corfu, where they spent more than a week.[4] The Venetians were pleased to describe the Emperor John VIII as 'an intimate friend of Venice'. But when they heard that he was coming their way again, they thought it proper to recall that they had lent him 1500 ducats on his last visit of which he had repaid

[1] Jorga, 'Notes', VI 380–1 and 381 n. 1; Thiriet, Sénat, III, nos. 2418 (28 June 1436), 2435 (18 February 1437). DR, V, nos. 3437–40, 3443–52, 3454, 3466.
[2] Thiriet, Sénat, III, no. 2445 (June 1437).
[3] The Venetian galley from Trebizoned would also travel with them. Jorga, 'Notes', VI, 391 and n. 5, 392–3; Thiriet, Sénat, III, no. 2455. The emperor left his son Constantine as regent in Constantinople.
[4] Jorga, 'Notes', VI, 393–4. Gill, Council of Florence, pp. 89–91.

no more than 500. This small embarrassment was removed when the son of Francesco Morosini settled the debt on the emperor's behalf.[1] John's father Manuel II and his grandfather John V had both visited Venice as emperors. The Doge, Francesco Foscari, was determined that the visit of John VIII should be the grandest of all such occasions. He was assured of the emperor's goodwill towards Venice and towards its interests in Constantinople. In October 1436 his emissaries had encountered no reluctance on John's part to renew the time-honoured treaty between Byzantium and Venice for another five years.[2] In December 1437 the Senate made plans for the emperor's reception and wrote to the pope to reassure him of their full support.[3]

As it happened, the ships carrying the emperor and the patriarch sailed into Venice an hour or two before their advance party. They tied up at the Lido on the morning of 8 February 1438, rather earlier than expected. They were politely asked to stay on board overnight. Nothing must go wrong with the pageantry of their official reception. The Doge, however, knowing that the emperor was unwell, went aboard his ship later in the day to make an unofficial call. The next morning dawned wet and misty, but the show went on. The Doge sailed out to the Lido in the state barge with an escort of smaller ships. One of them carried a tableau of the might of Venice. Its sides were hung with bright Byzantine banners; its prow bore two golden lions of St Mark flanking the Byzantine eagle; its upper deck was a stage for allegorical figures; and its oarsmen wore caps decorated with the emblems of Byzantium and Venice. It circled the emperor's ship to the sound of trumpets while the Doge paid his official respects. The air was full of the pealing of all the bells of Venice. The sea was covered with boats scurrying hither and thither. The Greeks, who loved a show no less than the Venetians, were enchanted. The patriarch and his suite were treated to a little pageant of their own. Their minds were on higher things and they had disembarked the night before to sleep in their appointed rooms in the monastery of San Giorgio Maggiore. But they were taken there in two small boats whose sides were adorned with the patriarchal insignia and whose decks were shaded by cedar branches. The emperor welcomed the Doge aboard his own ship. His brother, the Despot Demetrios, sat beside him. After polite conversation, the Doge invited the emperor to accompany him into Venice on his state barge. For reasons of protocol, however, or because of his gout, the emperor preferred to land from his

[1] Jorga, 'Notes', VI, 380 (10 January 1437).
[2] Greek text in *MM*, III, pp. 186–95. *DVL*, II, no. 185, pp. 346–7; *DR*, V, no. 3464 (30 October 1436).
[3] Jorga, 'Notes', VI, 391; Thiriet, *Sénat*, III, nos. 2455–6 (3 and 12 December 1437).

own ship, which was accordingly towed to the quay. For the rest of the day the Byzantine delegation enjoyed the grand tour of the canals of Venice which were alive with festive crowds and music. The Rialto Bridge on the Grand Canal was raised in their honour; and when at sunset they disembarked they had been mesmerised by the glory and the wonder of the city. It was indeed, as one of them recalled, 'marvellous in the extreme, rich and varied and golden and highly finished and variegated and worthy of limitless praise'.[1]

The emperor was accommodated in the palace of the Marquis of Ferrara on the Grand Canal, where his father had stayed in 1400. Rooms had been prepared for his entourage in the palace of Lodovico dal Verme and for the patriarch and his bishops in San Giorgio and elsewhere. On 14 February, at the pope's request, the senators informed the Kings of France, Hungary and England of the safe and happy arrival in Venice of the Emperor John VIII, his Patriarch Joseph, and others Byzantine bishops and noblemen.[2] They had voted 1000 ducats for the lodging and entertainment of their guests. The sum had to be raised to a maximum of 3000 ducats as time went on. For the emperor and his delegation seemed in no hurry to leave the 'marvellous city' of Venice. The Venetians had perhaps learnt from their experience of entertaining Manuel II that the Greek sense of time and urgency was different from their own. But there were other factors that delayed them. Both the emperor and the patriarch were ill for a few days. Their long journey had tired them; and there were agents from Basel in Venice still trying to influence the emperor to go there rather than to Ferrara. He finally wrote to the fathers at Basel on 25 February to confirm that he was on his way to the pope's council and invited them to come too; and two days later, no doubt to the relief of the Venetian exchequer, he and most of his delegation set out for Ferrara by sea and river, the emperor claiming that he was too ridden by gout to mount a horse. The Patriarch Joseph followed him a few days later.[3]

Never before had Byzantium come to Venice and to Italy on a mission

---

[1] The emperor's reception in Venice is most vividly described by the Greek diarist of the Council of Ferrara–Florence, Sylvester Syropoulos, and by the Greek Acts of the Council. *Les Mémoires du Grand Ecclésiarque de l'Eglise de Constantinople Sylvestre Syropoulos*, iv. 16–25, pp. 212–14; *Quae supersunt actorum graecorum Concilii Florentini*, ed. J. Gill, Concilium Florentinum Documenta et Scriptores, Series B, v, 1 (Rome, 1953), pp. 1–5. Cf. Pseudo-Phrantzes, *Chronicon maius*, pp. 322–6; Sanudo, *Vitae Ducum*, cols. 1051–5. For other, unpublished, Venetian accounts, see Jorga, 'Notes', VI, 398 n. 3. The passage cited above (*Acta graeca*, p. 4) is as translated by Gill, *Council of Florence*, p. 100.

[2] Jorga, 'Notes', VI, 399; Thiriet, *Sénat*, III, no. 2461. Syropoulos, *Mémoires*, v. 25: p. 222, records the patriarch's visit to St Mark's to see the Treasury and the Pala d'Oro. See above, Chapter 10, pp. 183–4.

[3] Jorga, 'Notes', VI, 401; Thiriet, *Sénat*, III, no. 2462. Gill, *Council of Florence*, pp. 104–5.

of peace in such imposing style and such numbers. The council to which
they were going was to be a very different event from the Council of
Lyons in 1274 or the personal conversion of John V in 1369. Apart
from the Emperor and the Patriarch of Constantinople, there were representatives of the ancient patriarchates of Alexandria, Antioch and Jerusalem. Few of the Byzantine delegates could compete with the refined
sophistry of the assembled Latin clerics; but among them were the
Bishops Bessarion of Nicaea, Isidore of Kiev, and Mark Eugenikos of
Ephesos. The laymen whom the emperor had brought to the council
included George Scholarios, later to become Patriarch of Constantinople,
and George Gemistos Plethon, the eminent platonist and philosopher
from Mistra. The party in Byzantium favourable to union with the Roman
Church had gained some ground over the years, inspired by the followers
of Demetrios Kydones. They were still a small minority, however, and
their conversion was more intellectual than spiritual. This might have
fitted them for the long and often bitter debates on matters of faith,
doctrine and authority in the church which took place at Ferrara and
then at Florence, whither the council moved in 1439. At the Council
of Lyons there had been no debate and no discussion about the issues
dividing the churches of east and west. At the Council of Florence there
was perhaps too much; and before it was over the Byzantines were weary
of it all, nostalgic and bewildered. They were also worried about the
fate of their relatives and their property in Constantinople, though many
of them had sent or brought personal possessions with them which they
had deposited in Venice along with much of the church plate of St Sophia.[1]
At the beginning of May 1438 word had come from Venice, confirmed by letters from Constantinople, that the Sultan Murad was
equipping a fleet of 150 ships and a vast army to attack Constantinople.
The Venetian merchants there were said to have taken refuge behind
the walls of Galata. The emperor and the patriarch urged the pope and
his cardinals to send help. Several weeks went by before the pope passed
the message on to Venice. On 24 May the Senate agreed to dispatch
three galleys to Constantinople, on certain conditions: their armament
must be paid for by the pope or the emperor; and their commanders
must be Venetians, though they might fly the Byzantine flag. There
is no evidence that the ships were ever sent or that the reported Turkish
attack ever took place.[2]

The theological debates at Ferrara and Florence had little to do with
relations between Byzantium and Venice. Their outcome, however, was

[1] Syropoulos, *Mémoires*, v. 24: p. 278.
[2] Jorga, 'Notes', vi, 404 and n. 3; Thiriet, *Sénat*, iii, nos. 2471–3; *DR*, v, nos. 3480–2; Syropoulos, *Mémoires*, v. 22–3: pp. 266–8. Gill, *Council of Florence*, pp. 116–17.

of concern to both. For the emperor believed that the success of the council was the last hope of salvation for Constantinople. He worked hard to allay the suspicions and to control the temper of some of his delegates. But towards the end he began to lose his own patience. In June 1439 he announced to the pope that he could waste no more time over the minutiae of the matter and that he had already sent a messenger to Venice to prepare for his return voyage. He thought that he might be able to go back in convoy with the merchant fleet bound for Romania and Tana. But the Venetians declined to delay its departure any longer. Instead they would lend him three warships, in spite of their pressing financial difficulties.[1] The Patriarch Joseph had died in the course of the discussions at Florence. But in the end the emperor stayed long enough to witness the conclusion of the council on which he had set such store. On 5 July 1439 the document proclaiming the union of the churches was signed by the emperor and the pope; and on the following day it was read out in the cathedral in Florence, first in Latin and then in Greek, to announce to God and man that the wall which had for so long separated eastern from western Christians had been demolished.[2]

Most of the Byzantine delegates left Florence about a fortnight later, though the emperor's brother Demetrios with George Scholarios and Gemistos Plethon had already gone. As laymen they had not been required to sign the document of union. The only Greek bishop who refused to sign it was Mark Eugenikos of Ephesos. He was later to be hailed as the only honest man among them. The Emperor John stayed on in Florence for about a month. He left for Venice on 26 August, taking with him Mark of Ephesos, with whom he was none too pleased. Like his father before him, John annoyed the Venetians by his indecision about the date of his departure. His own ship was fit to sail but the ships for which he had asked were not quite ready. He was offered two galleys bound for Romania which would take him as far as Lemnos, provided that he paid his way. While waiting, he made a visit to Padua; and when he got back the Doge asked him to permit his clergy to celebrate the Orthodox liturgy in St Mark's. Under protest they did so, though noticeably refraining from reciting the Latin form of the Creed and praying for the pope. Even so, there was a storm of protest when they got back to Constantinople. It was one of the first signs that the union of the churches proclaimed at Florence was little more than a piece of paper.

On 14 October the emperor and his suite finally embarked at Venice.

---

[1] Jorga, 'Notes', VI, 416 (1 August 1439); Thiriet, *Sénat*, III, nos. 2500, 2507. Gill, *Council of Florence*, pp. 276–7.

[2] Gill, *Council of Florence*, pp. 289–96.

But still they could not set out. It was a stormy night in the harbour
and three more days were needed to repair the damage done. The Greeks
also protested that they were going to be overcharged for their meals
aboard during the voyage. The Senate sent instructions to their baillie
in Constantinople to sort the matter out by refunding those who complained.[1] On 19 October the convoy set sail. The weather was bad;
the sea was rough. The news of what they had done at Florence had
gone before them. At Corfu and again at Modon the local Greeks accused
them of having betrayed their faith.[2] Not until February 1440 did the
emperor get to Constantinople; and there the news was brought to him
that his wife had died. His homecoming was mournful enough without
that tragedy. For most of the clergy and people of the capital felt that
the union of Florence had been a sad and shameful business; and the
men who had signed it found themselves denounced and shunned as
traitors who had sold their souls to the Latins. The Venetians, who
had brought the emperor home, added to his miseries by filing a complaint
about the maltreatment of their subjects and property in Constantinople
during his absence.[3]

[1] Jorga, 'Notes', VI, 416–17; Thiriet, *Sénat*, III, nos. 2510–13.
[2] Syropoulos, *Mémoires*, xi. 2–9, 13–14: pp. 524, 526–30, 532, 534–6.
[3] Thiriet, *Sénat*, III, no. 2531 (29 July 1440). Gill, *Council of Florence*, pp. 300–4.

21

THE WORST NEWS FOR ALL
OF CHRISTENDOM: VENICE AND
THE FALL OF CONSTANTINOPLE

THE emperor, his patriarch and his bishops had gone to Italy in 1437 on the understanding that, if and when the union of the churches was proclaimed, they would be accepted as full members of western Christendom. They would then qualify as the beneficiaries of a holy war against the Turks in which all their Christian brethren in the west would participate with wholehearted enthusiasm. Three months after the declaration of union, in October 1439, the pope outlined his proposals for the promised crusade. But the Christians of the west were far from wholehearted and it took months of painful diplomacy before a crusading army could be assembled. Once again the natural starting-point was Hungary. In 1440 the Kingdom of Hungary was united with that of Poland by the young Polish King Ladislas III. He was supported by the Hungarian general John Hunyadi, who had formerly been in the service of King Sigismund. Hunyadi was a brilliant soldier who had already fought valiantly against the Turks. Ladislas made him governor of Belgrade and Voivode of Transylvania. The Venetians had taken little part in the Council of Florence except as ferrymen and moneylenders. They were sceptical as well as anxious about its consequences. At the end of 1440 King Ladislas sent an envoy to enlist their sympathy for a crusade. They told him that they were at peace with the Turks and could not honourably join in war against them.[1] The Emperor John VIII, who was well informed about events in eastern Europe, sent an ambassador to Venice and to Rome early in 1442. He was Zanachio or Giovanni Torcello, who came from Crete, though he was described as a citizen of Constantinople. He was well known to the pope and to the emperor; and at the Council of Florence he had put forward a plan for a crusade against the Turks which would march overland from Hungary.[2] Torcello conveyed to the Doge the emperor's anxiety about the safety of Hungary, in view

---

[1] Setton, *Papacy and the Levant*, II, p. 66.
[2] Text in *Bertrandon de la Broquière, Voyage d'Outremer*, ed. C. Schefer (Paris, 1892), with Broquière's comments on the plan, pp. 263–74.

of the clear intentions of the Sultan Murad. The Venetians were surprised
at the alarmist tone of Torcello's report. They urged him to go to Hungary
and then to the pope and to come back to them with further news.
It was, as always, their sincere wish to do all that they could for the
good of the Christian religion and the propagation and defence of the
faith. But it would be helpful to have first-hand intelligence from Hungary
and from Pope Eugenius.[1]

The pope sincerely wanted to mount a crusade. But he found it hard
to stimulate enthusiasm. Apart from Hungary, Poland and Wallachia,
the only response came from France. The Duke of Burgundy, Philip
III, was the one western ruler eager to take the cross. The pope appointed
Cardinal Giuliano Cesarini to be in charge of arrangements. The crusading army would go by land from Hungary. The Venetians were expected
to provide a fleet. In August 1442, however, they complained to the
pope that, while they were ready to supply the ships, he had not given
them enough money to arm them.[2] Meanwhile the news from Constantinople was alarming. The Senate took special measures to protect its
convoy of merchantmen on their way to Tana; and the emperor begged
that the warships in the convoy might be allowed to stay for a week
at Constantinople to frighten the Turks. Alternatively, he suggested that
Venice might station three galleys there throughout the winter. The situation seemed so critical that the Captain of the Gulf, after talks with
the baillie, Marino Soranzo, was authorised to adopt the second of these
courses and to leave two or three ships at Constantinople. Their main
purpose, however, was stated to be the protection of Venetian merchants.
The baillie was also authorised to try to mediate between the emperor
and the Sultan.[3] Come what may, Venetian trade and profit must not
be interrupted. On 19 September 1442 the hard-pressed Emperor John
VIII was induced to sign a document extending for another five years
the privileges of the Venetian colony in his city. Five years was an optimistic projection in the circumstances. The treaty of 1442 was indeed almost
the last between Byzantium and Venice.[4]

On 1 January 1443 the pope announced to all the world that tithes
were to be collected for a crusade in defence of the eastern Christians
against the Turks. Almost at the same time the emperor in Constantinople, with or without Venetian mediation, signed a truce with the Sultan.[5]

---

[1] Jorga, 'Notes', ROL, VII (1899–1900), 56 (21 February 1442); Thiriet, Sénat, III, no. 2568;
DR, v, no. 3494. Setton, Papacy and the Levant, II, pp. 67–9.

[2] Jorga, 'Notes', VII, 73–4.

[3] Jorga, 'Notes', VII, 65, 74, 90–2; Thiriet, Sénat, III, nos. 2579, 2584, 2588, 2590–2 (June
to September 1442).

[4] Greek text in MM, III, pp. 207–15. DVL, II, no. 188, p. 352; DR, v, no. 3497.

[5] Chalkokondyles, II, p. 81. DR, v, no. 3501.

He can hardly have been surprised that it was not observed. It had suited the Sultan's purpose since he was called away to suppress a rebellion in Asia Minor. But his troops continued to harass the Byzantines, as their ambassador to Venice had cause to complain later in the year. He gave it as his emperor's opinion that the Turks could still be driven out of Europe if the Venetians would arm a really substantial fleet. The Senate patiently assured him that Venice had already undertaken to supply ten galleys at the pope's request. Everything now depended on the response from other Christian powers.[1] The Venetians did not see eye to eye with the pope. On 25 May 1443 they confirmed their goodwill on his behalf but they warned him that he must find the money to honour his agreement to arm all ten galleys and not just six of them. The ships were, after all, to fly the papal standard. They should be paid for and sent to the Hellespont without further delay if the Christian cause were not to be lost. The Venetians observed that they were already doing more than their share by spending 20,000 ducats in addition to 2000 for each of the four galleys which they were preparing for the Duke of Burgundy.[2]

The crusade, led by Ladislas and Hunyadi and accompanied by Cardinal Cesarini, set out from Hungary in the early summer of 1443. They were joined by a Serbian contingent under the Despot George Branković. The plan of campaign was much the same as in the Crusade of Nikopolis in 1396. While the army of about 25,000 men marched down the Danube valley, the fleet would sail up the river from the Black Sea. The crusaders won two promising victories at the start by recapturing first Niš and then Sofia. The Sultan was alarmed. He opted to play for time. A truce was arranged for a period of ten years. The terms were agreed in July 1444. It is doubtful if either party expected them to be kept. On the Christian side George Branković felt bound to observe them. Cardinal Cesarini, however, could not bear to think that the crusade which he had done so much to organise would have to be disbanded; and he absolved King Ladislas from the oath that he had sworn to the infidel. In September the crusade was on its way again. By then the long-delayed fleet had sailed from Venice. It was commanded by Cardinal Francesco Condulmer and its ships flew the pope's standard. There were eight from Venice led by Alvise Loredan and four from the Duke of Burgundy. The Venetian plan was that when they reached the straits at Gallipoli eight or more of them should sail on to the Black Sea and up the Danube

[1] The imperial ambassador was Theodore Karystenos. Jorga, 'Notes', VII, 95–6; Thiriet, Sénat, III, no. 2603 (3 May 1443); DR, V, nos. 3498–9. Setton, Papacy and the Levant, II, pp. 75–6.

[2] Jorga, 'Notes', VII, 101–2; Thiriet, Sénat, III, no. 2608.

to meet the crusaders and ferry them over the river. Venice was already anticipating the outcome by claiming the right to future ownership of Gallipoli and of Thessalonica as a just reward for the great expense of equipping the fleet.[1]

This claim illustrated the fact that those involved in the crusade had different objectives. The Hungarians and the Poles had in mind the expulsion of the Turks from the Balkans; the pope expected the rescue of Constantinople; while the Venetians thought of the protection and expansion of their colonial empire in Romania. By August 1444 the fleet had reached the Hellespont. Meanwhile, however, the Venetians had been informed of the truce between the crusaders and the Turks. At once they sent instructions to their admiral Loredan to hold his fire. Venice could not and should not carry on the war alone. Loredan must explain to the Sultan that the warships off Gallipoli belonged to the pope and not to Venice. He should try to make an armistice with the Turks and bring his ships home.[2] The crusaders, however, succeeded in crossing the Danube on 20 September; and new orders were sent to Loredan. They reached him too late. They were written in Venice on 9 November.[3] On the very next day the crusade came to grief. The Sultan Murad had been horrified by the perfidy of its Christian leaders. He rushed back from Asia Minor to do battle with them. The Venetian fleet held the Hellespont but made little effort to prevent the Sultan crossing the Bosporos. The ships may have been thwarted by adverse winds; but it seems that the Genoese and perhaps some Venetians accepted bribes to help the Turks over the water.[4] The battle was fought at Varna on the Black Sea coast. The crusaders were outnumbered by three to one. They fought with gallant desperation until Ladislas and then Cardinal Cesarini were killed. There were few survivors on the Christian side, though Hunyadi got away with some of his Hungarian troops. Those that escaped found no Venetian ships on hand to rescue them.[5]

The Crusade of Varna was the last attempt by western Christendom to drive the Turks out of Europe. One of its aims had been the salvation

[1] Jorga, 'Notes', VII, 417–19; Sathas, Documents, I, nos. 138–40, pp. 208–11; Thiriet, Sénat, III, no. 2656 (4 July 1444). Venice assessed the expense at 30,000 ducats.

[2] Thiriet, Sénat, III, no. 2668 (9 September 1444).

[3] Thiriet, Sénat, III, nos. 2670, 2671; Sathas, Documents, I, no. 140, pp. 208–11.

[4] Chalkokondyles, II, p. 99. Pope Eugenius IV later excommunicated the culprits. Setton, Papacy and the Levant, II, p. 89.

[5] On the Crusade of Varna, see: O. Halecki, The Crusade of Varna. A Discussion of Controversial Problems (New York, 1943); F. Babinger, Mehmed the Conqueror and his Time, trans. R. Manheim, ed. W. C. Hickman, Bollingen Series, xcvi (Princeton, N.J., 1978), pp. 27–41; Setton, Papacy and the Levant, II, pp. 66–107. The Venetian part in it is summarised by Thiriet, Romanie vénitienne, pp. 377–9.

of Constantinople. It had never reached there; and many of the city's Greek inhabitants were not sorry that it had failed. For its failure proved that no good could come to them from those who had forced them to adulterate the faith of their fathers. They would sooner pray for a miracle of divine intervention than expect a material reward for perpetuating a union which was so displeasing in the sight of God. The Emperor John VIII may have recalled his father's advice, that union with Rome would only alienate his own subjects and infuriate the Turks. So it had come about. His only part in the crusade had been to ignore the Sultan's summons to provide troops before the battle at Varna. There were, it seems, some Byzantine warships with the Venetian fleet patrolling the straits. But once again the emperor had been a passive spectator of events, unable to influence their course and reduced to despair by their outcome. He must have sensed that the Turkish victory at Varna was the prelude to the conquest of Constantinople. No more help could be expected from the west. The impetus provided by the Council of Florence, such as it was, had spent its force.

The crusade had foundered mainly because of poor organisation, division of purpose and lack of co-ordination. Some in the west blamed the perjury of Cardinal Cesarini. The pope blamed the Venetians for not doing their job properly in the straits. He refused to pay the crews of the ships which he had hired because they were all Venetians. They were self-righteously indignant. They pointed out that two of their ships had spent a miserable winter in the area, one at Tenedos and the other at Constantinople, suffering greatly from the cold and from Turkish attacks. The pope should consider it an honour to remunerate the sailors who had endured such hardships.[1] The emperor too complained to the pope about the way in which the Venetians had held back. He had not completely lost heart. In 1445 he sent an ambassador to Venice to announce that he was appealing to Charles VII of France, Philip of Burgundy and the pope. Cardinal Condulmer had expressed his willingness to stay at Constantinople with a few ships in the belief that the Hungarians were planning to try again.[2] The Venetians were rightly sceptical on this point. They could not wait for miracles. Towards the end of 1445 they began to negotiate peace with the Turks. In May they had advised Alvise Loredan to stay in the straits with the papal legate until peace was concluded. He was to consult with the baillie of Constantinople about the method of procedure to ensure freedom for their merchants

---

[1] Jorga, 'Notes', ROL, VIII (1900–1901), 8–9; Thiriet, Sénat, III, no. 2675 (15 February 1445); DR, v, no. 3508. Setton, Papacy and the Levant, II, pp. 91–2.
[2] The emperor's ambassador was the Archbishop Pachomios. Jorga, 'Notes', VIII, 11, 17; Thiriet, Sénat, III, nos. 2682 (3 April 1445), 2702 (19 October 1445); DR, v, no. 3510.

in the Sultan's dominions on the lines laid down in their treaty with
Murad in 1430. If a new truce or treaty was drafted, it would have to
be agreed by the Sultan 'in Europe' and the Sultan 'in Asia'. For after
the battle at Varna, Murad had unexpectedly opted to retire and to hand
over to his son Mehmed II Çelebi. It was a strange and, as it turned
out, a premature decision. Murad was no more than forty years old.
His son was not yet thirteen. To be on the safe side, the Venetians thought
it wise to make peace with both. Despite the pope's displeasure, a treaty
was agreed with the young Mehmed at Adrianople on 23 February 1446.
The text, in Greek, was taken to the Doge in Venice on 9 March. Its
terms were very similar to those of the Venetian–Turkish treaty of 1430.[1]

While others dreamt of holy wars against the infidel the Venetians
concentrated on the realities of trade and profit. When in October 1446
a papal legate asked them for some ships to continue the good fight,
the Senate tartly replied that Venice had done enough for the cause of
the crusade. The pope had still not defrayed the cost of the galleys lent
him in 1444. Venice had made peace with the Sultan. To renounce that
peace would greatly endanger Venetian interests in Romania. Venice was
not averse to fighting for the cause of Christendom. But past experience
and recent events were not very encouraging.[2]

The Venetians tended to regard the activities of the Byzantine Despots
of the Morea, the brothers of the Emperor John VIII, as no less of a
menace to their interests than the Turks. In the autumn of 1446 Murad
had come out of his retirement to lead his own army into Greece to
put an end to the pretensions of the Despot Constantine. He descended
on the Hexamilion wall at the Isthmus of Corinth. The heavy artillery
that he had brought made short work of it. Part of his army then marched
south to Mistra. His purpose was not to conquer the Morea, only to
teach the Greeks and their Despots a punitive lesson. But the province
was ruined and depopulated; 60,000 prisoners were taken; and Constantine and his brother Thomas had to swear oaths as tribute-paying vassals
of the Sultan. The Venetians were not disposed to help those who had
caused them so much trouble. A later Greek account records that the
Doge Francesco Foscari proposed that one of his daughters should marry
the Despot Constantine. There is no hint of any such proposal in the
abundant Venetian archives; and it would surely have been unacceptable
to Venice. For the Despot is said to have welcomed it mainly because

[1] Text in F. Babinger and F. Dölger, 'Mehmed's II frühester Staatsvertrag', OCP, xv (1949),
225–58 (reprinted in Dölger, Byzantinische Diplomatik, Ettal, 1956, pp. 262–91). Sanudo,
Vitae Ducum, col. 1120; Jorga, 'Notes', VIII, 13–14; Thiriet, Sénat, III, no. 2689 (11 May
1445). Babinger, Mehmed the Conqueror, pp. 41–4.
[2] Jorga, 'Notes', VIII, 21; Thiriet, Sénat, III, no. 2734 (25 October 1446).

it would have made him master of the Venetian possessions in the Morea.[1]

Having taught the Greeks a lesson, the Sultan turned to settling his accounts with John Hunyadi, the only leader of the Varna crusade who had eluded him. Hunyadi had made friends with the Albanian warrior Skanderbeg, whose prowess as a resistance leader worried the Turks. Skanderbeg had a generous patron in the King of Aragon, Alfonso V, who had made his capital at Naples in 1443 and inherited the former Angevin Kingdom of Albania. Alfonso dreamt of resurrecting the Latin Empire of Constantinople with himself as emperor; and Pope Nicholas V, who succeeded Eugenius in 1447, seemed eager to promote the dream without encouraging its realisation. In April 1448 he preached another crusade. The Venetians would have nothing to do with it. They distrusted Alfonso of Naples. They regarded Skanderbeg as a nuisance and a threat to their properties in Albania. They spent the best part of a year trying to curb his ardour by diplomacy and even contemplated inviting the Turks to join them in getting rid of him.[2] George Branković of Serbia flatly declined to become involved in another crusade. Nevertheless, Hunyadi marched into Serbia with his own army in September 1448, in the belief that Skanderbeg would catch up with him. He got as far as the plain of Kossovo, the battlefield on which, nearly eighty years before, the Serbians had gone down fighting against the Turks. There Murad and his son Mehmed waited for him. For three days the battle raged, until on 20 October the Hungarians were routed. Skanderbeg never arrived. Hunyadi escaped, as he had done from Varna. But his hopes had been dashed. There would be no more crusades. Defence was now more important than attack. The only active crusader left in the Balkans was Skanderbeg of Albania.[3]

The Venetians disapproved of all schemes that might upset the Turks and so disrupt their trade. Neutrality was more prudent and more profitable than heroism. They had made their peace with Mehmed II and his father. They evidently felt that Constantinople still had some future as a Christian city. In 1446 they sought the co-operation of the Grand Duke, Loukas Notaras, in the construction of a new pier for the convenience of their cargo ships. Even if the city changed hands their commercial quarter would, they hoped, be secured by their treaty with the Turks. Their treaty with Byzantium, however, must not be allowed to lapse. Discussions about renewing it were initiated by their baillie, Dardi Moro,

---

[1] Pseudo-Phrantzes, *Chronicon Maius*, p. 470. Zakythenos, *Despotat grec de Morée*, II, pp. 236–8; Nicol, *Last Centuries of Byzantium*, pp. 381–2; Setton, *Papacy and the Levant*, II, pp. 96–7.

[2] Thiriet, *Sénat*, III, nos. 2759–60, 2779, 2784, 2789.

[3] Babinger, *Mehmed the Conqueror*, pp. 51–6; Setton, *Papacy and the Levant*, II, pp. 98–100.

in 1446.[1] In July 1447 it was redrafted. The formalities were delayed by an outbreak of plague; but on 21 April 1448 the treaty was sealed with his golden bull by the Emperor John VIII in the Blachernai palace. Its term was set at five years. But there would be no more like it. Five years later Constantinople was at the mercy of the Sultan Mehmed. The final siege of the city had begun.[2]

To read the text of the last treaty between Byzantium and Venice is to read what was even then past history. It is as if the world had stopped at the year 1390. Since then the treaty had been confirmed seven times, in 1406, 1412, 1418, 1423, 1431, 1436 and 1442. On each occasion its text was almost word for word that enshrined in the chrysobull issued by the Emperor John VII, in June 1390. John was not otherwise remarkable as an emperor. He reigned for little more than four months. But his lasting memorial was the treaty which he signed with the Doge Antonio Venier; for it became the prototype and the basis of all subsequent agreements between Byzantium and Venice.[3] The only modification was that written in to Manuel II's treaty in 1406; and it referred to the possession of the island of Tenedos. Manuel had made the Venetians concede that this matter should remain 'in the air' or open to further discussion. In 1406 that had been a reasonable proposition. In 1448 it was meaningless. Yet it is slavishly reiterated, as though Venice would be likely to reopen the question or the emperor be able to make use of the island even if he could get it back.

The Byzantine debt to Venice in monetary terms had not changed since 1390, nor indeed since 1343, for all the promises sworn by previous emperors 'on the holy and life-giving Cross and the Gospels'. In 1390 John VII had contracted to pay damages to Venice amounting to 17,163 *hyperpyra*, at the annual rate of 3432 for five years. In 1448 John VIII agreed precisely the same; and he acknowledged that 30,000 ducats with interest were still required to redeem the crown jewels pawned 105 years earlier, as well as the 5000 ducats lent on other security to his grandfather John V in 1352. Both sides must have known that these debts would never now be settled. But they had to be recorded if only to emphasise the more general indebtedness of Byzantium to Venice over so many years. This by itself qualified the Venetian merchants in Constantinople

---

[1] Documents of May and June 1446 in Maltézou, *Thesmos*, pp. 190–4. Jorga, 'Notes', VIII, 20, 23–8; Thiriet, *Sénat*, III, no. 2726 (28 July 1446).

[2] Greek text in *MM*, III, pp. 216–24. Greek and partial Latin texts in Sp. P. Lambros, 'Treaty between John VIII Palaiologos and the Doge of Venice Francesco Foscari' (in Greek), *Neos Hellenomnenon*, XII (1915), 153–70. *DVL*, II, no. 204, p. 372; Jorga, 'Notes', VIII, 43; *DR*, V, no. 3516.

[3] See above pp. 329–30.

for confirmation of their freedom of trade and other privileges. These too had changed little. The items that most annoyed the Venetians were the restrictions which earlier emperors had tried to impose upon them in the matters of the ownership of property and real estate, of the import and sale of corn and wine, and of the number of taverns in the city where they could sell wine duty free. In a rare fit of determination, John V had bullied the Venetians into limiting to fifteen the number of such drinking houses in Constantinople. He had also argued with them over their claim that previous treaties had given them the right to purchase and hold private property in the city without payment of ground rent. It was harder to argue with them over the import of corn and the operation of Venetian corn-markets and granaries, since without such imports the people would starve. Without the revenue accruing from private property and from the sale of imported corn and wine, however, the Byzantine economy would wither and die and the emperors would never be able to pay their overdue debts to Venice. The Venetians were not indulgent creditors. They were always quick to protest at any suggestion that their rights in Constantinople were being violated or diminished; and their lawyers were adept at making favourable interpretations of what those rights were, dating back to their origin in 1277. Occasionally they would allow some compromise for a limited period of years, in recognition of the emperor's financial embarrassment and for the sake of amicable relationships. A number of such concessions, formulated in earlier versions of their treaties with Byzantium, are repeated in the last version signed in 1448.[1] Venice can be charged with having milked Byzantium dry, though with the most lofty and legally unimpeachable motives of self interest. On the other hand, Byzantium could not have survived so long without the support and the forbearance of Venice.

A few months after he had signed the treaty, John VIII died, on 31 October 1448. None of his three wives had borne him a child. His three surviving brothers were Constantine, Demetrios and Thomas. In his will John nominated Constantine as his successor. But they were a quarrelsome family; and it was mainly due to the firmness of their elderly mother Helena, the Serbian widow of Manuel II, that their jealousies were resolved. For in November 1448 Demetrios hurried to Constantinople from his appanage in Thrace, while Thomas was on his way there from the Morea. Demetrios had some following, since he posed as champion of the anti-unionist party. The dowager-empress Helena, however, overruled them all and asserted her right to act as regent until her eldest

[1] Chrysostomides, 'Venetian commercial privileges', 267–329.

surviving son Constantine arrived from Greece. In December she sent George Sphrantzes to the Sultan Murad to ask him to recognise Constantine as the new emperor. Constantine himself wrote to the Venetian Duke of Crete, Antonio Diedo, announcing the fact of his father's death.[1] Two prominent court officials were sent from Constantinople to the Morea carrying the imperial regalia; and on 6 January 1449 Constantine was crowned in the cathedral at Mistra by the local bishop. It was rare but not unprecedented for an emperor to be crowned in a provincial city. The founder of the dynasty of Palaiologos had been crowned at Nicaea, John Cantacuzene at Adrianople. But in all such cases in the past it had been thought proper that a second coronation ceremony be held at Constantinople, performed by the patriarch. Constantine Palaiologos was the exception. The patriarch at the time, Gregory III, was a unionist, shunned by most of his clergy. Constantine knew that to receive his crown from Gregory would add fuel to the existing fires of religious discord in the capital.[2]

He sailed from Greece on a Venetian ship and entered Constantinople on 12 March 1449. Almost at once he sent an ambassador to the Sultan to pay his compliments and to ask for a treaty of peace.[3] His brothers agreed to share the government and defence of the Despotate of the Morea between them and left for Greece in the summer. Within a few months they had quarrelled. Each in his turn called on the Turks for help; and both fell foul of Venice. Their departure left Constantine in sole charge of Constantinople. There too society was divided. The union of Florence was increasingly unpopular. No one had yet dared to celebrate it in St Sophia. Constantine himself upheld it. It was the last frail link with the western world from which rescue might yet come. But he did not thrust it upon his unwilling subjects, among whom he was in other respects admired. The Venetians, for all their professed piety, had never much cared whether the Byzantines were unionists or not. They were, however, deeply offended when Constantine decided to impose a whole new range of taxes on trade and goods imported into Constantinople, including wine and hides brought in from the Turkish capital of Adrianople. In August 1450 they sent Nicolò da Canale to the emperor to protest in the strongest terms about these 'innovations' which, they claimed, violated his brother's treaty with them. If the emperor refused to revoke them, Canale was to instruct the baillie and the merchants living in

---

[1] Pseudo-Phrantzes, *Chronicon Maius*, p. 348; *DR*, v, nos. 3519, 3520.
[2] Sphrantzes, *Chronicon Minus*, pp. 72–4; Pseudo-Phrantzes, *Chronicon Maius*, pp. 348–50. Nicol, *Last Centuries of Byzantium*, pp. 390–1.
[3] Doukas, XXXIII, 1–2: p. 279; Chalkokondyles, II, p. 141; *Chron. Brev.*, II, p. 475. *DR*, v, no. 3524.

Constantinople to pack their bags and leave for some safer place. To rub salt in the wound he was to remind the emperor that he owed Venice 17,163 *hyperpyra* and that none of the promised instalments had been paid. Two weeks later the Senate issued further orders to Canale, suggesting that he might be less peremptory in his demands. But if he could get no satisfaction from the emperor he was to call on the Sultan Murad to discuss the possibility of Venetian merchants using the port of Herakleia, presumably as a substitute for Constantinople. If the emperor would make no compromise, he must be told that the baillie and the Venetian community in his city would transfer their business to Galata and forbid the unloading of merchandise at Constantinople.[1]

In October Constantine wrote to the Doge, Francesco Foscari, to report on his talks with Nicolò da Canale. He assured the Doge that he cherished the friendship between Byzantium and Venice which his forebears had cultivated and that he confirmed every item of the treaty signed by his late brother John, as if he had signed it with his own hand. The taxes which he had imposed in no way contravened that treaty. They were designed to bring revenue to the imperial treasury and would hardly affect Venetian merchants at all. He also promised to do all that he could to make his fractious brothers in the Morea keep the peace with Venice.[2] The Venetians were not convinced. They were still more indignant when, in April 1451, another Byzantine envoy, Andronikos Leondaris, arrived to explain that some of the new taxes would continue to be levied in spite of their protests. Their baillie in Constantinople was ordered to defend the rights of their merchants against this flagrant disregard of past treaty agreements. In July they sent another ambassador, Lorenzo Moro, to make further complaints to the emperor. The petty grievances of the Venetian community in Constantinople seemed to be of more urgent importance than the fate of the city.[3]

In February 1451 the Sultan Murad II died at Adrianople. His son Mehmed II at once succeeded him, as had been arranged. He was only nineteen years of age. Christians in east and west alike were inclined to dismiss him as a feeble young man of no experience. They were slow to appreciate that Mehmed was their most dangerous and formidable enemy since the great Sultan Bajezid. From the moment of his accession Mehmed was obsessed with the conquest of Constantinople. For a while he concealed his obsession behind a smoke-screen of bland goodwill. The Venetians were confident that he would confirm his treaty with them. Lorenzo Moro, their ambassador to Constantinople in July, went

[1] Jorga, 'Notes', VIII, 67–8; Thiriet, *Sénat*, III, nos. 2830–1, 2834 (2–17 August 1450).
[2] *DVL*, II, no. 207, p. 380; Jorga, 'Notes', VIII, 70–1; *DR*, v, no. 3527.
[3] Jorga, 'Notes', VIII, 77–8; Thiriet, *Sénat*, III, nos. 2856, 2863; *DR*, v, no. 3527.

to salute him as Sultan and to offer their condolences on the death of his father.[1] The Byzantines had been even quicker off the mark in paying their respects. Mehmed is reported to have received the emperor's ambassadors with great honour and to have allayed their suspicions by dramatic declarations of good intent. He swore by Allah and the Prophet, by the Koran, by the angels and archangels to live at peace with the city of Constantinople and with its ruler Constantine for the rest of his life, maintaining the friendship that his late father had enjoyed with Constantine's brother John.[2]

No wonder that Mehmed was generally supposed to be immature and ineffectual. The illusion was shared by old enemies of the Ottomans in Asia Minor. In the autumn of 1451 the Emir of the Karamans led a revolt whose aim was to reconstitute the former emirates of Aydin and Menteshe, which the Ottomans had subjected. It was crushed as soon as Mehmed arrived on the scene; and any remaining illusions about his weakness or incompetence should have been shattered. He may have known that Venice had been in touch with the Karaman ruler, though more to dissuade him from invading Cyprus than to support his rebellion.[3] He was infuriated, however, when messengers from the Byzantine Emperor came to his camp at Prousa with certain demands. A grandson of the late Suleiman, called Orchan, was living as a refugee in Constantinople. He was the only other known member of the Ottoman dynasty. Mehmed had agreed to continue to pay an annuity for his subsistence. The emperor now complained to the Sultan's vizir that the annuity was not sufficient; and he hinted that in the person of Orchan he held a pretender to the Ottoman sultanate who might be let loose to substantiate his claim.

Constantine's father Manuel II had tried this form of blackmail on the Turks, not always with success. It was too dangerous a game to play with the Sultan Mehmed. His vizir was appalled by the ineptitude of the emperor's threats. He lost his temper with those who had brought the message. 'You stupid Greeks,' he shouted, 'I have known your cunning ways for long enough. The late Sultan was a tolerant and conscientious friend to you. The present Sultan Mehmed is not of the same mind. If Constantinople eludes his bold and impetuous grasp, it will only be

---

[1] Jorga, 'Notes', VIII, 77–8; Thiriet, *Sénat*, III, nos. 2857, 2862 (22 June and 8 July 1451). The treaty between Venice and the Sultan was confirmed on 10 September 1451. Text in *DVL*, II, no. 209, pp. 382–4; Jorga, 'Notes', VIII, 82–3.

[2] Doukas, xxxiii. 12: p. 289; Chalkokondyles, II, p. 142; Kritoboulos of Imbros, ed. D. R. Reinsch, *Critobuli Imbriotae Historiae*, CFHB, XXII (Berlin–New York, 1983), i. 5.3: p. 18. *DR*, V, no. 3530.

[3] Jorga, 'Notes', VIII, 78–9; Thiriet, *Sénat*, III, nos. 2582, 2864 (March and July 1451).

because God continues to overlook your devious and wicked schemes.'[1]
Mehmed's own reply to the emperor was more terse. He would look
into the matter when he got back to Adrianople. His mood did not
improve when he found that his sea crossing to Gallipoli was blocked
by Christian ships. He and his retinue had to cross the Bosporos near
the castle of Anadolu Hisar which his great-grandfather had built. It
is said that it was now that Mehmed conceived the plan to build another
castle on the European shore as the first step towards the conquest of
Constantinople.[2] Constantine had fatally misjudged his enemy. He had
given the Sultan the excuse to revoke his treaty and to begin the encirclement and siege of the city. The only practical measure that he could
take was to lay in all the provisions that he could find and see to the
repair and defence of the walls.

At the end of the year 1451 he sent a messenger to Venice to report
on the gigantic preparations that the Sultan was making by land and
sea for the siege and conquest of Constantinople. The city would fall
to the Turks unless reinforcements were sent at once. The senators gave
their answer on 14 February 1452. They well understood the emperor's
anxiety. They hoped to be able to help him, but they were heavily committed to war in Italy. They knew that the emperor's envoy was going
to tell the same agonising tale in Florence and then to the pope. The
Venetians would find it easier to join in the defence of Constantinople
if these and other western powers would commit themselves to the cause.
They would, however, authorise the dispatch of the gunpowder and
breastplates which the emperor had asked for.[3] The answer was tiresomely familiar. But now in addition it appeared that the Venetians had
lost interest in the fate of Christian Constantinople. Its conquest was
inevitable. Better look to the future than try to thwart the course of
history. Their merchants were already doing brisk trade in the Turkish
markets of Adrianople. Their Doge was on excellent terms with the Sultan. It would be prudent to take no risks by seeming to interfere with
the Sultan's plans.

Work on the construction of Mehmed's new castle on the Bosporos
began in April 1452. It was finished in August. It came to be known
as Rumeli Hisar, the European fortress across the water from the Asiatic

[1] Doukas, xxxiv. 2: pp. 393–5.
[2] Doukas, xxxiv. 3–4: pp. 295–7. S. Runciman, *The Fall of Constantinople 1453* (Cambridge,
1965), pp. 65–6; Babinger, *Mehmed the Conqueror*, p. 72.
[3] Thiriet, *Sénat*, III, no. 2881 (14 February 1452); *DR*, v, nos. 3539, 3541. R. Guilland,
'Les appels de Constantin XII Paléologue à Rome et à Venise pour sauver Constantinople
(1452–1453)', *Etudes byzantines* (Paris, 1959), pp. 151–75. M.-M. Alexandru-Dersca Bulgaru,
'L'action diplomatique et militaire de Venise pour la défense de Constantinople', *Revue
Roumaine d'Histoire*, XII (1974), 247–67, especially 250–1.

fortress of Anadolu Hisar. The Ottomans called it Boghaz-kesen, the cutter of the channel. The news of its completion and its purpose was known in Venice by the end of August. Constantinople was now completely encircled by land and sea. The first thought in Venice was the protection of the merchant convoys going up and down the Bosporos. The Vice-Captain of the Gulf, Gabriele Trevisan, was sent post-haste by way of Corfu and Modon to Negroponte and the straits. But only if it seemed that Constantinople was directly threatened by the Turks was he authorised to stay, with all or some of his ships, to assist in its defence. Some of the senators moved that the moment had come to abandon Constantinople to its fate.[1] The motion was rejected. But it is instructive that it was proposed. The last Byzantine ambassador to ask for immediate help from Venice got his reply from the Senate on 16 November 1452. He was told that Venice had already made contingency plans but that it would be better if he applied to the pope to organise a united effort of all Christian powers. The senators promised to use their good offices with the pope and the Venetian cardinals and kindly gave him a letter to take to the Curia emphasising the extreme danger facing Constantinople.[2]

Pope Nicholas V was full of sincere sympathy for the Christians of the east. But he was upset that the union of Florence had still not been proclaimed and celebrated in Constantinople. The unionist Patriarch Gregory III had despaired of winning over the opposition and had retired to Rome. In October 1452, however, Isidore of Kiev arrived in Constantinople as the pope's legate. He was a signatory and a staunch supporter of the union and had recently been made a cardinal of the Roman church. He brought a company of 200 archers from Naples and he had with him Leonardo, the Genoese Archbishop of Chios. He was welcomed by the emperor and even by some of the people, who fondly supposed that the 200 men he had brought were the advance guard of a larger army that was coming from Italy. Isidore's mission, however, was religious and not military. He had come to save the souls of the Byzantines by proclaiming the union of the churches in their midst. On 12 December a concelebration of the Catholic and Orthodox liturgies was conducted in St Sophia. The emperor and his court were present and the decree of union as recited at Florence was read out. To many of the Orthodox clergy and people it was the ultimate betrayal. The Latins had won the last round in the battle of wits that had begun with the Fourth Crusade. God would now assuredly abandon Constantinople to the infidel. The

---

[1] Thiriet, *Sénat*, III, no. 2896 (30 August 1452).

[2] Thiriet, *Sénat*, III, no. 2905 (16 November 1452); *DR*, v, no. 3548. Guilland, 'Les appels', pp. 169–70; Alexandru-Dersca Bulgaru, 'L'action diplomatique', 252–3.

scholar George Scholarios, now the monk Gennadios, was passionate in his denunciation. He pinned a declaration to the door of his monastic cell testifying that he would sooner die than abjure the Orthodox faith which was his heritage.[1]

In June 1452 some Greek peasants dared to protest at the ruination of their land by the construction work at Rumeli Hisar. They were massacred by the Turks. The incident led the emperor formally to declare war on the Sultan. He closed the gates of his city and arrested all Turks inside it. It was a futile gesture and he released them after three days.[2] When his fortress was finished and its guns were in position, Mehmed issued a proclamation that every ship of whatever origin passing up or down the Bosporos must stop at that point, pay a toll and ask permission to proceed. Any that refused to obey would be sunk by gunfire from the huge cannons sited on the walls of the castle. On 10 November two Venetian ships sailed down from Caffa and the Black Sea, one commanded by Girolamo Morosini. They may have thought that they were protected by treaty and sailed on. The guns were turned on them but they got through safely to the Golden Horn. Two weeks later a Venetian merchantman carrying barley from the Black Sea disregarded a Turkish command to heave to. The guns from Rumeli Hisar struck it amidships. Its captain, Antonio Rizzo, and thirty of his sailors got to the shore on a raft and were arrested. Chained together they were led before the Sultan. He decreed that they should be decapitated, though one lucky and presumably handsome young sailor was taken into the seraglio as a slave. Rizzo was impaled and his body lay unburied by the roadside. The Venetian baillie in Constantinople, Girolamo Minotto, had sent Fabruzzi Corner to plead with the Sultan, but to no avail. Corner returned with the two light galleys of Gabriele Trevisan, which were escorting three cargo ships on their way south from Tana, under the command of Alvise Diedo. Venice too was now technically at war with the Turks.[3]

The tragic and dramatic story of the Ottoman siege, capture and sack of Constantinople has been often and eloquently told.[4] This is not the place to tell it yet again in all its detail and complexity. But it may

---

[1] Doukas, xxxvi. 1–6: pp. 315–19. Gill, *Council of Florence*, pp. 383–7; Runciman, *Fall of Constantinople*, pp. 69–72.

[2] Doukas, xxxiv. 11: pp. 305–6.

[3] Doukas, xxxiv. 12; xxxv. 2: pp. 307, 309. (Doukas was at the Sultan's camp at Didymoteichon at the time and witnessed the executions.) Nicolò Barbaro, *Giornale dell'assedio di Costantinopoli 1453*, ed. E. Cornet (Vienna, 1856), p. 2. Runciman, *Fall of Constantinople*, pp. 66–7.

[4] See, most notably, E. Pears, *The Destruction of the Greek Empire and the Story of the Capture of Constantinople by the Turks* (London, 1903); Runciman, *Fall of Constantinople*; Setton, *Papacy and the Levant*, II, pp. 108–37.

be of interest to consider it as the last act in the long history of relations between Byzantium and Venice. One of the fullest eye-witness accounts was written by a Venetian, Nicolò Barbaro. He had been travelling as a ship's surgeon and he kept a day-to-day diary of the siege, which he wrote up when he got back to Venice in July 1453.[1] Barbaro's clear and lively narrative, combined with other Italian and Greek sources, makes it possible to assess what part the Venetians played in the final defence of Constantinople against the Turks. Some were there by chance or by accident, like Barbaro himself. Gabriele Trevisan, in command of two light galleys, and Giacomo Coco, captain of a ship which managed to run the gauntlet and get through from Trebizond in December 1452, were on their way west. Both were persuaded to stay and fight. Trevisan was under orders to return to Venice within ten days of the arrival of the ship from Trebizond. It was the baillie, Girolamo Minotto, who prevailed upon him to disobey his orders. Minotto called a meeting of his council in December. The Emperor Constantine and Cardinal Isidore were present; and the majority of the leading Venetians in Constantinople voted to stay and share in the defence of the city. They agreed that no Venetian ships should leave the harbour without the baillie's permission, on pain of a fine of 3000 ducats.[2]

There were five galleys at anchor in the Golden Horn, three commanded by Alvise Diedo and two by Gabriele Trevisan. Six other Venetian vessels and three from Crete were armed as warships. There were some defectors. On 26 February Pietro Davanzano and his ship slipped out of the harbour by night, followed by six cargo ships from Crete laden with cloth. About 700 people were aboard them. Blessed by a following wind they were blown past Gallipoli to Tenedos without being sighted by the Turks. Davanzano got safely home and the others to Crete. Those that had agreed to stay behind sent a messenger to Venice bearing letters from the baillie, from Diedo and from Trevisan, to be sure that their government knew what they were doing. Separate dispatches were also sent by land and by way of Chios. In January the baillie and a deputation of captains and merchants asked the emperor if they might load their wares and property on to their ships in the harbour rather than leaving them in warehouses in the city. The emperor was suspicious. He feared that once they had loaded their ships they

[1] See above, p. 395 n. 3. Extracts from the journal of Nicolò Barbaro, with a valuable commentary, are also in A. Pertusi, *La caduta di Costantinopoli*, 1: *Le testimonianze dei contemporanei*, Fondazione Lorenzo Valla (Verona, 1976), pp. 5–38, 345–71. There is an English translation by J. R. Jones, *Nicolò Barbaro, Diary of the Siege of Constantinople* (New York, 1969).
[2] Barbaro, ed. Cornet, pp. 5–11. Guilland, 'Les appels', pp. 170–1; Alexandru-Dersca Bulgaru, 'L'action diplomatique', 254–5. Runciman, *Fall of Constantinople*, pp. 84–5, gives the total number of warships in the harbour as 26.

would sail off by night and leave him stranded. He gave his consent only after Trevisan had sworn an oath that they would not sail away without first getting his permission.[1]

The reports coming in from Constantinople caused a flurry of activity in Venice. On 19 February the senators decided at once to arm two transport ships, each to carry 400 soldiers, to be ready to sail on 8 April. They would be commanded by a captain who would also be responsible for fifteen galleys which were being prepared. The expense of this armada would be met by taxes levied on merchants who had investments in Romania and the Black Sea, to a total of 16,000 ducats. Meanwhile, the government of Crete was to send two warships to Negroponte to be under the orders of Zaccaria Grioni who, having escaped from Constantinople, would have the latest news from there. The Senate also resolved to send an ambassador to the Sultan Mehmed to sound his intentions. These measures were taken 'for the good of Christendom, for the honour of Venice and for the benefit of Venetian merchants, lest the city of Constantinople, which could be regarded as under the dominion of Venice, should fall into the hands of the infidel'. At the same time the Doge sent letters to the pope, to the Western Emperor, to Alfonso of Aragon and to Ladislas of Hungary to urge them to take prompt action. Otherwise Constantinople would be lost.[2]

For once the Venetians seemed to be taking the initiative instead of waiting for the rest of Christendom to show the way. But their preparations were painfully slow. On 2 March the senators decided that it would be better to entrust command of the fifteen galleys still being equipped to a Captain-General of the Sea, yet to be appointed. A week later they declared that the galleys must be fit to sail within a few days. Their Captain-General was to be Giacomo Loredan who was on his way back from Constantinople. He was to wait at Modon with all his fleet. The galleys from Venice would set out under the command of Alvise Longo. But still there were delays. It was not until 13 April that Longo was commissioned to sail with all possible speed for Tenedos with only one ship. He was to wait there until 20 May when, it was hoped, Giacomo Loredan and the ships from Crete would have joined him. From Tenedos he could observe the movements of the Turkish fleet. After 20 May he could sail on to Constantinople if he thought the way was safe. Above all, he must avoid a confrontation with the Turks in the straits. At Constantinople he would serve in the defence of the city under the orders of the baillie and the captain of the fleet

---

[1] Barbaro, pp. 11–12. The messenger sent to Venice was Zuan Diusnaigi.
[2] Barbaro, p. 82. Jorga, 'Notes', VIII, 94–5; Thiriet, *Sénat*, III, nos. 2908–11. Sanudo, *Vitae Ducum*, col. 1148, puts the number of galleys at ten, not fifteen.

of Romania until such time as Loredan arrived to take overall command. Longo was due to sail on 17 April. He left Venice two days late.[1]

The departure of the fifteen ships was still further delayed. Many of the merchants who were supposed to be contributing to their cost had failed to subscribe. They had to be threatened with fines and penalties.[2] Finally, on 7 May, the Senate commissioned Giacomo Loredan to set out at once for Corfu with only five ships. At Corfu he would pick up the island's warship and proceed to Modon, where he would be joined by two galleys from Crete, and then to Negroponte, where he would find provisions. At Tenedos he would pick up one more ship and then sail on to Constantinople. He was specifically instructed not to give offence to the Turks or attack their property in the straits except in self-defence or under provocation. In Constantinople he would offer his services to the emperor, impressing upon him the great sacrifice that Venice was making in nobly and generously neglecting its interests in Italy to come to his aid. Loredan would then see to it that the warships of Romania, which had been stationed at Constantinople for a long time, were led to safer waters and that Gabriele Trevisan was relieved. If he found that the emperor had come to terms with the Sultan he should go back to Corfu, leaving one vessel to patrol the sea between Modon and Cape Malea.[3]

On 8 May the ambassador to the Sultan, Bartolomeo Marcello, was given his orders. He was to sail with Loredan either to Constantinople or, if that proved to be impossible, to a port in Greece. He was to emphasise the peaceful intentions of the Venetians. The warships which they had sent to Constantinople were there simply to protect their commerce and the interests of Venice, 'to whom, it could be said, the city belonged through the rights and privileges which Venetians had always enjoyed in it, flying their own flag and living under the jurisdiction of their own baillies and rectors, who imposed their own taxes in the name of the Republic'. Marcello should, with the help of Loredan and the baillie Girolamo Minotto, try to mediate between the emperor and the Sultan. But he should make no effort to deflect the Sultan from his purpose if his mind was set on war.[4] It was a hopeless mission. Mehmed's mind was firmly set on the conquest of Constantinople. He

[1] Thiriet, Sénat, III, nos. 2912, 2914, 2918–19; Jorga, 'Notes', VIII, 95–6. Alexandru-Dersca Bulgaru, 'L'action diplomatique', 256–7.

[2] Thiriet, Sénat, III, no. 2920.

[3] Thiriet, Sénat, III, no. 2922 (7 May); Jorga, 'Notes', VIII, 96–8. Loredan was instructed not to attack the Catalans, since Venice was at peace with the King of Aragon; though he should seek redress for the damage done by their pirates.

[4] Thiriet, Sénat, III, no. 2923; Jorga, 'Notes', VIII, 98–9. Alexandru-Dersca Bulgaru, 'L'action diplomatique', 258–60.

would rather take it by consent than by rape. He had no wish to see it destroyed by his own guns and pillaged by his own soldiers. In the middle of May, when the siege of the city had been going on for some weeks, he made an offer to the Emperor Constantine. The Greeks could either live under Turkish rule on payment of an annual tribute, or they could evacuate the city and find somewhere else to live. The emperor replied that the Sultan could have anything he wanted except for the city of Constantinople. He and his people would sooner die than surrender that. It was the last communication between a Byzantine Emperor and an Ottoman Sultan.[1]

A few weeks earlier, in April, the pope announced his growing concern. He had already sent three Genoese ships loaded with arms and provisions to Constantinople. He would now pay for five galleys to go to its defence. They would be armed at Venice. The Venetians responded with joy to this tardy gesture. It gave them occasion to send a testy reminder to the pope that he had never honoured his agreement to pay the crews of the ships which they had provided for him in 1444. If, however, a papal fleet was now to set out, it must leave without delay, not only to reinforce the defences but above all to take food to the starving inhabitants of Constantinople. It must at all events get there before the end of May. Otherwise it would run into the seasonal northerly winds blowing down the Hellespont and get no further. The Genoese ships that the pope had sent were indeed storm-bound at Chios for some weeks. But it was not only the elements that delayed the departure of the pope's fleet from Venice until it was too late. It was the unseemly haggling about the financial arrangements for arming and manning them. The Venetian fleet too, hurriedly put together, failed to reach its destination in time to save the city.[2]

If Venice earned any glory in the heroic defence of Constantinople against the Turks in 1453 it was through the action of its citizens and sailors who were there. The Republic may have lost heart in the cause. Its residents in the city had all their livelihood to lose. The Genoese at Galata lived behind their own walls. They could opt for neutrality rather than heroism. The Venetians were in the thick of it and had no option. Under the inspired leadership of their baillie, Girolamo Minotto, they fought with desperation but with courage; and they had the full support of the Venetian ships' captains who were present. Loredan had orders from his government to effect the escape from the Golden Horn

[1] Doukas, xxix. 1: p. 351; Kritoboulos, i. 26: pp. 41–2. DR, v, nos. 3553–4. Babinger, Mehmed the Conqueror, p. 90.
[2] Thiriet, Sénat, III, no. 2917 (10 April). Guilland, 'Les appels', pp. 165–6, 173–5; Alexandru-Dersca Bulgaru, 'L'action diplomatique', 260.

of the warships that had been there for so long and to see that Gabriele Trevisan was relieved and went back with his galley to Negroponte. The orders were never obeyed since Loredan arrived too late. But they indicate the lack of vital communication between Venice and the Venetians in Constantinople. For Trevisan and his colleagues had already agreed to take their orders from the baillie and to stay where they were. A few days after Loredan had left, on 11 May, news brought from Modon about events at Constantinople created panic in the Senate. Three more warships must be sent at once, one from Negroponte, one from Corfu and one from Crete, to join up with Loredan's fleet at Tenedos.[1] There were undoubtedly problems of communication between Constantinople and Venice. It took at least a month for messages to get from one to the other by way of Negroponte and Corfu. But Venice had been alerted to the imminent threat from the Turks many months earlier. The Venetians who really saved the honour of the Republic when the moment came were not those of the motherland but those on the spot at Constantinople.

The Emperor Constantine had great faith in them. When he asked Trevisan to advertise the Venetian commitment by allowing his sailors, about 1000 in number, to parade along the walls in sight of the Turks, they gladly agreed.[2] When they offered to stand guard at the four gates in the land walls, the emperor remarked that Constantinople had come to belong more to the Venetians than to the Greeks and that he would trust them with the keys of the gates. One was allotted to Catarino Contarini; the second to Fabruzzi Corner; the third to Nicolò Mocenigo; the fourth, that of the Blachernai Palace, to Dolfin Dolfin. The defence of the palace itself was entrusted to the baillie, Girolamo Minotto, with a number of patrician merchants. Sections of the land walls were also defended by Venetians. Filippo Contarini held the stretch between the Pegai Gate and the Golden Gate. Jacopo Contarini was stationed at Stoudion towards the Sea of Marmora. The shores of the Golden Horn were defended by Venetian and Genoese sailors commanded by Gabriele Trevisan; and Alvise Diedo was put in command of all the ships in the harbour. The entrance to the harbour was guarded by nine or ten ships, three of them from Crete under Zuan Venier. On 2 April the emperor had ordered that the chain or boom be placed in position across the harbour entrance, from Constantinople to Galata. Safe behind it lay seventeen square-rigged ships, the three galleys from Tana, the two light galleys from Venice and five unarmed galleys of the emperor's fleet. The Vene-

---

[1] Thiriet, *Sénat*, III, no. 2924; Jorga, 'Notes', VIII, 99.
[2] Barbaro, pp. 19–20.

tians were confident that they could hold the harbour against the enemy.[1]

There were men from Genoa too who volunteered to join in the defence. The most celebrated and the most heroic was Giovanni Giustiniani Longo, a soldier of fortune, who arrived in January bringing 700 troops recruited from Genoa, Chios and Rhodes. Giustiniani was renowned for his skill in siege warfare and the emperor was glad to give him general command of the defence of the land walls. The Genoese living in Galata were in a difficult position. They had the future of their colony to think of; and it went against their grain to collaborate with the Venetians. But many of them came over in secret to swell the Christian ranks and some of their ships fought alongside those of Venice. Nicolò Barbaro, the diarist of the siege, had little time for them. In his view even the Greeks, who fought with singular bravery, were cowards.[2]

The Ottoman army began to assemble on 5 April. The Sultan Mehmed had taken the field in person with 160,000 men and encamped within sight of the land walls. The confidence that the Venetians felt was strengthened when, on 12 April, the Sultan's fleet tried and failed to force an entry into the Golden Horn. Ten days later, however, the Turks contrived to haul some of their smaller ships overland and launch them into the harbour of Galata. This remarkable operation is described in detail by the Greek as well as the Italian sources. It could hardly have succeeded without the goodwill or at least the connivance of the Genoese at Galata. On the morning of 23 April the Byzantines and the Venetians were horrified to see no less than seventy-two small Turkish vessels in the Golden Horn, well behind the chain that blocked its entrance. The chain still had its uses, for the bigger Turkish warships were on the other side of it, anchored at the harbour known as the Diplokionion or Double Columns. The Venetians should not have been too surprised. They had employed the same tactics at one stage in the course of their war in northern Italy. They had always underestimated the maritime expertise and the initiative of the Turks.[3]

Their first reaction was to send fireships among the intruders. It was a rash decision; and Barbaro is not alone in recording that their plan was betrayed to the Sultan by a Genoese spy. On 28 April, two hours before dawn, a raiding party set out, enthusiastically led by Giacomo

[1] Barbaro, pp. 15–16, 20; Doukas, xxxviii. 8: p. 337; Pseudo-Phrantzes, *Chronicon Maius*, pp. 382–4; Kritoboulos, i. 24: p. 40. Alexandru-Dersca Bulgaru, 'L'action diplomatique', 261. 'Teodoro Caristo', whom some have taken to be a Venetian, was in fact Theodore Karystenos, Byzantine ambassador to Venice in 1443. He took charge of the section between the Caligaria Gate and the Theodosian wall. Pseudo-Phrantzes, *Chronicon Maius*, p. 398.
[2] Runciman, *Fall of Constantinople*, pp. 83–4.
[3] Runciman, *Fall of Constantinople*, pp. 100–11.

Coco, master of the galley of Trebizond. There were two large transport
ships, one Venetian and one Genoese, packed with sacks of cotton and
wool to resist gunfire. They were accompanied by the galleys of Gabriele
Trevisan and Zaccaria Grioni, with three smaller ships, one commanded
by Coco. It was he who spoilt the plan by impetuously sailing ahead
to strike the first blow at the enemy. The Turks opened fire on his
ship and it was sunk with all hands. Trevisan's galley was also hit but
managed to limp back to the shore half submerged. A violent battle
then took place between the remaining Venetian ships and the Turks.
After an hour and a half both sides abandoned the struggle. But it was
without doubt a Turkish victory and there were great celebrations in
the Sultan's camp. On the following day the Venetians mourned the
death of the brave Giacomo Coco and his crew and appointed Dolfin
Dolfin in his place as captain of the galley of Trebizond.[1]

The bombardment of the city walls had by then been almost continuous
for nearly four weeks. The inhabitants were suffering from nervous
exhaustion and starvation. The tension provoked quarrels between the
Venetians and the Genoese, who blamed the failure of the raid on 28
April on the impetuosity of Giacomo Coco and Venetian incompetence.
The emperor had to intervene to prevent fighting among those who were
supposed to be united in war against the Turks.[2] Still there was no
sign of the promised reinforcements and relief coming from Italy. On
3 May, at the emperor's suggestion, a small boat was sent out to Negroponte to see if Giacomo Loredan and his armada were on their way.
The twelve volunteers aboard were dressed as Turks and flew the Turkish
ensign. They got safely through into the open sea; but nowhere could
they find any trace of Loredan. Some of them then voted to choose
freedom and not go back to the doomed city of Constantinople. But
the more honourable of them felt it was their duty to obey the emperor's
orders; and they returned to report that they had sighted no Venetian
fleet. At this news the emperor broke down and wept. The whole of
Christendom, it seemed, had proved unwilling to come to his help against
its enemy, the infidel.[3]

On 8 May an incident occurred which showed the desperate mood
of some of those trapped in the Golden Horn. The baillie's council decreed
that the three galleys from Tana should be unloaded and scuppered.
Their crews angrily refused to allow their cargoes to be touched. 'Where
our property is,' they cried, 'there are our homes too.' They were afraid

[1] Barbaro, pp. 28–33; Doukas, xxxviii. 19: p. 347, credits Giustiniani Longo with the plan
of setting fire to the Turkish ships.
[2] Pseudo-Phrantzes, *Chronicon Maius*, p. 402.   [3] Barbaro, pp. 34–5.

that they would have no means of escape if their ships were emptied and sunk; and they would sooner die aboard them than be slaughtered or enslaved on land. Their protests were so effective that the authorities had to yield and they stayed where they were by the quay at Galata. Two days later Alvise Diedo, captain of the Tana galleys, was given supreme command of all ships of whatever origin lying in the harbour; and Gabriele Trevisan took forty of his men to help guard the city walls by land, leaving his two galleys, unarmed, at Diedo's disposition. He stayed at the walls until the end.[1]

The weight of the Turkish attack was directed against the land walls, where the Venetians tirelessly assisted in repairing and filling in the breaches opened by the Sultan's guns. There were skirmishes by sea but no decisive engagements, though the Venetians moved their ships, except for those guarding the boom, to the shelter of the small harbour of Neorion under the lee of the acropolis. The Turkish battleships still lay at anchor off the Double Columns. On 21 May, however, they made another attempt to force their way in to the Golden Horn. The ten ships guarding the entrance were in battle order and well armed and the rest of the ships were seen to be ready to fight. When the alarm was sounded in the city, the Turks realised that they had failed to take the defenders by surprise. They turned and rowed back to their station at the Double Columns. Two days later, just before daybreak, a small boat flying the Turkish flag sailed up the Sea of Marmora. It contained the brave souls who had been sent out to look for the reinforcements from Venice. The Turks knew that it was not one of theirs and tried to apprehend it. But when they saw the boom being opened to let it into the harbour they retreated to their anchorage. They had been alarmed that it might be the vanguard of the expected fleet from Venice.[2]

On 28 May the word went round that the Sultan was planning his final assault for the following day. Barbaro records with pride how the baillie ordered that every man who called himself a Venetian should make for the land walls, 'for the love of God and for the sake of the city and the honour of the Christian faith. Everyone should be of good heart and ready to die at his post.'[3] The attack began three hours before dawn on Tuesday 29 May. As wave upon wave of Turks hurled themselves against the walls, Greeks and Venetians fought side by side. The Genoese soldier, Giustiniani, had command of the weakest section of the land walls and for a long time held his ground. The Sultan's plan was to give the Christians no respite. Each new wave of his soldiers was fresh

---

[1] Barbaro, pp. 37–8.   [2] Barbaro, pp. 44–7. Runciman, *Fall of Constantinople*, p. 117.
[3] Barbaro, p. 50.

and eager. He kept his janissaries till the last. By the time they came rushing forward yelling their battle cry, the defenders had been fighting without rest for more than six hours. Just before daybreak Giustiniani was wounded in the chest and forced to retire. His troops at once lost heart and the janissaries saw their chance. Some of them beat their way through to the inner wall and scaled it. But another company of Turks had already broken in to the city through a little gate, climbed a tower and planted the Ottoman standard. The janissaries recognised the signal and pressed their attack, some through the gaps in the wall, others through the open gate. The defenders were surrounded with no way of escape. The baillie Minotto and his son Giorgio, Giovanni Loredan and others of the Venetian community had defended their allotted positions with fierce energy. But they were exhausted and finally overwhelmed. At the last the Byzantine Empire was reduced to a muddy patch of land by the gate of St Romanos where a handful of brave men fought hand to hand with the Turks. It was there that the Emperor Constantine was last seen. He had thrown away his regalia. He was killed fighting as a common soldier.[1] The last to go on fighting were the Cretan sailors stationed in a tower by the gate called Horaia in what had once been the Venetian quarter. The Sultan was so impressed by their determination that he guaranteed them their liberty.[2]

When all hope was lost, the surviving Venetians looked for means of escaping. The merchants in the city had taken refuge from the slaughter that followed its capture by hiding in cellars and basements. Sooner or later they were all found and rounded up by the Turks to be sold as slaves. The ships and their crews in the harbour were more fortunate. During the attack the seventy-odd Turkish boats there had sailed over from the Galata side to attack the sea walls. But when the sailors saw their Sultan's standard raised in the city they quickly leapt ashore to join in the plunder. The main Turkish fleet, finding the boom across the harbour well guarded, had sailed on round the point to fight on the side of the Sea of Marmora. At the cry of victory from the city all their sailors too disembarked to get their share of booty. The way was thus open for the Venetians and any other Christian refugees to escape by sea. Gabriele Trevisan had been captured fighting at the walls. Alvise Diedo, as commander of the fleet, took responsibility for the escape. He sailed over to Galata to consult the Genoese authorities. They had tried to remain neutral so far as was possible. But they would take no chances with the conquering Sultan after Constantinople had fallen. They closed the gates of Galata. Diedo was a prisoner. With him was

---

[1] Runciman, *Fall of Constantinople*, pp. 133–44.
[2] Pseudo-Phrantzes, *Chronicon Maius*, p. 430.

Nicolò Barbaro, who recorded these events. The Genoese sailors anchored off Galata, however, meant to get away while they could and they wanted to go in convoy with the Venetians. Thanks to their insistence Diedo and Barbaro were allowed to return to their ship.[1]

The boom across the harbour entrance was still in place. Two brave sailors from Diedo's crew climbed down and hacked it with axes until it broke. The exodus then began with Diedo leading the way. Behind him came most of the Venetian warships. Girolamo Morosini captained his own. The galley from Trebizond under Dolfin Dolfin had great trouble getting under way. Of her crew, 164 members had been killed or lost and there were hardly enough sailors to raise her sails. The galley of Trevisan left without him, for he was a prisoner. Seven or eight Genoese ships left later in the day, one of them carrying the wounded Giustiniani; and a small number of Cretan vessels sailed with the Venetians. That of Zaccaria Grioni was taken by the Turks; but those of Zuan Venier, Pietro Sgouros, Antonio Yalinas (or Hyalinos) and Antonio Philomati got through. Their decks were crowded with refugees, many of whom had swum out from the shore. A following wind blew them down the Sea of Marmora and the Hellespont and out into the freedom of the open sea. The ships that were left behind in the Golden Horn were at the mercy of the Turkish fleet once the boom had been broken. All the Venetian merchantmen were captured, as well as four or five of the emperor's galleys and two or three Genoese ships. They were so packed with refugees that they would have sunk if they had put to sea. The Cretan ships were the first to reach their destination, on 9 June 1453, and so the first to announce to a wider world the dreadful news that Constantinople had fallen. It was known in Venice by the end of the month. It was, as Sanudo said, 'the worst news for all of Christendom'.[2]

When the Venetians were turned out of Constantinople in 1261 some of them lined the decks of their ships as they left, shouting farewell to the land that they had come to call their own. In 1453 it was another story. The Greeks in 1261 had not ruthlessly slaughtered those Venetians who remained in the city. The Turks showed no mercy. Girolamo Minotto, the baillie, was executed along with his son and seven Venetian noblemen. Twenty-nine others were taken prisoner, among them Gabriele Trevisan, Zaccaria Grioni and Catarino Contarini. Another 600 Venetian soldiers and sailors were rounded up; some were put to death,

[1] Barbaro, pp. 57–8.
[2] Sanudo, *Vitae Ducum*, col. 1151: 'e fu pessima nuova a tutta la Cristianità'. Barbaro, pp. 58–9. R. Browning, 'A note on the capture of Constantinople in 1453', *B*, XXII (1952), 379–86; M. Manoussakas, 'Les derniers défenseurs crétois de Constantinople d'après les documents vénitiens', *Akten des XI. Internationalen Byzantinisten-Kongresses, München 1958* (Munich, 1960), pp. 331–40.

others sold as slaves. All the twenty-nine noblemen were ransomed within
the year, having purchased their freedom for anything between 800 to
2000 ducats each. At the end of his diary, Nicolò Barbaro proudly presents roll-calls of the quick and the dead among his compatriots. Marino
Sanudo records another list of names.[1] The Senate voted to provide
pensions for the bereaved families of those who had been killed and
to pay damages to all those who had suffered loss of property. The total
losses amounted to 200,000 ducats. Gabriele Trevisan, once he had been
ransomed, was rewarded for his outstanding bravery with an honorarium
of 350 ducats. The last Christian Emperor of Constantinople died at
the walls of his city still owing 17,163 *hyperpyra* to Venice.[2]

The Venetians looked after their own. But there was little that they
could do for the Greeks. The question remains whether they could have
done more to prevent the end of the world for Byzantium. The answer
must be yes. But they left it too late. The Venetian galleys which the
pope had financed failed to get to Constantinople in time. They were
waiting at Chios for the wind to change when some of the Genoese
ships that had escaped sailed in to tell them that it was all over. Loredan
with his long-expected reinforcements from Venice never got anywhere
near the city. He put into Negroponte to await further orders. The great
historian of Venice, H. Kretschmayr, concludes that it was the tragedy,
though not the fault, of Venice to have been unable to avert the fall
of Constantinople.[3] The Venetians would have agreed. This is the verdict
of a historian who was partial to Venice. A historian whose sympathies
are with the Byzantines will take a different view. He will recall how
the Venetians exploited the wealth and sapped the strength of Byzantium
over many centuries. Above all, he will bear in mind the Fourth Crusade
and the greed of Venice in it. He will listen to the voices, no less patriotic
than those of the Venetians, of the Byzantine historians who had to
live with these selfish and arrogant foreigners in Constantinople and in
the Romania which they called their own. And he may feel that they
tell the truth. Modern western historians think of the Venetians as
admirable because of the beauty of their city. They find it harder
to admire or appreciate the Byzantines. The beauty of their city was
wrecked by the conquering Turks. The Byzantines were foreigners. The

[1] Barbaro, pp. 59–65. On the fate of the baillie Minotto and his son, on which Barbaro and
the other sources give contradictory information, see Barbaro, ed. Pertusi, *La caduta*, I,
p. 369, n. 182. The Venetian Senate reported that 40 nobles and more than 500 citizens
perished in the siege. Thiriet, *Sénat*, III, no. 2936. Sanudo, *Vitae Ducum*, col. 1150, gives
the number of nobles as 47.
[2] Cretan losses amounted to 100,000 ducats. Special arrangements were made to provide for
the children of Giacomo Cocco. Barbaro, pp. 59, 65–6. Jorga, 'Notes', VIII, 101–3.
[3] Kretschmayr, II, p. 363.

Venetians thought so too. One forgets that so much of the beauty of Venice was fashioned at the expense of Byzantium. There is little that is lovely about the remaining monuments of the commercial empire which they held for so long in Romania and the Levant. Most of them are ruins of grim fortresses, fortified harbours and bastilles emblazoned with the Lion of St Mark, which have no aesthetic beauty save that imparted to all the ruins in Greece by the dawn or the sunset.

22

LEGACIES AND DEBTS

⊰∞————————————————————∞⊱

THE Venetians, who had made most out of the Fourth Crusade and the Latin conquest of Byzantium in 1204, and the Genoese, who had made most out of the empire's restoration in 1261, were the last of the Christians to abandon their possessions in the ruin of that empire. The Genoese in Galata made their own terms with the Turks, opening the gates to the Sultan's troops as soon as Constantinople had fallen and sending ambassadors to Mehmed II to congratulate him on his great victory. On 1 June 1453 the Sultan sent them their orders. They must demolish their walls and hand over their weapons. Galata would not be destroyed. Its Genoese merchants could trade safely and freely within the Ottoman Empire. But a Turkish governor would be installed and every male inhabitant must pay a poll tax. The Genoese had expected better things as a reward for their neutrality. They found it impossible to maintain their trade in the Black Sea now that the Turks controlled Constantinople and the Bosporos. For a time the Bank of St George in Genoa assumed the administration of the trading stations in the Crimea. But the risks were too great and the tolls that the Turks demanded were too high. Before the end of the fifteenth century all Genoese trade in the Black Sea, at Caffa, Tana and Trebizond, had ceased. Some of the other Genoese colonies in the Byzantine world, such as Lesbos and Chios, survived a while longer by paying tribute to the Sultan. No more is heard of the island of Tenedos over which so much blood had been spilt.[1]

The Venetians had sunk more of their capital in the Byzantine Empire. They did not lose heart quite so easily as the Genoese. They were even ready to pick up some of the pieces abandoned by other colonists, notably the island of Cyprus which they acquired in 1489. They too had at first hoped to reach an understanding with the Turks and the Sultan seemed to be amenable so long as it suited his plans. The Venetians were old hands at negotiating with the infidel while discussing plans for crusades

[1] Runciman, *Fall of Constantinople*, pp. 162–3; Babinger, *Mehmed the Conqueror*, pp. 119–20, 343–6.

408

against him; and plans for crusades were not lacking in the west after 1453. Their object, too late in the day, was the recovery of Constantinople rather than the liberation of Jerusalem; though, as usual, the Venetians refused to commit themselves unless they were certain of the whole-hearted commitment of the rest of Christendom. The rest of Christendom was not interested. Nor were the Turks much interested in promoting Venetian trade. They preferred conquest to commerce. One by one the Venetian colonies in Romania were absorbed into the Ottoman Empire, often after bitter assaults and sieges and epic battles. Negroponte fell in 1470, Modon and Coron in 1500; and with the two eyes of the Republic blinded, Venetian ships had to grope their way round to the few Greek ports and islands that they still owned. Monemvasia was lost in 1540. The Duchy of Naxos, which Marco Sanudo had created out of the Fourth Crusade, had been usurped from his descendants in 1383 by the Crispi family from Verona. They lived as vassals first of Venice and then of the Turks until the Sultan Selim II appropriated Naxos and its neighbour-ing islands in 1566. The last to go was the Venetian Duchy of Crete in 1669, after a siege lasting for twenty-two years. The dissolution of the Venetian empire was a long process. For a moment it seemed to be halted by the famous battle at Lepanto in 1571. But in the same year Cyprus was lost to the Turks. All that then remained was the island of Corfu, which Venice had acquired as late as 1386. Corfu was Venetian until the end of the Republic in 1797, when it passed not to the Turks but to the French. It was the only Greek island which Venice had saved from absorption into the Ottoman Empire.[1]

The remnants of the Byzantine Empire went down more quickly after 1453. The Greek Despots of the Morea and the Italian Despots of Epiros brought destruction upon themselves by calling on the Turks to help them in their petty struggles for power. Mistra, the capital of the Morea, which might well have served as a rallying-point and seat of a Byzantine government in exile, surrendered to the Turks on 29 May 1460, seven years to the day after the fall of Constantinople. The cities of Epiros had by then already succumbed. Ioannina capitulated in 1430, Arta in 1449. The offshore Ionian islands sought the protection of Venice, but they too were taken by the Turks in 1479. The independent Byzantine Empire of Trebizond on the Black Sea, where the Venetians had done much trade, surrendered to the Sultan Mehmed in 1461. The Sultan was now the undisputed master of Rum and of Rumelia, of Europe and of Asia. In 1480 Lorenzo de Medici had a medal engraved in the Sultan's

---

[1] The later history of the Italian colonies in Greece and the Greek islands is narrated by Miller, *Latins in the Levant*.

honour. The inscription round his portrait entitles him 'Emperor of Asia, Trebizond and Great Greece'; and on the reverse of the medal are depicted three captive princesses described as Greece, Trebizond and Asia.[1]

The Byzantine Empire was violently laid to rest. The Venetian empire within it had greater spirit to resist. The profit and honour of Venice depended on its survival. But in the end the wings of the Lion of St Mark were clipped by the conquering Turks. The Venetian empire would probably have crumbled even without the Turks, simply for lack of customers. For in the fifteenth century new trade routes were being opened up in other seas. Without control of Constantinople, the Hellespont and the Bosporos, the scattered Venetian colonies in the Aegean Sea had no focal point. At least since the eleventh century the wealth of Venice had been drawn from Byzantium. But it had been channelled through Constantinople; and it was to the emperors at Constantinople that the Doges applied for every pound of flesh. The emperors' debts to Venice were meticulously recorded to the last coin and never waived. Constantine XI died still owing 17,163 *hyperpyra*, quite apart from the capital and interest on the unredeemed pledges of his ancestors. It has been calculated that, in the 110 years since 1343, the loan of 30,000 ducats made to his great-great-grandmother, Anne of Savoy, on the security of the crown jewels, would have attracted 165,000 ducats at simple interest, making a total of 195,000. At compound interest his debt to Venice would have amounted to 6,425,000 ducats, the equivalent at fifteenth-century rates of 19,275,000 *hyperpyra*.[2]

The debt of Venice to Byzantium cannot be so nicely calculated. The Treasury of St Mark's bore and still bears witness to the wealth in gold, silver, jewels and relics which the Venetians acquired from Byzantium. The church of St Mark, its decoration, the Pala d'Oro, the Piazza outside it, might constantly have reminded the people of Venice of what they owed to Byzantium. They took it all for granted as part of their heritage and environment. They shed no tears for the sins of their fathers who had so ruthlessly purloined the riches of Byzantium to make their own city so rich and beautiful. Nor did they admit to guilt about keeping the works of art which they had stolen from others. They had little sense of indebtedness. Some of the precious objects in their Treasury were indeed gifts from grateful emperors of Byzantium or from refugees who found asylum in Venice after 1453. Most, however, were brought there after the sack of Constantinople by the Fourth Crusade. It made no difference. They were spoils of war, of a just war against perfidious schismatics, and therefore justly taken. The holy relics that they collected

---

[1] Babinger, *Mehmed the Conqueror*, pp. 386–7.   [2] Bertelè, 'Gioielli', p. 135.

to make their city a profitable place of pilgrimage were also justly obtained, since they were safer in the hands of true Christians of the Roman faith than in those of deviationists or worse still of infidels.

Most of the wealth that Venice made out of Byzantium, however, was ploughed back into the business of making more, invested in commercial enterprises in Constantinople, Romania and latterly the Black Sea. Since the chrysobull granted to the Venetians by Alexios I in 1082 their investments and their rights in Byzantium had been legally protected. For a time the emperors were strong enough to restrict them or to annul them if they seemed to be getting out of hand. Alexios's son John II did so in 1119, not because he feared that the Venetians were holding his economy to ransom but because their residents in Constantinople were disorderly. He changed his mind in 1126, but only after reminding them that their privileges in his empire depended upon their correct behaviour. In 1148 his son Manuel I confirmed and extended those privileges. Venice and Byzantium needed each other, though for different reasons. The emperors dispensed their favours to Venice as a means of perpetuating a valuable partnership for mutual assistance against the Arabs or the Normans in the western Mediterranean and the Adriatic. The Doges were keen to keep the Adriatic free, but more and more on their own behalf rather than for the sake of the Byzantine Empire. Their greatest asset in Byzantium was their commercial quarter in Constantinople, which Manuel was persuaded to enlarge. It was there, however, that they rubbed shoulders with the Byzantine people and earned their reputation for arrogance and offensiveness. Greeks and Venetians did not get on together. Their mutual dislike was shown during Manuel's siege of Corfu in 1149. He felt obliged to register official disapproval of their lawlessness by having them arrested and imprisoned in their thousands in 1171. Nothing was ever the same again between Byzantium and Venice. Manuel's successor Andronikos Komnenos rose to power on a wave of anti-Latin animosity in Constantinople, though it was the Genoese and the Pisans who suffered most in the massacre of 1182. The three chrysobulls that Isaac II issued in favour of Venice five years later redressed the balance which Manuel had upset. But the balance was now weighted in Venetian favour; and the Doges were justified in mounting what was to be an endless campaign for the settlement of damages and compensation for lost property. Isaac II was no match for the Doges of Venice, nor for any other western power, and his still more feeble successor Alexios III was naive in supposing that he could offset the greed of Venice by encouraging the ambitions of Genoa and Pisa. The Venetians kept their patience and extracted yet another charter of privileges from Alexios, which made their colony in Constantinople stronger and more nearly independent than ever before.

Yet their patience had been sorely tried. The Fourth Crusade offered them the opportunity to right the wrongs done to their profit and honour by the Greeks. The Doge Enrico Dandolo made sure that the privileges of his people in the Byzantine world were spelt out *in extenso* by Alexios III in 1198. It might be a useful document for reference if and when Constantinople came under western management. This possibility was no new idea. It had been in the air in western Europe for some time. If the Fourth Crusade had not achieved it other means might well have been found. In the twelfth century the Byzantines lived with the expectation of invasion from the west. The Normans had shown the way more than once. The German Emperors had boasted of their plans to conquer Constantinople. It was a pity that in the end the deed had to be done by the soldiers of Christ. But the end justified the means; for, as Pope Innocent III declared, it was God's way of bringing the wayward Greeks into the fold of Rome. In western eyes no one was to blame for the diversion of the Fourth Crusade. It was more a matter for congratulation, once the dust of plunder had settled and Byzantium was under Latin control. Only latterday historians have agonised about apportioning blame among the leaders of the Crusade. If, on the other hand, prizes were to be offered to those who ran the race to Constantinople, the Venetians would surely be the winners. They alone knew in advance what the prizes were likely to be. The Greeks at the time were right in suspecting that it was Enrico Dandolo who led the crusaders to Constantinople and then arranged things in such a way that they had a moral pretext for conquering it. Only once before had a Doge of Venice so enthusiastically supported a crusade. In 1122 Domenico Michiel had answered the pope's call and led a great fleet out of Venice to go to the rescue of Jerusalem. His flagship flew the banner of St Peter; but his prime purpose had been to put the fear of God into the Emperor John II who had cut short the privileges of Venetian merchants. Crusades to the Holy Land, still more to Egypt for which the Fourth Crusade was destined, were bad for business. Dandolo, like his predecessor Michiel, hid his purpose under a cloak of piety. But Constantinople was in his mind from the outset.

The Fourth Crusade, the most expensive gamble that Venice had ever undertaken, proved unbelievably good for business. For fifty-seven years the Doges did not have to worry about protecting the rights of their merchants in Byzantium. The colonial empire of Romania came into existence. A fruitful combination of state and private enterprise added untold wealth to the city of Venice. While it lasted, the Latin Empire of Constantinople was by far the most profitable investment that the Venetians had ever underwritten. They did all that they could to keep it alive. It was their fellow Latins who let the jewel slip from their hands in 1261. The Venetians were heartbroken. They had come to regard Constantinople as their city. They would join in any war, holy or unholy, to get it back. They could not bear the thought of having to court the favour of a Greek emperor to recover only a fraction of the freedom that they had enjoyed there. Their evident resentment did not endear them to the new Emperor Michael VIII. After the Fourth Crusade there could in any case be no real trust between Byzantium and Venice. For years they were technically at war. Doges no longer sent their sons to be educated at Constantinople, as they had once been wont to do. Byzantine ladies were no longer given as brides to Venetian noblemen. Perhaps the greatest mistake that the Venetians made in the thirteenth century was to stand on their dignity and spurn the Emperor Michael's offer of a truce in 1265. Three years later they had to settle for less in order to be sure of a foothold in Constantinople for a mere five years. Thereafter they were held to the irksome but necessary formality of persuading or bullying successive emperors into confirming the legal rights of Venetian residents in Byzantium every few years.

The first such confirmation, in 1277, gave them two important new privileges: the right to trade in the Black Sea and a commercial quarter to call their own in Constantinople. The opening up of the Black Sea brought them immense profits but almost inevitably provoked war with the Genoese, who had got there first. It was a war, or a series of wars, that brought little credit and no gain to either side. The chief victims of the commercial rivalry between Venice and Genoa were the Byzantines. If, as the Italians boasted, they could reduce the people of Constantinople to starvation by withholding imports of corn from the Black Sea, it was because they had so drained the economic resources of Byzantium that the emperors could not afford to build ships of their own. When they tried to do so they were thwarted. The Italians as well as the Turks must take some of the blame for the disastrous series of civil wars that divided Byzantium in the fourteenth century. By supporting one pretender against another they fomented discord and brought the empire to bankruptcy. The pawning of the Byzantine crown jewels to Venice and the squabble between Venice and Genoa over the tiny island of Tenedos would scarcely be credible in a work of fiction. The niggling and apparently interminable complaints of Venetian ambassadors to Byzantine Emperors about the settlement of damages, the import of corn and the sale of wine in Constantinople make tedious reading. But they were the necessary preludes to every renewal of the always temporary peace between Byzantium and Venice; and without that peace Venetian profits were likely to suffer.

The protection of those profits depended upon the defence of their colonies in Romania against the growing might of the Turks. Corfu, Modon, Coron and Negroponte were the vital stepping-stones on the way to Constantinople and the Black Sea. The Venetians were usually careful not to overstretch their resources. The greatest mistake that they made in the fifteenth century was to take over the city of Thessalonica. It cost them vast sums of money to no advantage and it antagonised the Turks. The lesson that they learnt was that the goodwill of the Sultans was far more important than that of the emperors. They took to instructing their ambassadors to Constantinople to use their initiative if they found that the city was already under Turkish rule. They anticipated the inevitable; but they were loth to partake in crusading ventures to forestall it. There was always the hope that, by appeasing the Turks, they might continue to make profit after the Byzantine Empire had changed hands. In 1453 the Venetians who happened to be there fought bravely in the defence of Christian Constantinople. But their Doge did not take the Cross to save it from the infidel; and his fleet set out too late.

In monetary terms the profit that Venice made out of Byzantium was incalculable. The Venetians would not have been ashamed to admit it. They were given to counting their money and dunning their creditors. They could even put a price on the Crown of Thorns. In a competitive world of trade and commerce it was natural that some should succeed at the expense of others. They would probably have disputed the charge that they were in part the agents of the ruin of Byzantium. Yet sometimes they showed signs of remorse. They were scrupulously protective of the welfare of the Greeks from Tenedos when they had to be evicted from their island; and after 1453 they were as generous as they could be to the Greek refugees who fled to Venice from Constantinople. It was some compensation for all that they had inflicted on the Greeks in times past; and as things turned out it brought some added glory and even profit to Venice and to Italy. The refugees came in dribs and drabs, often by way of Crete, to be washed up in the lagoons of Venice. Not all of them were destitute, though most were rootless and dis-heartened, and few had come that way before.

The Venetians had often proposed that they might spirit the emperor away from his doomed city and give him asylum. The last of the emperors, Constantine Palaiologos, preferred to die fighting at the walls. Many of his courtiers and officers died less heroic deaths as victims of the Sultan's wrath. The Grand Duke, Loukas Notaras, who had commanded the

Greek resistance in the last days of Byzantine Constantinople, and the Grand Domestic, Andronikos Palaiologos Cantacuzene, who had been a signatory of the last treaty between Byzantium and Venice, were both executed.[1] The Sultan was persuaded that it would be safer to liquidate the cream of the Byzantine aristocracy than to let them live to form a government in exile. A number of them managed to escape. A passenger list has been preserved of the refugees taken aboard one of the Genoese ships that got away from the Golden Horn on 29 May 1453. It includes the names of six members of the Palaiologos family, two Cantacuzenes, two Laskarids, two Komnenoi, two of the Notaras family and several others of less exalted birth. The ship's captain, Zorzi Doria, carried them first to Chios where some of them disembarked. Others transferred to a Venetian ship whose master, Tommaso Celsi, took them on to Crete, whence they made their different ways to the Morea, to Corfu and the Ionian islands, or to Italy. It was the beginning of the Byzantine diaspora which brought so many Greek refugees to the Venetian colonies in Romania and to Venice itself.[2]

Some who had wealth and influence had long before taken the precaution of sending their families and their treasures to the safety of Italy. The Grand Duke Notaras was forced to watch the Sultan's butchers murder his sons before meeting his own death. But he died in the knowledge that his three daughters and much of his private fortune were already safely settled and banked in Venice. Anna Palaiologina Notaras and her niece Eudokia Cantacuzene, who had settled there with her, were helpful and influential intermediaries between the Venetian authorities and the Greek émigrés seeking asylum in Venice. Some of them played on the sympathies of their hosts by declaring themselves to be fellow Christians and loyal adherents of the union of Florence. Most of them, however, felt that the only identity that they had left was their Orthodox faith. Their material world had been shattered. Their only link with the past and their main hope for the future was their inherited religion. Three years after the fall of Constantinople the Greeks in Venice asked permission to establish a church of their own. In June 1456 the senators considered the request. It had been put to them on behalf of the Greek community by Isidore of Kiev, who had been made a cardinal of the Roman Church for his stalwart work at the Council of Florence. Unionist

---

[1] Runciman, *Fall of Constantinople*, pp. 151-2; Nicol, *Byzantine Family of Kantakouzenos*, pp. 179-81.

[2] One version of the passenger list is published by K. D. Mertzios in *Actes du XIIᵉ Congrès International des Etudes Byzantines, Ochride, 10-16 Septembre, 1961*, II (Belgrade, 1964), pp. 171-6. A. E. Vacalopoulos, *Origins of the Greek Nation* (New Brunswick, N.J., 1970), pp. 201-2; Nicol, *Byzantine Family of Kantakouzenos*, p. 194.

though he was, Isidore appreciated the need for the Greeks to worship in their own fashion and their own language. The senators were not unsympathetic but they did not wish to offend their own Patriarch of Venice. A few years later, in 1470, the Greek community was granted the use of a side chapel in the church of San Biagio in Venice, on condition that Greek priests would cease celebrating the liturgy elsewhere on pain of a fine. An exception was made for the aristocratic Anna Notaras, who had become patroness of the Greeks in Venice. In June 1475 she and her niece Eudokia were given special permission to construct an oratory in their own house, though strictly for their private use and not to be frequented by others.[1]

By 1478 the number of Greeks in Venice had risen to over 4000. They were accepted as a foreign community with their own quarter in the city, though they had no charter of their rights to which they could appeal. Nor could they afford to be rude and arrogant as the Venetians had been in Constantinople. They knew that they were in Venice under sufferance and they were often made aware of it. There was a long history of mutual antipathy. The ordinary Greeks kept their distance. They found the Venetian dialect coarse and unfamiliar. Very few of them attempted to master Latin. The Venetians were inclined to distrust and despise them. Men soon forgot that they had fought side by side at the siege of Constantinople. The Constantinople that the Venetians remembered was a run down and impoverished city. The Venice that took in the Greek refugees in the fifteenth century was at the height of its glory and riches. They must be made to respect this fact. The Greeks knew that the ecclesiastical authorities in Venice expected them to honour the union of Florence and to worship in churches of the Latin rite in a foreign language. The secular authorities were more flexible. In November 1494 the Greeks asked permission to form a Brotherhood of the Greek race, on the lines of the brotherhoods or sodalities set up by other foreign communities in Venice, the Slavs, the Albanians and the Armenians. Their request was granted and there came into being a philanthropic and religious society with its own officers and councils to care for and promote the interests of the Greek community. Its numbers were limited to 250 and it was declared to be under the patronage of St Nicholas of Myra, an impartial protector of Venetians and Greeks alike. This was the first formal recognition by Venice of the legal status of the Greek colony. The Brotherhood was able to press the point that the Greeks

[1] Geanakoplos, *Greek Scholars in Venice*, pp. 61–2; Geanakoplos, *Byzantine East and Latin West* (Oxford, 1966), pp. 116–18; Nicol, *Byzantine Family of Kantakouzenos*, pp. 230–3.

still needed a church to call their own. But it was not until 1539 that they were authorised to begin building the church of San Giorgio dei Greci which still stands in the centre of the city on the canal known as the Rio dei Greci. It was completed in 1573 and is the oldest of the churches of the Greek diaspora in western Europe. Its construction was authorised by the popes and the clergy of Venice only on the understanding that its services, though in Greek, would be conducted according to the Latin rite as decreed by the Council of Florence. But as early as 1577 the Venetian government, tired of the trouble caused by this stipulation, tacitly allowed the Greeks to place their church directly under the jurisdiction of the Orthodox Patriarch of Constantinople.[1]

By then, 120 years after the fall of Byzantium, the Greeks in Venice had proved their worth in a number of ways. They had shown themselves to be an industrious and on the whole law-abiding community, willing to serve their hosts as soldiers and sailors. To preserve what was left of their empire in Romania from the Turks, the Venetians formed companies of light-armed cavalrymen, young men recruited from among the Greeks and Albanians. They were known as the *stradioti* from the Greek word for soldier; and many of the sons and grandsons of the émigrés took service in their ranks to fight for Venice against the common enemy in the east. One of the more distinguished of the *stradioti* was Matthew Spandounes or Spandugnino, who married the wealthy Eudokia Cantacuzene and was to be honoured by the Hapsburg Emperor Frederick III with the title of Count and Knight of the Roman Empire. One of his three sons was Theodore Spandounes who in 1538 wrote one of the earliest accounts of the origins of the Ottoman Empire.[2] Other Greeks served the state of Venice as sailors, merchants, shopkeepers, craftsmen, or artists, who made their living by painting icons. The worst and the most prolific of these were known as the Madonneri, churning out icons of the Virgin either in traditional Byzantine style or in an Italianate version more palatable to western tastes. There was a huge demand for these products. Every fashionable Venetian household in the fifteenth century had at least one. Hundreds were mass produced in Crete where orders were placed for them through Venetian dealers for the export market in other parts of western Europe. In the sixteenth century there were of course more talented artists in the Greek community, such as the Cretan Michael Damaskinos, many of whose works are in the museum of San Giorgio dei Greci, and the Cretan icon painter Domenikos

---

[1] Geanakoplos, *Greek Scholars in Venice*, pp. 63–9.
[2] Geanakoplos, *Byzantine East and Latin West*, pp. 119–23; Geanakoplos, *Greek Scholars in Venice*, pp. 55–6; Nicol, *Byzantine Family of Kantakouzenos*, pp. xv–xvii, 230–1.

Theotokopoulos, known as El Greco, who spent four years in Venice
as a young man.[1]

Long before their time, however, Greeks emigrating to Venice found
there a home from home, a community which gave them a sense of
security and to which they belonged by speech, race and religion. Not
the least important among them were the scholars and intellectuals, for
whom one man in particular set the example. Bessarion of Trebizond,
Bishop of Nicaea, settled in Italy about 1440. He had made a great impression in Florence at the time of the council and he too was made a cardinal.
Like Demetrios Kydones in an earlier generation, Bessarion was an intellectual convert to the Roman Church; and it was the intellectual and
philosophical legacy of the Greek world that he was concerned to impart
to his Latin friends. The revival of classical Greek studies in Italy had
been much stimulated by Manuel Chrysoloras, the pupil of Kydones
and friend of the Emperor Manuel II, who had been appointed to teach
Greek at Florence in 1396. He inspired a number of Italian scholars
to go to Constantinople to study the Greek language and literature on
the spot, among them Guarino of Verona and Francesco Filelfo, who
became a lifelong friend of Bessarion and married into the Chrysoloras
family. Aeneas Sylvius, the future Pope Pius II, naively declared that
no aspiring scholar could perfect his education without a visit to Constantinople.[2]

The new enthusiasm for the study of Greek in Italy soon spread to
the University of Padua, which was near enough to Venice to excite
interest among the Republic's intellectuals. They were not as numerous
as the scholars of the new humanism in Florence. The Venetians were
hard-headed practical men, not much given to philosophical pursuits.
But their administration needed lawyers and doctors and it was to Padua
that they went for their training and education. The first school in Venice
at which Greek was a part of the curriculum was founded by Guarino
of Verona in 1414; and one of his pupils was the humanist Francesco
Barbaro, who translated some of Plutarch's *Lives* and collected a library
of Greek manuscripts. Barbaro's friend, Leonardo Giustiniani, was
another pupil of Guarino; and Barbaro was responsible for bringing to
Venice the Cretan philosopher George of Trebizond, who was to become
a celebrated if opinionated and cantankerous purveyor of Greek learning

[1] Geanakoplos, *Byzantine East and Latin West*, pp. 133–4. Venetian painters were working
in Crete as early as the thirteenth and fourteenth centuries, sometimes in co-operation with
Greek artists; and there was some interchange of skills in glass-working. Angeliki E. Laiou,
'Venice as a centre of trade and of artistic production in the thirteenth century', in H. Belting,
ed., *Il Medio Oriente e l'Occidente nell' arte del XIII secolo* (Bologna, 1982), pp. 11–26,
especially pp. 17–19.
[2] Aeneas Sylvius, in Pertusi, *La caduta di Costantinopoli*, II, p. 52.

in Italy. George soon fell out with Guarino, who had tried to teach him Latin, and also with Bessarion, who condemned the inaccuracy of his translation of *The Laws* of Plato. This was unfortunate, for George had dedicated his translation to the Doge Francesco Foscari in the belief that it might serve as a guide for the conduct of Venetian policy. It was against George of Trebizond that Bessarion directed his treatise *In Calumniatorem Platonis*. This was the first balanced exposition of Platonic thought to appear in the west and it made a great impression.[1] Bessarion did not engage in the bitter invective employed by many of his contemporaries in the sterile controversy over the comparative merits of Plato and Aristotle. Nor was he carried away by the heretical idea of a reversion to pagan Hellenism advocated by his teacher, George Gemistos Plethon, who, after a brief stay in Italy for the Council of Florence, preferred to live and die at Mistra in Greece.[2] Bessarion's concern was to bring the Hellenic philosophers to the attention of the Latin Christian world and to bridge the gap between the Greek east and the Latin west. Lorenzo Valla indeed described him as *Latinorum graecissimus, Graecorum latinissimus*. Bessarion lived in Rome but he loved the city of Venice. To Greeks like himself who had lost their homeland it seemed 'like another Byzantium'. He made it his business to collect as many Greek books as he could from the wreck of the first Byzantium; and in 1468, before he died, he presented his whole library to the Venetian Senate. There were between 800 and 900 manuscripts, some 600 of which were Greek; and they formed the nucleus of the Biblioteca Marciana, a public library for the preservation and dissemination of knowledge.[3]

The Greeks coming to Venice bore many gifts as their passports to freedom. The Venetians were always eager to add to their collection of holy relics and similar treasures. In 1457 the Senate negotiated with 'a certain Greek' who was offering the tunic of Christ for 10,000 ducats along with some other relics at an unspecified price.[4] But the Greeks were sharp enough to learn that they would fare better in Italy if they presented themselves as heirs of Plato and Pericles rather than as pitiable and beggarly Byzantines. The philosophy and literature of the ancient world excited the minds of western scholars in the fifteenth century much more than the tales of woe brought by contemporaries who had lost

[1] K. M. Setton, 'The Byzantine background to the Italian Renaissance', *Proceedings of the American Philosophical Society*, C (1956), 1–76, especially 72–6. On Bessarion, see also D. M. Nicol, *Church and Society in the Last Centuries of Byzantium* (Cambridge, 1979), pp. 111–13 and references; Geanakoplos, *Greek Scholars in Venice*, pp. 28–33.
[2] C. M. Woodhouse, *Gemistos Plethon. The Last of the Hellenes* (Oxford, 1986).
[3] Setton, 'The Byzantine background to the Italian Renaissance', 74.
[4] Jorga, 'Notes', VIII, 103 n. 1.

their medieval roots. When Aeneas Sylvius heard of the fall of Constantinople he lamented 'the second death of Homer and Plato, of Pindar and Menander and the Greek philosophers'.[1] There were many like him in Italy, humanists with a growing taste for the long-lost treasures of classical antiquity. They mourned the loss of books which they had never had a chance to read. They shed few tears for the end of the Byzantine world and the fate of Orthodox Christianity.

The Venetians felt differently. They had made their fortune from Byzantium, not from ancient Athens. The fall of Constantinople affected them directly and in material ways. The banner of St Mark still flew in numerous ports and islands of Romania. There was still business to be done in a Greek-speaking world in which the language and the thought of Plato and Aristotle were irrelevant and hardly intelligible. The Greek that Venetian traders acquired was limited to seafaring and bargaining in the markets. As the movement to the Italian Renaissance gathered strength, however, some Venetians began to see that there was profit and honour to be made out of the thirst for Greek learning in Italy. By the middle of the fifteenth century the University of Padua vied with Florence as a centre of academic Greek studies. Its first Chair of Greek was instituted in 1463 and filled by a Greek from Athens, Demetrios Chalkokondyles. Bessarion's bequest of his manuscripts to Venice brought scholars to its library. When in 1495 Aldus Manutius set up his Greek printing press at Venice he had assessed the market for the first printed editions of the Greek classics. Aldus knew that no other Italian city could provide all the requirements to make it a profitable venture. Venice alone had the raw material in the form of Greek manuscripts, a rich and leisured class who could afford the money to buy and the time to read the classics in print, and above all the native Greek copyists, editors and typesetters.

Aldus was not the first in the field. The way had already been shown by two Cretans, Laonikos and Alexander, who set up a Greek press in Venice in 1486, and by an Italian printer two years before who had published the very useful and saleable Greek grammar (*Erotemata*) of Manuel Chrysoloras. Another Cretan, Zacharias Kalliergis, had gone into business as a printer in Venice perhaps as early as 1493, employing exclusively Greeks resident in the city; and in 1499 he produced the first edition of the *Etymologicum Magnum*, the great Greek dictionary of Byzantium. Aldus Manutius, however, thought on a grander scale, turning into print as many manuscripts of the Greek classics as he could find. To this end he founded an Academy, an association of Greek and

---

[1] Pertusi, *La caduta di Costantinopoli*, II, pp. 46, 54.

western scholars to exchange ideas for publication and to discuss the collation of manuscripts. The Academy's business was conducted entirely in Greek and its members included many of the Greek community in Venice. The Aldine Press and its later imitators provided employment for the expatriate scholars of Byzantium. Much of it was hack work. Few of them were of the academic stature of Cardinal Bessarion. But they had the satisfaction of knowing that they were helping to bring Greek literature and thought to a wider public and in a form more enduring than handwriting. The Renaissance in Italy owed much to the Venetian link with Byzantium which had caused so many Greeks to gravitate almost instinctively to Venice after the collapse of their civilisation. Venice was a gateway to the east. It was also a gateway from the Greek east to the western world; and through this gateway much of the material flowed, in the form of manuscripts and scholars, for the revival of Greek learning in the west and for the Italian Renaissance.[1]

The Greek contribution to the Renaissance was less spectacular than has sometimes been claimed. But it helped repay some of the debt of Venice to Byzantium, for Venice had given the Greeks a home. It made up too for the curious fact that, after so many centuries of close and often personal contact, there was so little fruitful rapport between Byzantines and Venetians, so little cultural exchange to produce a hybrid literature or art.[2] Though frequently thrown together in Constantinople and Romania they kept their distance, as did the Greek émigrés to Venice. Mixed marriages were frowned on, indeed for long forbidden in Venetian Crete. The Venetian merchants and sailors who thronged the docks on the Golden Horn or at Modon were not the elite of Venetian society. Very few Byzantines, whether sailors or merchants, ever went to Venice. No Doge of Venice was ever received in Constantinople after Enrico Dandolo, who staged his own reception. The only Byzantines to be received in Venice were emperors or their ambassadors, and their reception gave the Venetians the chance to put on the kind of show that they loved. The emperors might talk of the ancient trust and friendship between Byzantines and Venetians. At a humbler level there was mutual incomprehension and dislike. Itinerant sailors or traders are seldom purveyors of culture. Such were the Venetians that most Byzantines knew. They were divided also by religion. Andrea Dandolo saw the

---

[1] On Laonikos, Alexander and Aldus Manutius, see Geanakoplos, *Greek Scholars in Venice*, pp. 57–8, 116–20, 128–31, 201–22, 284–6, and *Byzantine East and Latin West*, pp. 126–8. On Demetrios Chalkokondyles (Chalcondyles), see D. J. Geanakoplos, *Interaction of the 'Sibling' Byzantine and Western Cultures in the Middle Ages and Italian Renaissance (330–1600)* (New Haven–London, 1976), pp. 231–64.

[2] Not until the sixteenth and seventeenth centuries, and again in Venetian Crete, did the fruits of a cultural symbiosis mature in Greek literature and poetry.

progressive separation of the Orthodox Christians from Rome as the force that destroyed the harmony between Byzantium and Venice.[1] The Venetians boasted that they put their race before their faith. They were Venetians first and Christians afterwards. But, like the Byzantines, they knew that religion is the deepest and too often the most intolerant emotion of all.

---

[1] F. Thiriet, 'Byzance et les Byzantins vus par le vénitien Andrea Dandolo', 5–15.

BYZANTINE EMPERORS (500–1453)

Anastasios I	491–518	Constantine VII	913–959
Justin I	518–527	Romanos I Lakapenos	920–944
Justinian I	527–565	Romanos II	959–963
Justin II	565–578	Nikephoros II Phokas	963–969
Tiberius I	578–582	John I Tzimiskes	969–976
Maurice	582–602	Basil II	976–1025
Phokas	602–610	Constantine VIII	1025–1028
Heraclius	610–641	Romanos III Argyros	1028–1034
Constantine III and		Michael IV	1034–1041
Heraclonas	641	Michael V	1041–1042
Heraclonas	641	Zoe and Theodora	1042
Constans II	641–668	Constantine IX	
Constantine IV	668–685	Monomachos	1042–1055
Justinian II	685–695	Theodora (again)	1055–1056
Leontios	695–698	Michael VI	1056–1057
Tiberius II	698–705	Isaac I Komnenos	1057–1059
Justinian II (again)	705–711	Constantine X Doukas	1059–1067
Philippicus Bardanes	711–713	Romanos IV Diogenes	1068–1071
Anastasios II	713–715	Michael VII Doukas	1071–1078
Theodosios III	715–717	Nikephoros III Botaneiates	1078–1081
Leo III	717–741	Alexios I Komnenos	1081–1118
Constantine V	741–775	John II Komnenos	1118–1143
Leo IV	775–780	Manuel I Komnenos	1143–1180
Constantine VI	780–797	Alexios II Komnenos	1180–1183
Eirene	797–802	Andronikos I Komnenos	1183–1185
Nikephoros I	802–811	Isaac II Angelos	1185–1195
Staurakios	811	Alexios III Angelos	1195–1203
Michael I Rangabe	811–813	Isaac II (again) and	
Leo V	813–820	Alexios IV	1203–1204
Michael II	820–829	Alexios V Mourtzouphlos	1204
Theophilos	829–842	Emperors in exile at	
Michael III	842–867	Nicaea:	
Basil I	867–886	Theodore I Laskaris	1204–1222
Leo VI	886–912	John III Doukas	
Alexander	912–913	Vatatzes	1222–1254

Theodore II Laskaris	1254–1258	John VI Kantakouzenos	
John IV Laskaris	1258–1261	(Cantacuzene)	1347–1354
Michael VIII Palaiologos	1261–1282	Andronikos IV Palaiologos	1376–1379
Andronikos II Palaiologos	1282–1328	John VII Palaiologos	1390
Andronikos III Palaiologos	1328–1341	Manuel II Palaiologos	1391–1425
John V Palaiologos	1341–1391	John VIII Palaiologos	1425–1448
		Constantine XI Palaiologos	1449–1453

DOGES OF VENICE

Orso (Ursus)	727–738	Vitale I Michiel	1096–1101
Teodato (Deusdedit)	742, 744–756	Ordelafo Falier	1101–1118
Galla Gaulo	756	Domenico Michiel	1118–1129
Domenico Monegaurio	756–765	Pietro Polani	1129–1148
Maurizio Galbaio	765–787	Domenico Morosini	1148–1155
Giovanni and Maurizio II		Vitale II Michiel	1155–1172
Galbaio	787–802	Sebastiano Ziani	1172–1178
Obelerio	802–811	Orio Mastropiero	
Beato	808–811	(Malipiero)	1178–1192
Agnello Partecipazio	811–827	Enrico Dandolo	1192–1205
Giustiniano Partecipazio	827–829	Pietro Ziani	1205–1229
Giovanni Partecipazio	829–836	Giacomo Tiepolo	1229–1249
Pietro Tradonico	836–864	Marino Morosini	1249–1253
Orso I Badoer		Reniero Zeno	1253–1268
(Partecipazio)	864–881	Lorenzo Tiepolo	1268–1275
Giovanni Badoer	881–888	Jacopo Contarini	1275–1280
Pietro I Candiano	887	Giovanni Dandolo	1280–1289
Pietro Tribuno	888–912	Pietro Gradenigo	1289–1311
Orso II Badoer	912–932	Marino Zorzi	1311–1312
Pietro II Candiano	932–939	Giovanni Soranzo	1312–1328
Pietro Badoer	939–942	Francesco Dandolo	1328–1339
Pietro III Candiano	942–959	Bartolomeo Gradenigo	1339–1342
Pietro IV Candiano	959–976	Andrea Dandolo	1343–1354
Pietro I Orseolo	976–978	Marino Falier	1354–1355
Vitale Candiano	978–979	Giovanni Gradenigo	1355–1356
Tribuno Menio	979–991	Giovanni Dolfin	1356–1361
Pietro II Orseolo	991–1008	Lorenzo Celsi	1361–1365
Otto Orseolo	1008–1026	Marco Corner	1365–1368
Pietro Centranico		Andrea Contarini	1368–1382
(Barbolano)	1026–1030	Michele Morosini	1382
Otto Orseolo	1030–1032	Antonio Venier	1382–1400
Domenico Flabianico	1032–1043	Michele Steno	1400–1413
Domenico Contarini	1043–1070	Tommaso Mocenigo	1414–1423
Domenico Silvio (Selvo)	1070–1084	Francesco Foscari	1423–1457
Vitale Falier	1084–1096		

BIBLIOGRAPHY

COLLECTIONS OF SOURCES

Acta Albaniae Veneta Saeculorum XIV et XV, ed. J. Valentini, I–XXIV (Palermo–Milan–Rome, 1967–77) (cited as *ActAlbVen*)

Acta et Diplomata res Albaniae mediae aetatis illustrantia, ed. L. de Thallóczy, C. Jireček, E. de Šufflay, I–II (Vienna, 1913, 1918) (cited at *ActAlb*)

Acta graeca Concilii Florentini, ed. J. Gill, *Quae supersunt actorum graecorum Concilii Florentini*, Concilium Florentinum Documenta et Scriptores, Series B, V, I (Rome, 1953)

Acta Sanctorum Bollandiana, in progress (Brussels, Paris, Rome)

Cessi, R., *Deliberazioni del Maggior Consiglio di Venezia*, I–III, Reale Accademia dei Lincei, Commissione per gli atti delle assemblee costituzionali italiane (Bologna, 1931–50)

    Documenti relativi alla storia di Venezia anteriore al mille, I–II (Padua, 1942)

    Le origini del ducato veneziano, Collana storica, IV (Naples, 1951), pp. 175–243: *Pacta Veneta*, I, *Pacta Carolina*; pp. 245–321: *Pacta Veneta*, II, *Dal 'Pactum Lotharii' al 'Foedus Octonis'*; earlier edition by R. Cessi, in *Archivio veneto*, ser. 5, III (1928), 118–24 and V (1929), 1–77

Cessi, R. and Sambin, P., *Le deliberazioni del Consiglio dei Rogati (Senato) serie Mixtorum*, Deputazione di Storia Patria per le Venezie: Monumenti Storici. Nuova serie, XV, XVI. I: Libri I–XIV (Venice, 1960); II: Libri XV–XVI, ed. R. Cessi and M. Brunetti (Venice, 1961)

Chronica Byzantina breviora, ed. P. Schreiner, *Die byzantinischen Kleinchroniken*, I–III, *CFHB*, XIII/1–3 (Vienna, 1975–9) (cited as *Chron. brev.*)

Diplomatarium Veneto-Levantinum, sive Acta et Diplomata res Venetas, Graecas atque Levantis illustrantia a 1330–1454, I–II, ed. G. M. Thomas and R. Predelli, Monumenti storici pubblicati dalla Reale Deputazione Veneta di Storia Patria, serie prima. Documenti, V, IX (Venice, 1880, 1889) (cited as *DVL*)

Dölger, F., *Regesten der Kaiserurkunden des oströmischen Reiches*, I: *565–1025*; II: *1025–1204*; III: *1204–1282* (2nd edn, P. Wirth: Munich, 1977); IV: *1282–1341*; V: *1341–1453* (Munich–Berlin, 1924–65) (cited as *DR*)

Giomo, G., *Rubriche dei libri perduti dei Misti* (Venice, 1887); also in *Archivio veneto*, XVII (1879), 126–32; XVIII (1879), 40–338; XIX (1880), 90–117; XX (1880), 81–95

Hopf, C., *Chroniques gréco-romanes inédites ou peu connues* (Berlin, 1873)

Jorga, N., 'Notes et extraits pour servir à l'histoire des Croisades au xve siècle', *ROL*, iv (1896), 226–30: 1400–10; 503–622: 1411–20; v (1897), 108–212: 1421–25; 311–88: 1426–9; vi (1898), 50–143: 1429–36; 370–434: 1436–40; vii (1899–1900), 38–107: 1441–3; 375–429: 1443–4; viii (1900–1), 1–115: 1444–53; 267–310: 1454–1500. Cited as Jorga, 'Notes', i–viii. Also published separately, with different pagination, in 3 vols. (Paris, 1899–1902)

Krekić, B., *Dubrovnik (Raguse) et le Levant au moyen âge*, Documents et Recherches, v (Paris–The Hague, 1961)

Lambros, Sp. P., Παλαιολογεῖα καὶ Πελοποννησιακά, i–iv (Athens, 1912–30)

Ljubić, S., *Monumenta spectantia historiam Slavorum meridionalium. Listine o odnošajih izmedju Južnoga Slaventsva i Mletačke Republike*, i–x (Zagreb, 1868–91) (cited as Ljubić, *Monumenta*)

Migne, J. P., *Patrologiae Cursus Completus. Series Graeco-latina* (Paris, 1857–66); *Series Latina* (Paris, 1844–55) (cited as *MPG, MPL*)

Miklosich, F. and Müller, J., *Acta et Diplomata graeca medii aevi sacra et profana*, i–vi (Vienna, 1860–90) (cited as *MM*)

Morozzo della Rocca, R., ed., *Lettere di mercanti a Pignol Zucchello (1336–1350)*, Fonti per la Storia di Venezia, sez. 4. Archivi privati (Venice, 1957)

Morozzo della Rocca, R. and Lombardo, A., *Documenti del commercio veneziano nei secolo XI–XIII*, i–11, Regesta Chartarum Italiae (Turin, 1940)
Nuovi documenti del commercio veneto nei secoli XI–XIII, Deputazione di Storia Patria per le Venezie: Monumenti Storici. Nuova serie, vii (Venice, 1953)

Muratori, L. A., *Rerum Italicarum Scriptores*, i–xxv (Milan, 1723–51) (New editions in progress) (cited as *RIS*)

Pertusi, A., *La caduta di Costantinopoli*, i: *Le testimonianze dei contemporanei*. ii: *L'eco nel mondo*, Fondazione Lorenzo Valla (Verona, 1976)

Predelli, R., *I Libri Commemoriali della Republica di Venezia: Regesti*, i–vi (Venice, 1876–8)

Predelli, R., ed. *Il Liber Communis detto anche Plegiorum del Reale Archivio generale di Venezia: Regesti* (Venice, 1872)

Recueil des historiens des Croisades, Historiens occidentaux, i–v, Académie des Inscriptions et Belles-Lettres (Paris, 1844–95) (cited as *RHC*)

Riant, P. E. D., *Exuviae Sacrae Constantinopolitanae*, i–iii (Paris, 1877–1904)

San Giorgio Maggiore, ii. *Documenti 982–1159* (nos. 1–288); iii: *Documenti 1160–1199* (nos. 289–614), ed. L. Lanfranchi, Fonti per la Storia di Venezia, Sezione 2. Archivi Ecclesiastici – Diocesi Castellana (Venice, 1968)

Sathas, K. N., Μνημεῖα Ἑλληνικῆς Ἱστορίας. *Monumenta Hellenicae Historiae. Documents inédits relatifs à l'histoire de la Grèce au moyen âge*, i–ix (Venice–Paris, 1880–96)

Tafel, T. L. F. and Thomas, G. M., *Urkunden zur älteren Handels- und Staatsgeschichte der Republik Venedig mit besonderen Beziehungen auf Byzanz und die Levante*, i–111, Fontes Rerum Austriacarum, Abt. ii: Diplomata, xii–xiv (Vienna, 1856–7) (cited as *TTh*)

Teulet, A., *Layette du Trésor des Chartes*, i–11 (Paris, 1866)

Thiriet, F., *Délibérations des assemblées vénitiennes concernant la Romanie*, i–ii, Documents et Recherches, viii, xi (Paris–The Hague, 1966, 1971)

Régestes des délibérations du Sénat de Venise concernant la Romanie, I, II, III, Documents et Recherches, I, II, IV (Paris–The Hague, 1958–61)
Thomas, G. M. and Predelli, R., *see Diplomatarium*...

INDIVIDUAL SOURCES

Greek

Akropolites, George, *Historia*, ed. A. Heisenberg, *Georgii Acropolitae Opera*, I (Leipzig, 1903); ed. P. Wirth (Stuttgart, 1978)

Anagnostes, John, *De Thessalonicensi excidio narratio*, ed. I. Bekker in Georgius Phrantzes, *CSHB* (1838), pp. 481–528; ed. G. Tsaras, Ἰωάννου Ἀναγνώστου διήγησις περὶ τῆς τελευταίας ἁλώσεως τῆς Θεσσαλονίκης (Thessaloniki, 1957)

Anna Comnena, *Alexiad*, ed. B. Leib, I–III (Paris, 1937–45)

Athanasios I, Patriarch, Letters. *The Correspondence of Athanasius I Patriarch of Constantinople. Letters to the Emperor Andronicus II, Members of the Imperial Family, and Officials*, ed. Alice-Mary Maffry Talbot, Dumbarton Oaks Texts, III, *CFHB*, VII (Washington, D.C., 1975)

Cantacuzenus (Kantakouzenos), John, *Historiae. Ioannis Cantacuzeni Eximperatoris Historiarum Libri IV*, ed. L. Schopen, I–III, *CSHB* (1828–32)

Cedrenus (Skylitzes-Kedrenos), *Compendium historiarum*, ed. I. Bekker, *CSHB* (1838)

Chalkokondyles, Laonikos. *Laonici Chalcocondylae Historiarum Demonstrationes*, ed. E. Darkó, I–II (Budapest, 1922–7)

Constantine Porphyrogenitus, *De administrando imperio*, ed. Gy. Moravcsik and R. J. H. Jenkins, Dumbarton Oaks Texts, I, *CFHB*, I (Washington, D.C., 1967); II, *Commentary* (London, 1962) (cited as *DAI*)
De Thematibus, ed. A. Pertusi, Studi et Testi, 160 (Vatican City, 1952)

Doukas. *Ducas, Istoria turco-bizantină (1341–1462)*, ed. V. Grecu (Bucharest, 1958). Translated by H. J. Magoulias, *Decline and Fall of Byzantium to the Ottoman Turks by Doukas* (Detroit, 1975)

Eustathios of Thessalonica, *De capta Thessalonica narratio*, ed. I. Bekker in *Leonis Grammatici Chronographia*, pp. 365–512, *CSHB* (1842); S. Kyriakides, *La espugnazione di Tessalonica*, ed. V. Rotolo, Istituto Siciliano di Studi Bizantini e Neoellenici. Testi, 5 (Palermo, 1961)

Gregoras, Nikephoros, *Byzantina Historia*, ed. L. Schopen, I–III, *CSHB* (1829–55)

Hierokles. *Le Synekdèmos d'Hiéroklès et l'opuscule géographique de Georges de Chypre*, ed. E. Honigmann (Brussels, 1939)

Kananos (Cananus), John, *De Constantinopoli Oppugnata (1422)*, ed. I. Bekker in *Georgius Phrantzes*, *CSHB* (1838), pp. 457–79

Kinnamos (Cinnamus), John. *Ioannis Cinnami Epitome rerum ab Ioanne et Alexio Comnenis gestarum*, ed. A. Meineke, *CSHB* (1836). Translated by C. M. Brand, *The Deeds of John and Manuel Comnenus by John Cinnamus*, Records of Civilisation, Sources and Studies, 45 (New York, 1976)

Kritoboulos of Imbros. *Critobuli Imbriotae Historiae*, ed. D. R. Reinsch, *CFHB*, XXII (Berlin–New York, 1983)

Kydones, Demetrios, Letters. *Démétrius Cydonès, Correspondance*, I–II, ed. R.-J. Loenertz, Studi e Testi, 186, 208 (Vatican City, 1956, 1960)

Lambros, Sp. P., Συνθήκη μεταξὺ Ἰωάννου Η′ Παλαιολόγου καὶ τοῦ δουκὸς τῆς Βενετίας Φραγκίσκου Φόσκαρη, *Neos Hellenomnenon*, XII (1915), 153–97

Makrembolites, Alexios, Λόγος Ἱστορικός (*Historical Discourse on the Genoese*), ed. A. Papadopoulos- Kerameus, Ἀνάλεκτα Ἱεροσολυμιτικῆς Σταχυολογίας, I (St Petersburg, 1891), pp. 144–59

Manuel II. *Manuel II Palaeologus, Funeral Oration on his Brother Theodore*, ed. J. Chrysostomides, *CFHB*, XXVI (Thessaloniki, 1985)

Mesarites, Nicholas, *Epitaphios*, ed. A. Heisenberg, *Neue Quellen zur Geschichte des lateinischen Kaisertums und der Kirchenunion*. I: *Der Epitaphios des Nikolaos Mesarites auf seinen Bruder Johannes*, Sitzungsberichte der Bayerischen Akademie der Wissenschaften, Philosophisch-philologische und historische Klasse, V (1922) (reprinted in A. Heisenberg, *Quellen und Studien zur spätbyzantinischen Geschichte*, London, 1973, no. II)

Michael VIII Palaiologos. *Imperatoris Michaelis Palaeologi De Vita Sua*, ed. H. Grégoire, *B*, XXIX–XXX (1959–60) (*Hommage à la Mémoire de Cirò Giannelli*), 447–76

Niketas Choniates, *Historia*, ed. J.-L. van Dieten, *CFHB*, XI/1, XI/2 (Berlin–New York, 1975)

Pachymeres, George, *De Michaele Palaeologo; De Andronico Palaeologo*, ed. I. Bekker, I–II, *CSHB* (1835). *Georges Pachymeres Relations Historiques*, I: Livres I–III; II: Livres IV–VI, ed. A. Failler, trans. V. Laurent, *CFHB*, XXIV/1–2 (Paris, 1984) (in progress)

Philotheos (Kokkinos), Patriarch, Λόγος Ἱστορικός ('Historical Discourse on the Siege and Capture by the Latins of Herakleia, 1352')', ed. C. Triantafillis and A. Grapputo, Anecdota Graeca e Codicibus Manu Scriptis Bibliothecae S. Marci, I (Venice, 1874), pp. 1–33; ed. B. S. Psevtongas, Φιλοθέου Κόκκινου Λόγοι καὶ Ὁμιλίες, Θεσσαλονικεῖς Βυζαντινοὶ Συγγραφεῖς, II (Thessaloniki, 1981), pp. 235–64

Planoudes, Maximos, *Letters*, ed. M. Treu, *Maximi monachi Planudis epistulae* (Breslau, 1890)

Procopius, *De Bello Gothico*, ed. J. Haury, *Procopii Caesariensis opera omnia*, II (Leipzig, 1905)

Pseudo-Kodinos, *De Officiis*, ed. J. Verpeaux, *Pseudo-Kodinos, Traité des Offices* (Paris, 1966)

Sphrantzes, George. *Chronicon Minus*, ed. together with the *Chronicon Maius* of Pseudo-Phrantzes (Makarios Melissenos) by V. Grecu, *Georgios Sphrantzes, Memorii 1401–1477: în anexă Pseudo-Phrantzes: Macarie Melissenos Cronica 1258–1481* (Bucharest, 1966)

Symeon of Thessalonica, *Discourse on the Miracles of St Demetrios*, ed. D. Balfour, *Politico-Historical Works of Symeon Archbishop of Thessalonica (1416/17 to 1429)*, Wiener byzantinische Studien, XIII (Vienna, 1979)

Syropoulos, Sylvester, ed. V. Laurent, *Les 'Mémoires' du Grand Ecclésiarque de l'Eglise de Constantinople Sylvestre Syropoulos sur le Concile de Florence (1438–1439)* (Paris, 1971)

Theophanes, *Chronographia*, ed. C. de Boor, I–II (Leipzig, 1883–5)

Theophanes Continuatus, *Chronographia*, ed. I. Bekker, *CSHB* (1838)

Venetian

Andrea de Redusiis, *Chronicon Tarvisinum*, *RIS*, xix (Milan, 1731)

Annales Venetici breves, ed. H. Simonsfeld, *MGH, Scriptores*, xiv (Hanover, 1883), pp. 69–72

Badoer, Giacomo. *Il Libro dei Conti di Giacomo Badoer (Costantinopoli 1436–1440)*, ed. V. Dorini and T. Bertelè, Il Nuovo Ramusio, Raccolta di Viaggi, Testi e Documenti relativi ai Rapporti fra l'Europa e l'Oriente a cura dell' Istituto Italiano per il Medio e Estremo Oriente, iii (Rome, 1956)

Barbaro, Nicolò, *Giornale dell' assedio di Costantinopoli 1453*, ed. E. Cornet (Vienna, 1856). Translated by J. R. Jones, *Nicolo Barbaro, Diary of the Siege of Constantinople* (New York, 1969)

Caresini, Raffaino. *Raphayni de Caresinis Cancellarii Venetiarum, Cronica AA. 1343–1388*, ed. E. Pastorello, *RIS*, xii/2 (Bologna, 1923); earlier ed. Muratori, *RIS*, xii (Milan, 1728, cols. 417–523 (*Andreae Danduli Tomus Secundus cum continuatione Raphayni Caresini...*)

Caroldo, Gian Giacomo, *Chronicle*. Partially ed. Julian Chrysostomides, 'Studies on the Chronicle of Caroldo' (q.v.)

Chinazzo, Daniele di, *Cronica de la guerra da Veniciani a Zenovesi*, ed. V. Lazzarini, Deputazione di Storia Patria per le Venezie: Monumenti Storici. Nuova serie, xi (Venice, 1958); earlier ed. Muratori, *RIS*, xv (Milan, 1729), cols. 695–804

Chronicon Altinate. Chronicon Venetum quod vulgo dicunt Altinate, ed. H. Simonsfeld, *MGH, Scriptores*, xiv (Hanover, 1883), pp. 1–69; ed. R. Cessi, *Origo Civitatum Italiae seu Venetiarum (Chronicon Altinate et Chronicon Gradense)*, Fonti per la Storia d'Italia. Scrittori, secoli xi–xii (Rome, 1933)

Chronicon Gradense, ed. G. Monticolo, *Cronache veneziane antichissime*, i, Fonti per la Storia d'Italia. Scrittori, secoli x–xi (Rome, 1890), pp. 17–51; ed. R. Cessi, *Origo Civitatum Italiae... (Rome, 1933)*

Cronaca di Marco. Estratti dall' opera MS. in lingua latina del cronista Marco, in *ASI*, viii (1845), 259–67

Dandolo, Andrea, *Chronicon Venetum. Andreae Danduli Ducis Venetiarum Chronica per extensum descripta aa. 46–1280*, ed. E. Pastorello, *RIS*, xii/1 (Bologna, 1938); ed. Muratori, *RIS*, xii (Milan, 1728), cols. 399–417 (*1280–1339*)

Famiglia Zusto, ed. L. Lanfranchi, Fonti per la Storia di Venezia, Sez. 4. Archivi Privati (Venice, 1955)

Gataro, Andrea, *Istoria Padovana (Chronicon Patavinum ... auctore Andrea de Gataris)*, *RIS*, xvii (Milan, 1730)

Historia Ducum Veneticorum, ed. H. Simonsfeld, *MGH, Scriptores*, xiv (Hanover, 1883), pp. 72–97

John the Deacon. *Giovanni Diacono, Cronaca veneziana*, ed. G. Monticolo, *Cronache veneziane antichissime*, i, Fonti per la Storia d'Italia. Scrittori, secoli x–xi (Rome, 1890), pp. 57–171

Jorga, N., 'Veneţia in Mare neagră', *Analele Academiei Române, Memoriile secţiunii istorice*, ser. 2, xxxvi (1913–14), *Apendice, 1058–1070* (Documents i–xxi); *Anexe, 1093–1118* (Documents i–lix)

Lazzarini, V., ed. 'Due documenti sulla guerra di Chioggia', *Nuovo archivio veneto*, XII (1896), 137–47

Lorenzo de Monacis, *Chronicon de rebus venetis*, ed. F. Cornelius, *Laurentii de Monacis Veneti Cretae Cancellarii Chronicon de Rebus Venetis ... ab u. c. usque ad Annum MCCCLIV, RIS*, Appendix to Vol. VIII, pp. 1–320 (Venice, 1758)

Martin da Canal, *Les Estoires de Venise. Cronaca veneziana in lingua francese dalle origini al 1275*, ed. A. Limentani, Civiltà Veneziana, Fonti e Testi, XII, serie terza (Florence, 1972); ed. F. L. Polidori with Italian translation by G. Galvani, *La Cronique des Veniciens de maistre Martin da Canal: Cronaca Veneta del Maestro Martino da Canale dall' origine della Citta sino all' anno MCCLXXV*, in *ASI*, ser. I, VIII (1845), 229–56, 268–798

Minieri-Riccio, C., 'Memorie della Guerra di Sicilia negli anni 1282, 1283, 1284', *Archivio storico per le province napoletane*, I (1876), 85–105, 275–315, 499–530

Sabellico, Marco Antonio, *Historia Vinitiana* (Venice, 1544, 1558)

Sanudo, Marino, *Vitae Ducum Venetorum (Vite dei duchi di Venezia), RIS*, XXII (Milan, 1733), cols. 405–1252; *Le vite dei Dogi di Venezia*, ed., G. Monticolo, *RIS*, XXII, part IV (1900)

Sanudo Torsello, Marino, *Istoria del Regno di Romania*, ed. C. Hopf, *Chroniques gréco-romanes* (Berlin, 1873), pp. 99–170. *Fragmentum Marini Sanuti Torselli*, ed., Hopf, *Chroniques...*, pp. 171–4; ed. R. L. Wolff, 'Hopf's So-Called "Fragmentum" of Marino Sanudo Torsello', *The Joshua Starr Memorial Volume* (New York, 1953), pp. 149–59

Translatio Isidori. Cerbani Cerbani, clerici Veneti, Translatio mirifici Martyris Isidori a Chio insula in civitatem Venetam (Jun. 1125), in *RHC, Historiens occidentaux*, V (1895), pp. 321–34

Translatio Sancti Nicolai. Monachi anonymi Littorensis, Historia de Translatione Sanctorum magni Nicolai, terra marique miraculis gloriosi, eiusdem avunculi, alterius Nicolai, Theodorique, martyris pretiosi, de civitate Mirea in monasterium S. Nicolai de Littore Venetiarum, 6 Dec. 1100, in *RHC, Historiens occidentaux*, V (1895), pp. 253–92

Zeno, Jacobus, *Vita Caroli Zeni*, ed. G. Zonta, *RIS*, XIX/6 (Bologna, 1940)

Zibaldone da Canal. *Zibaldone da Canal, manoscritto mercantile del sec. XIV*, a cura di A. Stussi, con studi di F. C. Lane, Th. E. Marston, O. Ore, Comitato per la pubblicazione delle fonti relative alla storia di Venezia, ser. V. Fondi vari (Venice, 1967)

Other

Albert of Aix, *Historia Hierosolymitana. Liber Christianae Expeditionis pro Ereptione, Emundatione, Restitutione Sanctae Hierosolymitanae Ecclesiae*, in *RHC, Historiens occidentaux*, IV (1879), pp. 265–713

Annales Ianuenses. Annali genovesi di Caffaro e de' suoi continuatori, ed. L. T. Belgrano and C. Imperiale, I–V, Fonti per la Storia d'Italia. Scrittori, secoli XII–XIII (Genoa, 1890, 1901; Rome, 1923, 1926, 1929)

Annales Regni Francorum inde ab a. 741 usque ad a. 829, ed. F. Kurze, *MGH, SGUS* (Hanover, 1895). Translated by W. Scholtz and Barbara Rogers,

Carolingian Chronicles: Royal Frankish Annals and Nithard's Histories (Ann Arbor, Michigan, 1972)

Bertrandon de la Broquière, ed. C. Schefer, *Bertrandon de la Broquière, Voyage d'Outremer* (Paris, 1892)

Boucicaut. *Le Livre des faicts du Bon Messire Jean le Meingre dit Boucicaut, Mareschal de France et Gouverneur de Gennes*, in J. F. Michaud and J. J. F. Poujoulat, ed., *Nouvelle Collection des mémoires pour servir à l'histoire de France*, VII–IX (Paris, 1825)

Caffaro. *See Annales Ianuenses*

Cassiodorus. *Magni Aurelii Cassiodori Variarum Libri XII*, ed. Å. J. Fridh, Corpus Christianorum Series Latina, XCVI (Turnholt, 1973)

Chronicle of Novgorod, 1016–1471, Translated by R. Michell and N. Forbes, Camden Society, 3rd series, XXV (London, 1914)

Chronicon Estense. Chronicon Estense Marchionum Estensium, *RIS*, XV (Milan, 1729)

Fulcher of Chartres. *Fulcheri Carontensis Historia Hierosolymitana (1095–1127)*, ed. H. Hagenmayer (Heidelberg, 1913)

Geoffrey of Malaterra, *De Rebus Gestis Rogerii ... et Roberti Guiscardi...*, ed. E. Pontieri, *RIS*, V/1 (Bologna, 1927)

del Giudice, G., *Codice diplomatico del regno di Carlo I.° e II.° d'Angiò*, 1 (Naples, 1863)

Innocent III, Pope, Letters and Acts. *MPL*, CCXIV–CCXVII; *Acta Innocentii PP. III (1198–1216)*, ed. P. T. Haluščynskyj, Pontificia Commissio ad Redigendum Codicem Juris Canonici Orientalis: Fontes, Series III, Vol. II: (Vatican City, 1944)

Jacopo da Varagine, ed. C. Monleone, *Iacopo da Varagine e la sua Cronaca di Genova dalle origini al MCCXCVII*, I–III, Fonti per la Storia d'Italia. Scrittori, secolo XIII (Rome, 1941)

Liber iurium reipublicae Genuensis, I–III, ed. E. Ricotti, Monumenta Historiae Patriae, VII–IX (Turin, 1854)

Maragone, Bernardo, *Annales Pisani*, ed. M. L. Gentile, *RIS*, VI/2 (Bologna, 1936), pp. 1–74

Martin IV, Pope. *Les Registres de Martin IV (1281–1285)*, ed. F. Olivier-Martin (Paris, 1935)

Paul the Deacon. *Pauli Historia Langobardorum*, ed. L. Bethman and G. Waitz, *MGH, Scriptores rerum Langobardorum* (Hanover, 1878), pp. 12–187. Translated by W. D. Foulke, *Paul the Deacon: History of the Lombards* (University of Pennsylvania, 1907; reprinted, 1974)

Pegolotti. Francesco Balducci Pegolotti, *La pratica della mercatura*, ed. A. Evans (Cambridge, Mass., 1936)

Peter Damian, *Opuscula varia*, *MPL*, CXLV, part 2

Pokorny, R., 'Zwei unedierte Briefe aus der Frühzeit des lateinischen Kaiserreichs von Konstantinopel', *B*, LV (1985), 180–209

Robert of Auxerre. *Ex Chronologia Roberti Altissiodorensis*, in *Recueil des historiens des Gaules et de la France*, ed. M.-J.-J. Brial (Bouquet) and L. Delisle, XVIII (Paris, 1879)

Robert of Clari, *La Conquête de Constantinople*, ed. P. Lauer (Paris, 1924). Italian

translation and commentary by Anna Maria Nada Patrone, *La conquista di Costantinopoli (1198–1216)*, Collana Storica di Fonti e Studi, 13 (Genoa, 1972)
Stella. *Georgii et Iohannis Stellae, Annales Genuenses*, ed. Giovanna Petti Balbi, *RIS*, xvii/2 (Bologna, 1975; earlier edn *RIS*, xvii (Milan, 1730)
Villani, Matteo. *Chroniche di Giovanni, Matteo e Filippo Villani*, ed. A. Racheli, ii (Trieste, 1858); and in *RIS*, xiv.
Villehardouin, Geoffrey of, *La Conquête de Constantinople*, ed. E. Faral, i–ii, Les Classiques de l'Histoire de France au Moyen Age, 18–19 (Paris, 1938–9)
William of Apulia. *Guillaume de Pouille, La Geste de Robert Guiscard*, ed. Marguerite Mathieu, Istituto Siciliano di Studi Bizantini e Neoellenici. Testi, 4 (Palermo, 1961)
William of Tyre. *Historia rerum in partibus transmarinis gestarum a tempore successorum Mahumeth usque ad annum domini MCLXXXIV, edita a Venerabili Willermo Tyrensi Archiepiscopo*, in *RHC, Historiens occidentaux*, i/1 (Paris, 1844)
Zurita, Gieronimo, *Los cinco libros postreros de la primera parte de los Anales de la Corona de Aragón*, i–vi (Saragossa, 1562–80)

MODERN WORKS

Abulafia, D., *The Two Italies. Economic Relations Between the Norman Kingdom of Sicily and the Northern Communes* (Cambridge, 1977)
Ahrweiler, Hélène, *Byzance et la mer* (Paris, 1966)
Alexandru-Dersca, Marie-Mathilde, *La Campagne de Timur en Anatolie (1402)* (Bucharest, 1942)
Alexandru-Dersca Bulgaru, M.-M., 'L'action diplomatique et militaire de Venise pour la défense de Constantinople', *Revue Roumaine d'Histoire*, xii (1974), 247–67
Anastos, M. V., 'Iconoclasm and imperial rule 717–842', in *CMH*, iv (1966), pp. 61–104
Angold, M., *The Byzantine Empire 1025–1204. A Political History* (London, 1984)
A Byzantine Government in Exile. Government and Society under the Laskarids of Nicaea (1204–1261) (Oxford, 1975)
Antoniadis-Bibicou, H., 'Notes sur les relations de Byzance avec Venise. De la dépendance à l'autonomie et à l'alliance: un point de vue byzantin', *Thesaurismata*, i (1962), 162–78
Argenti, P., *The Occupation of Chios by the Genoese and their Administration of the Island (1346–1566)*, i–iii (Cambridge, 1958)
Armingaud, M. J., *Venise et le Bas-Empire. Histoire des relations de Venise avec l'Empire d'Orient*, Archives des Missions Scientifiques et Littéraires, 2me série, iv (Paris, 1868)
Arnakis, G. G., Οἱ Πρῶτοι 'Οθωμανοί ('The Early Osmanlis') (Athens, 1947)
Atiya, A. S., *The Crusade in the Later Middle Ages*, 2nd edn (New York, 1965)
The Crusade of Nicopolis (London, 1934)
Avramea(s), Anna, 'The cartography of the Greek coastlands', in *The Greek Merchant Marine* (National Bank of Greece: Athens, 1972), pp. 175–80
'Maps of the Aegean', in *Maps and Mapmakers of the Aegean*, ed. V. Sphyroeras, Anna Avramea, S. Asdrachas (Athens, 1985), pp. 22–32

Babinger, F., *Mehmed the Conqueror and his Time*. Translated from the German by R. Manheim, ed. by W. C. Hickman, Bollingen Series, xcvi (Princeton, N.J., 1978)

Babinger, F. and Dölger, F., 'Mehmed's II frühester Staatsvertrag', *OCP*, xv (1949), 225–58 (reprinted in Dölger, *Byzantinische Diplomatik*, Ettal, 1956, pp. 262–91)

Balard, M., 'Amalfi et Byzance (xᵉ–xiiiᵉ siècles)', *TM*, vi (1976), 85–95

'A propos de la bataille du Bosphore. L'expédition génoise de Paganino Doria à Constantinople (1351–1352)', *TM*, iv (1970), 431–69

Barker, J. W., 'John VII in Genoa: a problem in late Byzantine source confusion', *OCP*, xxviii (1962), 213–38

Manuel II Palaeologus (1391–1425). A Study in Late Byzantine Statesmanship (New Brunswick, N.J., 1968)

Bertelè, T., 'I gioielli della corona bizantina dati in pegno alla Repubblica veneta nel sec. xiv e Mastino della Scala', *Studi in onore di Amintore Fanfani*, ii: *Medioevo* (Milan, 1962), pp. 90–177

'L'iperpero bizantino dal 1261 al 1453', *Rivista italiana di numismatica*, v, serie 5, lix (1957), 78–89

'Moneta veneziana e moneta bizantina (secoli xii–xv)', in *Venezia e il Levante fino al secolo XV*, i: *Storia–Diritto–Economia*, ed. A. Pertusi, i, pp. 3–146

Bertolini, A., 'Quale fu il vero oggiettivo assegnato da Leone III "Isaurico" all' armata di Manes, stratego dei Cibyrreoti?', *BF*, ii (1967) (*Polychordia. Festschrift F. Dölger*, ii), 15–49

Besta, E., 'La cattura dei Veneziani in oriente per ordine dell' imperatore Emanuele Comneno e le sue conseguenze nella politica interna ed esterna del commune di Venezia', in *Antologia veneta*, i, 1–2 (1900), pp. 35–46, 111–23

Bettini, S., 'Le opere d'arte importate a Venezia durante le Crociate', in *Venezia dalla Prima Crociata alla conquista di Costantinopoli del 1204* (Florence, 1965), pp. 157–90; translated as S. Bettini, 'Venice, the Pala d'Oro, and Constantinople', in *The Treasury of San Marco Venice*, Exhibition Catalogue, The British Museum (Olivetti, Milan, 1984), pp. 35–64

Bon, A., *La Morée franque. Recherches historiques, topographiques et archéologiques sur la principauté d'Achaïe (1205–1430)* (Paris, 1969)

Borsari, S., 'Il commercio veneziano nell' impero bizantino nel xii secolo', *RSI*, lxxvi (1964), 982–1011

'Il crisobullo di Alessio I per Venezia', *Annali dell' Istituto Italiano per gli studi storici*, ii (1969–70), 111–31

'Per la storia del commercio veneziano col mondo bizantino nel xii secolo', *RSI*, lxxxviii (1976), 104–26

Studi sulle colonie veneziane in Romania nel XIII secolo (Naples, 1966)

Bosch, Ursula V., *Kaiser Andronikos III. Palaiologos. Versuch einer Darstellung der byzantinischen Geschichte in den Jahren 1321–1341* (Amsterdam, 1965)

Bowman, S. B., *The Jews of Byzantium 1204–1453* (Alabama, 1985)

Branca, V., ed., *Storia della civiltà veneziana*, i: *Dalle origini al secolo di Marco Polo* (Florence, 1979)

Brand, C. M., *Byzantium Confronts the West, 1180–1204* (Cambridge, Mass., 1968)

Brătianu, G. I., *Etudes byzantines d'histoire économique et sociale* (Paris, 1938)

'Etudes sur l'approvisionnement de Constantinople et le monopole du blé à l'époque byzantine et ottomane', in *Etudes byzantines*, pp. 127–81

'L'hyperpère byzantin et la monnaie d'or des républiques italiennes au xiiiᵉ siècle', *Mélanges Charles Diehl*, i (Paris, 1930), pp. 37–48 (reprinted in *Etudes byzantines*, pp. 217–39)

Recherches sur le commerce génois dans la Mer Noire au XIIIᵉ siècle (Paris, 1929)

Brezeanu, S., 'Le premier traité économique entre Venise et Nicée, *RHSEE*, xii (1974), 143–6

Brown, H. F., 'The Venetians and the Venetian Quarter in Constantinople to the close of the twelfth century', *JHS*, xl (1920), 68–88

Venice. An Historical Sketch of the Republic (London, 1893)

Brown, T. S., *Gentlemen and Officers. Imperial Administration and Aristocratic Power in Byzantine Italy, A.D. 554–800* (British School at Rome, 1984)

Brown, T. S., Bryer, A. and Winfield, D., 'Cities of Heraclius', *Byzantine and Modern Greek Studies*, iv (1978) (*Essays Presented to Sir Steven Runciman*), 15–38

Browning, R., *Byzantium and Bulgaria. A Comparative Study Across the Early Medieval Frontier* (London, 1975)

'A note on the capture of Constantinople in 1453', *B*, xxii (1952), 379–86

Brunetti, M., *Contributo alla storia delle relazioni veneti–genovese dal 1348 al 1350*, Miscellanea di Storia Veneta, serie 3, ix/2 (Venice, 1916)

Bury, J. B., *History of the Eastern Empire from the Fall of Irene to the Accession of Basil I (802–867)* (London, 1912)

History of the Later Roman Empire from the Death of Theodosius I to the Death of Justinian, i–ii (London, 1923)

The Imperial Administrative System in the Ninth Century (London, 1911)

Cammelli, G., *I dotti bizantini e le origini dell' umanesimo*, i: *Manuele Crisolora* (Florence, 1941)

Carile, A., 'Federico Barbarossa, i Veneziani e l'assedio di Ancona del 1173. Contributo alla storia politica e sociale della città nel secolo xii', *Studi veneziani*, xvi (1974), 3–31

'Partitio Terrarum Imperii Romanie', *Studi veneziani*, vii (1965), 125–305

Carile, A. and Fedalto, G., *Le origini di Venezia* (Bologna, 1978)

Casati, L. A., *La guerra di Chioggia e la pace di Torino* (Florence, 1866)

Cessi, R., 'Bizantinismo veneziano', *Archivio veneto*, ser. 5, lxix (1961), 3–22

'Da Roma a Bisanzio', in *Storia di Venezia*, ed. P. Marinotti, i (Venice, 1957), pp. 179–401

Le origini del ducato veneziano (Naples, 1951)

Storia della Repubblica di Venezia, i–ii, 2nd edn (Milan, 1968)

'Venetiarum provincia', *BF*, ii (1967) (*Polychordia. Festschrift F. Dölger*, ii), 91–9

Venezia ducale, i: *Duca e popolo*; ii, 1: *Commune Venetiarum* (Venice, 1963, 1965)

'Venice to the eve of the Fourth Crusade', in *CMH*, iv/1 (1966), pp. 250–74

Chalandon, F., *Les Comnènes. Etudes sur l'empire byzantin aux XIᵉ et XIIᵉ siècles*. i: *Essai sur le règne d'Alexis Comnène (1081–1118)* (Paris, 1900); ii: *Jean II Comnène (1118–1143) et Manuel I Comnène (1143–1180)* (Paris, 1912)

Histoire de la domination normande en Italie et en Sicilie, i–ii (Paris, 1907)

Charanis, P., 'Byzantium, the west and the origins of the First Crusade', *B*, XIX (1949), 17–24 (reprinted in *Social, Economic and Political Life*, no. XIV)

'Piracy in the Aegean during the reign of Michael VIII Palaeologus', *Mélanges Henri Grégoire*, II (Brussels, 1950) (*Annuaire de l'Institut de Philologie et d'Histoire Orientales et Slaves*, X, 1950, 127–36; reprinted in *Social, Economic and Political Life*, no. XII)

Social, Economic and Political Life in the Byzantine Empire (London, 1973)

Chrysostomides, Julian, 'John V Palaeologus in Venice (1370–1371) and the Chronicle of Caroldo: a reinterpretation', *OCP*, XXXI (1965), 76–84

'Studies on the Chronicle of Caroldo, with special reference to the history of Byzantium from 1370 to 1377', *OCP*, XXXV (1969), 123–82

'Venetian commercial privileges under the Palaeologi', *Studi veneziani*, XII (1970), 267–356

Danstrup, J., 'Manuel I's coup against Genoa and Venice in the light of Byzantine commercial policy', *Classica et Mediaevalia*, X (1948), 195–219

Deér, J., 'Die Pala d'Oro in neuer Sicht', *BZ*, LXII (1969), 308–44

Deichmann, F. W., *Corpus der Kapitelle der Kirche von San Marco zu Venedig* (Wiesbaden, 1981)

Delatte, A., *Les Portulans grecs*, I (Liège–Paris, 1947); II (Brussels, 1958)

Demus, O., *The Church of San Marco in Venice. History, Architecture, Sculpture* (Dumbarton Oaks, Washington, D.C., 1960)

Dennis, G. T., *Byzantium and the Franks 1350–1420* (London, 1982)

'The Byzantine–Turkish treaty of 1403', *OCP*, XXXIII (1967), 72–88

'Official documents of Manuel II Palaeologus', *B*, XLI (1971), 45–58 (reprinted in *Byzantium and the Franks*, no. IX)

The Reign of Manuel II Palaeologus in Thessalonica, 1382–1387, OCA, 159 (Rome, 1960)

Diehl, C., 'La colonie vénitienne à Constantinople à la fin du XIVe siècle', *Mélanges de l'Ecole Française de Rome*, III (1883), 90–131 (reprinted in *Etudes byzantines*, pp. 241–75)

Etudes byzantines (Paris, 1905)

Etudes sur l'administration byzantine dans l'Exarchat de Ravenne (568–751) (Paris, 1888)

Dölger, F., *Byzantinische Diplomatik. 20 Aufsätze zum Urkundenwesen der Byzantiner* (Ettal, 1956)

Byzanz und die europäische Staatenwelt. Ausgewählte Vorträge und Aufsätze (Ettal, 1953)

'Europas Gestaltung im Spiegel der Fränkisch–byzantinischen Auseinandersetzungen des 9. Jahrhunderts', in *Byzanz*, pp. 282–369

Facsimiles byzantinischer Kaiserurkunden (Munich, 1931)

'Die "Familie der Könige" im Mittelalter', *Historisches Jahrbuch*, LX (1940), 397–420 (reprinted in *Byzanz*, pp. 34–69)

'Die Kaiserurkunden der Byzantiner als Ausdruck ihrer politischen Anschauungen', in *Byzanz*, pp. 9–33

Dölger, F. and Karayannopoulos, J., *Byzantinische Urkundenlehre*, I: *Die Kaiserurkunden* (Munich, 1968)

Ducellier, A., *La Façade maritime de l'Albanie au moyen âge. Durazzo et Valona du XIe au XVe siècle* (Thessaloniki, 1981)

Dvornik, F., *The Photian Schism. History and Legend* (Cambridge, 1948)

Failler, A., 'Note sur la chronologie du règne de Jean VI Cantacuzène', *REB*, xxix (1971), 293–302

'Nouvelle note sur la chronologie du règne de Jean VI Cantacuzène', *REB*, xxxiv (1976), 119–24

Falkenhausen, V. von, *Untersuchungen über die byzantinische Herrschaft in Süditalien vom 9. bis 11. Jahrhundert* (Wiesbaden, 1967)

Ferjančić, B., *Despoti u Vizantiji i južnoslovenskim zemljama* (Belgrade, 1960)

Ferluga, J., *L'amministrazione bizantina in Dalmazia* (Venice, 1978)

Byzantium on the Balkans. Studies on the Byzantine Administration and the Southern Slavs from the VIIIth to the XIIth Centuries (Amsterdam, 1976)

'La ligesse dans l'empire byzantin. Contribution à l'étude de la féodalité à Byzance', *ZRVI*, vii (Belgrade, 1961), 97–123 (reprinted in *Byzantium on the Balkans*, pp. 399–425)

Foss, C., *Ephesus after Antiquity. A Late Antique, Byzantine and Turkish City* (Cambridge, 1979)

Fotheringham, J. N., *Marco Sanudo Conqueror of the Archipelago* (Oxford, 1915)

Frances, E., 'Alexis Comnène et les privilèges octroyés à Venise', *BS*, xxix (1968), 17–23

Frolow, A., 'Notes sur les reliques et les reliquaires byzantins de Saint-Marc de Venise', Δελτίον τῆς Χριστιανικῆς Ἀρχαιολογικῆς Ἑταιρείας Ἀθηνῶν, iv/4 (1964–5), 205–26

Gadolin, Anitra R., 'Alexius Comnenus and the Venetian trade privileges. A new interpretation', *B*, l (1980), 439–46

Gallo, R., *Il Tesoro di San Marco e la sua storia*, Civiltà Veneziana, Saggi, xvi (Venice–Florence, 1967)

Gardner, Alice, *The Lascarids of Nicaea. The Story of an Empire in Exile* (London, 1912)

Gay, J., *L'Italie méridionale et l'empire byzantin depuis l'avènement de Basile Ier jusqu'à la prise de Bari par les Normands (867–1071)* (Paris, 1904)

Geanakoplos, D. J., *Byzantine East and Latin West: Two Worlds of Christendom in Middle Ages and Renaissance. Studies in Ecclesiastical and Cultural History* (Oxford, 1966)

Emperor Michael Palaeologus and the West 1258–1282. A study in Byzantine–Latin relations (Cambridge, Mass., 1959)

Greek Scholars in Venice. Studies in the Dissemination of Greek Learning from Byzantium to Western Europe (Cambridge, Mass., 1962)

Interaction of the 'Sibling' Byzantine and Western Cultures in the Middle Ages and Italian Renaissance (New Haven–London, 1976)

Gill, J., *Byzantium and the Papacy 1198–1499* (New Brunswick, N.J., 1979)

The Council of Florence (Cambridge, 1958)

Godfrey, J., *1204. The Unholy Crusade* (Oxford, 1980)

Goubert, P., *Byzance avant l'Islam*, ii: *Byzance et l'Occident sous les successeurs de Justinien*, 2: *Rome, Byzance et Carthage* (Paris, 1965)

Grabar, A., 'Byzance et Venise', in *Venezia e l'Europa, Atti del XVIII Congresso internazionale di Storia dell' Arte, Venezia 12–18 sett. 1955* (Venice, 1956), 45–55

'La Sedia di San Marco à Venise', *Cahiers Archéologiques*, VII (1954), 19–34

Grumel, V., *La Chronologie*, Bibliothèque Byzantine, Traité d'Etudes Byzantines, I (Paris, 1958)

Guilland, R., 'Les appels de Constantin XII Paléologue à Rome et à Venise pour sauver Constantinople (1452–1453)', *BS*, XIV (1953), 226–44 (reprinted in *Etudes byzantines*, Paris, 1959, pp. 151–75)

Halecki, O., *The Crusade of Varna. A Discussion of Controversial Problems* (New York, 1943)

Un Empereur de Byzance à Rome. Vingt ans de travail pour l'union des églises et pour la défense de l'empire d'Orient, 1355–1375 (Warsaw, 1930, reprinted London, 1972)

Hartmann, L. M., *Geschichte Italiens im Mittelalter*, I–IV (Gotha, 1897–1915)

Untersuchungen zur Geschichte der byzantinischen Verwaltung in Italien (540–750) (Leipzig, 1889)

Heinemeyer, W., 'Die Verträge zwischen dem oströmischen Reiche und den italienischen Städten Genua, Pisa und Venedig von 10. bis 12. Jahrhundert', *Archiv für Diplomatik*, III (1957), 79–161

Hemmerdinger, B., 'Deux Notes d'héraldique', *BZ*, LXI (1968), 304–9

Hendy, M. F., *Studies in the Byzantine Monetary Economy c. 300–1450* (Cambridge, 1985)

Herrin, Judith, 'The collapse of the Byzantine Empire in the twelfth century: a study of a medieval economy', *University of Birmingham Historical Journal*, XII/2 (1970), 188–203

Heyd, W., *Histoire du commerce du Levant au Moyen Age*, I–II (Leipzig, 1885–6, reprinted Amsterdam, 1967)

Heynen, R., *Zur Entstehung des Kapitalismus in Venedig*, Münchner Volkswirtschaftliche Studien, 71 (Stuttgart–Berlin, 1905)

Hocquet, J.-Cl., *Le sel et la fortune de Venise*, I: *Production et monopole*; II: *Voiliers et commerce en Méditerranée 1200–1650* (Lille, 1979)

Hodgson, F. C., *The Early History of Venice from the Foundation to the Conquest of Constantinople* (London, 1901)

Venice in the Thirteenth and Fourteenth Centuries (London, 1914)

Hoffman, J., *Rudimente von Territorialstaaten im byzantinischen Reich*, Miscellanea Byzantina Monacensia, 17 (Munich, 1974)

Hopf, K., *Geschichte Griechenlands vom Beginn des Mittelalters bis auf unserer Zeit*, I–II, in J. S. Ersch and J. G. Gruber, *Allgemeine Encyklopädie der Wissenschaften und Künste*, LXXXV, LXXXVI (Leipzig, 1867, 1868)

Veneto-Byzantinische Analekten, Sitzungsberichte der k. Akademie der Wissenschaften, phil.-hist. Classe, XXXII, 3 (Vienna, 1859)

The Horses of San Marco Venice, translated by John and Valerie Wilton-Ely, Procuratorio di San Marco, and Olivetti (Milan and London, 1979)

Housley, N. J. 'Angevin Naples and the defence of the Latin East, Robert the Wise and the Naval League of 1344', *B*, LI (1981), 549–56

Howse, D. and Sanderson, M., *The Sea Chart* (Newton Abbot, 1973)

Hunger, H., 'Thukydides bei Johannes Kantakuzenos. Beobachtungen zur Mimesis', *JÖB*, xxv (1976), 181–93

Jacoby, D., 'Les Juifs vénitiens de Constantinople et leur communauté du xiiiᵉ au milieu du xvᵉ siècle', *Revue des Etudes Juives*, cxxxi (1972), 397–410

Société et démographie à Byzance et en Romanie latine (London, 1975)

'Les quartiers juifs de Constantinople à l'époque byzantine', *B*, xxxvi (1967), 167–227 (reprinted in *Société et démographie*, no. ii)

'Les Vénitiens naturalisés dans l'empire byzantin: un aspect de l'expansion de Venise en Romanie du xiiiᵉ au milieu du xvᵉ siècle', *TM*, viii (1981), 207–35

Janin, R., *Constantinople byzantine. Développement urbain et répertoire topographique*, 2nd edn (Paris, 1964)

La Géographie ecclésiastique de l'empire byzantin, i: *Le Siège de Constantinople et le patriarcat oecuménique*, iii: *Les Eglises et les monastères*, 2nd edn (Paris, 1969)

'Les sanctuaires de Byzance sous la domination latine (1204–1261)', *Etudes Byzantines*, ii (1944), 134–84

Jegerlehner, J., 'Der Aufstand der kandiotischen Ritterschaft gegen das Mutterland Venedig', *BZ*, xii (1903), 78–125

Jenkins, R. J. H., *Byzantium. The Imperial Centuries, AD 610–1071* (London, 1966)

Jorga, N., 'Latins et Grecs d'Orient et l'établissement des Turcs en Europe, 1342–62', *BZ*, xv (1906), 179–222

'Veneţia in Mare neagră', *Analele Academiei Române*, Memoriile secţiunii istorice, ser. 2, xxxvi (1913–14), 1043–1118

Jurewicz, O., *Andronikos I. Komnenos* (Amsterdam, 1970)

Kazhdan, A. P. and Epstein, Ann W., *Change in Byzantine Culture in the Eleventh and Twelfth Centuries* (Berkeley–Los Angeles–London, 1985)

Koder, J., *Negroponte. Untersuchungen zur Topographie und Siedlungsgeschichte der Insel Euboia während der Zeit der Venezianerherrschaft* (Vienna, 1973)

Koder, J. and Hild, F., *Hellas und Thessalia*, Tabula Imperii Byzantini, i (Vienna, 1976)

Kretschmayr, H., 'Die Beschreibung der venezianischen Inseln bei Konstantin Porphyrogennetos', *BZ*, xiii (1904), 482–9

Geschichte von Venedig, i–ii (Gotha, 1905, 1920)

Kyrris, C. P., 'John Cantacuzenus, the Genoese, the Venetians and the Catalans (1348–1354)', *Byzantina*, iv (1972), 331–56

Laiou, Angeliki E., *Constantinople and the Latins. The Foreign Policy of Andronicus II, 1282–1328* (Cambridge, Mass., 1972)

'Marino Sanudo Torsello, Byzantium and the Turks: the background to the Anti-Turkish League of 1332–1334', *Speculum*, xlv (1970), 374–92

'The provisioning of Constantinople during the winter of 1306–1307', *B*, xxxvii (1967), 91–113

'Un notaire vénitien à Constantinople: Antonio Bresciano et le commerce international en 1350', in M. Balard, Angeliki E. Laiou and Catherine Otten-Froux, *Les Italiens à Byzance. Edition et présentation de documents*. Byzantina Sorbonensia, 6 (Paris, 1987), pp. 79–151

'Venice as a centre of trade and of artistic production in the thirteenth century', in H. Belting, ed., *Il Medio Oriente e l'Occidente nell' arte del XIII secolo* (Bologna, 1982), pp. 11–26

Laiou-Thomadakis, Angeliki E., 'The Byzantine economy and the medieval trade system: thirteenth–fifteenth centuries', *DOP*, XXXIV–XXXV (1982), 177–222

'The Greek merchant of the Palaeologan period: a collective portrait', Πρακτικὰ τῆς 'Ακαδημίας 'Αθηνῶν, LVII (1982), 96–132

Lamma, P., *Commeni e Staufer. Ricerche sui rapporti fra Bisanzio e l'Occidente nel secolo XII*, I–II, Istituto Storico Italiano per il medio evo. Studi storici, fasc. 14–18 (Rome, 1955, 1957)

'Venezia nel giudizio delle fonti bizantine', *RSI*, LXXIV (1962), 457–78

Lane, F. C., 'Manuali di mercatura e prontuari di informazioni pratiche', in A. Stussi, ed., *Zibaldone da Canal, manoscritto mercantile del secolo XIV* (Venice, 1967)

'Venetian merchant galleys 1300–1334: private and commercial operation', *Speculum*, XXXVIII (1963), 179–205

Venice and History. The Collected Papers of Frederic C. Lane (Baltimore, 1966)

Venice. A Maritime Republic (Baltimore–London, 1973)

Lazzarini, V., 'La battaglia di Porto Lungo nell' isola di Sapienza', *Nuovo archivio veneto*, VIII (1894), 5–45

'Un' iscrizione torcellana del sec. VII', *Istituto Veneto di Scienze, Lettere ed Arte, Atti*, LXXIII (1913–14), 2, 387–97; reprinted in *Scritti di paleografia e diplomatica* (Venice, 1938), pp. 120–31

'I titoli dei dogi di Venezia', *Nuovo archivio veneto*, n. s., V/2 (1903), 271–313

Lemerle, P., *Cinq études sur le XIᵉ siècle byzantin* (Paris, 1977)

'La domination vénitienne à Thessalonique', *Miscellanea Giovanni Galbiati*, III (*Fontes Ambrosiani*, XXVII) (Milan, 1951), 219–25

L'Emirat d'Aydin. Byzance et l'Occident: Recherches sur «La Geste d'Umur Pacha» (Paris, 1957)

Lentz, E., 'Der allmähliche Übergang Venedigs von faktischer zu nomineller Abhängigkeit von Byzanz', *BZ*, III (1894), 64–115

Das Verhältnis Venedigs zu Byzanz nach dem Fall des Exarchats bis zum Ausgang des 9. Jahrh. (Berlin, 1891)

Leyser, K., 'The tenth century in Byzantine–Western relationships', in *Relations between East and West in the Middle Ages*, ed. D. Baker (Edinburgh, 1973), pp. 29–63

Lilie, R.-J., *Handel und Politik zwischen dem byzantinischen Reich und den italienischen Kommunen Venedig, Pisa und Genua in der Epoche der Komnenen und der Angeloi (1081–1204)* (Amsterdam, 1984)

Loenertz, R.-J., *Byzantina et Franco-Graeca*, I–II, Storia e Letteratura, Raccolta di Studi e Testi, 118, 145 (Rome, 1970, 1978)

'Fragment d'une lettre de Jean V Paléologue à la Commune de Gênes 1387–1391', *BZ*, LI (1958), 37–40

'Jean V Paléologue à Venise (1370–1371)', *REB*, XVI (1958) (*Mélanges S. Salaville*), 217–32

'Notes d'histoire et de chronologie byzantines', *REB*, XVII (1959), 158–78 (reprinted in *Byzantina et Franco-Graeca*, I, pp. 421–39)

Longnon, J., *L'Empire latin de Constantinople et la principauté de Morée* (Paris, 1949)

Lopez, R. S., 'Venezia e le grandi linee dell' espansione commerciale nel secolo XIII', in *La civiltà veneziana del secolo di Marco Polo* (Florence, 1955)

Lopez, R. S. and Raymond, I. W., *Medieval Trade in the Mediterranean World* (New York–London, 1955)

Lounghis, T. C., *Les Ambassades byzantines en Occident depuis la fondation des états barbares jusqu'aux Croisades (407–1096)* (Athens, 1980)

Luzzato, G., *Storia economica di Venezia dall' XI al XVI secolo* (Venice, 1961)

Magdalino, P., 'Notes on the last years of John Palaiologos, brother of Michael VIII', *REB*, xxxiv (1976), 143–9

Maltézou, Chrysa A., Ὁ θεσμὸς τοῦ ἐν Κωνσταντινουπόλει Βενετοῦ Βαΐλου (*1268–1453*) (Athens, 1970)

Παρατηρήσεις στὸν θεσμὸ τῆς Βενετικῆς ὑπηκοότητας, Σύμμεικτα, IV (1981), 1–16

'Il quartiere veneziano di Costantinopoli (Scali marittimi)', *Thesaurismata*, XV (1978), 30–61

Mandić, D., 'Gregorio VII e l'occupazione veneta della Dalmazia nell' anno 1076', in A. Pertusi, ed., *Venezia e il Levante*, I/1, pp. 453–71

Manfroni, C., 'La battaglia di Gallipoli e la politica veneto-turca 1381–1420', *Ateneo veneto*, xxv/2, fasc. 1–2 (1902)

'La marina veneziana alla difesa di Salonicco (1423–1430)', *Nuovo archivio veneto*, n. s., anno x (1910), xx/1, 5–68

Manoussakas, M., 'Les derniers défenseurs crétois de Constantinople d'après les documents vénitiens', *Akten des XI. Internationalen Byzantinisten-Kongresses, München 1958* (Munich, 1960), pp. 331–40

Marinotti, P., ed., *Storia di Venezia*, I: *Dalla preistoria alla storia*; II: *Dalle origini del ducato alla IV Crociata* (Venice, 1957, 1958)

Markl, O., *Ortsnamen Griechenlands in "fränkischer" Zeit*, Byzantina Vindobonensia, I (Graz–Köln, 1966)

Martin, M. E., 'The Chrysobull of Alexius I Comnenus to the Venetians and the Early Venetian Quarter in Constantinople', *BS*, xxxix (1978), 19–23

'The first Venetians in the Black Sea', *Archeion Pontou*, xxxv (1979), 111–22

McNeal, E. H. and Wolff, R. L., 'The Fourth Crusade', in K. M. Setton, ed., *A History of the Crusades*, II (Philadelphia, 1962), pp. 153–85

McNeill, W. H., *Venice the Hinge of Europe 1081–1797* (Chicago–London, 1974)

Matschke, K.-P., *Die Schlacht bei Ankara und das Schicksal von Byzanz. Studien zur spätbyzantinischen Geschichte zwischen 1402 und 1422*, Forschungen zur mittelalterlichen Geschichte, 29 (Weimar, 1981)

Mély, F. de, *Les Reliques de Constantinople au XIIIᵉ siècle*, II: *La Sainte Couronne* (Lille, 1901) (from *Revue de l'Art Chrétien*, 1899, 35–133)

Mertzios, K. D., Μνημεῖα Μακεδονικῆς Ἱστορίας, Μακεδονικὴ Βιβλιοθήκη, 7 (Thessaloniki, 1947)

Mertzios, K. D., Περὶ τῶν ἐκ Κωνσταντινουπόλεως διαφυγόντων τὸ 1453 Παλαιολόγων καὶ ἀποβιβασθέντων εἰς Κρήτην, *Actes du XIIᵉ Congrès International d'Etudes Byzantines, Ochride, 10–16 septembre 1961* (Belgrade, 1964), pp. 171–6

Miller, T. S., 'The Plague in John VI Cantacuzenus and Thucydides', *GRBS*, xviii (1976), 385–95

Miller, W., *Essays on the Latin Orient* (Cambridge, 1921)

The Latins in the Levant. A History of Frankish Greece (1204–1566) (London, 1908)

Momferratos, A., Μεθώνη και Κορώνη ἐπι Ἐνετοκρατίας ὑπὸ κοινωνικὴν πολιτικὴν καὶ δημοσιακὴν ἔποψιν (Athens, 1914)

Morgan, G., 'The Venetian claims commission of 1278', *BZ*, lxix (1976), 411–38

Neumann, C., 'Über die urkundlichen Quellen zur Geschichte der byzantinisch-venezianischen Beziehungen vornehmlich im Zeitalter der Komnenen', *BZ*, i (1892), 366–78

Nicol, D. M., *Byzantium: its Ecclesiastical History and Relations with the Western World* (London, 1972)

Studies in Late Byzantine History and Prosopography (London, 1986)

'The abdication of John VI Cantacuzene', *BF*, ii (1976) (*Polychordia. Festschrift F. Dölger*), 269–83 (reprinted in *Studies*, no. vi)

'A Byzantine Emperor in England. Manuel II's visit to London in 1400–1401', *University of Birmingham Historical Journal*, xii/2 (1971), 204–25 (reprinted in *Byzantium*, no. x)

The Byzantine Family of Kantakouzenos (Cantacuzenus) ca. 1100–1460. A Genealogical and Prosopographical Study, Dumbarton Oaks Studies, xi (Washington D.C., 1968)

'The Byzantine reaction to the Second Council of Lyons, 1274', *Studies in Church History*, vii: *Councils and Assemblies*, ed. G. J. Cuming and D. Baker (Cambridge, 1971), pp. 113–46 (reprinted in Nicol, *Byzantium*, no. vi.)

Church and Society in the Last Centuries of Byzantium (Cambridge, 1979)

The Despotate of Epiros [1204–1267] (Oxford, 1957)

The Despotate of Epiros 1267–1479. A Contribution to the History of Greece in the Middle Ages (Cambridge, 1984)

'The Fourth Crusade and the Greek and Latin Empires', in *CMH*, iv (1966), pp. 275–330

The Last Centuries of Byzantium, 1261–1453 (London, 1972)

'The Papal scandal', *Studies in Church History*, xiii: *The Orthodox Churches and the West*, ed. D. Baker (Oxford, 1976), pp. 141–68 (reprinted in *Studies*, no. ii)

Norden, W., *Das Papsttum und Byzanz. Die Trennung der beiden Mächte und das Problem ihrer Wiedervereinigung bis zum Untergang des byzantinischen Reichs (1453)* (Berlin, 1903)

Norwich, J. J., *Venice. The Rise to Empire* (London, 1977); *Venice. The Greatness and the Fall* (London, 1981); the two published as one volume: *A History of Venice* (London, 1982; Harmondsworth, 1983)

Nystazopoulou-Pélékides, Marie, 'Listes des bailes de Trébizonde et des consuls de Tana', in *Venezia e il Levante fino al secolo XV*, ed. A. Pertusi, I/2 (Florence, 1973), pp. 576–82

'Venise et la Mer Noire du xiᵉ au xvᵉ siècle', *Thesaurismata*, vii (1970), 15–51 (reprinted in *Venezia e il Levante*, pp. 571–85)

Obolensky, D., *The Byzantine Commonwealth. Eastern Europe, 500–1453* (London, 1971)

Ohnsorge, W., *Abendland und Byzanz* (Darmstadt, 1958)

Das Zweikaiserproblem im früheren Mittelalter (Hildesheim, 1947)

Oikonomides, N., *Hommes d'affaires grecs et latins à Constantinople (XIIIᵉ–XVᵉ siècles)*, Conférence Albert-le-Grand (Montreal, 1979)

Les Listes de Préséance byzantines des IXᵉ et Xᵉ siècles (Paris, 1972)

Le origini di Venezia, Centro di Cultura e Civiltà della Fondazione Giorgio Cini (Florence, 1964)

Ostrogorsky, G., 'Byzance, état tributaire de l'empire turc', *ZRVI*, v (1958), 49–58

'Die byzantinische Staatenhierarchie', *Seminarium Kondakovianum*, VIII (1936), 41–61

'The Byzantine Empire and the hierarchical world order', *Slavonic and East European Review*, XXXV (1965), 1–14

History of the Byzantine State (Oxford, 1968)

Pasini, A., *Il Tesoro di San Marco a Venezia* (Venice, 1885–6)

Pears, E., *The Destruction of the Greek Empire and the Story of the Capture of Constantinople by the Turks* (London, 1903)

Pertusi, A., 'Ai confini tra religione e politica: la contesa per le reliquie di San Nicola tra Bari, Venezia e Genova', *Quaderni medievali*, v (1978), 6–58

'Bisanzio e le insegne regali dei Dogi di Venezia', *RSBN*, n.s. II–III (1965–6), 277–84

'Cultura bizantina a Venezia', in *Storia della cultura veneta*, I, ed. N. Pozza (Vicenza, 1976), pp. 326–49

'Exuviae sacrae Constantinopolitanae. A proposito degli oggetti bizantini esistenti oggi nel Tesoro di San Marco', *Studi Veneziani*, n.s., II (1978), 251–5

'L'impero bizantino e l'evolvere dei suoi interessi nell'alto Adriatico', in *Le origini di Venezia* (Florence, 1964), pp. 59–63; reprinted in V. Branca, ed., *Storia della civiltà veneziana*, I, (Florence, 1979), pp. 297–305

'Insigne del potere sovrano e delegato a Bisanzio e nei paesi di influenza bizantina', *Simboli e simbologia nell' alto medioevo. Spoleto, 3–9 April 1975*, Centro italiano di studi sull' alto medioevo, 23 (Spoleto, 1976), pp. 481–563

'L'iscrizione torcellana dei tempi di Eraclio', *Bollettino dell' Istituto di Storia della Società e dello Stato*, IV (1962), 9–38; also in *ZRVI*, VIII (1964) (*Mélanges G. Ostrogorsky*, II), 317–39

'Quedam regalia insignia. Ricerche sulle insegne del potere ducale a Venezia durante il medioevo', *Studi veneziani*, VII (1965), 3–123

La storiografia veneziano fino al secolo XVI. Aspetti e problemi (Florence, 1970)

'Venezia e Bisanzio nel secolo XI', in *La Venezia del Mille* (Florence, 1965), pp. 117–60; reprinted in V. Branca, ed., *Storia della civiltà veneziana*, I (Florence, 1979), pp. 175–98.

'Venezia e Bisanzio: 1000–1204', *DOP*, XXXIII (1979), 1–22

ed., *Venezia e il Levante fino al secolo XV*, I/1–2: *Storia–Diritto–Economia*; II: *Arte–Letteratura–Linguistica* (Florence, 1973, 1974)

Polemis, D. I., *The Doukai. A Contribution to Byzantine Prosopography* (London, 1968)

Pozza, N., ed., *Storia della cultura veneta*, I: *Dalle origini al Trecento* (Vicenza, 1976)

Prawer, J., *Histoire du Royaume latin de Jérusalem*, I–II (Paris, 1969, 1970)

Queller, D. E., *The Fourth Crusade. The Conquest of Constantinople, 1201–1204* (Philadelphia, 1977)

Renouard, Y., *Les Hommes d'affaires italiens du moyen âge* (Paris, 1949); revised edn by B. Guillemain (Paris, 1968)

'Mercati e mercanti veneziani alla fine del duecento', in *La civiltà veneziana del secolo di Marco Polo* (Florence, 1955), pp. 83–108; reprinted in V. Branca, ed., *Storia della civiltà veneziana: il secolo di Marco Polo* (Florence, 1979), pp. 387–97

Rhamnusius (Rannusio), Paulus, *De Bello Constantinopolitano et Imperatoribus Comnenis per Gallos, et Venetos restitutis Historia Pauli Ramnusij*. Editio altera (Venice, 1634)

Riant, P. E. D., *Des Dépouilles religieuses enlevées à Constantinople au XIIIᵉ siècle par les Latins, et des documents historiques nés de leur transport en Occident*, Mémoires de la Société Nationale des Antiquaires de France, sér. 4/vi (Paris, 1875)

ed., *Exuviae sacrae Constantinopolitanae*, I–III (Paris, 1877–1904)

Roberti, M., 'Richerche intorno alla colonia veneziana di Costantinopli nel sec. XII', in *Scritti storici in onore di C. Manfroni nel XL anno d'insegnamento* (Padua, 1925), pp. 137–47

Romanin, S., *Storia documentata della Repubblica di Venezia*, 2nd edn, I–X (Venice, 1912–21)

Runciman, S., *The Eastern Schism* (Oxford, 1955)

The Fall of Constantinople 1453 (Cambridge, 1965)

A History of the Crusades, I–III (Cambridge, 1951–4)

'L'intervento di Venezia dalla prima alla terza Crociata', in *Venezia dalla Prima Crociata alla Conquista di Costantinopoli del 1204* (Florence, 1965), pp. 3–22

The Sicilian Vespers. A history of the Mediterranean world in the later thirteenth century (Cambridge, 1958)

Saccardo, G., 'L'anticha chiesa di S. Teodoro in Venezia', *Archivio Veneto*, XXXIV (1887), 91–113

Schlosser, J. von, 'Die Entstehung Venedigs', reprinted in *Präludien. Vorträge und Aufsätze von Julius Schlosser* (Berlin, 1927), 82–111

Schlumberger, G., *Un Empereur de Byzance à Paris et à Londres* (Paris, 1916) (reprinted in Schlumberger, *Byzance et Croisades. Pages médiévales*, Paris, 1927, pp. 87–147)

L'Epopée byzantine à la fin du Xᵉ siècle, II: *Basile II (989–1025)* (Paris, 1900)

Schneider, A.-M., *Mauern und Tore am Goldenen Horn zu Konstantinopel*, Nachrichten der Akademie der Wissenschaften in Göttingen, 5 (Göttingen, 1950)

Schreiner, P., 'La Chronique brève de 1352, IVᵐᵉ partie (1348–1352)', *OCP*, XXXIV (1968), 38–61

'Untersuchungen zu den Niederlassungen westlicher Kaufleute im byzantinischen Reich des 11. und 12. Jahrhunderte', *BF*, VII (1979), 175–91

Setton, K. M., 'The Byzantine Background to the Italian Renaissance', *Proceedings of the American Philosophical Society*, C (1956), 1–76 (reprinted in Setton, *Europe and the Levant in the Middle Ages and the Renaissance*, London, 1974, no. 1)

Catalan Domination of Athens 1311–1388, 2nd edn (London, 1975)

ed. *A History of the Crusades*, 2nd edn (Milwaukee-London, 1969): I: *The First Hundred Years*, ed. M. W. Baldwin; II: *The Later Crusades*, ed. R. L. Wolff and H. W. Hazard; III: *The Fourteenth and Fifteenth Centuries*, ed. H. W. Hazard (Madison, Wisconsin, 1975)

The Papacy and the Levant (1204–1571), I: *The Thirteenth and Fourteenth Centuries*; II: *The Fifteenth Century*, Memoirs of the American Philosophical Society (Philadelphia, 1976, 1978)

Silberschmidt, M., *Das orientalische Problem zur Zeit der Entstehung des türkischen Reiches nach venezianischen Quellen. Ein Beitrag zur Geschichte der Beziehungen Venedigs zu Sultan Bajezid I., zu Byzanz, Ungarn und Genua und zum Reiche von Kiptschak (1381–1400)*, Beiträge zur Kulturgeschichte des Mittelalters und der Renaissance, herausgegeben von Walter Goetz, 27 (Leipzig–Berlin, 1923)

Sokolov, N. P., 'K voprosu o vzaimootnošenijach Vizantii i Venecii v poslednie godu pravlenija Komninov (1171–1185)', *VV*, V (1952), 139–51

'Venecija i Vizantija pri pervych Paleologach (1263–1328)', *VV*, XII (1957), 75–96

Sorbelli, A., *La lotta tra Genova e Venezia per il predominio del Mediterraneo*, Memorie della Reale Accademia delle Scienze dell'Istituto di Bologna, Classe di Scienze Morali, sezione I, vol. 5 (Bologna, 1911)

Stein, E., *Histoire du Bas-Empire*, II: *De la Disparition de l'Empire d'Occident à la mort de Justinien* (Paris–Brussels–Amsterdam, 1949)

Untersuchungen zur spätbyzantinischen Verfassungs- und Wirtschaftsgeschichte, Mitteilungen zur osmanischen Geschichte, II, 1–2 (Hanover, 1925; reprinted Amsterdam, 1962)

Tafrali, O., *Thessalonique au quatorzième siècle* (Paris, 1913)

Thiriet, F., 'Byzance et les byzantins vus par le Vénitien Andrea Dandolo', *Revue des Études Sud-Est Européennes*, X (1972), 5–15

'Les chroniques vénitiennes de la Marcienne et leur importance pour l'histoire de la Romanie gréco-vénitienne', *Mélanges de l'Ecole Française de Rome*, LXVI (Paris, 1954), 241–92 (reprinted in *Etudes*, no. III)

Etudes sur la Romanie gréco-vénitienne (X^e–XVe siècles) (London, 1977)

'Les interventions vénitiennes dans les Iles Ioniennes au XIVe siècle', *Actes du 3ème Congrès Panionien 1965* (Athens, 1967), 374–85 (reprinted in *Etudes*, no. X)

'Una proposta di lega antiturca tra Venezia, Genova e Bisanzio nel 1362', *ASI*, CXIII (1955), 321–34

La Romanie vénitienne au Moyen Age. Le développement et l'exploitation du domaine colonial vénitien (XIIe–XVe siècles), Ecoles Françaises d'Athènes et de Rome, 193 (Paris, 1959)

'Venise et l'occupation de Ténédos au XIVe siècle', *Mélanges de l'Ecole Française de Rome*, LXV (Paris, 1953), 219–45 (reprinted in *Etudes*, no. II)

'Les Vénitiens en Mer Noire: organisation et trafics (XIIIe–XVe siècles)', *Archeion Pontou*, XXXV (1979), 38–53

'Les Vénitiens à Thessalonique dans la première moitié du XIVe siècle', *B*, XXII (1952), 323–32 (reprinted in *Etudes*, no. I)

Thomson, J., 'Manuel Chrysoloras and the early Italian Renaissance', *GRBS*, VII (1966), 63–82

Tramontin, S., 'Influsso orientale nel culto dei Santi a Venezia fino al secolo XV', in A. Pertusi, ed., *Venezia e il Levante fino al secolo XV*, I/2 (Florence, 1973), pp. 801–20

The Treasury of San Marco in Venice. Exhibition Catalogue, The British Museum (Olivetti, Milan, 1984)

Tuilier, A., 'La date exacte du chrysobule d'Alexios I Comnène en faveur des Vénitiens et son contexte historique', *RSBN*, n. s., IV (1967), 27–48

Tůma, O., 'The dating of Alexius's chrysobull to the Venetians: 1082, 1084, or 1092?', *BS*, XLII (1981), 171–85

'Some notes on the significance of the imperial chrysobull to the Venetians of 992', *B*, LIV (1984), 358–66

Vakalopoulos (Vacalopoulos), A. E., *A History of Thessaloniki*, translated by T. F. Carney (Thessaloniki, 1963); 2nd Greek edn (in Greek) (Thessaloniki, 1983)

Origins of the Greek Nation. The Byzantine Period, 1204–1261 (New Brunswick, N.J., 1970)

Συμβολὴ στὴν ʿστορια τῆς Θεσσαλονικης ἐπὶ Βενετοκρατίας (1423–1430), Τόμος Κωνσταντινου ʿΑρμενοπούλου (Thessaloniki, 1952), pp. 127–49

Vannier, J.-F., *Familles byzantines. Les Argyroi (IXᵉ–XIIᵉ siècles)* (Paris, 1975)

Vasiliev, A. A., *Byzance et les Arabes*, I: *La dynastie d'Amorium (820–867)* (Brussels, 1935)

Byzance et les Arabes, II/1: *La dynastie macédonienne (867–959)* (Brussels, 1968)

'Putešestvie vizantijskago imperatora Manuila II Paleologa na zapadnoj Evrope (1399–1403 g.)', *Žurnal ministerstva narodnago prosveščenija*, XXXIX (1912), 41–78, 260–304

Venezia dalla Prima Crociata alla Conquista di Costantinopoli del 1204, Centro di Cultura e Civiltà della Fondazione Giorgio Cini (Florence, 1965)

La Venezia del Mille, Centro di Cultura e Civiltà della Fondazione Giorgio Cini (Florence, 1965)

Verlinden, C., 'Venezia e il commercio degli schiavi provenienti dalle coste orientali del Mediterraneo', in *Venezia e il Levante fino al secolo XV*, ed. A. Pertusi, I/2 (Florence, 1973), pp. 911–29

Volbach, W. F., Pertusi, A., Bischoff, B. and Hahnloser, H. R., *Il Tesoro di San Marco: La Pala d'Oro*, Fondazione Giorgio Cini (Florence, 1965)

Vryonis, S., *The Decline of Medieval Hellenism in Asia Minor and the Process of Islamization from the Eleventh through the Fifteenth Century* (Los Angeles, 1971)

'The Ottoman conquest of Thessaloniki in 1430', in A. Bryer and H. Lowry, eds., *Continuity and Change in Late Byzantine and Early Ottoman Society* (Birmingham and Dumbarton Oaks, Washington, D.C., 1986), pp. 281–321

Wirth, P., 'Zum Geschichtsbild Johannes' VII Palaiologos', *B*, XXV (1965), 592–600

'Zum Verzeichnis der venezianischen Baili von Konstantinopel', *BZ*, LIV (1961), 324–8

Wolff, R. L., 'Footnote to an incident of the Latin occupation of Constantinople: the Church and the Icon of the Hodegetria', *Traditio*, VI (1948), 319–28

'Hopf's so-called "Fragmentum" of Marino Sanudo Torsello', *The Joshua Starr Memorial Volume* (New York, 1953), pp. 149–59 (reprinted in *Studies*, no. x)

'The Latin Empire of Constantinople', in *A History of the Crusades*, ed. K. M. Setton, II (1969), pp. 187–233 (reprinted in *Studies*, no. II).

'Mortgage and redemption of an Emperor's son: Castile and the Latin empire of Constantinople', *Speculum*, XXIX (1954), 45–84 (reprinted in *Studies*, no. V)

'A New Document from the Period of the Latin Empire of Constantinople: The

Oath of the Venetian Podestà', *Pankarpeia. Mélanges Henri Grégoire*, IV (*Annuaire de l'Institut de Philologie et d'Histoire Orientales et Slaves*, XII, Brussels, 1953), 539–73 (reprinted in *Studies*, no. VI)

'The organisation of the Latin Patriarchate of Constantinople, 1204–1261: social and administrative consequences of the Latin conquest', *Traditio*, VI (1948), 33–60 (reprinted in *Studies*, no. VIII)

'Politics in the Latin Patriarchate of Constantinople, 1204–1261', *DOP*, VIII (1954), 225–303 (reprinted in *Studies*, no. IX)

'Romania: The Latin Empire of Constantinople', *Speculum*, XXIII (1948), 1–34 (reprinted in *Studies*, no. II)

Studies in the Latin Empire of Constantinople (London, 1976)

Woodhouse, C. M. *Gemistos Plethon. The Last of the Hellenes* (Oxford, 1986)

Xanthoudides, S., ʿΗ Ἐνετοκρατία ἐν Κρήτῃ καὶ οι κατὰ τῶν Ἐνετων ἀγῶνες τῶν Κρητῶν, Texte und Forschungen zur byzantinisch-neugriechischen Jahrbücher, 34 (Athens, 1939), pp. 81–110

Zachariadou, Elizabeth A., *Trade and Crusade. Venetian Crete and the Emirates of Menteshe and Aydin (1300–1415)*, Library of the Hellenic Institute of Byzantine and Post-Byzantine Studies, 11 (Venice, 1983)

Zakythenos, D. A., *Byzance: Etat–Société–Economie* (London, 1973)

'Crise monétaire et crise économique à Byzance du XIIIe au XVe siècle', *L'Hellénisme contemporain* (Athens, 1947–8), 1–160 (reprinted in *Byzance*, no. XI)

Le Despotat grec de Morée, I–II, édition revue et augmentée par Chryssa Maltézou (London, 1975)

Ziegler, P., *The Black Death* (London, 1969)

INDEX

1034656R0

Printed in Great Britain by
Amazon.co.uk, Ltd.,
Marston Gate.